DOCUMENTARY HISTORY OF THE FIRST FEDERAL CONGRESS OF THE UNITED STATES OF AMERICA

March 4, 1789–March 3, 1791

Linda Grant De Pauw, Editor

SPONSORED BY

THE NATIONAL HISTORICAL PUBLICATIONS COMMISSION

AND

THE GEORGE WASHINGTON UNIVERSITY

VOLUME I

SENATE

LEGISLATIVE

JOURNAL

LINDA GRANT DE PAUW, Editor

CHARLENE BANGS BICKFORD, Assistant Editor

LAVONNE MARLENE SIEGEL, Assistant Editor

The Johns Hopkins University Press, Baltimore and London

Library of Congress Catalog Card Number 73-155164
ISBN 0-8018-1280-1

CONTENTS

INTRODUCTION   vii
SYMBOLS   xv
GLOSSARY   xvii
MEMBERS OF THE SENATE   xxiii

JOURNAL OF THE FIRST SESSION
OF THE SENATE OF THE UNITED STATES

MARCH 1789   3
APRIL 1789   7
MAY 1789   34
JUNE 1789   56
JULY 1789   77
AUGUST 1789   104
SEPTEMBER 1789   148
APPENDIX TO THE FIRST SESSION   208

JOURNAL OF THE SECOND SESSION
OF THE SENATE OF THE UNITED STATES

JANUARY 1790   213
FEBRUARY 1790   233
MARCH 1790   250
APRIL 1790   274
MAY 1790   299
JUNE 1790   331
JULY 1790   394
AUGUST 1790   460

JOURNAL OF THE THIRD SESSION
OF THE SENATE OF THE UNITED STATES

DECEMBER 1790   495
JANUARY 1791   520
FEBRUARY 1791   545
MARCH 1791   660
APPENDIX TO THE THIRD SESSION   709
SUPPLEMENT TO THE APPENDIX
  TO THE THIRD SESSION   717

SENATE BILLS   719
HOUSE BILLS   723
INDEX   741

v

INTRODUCTION

When the First Federal Congress convened in March 1789, it seemed unlikely that the experiment represented by the new Federal Constitution would succeed. The United States had a population of four million and its area was larger than any European state except Russia. There was no example in history and no support in traditional political theory to encourage those who would attempt to govern such a nation by a republican form of government based on the consent of the governed. Many Federalist supporters of the Constitution, as well as Antifederalist critics, doubted that the plan of government devised by the Philadelphia Convention would work in practice, unless changes were made—either formally by amendment or informally by interpretation—to bring the new Constitution closer to their sometimes-conflicting standards of perfection.

Yet the American experiment did succeed. For almost two centuries, this has astonished skeptics. "God," a familiar epigram observes, "looks after fools, drunkards, and the United States of America." Indeed, the success of the American form of government has been remarkable; not only has the U.S. Constitution operated to provide a greater degree of justice, prosperity, and liberty to its citizens than that realized by any nation in recorded history, but it has also shown such impressive stability that it is now the oldest written constitution in operation in any modern state.

How can we account for this success? Much credit belongs to the genius of the framers of the Constitution—their historical and intuitive knowledge of man and politics. Yet that is not the full explanation. Many nations have come to ruin under constitutions deliberately patterned on the American model. It was the way in which the American people implemented their Constitution that made a functioning system from the document's abstractions. Nothing was more essential to the enduring success of that system than the First Federal Congress, which held its first and second sessions in New York City from March 1789 to August 1790, and then held a final third session in Philadelphia from December 1790 to March 1791.

The Congress was the first of the institutions created by the Constitution to take solid form. It antedated the Presidency, for the Congress made the arrangements for counting the ballots of the first electoral college and for inaugurating George Washington and John Adams as the first executive officers. The first executive departments—War, State, and Treasury—and the office of Attorney General were set up by acts of the First Congress. The Congress antedated the judicial branch of the government as well, for Congressional legislation was needed to erect the system of federal courts and establish the Supreme Court, implementing the general provisions of the Constitution's third article. The Congress was also the first to act under the U.S. Constitution; thus, even when it dealt with routine and trivial matters, or followed practices established by the British Parliament, state legislatures, or the old Continental Congress, it was setting precedent.

The First Federal Congress convened in a time of national crisis. The first nation to win independence from a European colonial empire and a new nation less than a decade removed from its Revolution, the United States faced real dangers of falling into anarchy or despotism. In fact, the First Congress confronted in one form or another almost every problem that would rise to plague or threaten the Union of the States in the future: secession (two states, North Carolina and Rhode Island, were out of the Union when the First Congress convened), States' rights, constitutional amendment, admission of new states, threat of war, military preparedness, inflation, depression, unfavorable trade balance and tariff reform, taxation, speculation, sectionalism, slavery, Indian affairs, veterans' pensions, congressional salaries, election irregularities, government support of science, government patronage of the arts, administration of public lands, and many others. Some of the problems it solved; some it merely postponed. Yet, despite its difficulties, the Congress survived, leaving to the future a sturdy foundation on which a great nation could build.

The *Documentary History of the First Federal Congress* will provide a full record of the debates and actions of the First Congress. The nature of the record suggests a division into two parts, the first presenting the official papers of the Congress and the second comprising all unofficial material (letters to or from Congressmen, newspaper accounts, shorthand transcriptions of debates, diary entries, etc.) that may illuminate the proceedings. This documentary history presents special problems; because their focus is an institution rather than an individual, the documents lack the obvious unity that the life of a particular person would provide. It would be impractical, therefore, to impose a single set of editorial procedures on the diversity of materials handled in these volumes.

While editorial consistency will be maintained as far as possible, we do not wish to be consistent at the expense of clarity or convenience to the reader. An editorial note in the introduction of each volume will explain the practices peculiar to it. The editorial apparatus will be sparser in the official volumes than in the unofficial. We will attempt to place editorial aids—glossaries, biographies, maps, tables, and extended explanatory notes—in the volumes where they seem most useful. But, as far as possible, extensive aids and elaborate annotation will be excluded from the volumes of official records. Since the entire collection of documents serves, in fact, as a gloss on the official materials, any relaxation of a policy of sparse annotation in these volumes would swell them to an impractical bulk.

This volume, the Senate Legislative Journal, begins the series of official documents. These Senate records, which were the Secretary's charge from the earliest days of the office, include all documents produced by the order of the Senate or directed to the Senate. Other documents for which the Secretary of the Senate is today responsible were specified by rule 32 of the standing rules of the Senate. That rule as amended December 14, 1887, which probably reflects earlier practice, requires that "all papers referred to Senate committees and not reported on at the close of a session of Congress" would be returned to the Secretary. Note that this rule does not include documents produced by a Senate committee and that committee documents were often not deposited with the Secretary. Many of these, however, were returned to Senate files after the passage of the Congressional Reorganization Act of August 2, 1946. Section 140a of that act provided that "the Secretary of the Senate and the Clerk of the House of Representatives are authorized and directed, acting jointly, to obtain at the close of each Congress all of the noncurrent records of the Congress and of each committee." We shall therefore consider all of these documents, including those produced by committees, to be official records of the Senate, whether they are now found in the National Archives or in private repositories.

The original custodians of the official documents of the Senate were Samuel A. Otis, the Secretary of the Senate, and his staff: Benjamin Bankson, principal clerk, and Robert Heysham and Samuel A. Otis, Jr., engrossing clerks.[1] Mr. Otis would doubtless have been pleased to learn how well his files have survived the years. The Senate records have not always enjoyed the careful, even reverential, handling they enjoy today; yet despite some damage sustained with the passage of time, they are essentially intact.

The files of the Senate were moved several times. In 1790, when the First Congress adjourned from New York to Philadelphia for its third session, Mr. Otis moved his records. A second move occurred ten years later when the national capital was permanently established in Washington, D.C. An emergency evacuation of the Senate records from the Capitol was accomplished safely in 1814, although the House lost almost all its earliest records when the British burned the building.[2] As the years passed, storage of Senate records taxed the capacity of the Capitol; papers were crammed into out-of-the-way storage rooms and overflowed into the attic and basement of the Old State Department building. The pressure was relieved by Senate Resolution No. 99,

[1] Senate Journal, August 28, 1789; Office of the Financial Clerk of the Senate, RG 46, Records of the United States Senate, National Archives, Washington, D.C.; Accounts of Receipts and Expenditures of Public Monies by the Treaurer of the United States, RG 233, Records of the United States House of Representatives, National Archives, Washington, D.C.

[2] An account of the British burning of the Capitol may be found in the [Washington] *National Intelligencer*, September 6, 1814.

Seventy-fifth Congress, first session, which was adopted on March 29, 1937, and which authorized the transfer of official Senate files that were not currently needed to the National Archives where they are now housed.

The Senate Legislative Journal was the Secretary's special trust. The keeping of a journal is a duty imposed by the Constitution itself,[3] and preparation of this record was among the chief occupations of Otis and his staff. Otis began the work by keeping minutes—a rough journal—at every session of the Senate. Since the minutes for each day were recorded in his hand, it seems clear that he took this responsibility seriously and never missed a session. The rough journal was read in the Senate each day in accordance with Senate standing rule 1 "to the end that any mistake may be corrected that shall have been made in the entries,"[4] and Otis revised the notes and inked in directions for the clerks. The lads in the Senate office were then set to copying out the smooth journal in a fine round hand. Their completed manuscript would be signed by Otis and sent to the printer.

One day, late in the first session, before the printer had received the copy, an accident befell the smooth journal. The exact nature of the accident is unknown, but it involved large amounts of some kind of liquid. Whether it was damaged by a sudden rainstorm when it was being taken to Thomas Greenleaf's shop, or whether someone carelessly upset a teapot, or whether the roof of Otis's office leaked during the night, the entire manuscript became so sodden that every page was damaged and some parts became completely illegible. The journal, which had already been copied at least through the session of September 9, had to be completely redone.

The water-damaged manuscript was not discarded, but preserved in a bound volume entitled "Journal/Senate/U.S.A./Fol. 1/Preliminary/draft/Office of the/Secretary Senate/1789." It was clearly intended as a smooth journal and had no characteristics of a "rough journal" or "minutes book." There is no "preliminary journal" for the second or third sessions; such an accident was not apt to be repeated. The damage must have occurred before the copy was delivered to the printer because Greenleaf's printed version is unquestionably based on the second clean copy, now known as the "smooth journal," of the first session.

The Constitution ordered that the Senate Journal should be printed, and a joint resolution effective June 3, 1789 authorized Otis to make the necessary arrangements. The work was contracted to Thomas Greenleaf for the first session[5] and to John Fenno for the second. Fenno continued to serve as printer

---

[3] Article I, Section 5.

[4] Senate Journal, April 16, 1789.

[5] The printed documents of the first session are discussed in detail in James B. Childs, "The Story of the United States Senate Documents, 1st Congress, 1st Session, New York, 1789," *Papers of the Bibliographical Society of America* 56 (1962): 175–94.

to the Senate during the third session after the move to Philadelphia. Their printed journals have been taken as the basic text for this edition.[6] Technically, of course, the smooth manuscript journal, signed by Otis, is the official text. But the printed volumes, which were meant to be a true copy of the manuscript, were the texts actually used for reference in the office of the Secretary of the Senate[7] and in the offices of other federal and state officials. It is the printed version that Senators in the First Congress themselves had at hand when they cited the Journal.

The primary aim of the annotation in this volume is to establish an accurate text. Variations between the four forms of the journal—rough, preliminary, smooth, and printed—are noted. Particular care has been given to recording every variation from the official smooth journal and, for the first session, from the preliminary journal as well, since deviations from the copy signed by Otis, however slight, were introduced by the printer as a departure from the form authorized by the official order of the Senate. Therefore, while notation of obviously trivial matters (broken letters, insignificant typographical errors such as the omission of a single quotation mark at the end of a line, slight variations in type face or capitalization, and consistent misspellings) has been avoided, any actual alteration of even a single word or the order of phrasing has been noted.

The rough journal could not practically be handled in this manner, since variations in phrasing, vocabulary, and even the order of paragraphs appear on almost every page; noting each variation would double the size of this volume for no essential purpose. Variations from the rough journal are therefore noted only when the rough form includes some matter omitted from the printed text or when the variation changes the sense from that in the printed form.

Finally, the printed version was silently edited to correct obvious typographical errors, to delete archaic punctuation at the ends of display lines (such as titles, signatures, and lists of names) that does not affect the sense of the text, to adjust quotation marks for the sake of clarity, and to regularize spelling of proper names of Senators to conform to that used by the Senators themselves in contemporary signed documents. The appendix to the first session Journal, the proposed amendments to the Constitution as sent to the states, has been retained. But the appendix to the third session has not been

---

[6] *Journal of the First Session of the Senate of the United States of America* (New York: Thomas Greenleaf, 1789). E–22207. *Journal of the Second Session of the Senate of the United States of America* (New York: John Fenno, 1790). E–22982. *Journal of the Third Session of the Senate of the United States of America* (Philadelphia: John Fenno, 1791). E–23901.

[7] An extended discussion of the nature and functions of the Journal occurred on the floor of the Senate during the first session of the Twenty-fourth Congress in 1836. See *Register of Debates in Congress* (Washington: Gales and Seaton, 1836), pp. 877–933, 1593–98, 1884–97.

printed in its entirety. Originally it included a list of bills passed in that session, and indexes to the Journal. These have been omitted and replaced by our own more complete versions.

In addition to clarifying the text, notes have been provided to identify all official documents. Most of these documents were retained by the Secretary of the Senate or the Clerk of the House and are housed today in the National Archives. Occasionally a document mentioned in the Journal or a document whose existence can be implied from a reference in the Journal, could not be found in these official files. Where we have located the original or a copy in another repository it is noted. We have also noted copies that include annotations, such as amendments to a bill, which provide documentation not available in the official versions.

Documents are identified in a footnote at the first point they are mentioned in the Journal. All items have been connected to the journal text as far as possible. The "journalized date" for these items will be used as identification when official records are published in later volumes. Evans numbers[8] are included for readers who may wish to consult the documents on Readex microcards.

Documents mentioned in the Journal that have not been located are noted as missing, but a continuing search for these items is in progress and any that are found will be included in the appropriate volume.

Such items as simple resolves or House messages are not necessarily documentary in character. They may have been delivered orally, never having existed in a written form. These are not considered "missing" unless there is good reason to believe that they did exist in writing at one time.

A final form of annotation in this volume is journal cross-referencing. The reader who wishes to trace congressional action on any particular subject through the three congressional journals—Senate, Senate Executive, and House —may do so without consulting the index, by following the cross-reference notes. These notes trace the action on any subject through all three sessions and both Houses of Congress. They lead from date to date, not from action to action. Thus if the Senate read a bill one morning and later during the same day read it a second time, there will be no note leading from the first to the second reading. The reader should also be aware that the Senate frequently

---

[8] We use the term "Evans numbers" to apply to the numbers assigned to printed documents in any one of the three related bibliographies of early American imprints: Charles Evans, *American Bibliography*, vols. 7 and 8 (New York: Peter Smith, 1942); Clifford Shipton and James Mooney, *National Index of American Imprints through 1800, The Short-Title Evans* (Worcester: The American Antiquarian Society and Barre Publishers, 1969); Roger Bristol, *Supplement to Charles Evans' American Bibliography* (Charlottesville: University Press of Virginia, 1970). The Readex Microprint Corporation's edition of *Early American Imprints, 1639–1800*, edited by Clifford Shipton, is keyed to these numbers.

considered several bills on related topics, all of which must be followed separately, since the cross-reference notes do not lead from one bill to another on a related topic unless one of them is introduced as a substitute for another.

Far more than most scholarly undertakings, a large-scale documentary history is a cooperative product. It is produced by blending thousands of individual acts of judgment on all levels of significance by many different persons and by careful performance of clerical routine by everyone who has contact with the project's files. Every trivial error can flaw the final product. As editors, we of course, assume full responsibility for this volume's imperfections, but we wish to acknowledge our indebtedness to the many persons whose contributions to the project have, we trust, kept these to a minimum.

We thank our sponsors, The George Washington University and The National Historical Publications Commission, for the support that keeps our offices functioning.

We congratulate the present and former members of the First Federal Congress project staff for their patience and perseverance: Judith Hendren, Judith Freeman, John Rowland, William Weneta, Christine Waters, Frances Falt, John Wilson, Joanne Bodnar, Mary Sittig, Rona Rosenblatt, and Mary Barnes.

We salute The George Washington University First Federal Congress research fellows who have performed many of our office's most boring and essential tasks: Rosemary Fry, Gail Ross, Harold Williams, and especially Roger Davis and James Holmes who created the index for this volume.

We recognize our heavy debt to the editors and staff of the *Documentary History of the Ratification of the Constitution and the First Ten Amendments* and the *Documentary History of the First Federal Elections*, both now directed by Merrill Jensen. We particularly thank Gaspare Saladino for allowing us to share the benefits of their very efficient searching and splendidly organized files.

We also appreciate the labors of many workers in the National Archives, particularly the staff of the National Historical Publications Commission, who did much preliminary work on the Congress records before this project was organized. Our thanks particularly to Buford Rowland, George Perros, H. B. Fant, Marion Tinling, and James Masterson.

Finally, we are profoundly grateful for the support and advice of two men who stand outside categories: Leonard Rapport and Kenneth Bowling. We have shamelessly exploited Mr. Rapport's unmatched expertise on archival matters and his extraordinarily catholic knowledge of late eighteenth-century documents. Mr. Bowling has done much of the searching for this project and has shared his expert knowledge of First Congress documents and his scholarly insights into early federal politics.

SYMBOLS

CSmH	Henry E. Huntington Library, San Marino, California
DeHi	Historical Society of Delaware, Wilmington, Delaware
DLC	United States Library of Congress, Washington, D.C.
DNA	United States National Archives, Washington, D.C.
E	Evans number
HR	House of Representatives
InU	Indiana University, Lilly Library, Bloomington, Indiana
M-Ar	Archives Division, Secretary of State, Boston, Massachusetts
MHi	Massachusetts Historical Society, Boston, Massachusetts
NcD	Duke University, Durham, North Carolina
NHi	New York Historical Society, New York, New York
NN	New York Public Library, New York, New York
PHi	Historical Society of Pennsylvania, Philadelphia, Pennsylvania
RBkRm	Rare Book Room, Library of Congress, Washington, D.C.
RG	Record Group, located in the National Archives, Washington, D.C.

     11 United States Government Documents Having a General Legal Effect

     46 Records of the United States Senate

     59 General Records of the Department of State

    128 Records of the Joint Committees of Congress

    233 Records of the United States House of Representatives

    360 Records of the Continental Congress and the Constitutional Convention

RHi	Rhode Island Historical Society, Providence, Rhode Island
S	Senate
Vi-Ar	Virginia State Library, Archives Division, Richmond, Virginia
ViHi	Virginia Historical Society, Richmond, Virginia

ACT: (1) A bill that has been passed by one or both Houses of Congress. (2) A bill that has been passed by both Houses of Congress and signed by the President or passed over his veto.

AMENDMENT: (1) A proposal to alter a bill, act, amendment, or resolution after it has been formally introduced. Amendments vary in importance from slight word changes to major substantive alterations. To be adopted, an amendment must be agreed to by a majority of the Members voting. (2) A change in the Constitution. Such an amendment is usually proposed in the form of a joint resolution of Congress, which may originate in either House. If passed, it does not go to the President for his approval but is submitted directly to the states for ratification.

BILL: A proposal of specific legislation presented to Congress for enactment into law. Bills may originate in either House; two exceptions, however, are those for raising revenue, which, according to the Constitution, must originate in the House of Representatives, and those for appropriating money, which customarily originate in the House. Before becoming law, a bill must be passed by both Houses and approved by the President; if vetoed by the President, it must be passed over his veto by two-thirds of each House. Although there does not appear to be a rule prohibiting the introduction of bills by individual congressmen, in the Senate of the First Congress, bills were commonly introduced by committees appointed to bring in legislation on a subject.

Engrossed bill: The final copy of a bill that has passed the House of origin and is sent to the other House for further action. Such a bill bears the certification of the Clerk of the House of Representatives or of the Secretary of the Senate. The engrossed copy of a bill that has passed both Houses, together with its engrossed amendments, is the official working copy from which an enrolled bill is prepared.

Enrolled bill: The final copy of an engrossed bill that has passed both Houses and that embodies all amendments. Such a bill is on parchment and is signed by the Speaker of the House and by the President of the Senate. It bears the attestation of an officer of the House of origin, that is, the Clerk of the House of Representatives or the Secretary of the Senate. This final copy is then presented to the President for approval or disapproval. No bills of the First Congress were vetoed by Washington.

CLASSIFICATION: Designates the term of office of a Senator. Senators from each state drew lots to determine the length of their first term in Congress.

CLERK OF THE HOUSE: The chief administrative officer of the House of Representatives, elected by a ballot of its Members. John Beckley held this position during the First Congress.

COMMITTEE: A body of Members, limited in number, that is selected according to rules or by resolution of each respective House to consider some matter of business and to report thereon for further action. With few exceptions, committees of the First Congress were ad hoc; when their purpose had been accomplished, they ceased to exist.

Committee of the whole: The entire House acting as a committee to facilitate the work of the House.

Conference committee: A committee whose Members are designated by order or resolve and whose purpose is to consider the points of conflict between the two Houses on a specific bill or joint resolution in an attempt to reach an agreement. The Members are referred to as "managers." Bills and resolutions that are passed by the House and the Senate with slightly different provisions need not be sent to conference; either body may agree to the other's amendments. Few bills of the First Congress went to conference.

Joint committee: A committee consisting of Members of both Houses and having jurisdiction over matters of common interest. Most of the joint committees of the First Congress were ad hoc; when their purpose had been accomplished, they ceased to exist.

Joint (standing) committee for enrolled bills: A committee composed of two Members of the House of Representatives and one Member of the Senate and charged with examining enrolled bills to assure their accuracy, with reporting thereon to both Houses, with presenting the truly enrolled bill to the President, and with notifying both Houses of such presentation. The committee dates from July 31, 1789.

CONGRESS: (1) The national legislature as a whole, including both the House and the Senate. (2) The united body of Senators and Representatives for any term of two years for which the whole body is chosen. A Congress lasts for a period of two years and is divided into sessions.

CREDENTIALS OF SENATORS: Certificates of election of Senators. Properly executed certificates are prima facie evidence of the lawful election of Members that entitles them to their respective seats. Article I, Section 5 of the Constitution states that "each House shall be the Judge of the Elections, Returns and Qualifications of its own Members."

JOURNAL: The official record of the proceedings of the Senate. Article I, Section 5 of the Constitution provides that "each House shall keep a Journal of its Proceedings, and from time to time publish the same, excepting such Parts as may in their Judgment require Secrecy. . . ." The Journal does not report speeches and debates.

LIE FOR CONSIDERATION: Action of postponing the consideration of a subject to a later date. In the case of petitions and memorials, such action often resulted in the adverse disposition of the document.

MEMORIAL: A document in the form of a petition, but differing from a petition insofar as it usually opposes a contemplated or proposed action and carries no prayer (plea). Some petitions, especially those from state legislatures, are termed "memorials."

MOTION: A proposal made to Congress for its approval or disapproval.

ORDER: A directive of the Senate.

PASSED IN THE AFFIRMATIVE: Agreed to.

PASSED IN THE NEGATIVE: Disagreed to.

PETITION: A written request for action addressed to either House of Congress and containing a prayer that the action be taken. *See also* Memorial.

PRESIDENT PRO TEMPORE: The presiding officer of the Senate when the Vice President is absent. John Langdon held this position during the First Congress.

PREVIOUS QUESTION: The principle of previous question was inherited from the Parliament of England where it was used as a device for removing a question from consideration.

An amended rule adopted by the Continental Congress in 1784 stated: "The previous question (which is always to be understood in this sense, that the main question be *not* now put) shall only be admitted when in the judgement of two Members, at least, the subject moved is in its nature, or from the circumstances of time or place, improper to be debated or decided, and shall therefore preclude all amendments and further debates on the subject until it is decided." (See Continental Congress Journal, July 8, 1784.) The Senate retained this form of the previous question except that it omitted the word *not* and thus reversed the formula. Rule 9 reads: "The previous question being moved and seconded, the question from the Chair shall be—'Shall the main question be now put?' And if the nays prevail, the main question shall not then be put."

In the Senate previous question was employed to stop debate on a certain line of discussion but not necessarily on the entire bill. It was used infrequently and inconsistently.

QUORUM: A majority of the membership of the House. Article I, Section 5 of the Constitution provides that ". . . a Majority of each [House] shall constitute a Quorum to do Business. . . ."

READING OF BILLS: The Senate followed the traditional parliamentary practice that all bills must be read three times before passage. In the rules of the Senate for the First Congress, adopted on April 16, 1789, it was specified that "every bill shall receive three readings previous to its being passed; and the President shall give notice at each, whether it be the first, second or third; which readings shall be on three different days, unless the Senate unanimously direct otherwise."

RECOMMIT: To return business to a committee that has already considered it.

REFER-TO: Assignment of a bill, communication, or other document to a committee for consideration. The Senate Journal indicates the committee to which any bill or document was referred.

RESOLUTION: Although not formally designated as such, resolutions of the First Congress fell into three categories: (1) concurrent, (2) joint, and (3) simple.

Concurrent resolution: A resolution that indicates joint action and requires the concurrence of both Houses. It contains no legislation, its authority does not extend beyond Congress, and it does not require Presidential approval. For example, in the First Congress, this type of resolution was used (1) to establish certain joint rules between the two Houses, (2) to furnish Members with copies of the Journals of the Continental Congress, and (3) for the appointment of chaplains, etc.

Joint resolution: A form of proposed legislation similar to a bill but usually serving a limited purpose or being temporary in effect. A joint resolution (except a joint resolution proposing an amendment to the Constitution) requires the signature of the President or passage over his veto before it becomes law. For example, in the First Congress joint resolutions were used to direct the Secretary of State to procure the statutes of the several states and to complete a survey ordered by the Continental Congress. For the most part, joint resolutions did not embrace comprehensive laws.

Simple resolution: A resolve whose authority extends only to the House in which it originates. It does not contain legislation and does not require concurrence of the other House, or Presidential approval. In the First Congress, such resolutions were used to express the sentiments of the Senate, to establish rules of procedure, to secure information from executive departments, etc.

SECRETARY OF THE SENATE: The chief administrative officer of the Senate, elected by a ballot of its Members. Samuel Otis held this position during the First Congress.

SESSION: A meeting of the Congress that continues from day to day until adjournment to a specified day. The Constitution provides that "the Congress shall assemble at least once in every Year...." The First Congress had three sessions: March 4, 1789–September 29, 1789; January 4, 1790–August 12, 1790; and December 6, 1790–March 3, 1791.

SPEAKER: The presiding officer of the House of Representatives, elected by a ballot of its Members. During the First Congress, this position was held by Frederick Augustus Muhlenberg.

TABLE: In the First Congress, the Senate followed general parliamentary law and used the motion "to lay on the table" as a means to put aside a matter temporarily; the issue could later be considered at any time, if the Senate desired.

YEAS AND NAYS (AYES AND NOES): The record of the vote on a matter by the Members of the House or Senate. Article I, Section 5 of the Constitution provides that ". . . the Yeas and Nays of the Members of either House on any question shall, at the Desire of one-fifth of those Present, be entered on the Journal."

Bassett, Richard	Delaware
Butler, Pierce	South Carolina
Carroll, Charles	Maryland
Dalton, Tristram	Massachusetts
Dickinson, Philemon	New Jersey

(Took his seat on December 6, 1790, after being elected to
fill the vacancy caused by the resignation of
William Paterson.)

Ellsworth, Oliver	Connecticut
Elmer, Jonathan	New Jersey
Few, William	Georgia
Foster, Theodore	Rhode Island
Grayson, William	Virginia

(Died March 12, 1790.)

Gunn, James	Georgia
Hawkins, Benjamin	North Carolina
Henry, John	Maryland
Izard, Ralph	South Carolina
Johnson, William Samuel	Connecticut
Johnston, Samuel	North Carolina
King, Rufus	New York
Langdon, John	New Hampshire
Lee, Richard Henry	Virginia
Maclay, William	Pennsylvania
Monroe, James	Virginia

(Took his seat on December 6, 1790, after being elected to
fill the vacancy caused by the death of
William Grayson.)

Morris, Robert	Pennsylvania
Paterson, William	New Jersey

(Resigned on November 13, 1790, after being elected
Governor of New Jersey.)

Read, George	Delaware
Schuyler, Philip	New York
Stanton, Joseph, Jr.	Rhode Island

Strong, Caleb   Massachusetts

Walker, John   Virginia
   (Appointed to fill the vacancy caused by the death of
   William Grayson. Served from March 31 through
   November 9, 1790.)

Wingate, Paine   New Hampshire

FIRST SESSION
March 4, 1789–September 29, 1789
New York City

SECOND SESSION
January 4, 1790–August 12, 1790
New York City

THIRD SESSION
December 6, 1790–March 3, 1791
Philadelphia

JOURNAL

OF THE FIRST SESSION OF THE

SENATE OF THE UNITED STATES

V I Z.

NEW-HAMPSHIRE	NEW-JERSEY	VIRGINIA
MASSACHUSETTS	PENNSYLVANIA	SOUTH-CAROLINA
CONNECTICUT	DELAWARE	AND
NEW-YORK	MARYLAND	GEORGIA

Being the ELEVEN STATES that have respectively ratified the Constitution of Government for the UNITED STATES, proposed by the CONVENTION, held at Philadelphia, on the 17th September, 1787.

WEDNESDAY, MARCH 4, 1789

THE following members of Senate appeared and took their seats:—From

New-Hampshire	The Honorable	{ John Langdon and Paine Wingate
Massachusetts	The Honorable	Caleb Strong
Connecticut	The Honorable	{ William S. Johnson and Oliver Ellsworth
Pennsylvania	The Honorable	{ William Maclay and Robert Morris
Georgia	The Honorable	William Few

The number not being sufficient to constitute a quorum, they adjourned from day to day, until[1]

WEDNESDAY, MARCH 11, 1789

The same members present as on the 4th; Agreed that the following circular letter should be written to the absent members, requesting their immediate attendance.[2]

---

[1] In the preliminary journal the entry for this date is as follows: "By authenticated Returns it appears that, the following Senators were appointed, in the Time and Manner, prescribed by the Legislatures of those States to which they respectively belong, to serve in the Congress of the United States, as the Constitution provides—and accordingly assembled

    From New Hampshire ....John Langdon } Esqrs.
                              Paine Wingate }

    From Massachusetts ....Caleb Strong, Esqr.

                                William Samuel Johnson } Esqrs.
    From Connecticut ....Oliver Ellsworth }

                              William Maclay }
    From Pensylvania ....   } Esqrs.
                              Robert Morris }

    From Georgia ....William Few, Esqr.

But the number not being sufficient to constitute [*illegible*] adjourned from day to day until."

[2] The official form letter is in the Office of the Financial Clerk of the Senate: Quorums, Letters relating thereto, RG 46, Records of the United States Senate, DNA. (Hereinafter, RG 46 will be referred to as Senate Records, DNA.)

The original of a letter dated March 11, 1789 and signed by the eight Senators present was sent to George Read and is in the Read Manuscript Collections, PHi. Presumably, similar letters were sent to the absent Senators whose names follow: Richard Bassett, Pierce Butler, Charles Carroll, Tristram Dalton, Jonathan Elmer, William Grayson, James Gunn, John Henry, Ralph Izard, Richard Henry Lee, and William Paterson.

New-York, March 11, 1789

SIR,

AGREEABLY to the Constitution of the United States, eight members of the Senate, and eighteen of the House of Representatives, have attended here since the 4th of March. It being of the utmost importance that a quorum sufficient to proceed to business be assembled as soon as possible, it is the opinion of the gentlemen of both Houses, that information of their situation be immediately communicated to the absent members.

We apprehend that no arguments are necessary to evince to you the indispensable necessity of putting the Government into immediate operation; and therefore earnestly request, that you will be so obliging as to attend as soon as possible.

We have the honor to be, Sir,

Your obedient humble servants,

JOHN LANGDON
PAINE WINGATE
CALEB STRONG
WILLIAM S. JOHNSON
OLIVER ELLSWORTH
ROBERT MORRIS
WILLLIAM MACLAY
WILLIAM FEW

TO THE HON. TRISTRAM DALTON
WILLIAM PATERSON
JONATHAN ELMER
GEORGE READ
RICHARD BASSETT
CHARLES CARROLL
JOHN HENRY
RICHARD HENRY LEE
WILLIAM GRAYSON
RALPH IZARD
PIERCE BUTLER
JAMES GUNN

Adjourned to 11 o'clock to-morrow morning.

THURSDAY, MARCH 12, 1789

Present as yesterday.

The number sufficient to make a quorum not appearing, they adjourned from day to day, until

WEDNESDAY, MARCH 18, 1789

Present, the same as on the 12th.

Agreed that the following circular letter should be written to eight of the absent members, urging their immediate attendance.[3]

New-York, March 18, 1789

SIR,

WE addressed a letter to you the 11th instant, since which no Senator has arrived. The House of Representatives will probably be formed in two or three days. Your presence is indispensably necessary. We therefore again earnestly request your immediate attendance, and are confident you will not suffer our, and the public anxious expectations to be disappointed.

We have the honor to be, Sir,

Your obedient humble servants,

JOHN LANGDON
PAINE WINGATE
CALEB STRONG
WILLIAM S. JOHNSON
OLIVER ELLSWORTH
ROBERT MORRIS
WILLIAM MACLAY
WILLIAM FEW

To the Hon.   JONATHAN ELMER
WILLIAM PATERSON
GEORGE READ
RICHARD BASSETT
CHARLES CARROLL
JOHN HENRY
RICHARD HENRY LEE
WILLIAM GRAYSON

Adjourned to 11 o'clock to-morrow morning.

THURSDAY, MARCH 19, 1789

Present as yesterday;

The Honorable William Paterson, from the State of New-Jersey, appeared and took his seat.

Adjourned to 11 o'clock to-morrow morning.

---

[3] The official form letter is in the Office of the Financial Clerk of the Senate: Quorums, Letters relating thereto, Senate Records, DNA. The original of the circular letter to George Read is in the George Read Papers, folder 3, DeHi. Presumably, seven others were sent but have not been located.

FRIDAY, March 20, 1789

Present as yesterday;
Adjourned to 11 o'clock to-morrow morning.

SATURDAY, March 21, 1789

Present as yesterday;
The Honorable Richard Bassett, from the State of Delaware, appeared and took his seat.

The number sufficient to constitute a quorum not appearing—adjourned from day to day, until

SATURDAY, March 28, 1789

Present as on the 21st.
The Honorable Jonathan Elmer, from the State of New-Jersey, appeared and took his seat.

The number sufficient to constitute a quorum not appearing, adjourned from day to day, until April the 6th; when the Honorable Richard Henry Lee, from the State of Virginia, appeared and took his seat in the Senate.[4]

---

[4] In the preliminary journal the entry for this date is as follows: "Present as on the 21st/With the addition of Jonathan Elmer, Esqr. from the State of New Jersey, who produced his Credentials and took his Seat in the Senate—/But not being a number sufficient to constitute a Quorum, they adjourned from day to day, until the 6 of April—When, Richard Henry Lee, Esqr. from the State of Virginia, produced his Credentials, and took his Seat in the Senate—"

M O N D A Y, April 6, 1789

The Senate assembled.

Present

From New-Hampshire	{ Mr. Langdon and { Mr. Wingate
Massachusetts	Mr. Strong
Connecticut	{ Mr. Johnson and { Mr. Ellsworth
New-Jersey	{ Mr. Paterson and { Mr. Elmer
Pennsylvania	{ Mr. Maclay and { Mr. Morris
Delaware	Mr. Bassett
Virginia	Mr. Lee
Georgia	Mr. Few

Being a Quorum, consisting of a majority of the whole number of Senators of the United States.

The credentials of the afore-mentioned members were read,[1] and ordered to be filed.

The Senate proceeded by ballot to the choice of a President, for the sole purpose of opening and counting the votes for President of the United States.

John Langdon, Esquire, was elected.

Ordered, That Mr. Ellsworth inform the House of Representatives that a quorum of the Senate is formed; that a President is elected for the sole purpose of opening the certificates and counting the votes of the Electors of the several States in the choice of a President and Vice President of the United States; and that the Senate is now ready in the Senate Chamber, to proceed, in the presence of the House, to discharge that duty: And that the Senate have appointed one of their members to sit at the Clerk's table to make a list of the votes as they shall be declared; submitting it to the wisdom of the House to appoint one or more of their members for the like purpose—Who reported, that he had delivered the message.

Mr. Boudinot, from the House of Representatives, communicated the following verbal message to the Senate:—

"Mr. President,

"I am directed by the House of Representatives to inform the Senate, that

---

[1] The credentials of John Langdon, Paine Wingate, Caleb Strong, Samuel Johnson, Oliver Ellsworth, William Paterson, Jonathan Elmer, William Maclay, Robert Morris, Richard Bassett, Richard Henry Lee, and William Few are in Election Records: Credentials of Senators, Senate Records, DNA.

the House is ready forthwith to meet the Senate, to attend the opening and counting the votes of the Electors for President and Vice President of the United States."—And he withdrew.

ORDERED, That Mr. Paterson be a teller on the part of the Senate.

The Speaker and the House of Representatives attended in the Senate Chamber, for the purpose expressed in the message delivered by Mr. Ellsworth— And after some time withdrew.

The Senate then proceeded by ballot to the choice of a President of their body PRO TEMPORE.

JOHN LANGDON, Esq. was duly elected.

The President elected for the purpose of counting the votes, declared to the Senate, that the Senate and House of Representatives had met, and that he, in their presence, had opened and counted the votes of the Electors for President and Vice President of the United States—which were as follow:—

	George Washington, Esq.	John Adams, Esq.	Samuel Huntington, Esq.	John Jay, Esq.	John Hancock, Esq.	Robert H. Harrison, Esq.	George Clinton, Esq.	John Rutledge, Esq.	John Milton, Esq.	James Armstrong, Esq.	Edward Telfair, Esq.	Benjamin Lincoln, Esq.
New-Hampshire	5	5	—	—	—	—	—	—	—	—	—	—
Massachusetts	10	10	—	—	—	—	—	—	—	—	—	—
Connecticut	7	5	2	—	—	—	—	—	—	—	—	—
New-Jersey	6	1	—	5	—	—	—	—	—	—	—	—
Pennsylvania	10	8	—	—	2	—	—	—	—	—	—	—
Delaware	3	—	—	3	—	—	—	—	—	—	—	—
Maryland	6	—	—	—	—	6	—	—	—	—	—	—
Virginia	10	5	—	1	1	—	3	—	—	—	—	—
South-Carolina	7	—	—	—	1	—	—	6	—	—	—	—
Georgia	5	—	—	—	—	—	—	—	—	2	1	1	1
	69	34	2	9	4	6	3	6	2	1	1	1[2]

Whereby it appears, that
GEORGE WASHINGTON, ESQ.
Was unanimously elected PRESIDENT,—And
JOHN ADAMS, ESQ.
Was duly elected VICE PRESIDENT,
OF THE UNITED STATES OF AMERICA.

---

[2] The votes are in Election Records: Electoral votes, Senate Records, DNA.

Mr. Madison came from the House of Representatives with the following verbal message:—

MR. PRESIDENT,

"I AM directed by the House of Representatives to inform the Senate, that the House have agreed, that the notifications of the election of the President and of the Vice President of the United States, should be made by such persons, and in such manner, as the Senate shall be pleased to direct."[3]—And he withdrew.

Whereupon the Senate appointed Charles Thomson, Esq. to notify George Washington, Esq. of his election to the Office of President of the United States of America, and Mr. Sylvanus Bourn to notify John Adams, Esq. of his election to the Office of Vice President of the said United States.

The instructions to the Messengers are in the following words.

In SENATE, April 6, 1789

SIR,

THE Senate of the United States have appointed you to wait upon General Washington, with a certificate of his being elected to the Office of President of the United States of America. You will therefore prepare to set out as soon as possible, and apply to the Board of Treasury for such sums as you may judge necessary for the expenses of the journey.

JOHN LANGDON, President pro tem.

To CHARLES THOMSON, Esq.

In SENATE, April 6, 1789

SIR,

THE Senate of the United States have appointed you to wait on John Adams, Esq. with a certificate of his being elected to the Office of Vice President of the United States. You are therefore to set out with the dispatches herewith sent you as soon as possible, and to apply to the Treasury Board for one hundred dollars towards defraying the expenses of your journey.

JOHN LANGDON, President pro tem.

To Mr. SYLVANUS BOURN[4]

ORDERED, That Mr. Paterson, Mr. Johnson, Mr. Lee, and Mr. Ellsworth be a committee to prepare the certificates of the election of the President and of the Vice President of the United States; and to prepare letters to George Washington, Esq. and to John Adams, Esq. to accompany the said certificates respectively.

---

[3] This message, a Journal extract, is in Papers Pertaining to the Notification of the President and Vice President of Their Election, Senate Records, DNA.

[4] A copy of these instructions is in Papers Pertaining to the Notification of the President and Vice President of Their Election, Senate Records, DNA. A memorial from Charles Stoner asking to be selected to notify John Adams is in Petitions and Memorials: Applications for jobs, Senate Records, DNA.

The certificates and letters are as follow:—

BE IT KNOWN, That the Senate and House of Representatives of the United States of America, being convened in the City and State of New-York, the sixth day of April, in the year of our Lord, one thousand seven hundred and eighty-nine, the under-written, appointed President of the Senate, for the sole purpose of receiving, opening, and counting the votes of the Electors, did, in the presence of the said Senate and House of Representatives, open all the certificates, and count all the votes of the Electors for a President and for a Vice President; by which it appears, that GEORGE WASHINGTON, Esq. was unanimously elected, agreeably to the Constitution, to the Office of President of the United States of America.

In testimony whereof, I have hereunto set my hand and seal.

JOHN LANGDON

New-York, April 6, 1789

SIR,

I HAVE the honor to transmit to your Excellency the information of your unanimous election to the Office of President of the United States of America. Suffer me, Sir, to indulge the hope, that so auspicious a mark of public confidence will meet your approbation, and be considered as a sure pledge of the affection and support you are to expect from a free and an enlightened people.

I am, Sir, with sentiments of respect,
Your obedient, humble servant,
JOHN LANGDON

To his Excellency GEORGE WASHINGTON, Esq.

BE IT KNOWN, That the Senate and House of Representatives of the United States of America, being convened in the City and State of New-York, the sixth day of April, in the year of our Lord, one thousand seven hundred and eighty-nine, the under-written, appointed President of the Senate, for the sole purpose of receiving, opening, and counting the votes of the Electors, did, in the presence of the said Senate and House of Representatives, open all the certificates, and count all the votes of the Electors for a President and for a Vice President; by which it appears, that JOHN ADAMS, Esq. was duly elected, agreeably to the Constitution, to the Office of Vice President of the United States of America.

In testimony whereof, I have hereunto set my hand and seal.

JOHN LANGDON

New-York, April 6, 1789

SIR,

I HAVE the honor to transmit to you the information of your being elected to the Office of Vice President of the United States of America. Permit me, Sir, to hope, that you will soon safely arrive here, to take upon you the discharge of the important duties, to which you are so honorably called by the voice of your Country.

I am, Sir, with sentiments of respect,
Your obedient, humble servant,
JOHN LANGDON

TO JOHN ADAMS, Esq.[5]

A letter from James Duane, Esq. was read,[6] enclosing resolutions of the Mayor, Aldermen, and Commonalty of the City of New-York, tendering to Congress the use of the City-Hall.[7]

The Senate adjourned to 11 o'clock, to-morrow morning.

TUESDAY, APRIL 7, 1789

The SENATE assembled,
Present as yesterday.

The Senate proceeded to elect a Door-Keeper, and James Mathers was chosen.[8]

ORDERED, That Mr. Ellsworth, Mr. Paterson, Mr. Maclay, Mr. Strong, Mr. Lee, Mr. Basset, Mr. Few, and Mr. Wingate be a Committee, to bring in a bill for organizing the JUDICIARY of the United States.[9]

---

[5] Copies of the letters to Washington and Adams are in Papers Pertaining to the Notification of the President and Vice President of Their Election, Senate Records, DNA. The original letter to Washington is in the George Washington Papers, series 4, reel 98, Manuscript Division, DLC. The original of the letter to Adams and his certificate of election is in the Loose Papers of the Adams Family Papers, reel 372, Manuscript Division, DLC. The original certificate for Washington has not been located. On April 25 Charles Thomson reported that the letter to the President had been delivered.

[6] This letter is in Reports and Communications, Senate Records, DNA.

[7] On April 13 a committee was appointed to consider these communications.

[8] The petition of James Mathers and his letter of thanks for his appointment as Door-Keeper, along with petitions from David Eliot and Thomas Claxton (which included an endorsement by Alexander Hamilton), are in Petitions and Memorials: Applications for jobs, Senate Records, DNA. A memorandum from the Secretary of the Treasury to Samuel Otis asking for extracts from the Journal and designating the appointments of Door-Keeper and assistants is in Records of the Secretary: Letters concerning fiscal policy, Senate Records, DNA. A letter from the office of the Door-Keeper written after the first session had adjourned is in Records of the Secretary: Letters concerning accommodations, Senate Records, DNA.

[9] On April 13 additional members were appointed to this committee.

ORDERED, That Mr. Ellsworth, Mr. Lee, Mr. Strong, Mr. Maclay, and Mr. Bassett be a Committee to prepare a system of rules to govern the two Houses in cases of conference, and to take under consideration the manner of electing Chaplains, and to confer thereupon with a Committee of the House of Representatives.

ORDERED, That the same Committee prepare a system of rules for conducting business in the Senate.[10]

The Senate adjourned to 11 o'clock to-morrow.

WEDNESDAY, APRIL 8, 1789

The SENATE assembled,
Present as yesterday.

The Senate proceeded by ballot to the choice of a SECRETARY. SAMUEL ALLYNE OTIS, Esq. was elected.

The respective petitions of Abraham Okee, Cornelius Maxwell, and Abraham Mitchell, praying to be employed as attendants on the Senate, were read,[11] and ordered to lie on the table.

The Senate proceeded to elect a Messenger, and Cornelius Maxwell was appointed.[12]

The Senate adjourned to 11 o'clock to-morrow.

THURSDAY, APRIL 9, 1789

The SENATE assembled,
Present as yesterday.

The memorial of John Bryce was read,[13] praying to be employed as Bookbinder, &c. to the Senate and House of Representatives.

ORDERED, That Mr. Langdon, Mr. Johnson, and Mr. Few be a Committee to make the necessary arrangements for receiving the President; and that they be empowered to confer with any Committee of the House of Representatives that may be appointed for that purpose.[14]

The Senate adjourned until Saturday next, at 11 o'clock, A.M.

---

[10] On April 13 this committee reported on rules for the Senate. On April 15 it reported on conference committee rules and the election of chaplains.

[11] These petitions are in Petitions and Memorials: Applications for jobs, Senate Records, DNA.

[12] The smooth journal inserts the following at this point: "Ordered, That the chains at each end of the federal building be extended across the Street, from the commencement of the Session in the morning, until the adjournment of the Senate, to prevent disturbance by Carriages."

[13] This petition is in Petitions and Memorials: Applications for jobs, Senate Records, DNA.

[14] On April 13 the instructions of this committee were enlarged to include consideration of the Vice President's reception.

SATURDAY, April 11, 1789

The SENATE assembled;

Present

From New-Hampshire	Mr. Langdon and Mr. Wingate
Massachusetts	Mr. Strong
Connecticut	Mr. Johnson and Mr. Ellsworth
New-Jersey	Mr. Paterson and Mr. Elmer
Pennsylvania	Mr. Maclay
Delaware	Mr. Bassett
Virginia	Mr. Lee
Georgia	Mr. Few

The Senate adjourned until Monday next, at 11 o'clock.

MONDAY, April 13, 1789

The SENATE assembled;

Present, as on Saturday,

Except Mr. Paterson, who had leave of absence;[15]—And

The Honorable Ralph Izard, from the State of South-Carolina, the Honorable Charles Carroll, from the State of Maryland, and the Honorable George Read, from the State of Delaware, severally produced their credentials,[16] and took their seats in the Senate.

The report of the Committee appointed the 7th instant, upon a system of rules for conducting business in the Senate, was read,[17] and ordered to lie until to-morrow for consideration.[18]

On motion, ORDERED,[19] That a Committee of three, on the part of the Senate, be appointed to confer with any Committee, on the part of the House of Representatives, instructed to that purpose, upon the future disposition of the papers in the office of the late Secretary of Congress, and report; and that

---

[15] In the preliminary journal, this entry, in the hand of Samuel Otis, begins: "The Senate met agreeably to adjournment—/———Present,———." Then follows a tabulated list of members present and the marginal note, "Say Present as on Saturday Except Mr. Paterson had leave of absence. 11th."

[16] These credentials are in Election Records: Credentials of Senators, Senate Records, DNA.

[17] This report is in Various Select Committee Reports, Senate Records, DNA.

[18] On April 14 this report was read again and ordered to lie for consideration.

[19] The preliminary journal reads: "On motion by Mr. Johnson, 2d by Mr. Maclay Ordered."

Mr. Johnson, Mr. Izard, and Mr. Maclay be the Committee on the part of the Senate.[20]

On motion, ORDERED,[21] That the Committee appointed the 9th instant, to determine the ceremonial proper to be observed on the reception of the President, be empowered to consider what arrangements are necessary for the reception of the Vice President, and to confer with any Committee the House may instruct to that purpose.[22]

On motion, ORDERED,[23] That Mr. Lee, Mr. Ellsworth, and Mr. Few be a Committee to consider and report upon the communications made on the 6th instant, from the Mayor, &c. of the city of New-York, tendering to Congress the use of the City-Hall.[24]

On motion, ORDERED,[25] That an addition of one from each State not having a member already on the Committee, be added to the Committee of the 7th of April, to bring in a bill for organizing the Judiciary of the United States; and Mr. Carroll, and Mr. Izard were joined.[26]

The Senate adjourned to 11 o'clock to-morrow morning.

TUESDAY, APRIL 14, 1789

The SENATE assembled;

Present

From New-Hampshire	Mr. Langdon and Mr. Wingate
Massachusetts	Mr. Strong
Connecticut	Mr. Johnson and Mr. Ellsworth
New-Jersey	Mr. Elmer
Delaware	Mr. Read and Mr. Bassett

---

[20] A copy of this order, varying considerably from the wording in the Journal, is in RG 128 (which is included in Senate Records for the First Congress), Records of the Joint Committees of Congress (hereinafter referred to as Joint Committee Reports), Senate Records, DNA. On April 29 the Senate was notified that the House had appointed a committee to confer with this committee.

[21] The preliminary journal reads: "On motion by Mr. Maclay, 2d by Mr. Few, Ordered."

[22] On April 15 the report of this committee was printed in the Journal and accepted.

[23] The preliminary journal reads: "On motion by Mr. Few, seconded by Mr. Johnson, Ordered."

[24] On April 14 this committee reported and recommended a letter to be written to the Mayor of New York City.

[25] The preliminary journal reads: "On motion by Mr. Ellsworth, seconded by Mr. Johnson, Ordered."

[26] On June 12 this committee reported a bill to establish the Judicial Courts.

Maryland	Mr. Carroll
South-Carolina	Mr. Izard
Georgia	Mr. Few

The Honorable Tristram Dalton, from the State of Massachusetts, appeared, produced his credentials,[27] and took his seat in the Senate.

On the report of the Committee appointed the 13th instant, to take into consideration the letter and communications from the Mayor of the City of New-York,

ORDERED, That the following letter be written to the Mayor of the City of New-York by the President; and that nothing further for the present be done in the business.

New-York, April 14, 1789

SIR,

THE Senate have considered the letter that you were pleased to address to their House on the 6th instant; and they entertain a proper sense of the respect shewn to the General Government of the United States, by providing so commodious a building for the accommodation of Congress, as the Mayor, Aldermen, and Commonalty of the city have appropriated to that use. The appointment of Mr. Skaats to the care of the public Hall would be very agreeable to the Senate; but in their idea such appointment must depend upon a legislative act for creating the office, and then the officer to fill it will come constitutionally from the nomination of the President of the United States, with the approbation of Senate. In the mean time the Senate have no objection to the Mayor and Aldermen appointing such person to the care of the Hall as they deem worthy of such trust.

I have the honor to be, &c.
Signed by
The PRESIDENT of the SENATE

The Hon. JAMES DUANE, Esq.[28]

The rules and orders as reported by the Committee were again read, and ordered to lie for consideration.[29]

On motion, a Committee, consisting of Mr. Read, Mr. Ellsworth, and Mr. Lee, were appointed to consider of the utility of printing the Journals weekly, and furnishing the members with copies; and the same Committee are in-

---

[27] The credentials are in Election Records: Credentials of Senators, Senate Records, DNA.

[28] This report, in the form of a letter, is in Various Select Committee Reports, Senate Records, DNA. On May 9 a committee on the use of City Hall was appointed.

[29] On April 15 this report was considered again.

structed to determine the mode of keeping the Journals, and report.[30]

The Senate adjourned to 11 o'clock to-morrow.

WEDNESDAY, APRIL 15, 1789

The SENATE assembled,

Present as yesterday:

Also, Mr. Dalton and Mr. Paterson.

The Committee appointed the 7th of April, to prepare a system of rules to govern the two Houses in cases of conference, to take into consideration the manner of electing Chaplains, and to confer thereon with a Committee of the House of Representatives, REPORTED,[31] That they had conferred on the business with a Committee of the House of Representatives for that purpose appointed. Whereupon,

RESOLVED, That in every case of an amendment to a bill agreed to in one House and dissented to in the other, if either House shall request a conference, and appoint a Committee for that purpose, and the other House shall also appoint a committee to confer, such Committees shall, at a convenient time to be agreed on by their Chairman, meet in the conference Chamber and state to each other, verbally or in writing, as either shall choose, the reasons of their respective Houses, for and against the amendment, and confer freely thereon.

The Committee above mentioned further reported,

"That two Chaplains of different denominations be appointed to Congress, for the present session, the Senate to appoint one, and give notice thereof to the House of Representatives, who shall thereupon appoint the other, which Chaplains shall commence their services in the Houses that appoint them, but shall interchange weekly."

Which was also accepted.[32]

The Committee to whom it was referred to consider of and report respecting the ceremonial of receiving the President, and the arrangements necessary

---

[30] The preliminary journal gives the following text of this paragraph and a second paragraph canceled by the marginal notation "Comte. discharged":

On motion, *by Mr. Lee, seconded by Mr. Izard,* a Committee, consisting of Mr. Read, Mr. Ellsworth, & Mr. Lee, were appointed to consider of the utility of printing the Journals weekly, & furnishing the members with Copies, And the same Committee are instructed to determine the mode of keeping the Journals, & report.

On motion *by Mr. Ellsworth, seconded by Mr. Johnson,* a Committee, consisting of Mr. Ellsworth, Mr. Bassett, & Mr. Wingate was appointed, to report a bill prescribing the form of the oath required to be taken by the third Section, of 6th Art. of the Constitution, & the time within which, the same has to be taken.

The first committee was further instructed on April 25.

[31] The annotated report is in Joint Committee Reports, Senate Records, DNA.

[32] On April 18 the Senate resolutions on rules for conference committees and the election of chaplains were agreed to by the House.

for the reception of the Vice President, agreed to the following REPORT, viz.[33]

"That Mr. Osgood, the proprietor of the house lately occupied by the President of Congress, be requested to put the same, and the furniture thereof, in proper condition for the residence and use of the President of the United States, and otherwise, at the expense of the United States, to provide for his temporary accommodation.

"That it will be more eligible in the first instance, that a Committee of three members from the Senate, and five members from the House of Representatives, to be appointed by the two Houses respectively, attend to receive the President, at such place as he shall embark from New-Jersey for this city, and conduct him without form, to the House lately occupied by the President of Congress; and that at such time thereafter the President shall signify, it will be most convenient for him, he be formally received by both Houses.

"That a Committee of two members from the Senate, and three members from the House of Representatives, to be appointed by the Houses respectively, wait on the Vice President of the United States, as soon as he shall come to this city, and in the name of the Congress of the United States, congratulate him on his arrival."

Which report was read and accepted.[34]

The Senate proceeded to the consideration of the REPORT of the Committee upon rules for conducting business in the Senate, and after some progress, adjourned to 11 o'clock to-morrow morning.[35]

THURSDAY, APRIL 16, 1789

The SENATE assembled,
Present as yesterday.

The Senate proceeded BY BALLOT to the choice of the Committees conformably to the report of the Committee of both Houses, agreed to the 15th instant.—Mr. Langdon, Mr. Carroll, and Mr. Johnson, were appointed to wait on the President, and Mr. Ellsworth, and Mr. Dalton, were appointed to wait on the Vice-President.[36]

ORDERED, That Mr. Strong, Mr. Izard, and Mr. Lee, be a Committee to report a mode of communication to be observed between the Senate and House of Representatives with respect to papers, bills, and messages, and to

---

[33] The committee report of the House is in Various Select Committee Reports, vol. 1, RG 233, Records of the United States House of Representatives, DNA. (Hereinafter RG 233 will be referred to as House Records.) The Senate report has not been located.

[34] On April 16 committees to wait upon the President and Vice President were appointed.

[35] On April 16 the complete set of rules decided upon by this committee was printed in the Journal and accepted by the Senate.

[36] On April 20 a committee was appointed to escort the Vice President to the Senate chamber.

confer thereon with such Committee as may be appointed by the House of Representatives for that purpose.[37]

The petition of David Ramsay, that a law might pass, securing to him and his heirs an exclusive right of vending, &c. his "History of the American Revolution," was read.[38]

The REPORT of the Committee appointed to determine upon rules for conducting business in the Senate, was agreed to. Whereupon,

RESOLVED, That the following RULES, from No. I, to XIX, inclusive, be observed.

I

The President having taken the Chair and a quorum being present the Journal of the preceding day shall be read, to the end that any mistake may be corrected that shall have been made in the entries.

II

No member shall speak to another, or otherwise interrupt the business of the Senate, or read any printed paper while the Journals or public papers are reading, or when any member is speaking in any debate.

III

Every member when he speaks shall address the Chair standing in his place, and when he has finished shall sit down.

IV

No member shall speak more than twice in any one debate on the same day, without leave of the Senate.

V

When two members rise at the same time, the President shall name the person to speak; but in all cases the member first rising shall speak first.

VI

No motion shall be debated until the same shall be seconded.

VII

When a motion shall be made and seconded, it shall be reduced to writing, if desired by the President, or any member, delivered in at the table, and read by the President before the same shall be debated.

---

[37] On April 23 the report of this committee was printed in the Journal and accepted.

[38] This petition is in Petitions and Memorials: Various subjects, Senate Records, DNA. It was not taken up again by the Senate. On April 15 Dr. David Ramsay's petition was presented to the House which appointed a committee to consider it. This committee reported on April 20 and after the House accepted the report, it was referred to a committee on copyrights to be included in a general bill.

VIII

While a question is before the Senate, no motion shall be received unless for an amendment, for the previous question; or for postponing the main question, or to commit it, or to adjourn.

IX

The previous question being moved and seconded, the question from the Chair shall be—"Shall the main question be now put?"—And if the nays prevail, the main question shall not then be put.

X

If a question in debate contain several points, any member may have the same divided.

XI

When the yeas and nays shall be called for by one fifth of the members present, each member called upon shall, unless for special reasons he be excused by the Senate, declare openly and without debate, his assent or dissent to the question—In taking the yeas and nays, and upon the call of the House, the names of the members shall be taken alphabetically.

XII

One day's notice at least shall be given of an intended motion for leave to bring in a bill.

XIII

Every bill shall receive three readings previous to its being passed; and the President shall give notice at each, whether it be the first, second, or third; which readings shall be on three different days, unless the Senate unanimously direct otherwise.

XIV

No bill shall be committed or amended until it shall have been twice read, after which it may be referred to a Committee.

XV

All Committees shall be appointed by BALLOT, and a plurality of votes shall make a choice.

XVI

When a member shall be called to order, he shall sit down until the President shall have determined whether he is in order or not; and every question of order shall be decided by the President without debate: but if there be a doubt in his mind, he may call for the sense of the Senate.

XVII

If a member be called to order for words spoken, the exceptionable words shall be immediately taken down in writing, that the President may be better enabled to judge of the matter.

XVIII

When a blank is to be filled, and different sums shall be proposed, the question shall be taken on the highest sum first.

XIX

No member shall absent himself from the service of the Senate without leave of the Senate first obtained.[39]

The Senate adjourned to 11 o'clock to-morrow morning.

FRIDAY, APRIL 17, 1789

The SENATE assembled,
Present as yesterday.

The petition of Leonard Bleecker, to be appointed Serjeant at Arms, was read,[40] and ordered to lie on the table.[41]

The Senate adjourned to 11 o'clock to-morrow morning.

SATURDAY, APRIL 18, 1789

The SENATE assembled,
Present as yesterday.

A letter from the Speaker of the House to the President was read, enclosing a concurrence of the House with the resolve of Senate of the 15th, upon the mode of conference between the Senate and House of Representatives; also, a concurrence upon the mode of choosing Chaplains.[42]

On motion,[43] RESOLVED, That the following be subjoined to the standing orders of the Senate:—

XXth RULE

Before any petition or memorial, addressed to the Senate, shall be received and read at the table, whether the same shall be introduced by the President, or a member, a brief statement of the contents of the petition or memorial shall verbally be made by the introducer.

The Senate adjourned until 11 o'clock on Monday morning.

[39] The rough report, including drafts of the rules, is in Various Select Committee Reports, Senate Records, DNA. E–46030. On April 18 an additional rule was adopted.

[40] This petition is in Petitions and Memorials: Applications for jobs, Senate Records, DNA.

[41] This petition was never taken up by the Senate.

[42] The letter from the Speaker and the enclosure, an extract from the Journal, are in Messages from the House, Senate Records, DNA. On April 22 the question of electing a chaplain was taken up.

[43] The preliminary journal reads: "On motion *by Mr. Lee, seconded by Mr. Paterson.*"

MONDAY, April 20, 1789

The SENATE assembled,
Present as on Saturday.

The Honorable John Henry, from the State of Maryland, produced his credentials,[44] and took his seat in the Senate.

The Honorable James Gunn, from the State of Georgia, produced his credentials,[45] and took his seat in the Senate.

On motion,[46] RESOLVED, That Mr. Strong and Mr. Izard be a Committee to wait on the Vice President, and conduct him to the Senate-Chamber.[47]

The Senate adjourned to 11 o'clock to-morrow morning.

TUESDAY, April 21, 1789

The SENATE assembled,
Present as yesterday.

The Committee appointed on the 20th instant, consisting of Mr. Strong and Mr. Izard, to conduct the Vice President to the Senate-Chamber, executed their commission: and Mr. Langdon, the President pro tempore, meeting the Vice President upon the floor of the Senate-Chamber, addressed him as follows:—

SIR,

I HAVE it in charge from the Senate, to introduce you to the Chair of this House; and also to congratulate you on your appointment to the Office of Vice President of the United States of America.

After which Mr. Langdon conducted the Vice President to the Chair, when the Vice President addressed the Senate as follows:

GENTLEMEN OF THE SENATE,

INVITED to this respectable situation by the suffrages of our fellow-citizens, according to the Constitution, I have thought it my duty cheerfully and readily to accept it. Unaccustomed to refuse any public service, however dangerous to my reputation, or disproportioned to my talents, it would have been inconsistent to have adopted another maxim of conduct, at this time, when the prosperity of the country, and the liberties of the people, require perhaps, as much as ever, the attention of those who possess any share of the public confidence.

I should be destitute of sensibility, if, upon my arrival in this city, and presentation to this Legislature, and especially to this Senate, I could see, with-

---

[44] These credentials are in Election Records: Credentials of Senators, Senate Records, DNA.

[45] These credentials are in Election Records: Credentials of Senators, Senate Records, DNA.

[46] The preliminary journal reads: "On motion by *Mr. Henry seconded by Mr. Few.*"

[47] On April 21 this committee received the Vice President, congratulated him, and escorted him to the chair for his inaugural address.

out emotion, so many of those characters, of whose virtuous exertions I have
so often been a witness—from whose countenances and examples I have ever
derived encouragement and animation—whose disinterested friendship has
supported me, in many intricate conjunctures of public affairs, at home and
abroad:—Those celebrated defenders of the liberties of this country, whom
menaces could not intimidate, corruption seduce, nor flattery allure: Those
intrepid assertors of the rights of mankind, whose philosophy and policy, have
enlightened the world, in twenty years, more than it was ever before enlightened in many centuries, by ancient schools, or modern universities.

I must have been inattentive to the course of events, if I were either
ignorant of the same, or insensible to the merit of those other characters in the
Senate, to whom it has been my misfortune to have been, hitherto, personally
unknown.

It is with satisfaction, that I congratulate the people of America on the
formation of a national Constitution, and the fair prospect of a consistent
administration of a government of laws. On the acquisition of an House of
Representatives, chosen by themselves; of a Senate thus composed by their
own State Legislatures; and on the prospect of an executive authority, in the
hands of one whose portrait I shall not presume to draw—Were I blessed
with powers to do justice to his character, it would be impossible to increase
the confidence or affection of his country, or make the smallest addition to his
glory. This can only be effected by a discharge of the present exalted trust on
the same principles, with the same abilities and virtues, which have uniformly
appeared in all his former conduct, public or private. May I nevertheless, be
indulged to enquire, if we look over the catalogue of the first magistrates of
nations, whether they have been denominated Presidents or Consuls, Kings or
Princes, where shall we find one, whose commanding talents and virtues,
whose over-ruling good fortune have so completely united all hearts and
voices in his favor? who enjoyed the esteem and admiration of foreign nations
and fellow-citizens with equal unanimity? Qualities so uncommon, are no
common blessings to the country that possesses them. By those great qualities,
and their benign effects, has Providence marked out the head of this nation,
with an hand so distinctly visible, as to have been seen by all men, and mis-
taken by none.

It is not for me to interrupt your deliberations by any general observations
on the state of the nation, or by recommending, or proposing any particular
measures. It would be superfluous, to gentlemen of your great experience, to
urge the necessity of order.—It is only necessary to make an apology for myself. Not wholly without experience in public assemblies, I have been more
accustomed to take a share in their debates, than to preside in their deliberations. It shall be my constant endeavor to behave towards every member of
this MOST HONORABLE body with all that consideration, delicacy, and decorum

which becomes the dignity of his station and character: But, if from inexperience, or inadvertency, any thing should ever escape me, inconsistent with propriety, I must entreat you, by imputing it to its true cause, and not to any want of respect, to pardon and excuse it.

A trust of the greatest magnitude is committed to this Legislature—and the eyes of the world are upon you. Your country expects, from the results of your deliberations, in concurrence with the other branches of government, consideration abroad, and contentment at home—prosperity, order, justice, peace, and liberty:—And may God Almighty's providence assist you to answer their just expectations.[48]

Adjourned[49] to 11 o'clock to-morrow morning.

WEDNESDAY, APRIL 22, 1789
The SENATE assembled,
Present as yesterday.

On motion,[50] The sense of the Senate was taken, Whether in the choice of a Chaplain, they shall be confined to the list of such gentlemen as may be previously nominated?—Passed in the negative.

AGREED, That Saturday next be assigned to proceed to the election of a Chaplain, and that in the mean time, the members be at liberty to make their nomination.[51]

The PETITION of William Finnie, praying that he might be appointed Serjeant at Arms, was read.[52]

Adjourned to 11 o'clock to-morrow morning.

THURSDAY, APRIL 23, 1789
The SENATE assembled,
Present as yesterday.

The Committee appointed on the 16th of April, to report a mode of communication to be observed between the Senate and House of Representatives, with respect to papers, bills and messages, and to confer thereon with such Committee as may be appointed, by the House of Representatives for that purpose, have conferred with a Committee of the House, and have agreed to the following REPORT:[53]—

---

[48] John Adams's address to Congress has not been located.

[49] The smooth journal reads: "The Senate adjourned."

[50] The preliminary journal reads: "On motion *by Mr. Maclay, seconded by Mr. Lee.*"

[51] On April 25 the Senate appointed Samuel Provoost to be chaplain.

[52] This petition is in Petitions and Memorials: Applications for jobs, Senate Records, DNA. A cover letter is in Other Records: Various papers, Senate Records, DNA. It was not taken up by the Senate.

[53] A true copy and a draft copy noted as accepted are in Joint Committee Reports, Senate Records, DNA. E–45672. An undated fragment which may have been a suggested rule is in Other Records: Various papers, Senate Records, DNA.

When a bill or other message shall be sent from the Senate to the House of Representatives, it shall be carried by the Secretary, who shall make one obeisance to the Chair on entering the door of the House of Representatives, and another, on delivering it at the table into the hands of the Speaker—After he shall have delivered it, he shall make an obeisance to the Speaker, and repeat it as he retires from the House.

When a bill shall be sent up by the House of Representatives to the Senate, it shall be carried by two members, who, at the bar of the Senate, shall make their obeisance to the President, and thence advancing to the Chair, make a second obeisance, and deliver it into the hands of the President—After having delivered the bill, they shall make their obeisance to the President, and repeat it as they retire from the bar: The Senate shall rise on the entrance of the members within the bar, and continue standing until they retire.

All other messages from the House of Representatives, shall be carried by one member, who shall make his obeisance as above mentioned—but the President of the Senate, alone, shall rise.

READ AND ACCEPTED.[54]

On motion,[55] RESOLVED, That a Committee, consisting of three members, be appointed to consider and report, what STYLE or TITLES it will be proper to annex to the OFFICES of President and of Vice President of the United States—if any other than those given in the Constitution. Also to consider of the time, place, and manner in which, and the person by whom the oath prescribed by the Constitution, shall be administered to the President; and to confer thereon with such Committee as the House of Representatives shall appoint for that purpose.—

Mr. Lee

Mr. Izard and

Mr. Dalton were chosen.[56]

Adjourned to 11 o'clock to-morrow morning.

FRIDAY, APRIL 24, 1789

The SENATE assembled,

Present as yesterday.

On motion, The question was taken,[57] Whether the report of the Committee upon the mode of communication between the two Houses of Legislature, as yesterday read and accepted in the Senate, shall at this time be sent to the House of Representatives?—

---

[54] On April 24 a motion was made on this report.

[55] The preliminary journal reads: *"On motion by Mr. Lee seconded by Mr. Wingate."*

[56] On April 24 the instructions to this committee were changed.

[57] The preliminary journal reads: "On motion (*by Mr. Maclay, seconded by Mr. Bassett*), The sense of the Senate was taken."

Passed in the negative.[58]

On motion,[59] To re-consider the commission of the Committee appointed the 23d instant, to report what TITLES shall be annexed to the OFFICES of President and Vice President—

Passed in the affirmative.

On motion, That the following words, "What TITLES it will be proper to annex to the offices of President and of Vice President of the United States— if any other than those given in the Constitution," be struck out—

Passed in the negative.

On motion, That the words "STYLE or," before the word "TITLE," be added—

Passed in the affirmative.[60]

Adjourned to 11 o'clock to-morrow morning.

S A T U R D A Y, APRIL 25, 1789

The SENATE assembled,
Present as yesterday.

An Order of the House of Representatives, for the recommitment of a Report upon the mode of communication between the two Houses, to the Committee originally appointed on the part of the House, and directed by the Speaker to the President, was read,[61] and, upon motion, the acceptance of the Report of the Committee of both Houses by the Senate the 23d instant, was reconsidered, and the recommitment was agreed to on the part of the Senate.[62]

The Senate proceeded to the appointment of a Chaplain, in the manner agreed upon the 15th of April: And

The Right Reverend SAMUEL PROVOOST, was elected.[63]

On motion,[64] The Committee appointed the 14th instant, to determine the mode of keeping the Journals, were instructed to consider, "Whether the Minutes be amended so as to record only the act, as it may be agreed on after the Journal shall be read on the day following."[65]

---

[58] On April 25 the House ordered this report recommitted and the Senate agreed.

[59] The preliminary journal reads: "On Motion (*by Mr. Carrol seconded by Mr. Paterson*)."

[60] On April 25 this committee reported. On the same date a committee was appointed by the House to consider titles for the President and Vice President. This committee was instructed to confer with a House Committee.

[61] The order of the House is in Messages from the House, Senate Records, DNA.

[62] On April 28 the second report of this committee was read and ordered for consideration.

[63] On April 27 the Reverend Mr. Provoost accepted the appointment.

[64] The preliminary journal reads: "On Motion (*by Mr. Few seconded by Mr. Henry*)."

[65] On May 16 this committee reported and its report was tabled.

A letter from Charles Thomson, Esq. dated the 24th of April, 1789, directed to the President of the Senate, purporting his having delivered to General Washington the certificate of his being elected President of the United States, was read,[66] and ordered to be filed.

The Committee appointed to consider of the time, place, and manner in which, and of the person by whom the oath prescribed by the Constitution shall be administered to the President of the United States, and to confer with a Committee of the House appointed for that purpose,

REPORT,[67] That the President hath been pleased to signify to them that any time or place which both Houses may think proper to appoint, and any manner which shall appear most eligible to them, will be convenient and acceptable to him—That requisite preparations cannot probably be made before Thursday next—That the President be on that day FORMALLY received by both Houses in the Senate Chamber—That the Representative's Chamber being capable of receiving the greater number of persons, that therefore the President do take the oath in that place, and in the presence of both Houses.

That after the formal reception of the President in the Senate Chamber, he be attended by both Houses to the Representative's Chamber, and that the oath be administered by the Chancellor of the State of New-York.

The Committee farther report it as their opinion, that it will be proper that a Committee of both Houses be appointed to take order for conducting the business—

READ and ACCEPTED.

Whereupon,   Mr. Lee

                      Mr. Izard and

                      Mr. Dalton, on the part of the Senate, together with a Committee that may be appointed on the part of the House of Representatives, were empowered to take order for conducting the business.[68]

An Order of the House of Representatives concurring in the appointment of a Committee on their part, to confer with a Committee appointed the 24th instant, on the part of the Senate, to consider and report what STYLE, &C. it will be proper to annex to the Offices of President and of Vice President, was read, by which it appeared that

                      Mr. Benson

                      Mr. Ames

                      Mr. Madison

---

[66] A copy of this letter is in Papers Pertaining to the Notification of the President and Vice President of Their Election, Senate Records, DNA. The Washington letter referred to in the report is in the Lilly Library, InU.

[67] The House report, with slight word variations, is in Various Select Committee Reports, vol. 1, House Records, DNA.

[68] On April 27 the report of this committee was read and accepted.

Mr. Carroll and

Mr. Sherman were appointed on the part of the
House.[69]

Adjourned to 11 o'clock on Monday morning.

MONDAY, APRIL 27, 1789

The SENATE assembled,

Present as on Saturday.

The Committee appointed to take order for conducting the ceremonial of the formal reception, &c. of the President, REPORTED,[70] That it appears to them more eligible, that the oath should be administered to the President in the outer gallery adjoining the Senate Chamber, than in the Representative's Chamber, and therefore, submit to the respective Houses the propriety of authorising their Committee to take order as to the place where the oath shall be administered to the President, the resolution of Saturday, assigning the Representative's Chamber as the place, notwithstanding—

READ and ACCEPTED.[71]

RESOLVED,[72] That after the oath shall have been administered to the President, he, attended by the Vice President and the members of the Senate and House of Representatives, proceed to St. Paul's Chapel, to hear Divine Service, to be performed by the Chaplain of Congress already appointed.[73]

Sent to the House of Representatives for concurrence.[74]

A LETTER of the 25th instant, from the Right Rev. Samuel Provoost, to the Secretary, signifying his acceptance of the appointment of Chaplain to Congress, was read,[75] and ordered to be filed.[76]

Adjourned to 11 o'clock to-morrow morning.

---

[69] An extract of the House order dated April 24, 1789 is in Messages from the House, Senate Records, DNA. On April 30 the President took the oath. The conference committee on oaths and titles reported on May 7, and the report was ordered to lie for consideration.

[70] The report is in Select Committee Reports, vol. 1, House Records, DNA.

[71] On April 27 this committee report was read in the House. The House notified the Senate of its acceptance of the report on April 28.

[72] The preliminary journal reads: "On motion (*by Mr. Lee seconded by Mr. Izard*) Resolved."

[73] This resolve has not been located.

[74] On April 30 the divine service was held immediately following the inauguration. The House sent its concurrence to this resolution to the Senate on May 2.

[75] This letter has not been located.

[76] This was the last time the subject of a Senate chaplain was considered in the first session. Chaplains are appointed for each session.

TUESDAY, April 28, 1789

The SENATE assembled,
Present as yesterday.

A LETTER was received from the Speaker of the House by the President of the Senate, containing the two following enclosures:

The REPORT of a joint Committee upon the ceremonial to be observed in administering the oath, &c. to the President, as accepted in the House of Representatives; and,

A BILL, entitled "An act to regulate the time and manner of administering certain oaths."[77]

The above mentioned report was read, and ordered to lie on the table.[78]

The BILL was read the first time, and to-morrow was assigned for a second reading.[79]

The Committee appointed to report a mode of communication to be observed between the Senate and House of Representatives, with respect to papers, bills, &c. and to whom the subject was recommitted, having again conferred with the Committee of the House of Representatives, agreed upon a report; which was read,[80] and ordered to lie for consideration.[81]

Adjourned to 11 o'clock to-morrow morning.

WEDNESDAY, April 29, 1789

The SENATE assembled,
Present as yesterday.

Proceeded to the SECOND reading of the Bill, entitled "An act to regulate the time and manner of administering certain oaths," and after debate,[82] it was COMMITTED to   Mr. Strong
                                 Mr. Paterson
                                 Mr. Read
                                 Mr. Johnson and
                                 Mr. Henry[83]

A LETTER from the Speaker of the House of Representatives to the Vice

---

[77] The letter from the Speaker is in Messages from the House, Senate Records, DNA. The joint report was not included but can be found in the Office of the Financial Clerk of the Senate, Senate Records, DNA. The bill has not been located.

[78] On April 30 the Senate members of this committee reported and the inauguration was held. On the same date the committee escorted the President to his home.

[79] On April 29 the Oath Bill was read for the second time and committed.

[80] The House report is in Select Committee Reports, vol. 1, House Records, DNA.

[81] On April 29 the House notified the Senate of its concurrence with this report.

[82] The preliminary journal reads: "And after debate on motion (by Mr. Lee seconded by Mr. Paterson)."

[83] On May 2 this committee reported amendments to the bill and consideration was postponed.

President was read,[84] communicating the concurrence of the House on a report of a joint Committee, on the mode of communicating papers, bills and messages, between the Senate and House of Representatives.[85]

ALSO, the concurrence of the House with the Senate on the appointment of a committee, respecting the future disposition of the papers, in the office of the late Secretary—and

> Mr. Trumbull
> Mr. Cadwalader and
> Mr. Jackson were joined.[86]

Adjourned to 11 o'clock to-morrow morning.

THURSDAY, APRIL 30, 1789

The SENATE assembled,
Present as yesterday.

The REPORT of the Committee on the mode of communication between the Senate and House of Representatives, was taken up, and after debate postponed.[87]

Mr. Lee, in behalf of the Committee appointed to take order for conducting the ceremonial of the formal reception,[88] &c. of the President of the United States, having informed the Senate, that the same was adjusted; the House of Representatives were notified, that the Senate were ready to receive them in the Senate Chamber, to attend the President of the United States while taking the oath required by the Constitution.—Whereupon, the House of Representatives, preceded by their Speaker, came into the Senate Chamber, and took the seats assigned them; and the joint Committee, preceded by their Chairman, agreeably to order, introduced the PRESIDENT of the UNITED STATES to the Senate Chamber, where he was received by the VICE PRESIDENT, who conducted him to the CHAIR; when the VICE PRESIDENT informed him, that "The SENATE and HOUSE of REPRESENTATIVES of the UNITED STATES were ready to attend him to take the oath required by the Constitution, and that it would be administered by the Chancellor of the State of New-York."—To which the PRESIDENT replied, HE WAS READY TO PROCEED:—

---

[84] This letter has not been located.

[85] On April 30 this report was considered and postponed by the Senate.

[86] At this point the preliminary journal includes the following canceled paragraph: "(John Ross upon request had leave to withdraw his petition.)" On May 11 this committee reported, and the report was ordered to lie until after the report of the joint committee on rules.

[87] On May 1 the Senate considered this report, the report of the House committee on messages between houses, and a motion on this subject. The motion was committed to a new joint committee on messages between houses.

[88] A printed copy of the ceremonial procedure for the inauguration is in the Broadside Collection, Rare Book Room (hereinafter cited as RBkRm), DLC. E–45671.

And being attended to the gallery in front of the Senate Chamber, by the Vice President and Senators, the Speaker and Representatives, and the other public characters present, the oath was administered.[89]—After which the Chancellor proclaimed, "LONG LIVE GEORGE WASHINGTON, PRESIDENT OF THE UNITED STATES."

The PRESIDENT having returned to his seat, after a short pause, arose and addressed the Senate and House of Representatives as follows:—

FELLOW-CITIZENS OF THE SENATE AND
    OF THE HOUSE OF REPRESENTATIVES:

AMONG the vicissitudes incident to life, no event could have filled me with greater anxieties than that of which the notification was transmitted by your order, and received on the 14th day of the present month.—On the one hand, I was summoned by my country, whose voice I can never hear but with veneration and love, from a retreat which I had chosen with the fondest predilection, and, in my flattering hopes, with an immutable decision, as the asylum of my declining years: A retreat which was rendered every day more necessary as well as more dear to me, by the addition of habit to inclination, and of frequent interruptions in my health to the gradual waste committed on it by time.—On the other hand, the magnitude and difficulty of the trust to which the voice of my country called me, being sufficient to awaken in the wisest and most experienced of her citizens, a distrustful scrutiny into his qualifications, could not but overwhelm with despondence, one, who, inheriting inferior endowments from nature and unpracticed in the duties of civil administration, ought to be peculiarly conscious of his own deficiencies.—In this conflict of emotions, all I dare aver, is, that it has been my faithful study to collect my duty from a just appreciation of every circumstance, by which it might be effected.—All I dare hope, is, that, if in executing this talk, I have been too much swayed by a grateful remembrance of former instances, or by an affectionate sensibility to this transcendant proof, of the confidence of my fellow-citizens; and have thence too little consulted my incapacity as well as disinclination for the weighty and untried cares before me; my ERROR will be palliated by the motives which misled me, and its consequences be judged by my country, with some share of the partiality in which they originated.

Such being the impressions under which I have, in obedience to the public summons, repaired to the present station; it would be peculiarly improper to omit in this first official act, my fervent supplications to that Almighty being who rules over the universe,—who presides in the Councils of nations,—and

---

[89] The oath is in the Office of the Financial Clerk of the Senate, Senate Records, DNA. On May 7 the question of Presidential titles was still unsettled and debate on the question was resumed.

whose providential aids can supply every human defect, that his benediction may consecrate to the liberties and happiness of the people of the United States, a government instituted by themselves for these essential purposes: and may enable every instrument employed in its administration, to execute with success, the functions allotted to his charge.—In tendering this homage to the Great Author of every public and private good, I assure myself that it expresses your sentiments not less than my own;—nor those of my fellow-citizens at large, less than either.—No people can be bound to acknowledge and adore the invisible hand, which conducts the affairs of men, more than the people of the United States.—Every step, by which they have advanced to the character of an independent nation, seems to have been distinguished by some token of providential agency—and in the important revolution just accomplished in the system of their united government, the tranquil deliberations and voluntary consent of so many distinct communities, from which the event has resulted, cannot be compared with the means by which most governments have been established, without some return of pious gratitude along with an humble anticipation of the future blessings which the past seem to presage.—These reflections, arising out of the present crisis, have forced themselves too strongly on my mind to be suppressed.—You will join with me I trust in thinking, that there are none under the influence of which, the proceedings of a new and free government can more auspiciously commence.

By the article establishing the executive department, it is made the duty of the President "To recommend to your consideration, such measures as he shall judge necessary and expedient."—The circumstances under which I now meet you, will acquit me from entering into that subject, farther than to refer to the great constitutional Charter under which you are assembled; and which, in defining your powers, designates the objects to which your attention is to be given.—It will be more consistent with those circumstances, and far more congenial with the feelings which actuate me, to substitute, in place of a recommendation of particular measures, the tribute that is due to the talents, the rectitude, and the patriotism which adorn the characters selected to devise and adopt them.—In these honorable qualifications, I behold the surest pledges, that as on one side, no local prejudices, or attachments; no separate views, nor party animosities, will misdirect the comprehensive and equal eye which ought to watch over this great assemblage of communities and interests: so, on another, that the foundations of our national policy will be laid in the pure and immutable principles of private morality; and the pre-eminence of free government, be exemplified, by all the attributes which can win the affections of its citizens, and command the respect of the world.—I dwell on this prospect with every satisfaction which an ardent love for my country can inspire: since there is no truth more thoroughly established, than that there exists in the economy and course of nature, an indissoluble union between virtue and happiness,—between duty and advantage,—between the genuine maxims of an honest and magnanimous policy, and the solid rewards of public prosperity and felicity:—since we ought to be no less persuaded that the propitious smiles of Heaven, can never be expected on a nation that disregards the eternal rules of order and right, which Heaven itself has ordained:—and since the preservation of the sacred fire of liberty, and the destiny of the republican model of government, are justly considered as DEEPLY, perhaps as FINALLY staked, on the experiment entrusted to the hands of the American people.

Besides the ordinary objects submitted to your care, it will remain with your judgment to decide, how far an exercise of the occasional power delegated by the fifth article of the constitution is rendered expedient at the present juncture by the nature of objections which have been urged against the system, or by the degree of inquietude which has given birth to them.—Instead of undertaking particular recommendations on this subject, in which I could be guided by no lights derived from official opportunities, I shall again give way to my entire confidence in your discernment and pursuit of the public good:—for I assure myself that whilst you carefully avoid every alteration which might endanger the benefits of an united and effective government, or which ought to await the future lessons of experience; a reverence for the characteristic rights of freemen, and a regard for the public harmony, will sufficiently influence your deliberations on the question how far the former can be more impregnably fortified, or the latter be safely and advantageously promoted.

To the preceding observations I have one to add, which will be most properly addressed to the House of Representatives.—It concerns myself, and will therefore be as brief as possible.—When I was first honored with a call into the service of my country, then on the eve of an arduous struggle for its liberties, the light in which I contemplated my duty required that I should renounce every pecuniary compensation.—From this resolution I have in no instance departed.—And being still under the impressions which produced it, I must decline, as inapplicable to myself, any share in the personal emoluments, which may be indispensably included in a permanent provision for the executive department: and must accordingly pray that the pecuniary estimates for the station in which I am placed, may, during my continuance in it, be limited to such actual expenditures as the public good may be thought to require.

Having thus imparted to you my sentiments, as they have been awakened by the occasion which brings us together,—I shall take my present leave; but not without resorting once more to the benign Parent of the human race, in humble supplication that since he has been pleased to favor the American people, with opportunities for deliberating in perfect tranquillity, and dispositions for deciding with unparalleled unanimity on a form of government, for the security of their union, and the advancement of their happiness; so his divine blessing may be equally CONSPICUOUS in the enlarged views,—the temperate consultations,—and the wise measures on which the success of this government must depend.

G. WASHINGTON

April 30[90]

The PRESIDENT, the Vice President, the Senate and House of Representatives, &c. then proceeded to St. Paul's Chapel, where divine service was performed by the Chaplain of Congress, after which the PRESIDENT was reconducted to his house, by the Committee appointed for that purpose.

The Vice President and Senate returned to the Senate Chamber, and,

Upon motion,[91] UNANIMOUSLY AGREED, that a committee of three should be appointed to prepare an answer to the President's Speech—

> Mr. Johnson
> Mr. Paterson and
> Mr. Carroll were elected.[92]

Adjourned to 11 o'clock to-morrow morning.

---

[90] The address is in President's Messages: Annual reports, Senate Records, DNA. Another copy is in George Washington Papers, series 4, reel 98, Manuscript Division, DLC.

[91] The preliminary journal reads: "Upon motion (*by Mr. Johnson seconded by Mr. Elsworth*)—."

[92] On May 7 this committee's report was read, printed in the Journal, accepted, and given to the Vice President for signature.

FRIDAY, MAY 1, 1789

The SENATE assembled,
Present as yesterday.[1]

The REPORT of the joint Committee, to whom was recommitted, the mode of communication between the Senate and House of Representatives, as made by the Committee, on the part of the Senate, was taken up and NOT accepted.

The SAME report of the Committee on the part of the House, and the acceptance thereof by the House was considered in the Senate, and it was determined that it should lie until further order.

A MOTION,[2] "That when a messenger shall come from the House of Representatives to the Senate, and shall be announced by the door-keeper, the messenger shall be received at the bar of this House by the Secretary, and the bill or paper that he may bring, shall there be received from him by the Secretary, who shall deliver it to the President of the Senate," was committed to

> Mr. Ellsworth
> Mr. Lee and
> Mr. Read

And[3] the Committee were instructed to report a mode of sending papers, bills and messages from the Senate, to the House of Representatives.[4]

Adjourned to 11 o'clock to-morrow morning.

SATURDAY, MAY 2, 1789

The SENATE assembled,
Present as yesterday.

AGREED, That until a permanent mode of communication shall be adopted between the Senate and House of Representatives, the Senate will receive messages by the Clerk of the House, if the House shall think proper to send him, and papers sent from the House, shall be delivered to the Secretary at the bar of the Senate, and by him be conveyed to the President.[5]

A message from the House of Representatives, by Mr. Beckley, their Clerk:

"Mr. PRESIDENT,

"I AM commanded by the House of Representatives, to bring to the Senate,

---

[1] At this point the smooth journal inserts the following: "ORDERED, that the Journals of yesterday be committed to the Committee appointed the 14th of April, to determine the mode of printing the Journals."

[2] The preliminary journal reads: "A Motion *by Mr. Lee seconded by Mr. Izard.*"

[3] The preliminary journal inserts: "Upon Motion *by Mr. Patterson seconded by Mr. Elsworth—.*"

[4] On May 2 a temporary procedure for delivering Senate messages to the House was devised.

[5] On May 4 the report of the committee on the procedure for delivering messages was read and ordered for consideration.

the proceedings of the House on a resolution of the Senate of the 27th of April;—Also, to communicate to the Senate the appointment of the Reverend WILLIAM LYNN, D.D. to be one of the Chaplains to Congress, agreeably to the resolves of the 15th of April."—And he withdrew.

The concurrence of the House of Representatives on the resolve of the 27th, is as follows:

"In the House of Representatives of the United States
"the 29th of April, 1789—

"The House proceeded to consider the following resolution of the Senate, to wit,

"In Senate, April 27th, 1789

"RESOLVED, That after the oath shall have been administered to the President, he attended by the Vice President, and the members of the Senate, and House of Representatives, proceed to St. Paul's Chapel, to hear divine service to be performed by the Chaplain of Congress, already appointed—whereupon,

"RESOLVED, That this House doth concur in the said resolution, amended to read as followeth, to wit,

"That after the oath shall have been administered to the President, the Vice President, and members of the Senate, the Speaker, and members of the House of Representatives, will accompany him to St. Paul's Chapel, to hear divine service performed by the Chaplain of Congress."[6]

Mr. Strong, by order of the Committee appointed the 28th of April, on a bill passed the House of Representatives, entitled "An act to regulate the time and manner of administering certain oaths," reported sundry AMENDMENTS;[7] and Monday next was assigned to take the same into consideration.[8]

Adjourned until Monday morning, 11 o'clock.

MONDAY, MAY 4, 1789

The SENATE assembled,
Present as on Saturday.[9]

Agreeably to the order of the day, the Senate proceeded in the second reading of a bill, entitled "An act to regulate the time and manner of administering certain oaths," and to the consideration of the amendments reported by the Committee, which are as follow:

In line 1, strike out the words "CONGRESS OF THE UNITED STATES," and

---

[6] The House resolve is in Messages from the House, Senate Records, DNA.

[7] These amendments have not been located.

[8] On May 4 these amendments were printed in the Journal, considered, and agreed upon; a third reading was then scheduled.

[9] The preliminary journal adds: "except Mr. Johnson, absent with leave."

insert, "Senate and Representatives of the United States of America in Congress assembled."

At the end of the second paragraph add the words "of the Senate," and insert the following clause, "And be it further enacted, That the members of the several state Legislatures, and all executive and judicial Officers of the several States, who have been heretofore chosen or appointed, or who shall be chosen or appointed before the first day of August next, and who shall then be in office, shall, within one month thereafter, take the same oath or affirmation, except where they shall have taken it before; which may be administered by any person authorised by the law of the State, in which such office shall be holden, to administer oaths. And the members of the several state Legislatures, and all executive and judicial Officers of the several States, who shall be chosen or appointed, after the said first day of August, shall, before they proceed to execute the duties of their respective offices, take the foregoing oath or affirmation, which shall be administered by the person or persons, who by the law of the State, shall be authorised to administer the oath of office; and the person or persons so administering the oath hereby required to be taken, shall cause a record or certificate thereof to be made, in the same manner as by the law of the State, he or they, shall be directed to record or certify the oath of office."

In the last paragraph, strike out the words "Of the UNITED STATES of AMERICA," in the third and fourth lines, and insert the same words in the fourth line next after the words "As the case may be;"—and which being accepted, Tuesday morning, 11 o'clock, was assigned for the THIRD READING of the bill.[10]

The REPORT of the Committee to whom was referred the motion made the 1st instant, upon the mode of sending messages to, and receiving them from the House of Representatives, was read,[11] and ordered to lie for consideration.[12]

Adjourned to 11 o'clock to-morrow morning.

TUESDAY, MAY 5, 1789

The SENATE assembled,
Present as yesterday.

Agreeably to the order of the day, the Bill, entitled "An act to regulate the time and manner of administering certain oaths," was read a third time, and PASSED the Senate with the amendments.

ORDERED, That the Secretary carry the afore-mentioned Bill to the House of

---

[10] On May 5 this bill with amendments was read for the third time and passed; a message was then sent to the House informing it of the Senate actions.

[11] This report has not been located.

[12] On May 7 this report was considered and the first paragraph accepted.

Representatives, together with the amendments, and address the Speaker in the words following:

SIR,

THE Senate have passed the Bill, entitled "An act to regulate the time and manner of administering certain oaths," with amendments, to which they desire the concurrence of your House.[13]—

ORDERED, That when a Bill has passed the Senate, the Secretary shall endorse the FINAL DETERMINATION thereon, and the day when such final question was taken, previous to its being transmitted to the House of Representatives.

Adjourned to 11 o'clock on Thursday morning.

THURSDAY, MAY 7, 1789

The SENATE assembled,
Present as on Tuesday.

The Committee, appointed to confer with such Committee as might be appointed on the part of the House of Representatives to report what STYLE or TITLES it will be proper to annex to the OFFICE of PRESIDENT and of VICE-PRESIDENT of the UNITED STATES, if any other than those given in the Constitution, REPORTED;[14]

Which Report was ordered to lie for consideration.[15]

The REPORT of the Committee upon the MOTION committed May 1st, was considered, and the first paragraph thereof accepted—Whereupon

ORDERED, that when a messenger shall come from the House of Representatives to the Senate, and shall be announced by the doorkeeper, the messenger or messengers, being a member or members of the House, shall be received within the bar, the President rising when the message is by one member, and the Senate also, when it is by two or more: If the messenger be not a member of the House, he shall be received at the bar, by the Secretary, and the bill or papers that he may bring, shall THERE be received from him by the Secretary, and be by him delivered to the President.[16]

The Committee appointed to prepare an answer to the President's Speech,

---

[13] On May 6 the House amended the Senate amendments and returned this bill to the Senate on May 7.

[14] A House report dated May 5, 1789 (there is no indication that it is a joint report) is in Select Committee Reports, vol. 1, House Records, DNA.

[15] On May 5 the House agreed to the report of this conference committee, but the Senate did not approve it and appointed a new committee to consider the titles of the President and Vice President on May 8.

[16] On May 9 the Senate notified the House of this decision.

delivered to the Senate and House of Representatives of the United States, reported as follows[17]—

SIR,

WE, the Senate of the United States, return you our sincere thanks for your excellent speech delivered to both Houses of Congress; congratulate you on the complete organization of the federal government, and felicitate ourselves and our fellow citizens on your elevation to the office of President; an office highly important by the powers constitutionally annexed to it, and extremely honorable from the manner in which the appointment is made. The unanimous suffrage of the elective body in your favor is peculiarly expressive of the gratitude, confidence and affection of the citizens of America, and is the highest testimonial at once of your merit and their esteem. We are sensible, Sir, that nothing but the voice of your fellow citizens could have called you from a retreat, chosen with the fondest predilection, endeared by habit, and consecrated to the repose of declining years. We rejoice, and with us all America, that, in obedience to the call of our common country, you have returned once more to public life. In you all parties confide; in you all interests unite; and we have no doubt that your past services, great as they have been, will be equalled by your future exertions; and that your prudence and sagacity as a statesman will tend to avert the dangers to which we were exposed, to give stability to the present government, and dignity and splendor to that country, which your skill and valor as a soldier, so eminently contributed to raise to independence and empire.

When we contemplate the coincidence of circumstances, and wonderful combination of causes, which gradually prepared the people of this country for independence; when we contemplate the rise, progress and termination of the late war, which gave them a name among the nations of the earth, we are, with you, unavoidably led to acknowledge and adore the great arbiter of the universe, by whom empires rise and fall. A review of the many signal instances of divine interposition in favor of this country claims our most pious gratitude:—and permit us, Sir, to observe, that among the great events, which have led to the formation and establishment of a federal government, we esteem your acceptance of the office of President as one of the most propitious and important.

In the execution of the trust reposed in us, we shall endeavor to pursue that enlarged and liberal policy, to which your speech so happily directs. We are conscious, that the prosperity of each State is inseparably connected with the welfare of all, and that in promoting the latter, we shall effectually advance the former. In full persuasion of this truth, it shall be our invariable aim to divest ourselves of local prejudices and attachments, and to view the great

---

[17] This committee report has not been located.

assemblage of communities and interests committed to our charge with an equal eye. We feel, Sir, the force, and acknowledge the justness of the observation, that the foundation of our national policy should be laid in private morality; if individuals be not influenced by moral principles, it is in vain to look for public virtue; it is, therefore, the duty of Legislators to enforce, both by precept and example, the utility as well as the necessity of a strict adherence to the rules of distributive justice. We beg you to be assured, that the Senate will, at all times, cheerfully co-operate in every measure, which may strengthen the union, conduce to the happiness, or secure and perpetuate the liberties of this great confederated republic.

We commend you, Sir, to the protection of Almighty God, earnestly beseeching him long to perserve a life so valuable and dear to the people of the United States, and that your administration may be prosperous to the nation and glorious to yourself.

In SENATE, May 16th, 1789

Read and accepted, and ordered that the Vice President should affix his signature to the address in behalf of the Senate.[18]

Mr. Beckley, the Clerk of the House of Representatives, delivered a message, purporting, "That the House had concurred with the Senate in the amendments proposed on a Bill, entitled 'An act to regulate the time and manner of administering certain oaths' "—and "That the House proposed an amendment, to the third amendment, by inserting after the word 'Legislatures in the first place,' the words 'At the next session of the said Legislatures respectively:' "

He also brought to the Senate a resolve of the House of Representatives, appointing   Mr. Bland

Mr. Trumbull and

Mr. Vining a Committee on the part of the House, to confer with any Committee to be appointed on the part of the Senate, and report "Joint rules to be established between the two Houses, for the enrollment, &c. of the acts of Congress, and to confer on the mode of presenting addresses, bills, &c. to the President."[19]—And he withdrew.

The Senate agreed to the amendment proposed by the House of Representatives to the amendment to the afore-mentioned Bill—

And appointed   Mr. Langdon

Mr. Read and

---

[18] In the preliminary journal the dateline and the order are omitted. The smooth journal corresponds to the printed journal. On May 12 a motion concerning this report was postponed.

[19] The resolve is in Messages from the House, Senate Records, DNA.

Mr. Henry a Committee on their part,[20] for the purpose expressed in the resolve of the House of Representatives received this day;[21] which, together with the concurrence of the Senate to the amendment on the amendment to the bill above-mentioned, was carried to the House by the Secretary.[22]

Adjourned to 11 o'clock to-morrow morning.

FRIDAY, MAY 8, 1789

The SENATE assembled,
Present as yesterday.[23]

The REPORT of the Committee appointed to determine "What STYLE or TITLES it will be proper to annex to the OFFICE of PRESIDENT and of VICE PRESIDENT of the UNITED STATES, if any other than those given in the Constitution,"—and, to confer with a Committee of the House of Representatives appointed for the same purpose—

Was considered, and DISAGREED to.

The question was taken "Whether the President of the United States shall be addressed by the title of HIS EXCELLENCY?"—and it passed in the negative.

On motion[24]—That a Committee of three be appointed to consider and report under what TITLE it will be proper for the Senate to address the PRESIDENT of the UNITED STATES,

Mr. Lee
Mr. Ellsworth and
Mr. Johnson were elected.[25]

Adjourned to 11 o'clock to-morrow.

---

[20] The appointment to committee noted on the House resolve is in United States Misc. Box, NHi.

[21] On May 11 the report of the committee on the disposition of the papers of the late Secretary of Congress was ordered to wait for the report of this committee.

[22] On May 18 a committee to present this bill to the President was appointed by the Senate.

[23] At this point, the preliminary journal includes the following, with the marginal notation "omit."

Ordered that the Committee appointed to draft an Answer to the President's Speech wait on him & request him to appoint the time when it will be agreeable formally to receive the Address of the Senate at his own House.

Ordered that the Committee defer proceeding upon the business assigned them until the further order of the Senate.

The first of these paragraphs appears in the smooth and printed journals on May 14. It also appears in the preliminary journal on this date but with a notation to delete and insert on May 8.

[24] The preliminary journal reads: "On Motion *by Mr. Lee seconded by Mr. Ellsworth*."

[25] On May 9 consideration of this committee's report was postponed, and on this same date a conference committee to settle the difference of opinion between the two Houses was appointed.

S A T U R D A Y, MAY 9, 1789

The SENATE assembled,

Present as yesterday.

Mr. Beckley, the Clerk of the House of Representatives, delivered a message, purporting, That the House had ACCEPTED the report of a Committee appointed to consider, what STYLE or TITLE it will be proper to annex to the Office of President and of Vice President of the United States, if any other than THOSE given in the Constitution. And he withdrew.

Ordered, That   Mr. Few

                     Mr. Maclay and

                     Mr. Strong be a Committee to view the apartments in the City Hall, and to confer with any Committee that may be appointed by the House of Representatives for that purpose, and report how the same shall be appropriated.[26]

The Committee appointed to consider under what TITLE it will be proper for the Senate to address the PRESIDENT of the United States, REPORTED[27]— The consideration of which was postponed until Monday next.

The Secretary was charged with a message to the House of Representatives, with the order of Senate passed the 7th instant, on the mode adopted by the Senate in receiving communications from that House.

Ordered, That   Mr. Lee

                     Mr. Ellsworth and

                     Mr. Johnson be a Committee, to confer with any committee, to be appointed by the House of Representatives, ON THE DIFFERENCE OF OPINION NOW SUBSISTING BETWEEN THE TWO HOUSES, RESPECTING THE TITLE OF THE PRESIDENT of the UNITED STATES—And on motion for RECONSIDERATION, the instruction of the Committee was agreed to as follows:

"That they consider and report under what TITLE it will be proper for the President of the United States in future to be addressed, and to confer thereon with such Committee as the House of Representatives may appoint for that purpose."

The Secretary carried to the House of Representatives the appointment of a Committee on the part of the Senate to view the rooms in the City Hall, and to confer upon THEIR appropriation,[28]—

The REJECTION of the report of the Committee appointed to consider what STLYE, &c. it will be proper to annex to the OFFICES of PRESIDENT and of Vice President,—

---

[26] On May 9 the Senate notified the House of the appointment of this committee and asked for a conference.

[27] This committee report has not been located.

[28] On May 12 the House appointed a conference committee on the use of the City Hall and notified the Senate of this action.

And the appointment of a Committee on the part of the Senate to confer, on a TITLE under which it will be proper to address the PRESIDENT of the UNITED STATES.[29]

Adjourned until 11 o'clock on Monday morning.

MONDAY, MAY 11, 1789

The SENATE assembled,
Present as on Saturday.

Ordered, That the consideration of the report of the Committee upon "the TITLE by which it will be proper for the Senate to address the President" be postponed until Tuesday next.[30]—

Ordered, That a Committee, to consist of

Mr. Ellsworth
Mr. Carroll and
Mr. Few be appointed to consider and report a mode of carrying into execution the second paragraph, of the third section, of the first article of the Constitution.[31]

The Committee appointed the 13th of April to confer with a Committee of the House of Representatives, upon the future disposition of the papers in the Office of the late Secretary of Congress, made a REPORT,[32] which was ordered to lie until a Committee appointed May 7, to confer with a Committee of the House "On joint rules to be established for the enrollment, &c. of the acts of Congress" SHOULD REPORT.[33]

Adjourned to 11 o'clock to-morrow morning.

TUESDAY, MAY 12, 1789

The SENATE assembled,
Present as yesterday;
And Mr. Morris, from the State of Pennsylvania.

Mr. Beckley, the Clerk of the House of Representatives, delivered a mes-

---

[29] On May 11 consideration of this committee's report was postponed.

[30] The preliminary journal includes the following paragraph canceled by the marginal notation "omit." "On Motion to proceed to the appointment of a Sergeant at Arms— After some debate the question was postponed—." On May 12 the Senate conference committee on this subject was ordered to confer with the House committee.

[31] On May 13 this committee reported and the report was ordered to lie for consideration.

[32] A draft of the report is in Joint Committee Reports, Senate Records, DNA. This committee is not mentioned again in the First Congress. On May 29 the House sent a resolution on the Journals of the Continental Congress of the Senate.

[33] The order for postponement noted on the report on the disposition of papers is in Joint Committee Reports, Senate Records, DNA. On May 14 the joint committee on enrollment reported, and the report was ordered to lie for consideration.

sage, purporting, that the House had concurred in the appointment of a Committee on THEIR part, consisting of

Mr. White

Mr. Scott and

Mr. Sturges to confer, with the Committee appointed on the part of the Senate, May the 9th, on the appropriation of the rooms in the City-Hall;[34]—

Also, that the House had appointed a Committee, consisting of

Mr. Madison

Mr. Trumbull

Mr. Page

Mr. Benson and

Mr. Sherman to confer with any Committee that the Senate shall appoint on the disagreeing votes of the Senate and House of Representatives upon the report of their joint Committee, appointed to consider, what TITLES shall be given to the President and to the Vice President of the United States, if any other than those given in the Constitution.[35]— And he withdrew.

ORDERED, that the Committee appointed the 9th of May to consider "By what TITLE it will be proper for the Senate to address the PRESIDENT of the UNITED STATES," be instructed to confer with the Committee of the House of Representatives, agreeably to the proposition in their message of this day.[36]

A motion for the Committee, appointed to address the PRESIDENT, to proceed, was postponed to Thursday next.[37]

Adjourned to 11 o'clock to-morrow morning.

WEDNESDAY, MAY 13, 1789

The SENATE assembled,

Present as yesterday;

And Mr. Paterson, from the State of New-Jersey.

The Committee appointed the 11th inst. on the mode of carrying into execution, the second paragraph, of the third section, of the first article of the Constitution, REPORTED[38]—

---

[34] An extract of the message concerning the appointment of the committee is in Messages from the House, Senate Records, DNA. On June 17 the committee on the use of City Hall reported, and the report was ordered to lie for consideration.

[35] The House order is in Messages from the House, Senate Records, DNA.

[36] On May 14 this committee's report was printed in the Journal and consideration was postponed. The question of titles for the President and Vice President was resolved by a Senate resolution on the same day.

[37] In the preliminary journal this paragraph is marked "Omit." On May 14 this committee was ordered to request an appointment with the President.

[38] This report has not been located. It is printed in the Journal on May 14.

And the report was ordered to lie for consideration.[39]

ORDERED, That   Mr. Langdon
                       Mr. Strong and
                       Mr. Carroll be a Committee, to confer with any Committee that may be appointed on the part of the House of Representatives, and report what news-papers the members of the Senate and House of Representatives shall be furnished with, at the public expense.[40]

A Committee consisting of
                       Mr. Johnson
                       Mr. Read
                       Mr. Langdon
                       Mr. Morris
                       Mr. Dalton
                       Mr. Elmer
                       Mr. Henry and
                       Mr. Gunn was appointed to report a bill, defining the crimes and offences that shall be cognizable under the authority of the United States, and their punishment.[41]

Adjourned to 11 o'clock to-morrow morning.

THURSDAY, MAY 14, 1789

The SENATE assembled,
Present as yesterday.

The petition of Archibald McLean, to be employed as a Printer to the Senate and House of Representatives, was read[42] and ordered to lie on the table.[43]

The Secretary carried to the House of Representatives the order of Senate passed yesterday, appointing a Committee to report, "What news-papers the members of Congress shall be furnished with at the public expense."[44]

The Committee appointed the 9th inst. to determine "Under what TITLE

---

[39] On May 14 this committee's report was read and printed in the Journal and passed in the form of a resolve.

[40] On May 14 the House was notified of this action.

[41] On May 21 William Grayson was added to this committee.

[42] This petition has not been located.

[43] On May 16 this petition was referred to the committee on what newspapers should be furnished at public expense to members of Congress and on the printing of bills.

[44] On May 15 the House appointed a committee to meet with this committee and also instructed them to receive proposals for printing acts and proceedings of Congress. On May 16 the Senate was notified of this action and agreed to instruct the Senate committee in the same way.

it will be proper for the Senate to address the PRESIDENT"—and to confer with a Committee of the House of Representatives "Upon the disagreeing votes of the Senate and House," informed the Senate, that they had conferred with a Committee of the House of Representatives, but could not agree upon a report.

The Committee appointed the 9th inst. "To consider and report under what TITLE it will be proper for the Senate to address the PRESIDENT of the UNITED STATES of AMERICA," REPORTED—That in the opinion of the Committee it will be proper thus to address the PRESIDENT—HIS HIGHNESS THE PRESIDENT OF THE UNITED STATES OF AMERICA, AND PROTECTOR OF THEIR LIBERTIES.—

Which report was postponed—

And the following resolve was agreed to; to wit:—

From a decent respect for the opinion and practice of civilized nations, whether under monarchical or republican forms of government, whose custom is to annex TITLES of respectability to the OFFICE of their CHIEF MAGISTRATE; and that, on intercourse with foreign nations, a due respect for the majesty of the people of the United States, may not be hazarded by an appearance of singularity; the Senate have been induced to be of opinion, that it would be proper to annex a RESPECTABLE TITLE to the OFFICE of PRESIDENT of the UNITED STATES: But the Senate, DESIROUS of PRESERVING HARMONY with the House of Representatives, where the practice lately observed in presenting an address to the PRESIDENT was without the addition of TITLES, think it proper for the present to act in conformity with the practice of that House:—

Therefore RESOLVED, that the present address be—"To the PRESIDENT of the UNITED STATES"—without addition of TITLE.[45]

A motion was made to strike out the preamble as far as the words "But the Senate"; which passed in the negative—

And on motion for the main question—It passed in the affirmative.

The Committee appointed to consider and report a mode of carrying into effect the provision in the second clause, of the third section, of the first article of the Constitution, reported,—

Whereupon RESOLVED, That the Senators be divided into THREE CLASSES, the FIRST to consist of Mr. Langdon
                        Mr. Johnson
                        Mr. Morris
                        Mr. Henry

---

[45] The resolve is in Various Select Committee Reports, Senate Records, DNA. A memo, probably in the hand of Richard Henry Lee, from the Committee on Titles, Presidential, is in Various Collections, HM 28824, CSmH.

	Mr. Izard and
	Mr. Gunn
The SECOND of	Mr. Wingate
	Mr. Strong
	Mr. Paterson
	Mr. Bassett
	Mr. Lee
	Mr. Butler and
	Mr. Few
And the THIRD of	Mr. Dalton
	Mr. Ellsworth
	Mr. Elmer
	Mr. Maclay
	Mr. Read
	Mr. Carroll and
	Mr. Grayson

That three papers of an equal size, numbered 1, 2, and 3, be by the Secretary rolled up and put into a box, and drawn by Mr. Langdon, Mr. Wingate and Mr. Dalton, in behalf of the respective classes in which each of them are placed; and that the classes shall vacate their seats in the Senate according to the order of numbers drawn for them, beginning with number one—

And that when Senators shall take their seats from States that have not yet appointed Senators, they shall be placed by lot in the foregoing classes, but in such manner as shall keep the classes as nearly equal as may be in numbers.[46]

The Committee, appointed to confer with a Committee of the House of Representatives, in preparing proper rules to be established for the enrollment, &c. of the acts of Congress—REPORTED[47]—Which report was ordered to lie for consideration.[48]

ORDERED, That the Committee appointed to draft an answer to the President's Speech wait on him, and request him to appoint the time when it will be agreeable to receive the Address of the Senate, at his own house.[49]—

Adjourned to 11 o'clock to-morrow.

---

[46] On May 15 the Senate drew lots in the manner established by this resolution.

[47] A printed copy of the House committee report is in the Broadside Collection, RBkRm, DLC.

[48] On May 15 the committee on joint rules reported in the House, and its report was committed to the committee of the whole. The report was postponed as the order of the day until July 27 when it was passed (with modifications) by the House. On August 4 the House returned this report to the Senate for approval of the modified version.

[49] In the preliminary journal, this paragraph, with minor differences in wording, was originally entered under May 8. On May 15 this committee reported further and was ordered to wait upon the President.

FRIDAY, MAY 15, 1789

The SENATE assembled,

Present as yesterday.

The Committee appointed to draft an answer to the President's Speech further Reported[50]—Whereupon it was

AGREED, That the Senate should wait on the President at his own house on Monday next, at a quarter after 11 o'clock, and that the Vice President then, present the address of the Senate, as agreed to on the 7th instant.[51]

The Senate proceeded to determine the CLASSES agreeably to the Resolve of yesterday, on the mode of carrying into effect the provision in the SECOND CLAUSE, of the THIRD SECTION, of the FIRST ARTICLE of the CONSTITUTION, and the numbers being drawn, the CLASSES were determined as follows:—

LOT NO. 1, drawn by MR. DALTON

Contained Mr. Dalton
    Mr. Ellsworth
    Mr. Elmer
    Mr. Maclay   Whose seats shall accordingly, be vacated in
    Mr. Read   the Senate, at the expiration of the second year
    Mr. Carroll and
    Mr. Grayson

LOT NO. 2, drawn by MR. WINGATE

Contained Mr. Wingate
    Mr. Strong
    Mr. Paterson
    Mr. Bassett   Whose seats shall accordingly, be vacated in
    Mr. Lee   the Senate, at the expiration of the fourth year
    Mr. Butler and
    Mr. Few

LOT NO. 3, drawn by MR. LANGDON

Contained Mr. Langdon
    Mr. Johnson
    Mr. Morris   Whose seats shall accordingly, be vacated in
    Mr. Henry   the Senate, at the expiration of the sixth year
    Mr. Izard and
    Mr. Gunn[52]

Adjourned to 11 o'clock to-morrow morning.

---

[50] The continuation of this report has not been located.

[51] On May 18 the Senate replied to the President's inaugural address and the President answered on the same date.

[52] On July 28 Philip Schuyler and Rufus King drew lots to determine their classification.

SATURDAY, May 16, 1789

The SENATE assembled,
Present as yesterday.

A message from the House of Representatives by Mr. Beckley, their Clerk, who informed the Senate that "The House had concurred in the appointment of a Committee, consisting of

Mr. Silvester
Mr. Wynkoop and
Mr. Smith (of South-Carolina) to confer with a

Committee appointed on the part of the Senate the 13th instant, and to report what newspapers the members of Congress shall be furnished with at the public expense; and that it was an instruction to the said Committee on the part of the House, to receive proposals for printing the acts and other proceedings of Congress."[53]—And he withdrew.

The question being taken, Whether the Senate will give a similar instruction to the Committee on their part? It passed in the affirmative—And the Secretary informed the House of Representatives of the concurrence.

ORDERED, that the Petitions from sundry Printers presented to the Senate, be referred to the Committee of the Senate appointed the 13th instant.[54]

The Committee appointed the 14th of April to consider the mode of keeping and publishing the Journals, &c. REPORTED[55]—And the report was ordered to lie on the table.[56]

Adjourned until 11 o'clock on Monday next.

MONDAY, May 18, 1789

The SENATE assembled,
Present as on Saturday.

Agreeably to the order of the 15th instant the Senate waited on the President of the United States, at his own house, when the Vice President in their name, delivered to the President the address agreed to on the 7th instant: To which the President of the United States was pleased to make the following reply:

GENTLEMEN,

I THANK you for your address, in which the most affectionate sentiments are expressed in the most obliging terms.—The coincidence of circumstances which led to this auspicious crisis, the confidence reposed in me by my fellow-

---

[53] The House order is in Messages from the House, Senate Records, DNA.

[54] On May 19 this committee reported.

[55] A draft of this committee report is in Various Select Committee Reports, Senate Records, DNA.

[56] On May 19 the committee's report was printed in the Journal and accepted.

citizens, and the assistance I may expect from counsels which will be dictated by an enlarged and liberal policy, seem to persage a more prosperous issue to my administration, than a diffidence of my abilities had taught me to antici-pate.—I now feel myself inexpressibly happy in a belief, that Heaven which has done so much for our infant nation will not withdraw its providential in-fluence before our political felicity shall have been completed; and in a con-viction, that the Senate will at all times co-operate in every measure, which may tend to promote the welfare of this confederated republic.—Thus sup-ported by a firm trust in the great arbiter of the universe, aided by the col-lected wisdom of the union, and imploring the Divine Benediction on our joint exertions in the service of our country, I readily engage with you in the arduous, but pleasing, task, of attempting to make a nation happy.

G. WASHINGTON[57]

The petition of Thomas Greenleaf, that he might be appointed Printer to Congress, was read,[58] and committed to the Committee, to whom petitions of a similar nature were referred on the 16th instant.[59]

The petition of Paul Pritchard, in behalf of himself, and other shipwrights of South-Carolina, was read,[60] and ordered to lie for consideration.[61]

A message by Mr. Beckley, the Clerk of the House of Representatives;—Who brought to the Senate a bill, entitled, "An act for laying a duty on goods, wares and merchandizes imported into the United States"[62]—which he informed the Senate the House had passed, and to which they desired the concurrence of the Senate,—

And he withdrew.

The bill above mentioned was read a first time, and Thursday next was assigned for the second reading; and it was ordered that fifty copies thereof be printed in the mean time for the use of the Senate.[63]

ORDERED, That Mr. Lee be a Committee on the part of the Senate, to join any Committee appointed for that purpose on the part of the House of Repre-sentatives, and lay before the President of the United States for his approba-tion, a bill, entitled, "An act to regulate the time and manner of administering

[57] The message is in President's Messages: Annual reports, Senate Records, DNA.

[58] The petition has not been located but the agreement in which Greenleaf was selected printer and records of his accounts, along with a letter from Sam Loudon requesting the job of printer, are in Records of the Secretary: Letters concerning print-ing, Senate Records, DNA.

[59] The committee referred to is the committee on newspapers.

[60] The petition is in Petitions and Memorials: Various subjects, Senate Records, DNA.

[61] No action was taken on this petition during the First Congress.

[62] An annotated printed copy is in House Bills, Senate Records, DNA. A clear printed copy is in the Broadside Collection, RBkRm, DLC. E–45674.

[63] On May 21 the second reading of this bill was postponed until May 25.

certain oaths," after it shall be enrolled, examined by the said Committee, and signed by the Speaker of the House of Representatives, and by the Vice President.[64]

Adjourned to 11 o'clock to-morrow morning.

TUESDAY, MAY 19, 1789

The SENATE assembled,
Present as yesterday.

The Secretary carried to the House of Representatives the resolve of Senate, passed the 18th instant, appointing a Committee on their part, to lay before the President a bill, entitled, "An act to regulate the time and manner of administering certain oaths," after it shall be enrolled, &c.[65]

The Committee to whom was referred the motion for printing the Journals of the Senate, and furnishing each member with a copy thereof, and also to report upon the mode of keeping the Journals, and who were instructed to consider whether the minutes be amended, so as to record only the acts of the Senate on the Journal, reported as follows:[66]—

"That one hundred and twenty copies of the Journals of the Legislative proceedings only, be printed once a month; commencing the first publication on the first day of June next; and that each member be furnished with a copy.— That the proceedings of the Senate when they shall act in their executive capacity, shall be entered, and kept in separate and distinct books.

"That every vote of the Senate shall be entered on the Journals, and that a brief statement of the contents of each petition, memorial or paper, presented to the Senate, be also inserted on the Journals.

"That the Journals previous to each publication be revised, by a Committee to be appointed from time to time, for that purpose:" Which REPORT was accepted.

The Committee appointed to confer with a Committee of the House of Representatives, and report, what newspapers the members of Congress shall be furnished with at the public expense, reported in part:[67]—Which report was ordered to lie on the table.[68]

---

[64] An extract of the Journal is in Messages from the House, Senate Records, DNA, where it is attached to the House reply. On May 19 the Senate notified the House of this resolve.

[65] On May 19 the House appointed a committee to deliver the bill to the President, and on May 21 the Speaker signed this bill. The Senate was notified of these actions on May 22. The Vice President then signed the bill and it was sent to the President.

[66] The draft of this committee report marked "accepted" is in Various Select Committee Reports, Senate Records, DNA.

[67] The report is in Joint Committee Reports, Senate Records, DNA.

[68] On May 29 this committee continued its report. On the same date the House sent over a resolution on this joint committee report; after this, the Senate considered the resolution and not the committee report.

ORDERED, That   Mr. Paterson
                   Mr. Carroll and
                   Mr. Wingate be a Committee to revise the Journal,
previous to its publication.

Adjourned to 11 o'clock to-morrow morning.

WEDNESDAY, MAY 20, 1789

The SENATE assembled,
Present as yesterday.

The petition of Thomas Allen, to supply the stationary that may be wanted for the use of Congress, was read,[69] and referred to the Committee on petitions of a similar nature.[70]

Adjourned to 11 o'clock to-morrow morning.

THURSDAY, MAY 21, 1789

The SENATE assembled,
Present as yesterday.—

The Honorable William Grayson, from the State of Virginia, appeared, produced his credentials,[71] and took his seat in the Senate.

RESOLVED, That all bills on a second reading shall be considered by the Senate in the same manner, as if the Senate were in a Committee of the whole, before they shall be taken up and proceeded on by the Senate agreeable to the standing rules, unless otherwise ordered.

Mr. Grayson was added to the Committee appointed the 13th, of May, "To define the crimes and offences that shall be cognizable under the authority of the United States, and their punishment."[72]

ORDERED, That the second reading of a bill, entitled, "An act for laying a duty on goods, wares and merchandizes imported into the United States," be postponed until Monday next.[73]

Adjourned to 11 o'clock to-morrow morning.

FRIDAY, MAY 22, 1789

The SENATE assembled,
Present as yesterday.

A message from the House of Representatives, by Mr. Beckley, their Clerk; —Who brought to the Senate an enrolled bill, entitled, "An act to regulate

---

[69] The petition has not been located.

[70] This petition was referred to the committee on newspapers which was appointed on May 16.

[71] The credentials are in Election Records: Credentials of Senators, Senate Records, DNA.

[72] On June 12 Pierce Butler was appointed to this committee.

[73] On May 25 this bill was considered.

the time and manner of administering certain oaths,"[74] signed by the Speaker of the House of Representatives, and informed the Senate, "That the House had agreed in the appointment of a Committee on their part, consisting of

Mr. Partridge and

Mr. Floyd,[75] to lay the bill before the President, after it shall have passed the formalities prescribed in the resolve of the 18th of May;"—

And he withdrew.

The Committee appointed to examine the afore-mentioned bill, reported, that they had performed the service,—Whereupon the bill was signed by the Vice President, and was, by the Committee thereunto appointed, laid before the President of the United States for his approbation.[76]

Adjourned until 11 o'clock on Monday next.

M O N D A Y, MAY 25, 1789

The SENATE assembled,

Present as on Saturday.

Mr. Elmer had leave of absence for three weeks.[77]

The Senate proceeded in the consideration of the bill, entitled, "An act for laying a duty on goods, wares and merchandizes, imported into the United States."—And after progress[78]—

Adjourned to 11 o'clock to-morrow morning.

T U E S D A Y, MAY 26, 1789

The SENATE assembled,

Present as yesterday.

A message was delivered from the House of Representatives, by Mr. Beckley, their Clerk, who delivered the following resolve—

And withdrew.

"In the House of Representatives of the United States

"Monday, the 25th of May, 1789

"RESOLVED, That a Committee be appointed to confer with any Committee

---

[74] The enrolled bill is in Enrolled Acts and Resolutions of the Congress of the United States: 1789–1823, vol. 1, microfilm, M–337, roll 1, RG 11, United States Government Documents Having a General Legal Effect, DNA (hereinafter cited as Enrolled Acts, RG 11, DNA). E–45715. All enrolled bills are signed by the Speaker, the Vice President, and the President and are certified by the Secretary of the house of origin.

[75] The House message is in Messages from the House, Senate Records, DNA.

[76] On June 1 the President signed this bill.

[77] At this point the preliminary journal includes three paragraphs marked for deletion, with the following note in Otis's hand: "Should not have been here as it is Entered in the Journal of the Executive Senate."

[78] On May 28 this bill was considered again.

which may be appointed by the Senate, on the proper method of receiving into either House, bills or messages, from the President of the United States.— The members appointed

> Mr. Partridge
> Mr. Floyd and
> Mr. Thatcher

> > "Extract from the Journal,
> > JOHN BECKLEY, Clerk"[79]

The message was considered, and the appointment of a committee on the part of the Senate, was concurred:—

> Mr. Lee and
> Mr. Izard were joined.[80]

Adjourned to 11 o'clock to-morrow morning.

WEDNESDAY, MAY 27, 1789

The SENATE assembled,
Present as yesterday.

The Secretary went to the House of Representatives with a message, purporting the concurrence on the part of the Senate, in the appointment of a Committee upon the mode of receiving messages from the President of the United States, agreeably to the proposition of the House of Representatives made yesterday.[81]

Adjourned to 11 o'clock to-morrow morning.

THURSDAY, MAY 28, 1789

The SENATE assembled,
Present as yesterday.

The Senate proceeded in the consideration of the bill, entitled, "An act for laying a duty on goods, wares and merchandizes imported into the United States."—And after debate,[82]

Adjourned to 11 o'clock to-morrow morning.

---

[79] The resolve, in the form of an extract from the House Journal, is in Messages from the House, Senate Records, DNA.

[80] On May 27 the Senate notified the House of the appointment of this committee.

[81] On May 29 the House committee reported. The report was printed in the Journal of the House, amended, and accepted. The House then sent the report to the Senate for concurrence and the Senate agreed to the report on the same date.

[82] On May 29 this bill was considered again.

FRIDAY, MAY 29, 1789

The SENATE assembled,

Present as yesterday.

Proceeded in the consideration of the bill, entitled, "An act for laying a duty on goods, wares and merchandizes imported into the United States."[83]

The Committee appointed the 13th instant, to confer with a Committee of the House of Representatives, and report "What newspapers the members of Congress shall be furnished with at the public expense," further reported;[84]— Which report was ordered to lie on the table.

A message from the House of Representatives, by Mr. Beckley, their Clerk; —Who brought to the Senate an engrossed bill, entitled, "An act imposing duties on tonnage;"[85]—

A resolve of the House of Representatives of the 28th, providing the members of the Senate and House of Representatives each, with a sett of the Journals of the late Congress;[86]—

A resolve of the 28th, on the report of a joint committee appointed "To confer on the mode of furnishing the members of the Senate and House of Representatives with newspapers, journals," &c.[87]

Also, a resolve of this day, on the report of a joint Committee appointed "To confer upon the mode of receiving in the Senate and House of Representatives, bills, &c. from the President of the United States," Desiring the concurrence of the Senate thereto,—

And he withdrew.

"In the House of Representatives of the United States

"The 29th of May, 1789

"Mr. Partridge, from the Committee appointed to confer with a Committee of the Senate on the proper method of receiving into either House, bills or messages from the President of the United States, made a report, and the said report being amended to read as followeth—

"That until the public offices are established, and the respective officers are appointed, any returns of bills and resolutions or other communications from the President, may be received by either House under cover directed to the President of the Senate or Speaker of the House of Representatives (as the

---

[83] On June 1 this bill was again taken up.

[84] The report is in Joint Committee Reports, Senate Records, DNA.

[85] The annotated engrossed printed bill is located in the Broadside Collection, RBkRm, DLC. E–45626. On June 9 this bill was read for the first time in the Senate and the time for the second reading was assigned.

[86] The resolve, in the form of a journal extract, is in Messages from the House, Senate Records, DNA. On June 8 this resolve was read and concurred in by the Senate.

[87] The resolve, in the form of an extract from the House Journal, is in Joint Committee Reports, Senate Records, DNA. On June 2 this resolve was considered and amended by the Senate.

case may be) and transmitted by such person as the President may think proper—

"RESOLVED, That this House doth agree to the said report.—

"Extract from the Journal,

JOHN BECKLEY, Clerk"[88]

In Senate, read and concurred.[89]

The bill and other resolutions were ordered to lie for consideration.

Adjourned until 11 o'clock on Monday morning.—

[88] The resolve, in the form of an extract from the House Journal, is in Joint Committee Reports, Senate Records, DNA.

[89] On June 1 the Senate notified the House of this concurrence.

MONDAY, June 1, 1789

The SENATE assembled,
Present as on Saturday.

The Secretary carried to the House of Representatives, the concurrence of the Senate upon a resolve of the House of the 29th of May, on the mode of receiving communications from the President of the United States.

A message from the House of Representatives, by Mr. Beckley, their Clerk—

"MR. PRESIDENT,

I AM directed to inform the Senate, that the President has affixed his signature to a bill, entitled, "An act to regulate the time and manner of administering certain oaths," and has returned it to the House of Representatives, from whence it originated;[1]—

And he withdrew.

The Senate proceeded in the consideration of the bill, entitled, "An act for laying a duty on goods, wares and merchandizes, imported into the United States," and after debate,[2]

Adjourned to 11 o'clock to-morrow morning.

TUESDAY, June 2, 1789

The SENATE assembled,
Present as yesterday.

The resolve of the House of Representatives of the 28th May, was considered, viz.

"In the House of Representatives of the United States
"Thursday, the 28th May, 1789

"The House proceeded to consider the two reports, one made the 19th instant, the other the 26th instant, by the Committee appointed to confer with a Committee of the Senate, to consider and report what newspapers the members of Congress shall be furnished with at the public expense, and to receive proposals for printing the Acts and other proceedings of Congress: And the first Report in the words following, to wit:

" 'That in their opinion public economy requires that the expense heretofore incurred by the public, of supplying every member of Congress with all the newspapers printed at the seat of Congress, should be retrenched in future; but as your Committee consider the publication of newspapers to be highly

---

[1] On June 3 the Senate requested that this act be sent to the House.
[2] On June 2 consideration of this bill was resumed.

beneficial in disseminating useful knowledge throughout the United States, and deserving of public encouragement, they recommend that each member of Congress be supplied at the public expense with one paper, leaving the choice of the same to each member, and that it be the duty of the Secretary of the Senate, and Clerk of the House of Representatives to give the necessary directions to the different printers to furnish each member with such papers as he shall choose,'—Being again read and debated—

"RESOLVED, That this House doth disagree to the said report:

"The other report being again read, and amended to read as follows:—

" 'That it would be proper that it should be left to the Secretary of the Senate and Clerk of the House of Representatives, to contract with such person as shall engage to execute the printing and binding business on the most reasonable terms, the paper being furnished by the said Secretary and Clerk to such person at the public expense. That such person as they shall contract with, shall be obliged to render a state of his accounts quarterly, and that six hundred copies of the Acts of Congress, and seven hundred copies of the Journals be printed, and distributed to the Executive and Judicial, and Heads of Departments of the Government of the United States, and the Executive, Legislative and Judicial of the several States.'

"RESOLVED, That this House doth agree to the said report.

"Extract from the Journal,
JOHN BECKLEY, Clerk"[3]

---

[3] An annotated extract of the House message is in Joint Committee Reports, Senate Records, DNA. An extract from the House Journal with the same message is in Records of the Secretary: Letters concerning printing, Senate Records, DNA.

In accordance with the resolve, Samuel Otis and John Beckley, Secretary of the Senate and Clerk of the House, respectively, issued a statement that each would choose the printer for his respective House and that Messrs. Francis Childs and John Swaine would print the laws of Congress while Thomas Greenleaf would print the other bills as necessary. A copy of this agreement is included with the documents in Joint Committee Reports, Senate Records, DNA. After the selection of Childs and Swaine, contracts were drawn up. These contracts, including the first drafts, and a letter from Childs and Swaine that outlined conditions for printing the laws of Congress are also in Joint Committee Reports.

A second session order for House Journals sent to Childs and Swaine and signed by Beckley, is in Messages from the House, Senate Records, DNA. A letter from John Fenno to Otis dated after the second session, regarding the printing of journals, is in Records of the Secretary: Letters concerning publications, Senate Records, DNA. After the selection of Greenleaf, Otis was contacted by Joseph Gilpin and Henry Kammerer about their supplying the paper necessary for the printing. Apparently Kammerer was chosen; there are numerous letters that he wrote to Otis about the type of paper he was sending and the amount of time the deliveries would take. These documents are located in Records of the Secretary: Letters concerning printing, Senate Records, DNA.

Also regarding the first mentioned resolution, there is evidence that Samuel Otis did send copies of the Journal of the Senate to the various state legislatures. These letters are located in Records of the Secretary: Letters concerning printing, Senate Records, DNA. There are several letters acknowledging receipt of the Journals as well as letters

And on the question of concurrence on the first report, it was postponed.

The other report was read and concurred with an amendment, viz. after the words "And distributed to the,"

Insert "Members of the Legislative, to the."[4]

The Senate proceeded in the consideration of the bill entitled, "An act for laying a duty on goods, wares and merchandizes imported into the United States."[5]

Adjourned to 11 o'clock to-morrow morning.

WEDNESDAY, JUNE 3, 1789

The SENATE assembled,
Present as yesterday.

Proceeded in the consideration of the bill, entitled, "An act for laying a duty on goods, wares and merchandizes imported into the United States,"—

And further postponed the SECOND reading until to-morrow at 11 o'clock.[6]

The Secretary informed the House of Representatives of the concurrence of the Senate in a resolve of the 28th of May, upon the mode of printing the Acts and Journals of Congress as agreed to yesterday—And requested the House of Representatives to send to the Senate, "An act to regulate the time and manner of administering certain oaths."

A message from the House of Representatives, by Mr. Beckley, their Clerk; —Who brought to the Senate the act last mentioned;—Informed the Senate of the concurrence of the House of Representatives in THEIR amendment on a

---

indicating that copies were forwarded to the Massachusetts legislature and the Virginia legislature; these documents are located in the Misc. Legislative Papers, M-Ar, and the Executive Papers, Vi-Ar. Two letters from Beckley sending copies of Journals are in Executive Papers, Vi-Ar, and Livingston Papers, MHi. For the first session, there are letters of acknowledgment from John Sullivan, J. Meriwether, and John Dart; for the second session, letters from Joseph Pearson, Charles Hay, Welcome Arnold, Wm. Williams, John Avery, David Cobb, H. Brooke, Jacob Read, and Abm. Bancker; for the third session, letters from A. Blaire and John Langdon. In addition, there is a letter, addressed to Otis and dated February 3, from Tobias Lear, writing for George Washington, that requests two copies of bills to be printed and two copies of the Journals. The Pearson letter is in Reports and Communications, Senate Records, DNA, and the other documents are in Records of the Secretary: Letters concerning publications, Senate Records, DNA. There is also a letter from H. Remsen to Otis regarding the return of extra journals; this is located in Records of the Secretary: Letters concerning publications, Senate Records, DNA.

[4] The amended extract with a note of concurrence is in Joint Committee Reports, Senate Records, DNA. On June 3 the House concurred with this amendment and notified the Senate.

[5] On June 3 consideration was resumed and the second reading of the bill was postponed until June 4.

[6] On June 4 this bill was read for the second time and consideration of it was postponed.

resolve of the 28th May, on the mode of printing the Acts and Journals of Congress;—

And he withdrew.

ORDERED, That Mr. Langdon administer the oath to the Vice President— Which was done accordingly:

And the Vice-President administered the oath, according to law, to the following members—

To Mr. Langdon	Mr. Paterson	Mr. Henry
Mr. Wingate	Mr. Maclay	Mr. Lee
Mr. Strong	Mr. Morris	Mr. Grayson
Mr. Dalton	Mr. Read	Mr. Izard
Mr. Johnson	Mr. Bassett	Mr. Few and
Mr. Ellsworth	Mr. Carroll	Mr. Gunn[7]

The same oath was by the Vice-President administered to the Secretary, together with the oath of Office.

ORDERED, That   Mr. Morris
    Mr. Carroll
    Mr. Langdon
    Mr. Read and
    Mr. Lee be a Committee, to consider and report the mode of communicating the Acts of Congress to the several States in the Union, and the number necessary for that purpose.[8]

Adjourned to 11 o'clock to-morrow morning.

THURSDAY, JUNE 4, 1789

The SENATE assembled,
Present as yesterday.

On the report of the Committee appointed the 3d June, to consider the mode of communicating the Acts of Congress to the several States in the Union—

RESOLVED, That in ten days after the passing of every Act of Congress during the present session, or until some other regulation shall be adopted, twenty two printed copies thereof, signed by the Secretary of the Senate, and Clerk of the House of Representatives, and certified by them to be true copies of the original Act, be lodged with the President of the United States, and that he be requested to cause to be transmitted, two of the said copies so at-

[7] Pierce Butler took the oath on June 8 and Jonathan Elmer on June 22. The oath was administered to Rufus King on July 25 and to Philip Schuyler on July 27.

[8] On June 4 this committee reported and a resolve on their report was passed by the Senate. The resolution was then sent to the House for concurrence.

tested as aforesaid, to each of the Supreme Executives in the several States.[9]

The Secretary carried the aforesaid resolve to the House of Representatives for their concurrence.[10]

The Senate proceeded to the SECOND reading of the bill, entitled, "An act for laying a duty on goods, wares and merchandizes imported into the United States."[11]—

And the further consideration of the bill was postponed until tomorrow.[12]

Adjourned to 11 o'clock to-morrow morning.

FRIDAY, JUNE 5, 1789

The SENATE assembled,

Present as yesterday.

A message from the House of Representatives, by Mr. Beckley, their Clerk —Who informed the Senate of the concurrence of the House on the resolution of the 4th June, upon the mode of communicating the acts of Congress to the Executives of the several States in the Union—

And he withdrew.

According to the order of the day, the Senate proceeded in the SECOND reading of the bill, entitled, "An act for laying a duty on goods, wares and merchandizes imported into the United States."[13]

Adjourned until Monday next at 11 o'clock.—

---

[9] The resolve is in Senate Joint and Concurrent Resolutions, Senate Records, DNA. It is followed by the concurrence of the House. A draft of a circular letter from George Washington addressed to the Executives states his agreement to the resolve referred to above. It is in Misc. Letters, M–179, roll 2, RG 59, General Records of the Department of State, DNA. See also the letter to the committee about printing 650 sets of laws, located in Misc. Legislative Papers, Senate Files, M-Ar.

[10] On June 5 the House concurred in this resolution and notified the Senate.

[11] At this point the preliminary journal adds:

And agree to the following amendments—

Amendt. 1.	Page 1.	Line 1st.	At A. insert, "for the discharge of the debts of the United States."
2d.		3d.	Strike out *Congress* and insert "Senate and Representatives" and after the words "United States" insert "of America in Congress assembled."
3d.		4.	Strike out *15th.* & insert "first" & in the same line strike out *June* & insert "July"
4th.		7.	Strike out from a to b
5th.		10.	Strike out *other*
6th.		11th.	Strike out *15* & insert "10."
7.		12.	Strike out *12* & insert "8."
8th.		13.	Strike out *5* & insert "3."

This material appears in the printed journal on June 11.

[12] On June 5 the second reading of this bill was resumed.

[13] At this point the preliminary journal adds:

MONDAY, JUNE 8, 1789

The SENATE assembled,

Present as on Friday.

The Honorable Pierce Butler, from the State of South-Carolina, appeared, presented his credentials,[14] and took his seat in the Senate.—

The Vice President administered the oath to Mr. Butler.

"In the House of Representatives of the United States

"Thursday, the 28th of May, 1789

"On motion,

"RESOLVED, That every such member of the present Congress, as is not yet furnished with a set of the journals of the late Congress, shall on application to the keeper of the records and papers of the said late Congress, be entitled to receive a complete set of such journals.

"Extract from the journal,

JOHN BECKLEY, Clerk"

Read and concurred—

And agree				
Amendt. 9th.	Page 1.	Line 14th.		To strike out 75. & insert "18"
10.		15th.		To strike out 15. & insert "10"
11th.		16th.		To strike out 8. & insert "5."
12th.		17.		To strike out 25. & insert "16."
13.	Page 2d.	Line 1st.		To strike out 75. & insert "60."
15th.		4th.		To strike out 200 & insert "150"
16th.		at B		insert "On Indigo per pound 16 Cents"
17.		Line 11th.		To strike out 3 & insert "1."
19th.		19th.		To strike out 10. & insert "12"
		21st.		To strike out the words from c to d.
21st.		at C		insert—"On gun powder ⎫ 10 per "On all paints, ⎬ centum ground in oil." ⎭ ad valorem
22d.		Line 32.		To strike out 7½. & insert "10." & in the same line to strike out "of Metal"
24th.		33d. 34.	⎫	To strike out 7½. & insert "10."
	Page 3d.	Lines 1. 2d. 3.	⎬	To strike out 7½. & insert "10."
25. 30.		6.		To strike out 7½. & insert "10."
		9.		To strike out 7½. & insert "10."
		10.		As above
32d.				And it was agreed to propose that all the Articles dutied ad Valorem be arranged together under their respective rates—
34th.	Page 3d.	Line 17.		Next after "Wool" insert "Cotton"
36th.		21.		"And on Cotton per pound 3 cents."

This material appears in the printed journal on June 11. On June 8 the Senate appointed a committee to consider adding a clause to this bill.

[14] The credentials are in Election Records: Credentials of Senators, Senate Records, DNA.

And the Secretary carried a message to the House of Representatives accordingly. ✐

The Senate proceeded in the second reading of the bill, entitled, "An act for laying a duty on goods, wares and merchandizes imported into the United States," And agreed,[15] that

> Mr. Ellsworth
> Mr. Morris
> Mr. Lee
> Mr. Butler and
> Mr. Dalton be a Committee to consider and report

the expediency of adding a clause, prohibiting the importation of goods from China or India, in ships or vessels, other than those belonging to the citizens of the United States.[16]

Adjourned to 11 o'clock to-morrow morning.

TUESDAY, JUNE 9, 1789

The SENATE assembled,
Present as yesterday.

The petitions of Brittingham Dickinson and others, in behalf of the shipwrights of Baltimore town,[17]—and of John Wharton and others, in behalf of the shipwrights of Philadelphia,[18] praying that such restrictions may take place, as to effect the revival of THEIR branch of business;—

The petition of Thomas Long and others, in behalf of the tradesmen and manufacturers of Baltimore town;[19]

Of Gibbons Sharp and others, in behalf of the manufacturers of the town of Boston;[20]

Of Anthony Post and others, in behalf of the manufacturers of the city of New-York,[21] praying that such regulations and restrictions may be adopted in relation to the importation of foreign articles, as may encourage home manufactures;

---

[15] The preliminary journal reads: "and agree Page & Line 1. to strike out from g to h Agreed that Mr. Ellsworth," etc.

[16] At this point the preliminary journal adds: "On Motion for reconsideration, Agreed, Page 1. Line 13. To strike out 3 & insert '2½.' " On June 9 the Senate resumed consideration of this bill.

[17] The petition is printed in the *New York Daily Gazette*, May 8, 1789.

[18] The petition is in Petitions and Memorials: Various subjects, Senate Records, DNA.

[19] The petition is in Petitions and Memorials: Various subjects, House Records, DNA.

[20] The petition is in Petitions and Memorials: Various subjects, Senate Records, DNA.

[21] The petition is in Petitions and Memorials: Various subjects, Senate Records, DNA.

Also, the petition of Jacob Morgan and others, in behalf of the distillers of Philadelphia;[22]

And of, John McLellan, in behalf of the merchants and traders of Portland,[23] praying that the proposed duty on molasses may be either abolished, or greatly reduced;—Were severally read, and ordered to lie for consideration.[24]

The bill, entitled, "An act imposing duties on tonnage," was read a FIRST time, and Thursday next was assigned for the SECOND reading.[25]

The Senate proceeded in the SECOND reading of the bill, entitled, "An act for laying a duty on goods, wares and merchandizes, imported into the United States,"[26] and Wednesday next was assigned for the THIRD reading of the bill.[27]

Adjourned to 11 o'clock to-morrow morning.

WEDNESDAY, JUNE 10, 1789

The SENATE assembled,
Present as yesterday.

Agreeably to the order of the day, proceeded to a THIRD reading of the

[22] The petition is in Petitions and Memorials: Various subjects, Senate Records, DNA.

[23] The petition is in Petitions and Memorials: Various subjects, Senate Records, DNA.

[24] No particular action was taken on any of these petitions during the First Congress.

[25] On June 11 the second reading of this bill was postponed until June 12.

[26] At this point the preliminary journal inserts:
and,

Upon the Report of the Committee to whom was referred the consideration of a farther Amendment, it was agreed to strike out in Amendt. 20th. Page 2d. from E to f being Lines 20 to 26 inclusive—& insert—'on all teas imported from Europe in Ships or Vessels built in the United States, and belonging wholly to a Citizen or Citizens thereof, or in Vessels built in foreign Countries and on the sixteenth day of May last, wholly the property of a Citizen or Citizens of the United States, and so continuing until the time of importation,—as follows:

On bohea tea. . . . . .per pound,   8 Cents
On all Souchong & other black teas. . . . . .per pound, 13 Cents
On all hyson teas. . . . . .per pound, 26 Cents
On all other green teas. . . . . .per pound, 16 Cents
On all teas imported in any other manner than as above mentioned as follows:

On bohea tea. . . . . .per pound, 15. Cents
On all Souchong or other black teas. . . . . .per pound, 22. Cents
On all hyson teas. . . . . .per pound, 45. Cents
On all other green teas. . . . . .per pound, 27. Cents
On all goods, wares & merchandizes other than teas imported *from China or India in Ships not built in the United States*, and not wholly the property of a Citizen or Citizens thereof, nor in Vessels built in foreign Countries and on the sixteenth day of May last, wholly the property of a Citizen or Citizens of the United States and so continuing until the time of importation Twelve & one half per Centum ad Valorem.
This material appears in the printed journal on June 11.

[27] On June 11 this bill was read for the third time.

bill, entitled, "An act for laying a duty on goods, wares and merchandizes imported into the United States."[28]

Adjourned to 11 o'clock to-morrow morning.

THURSDAY, JUNE 11, 1789

The SENATE assembled,

Present as yesterday.

Proceeded in the THIRD reading of the bill, entitled, "An act, for laying a duty on goods, wares and merchandizes imported into the United States."[29]

And the question being taken upon the bill, it was concurred, with the following amendments:—

Amendment	Page	Line	
1	1	1	At A. insert, "For the discharge of the debts of the United States."
2		3	Strike out "Congress," and insert, "Senate and Representatives," and after the words "United States," insert, "of America in Congress assembled."

---

[28] At this point the preliminary journal inserts:

Amendt.

And it was agreed to insert at E

18th. Page 2d. Line 15. "or in Vessels built in foreign Countries, and on the sixteenth day of May last, wholly the property of a Citizen or Citizens of the United States, and so continuing until the time of importation"—

23d. Page 2. at K insert "On Shoe & Knee buckles, ten per Centum ad Valorem"

31st. Page 3. at L. insert "On gold & silver lace ⎫ ten per Centum On gold & silver leaf." ⎭ ad Valorem

33d. at M insert "On playing cards per pack—10 cents"

These amendments appear in the printed journal for June 11. On June 11 the Senate resumed the third reading of the bill and several amendments were agreed upon and printed in the Journal.

[29] At this point the preliminary journal inserts:

And it was agreed to insert at N.

38th. Page 3. Line 23. "except on distilled Spirits other than Brandy & Geneva"

39th. 25. at O insert "as settled by the late treaty of peace."

40th. Page 4. Line 7. at P. insert "or in Vessels built in foreign Countries, and on the sixteenth day of May last, wholly the property of a Citizen or Citizens of the United States and so continuing, until the time of importation"—

The Question being taken upon the Bill, it was concurred with the amendments—

The preliminary journal does not include the other amendments since they were inserted in previous entries for the days on which they had been adopted.

Amendment	Page	Line	
3	1	4	Expunge "fifteenth day of June," and insert "first day of July."
4		7	Strike out the words following:—"On all distilled spirits of Jamaica proof, imported from the European dominions of any State or Kingdom, having a commercial treaty with the United States, per gallon, 12 cents. "On all other distilled spirits, imported from the European dominions of such State or Kingdom, per gallon, 10 cents."
5		10	Strike out the word "other."
6		11	Strike out "15" and insert "10."
7		12	Strike out "12" and insert "8."
8		13	Strike out "5" and insert "3."
9		14	Strike out "25" and insert "18."
10		15	Strike out "15" and insert "10."
11		16	Strike out "8" and insert "5."
12		17	Strike out "25" and insert "16."
{13 14	2	1} 2	Strike out "75," and insert, "60."
15		4	Strike out "200," and insert, "150."
16		do	At B. insert, "On indigo per pound, 16 cents."
17		11	Strike out "3," and insert, "1."
18		15	At E. insert, "Or in ships or vessels built in foreign countries and on the sixteenth day of May last, wholly the property of a citizen or citizens of the United States, and so continuing until the time of importation."
19		19	Strike out "10," and insert, "12."
20		20	Strike out the words following:—"On all teas imported from any country, other than China or India, in any ship or vessel whatsoever, or from China or India in any ship or vessel, which is not wholly the property of a citizen or citizens of the United States, as follows: "On bohea tea, per pound, 10 cents. "On all souchong or other black teas, per pound, 15 cents. "On all hyson teas, per pound, 30 cents. "On all other green teas, per pound, 18 cents." And insert, "On all teas imported from Europe, in ships or vessels built in the United States, and belonging wholly to a citizen or citizens thereof, or in ships or vessels built in foreign countries, and on the sixteenth day of May last wholly the property of a citizen or citizens of the United States, and so continuing until the time of importation, as follows:— "On bohea tea, per pound, 8 cents.

Amendment Page Line

"On all souchong and other black teas, per pound, 13 cents.

"On all hyson teas, per pound,   26 cents.

"On all other green teas, per pound,   16 cents.

"On all teas imported in any other manner than as above mentioned, as follows;

"On bohea tea, per pound,   15 cents.

"On all souchong and other black teas, per pound, 22 cents.

"On all hyson teas, per pound,   45 cents.

"On all other green teas, per pound,   27 cents.

"On all goods, wares and merchandizes, other than teas imported from China or India in ships not built in the United States, and not wholly the property of a citizen or citizens thereof, nor in vessels built in foreign countries and on the sixteenth day of May last wholly the property of a citizen or citizens of the United States, and so continuing until the time of importation,—Twelve and an half per centum ad valorem."

21   At C. insert,

"On gun powder,
"On all paints ground
in oil, } 10 per centum ad valorem."

22   32   Strike out "7½" and insert "10."
And in the same line strike out "of metal."

23   At K. insert, "On shoe and knee buckles ten per centum ad valorem."

24   2   { 33 and 34   Strike out "7½," and insert, "10."

25   3   1
26   2
27   3
28   6   } Strike out "7½," and insert "10."
29   9
30   10

31   At L. insert "On gold and silver lace, on gold and silver leaf, ten per centum ad valorem."

32   "And that all the articles dutied ad valorem be arranged together under their respective rates."

33   At M. insert "On playing cards per pack ten cents."

34   17   After "wool" insert "cotton," and strike out the words "other than indigo."

35 36 }   21   Insert after "sixty cents," "and on cotton per pound, three cents."

37   4   1   Strike out the following words, "And be it further enacted by the authority aforesaid, That there shall

Amendment	Page	Line	

be allowed and paid on every gallon of rum distilled within the United States, and exported beyond the limits of the same, in consideration of the duty on the importation of the molasses, from which the said rum shall have been distilled, six cents."

38	3	23	At N. insert "except on distilled spirits other than brandy and geneva."
39		25	At O. insert, "as settled by the late treaty of peace."
40	4	7	At P. insert, "or in vessels built in foreign countries, and on the sixteenth day of May last, wholly the property of a citizen or citizens of the United States, and so continuing until the time of importation."[30]

The SECOND reading of the bill, entitled, "An act imposing duties on tonnage," was postponed until to-morrow.[31]

Adjourned to 11 o'clock to-morrow morning.

FRIDAY, JUNE 12, 1789

The SENATE assembled,

Present as yesterday.

The SECOND reading of the bill, entitled, "An act imposing duties on tonnage," was farther postponed to Monday next.[32]

The Secretary carried to the House of Representatives the bill, entitled, "An act for laying a duty on goods, wares and merchandizes imported into the United States," as concurred with amendments.[33]

Mr. Lee, in behalf of the Committee thereto appointed, reported, "A bill to establish the Judicial Courts of the United States,"[34] which was read the FIRST time, and Monday the 22d of June, was assigned for the SECOND reading.[35]

ORDERED, That Mr. Butler be added to the Committee appointed, "To consider and report a bill defining the crimes and offences that shall be cognizable under the authority of the United States, and their punishment."[36]

Adjourned until Monday next, at 11 o'clock.

[30] The amendments noted with the bill are in House Bills, Senate Records, DNA. On June 12 this amended bill was carried to the House.

[31] On June 12 the second reading of this bill was postponed until June 15.

[32] On June 15 this bill was read for the second time.

[33] On June 16 the Senate amendments were considered by the House. Some were agreed to and others were disagreed to. The Senate was notified of these actions on June 17.

[34] The annotated manuscript copy of this bill is in Senate Bills, Senate Records, DNA. E-45657.

[35] On June 22 this bill was read again.

[36] On July 28 this committee introduced a bill. The bill was then read and scheduled for a second reading.

MONDAY, JUNE 15, 1789

The SENATE assembled,
Present as on Friday.

Proceeded to the SECOND reading a bill, entitled, "An act imposing duties on tonnage."—And after debate,[37]

Adjourned to 11 o'clock to-morrow morning.

TUESDAY, JUNE 16, 1789

The SENATE assembled,
Present as yesterday.

Proceeded in the SECOND reading of the bill, entitled, "An act imposing duties on tonnage."

Assigned to-morrow at 11 o'clock for the third reading.[38]

The petition of Richard Phillips, praying for consideration on account of his past services, was read,[39] and ordered to lie on the table.[40]

Adjourned to 11 o'clock to-morrow morning.

WEDNESDAY, JUNE 17, 1789

The SENATE assembled,
Present as yesterday.

Agreeably to the order of the day, proceeded to the THIRD reading of the bill, entitled, "An act imposing duties on tonnage," and concurred in the same with the amendments following:—

Amendment	Line	
1	1	Strike out "the Congress of the United States," and insert "the Senate and Representatives of the United States of America, in Congress assembled."
2	4	Strike out at A. "now belonging," and insert "on the 29th day of May, 1789, belonging and during the time such ships or vessels shall continue to belong."
3	{ 5 6 7	Strike out from c. to d. viz. "On all ships," &c. and and insert "on all ships or vessels hereafter built in the United States, belonging wholly or in part to subjects of foreign powers, at the rate of twenty cents per ton."
4	7	Next after the words "on all," insert "other."
5	8	Strike out from e. to f. viz. "belonging wholly or in part to subjects of other powers."

[37] On June 16 this bill was considered again and assigned a third reading.
[38] On June 17 this bill was read a third time and amended.
[39] This petition has not been located.
[40] On July 21 this petition was withdrawn.

Amendment	Line	
6	9 and 10	Strike out from g. to h. viz. "on all ships," &c.
7	14	Strike out "no" and "shall be," and insert "every."
8	17	Insert after "citizens thereof," "shall on each entry pay fifty cents per ton."
9	19	Strike out "June" and insert "July."[41]

On motion,

ORDERED, that a Committee, to consist of

> Mr. Butler
> Mr. Morris
> Mr. Langdon
> Mr. Dalton and
> Mr. Lee

be appointed to arrange and bring forward a system, for the regulation of the trade and intercourse between the United States and the territory of other powers in North-America, and the West-Indies, so as to place the same on a more beneficial and permanent footing.[42]

The Committee appointed May the 9th, to view the rooms in the City-Hall, and to confer with a Committee of the House of Representatives appointed for that purpose, reported:[43]—

ORDERED, That the report lie for consideration.[44]

Mr. Beckley, the Clerk of the House of Representatives, brought up the following resolve;—

In the House of Representatives of the United States

Monday, the 15th of June, 1789

The House proceeded to consider the amendments of the Senate to the bill, entitled, "An act for laying a duty on goods, wares and merchandizes imported into the United States."—Whereupon

RESOLVED, That this House doth agree to the 1st, 8th, 9th, 10th, 16th, 18th, 19th, 20th, 21st, 23d, 31st, 33d, 34th, 35th, 36th, 37th, 38th, 39th and 40th amendments—and doth disagree to the 2d, 4th, 5th, 6th, 7th, 11th, 12th, 13th, 14th, 15th, 17th, 22d, 24th, 25th, 26th, 27th, 28th, 29th, 30th and 32d amendments.

---

[41] The bill noting changes which correspond to amendments is in the Broadside Collection, RBkRm, DLC. E–45626. On June 18 this amended bill was returned to the House.

[42] On July 11 this committee presented its report.

[43] The report is in Joint Committee Reports, Senate Records, DNA. A copy of a note from John Beckley and Samuel Otis to the Mayor of New York regarding the report, and a House resolve to concur with this report are in Other Records: Various papers, Senate Records, DNA.

[44] On June 19 this committee's report was read, accepted, and sent to the House.

The third amendment was read and agreed to with an amendment, by striking out the word "July" proposed to be inserted by the Senate, and inserting in lieu thereof, the word "August."

Teste,   JOHN BECKLEY, Clerk[45]

And he withdrew.

ORDERED, That to-morrow be assigned for the consideration of the above message.[46]—

Adjourned to 11 o'clock to-morrow morning.

THURSDAY, JUNE 18, 1789

The SENATE assembled,
Present as yesterday.

The bill, entitled, "An act imposing duties on tonnage,"—with amendments, was carried to the House of Representatives by the Secretary.[47]

The Senate proceeded to the consideration of the message from the House of Representatives of yesterday, upon the proposed amendments to a bill, entitled, "An act for laying a duty on goods, wares and merchandizes imported into the United States;"—And after debate,[48]

Adjourned to 11 o'clock to-morrow morning.

FRIDAY, JUNE 19, 1789

The SENATE assembled,
Present as yesterday,
And Mr. Elmer from the State of New-Jersey.

Proceeded in the consideration of the message from the House of Representatives of the 17th, upon the amendments proposed by the Senate to a bill, entitled, "An act for laying a duty on goods, wares and merchandizes imported into the United States,"—and INSISTED on their amendments, as follow,—No. 2, 4, 5, 6, 7, 11, 12 and 17:—But RECEDED from the following amendments, No. 3, 13, 14, 15, 22, 24, 25, 26, 27, 28, 29, 30 and 32; and the Secretary delivered the message to the House of Representatives accordingly.[49]

The Committee, appointed May 9th, to view the rooms in the City-Hall,

---

[45] This resolve has not been located.

[46] On June 18 this message was considered.

[47] On June 24 the House disagreed to some of the Senate amendments to this bill and agreed to others. The House then appointed a committee to confer with a Senate committee on these amendments and notified the Senate of this action.

[48] On June 19 the Senate receded from some of its amendments to this bill and insisted on others. The House was then notified of this action.

[49] On June 23 the House considered this message and on June 24 it was resolved to agree to some amendments and insist on others. A conference committee was appointed and the Senate was notified of these actions.

and to confer with a Committee of the House of Representatives appointed for that purpose, reported in part—

That the two rooms on the first floor in the south-west angle of the said Hall, are not necessary for the accommodation of Congress, and that the Mayor of the City be notified thereof that the said rooms may be occupied by such persons as the Corporation may employ to take charge of the building.

Read and accepted, and sent to the House of Representatives for concurrence.[50]

Adjourned until 11 o'clock on Monday next.

MONDAY, JUNE 22, 1789

The SENATE assembled,
Present as on Friday.

The Vice President administered the oath to Mr. Elmer.

Proceeded to the SECOND reading of "A bill to establish the Judicial Courts of the United States;" And after progress,[51]—

Adjourned to 11 o'clock to-morrow morning.

TUESDAY, JUNE 23, 1789

The SENATE assembled,
Present as yesterday.

Proceeded in the second reading "A bill to establish the Judicial Courts of the United States;" And after progress,[52]

Adjourned to 11 o'clock to-morrow morning.

WEDNESDAY, JUNE 24, 1789

The SENATE assembled,
Present as yesterday.

Proceeded in the second reading, "A bill to establish the Judicial Courts of the United States."[53]

A message from the House of Representatives, by Mr. Beckley their Clerk; who brought to the Senate,

The concurrence of the House, upon the report of a Committee appointed May the 9th, to view the rooms in the City-Hall;[54]

A bill, entitled, "An act for establishing an Executive Department, to be

---

[50] On June 24 this report was approved by the House.
[51] On June 23 this bill was considered.
[52] On June 24 this bill was considered again.
[53] On June 25 this bill was considered again.
[54] On September 29 it was resolved that the City Hall of New York be the site of the second session of Congress.

denominated the Department of Foreign Affairs,"[55] which had passed the
House of Representatives, and to which the concurrence of the Senate was
desired:[56]

A bill, entitled, "An act for laying a duty on goods, wares and merchandizes imported into the United States," together with the concurrence of the
House of Representatives upon the SECOND amendment, and their concurrence
on the THIRD amendment insisted on by the Senate with an amendment, viz.

After the words "Senate and," to insert "House of;"

The non-concurrence of the House on the FOURTH and FIFTH amendments
insisted on by the Senate, and their desire of a conference with the Senate on
the subject matter of disagreement on the sixth, seventh, eleventh, twelfth
and seventeenth amendments—with the appointment of

> Mr. Boudinot
> Mr. Fitzsimons and
> Mr. Madison managers of the conference on the part

of the House;[57]

Also, a bill, entitled, "An act imposing duties on tonnage," and the agreement of the House of Representatives to the FIRST, SECOND and NINTH
amendments, with an amendment; and their disagreement to the THIRD,
FOURTH, FIFTH, SIXTH, SEVENTH and EIGHTH amendments proposed by the
Senate, together with the desire of the House of Representatives of a conference with the Senate upon the subject matter of the amendments disagreed to
with the appointment of

> Mr. Boudinot
> Mr. Fitzsimons and
> Mr. Madison managers of the conference on the part

of the House of Representatives[58]—

And he withdrew.

Adjourned to 11 o'clock to-morrow morning.

THURSDAY, JUNE 25, 1789

The SENATE assembled,
Present as yesterday.

Proceeded to consider the message from the House of Representatives, on
the amendments proposed by the Senate to a bill, entitled, "An act for

---

[55] The bill is in House Bills, Senate Records, DNA.

[56] On June 25 this bill was read for the first time and ordered to lie for consideration.

[57] On June 25 the Senate considered this message and appointed a committee to meet
with the House committee.

[58] On June 25 this message was considered and the Senate appointed a committee to
confer with the House committee.

laying a duty on goods, wares and merchandizes imported into the United States"—and

RESOLVED, to RECEDE from their SECOND amendment so far as to concur with the House of Representatives in inserting the words "HOUSE OF" next to the words "SENATE AND;"

RESOLVED, that the Senate do still INSIST on the fourth and fifth amendments, but have agreed to the proposed conference; and have charged their managers to confer with those of the House of Representatives, as well on the said fourth and fifth amendments, as on the other amendments, on which, the House of Representatives have requested a conference, and the Senate request that the House of Representatives will also charge their managers to confer with those of the Senate on the said fourth and fifth amendments; And that

> Mr. Morris
> Mr. Lee and
> Mr. Ellsworth be the managers on the part of the

Senate.[59]

And, a message was carried to the House of Representatives accordingly.[60]

Proceeded to consider the message from the House of Representatives of the 24th, upon their amendments proposed to a bill, entitled, "An act imposing duties on tonnage"—and, the Senate, agreed to recede from their FIRST amendment, so far as to concur with the House of Representatives in the insertion of the words "House of" after "Senate and;"

And in the NINTH amendment to strike out the word "July" and insert "August;"—And,

> RESOLVED, That   Mr. Morris
> Mr. Lee and
> Mr. Ellsworth be a Committee to confer with the

Committee appointed by the House of Representatives, upon the disagreement of the Senate and House on the third, fourth, fifth, sixth, seventh and eight amendments proposed by the Senate;

And a message was carried to the House of Representatives accordingly.[61]

The Senate proceeded to the consideration of a bill, entitled, "An act for establishing an Executive Department, to be denominated the Department of Foreign Affairs," which was read the first time, and ordered to lie for consideration.[62]

---

[59] The above resolves have not been located.

[60] On June 27 this committee reported, and the report was ordered to lie for consideration. On the same date the House resolved to recede from some of its amendments and agreed to some of the Senate amendments with amendments. The Senate resolved to agree to these House actions.

[61] On June 27 this committee reported, and the report was ordered to lie for consideration.

[62] On July 6 the second reading of this bill was postponed.

Proceeded in the SECOND reading, "A bill to establish the Judicial Courts of the United States."—And after debate,[63]

Adjourned to 11 o'clock to-morrow morning.

FRIDAY, JUNE 26, 1789

The SENATE assembled,
Present as yesterday.

Resumed the SECOND reading, "A bill to establish the Judicial Courts of the United States."[64]

Adjourned to 11 o'clock to-morrow morning.

SATURDAY, JUNE 27, 1789

The SENATE assembled,
Present as yesterday.

Mr. Morris, in behalf of the Committee appointed to confer with a Committee of the House of Representatives upon the amendments proposed to a bill, entitled, "An act for laying a duty on goods, wares and merchandizes imported into the United States;"[65] and upon a bill, entitled, "An act imposing duties on tonnage;"[66]—reported upon the respective bills; and the reports were ordered to lie for consideration.[67]

Resumed the SECOND reading, "A bill to establish the Judicial Courts of the United States."[68]

A message from the House of Representatives, by Mr. Beckley their Clerk—

"In the House of Representatives of the United States
"The 27th of June, 1789

"Mr. Boudinot, from the managers appointed on the part of this House, to attend the conference with the Senate on the subject matter of the amendments depending between the two Houses, to the bill, entitled, 'An act for laying a duty on goods, wares and merchandizes imported into the United States,' made a report; Whereupon,

"RESOLVED, That this House doth recede from their disagreement to the fourth, fifth, sixth, seventh, eleventh, twelfth, and seventeenth amendments,

---

[63] On June 26 this bill was considered again.

[64] On June 27 this bill was considered again.

[65] The report is in Joint Committee Reports, Senate Records, DNA.

[66] The report is in Joint Committee Reports, Senate Records, DNA.

[67] On June 27 the House acted on this report on the Tonnage Bill and notified the Senate of its resolutions on June 29.

[68] On June 29 this bill was considered again.

and doth agree to the said amendments respectively, with amendments to the said twelfth and seventeenth amendments, as follow: In the twelfth amendment, strike out 'sixteen' and insert 'twenty.' In the seventeenth amendment, strike out 'one' and insert 'two.'

"Teste,   JOHN BECKLEY, Clerk"[69]

And he withdrew.

The Senate agreed so far to recede from their twelfth and seventeenth amendments, proposed to the House of Representatives, as to concur in their propositions on those amendments.[70]

Adjourned until 11 o'clock on Monday morning.

MONDAY, JUNE 29, 1789

The SENATE assembled,
Present as on Saturday.

Resumed the SECOND reading of "A bill to establish the Judicial Courts of the United States."[71]

The bill entitled, "An act for laying a duty on goods, wares and merchandizes imported into the United States," was carried to the House of Representatives, with the amendments as agreed to on the 27th.[72]

A message from the House of Representatives, by Mr. Beckley, their Clerk;—

"In the House of Representatives of the United States
"The 27th of June, 1789

"Mr. Boudinot, from the managers appointed on the part of this House, to attend the conference with the Senate, on the subject matter of the amendments depending between the two Houses, to the bill, entitled, 'An act imposing duties on tonnage'—made a report;—Whereupon,

"RESOLVED, That this House doth recede from their disagreement to the third, seventh and eighth amendments; and doth agree to the said amendments, with an amendment to the third amendment, as followeth:—

"In lieu of striking out the clause as proposed by the Senate, to retain the same, and add to the end thereof, the words proposed to be inserted by the Senate, amended to read thus, 'On all ships or vessels hereafter built in the United States, belonging wholly or in part to subjects of foreign powers, at the rate of thirty cents per ton.'

---

[69] This House message has not been located.

[70] On June 29 this amended bill was carried back to the House.

[71] On June 30 this bill was considered again.

[72] On July 1 the House notified the Senate that it had appointed a committee to examine this enrolled bill and present it to the President. Mr. Wingate was appointed to join this committee.

"Resolved, That this House doth insist on their disagreement to the fourth, fifth and sixth amendments.

"Teste, John Beckley, Clerk"[73]

Adjourned to 11 o'clock to-morrow morning.

TUESDAY, June 30, 1789

The Senate assembled,
Present as yesterday.

The Senate proceeded to the consideration of the resolve of the House of Representatives of the 27th, and the report of a Committee of conference, on their disagreement to the amendments proposed by the Senate to a bill, entitled, "An act imposing duties on tonnage"—And

Resolved, to adhere to their third, fourth, fifth and sixth amendments:—But so far to concur in the amendment of the House of Representatives upon the third amendment, as to agree to the insertion of the following words, "On all ships or vessels hereafter built in the United States, belonging wholly or in part to subjects of foreign powers, at the rate of thirty cents per ton."[74]

The Senate resumed the second reading of "A bill to establish the Judicial Courts of the United States"—And after debate,[75]

Adjourned to 11 o'clock to-morrow morning.

---

[73] This House message containing two resolves has not been located. On June 30 the Senate adhered to some of its amendments and agreed to some of the House amendments to this bill.

[74] On July 1 this bill was carried to the House of Representatives. On the same date the House receded from some of its amendments to this bill and it was ordered to be enrolled. The House then notified the Senate of these actions.

[75] On July 1 this bill was considered again.

WEDNESDAY, July 1, 1789

The SENATE assembled,

Present as yesterday.

Resumed the SECOND reading of "A bill to establish the Judicial Courts of the United States."[1]

A message from the House of Representatives, by Mr. Beckley their Clerk; Who informed the Senate, that a Committee consisting of

Mr. Partridge and

Mr. White, was appointed on the part of the House, to join such Committee as may be appointed on the part of the Senate, to examine an enroled bill, entitled, "An act for laying a duty on goods, wares and merchandizes imported into the United States," and to lay the same before the President of the United States for his approbation—

And he withdrew.

Whereupon Mr. Wingate was appointed on the part of the Senate; and the House of Representatives was notified accordingly.[2]

The bill, entitled, "An act imposing duties on tonnage," was carried to the House of Representatives as agreed to on the 30th of June.

A message from the House of Representatives, by Mr. Beckley their Clerk; Who informed the Senate that the House had receded from their disagreement to the fourth, fifth, and sixth amendments of the Senate, to the bill, entitled, "An act imposing duties on tonnage"—And he withdrew.[3]

Adjourned to 11 o'clock to-morrow morning.

THURSDAY, July 2, 1789

The SENATE assembled,

Present as yesterday.

Mr. Wingate on the part of the joint Committee reported, that they had examined the enroled bill, entitled, "An act for laying a duty on goods, wares and merchandizes imported into the United States;"[4] And that the same was perfected.

The Senate resumed the SECOND reading of "A bill to establish the Judicial Courts of the United States."[5]

A message from the House of Representatives, by Mr. Beckley their Clerk;

---

[1] On July 2 this bill was considered again.

[2] On July 2 this bill, signed by the Speaker, was brought to the Senate and signed by the Vice President. It was then delivered to the President.

[3] On July 6 the House notified the Senate that it had appointed a committee to enroll this bill and present it to the President. Mr. Wingate was appointed by the Senate to join this committee.

[4] The enrolled bill is in Enrolled Acts, RG 11, DNA. E–22193, E–45693.

[5] On July 3 this bill was considered again.

Who brought up the enroled bill, entitled, "An act for laying a duty on goods, wares and merchandizes imported into the United States," signed by the Speaker;

Also, a bill, entitled, "An act to establish the Treasury Department;"[6] which had passed the House of Representatives, for the concurrence of the Senate thereon.

The enroled bill was signed by the Vice President, and delivered to the Chairman of the Committee, who laid it before the President of the United States for his approbation.[7]

Adjourned to 11 o'clock to-morrow morning.

FRIDAY, JULY 3, 1789

The SENATE assembled,
Present as yesterday.

Resumed the SECOND reading of "A bill to establish the Judicial Courts of the United States:" And after debate,[8]

Adjourned to 11 o'clock to-morrow morning.

MONDAY, JULY 6, 1789

The SENATE assembled,
Present as on Friday.

Resumed the SECOND reading "A bill to establish the Judicial Courts of the United States."—

Assigned to-morrow for the THIRD reading.[9]

The bill, entitled, "An act to establish the Treasury Department,"—was read a FIRST time, and Monday next was assigned for a SECOND reading.[10]

The SECOND reading of a bill entitled, "An act for establishing an Executive Department, to be denominated the Department of Foreign Affairs"—was deferred to Thursday next.[11]

A bill, entitled, "An act to establish an Executive Department, to be denominated the Department of War,"[12] was read a FIRST time, and Friday next was assigned for a second reading.[13]

---

[6] An annotated printed copy of the bill is in House Bills, Senate Records, DNA. E–45631. On July 6 this bill was read for the first time and the second reading was assigned.

[7] On July 4 the President signed this bill and the House notified the Senate of this action on July 6.

[8] On July 6 this bill was considered again.

[9] On July 7 this bill was read for the third time.

[10] On July 21 this bill was read for the second time and ordered to lie for consideration.

[11] On July 14 this bill was read a second time and debated.

[12] Two annotated printed copies of this bill are in House Bills, Senate Records, DNA and the Broadside Collection, RBkRm, DLC.

[13] On July 21 this bill was read a second time and considered.

A message from the House of Representatives, by Mr. Beckley their Clerk; Who informed the Senate, that the President of the United States had affixed his signature to a bill, entitled, "An act for laying a duty on goods, wares and merchandizes imported into the United States,"—and had returned it to the House of Representatives—

And that the House had appointed a Committee on their part, to be joined by a Committee on the part of the Senate, for the purpose of examining an enroled bill, entitled, "An act imposing duties on tonnage," and to lay the same before the President of the United States for his appropbation—

He also brought with him a resolve of the House of Representatives—

Providing, "That there be prefixed to the publication of the acts of the present session of Congress, a correct copy of the Constitution of the United States"[14]—

And he withdrew.

Mr. Wingate was appointed on the part of the Senate to join a Committee of the House of Representatives, in examining, &c. the bill, entitled, "An act imposing duties on tonnage."[15]

The resolve of the House of Representatives, providing, that a copy of the Constitution of the United States be prefixed to the publication of the acts of the present session of Congress, was read;

Whereupon,

Resolved, That the Senate do concur.

Adjourned to 11 o'clock to-morrow morning.

TUESDAY, JULY 7, 1789

The SENATE assembled,

Present as on Friday.

According to the order of the day, proceeded to a THIRD reading of "A bill to establish the Judicial Courts of the United States."[16]

Adjourned to 11 o'clock to-morrow morning.

WEDNESDAY, JULY 8, 1789

The SENATE assembled,

Present as yesterday.

Mr. Wingate in behalf of the Committee appointed to inspect an enroled bill, entitled, "An act imposing duties on Tonnage,"[17] reported, that they had

---

[14] The resolve of the House is in Messages from the House, Senate Records, DNA. It is also printed in the preliminary journal.

[15] On July 8 Mr. Wingate reported and the enrolled bill, signed by the Speaker, was brought to the Senate and signed by the Vice President.

[16] A copy of this printed bill, dated before the third reading on July 7, 1789 (probably in the wording decided on just prior to this date), is in the Broadside Collection, RBkRm, DLC. It was considered again on July 8.

[17] The inspected enrolled bill is in Enrolled Acts, RG 11, DNA. E–45700.

examined the same, and the errors being corrected, it was ready to be laid before the President for his approbation.

A message from the House of Representatives, by Mr. Beckley, their Clerk;—

Mr. President,

I am directed to bring to the Senate an enroled bill, entitled, "An act imposing duties on tonnage," Which having been examined by the Committee, is signed by the Speaker of the House of Representatives—

And he withdrew.

The Vice President affixed his signature to the above bill, and the Committee on the part of the Senate, was ordered to proceed.[18]

The Senate resumed the THIRD reading of "A bill to establish the Judicial Courts of the United States."[19]—

Adjourned to 11 o'clock to-morrow morning.

THURSDAY, JULY 9, 1789

The SENATE assembled,
Present as yesterday.

Mr. Wingate, in behalf of the joint Committee, appointed to lay before the President of the United States, an enroled bill, entitled, "An act imposing duties on tonnage," for his approbation, reported, that they yesterday executed the service assigned them.[20]

The Senate resumed the THIRD reading of "A bill to establish the Judicial Courts of the United States."

On motion to amend the paragraph, section 27th, line 6th, by inserting, "That Grand Jurors in all cases whatever, and petit Jurors in all cases not punishable with death"—Passed in the negative:

And in the same section, line 11th, to insert these words, "That petit Jurors, in all cases punishable with death, shall be returned from the body of the county in which the offence was committed"—Passed in the negative.[21]

Adjourned to 11 o'clock to-morrow.

FRIDAY, JULY 10, 1789

The SENATE assembled,
Present as yesterday.

Resumed the THIRD reading of "A bill to establish the Judicial Courts of the

---

[18] On July 9 Mr. Wingate reported that the committee had laid this bill before the President on July 8.

[19] On July 9 this bill was considered again and amendments to it were rejected.

[20] On July 20 the President signed this bill and the House notified the Senate of this action.

[21] On July 10 this bill was amended and considered again.

United States;" and agreed, in section twenty-ninth, line 11th, after the word "For," to insert "The executor or administrator," and to expunge the words "The estate of the deceased in the hands of such" and insert "The" line 12th, "or by."

In section thirtieth to add, "And may, at any time permit either of the parties to amend any defect in the process or pleadings, upon such conditions as the said courts respectively shall in their discretion, and by their rules prescribe:"

In section 31st, line 1st, to expunge the words "By the authority aforesaid." So in all cases where the words are redundant:

In line 2d, next after "That" inclusive, expunge the words "Every Justice, &c." as far as to, "Was committed:" in line 9th.

In section 31st, line 10th, after "By" insert these words, "Justice or Judge of the United States, or by."

On motion it was agreed to reconsider the amendment, page 13th, line 35th, "Or on any hearing of a cause in equity in a circuit court;" and in line 39th, to reconsider "Or supreme court, as the case may be—" So the words were struck out.[22]

Adjourned to 11 o'clock to-morrow morning.

SATURDAY, July 11, 1789

The SENATE assembled,
Present as yesterday.

Resumed the THIRD reading of "A bill to establish the Judicial Courts of the United States."

On motion to insert between section 17th, and 18th, "And be it further enacted, that it shall be the duty of Circuit Courts, in causes in equity, and of admiralty and maritime jurisdiction, to cause the facts on which they found their sentence or decree, fully to appear upon the record, either from the pleadings and decree itself, or a state of the case, agreed by the parties or their counsel; or if they disagree, by a stating of the case by the court."—

A motion was made to postpone THIS to take up the following: "And be it further enacted, That it shall be the duty of Circuit Courts, in the trial of causes in equity, and of admiralty jurisdiction, where facts are contested, to cause the evidence exhibited at the hearing, to be reduced to writing, if either of the parties require it, or a state of the facts to be made, if the parties agree thereto:"—

Passed in the negative.

---

[22] On July 11 this bill was again considered and amended.

On motion to expunge the word "Facts," and insert the word "Evidence;"
                    Passed in the negative:
And on the motion[23] for the MAIN question;
                    Passed in the affirmative.

Agreed to expunge the 15th section. "And be it further enacted, That suits in equity," &c.

Agreed, section 20th, page 8th, line 6th, to expunge "Containing;" and insert, "Whereto shall be annexed and returned therewith, at the day and place therein mentioned."

On motion, "That in the trial of causes in the Supreme Court upon a writ of error from a Circuit Court, the Justices who sat on the trial of the cause below, shall not vote in the decision of the cause, except where the court shall be equally divided, but may assign the reasons of their former decision;"
                    Passed in the negative.

On motion to insert the following clause, "But no Judge of the Supreme Court shall sit on any cause wherein he has given judgment in a Circuit Court;"[24]

                    Passed in the negative.[25]
Adjourned until 11 o'clock on Monday morning.

MONDAY, JULY 13, 1789

The SENATE assembled,
Present as on Saturday.

Mr. Butler, in behalf of the Committee, appointed the 17th of June, "To bring forward a system for the regulation of the trade and intercourse, between the United States and the territory of other powers in North-America and the West-Indies, so far as to place the same upon a more beneficial and permanent footing," REPORTED;[26] And the report was ordered to lie for consideration.[27]

Resumed the THIRD reading, of "A bill to establish the Judicial Courts of the United States."—And,

Agreed to strike out from the word "Where," line 3d, sec. 22d, to the words "Writ of error," in line 6th, and what follows the word "Supersedeas," in line 12th, to the word "Execution" inclusive, and insert instead thereof, "And where upon such writ or error:"

---

[23] The smooth journal reads: "And on motion."

[24] A draft of these motions covering through July 13 is in Senate Bills, Senate Records, DNA.

[25] On July 13 this bill was considered again, amended, and recommitted.

[26] This committee report has not been located.

[27] On July 14 consideration of this bill was postponed.

To expunge "Well as his costs," in the last line, and insert as follows; "Also single or double costs, in their discretion."

Agreed to restore the 15th section, adding the words "Plain, adequate, and," before "complete."

Section eighteenth, last line, agreed to expunge the word "Shall," and insert as follows, "But in the discretion of the court may be adjudged to."

Section ninth, last line, insert "Issues in."

On motion, by Mr. Lee, seconded by Mr. Grayson, to reconsider the twenty-seventh section, and insert, after the word "Services," in the 11th line, "Provided always, that in criminal cases where the punishment is capital, the petit jury shall come from the body of the county where the fact was committed:"

Passed in the negative.

Ordered that the bill be recommitted.[28]

Adjourned to 11 o'clock to-morrow morning.

TUESDAY, JULY 14, 1789

The SENATE assembled,
Present as yesterday.

The report of the Committee appointed the 17th of June, "To bring forward a system for the regulation of the trade, and intercourse, between the United States and the territory of other powers in North-America and the West-Indies, so far as to place the same upon a more beneficial and permanent footing," was further postponed to the 15th of July.[29]

Proceeded to the SECOND reading of a bill, entitled, "An act for establishing an Executive Department, to be denominated the Department of Foreign Affairs, and after debate[30]—

Adjourned to 11 o'clock to-morrow morning.

WEDNESDAY, JULY 15, 1789

The SENATE assembled,
Present as yesterday.

A message from the House of Representatives, by Mr. Beckley, their Clerk—

Mr. President,

The House of Representatives have passed the bill, entitled, "An act to

---

[28] On July 17 this bill was passed and ordered to be sent to the House of Representatives for concurrence. The committee to organize the judiciary reported on September 16, and the Judiciary Act was read for the first time.

[29] On August 5 this report was read and printed in the Journal. The Senate agreed to the first part of the report and ordered the second part recommitted. The committee is not mentioned again.

[30] On July 15 this bill was considered again.

regulate the collection of the duties imposed by law on the tonnage of ships or vessels, and on goods, wares and merchandizes, imported into the United States," to which they request the concurrence of the Senate[31]—

And he withdrew.

The above bill was read a FIRST time, and Friday next was assigned for a SECOND reading.[32]

Resumed the SECOND reading of the bill, entitled, "An act for establishing an Executive Department to be denominated the Department of Foreign Affairs."[33]

Adjourned to 11 o'clock to-morrow morning.

THURSDAY, JULY 16, 1789

The SENATE assembled,
Present as yesterday.

Resumed the SECOND reading of the bill, entitled, "An act for establishing an Executive Department to be denominated the Department of Foreign Affairs;" and after debate,[34]

Adjourned to 11 o'clock to-morrow morning.

FRIDAY, JULY 17, 1789

The SENATE assembled,
Present as yesterday.

Resumed the SECOND reading of the bill, entitled, "An act for establishing an Executive Department to be denominated the Department of Foreign Affairs;" And agreed line 1st to expunge the word "Congress of the United States," and insert, "Senate and House of Representatives of the United States of America in Congress assembled,"[35] and assigned to-morrow for a THIRD reading.[36]

On motion,

That on the final question upon a bill or resolve, any Member shall have a right to enter his PROTEST or dissent on the Journal, with reasons in support of such dissent, provided the same be offered within two days after the determination on such final question—

Passed in the negative.

The engrossed "Bill to establish the Judicial Courts of the United States,"

---

[31] An annotated printed copy of this bill is in House Bills, Senate Records, DNA.
[32] On July 18 the second reading of this bill was assigned.
[33] On July 16 this bill was considered again.
[34] On July 17 this bill was considered again and amended.
[35] This agreement to amend line 1 is in House Bills, Senate Records, DNA.
[36] On July 18 this bill was read a third time, amended, and passed.

was read,[37] and upon the question, "Shall the bill pass?" The yeas and nays being required by one-fifth of the Senators present, the determination was as follows:

Mr. Bassett	Yea	
Mr. Butler		Nay
Mr. Carroll	Yea	
Mr. Dalton	Yea	
Mr. Ellsworth	Yea	
Mr. Elmer	Yea	
Mr. Few	Yea	
Mr. Grayson		Nay
Mr. Gunn	Yea	
Mr. Henry	Yea	
Mr. Johnson	Yea	
Mr. Izard	Yea	
Mr. Langdon		Nay
Mr. Lee		Nay
Mr. Maclay		Nay
Mr. Morris	Yea	
Mr. Paterson	Yea	
Mr. Read	Yea	
Mr. Strong	Yea	
Mr. Wingate		Nay

So the BILL PASSED, and the Secretary was directed to carry the same to the House of Representatives for concurrence.[38]

Adjourned to 11 o'clock to-morrow morning.

SATURDAY, JULY 18, 1789

The SENATE assembled,

Present as yesterday.

Agreeably to the order of the day proceeded to a THIRD reading of the bill, entitled "An Act for establishing an Executive Department, to be denominated the Department of Foreign Affairs."

ORDERED, That in taking the yeas and nays, where the Vice-President is called upon to vote, the Secretary propose to him the question.

---

[37] The annotated engrossed bill is in Engrossed Senate Bills and Resolutions, Senate Records, DNA. A copy of the printed engrossed bill is in the Broadside Collection, RBkRm, DLC.

The motions journalized on the preceding pages are attached to the manuscript bill located in Senate Bills, Senate Records, DNA.

[38] On July 20 this bill was sent to the House.

On motion to strike out of the bill these words—Page 3d, line 15th, "By the President of the United States," and the yeas and nays being required thereupon by one fifth of the Senators present, the determination was as follows:—

Mr. Bassett		Nay
Mr. Carroll		Nay
Mr. Dalton		Nay
Mr. Elmer		Nay
Mr. Few	Yea	
Mr. Grayson	Yea	
Mr. Gunn	Yea	
Mr. Henry		Nay
Mr. Johnson	Yea	
Mr. Izard	Yea	
Mr. Langdon	Yea	
Mr. Lee	Yea	
Mr. Maclay	Yea	
Mr. Morris		Nay
Mr. Paterson		Nay
Mr. Read		Nay
Mr. Strong		Nay
Mr. Wingate	Yea	
The Vice President		Nay

So it passed in the negative, and the clause proposed to be struck out was retained.

On motion to strike out these words,

Line 4th, "Such duties as shall from time to time be enjoined on, or entrusted to him, by the President of the United States, agreeable to the Constitution, relative to correspondences, commissions or instructions to or with public Ministers or Consuls from the United States, or to negotiations with public Ministers from foreign States or Princes, or to memorials, or other applications, from foreign public Ministers, or other foreigners, or to such other matters respecting foreign affairs, as the President of the United States shall assign to the said department: And furthermore that the said principal officer shall conduct the business of said department, in such manner as the President of the United States shall, from time to time, order or instruct."

And insert in lieu thereof these words,

"The duties of his office with integrity, ability, and diligence"—

Passed in the negative.

On motion to strike out of line 13th these words,

"To be appointed by the said principal officer"—

Passed in the negative.

Agreed to expunge the proviso in lines 17th, 18th, and 19th, to wit:[39]—

"PROVIDED NEVERTHELESS, That no appointment of such chief Clerk shall be valid, until the same shall have been approved by the President of the United States."

Upon the question, "To concur in this bill as amended?" and one fifth of the Senators present requiring the yeas and nays, the determination was as follows:—

Mr. Bassett	Yea	
Mr. Carroll	Yea	
Mr. Dalton	Yea	
Mr. Ellsworth	Yea	
Mr. Elmer	Yea	
Mr. Few		Nay
Mr. Grayson		Nay
Mr. Gunn		Nay
Mr. Henry	Yea	
Mr. Johnson		Nay
Mr. Izard		Nay
Mr. Langdon		Nay
Mr. Lee		Nay
Mr. Maclay		Nay
Mr. Morris	Yea	
Mr. Paterson	Yea	
Mr. Read	Yea	
Mr. Strong	Yea	
Mr. Wingate		Nay

So the bill was concurred with amendments.[40]

The petition of Robert Sickles and others, Meters of the city of New-York,[41] praying that an augmentation of the rate for measuring grain, &c. may be made in the act for the collection of duties, was read and ordered to lie on the table.[42]

Assigned Monday next for the SECOND reading of the bill, entitled, "An act to regulate the collection of the duties imposed by law on the tonnage of ships or vessels, and on goods, wares and merchandizes imported into the United States."[43]

Adjourned to 11 o'clock on Monday morning.

---

[39] The agreement to amend lines 17, 18, and 19 is in House Bills, Senate Records, DNA.

[40] On July 20 this amended bill was carried to the House. On the same date the House notified the Senate of its concurrence in the Senate amendments.

[41] The petition is in Petitions and Memorials: Various subjects, Senate Records, DNA.

[42] This petition was not considered again in the First Congress.

[43] On July 20 this bill was read for the second time.

MONDAY, JULY 20, 1789

The SENATE assembled,

Present as on Saturday,

Except Mr. Ellsworth, and Mr. Bassett, who had leave of absence.

The Secretary carried to the House of Representatives for their concurrence, "A bill to establish the Judicial Courts of the United States," and[44]

"A bill for establishing an Executive Department, to be denominated the Department of Foreign Affairs;"

Concurred in by the Senate with amendments.

Agreeably to the order of the day, proceeded to the SECOND reading of the bill, entitled, "An act to regulate the collection of the duties imposed by law on the tonnage of ships or vessels, and on goods, wares and merchandizes imported into the United States."

And after debate it was committed to

> Mr. Morris
>
> Mr. Langdon
>
> Mr. Carroll
>
> Mr. Dalton and
>
> Mr. Lee to report such additions and alterations as

they may judge requisite.[45]

A message from the House of Representatives, by Mr. Beckley, their Clerk—

Mr. President,

The House of Representatives have passed a bill, entitled, "An act for the establishment and support of Light-Houses, Beacons and Buoys."[46]—They have concurred in the amendments proposed by the Senate to a bill, entitled, "An act for establishing an Executive Department, to be denominated the Department of Foreign Affairs."[47]—And they have received from the President of the United States an enroled bill, entitled, "An act imposing duties on tonnage," with his signature affixed thereto—

---

[44] On July 20 the House read this bill for the first time. Consideration of the bill was postponed from day to day until it was considered by a committee of the whole on August 24. Consideration was again postponed until August 29 and 31 when another meeting of the committee of the whole was held. After another series of postponements the bill was again considered by a committee of the whole on September 8 and 9. From September 11–17 the bill and amendments to it were considered in the House. On September 17 the House amended this bill and passed it. The amended bill was then sent to the Senate where a committee was appointed to consider the House amendments.

[45] On July 21 this bill was considered again and the third reading assigned.

[46] An annotated printed copy of the bill is in the Broadside Collection, RBkRm, DLC. This bill was read a first time and assigned to a second reading on July 21.

[47] On July 21 the House notified the Senate that it had appointed a committee to examine this bill and present it to the President. Mr. Strong was appointed by the Senate to join this committee.

And he withdrew.

Adjourned to 11 o'clock to-morrow morning.

TUESDAY, JULY 21, 1789

The SENATE assembled,

Present as yesterday,

Except Mr. Maclay, who had leave of absence.

Resumed the SECOND reading of a bill, entitled, "An act to regulate the collection of the duties imposed by law on the tonnage of ships or vessels, and on goods, wares, and merchandizes imported into the United States," and assigned to-morrow for a THIRD reading.[48]

A message from the House of Representatives, by Mr. Beckley, their Clerk;—

Who brought up a bill, entitled, "An act to provide for the government of the territory north-west of the river Ohio."[49]—

He also informed the Senate, that the House of Representatives had appointed a Committee, to be joined by a Committee on the part of the Senate, to examine an ENROLED bill, entitled, "An act for establishing an Executive Department to be denominated the Department of Foreign Affairs," and to lay the same before the President of the United States for his approbation.

Mr. Strong was appointed on the part of the Senate, to join the Committee on the part of the House, in examining, &c. the ENROLED bill above-mentioned; and the Secretary notified the House accordingly.[50]

The bill, entitled, "An act to provide for the government of the territory north west of the river Ohio;" was read a FIRST time, and Wednesday was assigned for a SECOND reading.[51]

The bill, entitled, "An act for the establishment and support of Light-Houses, Beacons, and Buoys," was read a first time, and tomorrow 11 o'clock was assigned for a SECOND reading.[52]

The bill, entitled, "An act to establish an Executive Department, to be denominated the Department of War," was read a second time, and the farther consideration of it was postponed until to-morrow.[53]

The bill, entitled, "An act to establish the Treasury Department," was read a SECOND time, and ordered to lie for consideration.[54]

---

[48] On July 23 a question on this bill was defeated.

[49] An annotated printed copy of the bill is in House Bills, Senate Records, DNA.

[50] On July 22 this bill, signed by the Speaker, was sent to the Senate for the Vice President's signature. It was then delivered to the President.

[51] On July 25 the second reading of this bill was postponed.

[52] On July 23 this bill was read a second time, considered, and committed.

[53] On August 3 this bill was considered again and a third reading was assigned.

[54] On July 29 this bill was considered again.

Richard Phillips had leave to withdraw his petition.

Adjourned to 12 o'clock to-morrow.

WEDNESDAY, JULY 22, 1789

The SENATE assembled,

Present as yesterday.

Mr. Strong, in behalf of the joint Committee, appointed to examine an ENROLED bill, entitled, "An act for establishing an Executive Department, to be denominated the Department of Foreign Affairs"[55]—

REPORTED, That they had performed that service.

A message from the House of Representatives, by Mr. Beckley, their Clerk: —Who brought up the above mentioned bill, signed by the Speaker of the House of Representatives—

And he withdrew.

The ENROLED bill being signed by the Vice President, was, by the Committee, laid before the President of the United States for his approbation.[56]

Adjourned to 11 o'clock to-morrow.

THURSDAY, JULY 23, 1789

The SENATE assembled,

Present as yesterday.

The bill, entitled, "An act for the establishment and support of Light-Houses, Beacons, and Buoys," was read a second time, and committed to

Mr. Morris

Mr. Langdon and

Mr. Dalton[57]

On the question, Whether the clauses in the bill, entitled, "An act to regulate the collection of the duties imposed by law on the tonnage of ships or vessels, and on goods, wares, and merchandizes imported into the United States," providing, "That oaths shall be administered to the master, or other persons having the charge or command of any ship or vessel," shall be expunged, and the words "And the owner and master's declaration, with penalties for false entry," be substituted?

Passed in the negative.[58]

Adjourned to 11 o'clock to-morrow.

---

[55] The inspected enrolled bill is in Enrolled Acts, RG 11, DNA. E–45691.

[56] On July 27 the President signed this bill and the House notified the Senate of this action.

[57] On July 24 the committee on this bill reported amendments.

[58] On July 27 this bill was read a third time and the Senate passed numerous amendments which are printed in the Journal.

FRIDAY, JULY 24, 1789

The SENATE assembled,

Present as yesterday.

The Committee appointed on the bill, entitled, "An act for the establishment and support of Light-Houses, Beacons, and Buoys"—

REPORTED amendments,[59] which were read, and ordered to be printed.[60]

The Committees requested a recess, to give opportunity to perfect their reports.

Adjourned to 11 o'clock to-morrow.

SATURDAY, JULY 25, 1789

The SENATE assembled,

Present as yesterday.

The honorable Rufus King, from the State of New-York, appeared, produced his credentials,[61] and took his seat—

And the oath was administered to him according to law.

The petition of Mathew Tallcott[62] and others, citizens of the State of Connecticut,[63] praying that the port of Middletown, in the said State, might be established a port of entry and delivery, was read, and ordered to lie for consideration.[64]

The SECOND reading of the bill, entitled, "An act to provide for the government of the territory north-west of the river Ohio," was further postponed to Monday next.[65]

Adjourned to 11 o'clock on Monday morning.

MONDAY, JULY 27, 1789

The SENATE assembled,

Present as on Saturday.

The honorable Philip Schuyler, from the State of New-York, appeared, produced his credentials,[66] and took his seat—And the oath was administered to him according to law.

---

[59] A copy of the printed bill, with amendments, is in the Broadside Collection, RBkRm, DLC. The report has not been located.

[60] On July 28 this bill was again considered.

[61] The credentials are in Election Records: Credentials of Senators, Senate Records, DNA.

[62] The smooth journal spells Tallcott incorrectly as "Talcott." In the preliminary journal the name is correct.

[63] The petition is in Petitions and Memorials: Various subjects, Senate Records, DNA.

[64] This petition was not considered in the First Congress.

[65] On July 31 this bill was read for the second time.

[66] The credentials are in Election Records: Credentials of Senators, Senate Records, DNA.

Mr. Paterson had leave of absence for four days.

A message from the House of Representatives, by Mr. Beckley their Clerk;
—Who brought up a bill, entitled, "An act for settling the accounts between
the United States and invidiual States,"[67] for concurrence—and informed the
Senate, that the President of the United States had affixed his signature to a
bill, entitled, "An act for the establishment of an Executive Department, to be
denominated the Department of Foreign Affairs;" and had returned the same
to the House of Representatives—

And he withdrew.

The first mentioned bill was read a FIRST time, and July the 29th was assigned for a SECOND reading.[68]

Proceeded to the THIRD reading of a bill, entitled, "An act to regulate the
collection of the duties imposed by law, on the tonnage of ships or vessels,
and on goods, wares and merchandizes imported into the United States;"—

And resolved that the Senate do concur therein with the following amendments:—

A.   P.   L.
     1.   4.   After "Law," strike out "Upon," and insert "On the tonnage of
                ships and vessels, and on."
          25. After "Medford," insert "Cohasset."
     4.   9.   After "Also," strike out "A," and insert "Two."
                Strike out "To reside at the city of Hudson," and insert,
          10. "One to reside at the city of Albany, and the other at the city of
                Hudson."
          13. After "Burlington, and" strike out "Greenwich," and insert
                "Bridgetown."
          24. Strike out "Greenwich," and insert "Bridgetown."
          27. After "Salem," insert "Port Elizabeth, or" And
                After "Maurice river," insert "Stillwell's landing on."
          28. Strike out "Greenwich," and insert "Bridgetown."
     5.   5.   After "Annexed," insert "Newcastle and."
                Strike out "A," after "As," and insert "S," after "port," in the
                second place.
          11. After "River shall be," strike out "Constituted."
          12. After "Baltimore," insert "Which shall be the sole port of entry."
          15. Strike out "Constituted."
          16. After "Chester," insert, "Which shall be the sole port of entry."
          17. After "Inclusive," insert "And Cambridge shall be a port of
                delivery only."
          18. After "Oxford," insert "Which shall be the sole port of entry."
          20. After "Inclusive," insert "And Salisbury shall be a port of delivery
                only."
          21. After "Vienna," insert "Which shall be the sole port of entry."
          24. Strike out "Constituted."

---

[67] This act, as it passed the House, has not been located.
[68] On July 29 this bill was read a second time and the third reading was assigned.

A.   P.   L.

    25.   After "Snow-Hill," insert "Which shall be the sole port of entry."

6.   11.   Strike out "Ten," and insert "Twelve."

         After "To wit:" insert "Hampton as one port."

    12.   After "Tappahannock," insert "Yeocomico River, including Kinsale."

    13.   After "Louisville," insert "The authority of the officers at Hampton shall extend over all the waters, shores, bays, harbours and inlets, between the south side of the mouth of York-River, along the west shore of Chesapeake-Bay to Hampton, and thence up James-River to the west side of Chicahomony River; and a Collector shall be appointed to reside at Hampton, which shall be the sole port of entry."

    16.   Strike out "The point of land forming the south shore at the mouth of York-River, thence up to Hampton," and insert "The mouth of James-River."

    17.   Strike out "Including both shores thereof," after "James-River."

    19.   Strike out "Or Portsmouth, as the Secretary of the Treasury shall direct."

    20.   Strike out "Hampton."

7.   8.   Strike out "To the district of Dumfries, including Newport, shall
to   be annexed Yeocomico-River, including Kinsale, as a port of
13.   delivery only; and a Collector for the district shall be appointed, to reside at Dumfries, which shall be the sole port of entry; also a Surveyor to reside at Barren-point, on Yeocomico-River, and the authority of the officers of the said district shall extend over all the waters, shores, bays, harbours and inlets, comprehended on the south side of Potowmac-River, from Smith's-point to Cockpit-point, on the said river,"

         And insert

         "The district of Yeocomico-River, including Kinsale, shall extend from Smith's-point, on the south side of Potowmac-River to Boyd's-hole,[69] on the same river, including all the waters, shores, bays, rivers, creeks, harbours and inlets along the south shore of Potowmac-River to Boyd's-hole, aforesaid, and Yeocomico, including Kinsale, shall be the sole port of entry, and a Collector shall be appointed to reside on Yeocomico-River. The district of Dumfries, including Newport, shall extend from Boyd's-hole to Cockpit-point, on the south side of Potowmac-River, and a Collector shall be appointed to reside at Dumfries, which shall be the sole port of entry, and the authority of the officers of this district shall extend over all the waters, shores, bays, harbours and inlets comprehended between Boyd's-hole and Cockpit-point, aforesaid."

8.   14.   After "Jekyl Island," insert "Frederica shall be a port of delivery only."

    21.   Strike out "Constituted."

---

[69] The following lines, to the repetition of the phrase "Potowmac-River to Boyd's-hole," are omitted in the smooth journal.

A.   P.   L.

             27.   After "Wilmington," insert "Newcastle and Port Penn."

             28.   After "Georgetown," insert "On Potowmac."

             29.   Strike out "Or," and insert "And."

    9.   4.   Strike out "Any port or place in India or China, or beyond."

             5.   Insert after "Cape of Good Hope," "Or from any place beyond the same."

             8.   After "Delaware," insert "Baltimore Town."

            12.   Strike out "And," and insert "Or."

            16.   Strike out "(Except the port of Hampton in the said district.)"

            21.   Strike out "Hampton."

            27.   After "Or," insert "The Collector."

    10.   5.   After "Portsmouth," insert "Or with the Collector for the port of Hampton."

            15.   Strike out "Making the same."

            18.   After "Of goods," insert "To employ proper persons as Weighers, Gaugers, Measurers and Inspectors, at the several ports within his district, together with such persons as shall be necessary to serve in the boats which may be provided for securing the collection of the revenue: To provide at the public expense, and with the approbation of the principal officer of the Treasury department, storehouses for the safe keeping of goods, together with such scales, weights and measures as shall be deemed necessary."

            22.   Strike out "And jointly with him to employ proper persons as
            to   Weighers, Gaugers, Measurers and Inspectors at the several ports
            27.   within their district, together with such persons as shall be necessary to serve in the boats which may be provided for securing the collection of the revenue; to provide at the public expense, and with the approbation of the principal Officer of the Treasury Departments, store-houses for the safe keeping of goods, together with such scales, weights and measures, as shall be deemed necessary."

    11.   6.   After "Naval Officer," insert "AND BE IT FURTHER, ENACTED, That every Collector appointed in virtue of this act, in case of his necessary absence, sickness, or inability to execute the duties of his office, may appoint a deputy, duly authorized under his hand and seal, to execute and perform on his behalf, all and singular the powers, functions and duties of Collector of the district to which he the said principal is attached, who shall be answerable for the neglect of duty, or other mal-conduct of his said deputy in the execution of the office.—

                "AND BE IT FURTHER ENACTED, That in case of the disability or death of any Collector, the duties and authorities vested in him by this act shall devolve on his deputy, if any such hath been appointed (for whose conduct the estate of such disabled or deceased Collector shall be liable) and the said deputy shall exercise the authority and perform all the duties until a successor shall be appointed. But in cases where no deputy is appointed, the authorities and duties of the disabled or deceased Collector shall devolve upon the Naval Officer of the same district until a

A.   P.   L.

successor duly authorised and sworn shall enter upon the execution of the duties of the said office."—

9.   After "Port," strike out "And the Surveyor shall in like manner, execute all the duties required of other Surveyors."

25.   After "Informer"—insert "And no Weigher, Gauger, Measurer, or Inspector shall execute the duties of his office, until he shall have taken the above oath or affirmation."—

12.   7.   After "Is bound," insert "And the name or names of the person or persons to whom the goods are consigned, or in cases where the goods are shipped to order, the names of the shippers, noting the goods consigned to their orders."—

19.   After "Authorised," insert "And required."—

27.   After "Ship or vessel," insert "But in open day or."

30.   Strike out "And if he be a pilot or officer of the Customs."

13.   1.   After "Years," insert, "And it shall be the duty of the Collector of the district, to advertise the names of all such persons in the public gazette of the State in which he resides, within twenty days after each respective conviction."

19.   Strike out "Credible witnesses," and insert "Reputable citizens of the neighbourhood, best acquainted with matters of that kind."

21.   Strike out "Within eight days next after the arrival of such ship or vessel."

24.   Strike out "Exact."

27.   Strike out "Thereon," and insert "On the said entry."

14.   3.   Strike out "Thirty," and insert "Ten."

25.   Strike out "Port," and insert "District, or to such person as he shall authorise or appoint on his behalf, to receive the said goods."

26.   Strike out "Goods," and insert "Packages, with their marks and numbers."

15.   1.   After "Discharged," insert "Provided always, that the said limitation of fifteen days shall not extend to vessels laden with salt or coal, but if the master or owner of such vessels require longer time to discharge their cargoes, the wages of the Inspector, for every day's attendance exceeding the said[70] fifteen days, shall be paid by the master or owner."

24.   Strike out "From India or China," and insert "From any place beyond the same."

25.   Strike out "Of packages and commissions."

16.   9.   Strike out "One hundred," and insert "Fifty."

14.   Strike out "Sufficient in," and insert "Of double the."

21.   Strike out "One hundred," and insert "Fifty."

27.   After "Clear out," insert "The register of which ship or vessel, at the time of entry, shall be lodged in the office of the Collector, and there remain until such clearance."

18.   5.   After "Equal to," insert "Double."

11.   After "By any," insert "Judge or."

---

[70] The smooth journal omits "said."

A.   P.   L.

21.   After "That is to say," strike out "Every Collector in the sum of
to   five thousand dollars; every Naval Officer in the sum of one
23.   thousand dollars, and every Surveyor in the sum of one thousand
        dollars," and insert—"The Collector of Philadelphia in the sum
        of sixty thousand dollars; the Collector of New-York fifty
        thousand dollars; the Collector of Boston forty thousand dollars;
        the Collectors of Baltimore-town and Charleston thirty thou-
        sand dollars; the Collectors of Norfolk and Portsmouth fifteen
        thousand dollars; the Collectors of Portsmouth, in New-Hamp-
        shire, of Salem and Beverly, Wilmington, Annapolis, George-
        town, in Maryland, Bermuda Hundred, and City-point, and
        Alexandria ten thousand dollars each; the Collectors of New-
        bury-port, Gloucester, Marblehead, Plymouth, Nantucket, Port-
        land and Falmouth, New-London, New-Haven, Fairfield, Perth-
        Amboy, Chester, Oxford, York-town, Dumfries, George-town
        in South-Carolina, Beaufort and Savannah each five thousand
        dollars; and all the other Collectors in the sum of two thousand
        dollars each; the Naval Officers for the ports of Boston, New-
        York, Philadelphia, Baltimore-town and Charleston ten thou-
        sand dollars each; and all the other Naval Officers in the sum of
        two thousand dollars each; the Surveyors of the ports of Boston,
        New-York, Philadelphia, Baltimore-town and Charleston five
        thousand dollars each; and all the other Surveyors one thousand
        dollars each."

24.   After "Vessel," strike out "Which is not wholly the property of a
to   citizen or citizens of the United States six dollars; for every
29.   entrance of any other ship or vessel of the burthen of one hun-
and   dred tons or upwards, arriving from any foreign port, four
19. 1. dollars; for every entrance of any such other ship or vessel under
     2. the burthen of one hundred tons, arriving from any foreign port,
        three dollars;" and insert "Of one hundred tons burthen and up-
        wards, two dollars and an half; for every clearance of any ship
        or vessel of one hundred tons burthen and upwards, two dollars
        and an half; for every entrance of any ship or vessel under the
        burthen of one hundred tons, one dollar and an half; for every
        clearance of a ship or vessel under one hundred tons burthen,
        one dollar and an half."

3.   After "Bond," strike out "To secure the payment of duties," and
        insert "Taken officially."

4.   After "Thirty cents," insert "For every official certificate twenty
        cents; for every bill of health twenty cents; for every other
        official document, registers excepted, required by the owner or
        master of every vessel not before enumerated, twenty cents."

6.   Strike out "A common," and insert "An office to be provided by
        the Collector, in the place of his residence, most convenient for
        the trade of the district, in which the said Collector and Naval
        Officer shall each have, at least, one separate room."
        After "Office," insert "And the said fees shall be received by the

A. P. L.

           Collector, who shall settle the accounts monthly, and pay to the Naval Officer, the balance which may be due to him on such monthly settlement.''

7. Strike out ''Any ship or vessel which is not wholly the property of a citizen or citizens of the United States, and having on board goods, wares or merchandize, subject to duty, four dollars; for the like services on board any other such ship or vessel, two dollars; for the like services on board any ship or vessel, wholly belonging to a citizen or citizens of the United States, and having on board goods, wares and merchandize subject to duty, three dollars; for the like services on board every other ship or vessel, one dollar,'' and insert ''Any ship or vessel of one hundred tons and upwards, and having on board goods, wares and merchandize, subject to duty, three dollars; for the like services on board any ship or vessel of less than one hundred tons burthen, having on board goods, wares and merchandize, subject to duty, one dollar and an half; on all vessels not having on board goods, wares and merchandize, subject to duty, two-thirds of a dollar.''

12. After ''Shall be paid,'' insert ''To the Collector.''

13. After ''Performed,'' insert ''And the said Collector shall pay weekly to the Surveyor the fees so received.''

16. After ''Paid by,'' strike out ''Owners thereof,'' and insert ''Collector out of the revenue.''

18. Strike out ''Two cents,'' and insert ''One cent.''

20. 25. After ''Such goods,'' insert ''A protest in due form of law made by the master and mate, or some of the seamen, or in case no such protest can be had.''

21. 19. After ''Recompence,'' insert ''For conniving.''

20. Strike out ''With intent to elude the payment of any debt, or the
to   performance of any duty established by law.''
21.

24. Strike out ''The sum of one hundred,'' and insert ''A sum not less than two hundred, nor more than two thousand.''

22. 15. After ''Merchandize and,'' insert ''Shall give bond to.''
After ''Thereof,'' insert ''And to respond the cost in case he shall not support his claim.''

23. 9. Strike out ''Two,'' and insert ''Three.''

24. 2. Strike out ''Of foreign,'' and insert ''Not of their own.''

10. After the end of the paragraph, insert ''And all goods, wares and merchandize brought into the United States by land, contrary to this act, shall be forfeited, together with the carriages, horses and oxen that shall be employed in conveying the same.''[71]

Adjourned to 11 o'clock to-morrow.

---

[71] The annotated printed copy of this bill which includes amendments is located in House Bills, Senate Records, DNA. On July 28 this bill was passed with amendments and sent to the House. On the same date the House concurred with all the amendments and notified the Senate.

TUESDAY, JULY 28, 1789

The SENATE assembled,

Present as yesterday.

Mr. Johnson, in behalf of the Committee appointed the 13th of May, reported a bill, entitled, "An act for the punishment of certain crimes against the United States;"[72] Which was read a FIRST TIME, and Monday next was assigned for a SECOND reading.[73]

The Secretary carried to the House of Representatives, the bill entitled, "An act to regulate the collection of the duties imposed by law on the tonnage of ships or vessels, and on goods, wares and merchandizes imported into the United States"—

Concurred in with amendments.

On MOTION, the Senators from the State of New-York proceeded to draw lots for their classes, in conformity to the resolve of the 14th of May: And two lots, No. 3 and a blank, being by the Secretary rolled up, and put into the box, Mr. Schuyler drew Blank, and Mr. King having drawn No. 3—His seat shall accordingly be vacated in the Senate, at the expiration of

The SIXTH year.

The Secretary proceeded to put two other lots into the box marked No. 1, and 2, and Mr. Schuyler having drawn lot No. 1—His seat shall accordingly be vacated in the Senate, at the expiration of

The SECOND year.[74]

Proceeded in a SECOND reading of the bill, entitled, "An act for the establishment and support of Light-Houses, Beacons and Buoys."[75]

A message from the House of Representatives, by Mr. Beckley, their Clerk—

"MR. PRESIDENT,

THE House of Representatives have considered the amendments proposed by the Senate upon the bill, entitled, "An act to regulate the collection of the duties imposed by law, on the tonnage of ships or vessels, and on goods, wares and merchandizes imported into the United States," and have concurred therein[76]—

And he withdrew.

Adjourned to 11 o'clock to-morrow.

---

[72] The bill is in Senate Bills, Senate Records, DNA. E–45679.

[73] On August 3 this bill was read a second time and its consideration was postponed.

[74] On January 29, 1790, the Senators from North Carolina drew lots to determine their classification.

[75] On July 29 this bill was considered again.

[76] On July 29 the House notified the Senate that it had appointed a committee to examine this bill and present it to the President. Mr. Few was appointed to join this committee.

WEDNESDAY, JULY 29, 1789

The SENATE assembled,
Present as yesterday,
And Mr. Ellsworth attended.

Resumed the SECOND reading of a bill, entitled, "An act for the establishment and support of Light-Houses, Beacons and Buoys."[77]

A message from the House of Representatives, by Mr. Beckley, their Clerk —Who informed the Senate, "That a Committee was appointed, with such Committee as the Senate on their part might appoint to examine an enroled bill, entitled, 'An Act to regulate the collection of the duties imposed by law, on the tonnage of ships or vessels, and on goods, wares and merchandizes imported into the United States,' and when signed by the Vice President, and Speaker, to lay the same before the President of the United States for his approbation"—

And he withdrew.

The Senate proceeded to the appointment of Mr. Few, a Committee on their part, for the purposes expressed in the above message—And the Secretary notified the House of Representatives accordingly.[78]

Resumed the SECOND reading of the bill, entitled, "An act to establish the Treasury Department"—

And postponed the further consideration thereof until to-morrow.[79]

Proceeded to the SECOND reading of the bill, entitled, "An act for settling the accounts between the United States and individual States," and assigned to-morrow for a THIRD reading.[80]

Adjourned to 11 o'clock to-morrow.

THURSDAY, JULY 30, 1789

The SENATE assembled,
Present as yesterday.

Proceeded to a THIRD reading of the bill, entitled, "An act for settling the accounts between the United States and individual States," and—

RESOLVED, That the Senate do concur therein—

And the Secretary notified the House of Representatives accordingly.[81]

[77] On July 30 this bill was considered again.
[78] On July 30 this committee reported and on the same date the bill, signed by the Speaker, was brought to the Senate for the Vice President's signature. It was then taken to the President.
[79] On July 30 this bill was considered again and assigned to a third reading.
[80] On July 30 this bill was read a third time, passed, and returned to the House.
[81] On August 4 this bill, signed by the Speaker, was sent back to the Senate. The Vice President then signed it and it was sent to the President.

Proceeded in the SECOND reading of the bill, entitled, "An act for the establishment and support of Light-Houses, Beacons and Buoys."[82]—

The Committee on the part of the Senate reported, that the joint Committee appointed to examine an ENROLED bill, entitled, "An act to regulate the collection of the duties imposed by law, on the tonnage of ships or vessels and on goods, wares and merchandizes imported into the United States," had performed that service[83]—

Mr. Beckley, the Clerk of the House of Representatives, brought up the above mentioned ENROLED bill, signed by the Speaker—

And withdrew.

The Vice President signed the enroled bill, and the Committee proceeded to lay it before the President of the United States.[84]

Proceeded in a SECOND reading of the bill, entitled, "An act to establish the Treasury Department"—And assigned to-morrow for a THIRD reading.[85]

On motion,

That the sense of the Senate should be taken on the following Resolve— to wit:

RESOLVED, That a clause passed, or amendment made in Committee, shall not be revised in the same Committee, but may be so done in the Senate— And no amendment or clause agreed to in the Senate shall be reconsidered until the next reading of the bill, except at the THIRD reading of a bill, when by the consent of the Senate it may be amended[86]—

Passed in the Negative.—

Adjourned to 11 o'clock to-morrow.

FRIDAY, JULY 31, 1789

The SENATE assembled,
Present as yesterday.

Proceeded to a THIRD reading of the bill, entitled, "An act to establish the Treasury Department."

On the question, shall the words "And an Assistant to the Secretary of the Treasury," At the end of the first paragraph, be stricken out?

Passed in the negative.

On motion,

---

[82] On July 31 this bill was read a third time and several amendments to it were passed by the Senate.

[83] The inspected enrolled bill is in Enrolled Acts, RG 11, DNA. E–45713.

[84] On July 31 the President signed this bill and the House notified the Senate of this action.

[85] On July 31 this bill was read for the third time and the Senate passed several amendments to it which are printed in the Journal. The bill was then sent to the House.

[86] This resolve has not been located.

To strike out the words, "Secretary of the Treasury," and insert, "Three Superintendants of the Treasury"—

It passed in the negative;—

And on the question upon the bill,

RESOLVED, That the Senate do concur therein with the following amendments:—To wit.

A.   P.   L.

1.   5.   After "Treasury," insert "Which Assistant shall be appointed by the said Secretary."—

20.   Strike out "Of."
Between the words, "Debts" and "Due," and insert "That are or shall be."—

2.   3.   Between the words "The," and "House," insert "Senate and."

15.   Strike out "Three," and insert "Six."

20.   Strike out "Certify upon," and insert "Record."

21.   After "Treasury," insert "Certify the same thereon."

23.   Strike out these words, "And be it further enacted, That the
to   Assistant to the Secretary of the Treasury shall be appointed by
27.   the President, and whenever the Secretary shall be removed from office by the President of the United States, or in any other case of vacancy in the office of the Secretary, the Assistant shall, during the vacancy, have the charge and custody of the records, books and papers appertaining to the said office.—

28.   Strike out "That shall be."

3.   5.   Strike out these words,
to   "On conviction be deemed guilty of a high misdemeanor, shall
10.   forfeit the penalty of five thousand dollars, and be forever incapable of holding any office under the United States; and any other officer herein mentioned, so offending, shall be removed from office, and pay a fine of two thousand dollars; the forfeitures under this act to go one half to the United States, the other half to him who will sue for it"—

And insert,
"Be deemed guilty of a high misdemeanor, and forfeit to the United States the penalty of three thousand dollars, and shall, upon conviction, be removed from office, and forever thereafter incapable of holding any office under the United States. PROVIDED, That if any other person than a public prosecutor shall give information of any such offense, upon which a prosecution and conviction shall be had, one half the aforesaid penalty of three thousand dollars, when recovered, shall be for the use of the person giving such information"[87]—

A message from the House of Representatives by Mr. Beckley, their Clerk, who informed the Senate, that

[87] The amendments are noted on the annotated printed copy of this bill and are found in House Bills, Senate Records, DNA.

"The House of Representatives had appointed Mr. White and Mr. Partridge with such as the Senate may join a standing Committee to examine the enrolment of all bills, as the same shall pass the two Houses, and after being signed by the President of the Senate and Speaker of the House of Representatives, to present them forthwith to the President of the United States:"[88]—

Also, that the President of the United States had affixed his signature to a bill, entitled, "An act to regulate the collection of the duties imposed by law, on the tonnage of ships or vessels, and on goods, wares and merchandizes imported into the United States," and had returned it to the House of Representatives—

And he withdrew.

The Senate proceeded to appoint Mr. Wingate a Committee on their part, to examine and present to the President of the United States the enroled bills, that may pass the Senate and House of Representatives from time to time.

Proceeded to a THIRD reading of the bill, entitled, "An act for the establishment and support of Light-Houses, Beacons and Buoys," and resolved to concur therein with the following amendments.—

A.   P.   L.

          In the title of the bill, after "Beacons," strike out "And," and after "Buoys," insert "And public Piers."—

1.   Strike out the whole of the section, except the word "That," and
to 10.   insert "All expenses which shall accrue from and after the 15th day of August, 1789, in the necessary support, maintenance and repairs of all Light-Houses, Beacons, Buoys, and Public Piers, erected, placed, or sunk before the passing of this act, at the entrance of, or within any bay, inlet, harbour, or port of the United States, for rendering the navigation thereof easy and safe, shall be defrayed out of the Treasury of the United States: PROVIDED NEVERTHELESS, That none of the said expenses shall continue to be so defrayed by the United States, after the expiration of one year from the day aforesaid, unless such Light-Houses, Beacons, Buoys, and Public Piers, shall in the mean time be ceded to and vested in the United States, by the State or States respectively in which the same may be, together with the Lands and Tenements thereunto belonging, and together with the jurisdiction of the same."

11.   Strike out the whole section.
to 13.

15.   After the word "States," insert "In manner aforesaid."

18.   After the word "Contracts," strike out the whole of the remaining
to   part of the section, and insert "Which shall be approved by the
22.   President of the United States for building a Light-House near the entrance of Chesapeake-Bay; and for rebuilding when necessary, and keeping in good repair the Light-Houses, Beacons,

[88] The resolve, in the form of an extract from the House Journal, is in Messages from the House, Senate Records, DNA.

A. P. L.

Buoys, and Public Piers in the several States, and for furnishing the same with all necessary supplies, and also to agree for the salaries, wages, or hire of the person or persons appointed by the President for the superintendance and care of the same."

"AND BE IT FURTHER ENACTED, That all pilots in the bays, inlets, rivers, harbours, and ports of the United States, shall continue to be regulated in conformity with the existing laws of the States respectively, wherein such pilots may be, or with such laws as the States may respectively hereafter enact for the purpose, until further Legislative provision shall be made by Congress."[89]

The Secretary carried the bill, entitled, "An act to establish the Treasury Department," to the House of Representatives, concurred in with the Amendments[90]—

Also the concurrence of the Senate in the resolve of the 31st July, and the appointment of Mr. Wingate a standing Committee, jointly with the Committee of the House, to examine and present the enroled bills that may pass the Senate and House of Representatives from time to time.

Proceeded to a SECOND reading of the bill, entitled, "An act to provide for the Government of the Territory north-west of the River Ohio,"—

And postponed the consideration thereof to Monday next.[91]

Adjourned to 11 o'clock on Monday morning.

---

[89] This amended bill was carried to the House on August 3.

[90] On August 3, 4, and 5, the House considered this bill, concurred with some Senate amendments, and disagreed to others. On August 5 it returned this bill to the Senate with the House resolutions which are printed in the Senate Journal. The Senate then considered this message and resolved to insist upon their eighth amendment.

[91] On August 3 this bill was considered again and assigned to a third reading.

MONDAY, AUGUST 3, 1789

The SENATE assembled,
Present as on Saturday.

Proceeded to the SECOND reading of a bill, entitled, "An act to provide for the Government of the Territory north-west of the River Ohio,"—And assigned to-morrow for a THIRD reading.[1]

The bill, entitled, "An act for the establishment and support of Light-Houses, Beacons and Buoys," concurred in with Amendments, was carried to the House of Representatives by the Secretary.[2]

A bill, entitled, "An act to establish an Executive Department, to be denominated, the Department of War," was considered, and a THIRD reading postponed until to-morrow.[3]

The bill, entitled, "An act for the punishment of certain Crimes against the United States," was read a SECOND time, and the further consideration thereof was postponed.[4]

Adjourned to 11 o'clock to-morrow.

TUESDAY, AUGUST 4, 1789

The SENATE assembled,
Present as yesterday,
And Mr. Morris attended.

Proceeded to a THIRD reading a bill, entitled, "An act to establish an Executive Department, to be denominated the Department of War."

On MOTION to strike out these words—in line 6th and 7th, "And Naval," "Ships," "Or Naval Affairs"—

Passed in the Negative.

On MOTION to strike out the words—line 14th, "And who, whenever the said principal officer shall be removed from office by the President of the United States"—

And the Yeas and Nays being required by one FIFTH of the Senators present, the determination was as follows:—

Mr. Butler	Yea	
Mr. Carroll		Nay
Mr. Dalton		Nay
Mr. Ellsworth		Nay

---

[1] On August 4 this bill was read a third time, passed with amendments, and returned to the House.

[2] On August 3 the House approved the amendments and notified the Senate of this concurrence on August 4.

[3] On August 4 this bill was read a third time, passed with amendments, and returned to the House.

[4] On August 11 this bill was considered again.

Mr. Elmer		Nay
Mr. Few	Yea	
Mr. Gunn	Yea	
Mr. Grayson	Yea	
Mr. Henry		Nay
Mr. Johnson	Yea	
Mr. Izard	Yea	
Mr. King		Nay
Mr. Langdon	Yea	
Mr. Lee	Yea	
Mr. Morris		Nay
Mr. Read		Nay
Mr. Schuyler		Nay
Mr. Strong		Nay
Mr. Wingate	Yea	

Yeas 9
Nays 10

So the question was lost, and the words proposed to be struck out, were retained;

And upon the question on the bill,

RESOLVED, That the Senate do concur therein with the following Amendments:—

A.   P.   L.
1. After "Be it enacted by the," strike out "Congress of the United States," and insert "Senate and House of Representatives of the United States of America in Congress assembled."
3. After "War," strike out "And."
to 8. Strike out "By reason of," and insert "For."
16. Strike out "Provided nevertheless, That no appointment of such
to chief Clerk shall be valid until the same shall have been approved
18. by the President of the United States"[5]—

Which Bill, with the Amendments, was carried to the House of Representatives.[6]

Proceeded to the THIRD reading of a bill, entitled,

"An act to provide for the Government of the Territory north-west of the River Ohio."

On MOTION to insert these words after the word "President," in the last line of the second section,

"By and with the consent of the Senate;"

---

[5] The amendments are noted on the engrossed bill sent from the House which is located in House Bills, Senate Records, DNA.

[6] On August 5 the House notified the Senate of its concurrence with these amendments.

And the Yeas and Nays being required by one fifth of the Senators present, the determination was as follows:

Mr. Butler	Yea	
Mr. Carroll		Nay
Mr. Dalton		Nay
Mr. Ellsworth		Nay
Mr. Elmer		Nay
Mr. Few	Yea	
Mr. Gunn	Yea	
Mr. Grayson	Yea	
Mr. Henry		Nay
Mr. Johnson	Yea	
Mr. Izard	Yea	
Mr. King		Nay
Mr. Langdon	Yea	
Mr. Morris		Nay
Mr. Read		Nay
Mr. Schuyler		Nay
Mr. Strong		Nay
Mr. Wingate	Yea	

Yeas 8
Nays 10

So it passed in the Negative:

And on the question upon the bill, it was

RESOLVED, to concur therein with the following Amendments, to wit:—

A. P. L.
10. After "United States; and" strike out "All appointments to offices
to which by the said ordinance were to have been made by the
12. United States in Congress assembled, shall be made by the President of the United States, with the advice and consent of the Senate," and insert

"The President shall nominate, and by and with the advice and consent of the Senate, shall appoint all officers which by the said ordinance were to have been appointed by the United States in Congress assembled."

17. After "Shall," insert "Be"[7]—

Which bill, with the Amendments, was carried to the House of Representatives.[8]

A message from the House of Representatives, by Mr. Beckley, their Clerk

---

[7] The amendments, noted on the annotated printed copy of this bill, are located in House Bills, Senate Records, DNA.

[8] On August 5 the House notified the Senate of its concurrence with these amendments.

—Who brought up a bill, entitled, "An act for making compensation to the President and Vice President of the United States,"[9] and desired the concurrence of the Senate therein;[10]

Informed the Senate that the House had agreed to the Amendments on the bill, entitled, "An act for the establishment and support of Light-Houses, Beacons, and Buoys"[11]—

Brought up the acceptance, by the House of Representatives, of a report of a joint Committee upon the mode of presenting addresses, the enrolment of bills, &c.[12]—

Also an enroled bill, entitled, "An act for settling the accounts between the United States and individual States,"[13] examined by the Committee, and signed by the Speaker of the House of Representatives—

Together with the appointment of

> Mr. Wadsworth
> Mr. Carroll and
> Mr. Hartley a Committee, to join with a Committee

of the Senate, to be appointed for the purpose "To consider of and report, WHEN it will be convenient and proper that an adjournment of the present session of Congress should take place; and to consider and report such business, now before Congress, necessary to be finished before the adjournment, and such as may be conveniently postponed to the next sessions; and also to consider and report such matters now before Congress, but which it will be necessary should be considered and determined by Congress, before an adjournment"[14]—

And he withdrew.

The Vice President affixed his signature to the enroled bill, entitled, "An act for settling the Accounts between the United States and Individual States," and the Committee proceeded to lay it before the President of the United States for his approbation.[15]

Adjourned to 11 o'clock to-morrow.

---

[9] This bill, as it passed the House, has not been located.

[10] On August 5 this bill was read for the first time and the second reading was assigned.

[11] On August 6 this bill, signed by the Speaker, was sent to the Senate for the Vice President's signature. It was then presented to the President.

[12] The acceptance, in the form of an amendatory House resolve, is in Messages from the House, Senate Records, DNA. This report and the House resolutions accompanying it were read and ordered to be printed on August 5.

[13] The inspected enrolled bill is in Enrolled Acts, RG 11, DNA. E–45697.

[14] An extract from the House Journal concerning the resolve to join a Senate committee to discuss the time of adjournment is in Messages from the House, Senate Records, DNA. On August 5 the Senate appointed a committee to meet with this committee.

[15] On August 5 the President signed this bill and the House notified the Senate of this action.

WEDNESDAY, AUGUST 5, 1789

The SENATE assembled,

Present as yesterday.

Proceeded to a FIRST reading of a bill, entitled, "An act for allowing a compensation to the President and Vice President of the United States," and assigned to-morrow for the SECOND reading.[16]

Appointed   Mr. Strong

                    Mr. Ellsworth and

                    Mr. Carroll, a Committee, jointly with the Committee of the House of Representatives, to that purpose appointed, to consider what business is necessary to be acted upon prior to an adjournment, and to report a proper time at which an adjournment shall take place, agreeably to a proposition from the House of Representatives of the 4th of August.[17]

The resolve of the House of Representatives, on the report of a joint Committee appointed the 8th of May, upon the enrolment and presentation of the acts of Congress, &c. was read, and ordered to be printed for the consideration of the Senate.[18]

A message from the House of Representatives, by Mr. Beckley, their Clerk; —Who brought up the concurrence of the House on the Amendments proposed by the Senate, to a bill, entitled, "An act to establish an Executive Department, to be denominated the Department of War"[19]—

Their concurrence on the proposed Amendments to a bill, entitled, "An act to provide for the Government of the Territory north-west of the River Ohio"[20]—

And he informed the Senate, that the President of the United States had affixed his signature to a bill, entitled, "An act for settling the Accounts between the United States and Individual States:"

He also brought up the following resolve, and the bill therein mentioned— And withdrew.

"CONGRESS OF THE UNITED STATES

"IN THE HOUSE OF REPRESENTATIVES

"MONDAY, THE 3D OF AUGUST, 1789

"The House proceeded to consider the Amendments proposed by the Senate to the bill, entitled, 'An act to establish the Treasury Department;'—

---

[16] On August 6 this bill was read a second time and committed.

[17] On August 6 the Senate notified the House of the appointment of this committee.

[18] On August 6 this report was printed in the Senate Journal and concurred in by the Senate.

[19] On August 6 this bill, signed by the Speaker, was returned to the Senate for the Vice President's signature. It was then presented to the President.

[20] On August 6 this bill, signed by the Speaker, was returned to the Senate for the Vice President's signature. It was then presented to the President.

"Whereupon,

"RESOLVED, That this House doth agree to the second, third, fourth, fifth, sixth, and seventh Amendments.

"T U E S D A Y, THE 4TH OF AUGUST, 1789[21]

"The House resumed the consideration of the Amendments proposed by the Senate to the bill, entitled, 'An act to establish the Treasury Department;'

"Whereupon,

"RESOLVED, That this House doth agree to the first Amendment, also to so much of the eighth Amendment as proposes to strike out the following words in the seventh clause of the bill, to wit:

" 'The Assistant to the Secretary of the Treasury shall be appointed by the President, and;'—and doth disagree to such other part of the said eighth Amendment, as proposes to strike out the rest of the clause.

"W E D N E S D A Y, THE 5TH OF AUGUST, 1789[22]

"The House resumed the further consideration of the Amendments proposed by the Senate, to the bill, entitled, 'An act to establish the Treasury Department;'—Whereupon,

"RESOLVED, That this House doth agree to the NINTH and TENTH Amendments."[23]

The Senate proceeded to the consideration of the above recited message, and RESOLVED to insist on their eighth Amendment proposed to the House of Representatives on the bill, entitled, "An act to establish the Treasury Department."[24]

Mr. Butler, in behalf of the Committee to whom it was referred "To arrange and bring forward a system to regulate the trade and intercourse between the United States, and the Territory of other Powers in North-America and the West-Indies"—

REPORTED,[25] That it will be expedient to pass a law for imposing an increased duty of tonnage, for a limited time, on all foreign ships and other vessels that shall load in the United States with the produce of the same, to any port or place in America whereto the vessels of the United States are not permitted to carry their own produce; but such a law being of the nature of a revenue law, your Committee conceive, that the originating a bill for that

---

21 The printed journal omits "1789."
22 The printed journal omits "1789."
23 This House message has not been located.
24 On August 6 this resolution was carried to the House.
25 This report has not been located.

purpose, is, by the Constitution, exclusively placed in the House of Representatives—

Your Committee beg leave further to report, as their opinion, that it will be expedient to direct a bill to be brought in, for imposing similar restraints upon the trade of the European settlements in America with the United States, that are imposed on the trade of the United States with those settlements.

RESOLVED, That the first clause of this report be accepted, and that the remainder of the report be recommitted, and that it be an instruction to the Committee, in case it shall be their opinion that a Legislative provision ought to be made on the subject of the commitment, to report a bill for that purpose
—And that   Mr. Ellsworth
                 Mr. King and
                 Mr. Read be added to the Committee.

Adjourned to 11 o'clock to-morrow.

THURSDAY, AUGUST 6, 1789

The SENATE assembled,
Present as yesterday.

Mr. Wingate, in behalf of the Committee of enrolment, reported, that they had examined

A bill, entitled, "An act for the support of Light Houses, Beacons, Buoys and public Piers"[26]—

A bill, entitled, "An act to provide for the Government of the Territory north-west of the River Ohio"[27]—

A bill, entitled, "An act to establish an Executive Department, to be denominated the Department of War;"[28]—and that the same were perfected.

The Senate proceeded to a SECOND reading of a bill, entitled, "An act for allowing a compensation to the President and Vice President of the United States," and committed it to

Mr. Morris	Mr. Ellsworth
Mr. Read	Mr. Strong
Mr. Elmer	Mr. Few
Mr. Schuyler	Mr. Izard[29]
Mr. Langdon	Mr. Lee[30]
Mr. Carroll	

---

[26] The inspected enrolled bill is in Enrolled Acts, RG 11, DNA. E–45698.
[27] The inspected enrolled bill is in Enrolled Acts, RG 11, DNA. E–22195.
[28] The inspected enrolled bill is in Enrolled Acts, RG 11, DNA. E–22194.
[29] The smooth journal adds "and."
[30] On August 7 this committee reported an amendment to this bill. Two motions on the bill were defeated on this date.

"CONGRESS of the UNITED STATES
"In the House of Representatives

"M O N D A Y, the 27th of July, 1789

"The House proceeded to consider the report of a Committee of the whole House, to whom was referred the report of the Committee appointed to confer with a Committee of the Senate, in preparing joint rules to be established between the two Houses, for the enrolment, attestation, publication, and preservation of the acts of Congress; and to regulate the mode of presenting addresses and other acts to the President of the United States:

"Whereupon,

"RESOLVED, That the following be established joint rules between the two Houses, to wit:—

"That while bills are on their passage between the two Houses, they shall be on paper, and under the signature of the Secretary or Clerk of each House respectively.

"After a bill shall have passed both Houses, it shall be duly enroled on parchment, by the Clerk of the House of Representatives, or the Secretary of the Senate, as the bill may have originated in the one or the other House, before it shall be presented to the President of the United States.

"When bills are enroled, they shall be examined by a joint Committee of one from the Senate, and two from the House of Representatives, appointed as a standing Committee for that purpose, who shall carefully compare the enrolment with the engrossed bills, as passed in the two Houses, and correcting any errors that may be discovered in the enroled bills, make their report forthwith to the respective Houses.

"After examination and report, each bill shall be signed in the respective Houses, first by the Speaker of the House of Representatives, and then by the President of the Senate.

"After a bill shall have thus been signed in each House, it shall be presented by the said Committee to the President of the United States for his approbation, it being first endorsed on the back of the roll, certifying in which House the same originated, which indorsement shall be signed by the Secretory or Clerk, as the case may be, of the House in which the same did originate, and shall be entered on the journal of each House. The said Committee shall report the day of presentation to the President, which time shall also be carefully entered on the journal of each House.

"All orders, resolutions, and votes, which are to be presented to the President of the United States for his approbation, shall also in the same manner be previously enroled, examined, and signed, and shall be presented in the same manner, and by the same Committee, as is provided in case of bills.

"That when the Senate and House of Representatives shall judge it proper to make a joint address to the President, it shall be presented to him in his audience Chamber by the President of the Senate, in the presence of the Speaker and both Houses."

Read, and RESOLVED, That the Senate do concur in the report.[31]

A message from the House of Representatives, by Mr. Beckley, their Clerk; —Who brought up a bill, entitled, "An act for registering and clearing Vessels, regulating the Coasting Trade, and for other purposes"[32]—

An enroled bill, entitled, "An act for the support of Light-Houses, Beacons, Buoys, and Public Piers"—

An enroled bill, entitled, "An act to provide for the Government of the Territory north-west of the River Ohio"—

An enroled bill, entitled, "An act to establish an Executive Department, to be denominated the Department of War:"—

Severally signed by the Speaker of the House of Representatives— And he withdrew.

The three last mentioned bills, were signed by the Vice President, and delivered to the Committee of enrolment for presentation—Which was accordingly done.[33]

Proceed to the FIRST reading of a bill, entitled, "An act for registering and clearing Vessels, regulating the Coasting Trade, and for other purposes,"

And assigned Monday next for a SECOND reading.[34]

The Secretary carried to the House of Representatives the bill, entitled, "An act to establish the Treasury Department," with the resolution of the Senate to INSIST on their eighth Amendment; Also,[35]

The concurrence of the Senate in the resolve of the House of Representatives, of the 4th of August, and the appointment of a Committee on the part of the Senate, to consider the business necessary to be transacted previous to a recess of Congress.[36]

Adjourned to 11 o'clock to-morrow.

---

[31] On August 7 this concurrence was carried to the House.

[32] A clear printed copy of this bill is in the Broadside Collection, RBkRm, DLC. An annotated copy of the same printing and an annotated printing of sections 25–29 are in American Imprints, 1789, Folio, United States Laws and Statutes, RBkRm, DLC. Another annotated printed copy of the bill is attached to several lists of amendments including an annotated printing of sections 25–29 and is located in House Bills, Senate Records, DNA. E–45644, E–45645.

[33] On August 7 the President signed these three bills and the Senate was notified of this action.

[34] On August 10 this bill was read a second time and committed.

[35] On August 10 the House requested a conference committee on this amendment and the Senate appointed a committee to join this committee.

[36] On August 10 this committee reported.

FRIDAY, AUGUST 7, 1789

The SENATE assembled,

Present as yesterday,

And Mr. Paterson from the State of New-Jersey attended.

In the absence of the Vice President, proceeded to elect a President pro tempore, and the votes being collected and counted, the Hon. John Langdon was unanimously appointed.

A message from the President of the United States, by General Knox—

"GENTLEMEN OF THE SENATE,

"THE business which has hitherto been under the consideration of Congress, has been of so much importance, that I was unwilling to draw their attention from it to any other subject.—But the disputes which exist between some of the United States and several powerful tribes of Indians within the limits of the Union, and the hostilities which have in several instances been committed on the frontiers seem to require the immediate interposition of the general Government.

"I have, therefore, directed the several statements and papers which have been submitted to me on this subject, by General Knox, to be laid before you for your information.

"While the measures of Government ought to be calculated to protect its citizens from all injury and violence, a due regard should be extended to those Indian Tribes, whose happiness, in the course of events so materially depends on the national justice and humanity of the United States.

"If it should be the judgment of Congress that it would be most expedient to terminate all differences in the southern district, and to lay the foundation for future confidence by an amicable Treaty with the Indian Tribes in that quarter, I think proper to suggest the consideration of the expediency of instituting a temporary commission for that purpose, to consist of three persons, whose authority should expire with the occasion. How far such a measure, unassisted by posts, would be competent to the establishment and preservation of peace and tranquility on the frontiers, is also a matter which merits your serious consideration.

"Along with this object I am induced to suggest another, with the national importance and necessity of which I am deeply impressed; I mean, some uniform and effective system for the militia of the United States. It is unnecessary to offer argument in recommendation of a measure, on which the honor, safety and well being of our country so evidently and so essentially depend:—But it may not be amiss to observe, that I am particularly anxious it should receive as early attention as circumstances will admit; because it is now in our power to avail ourselves of the military knowledge disseminated throughout the several

States by means of the many well instructed officers and soldiers of the late army; a resource which is daily diminishing by death and other causes. To suffer this peculiar advantage to pass away unimproved, would be to neglect an opportunity which will never again occur, unless, unfortunately, we should again be involved in a long and arduous war.

"GEO. WASHINGTON

"New-York, August 7, 1789"[37]

The above message was ordered to lie for consideration.

Mr. Morris, in behalf of the Committee on the bill, entitled, "An act for allowing a compensation to the President and Vice President of the United States,"—reported an Amendment, to wit:—

To expunge in the provision for the Vice President, "Five thousand Dollars," and insert "Six thousand Dollars."—

On motion, to reduce the provision for the President of the United States from twenty-five thousand to twenty thousand Dollars—

Passed in the Negative.

On motion to make the provision for the Vice President eight thousand Dollars instead of five thousand Dollars—

Passed in the Negative.

And on motion, the further consideration of this clause of the bill was postponed.[38]

A message from the House of Representatives, by Mr. Beckley, their Clerk; —Who informed the Senate, that the President of the United States had affixed his signature to the following bills;

"An act to provide for the Government of the Territory north-west of the River Ohio"—

"An act to establish an Executive Department, to be denominated the Department of War"—

"An act for the establishment and support of Light-Houses, Beacons, Buoys, and Public Piers"—And had returned them to the House of Representatives— And he withdrew.

Mr. Grayson requested leave of absence, for the recovery of his health.

The concurrence of the Senate, upon the resolve of the House on the mode of enrolment, and the presentation of bills, &c. was carried to the House of Representatives.

Adjourned to 11 o'clock on Monday morning.

---

[37] The message is in President's Messages: Transmitting reports from the Secretary of War, Senate Records, DNA. Included are numerous letters from Henry Knox about Indian Affairs.

[38] On September 7 this bill was read a third time and passed with amendments.

MONDAY, AUGUST 10, 1789

The SENATE assembled,

Present as on Friday.

Mr. Strong, on behalf of the joint Committee appointed the 5th of August, "To consider what business is necessary to be acted upon prior to an adjournment, and to report a proper time at which an adjournment shall take place," —reported,[39]—And the report was ordered to lie for consideration.[40]

A message from the House of Representatives, by Mr. Beckley, their Clerk; —Who brought up a bill, entitled, "An act for allowing compensation to the members of the Senate and House of Representatives of the United States, and to the officers of both Houses,"[41] and requested the concurrence of the Senate therein[42]—

And he withdrew.

A message from the President of the United States by General Knox:—

"GENTLEMEN OF THE SENATE,

"I HAVE directed a statement of the troops in the service of the United States to be laid before you for your information.

"These troops were raised by virtue of the resolves of Congress of the 20th October, 1786, and the 3d of October, 1787, in order to protect the frontiers from the depredations of the hostile Indians; to prevent all intrusions on the public lands; and to facilitate the surveying and selling of the same, for the purpose of reducing the public debt.

"As these important objects continue to require the aid of the troops, it is necessary that the establishment thereof should, in all respect, be conformed, by law, to the Constitution of the United States.

"GEO. WASHINGTON

"New York, August 10th, 1789"

A statement of the troops in the service of the United States.

The establishment as directed to be raised and organized by the acts of Congress, of the 3d of October, 1787, to wit:—

ONE REGIMENT OF INFANTRY

Consisting of   1 Lieutenant-Colonel Commandant

2 Majors

7 Captains

---

[39] The annotated report is in Joint Committee Reports, Senate Records, DNA.

[40] On August 24 the House resolved that Congress should adjourn on September 22. The Senate was notified on August 25 and concurred with this solution on the same date.

[41] The manuscript and printed copies of this bill are in House Bills, Senate Records, DNA. E–45634.

[42] On August 11 this bill was read a first time and the second reading was assigned.

    7 Lieutenants
    8 Ensigns
    1 Surgeon
    4 Mates

Eight companies, each of which to consist of four Serjeants, four Corporals, two Musicians, and sixty Privates............................ 560

ONE BATTALION OF ARTILLERY

    1 Major
    4 Captains
    8 Lieutenants
    1 Surgeon's Mate

Four companies, each of which to consist of four Serjeants, four Corporals, two Musicians, and sixty Privates............................ 280

Non-commissioned officers[43] and Privates..................... 840

That the pay of the troops was fixed by the act of Congress of the 12th of April, 1785, and confirmed by the acts of the 20th of October, 1786, and the 3d of October, 1787, to wit:—

LIEUTENANT COLONEL COMMANDANT

	at 50 Dollars per month—
Major	45 do.
Captain	35 do.
Lieutenant	26 do.
Ensign	20 do.
Surgeon	45 do.
Mate	30 do.
Serjeants	6 do.
Corporals	5 do.
Musicians	5 do.
Privates	4 do.

That the subsistence to the Officers, in lieu of rations, are the same as during the late war, to wit:—

LIEUTENANT COLONEL COMMANDANT

	at ——— Dollars per month—
Major	20 do.
Captain	12 do.
Lieutenant	8 do.

---

[43] The printed journal omits "Officers."

Ensign	8 do.
Surgeon	16 do.
Mate	8 do.

That Lieutenants, acting as Adjutant, Quarter-Master, and Paymaster, are allowed, by the act of Congress of the 12th of April, 1785, for their extra duty, ten Dollars per month.

That the allowance of forage is as follows:

3 Majors each	12 Dollars per month
1 Surgeon	6 do.
3 Regimental Staff, each	6 do.

That by the act of Congress of the 31st of July, 1787, Lieutenant Colonel Commandant Harmar was promoted to the rank of Brigadier General by brevet, with an allowance of the emoluments, but not the pay of said rank.

That the emoluments are as follows, to wit:—

Subsistence	64 Dollars per month
Forage	18 do.

That each non-commissioned officer and soldier are allowed annually, one suit of uniform cloaths, as follows:

1 coat
1 vest
2 pairs woolen overalls
2 pairs linen overalls
1 hat
4 shirts
4 pairs shoes
4 pairs socks
1 stock
1 stock clasp
1 pair shoe buckles
1 blanket

That each non-commissioned officer and soldier are also allowed one ration per day, to consist of the following articles,—

1 pound of bread or flour
1 pound of beef, or ¾ pound of pork
1 jill of common rum

1 quart of salt
2 quarts of vinegar   } to every hundred rations
2 pounds of soap
1 pound of candles

That the troops in actual service, are as follow;—

Two companies of Artillery, raised by virtue of the acts of Congress of the 20th of October, 1786, and continued by the act of Congress of the 9th of April, 1787, one of which is stationed at the arsenal at West-Point, on Hudson's River, and the other at the arsenal at Springfield, on Connecticut River   76

Troops stationed on the frontiers as follow:—

At the various posts north-west of the River Ohio   596
                                                                                                         ———
                                                                                                         672
Wanting to complete the establishment   168
Non-commissioned officers and privates   ———
                                                                                                         840

That all the troops are enlisted for three years.

That the engagements of the two companies of Artillery at West-Point and Springfield, will expire the beginning of the year 1790.

That of the troops on the frontiers, enlisted by virtue of the acts of Congress of the 3d of October, 1787, five hundred and twenty-eight non-commissioned officers and soldiers will have to serve generally to the middle of the year 1791, and two companies, consisting of sixty-eight non-commissioned and privates, until towards the month of May, 1792—

That the change in the Government of the United States, will require that the articles of war be revised and adapted to the Constitution—

That the oaths necessary to be taken by the troops be prescribed, and also the form of the commissions which are to be issued to the officers—

All which is humbly submitted to the President of the United States.

H. KNOX

War-Office, August 8th, 1789[44]

The Senate proceeded to the SECOND reading of a bill, entitled, "An act for registering and clearing of Vessels, regulating the Coasting Trade, and for other purposes"—

ORDERED, That it be committed to

Mr. Morris

Mr. Dalton

Mr. Langdon

Mr. Butler and

Mr. King[45]

A message from the House of Representatives—

Mr. Beckley, their Clerk, informed the Senate, that the House had desired a conference on so much of the eighth Amendment proposed by the Senate,

---

[44] The messages from George Washington and Henry Knox are in President's Messages: Transmitting reports from the Secretary of War, Senate Records, DNA.

[45] On August 17 this committee reported amendments to the bill.

on the bill, entitled, "An Act, to establish the Treasury Department," as was disagreed to by the House of Representatives, and had appointed

> Mr. Madison
> Mr. Fitzsimons and
> Mr. Boudinot[46]

Managers on the part of the House—
And he withdrew.
Whereupon,
RESOLVED, That the Senate do agree to the conference, and that

> Mr. Johnson
> Mr. Lee and
> Mr. Strong

Be the managers on the part of the Senate;[47]
And the House was notified thereof accordingly.[48]
Adjourned to 11 o'clock to-morrow.

T U E S D A Y, AUGUST 11, 1789

The SENATE assembled,
Present as yesterday.

Proceeded to the FIRST reading of the bill, entitled, "An Act for allowing Compensation to the Members of the Senate and House of Representatives of the United States, and to the Officers of both Houses," and assigned to-morrow for the SECOND reading.[49]

A message from the House of Representatives—

Mr. Beckley, their Clerk, brought up a resolve of the House, of the 10th of August, providing,

"That the Survey directed by Congress, in their Act of June the[50] 6th, 1788, be made, and returned into the Treasury without delay"[51]—

And he withdrew.

The above resolve was read in Senate, and the consideration thereof postponed to Friday next.[52]

---

[46] The resolve, in the form of a journal extract, is in Messages from the House, Senate Records, DNA.

[47] The appointment to committee is in the William S. Johnson Papers, Manuscript Division, DLC.

[48] On August 14 this committee announced that a report had not been agreed upon.

[49] On August 12 this bill was read a second time and consideration was postponed.

[50] The smooth journal omits "the."

[51] The resolve, in the form of an extract from the House Journal, is in Messages from the House, Senate Records, DNA.

[52] On August 14 this resolution and two petitions related to it were read, and consideration of them was postponed.

Proceeded in the SECOND reading of the bill, entitled, "An Act for the Punishment of certain Crimes against the United States,"[53]

And after progress,

Adjourned to 11 o'clock to-morrow.

WEDNESDAY, AUGUST 12, 1789

The SENATE assembled,

Present as yesterday.

Proceeded in the SECOND reading of the bill, entitled, "An Act for the Punishment of certain Crimes against the United States,"—and

Postponed the farther consideration thereof until to-morrow.[54]

Proceeded to a SECOND reading of the bill, entitled, "An Act for allowing Compensation to the Members of the Senate and House of Representatives of the United States, and to the Officers of both Houses;"

The further consideration of which was postponed.[55]

Adjourned to 11 o'clock to-morrow.

THURSDAY, AUGUST 13, 1789

The SENATE assembled,

Present as yesterday.

Proceeded in the SECOND reading of the bill, entitled, "An Act for the Punishment of certain Crimes against the United States,"—

ORDERED, That Monday next be assigned for a THIRD reading.[56]

A message from the House of Representatives—

Mr. Beckley, their Clerk, brought up a bill, entitled, "An Act providing for the Expenses which may attend Negotiations or Treaties with the Indian Tribes, and the Appointment of Commissioners for managing the same,"[57] together with the papers referred to in the President's message of the 7th of August—And he withdrew.

The bill entitled, "An Act providing for the Expenses which may attend Negotiations or Treaties with the Indian Tribes, and the Appointment of Commissioners for managing the same," was read a FIRST time—

ORDERED, That to-morrow be assigned for a SECOND reading.[58]

Adjourned to 11 o'clock to-morrow.

---

[53] On August 12 this bill was considered again.
[54] On August 13 this bill was considered again and assigned to a third reading.
[55] On August 25 this bill was considered again and committed.
[56] On August 18 this bill was read for the third time.
[57] This bill, as it passed the House, has not been located.
[58] On August 14 this bill was read a second time and committed.

F R I D A Y, August 14, 1789

The SENATE assembled,
Present as yesterday.

The petition of Nathaniel Gorham,[59] praying that a resolution of the House of Representatives of the United States, providing, "That the Survey directed by an Act of Congress of the 6th of June, 1788, be made," might not pass the Senate in its present form, for reasons set forth in the petition—

The resolve of the House of Representatives of the United States of the 11th of August, referred to in the said petition,—and

The petition of Andrew Ellicott,[60] on the same subject, were severally read; And the consideration of the BUSINESS was postponed until Wednesday next.[61]

Proceeded to a SECOND reading of the bill, entitled, "An Act providing for the Expenses which may attend Negotiations or Treaties with the Indian Tribes, and the Appointment of Commissioners for managing the same"—

ORDERED, That the bill be committed to

> Mr. Few
> Mr. Ellsworth
> Mr. King
> Mr. Lee and
> Mr. Butler[62]

Mr. Johnson, in behalf of the managers of the conference on the part of the Senate upon the bill, entitled, "An Act to establish the Treasury Department," informed the Senate, that they had conferred on the subject with the Committee on the part of the House of Representatives, but could not agree upon a report.[63]

Adjourned until 11 o'clock on Monday morning.

M O N D A Y, August 17, 1789

The SENATE assembled,
Present as on Friday.

Mr. Morris, on behalf of the Committee, to whom IT was referred, reported

---

[59] The petition is in Petitions and Memorials: Various subjects, Senate Records, DNA. A House document containing cessions referred to in the above petition is located in Various Select Committee Reports, House Records, DNA. The smooth journal spells this name or signature incorrectly as "Goreham."

[60] This petition has not been located.

[61] On August 19 this resolution was passed by the Senate after several motions on it were defeated.

[62] On August 17 this committee reported and the report was disagreed to. Several other resolutions on this bill were defeated and consideration was postponed.

[63] On August 24 the House resolved to adhere to its disagreement to part of the eighth amendment to this bill and notified the Senate. The Senate then resolved to recede from this part of the eighth amendment.

sundry Amendments to the bill, entitled, "An Act for registering and clearing of Vessels, regulating the Coasting Trade, and for other Purposes"[64]—

ORDERED, That the further consideration thereof be postponed.[65]

The Committee appointed to take into consideration the bill, entitled, "An Act providing for the Expenses which may attend Negotiations or Treaties with the Indian Tribes, and the appointment of Commissioners for managing the same," reported that it be

"RESOLVED, That there be allowed and paid to a Superintendant of Indian Affairs in the Southern Department, that may be nominated by the President, and appointed by, and with the advice and consent of the Senate, the sum of   per day, including his expenses, for the time he may be employed in attending a Treaty, proposed to be held by the Commissioners of the United States and the Creek Indians, at the Rock-Landing, in the State of Georgia, on the 15th day of September next—

"That in case the proposed Treaty should fail in the desired object, of establishing peace between the citizens of the United States and the Creek Indians, Congress will make such grants of money, and pursue such other measures, as will be necessary for the protection and safety of the inhabitants of the Southern frontiers, and best secure the peace of the United States"—

And on motion to accept the report,

It passed in the Negative.

On motion, that it be

"RESOLVED, That the President of the United States be requested to nominate a fit person for Superintendant of Indian Affairs in the Southern Department, in order that he may be sent forward as soon as may be, to act with the Commissioners of Indian Affairs in the Southern Department, appointed pursuant to a resolution of Congress, passed on the   day of   and aid them in carrying into effect a Treaty that is proposed to be held with the Creek Nation, on the 15th day of September next, in the State of Georgia, at the Rock-Landing—

"That the sum of   dollars be delivered to the said Superintendant, to be appropriated for the immediate purpose of the said Treaty, for which sum he shall be accountable—

"That the President of the United States be requested to instruct the said Superintendant and Commissioners, to hear and fully investigate all the complaints and grievances, of the said Creek Indians, and to use all the means in their power to quiet their minds and do them ample justice, agreeably to the aforesaid resolution of Congress, and instructions heretofore given for that purpose: That if the said Indians should prove refractory, or refuse to treat

---

[64] The report has not been located but a draft of amendments which are probably from the report is in House Bills, Senate Records, DNA. E–45681, amendments 25–29.

[65] On August 18 consideration of this bill was postponed again.

and establish peace on just and reasonable terms, then and in that case, the said Superintendant and Commissioners be directed to make immediate report thereof to the President of the United States, and Congress will make such grants of money, and pursue such other measures, as will be necessary for the safety and protection of the inhabitants of the Southern frontiers, and best secure the peace of the United States"—

It passed in the Negative.

On motion, that it be

"RESOLVED, That the President of the United States be authorised and empowered, and he is hereby authorised and empowered, should the Creek Indians decline to make peace with the State of Georgia, to take effectual measures for covering the State of Georgia from the incursions of the Indians, either by ordering some of the troops now at Fort Harmar to march to the frontiers of Georgia, or by embodying such a number of the militia as he shall think sufficient to insure to the citizens of Georgia protection, and the cultivation of their lands in peace and security, and that he be empowered to draw on the Treasury for defraying the expenses of the same"[66]—

And on motion for the previous question, to wit:

"Shall the main question be now put?"

It passed in the Negative.[67]

The Senate adjourned to 11 o'clock to-morrow.

TUESDAY, AUGUST 18, 1789

The SENATE assembled,

Present as yesterday,

And proceeded in a SECOND reading of the Bill, entitled, "An Act providing for the expenses which may attend Negotiations or Treaties with the Indian Tribes, and the appointment of Commissioners for managing the same"—

On motion,

To strike out "Eight dollars," from the clause providing for the compensation to the Commissioners, and insert FIVE DOLLARS, in line 8th—

It passed in the Negative.

On motion,

To insert after "Eight dollars per day," AT THE DISCRETION OF THE PRESIDENT—

It passed in the Negative.

---

[66] The report is in Various Select Committee Reports, Senate Records, DNA. Another version of this resolve, in which the wording varies slightly, is in the Pierce Butler Papers, PHi. The second resolve in this report has not been located.

[67] On August 18 this bill was passed with amendments.

On motion,

Upon the compensation to the Commissioners, to strike out "Eight dollars," and insert SIX DOLLARS,

It passed in the Negative.

Ordered, that the rules of the House be so far dispensed with, as that the said Bill shall have a THIRD reading at this time.

On motion,

To strike out in line 3d, "Forty," and insert TWENTY, in order thereby to limit the sum to be expended in negotiating a Treaty with the Indian Tribes, to twenty thousand dollars instead of forty thousand—

The yeas and nays being required by one fifth of the Senators present,

Mr. Butler		Nay
Mr. Carroll	Yea	
Mr. Dalton	Yea	
Mr. Ellsworth	Yea	
Mr. Elmer	Yea	
Mr. Few		Nay
Mr. Gunn		Nay
Mr. Henry	Yea	
Mr. Johnson	Yea	
Mr. Izard		Nay
Mr. King	Yea	
Mr. Langdon	Yea	
Mr. Lee		Nay
Mr. Maclay		Nay
Mr. Morris		Nay
Mr. Read	Yea	
Mr. Schuyler	Yea	
Mr. Strong	Yea	
Mr. Wingate	Yea	

Yeas 12
Nays 7

So it passed in the Affirmative.

On motion, that it be

RESOLVED, That Congress will make provision for the discharging of any expenses that may be incurred by such military arrangements, as the President of the United States may think proper to make, for the purpose of protecting the citizens of Georgia from the depredations of the Creek Indians, should peace not take place with them, or should they, having agreed to a peace, violate the same,[68]—

---

[68] This resolve has not been located.

And on motion for the previous question, to wit:
"Shall the main question be now put?"
It passed in the Negative;
And on the question upon the Bill, it was
RESOLVED, To concur therein with the Amendment:
ORDERED, That the Secretary carry the said bill to the House of Representatives for their concurrence in the Amendment.[69]
ORDERED, That the further consideration of the Bill, entitled, "An Act for registering and clearing of Vessels, regulating the Coasting Trade, and for other Purposes," be postponed until to-morrow.[70]
The Senate proceeded in a THIRD reading of the Bill, entitled, "An Act for the Punishment of certain Crimes against the United States"—And after progress,[71]
Adjourned to 11 o'clock to-morrow.

WEDNESDAY, AUGUST 19, 1789

The SENATE assembled,
Present as yesterday,
And Mr. Bassett attended.

Agreeably to the order of the day, the Senate proceeded to the consideration of a Resolve of the House of Representatives, of the 10th of August, providing, "That the Survey directed by Congress, in their Act of June the 6th, 1788, be made, and returned to the Secretary of the Treasury without delay; and that the President of the United States be requested to appoint a fit person to complete the same, who shall be allowed five dollars per day, whilst actually employed in the said service, with the expenses necessarily attending the execution thereof"—

And on motion,
"That the consideration of the Resolution be postponed to such time in the next Session of Congress, as that the Legislature of the State of New York may be afforded an opportunity of interposing their objections"—
It passed in the Negative.

On motion,
To insert OR PERSONS, after the word "Person"—
It passed in the Negative.

On motion,

---

[69] On August 19 the House concurred with the Senate amendments to this bill and notified the Senate.

[70] On August 20 this bill was read a second time and considered.

[71] On August 26 this bill was considered again.

To insert, BY AND WITH THE ADVICE AND CONSENT OF THE SENATE, after "President"—

It passed in the Negative.

And on the main question—

RESOLVED, That the Senate do concur in the said Resolution.

ORDERED, That the Secretary do carry a message to the House of Representatives accordingly.[72]

A message from the House of Representatives—

Mr. Beckley, their Clerk, informed the Senate, that the House had concurred in their Amendment[73] proposed to the Bill, entitled, "An Act providing for the expenses which may attend Negotiations or Treaties with the Indian Tribes, and the appointment of Commissioners for managing the same"[74]—

And he withdrew.

The Senate adjourned to 11 o'clock to-morrow.

THURSDAY, AUGUST 20, 1789

The SENATE assembled,

Present as yesterday,

Except Mr. Strong, absent with leave.

A message from the House of Representatives—

Mr. Beckley, their Clerk, brought up the enroled Bill, entitled, "An Act providing for the expenses which may attend Negotiations or Treaties with the Indian Tribes, and the appointment of Commissioners for managing the same,"[75] examined by the Committee of enrolment, and signed by the Speaker—

And he withdrew.

Whereupon the Bill was signed by the Vice President, and by the Committee of enrolment laid before the President of the United States for his approbation.

The Senate proceeded in the SECOND reading of a Bill, entitled, "An Act for registering and clearing of Vessels, regulating the Coasting Trade, and for other Purposes"—And after progress,

ORDERED, That the further consideration thereof be postponed.[76]

A message from the House of Representatives—

---

[72] On August 25 this resolve, signed by the Speaker, was brought to the Senate for the Vice President's signature. It was then presented to the President.

[73] The smooth journal reads "amendment."

[74] The resolve is in Messages from the House, Senate Records, DNA. On August 20 this bill, signed by the Speaker, was sent to the Senate for the Vice President's signature. It was then presented to the President who signed it on the same day.

[75] The inspected enrolled bill is in Enrolled Acts, RG 11, DNA. E-45703, E-22196.

[76] On August 21 this bill was considered again and the third reading was scheduled.

Mr. Beckley, their Clerk, informed the Senate, that the President of the United States had affixed his Signature to a Bill, entitled, "An Act providing for the Expenses which may attend Negotiations or Treaties with the Indian Tribes, and the Appointment of Commissioners for managing the same"— And had returned it to the House of Representatives.

The Senate adjourned to 11 o'clock to-morrow.

FRIDAY, AUGUST 21, 1789

The SENATE assembled,

Present as yesterday,

And proceeded in the SECOND reading of the bill, entitled, "An Act for registering and clearing of Vessels, regulating the Coasting Trade, and for other Purposes"[77]—

ORDERED, That the bill be read the[78] THIRD time to-morrow.[79]

The Senate adjourned to 11 o'clock to-morrow.

SATURDAY, AUGUST 22, 1789

The SENATE assembled,

Present as yesterday.

The memorial of John Cox, and others, citizens of the State of New-Jersey and of the State of Pennsylvania,[80] praying that the future Seat of Government might be established on the Banks of the Delaware, and proposing a cession of a tract of land of ten miles square, was read, and, together with a draught of the said tract, was laid on the table for consideration.[81]

Proceeded in the THIRD reading of the bill, entitled, "An Act for registering and clearing of Vessels, regulating the Coasting Trade, and for other Purposes"—And after progress,[82]

Adjourned until 10 o'clock on Monday morning.

MONDAY, AUGUST 24, 1789

The SENATE assembled,

Present as on Saturday.

Proceeded in the Executive business before the Senate—

Adjourned to 11 o'clock to-morrow.

---

[77] The amendments are attached to this bill located in House Bills, Senate Records, DNA.

[78] The smooth journal substitutes "a" for "the."

[79] On August 22 this bill was read a third time and considered.

[80] This petition is in Petitions and Memorials: Various subjects, Senate Records, DNA.

[81] This petition was not considered in the Senate or the House. There was a committee on the permanent seat of government.

[82] On August 25 the Senate concurred in sixty-nine amendments to this bill.

TUESDAY, AUGUST 25, 1789

The SENATE assembled,
Present as yesterday.

Mr. Maclay, presented a draught of ten miles square, including the borough of Lancaster, with a letter containing a description of the same, from Edward Hand,[83] directed to the Hon. Robert Morris and the Hon. William Maclay; Mr. Maclay likewise nominated Wright's Ferry, on the Susquehannah; York-Town, west of the Susquehannah; Carlisle, west of the Susquehannah; Harris-burgh, on the Susquehannah; Reading, on the Schuylkill, and Germantown, in the neighbourhood of Philadelphia, as different places in Pennsylvania, which had been proposed for the permanent Seat of Government of the United States—

The letter being read, was, together with the draught,
Ordered to lie for consideration.[84]

Proceeded to the THIRD reading of the bill, entitled, "An Act for registering and clearing of Vessels, regulating the Coasting Trade, and for other Purposes"—And

RESOLVED, That the Senate do concur therein with, sixty-nine Amendments.[85]

---

[83] The petition is in Petitions and Memorials: Various subjects, Senate Records, DNA.

[84] This letter and Mr. Maclay's suggestions were not considered again in the first Congress. There was a committee on the permanent seat of government.

[85] The smooth journal reads:

"RESOLVED, That the Senate do concur therein with the following Amendments

A.	P.	L.	
1.	1.	7.	Strike out "and chief mate shall be citizens," and insert "is a Citizen."
2.		8.	Strike out "hereafter," and insert "hereinafter."
3.	1.	15. a 18.	Strike out all the words between "Collector" and "In pursuance."
4.		20.	Strike off the letter "S" from the words "Names," "Occupations" and "Owners."
5.		21.	Strike out "(or they)"
6.		24.	Strike out "And (mates name) chief mate."
7.			Strike out "are Citizens," and insert "is a Citizen."
8.		26.	Strike out "being a Ship (or vessel) of the United States."
9.	2.	4.	Strike out all the words between "Port of," and "and it," and insert "Given under our Hands and Seals of Office at (Port) this day of in the year (words at full length) and the Collector shall transmit to the Secretary of the Treasury a duplicate of every such Certificate so granted."
10.		9.	After "appointed," insert "by the Collector."
11.		20. a 21.	Strike out all the words between "Port," and "at."
12.		24.	Strike out all the remaining part of the Section after "painted" and insert "on her Stern on a black ground with white Letters of not less than three inches in length."

A.	P.	L.	
13.		25. a 28.	Strike out all the words between "enacted," and "unless" and insert "That no Ship or Vessel owned in whole or in part by any Citizen of the United States usually residing in any foreign Country, shall during the time he shall continue so to reside be deemed a vessel of the United States entitled to be registered by virtue of this act."
14.	3.	3.	Strike out all the words between "If," and "owned."
15.		4.	Strike out "Joint"
16.		4. a 6.	Strike out all the words between "Owners," and "I"—and insert "Then by any one of such Owners; namely"
17.		12. a 13.	Strike out all the words between "Master," and "and that I," and insert "is a Citizen of the United States."
18.		20. a 28.	Strike out the whole of the enacting clause, and insert, "Provided always and be it further enacted, that when ever the Owner or Owners of such Ship or Vessel usually resides or reside out of the district within which such Ship or Vessel may be at the time of granting the Certificate of Registry, that such Owner, or where there are two or more Owners, any one of them, may take and subscribe the said oath or affirmation before the Collector of the district, within which he usually resides, omitting in the said oath or affirmation the description of such Ship or Vessel as expressed in the Certificate of the Surveyor, and inserting in lieu thereof, the Name of the Port and district within which such Ship or Vessel may then be; and the Collector before whom such oath or affirmation may be taken and subscribed, shall transmit the same to the Collector of the Port where such Ship or Vessel may be; upon the receipt whereof the said Collector shall proceed to register such Ship or Vessel in like manner as though the usual and regular oath or affirmation had been taken and subscribed before him."
19.	4.	12. a 13.	Strike out all the words between "Master," and "Such" and insert "And Owner or Owners, or by some other person or persons, on his, her or their behalf."
20.	5.	6. a 22.	Strike out the whole of the enacting clause—and insert "And be it further enacted, that whenever any Ship or Vessel registered in conformity with this Act, shall in whole or in part be sold or transferred to a Citizen or Citizens of the United States, the former Certificate of Registry shall be delivered up to the Collector, and by him without delay transmitted to the Secretary of the Treasury to be cancelled, and such Ship or Vessel shall be registered anew by her former Name, and a Certificate thereof shall be granted by the Collector in like manner as is herein before directed."
21.	5.	23. a 28.	Strike out the whole of the enacting Clause—And insert "And be it further enacted, That whenever any such Ship or Vessel shall in whole or in part be sold or transferred to any Person or Persons, the Certificate of the Registry of every such Ship or Vessel shall be recited at length in the Instrument of transfer or sale thereof, and in default thereof such instrument of sale or transfer shall be void, and such Ship or Vessel shall not be deemed or denominated a Ship or Vessel entitled to any of the benefits and advantages of a Ship or Vessel of the United States."
22.	6.	6.	After "Register," insert "and transmit a Copy thereof to the Secretary of the Treasury"
23.		13.	After "Law," insert "by the name of."

A.	P.	L.	
24.			After "That," Strike out "I had."
25.			After "Thereof," insert "Was."
26.		15.	After "Again," insert "and comes again within my power."
27.		16.	Strike out "Are," and insert "is a."
28.			Strike the letter "S," from the word "Citizens."
29.	6.	20.	After "anew," insert "By her former name."
30.		23. a 24.	Strike out all the words between "Vessel," (in the beginning of line 23) and "That."
31.	7.	4.	After "anew," insert "By her former name."
32.		18. a 19.	Strike out all the words between "power," and "shall."
33.		22.	Strike out all the words between "Affirmation," and "before," (in the latter part of the line.)
34.		23.	After "Who," strike out "are, or."
35.	8.	6. a 7.	Strike out all the words between "Collector" (in the beginning of the line) and "of the district."
36.		8. a 10.	Strike out all the words between "Entitled an act," and "I."
37.		21.	After "Witness," strike out "Our, or."
38.	9.	6.	After "Copy thereof," insert "Shall be."
39.		15. a 23.	After "Aforesaid," strike out the whole of the remaining part of the Section.
40.	10.	3.	After "Vessel," insert "Of the burthen of Twenty Tons or upwards."
41.		6.	Strike out "by Sea."
42.	10.	9.	After "Reside," insert "And every Vessel so enroled shall have her name and the name of the place to which she belongs painted on her Stern in manner directed by this act for registered Vessels."
43.		15.	After "Master," strike out "And chief mate."
44.		21.	After "Such," strike out "Purchase" and insert "Change."
45.		23.	Strike out all the words between "Certificate," and "Upon" and insert "of the enrolment of such Ship or Vessel by her former name to such Owner or Owners."
46.	10.	25.	After "Cancelled," insert "Provided that the Master or Owner of every Vessel of less than twenty tons burthen and not less than five tons which shall be employed between any of the districts in the United States, shall cause the name of such Vessel and of the place to which she belongs to be painted on her Stern in manner directed by this act for registered Vessels, and shall annually procure a license from the Collector of the district, to which such Vessel belongs, who is hereby authorised to give the same, purporting that such Vessel is exempt from clearing and entering for the Term of one year from the date thereof, and the Master or Owner of every such Vessel shall give Bond with sufficient security for the payment of Two hundred Dollars to the United States with condition that such Vessel shall not be employed in any illicit trade or commerce; and before any new License shall be given for a succeeding year to the Master of such Vessel, he shall on oath or affirmation declare that no illicit trade has been carried on in such Vessel to his knowledge or belief during the term for which she was licensed."
47.		27.	After "Vessel," insert "Of the burthen of Twenty Tons or upwards to be."
48.			After "Trade," strike out "By sea."

A.	P.	L.	
49.		28.	After "Vessel," insert "To be."
50.	II.	8.	After "Vessel," insert "Of the burthen of Twenty Tons or upwards"
51.		9.	After "and," insert "A."
52.			Strike out "By sea."
53.		13. a 14.	Strike out all the words between "To the Collector," and "where," and insert "Of the district."
54.		15.	After "Of the," insert "Said."
55.		15. a 16.	Strike out all the words between "Of the Collector," and "To grant."
56.		18.	After "Commander," insert "Consignee."
57.	II. a 13.	19. 23.	After "Offence," strike out three following enacting Clauses to the word "Manner" inclusive—And insert, "And be it further enacted, That the Master of every Ship or Vessel of the burthen of Twenty Tons on upwards licensed to Trade between the different districts of the United States, having on board goods, wares or merchandize of foreign growth or manufacture of the value of Two hundred dollars, or Rum or other ardent Spirits exceeding Four hundred gallons, and being bound from one district to another, shall deliver to the Collector and where the Collector and Surveyor reside at different places within the Same district, to the Collector or Surveyor, as the one or the other may reside at or nearest to the port where such Ship or Vessel may be duplicate manifests of the whole cargo on board such Ship or Vessel, whether such cargo shall consist wholly of goods, wares or merchandize of foreign growth or manufacture, or partly of such goods, wares or merchandize, and partly of goods, wares and merchandize, the growth or manufacture of the United States, specifying therein the name and place of residence of every Shipper and Consignee, together with the quantity of goods, wares or merchandize shipped by and to each; and upon the oath or affirmation of the said Master before the said Collector or Surveyor to the truth of such manifest, and that he doth not know, and hath no reason to believe that the revenue of the United States has been defrauded of any part of the duties imposed by Law upon the importations of any of the goods, wares or merchandize contained in the said manifest, it shall be duty of such Collector or Surveyor to return to the said Master one of the said Manifests, first certifying thereon that the same had been sworn to and delivered to him according to law, and also to grant to the said master a permit authorising such Ship or Vessel to proceed to the place of her destination. So always, and provided that where goods, wares or merchandize of foreign growth or manufacture are to be transported to and from the respective ports of Philadelphia and Baltimore unto each other through and across the State of Delaware, a manifest cerified as aforesaid by the Officers of that one said ports from whence the same goods, wares or merchandizes are to be so transported shall be sufficient to warrant the transportation thereof to the other of the said ports without an intermediate Entry in the district of Delaware.

"PROVIDED ALWAYS, That no Master of any Ship or Vessel, licensed to trade as aforesaid, having on board goods wares or merchandize of the growth or manufacture of the United States only. Rum and other ardent Spirits exceeding four hun-

dred gallons excepted, and being bound from one district to
another in the same State, or from a district in one State to a
district in the next adjoining State, shall be obliged to deliver
duplicate manifests, or to apply for a permit as aforesaid, but
any such Master may in such case lawfully proceed to any other
district in the same State, or in the next adjoining State freely
and without interruption.

"AND BE IT FURTHER ENACTED, That the Master of every
Ship or Vessel of the burthen of twenty Tons or upwards,
licensed to trade as aforesaid, having on board goods, wares or
merchandize of the growth or manufacture of the United States
only, and being bound from a district in one State to a district
in any other than an adjoining State, shall deliver to the Collector, or where the Collector and Surveyor reside at different
places within the same district, to the Collector or Surveyor as
the one or the other may reside at or nearest to the Port where
such Ship or Vessel may be, duplicate manifests of the whole
cargo on board such Ship or Vessel, specifying therein the
name and place of residence of every Shipper and Consignee,
together with the quantity of goods, wares or merchandize
shipped by and to each: And upon the oath or affirmation of
the said Master before the said Collector or Surveyor, to the
truth of such manifest it shall be the duty of such Collector or
Surveyor, to return to the said Master one of the said manifests, first certifying thereon, that the same had been sworn to
and delivered to him, according to law; and also to grant to
the said Master a permit, authorising such Ship or Vessel to
proceed to the place of her destination.

"AND BE IT FURTHER ENACTED, That the Master of every
Ship or Vessel of the burthen of twenty Tons or upwards
licensed to trade as aforesaid, not having on board Rum or
other ardent Spirits, exceeding four hundred gallons, and arriving from one district to another in the same State, or from a
district in one State to a district in the next adjoining State,
with goods, wares or merchandize, of the growth or manufacture of the United States only, shall, within twenty four hours,
Sundays excepted, next after his arrival at any place or port
where a Collector or Surveyor resides, and before any part of
the Cargo on board such Ship or Vessel be landed or unloaded, deliver to such Collector or Surveyor a manifest
thereof, and shall make oath before such Collector or Surveyor,
that such manifest contains a true account of all the goods,
wares and merchandize on board such Ship or Vessel, and
thereupon shall receive from such Collector or Surveyor a permit to land or unload the same.

"AND BE IT FURTHER ENACTED, That in all other cases the
Master of every Vessel of the burthen of twenty Tons or upwards licensed to trade as aforesaid, shall within twenty four
hours, Sundays excepted, next after his arrival at any port or
place within the United States, where a Collector or Surveyor
resides, and before any part of the cargo on board any such
Ship or Vessel be landed or unloaded, deliver to such Collector
or Surveyor the manifest thereof, authenticated before and received from the Collector or Surveyor of the port or place
where the said Cargo, was taken on board, together with his

A.   P.   L.

permit to depart from the place of lading, whereupon it shall be the duty of such Collector or Surveyor to grant a permit to land or unload such Cargo.

"AND BE IT FURTHER ENACTED, That if the Master of any Ship or Vessel of the burthen of twenty Tons or upwards licensed to trade as aforesaid, and having on board goods, wares or merchandize, of the value of Two hundred dollars, or upwards, shall depart with the said Ship or Vessel from any port, with intent to go to another district, without such manifest and permit, except as is hereinafter provided, the Master or Owner of such Ship or Vessel shall forfeit and pay the sum of four hundred dollars for every such offence; and all goods, wares, and merchandize, of the value of two hundred dollars or upwards, which shall be found on board any such Ship or Vessel after her departure from the port where the same were taken on board, without being contained in and accompanied with such manifest as is herein before directed, except as is herein after excepted, shall be subject to seizure and forfeiture.

"PROVIDED ALWAYS, That nothing herein contained shall be construed to subject the Master or Owner of any Ship or Vessel licensed to trade as aforesaid, having on board goods, wares and merchandize of the growth and manufacture of the United States only. Rum and other ardent Spirits exceeding four hundred gallons excepted, and bound from district to district in the same State, or from a district in one State to a district in the next adjoining State, to any penalty for having departed from the port of loading without such permit and manifest or to subject the said goods on board such Ship or Vessel to seizure or forfeiture, in case they are not accompanied with a manifest as aforesaid."

58.		27.	Strike out all the words between "Collector," (in the beginning of the line) and "of the Port."
59.		28.	Strike out "Or Surveyor."
60.			Strike out "S" in the word "Licenses."
61.		29.	Strike out "such."
62.	14.	6.	Strike out "Three," and insert "Two."
63.			Strike out "Two," and insert "One dollar and fifty cents."
64.		7.	Strike out "One dollar," and insert "fifty Cents."
65.		7.	Strike out all the words between "To trade," and "One dollar,"
		a	and insert "Between the different districts of the United States,
		8.	or to carry on the Bank or Whale fishery for one year, fifty Cents."
66.		10.	Strike out all the words between "Of Vessels," and "for" and
		a 11.	insert "Licensed to trade as aforesaid sixty Cents."
67.		12.	After "Cents," insert "and for taking every Bond required by this act twenty Cents."
68.		12.	Strike out all the words between "For every," (in the latter part
		a 15.	of the line) and "the whole."
69.	14.	20.	After "Appointed," insert "Provided always, that in all cases where the Tonnage of any Ship or Vessel shall be ascertained by any Person specially appointed for that purpose shall be allowed and paid by the Collector a reasonable compensation for the same out of the fees aforesaid before any distribution thereof as aforesaid."

On August 26 this amended bill was returned to the House for its concurrence.

A message from the House of Representatives—

Mr. Beckley, their Clerk, brought up an enroled Resolve, providing, "That the survey directed by Congress, in their act of June 6th, 1788, be made,"[86]— Signed by the Speaker of the House of Representatives—Also,

The bill, entitled, "An Act to establish the Treasury Department," with an adherence of the House of Representatives to a part of the eighth Amendment, to wit:

"Whenever the Secretary of the Treasury shall be removed from office by the President of the United States, or in any other case of vacancy in the office of Secretary, the Assistant shall, during the vacancy, have the charge and custody of the records, books, and papers appertaining to the said office"— He also brought up,

The Resolve of the House of Representatives of the 24th of August,

"That the Vice President and Speaker of the House of Representatives, do adjourn their respective Houses on the twenty-second day of September next, to meet again on the first Monday in December next"[87]—Also,

The Resolve of the House of Representatives, that certain "Articles be proposed to the Legislatures of the several States, as Amendments to the Constitution of the United States"[88]—and requested the concurrence of the Senate therein—

And he withdrew.

The Senate proceeded to consider the Resolve of the House of Representatives, of the 24th of August, "To adhere to the part of their eighth Amendment," before recited—And

On motion,

That the Senate do recede therefrom, the yeas and nays being required by one-fifth of the Senators present,

Mr. Bassett	Yea	
Mr. Butler		Nay
Mr. Carroll	Yea	
Mr. Dalton		Nay
Mr. Ellsworth	Yea	
Mr. Elmer	Yea	
Mr. Few		Nay
Mr. Gunn		Nay
Mr. Henry	Yea	
Mr. Johnson		Nay
Mr. Izard		Nay

[86] The inspected enrolled resolve is in Enrolled Acts, RG 11, DNA. E–45723.

[87] The House resolve is in Messages from the House, Senate Records, DNA.

[88] The annotated printed copy of the articles of amendment are in House Joint and Concurrent Resolutions, Senate Records, DNA. A clear printed copy is in the Broadside Collection, RBkRm, DLC.

	Mr. King	Yea	
	Mr. Langdon		Nay
	Mr. Lee		Nay
	Mr. Maclay		Nay
	Mr. Morris	Yea	
	Mr. Paterson	Yea	
	Mr. Read	Yea	
	Mr. Schuyler	Yea	
	Mr. Wingate		Nay

Yeas 10
Nays 10

The Senate being equally divided, the Vice President determined the question in the affirmative—So it was

RESOLVED, That the Senate do recede from so much of the eighth Amendment as was disagreed to by the House of Representatives.

ORDERED, That the Secretary do carry a Message to the House of Representatives accordingly.[89]

The Senate proceeded to consider the Resolve of the House of Representatives, of the 24th of August, proposing,

"That the Vice President and Speaker be empowered to adjourn the Senate and House of Representatives respectively, on the 22d of September, &c."—And

On motion,

That it should lie for consideration,

                    It passed in the Negative—

And upon the main question,

RESOLVED, That the Senate do concur therein.

ORDERED, That the Secretary do carry a Message to the House of Representatives accordingly.[90]

The Resolve of the House of Representatives of the 24th of August, was read as followeth:

"CONGRESS OF THE UNITED STATES
"IN THE HOUSE OF REPRESENTATIVES

"M O N D A Y, THE 24TH OF AUGUST, 1789

"RESOLVED, BY THE SENATE AND HOUSE OF REPRESENTATIVES OF THE UNITED STATES OF AMERICA IN CONGRESS ASSEMBLED, two thirds of both

---

[89] On August 28 this bill, signed by the Speaker, was returned to the Senate and signed by the Vice President on the same day. Then it was presented to the President.

[90] On September 22 the House ordered the date of adjournment changed to the twenty-sixth and the Senate agreed.

Houses deeming it necessary, That the following Articles be proposed to the Legislatures of the several States, as Amendments to the Constitution of the United States, all or any of which Articles, when ratified by three-fourths of the said Legislatures, to be valid, to all intents and purposes, as part of the said Constitution—to wit:

"ARTICLES in addition to, and Amendment of, the Constitution of the United States of America, proposed by Congress, and ratified by the Legislatures of the several States, pursuant to the fifth Article of the original Constitution.

"Article the First

"After the first enumeration, required by the first Article of the Constitution, there shall be one Representative for every thirty thousand, until the number shall amount to one hundred, after which the proportion shall be so regulated by Congress, that there shall be not less than one hundred Representatives, nor less than one Representative for every forty thousand persons, until the number of Representatives shall amount to two hundred, after which the proportion shall be so regulated by Congress, that there shall not be less than two hundred Representatives, nor less than one Representative for every fifty thousand persons.

"Article the Second

"No law, varying the compensation to the Members of Congress, shall take effect, until an election of Representatives shall have intervened.

"Article the Third

"Congress shall make no law establishing Religion, or prohibiting the free exercise thereof, nor shall the rights of conscience be infringed.

"Article the Fourth

"The freedom of speech, and of the press, and the right of the people peaceably to assemble, and consult for their common good, and to apply to the Government for redress of grievances, shall not be infringed.

"Article the Fifth

"A well regulated militia, composed of the body of the people, being the best security of a free State, the right of the people to keep and bear arms, shall not be infringed, but no one religiously scrupulous of bearing arms, shall be compelled to render military service in person.

"Article the Sixth

"No soldier shall, in time of peace, be quartered in any house without the consent of the owner, nor in time of war, but in a manner to be prescribed by law.

"Article the Seventh

"The right of the people to be secure in their persons, houses, papers and effects, against unreasonable searches and seizures, shall not be violated, and no warrants shall issue, but upon probable cause, supported by oath or affirmation, and particularly describing the place to be searched, and the persons or things to be seized.

"Article the Eighth

"No person shall be subject, except in case of impeachment, to more than one trial, or one punishment for the same offence, nor shall be compelled in any criminal case, to be a witness against himself, nor be deprived of life, liberty or property, without due process of law; nor shall private property be taken for public use without just compensation.

"Article the Ninth

"In all criminal prosecutions, the accused shall enjoy the right to a speedy and public trial, to be informed of the nature and cause of the accusation, to be confronted with the witnesses against him, to have compulsory process for obtaining witnesses in his favor, and to have the assistance of counsel for his defence.

"Article the Tenth

"The trial of all crimes (except in cases of impeachment, and in cases arising in the land or naval forces, or in the militia when in actual service in time of war or public danger) shall be by an impartial Jury of the vicinage, with the requisite of unanimity for conviction, the right of challenge, and other accustomed requisites; and no person shall be held to answer for a capital, or otherways[91] infamous crime, unless on a presentment or indictment by a Grand Jury; but if a crime be committed in a place in the possession of an enemy, or in which an insurrection may prevail, the indictment and trial may by law be authorised in some other place within the same State.

"Article the Eleventh

"No appeal to the Supreme Court of the United States, shall be allowed, where the value in controversy shall not amount to one thousand dollars, nor shall any fact, triable by a Jury according to the course of the common law, be otherwise re-examinable, than according to the rules of common law.

---

[91] The smooth journal reads "otherwise."

"Article the Twelfth

"In suits at common law, the right of trial by Jury shall be preserved.

"Article the Thirteenth

"Excessive bail shall not be required, nor excessive fines imposed, nor cruel and unusual punishments inflicted.

"Article the Fourteenth

"No State shall infringe the right of trial by Jury in criminal cases, nor the rights of conscience, nor the freedom of speech, or of the press.

"Article the Fifteenth

"The enumeration in the Constitution of certain rights, shall not be construed to deny or disparage others retained by the people.

"Article the Sixteenth

"The powers delegated by the Constitution to the Government of the United States, shall be exercised as therein appropriated, so that the Legislative shall never exercise the powers vested in the Executive or Judicial; nor the Executive the powers vested in the Legislative or Judicial; nor the Judicial the powers vested in the Legislative or Executive.

"Article the Seventeenth

"The powers not delegated by the Constitution, nor prohibited by it to the States, are reserved to the States respectively;"

On motion, to postpone the consideration of the Articles to the next session of Congress—

It passed in the Negative.

ORDERED, That Monday next be assigned to take them under consideration.[92]

The Vice President affixed his signature to the Resolve, directing "The Survey ordered to be made by the Act of Congress of June the 6th, 1788"—

And the Committee laid it before the President of the United States for his approbation.[93]

Resumed the SECOND reading of the Bill, entitled, "An Act for allowing Compensation to the Members of the Senate and House of Representatives of the United States, and to the Officers of both Houses"—

ORDERED, That it be committed to

Mr. King
Mr. Morris

---

[92] On September 2 the proposed amendments to the Constitution were considered and the first article was amended.

[93] On August 26 the President signed this resolve and the Senate was notified on August 28.

Mr. Carroll
Mr. Izard and
Mr. Lee[94]

The Senate adjourned to 11 o'clock to-morrow.

WEDNESDAY, AUGUST 26, 1789

The SENATE assembled,
Present as yesterday.

ORDERED, That the Secretary carry the Bill, entitled, "An Act for registering and clearing of Vessels, regulating the Coasting Trade, and for other Purposes," to the House of Representatives, with the Amendments, and request their concurrence therein.[95]

The Senate proceeded in the THIRD reading of the Bill, entitled, "An Act for the Punishment of certain Crimes against the United States"—And after progress,[96]

Adjourned to 11 o'clock to-morrow.

THURSDAY, AUGUST 27, 1789

The SENATE assembled,
Present as yesterday,
Except Mr. Langdon, absent with leave.

Mr. Wingate, on behalf of the Committee appointed to examine an enroled Bill, entitled, "An Act to establish the Treasury Department,"[97] reported, that they had performed that service.

The Senate proceeded in the THIRD reading of the Bill, entitled, "An Act for the Punishment of certain Crimes against the United States"—

ORDERED, That the Bill be engrossed.[98]

Mr. King, on behalf of the Committee to whom was referred the Bill, entitled, "An Act for allowing Compensation to the Members of the Senate and House of Representatives of the United States, and to the Officers of both Houses," reported Amendments.[99]

---

[94] On August 27 this committee reported amendments to this bill.

[95] On August 26 and 27 the House considered these amendments. On the twenty-seventh, it accepted all the Senate amendments with amendments to numbers three and fifty-seven. The Senate was notified of these actions on August 28 and concurred with the House amendments on the same date.

[96] On August 27 this bill was considered again and ordered engrossed.

[97] The inspected enrolled bill is in Enrolled Acts, RG 11, DNA. E–45708.

[98] On August 31 this bill was passed by resolution and sent to the House.

[99] The report is in House Bills, Senate Records, DNA. It is also printed on August 28 in the Journal.

ORDERED, That to-morrow be assigned for taking the same into consideration.[100]

The Senate adjourned to 11 o'clock to-morrow.

FRIDAY, AUGUST 28, 1789

The SENATE assembled,
Present as yesterday.

A Message from the House of Representatives—

Mr. Beckley, their Clerk, informed the Senate, that the President of the United States had signed an enroled Resolve, for carrying into effect "A Survey directed by an Act of the late Congress of the 6th of June, 1788"—He brought up an enroled Bill, entitled, "An Act to establish the Treasury Department," signed by the Speaker of the House of Representatives—And an engrossed Bill, entitled, "An Act to provide for the safe keeping of the Acts, Records and the Seal of the United States, and for other Purposes,"[101] And requested the concurrence of the Senate in the engrossed Bill[102]—He also informed the Senate, that the House of Representatives had concurred in the Amendments proposed to the Bill, entitled, "An Act for registering and clearing of[103] Vessels, regulating the Coasting Trade, and for other Purposes," with Amendments to the third and fifty-seventh Amendments proposed by the Senate—

And he withdrew.

The Senate proceeded in the SECOND reading of the Bill, entitled, "An Act for allowing Compensation to the Members of the Senate and House of Representatives of the United States, and to the Officers of both Houses"—

The report of the Committee thereon was also read; in which it was proposed to strike out the first enacting clause of the Bill—To wit:

"BE IT ENACTED BY THE SENATE AND HOUSE OF REPRESENTATIVES OF THE UNITED STATES OF AMERICA IN CONGRESS ASSEMBLED, That at every session of the Congress of the United States, or whenever the Senate shall assemble for the purpose of exercising any of the powers and duties in them vested by the Constitution, every member of each branch shall be entitled to receive at the rate of six dollars, and the Speaker of the House of Representatives, twelve dollars for every day he shall attend, and shall also be allowed at the commencement of every session, six dollars for every twenty-five miles of

---

[100] On August 28 this report was printed in the Journal and several motions on the bill were considered. The Senate then passed a series of amendments to the bill. The third reading was scheduled for August 31.

[101] An annotated printed copy of the bill is in House Bills, Senate Records, DNA. E–45675.

[102] On August 31 this bill was read for the first time and the second reading was scheduled.

[103] In the smooth journal the word "of" is omitted.

the estimated distance by the most usual route by land from his place of residence to the seat of Congress, and the same allowance at the end of every
session. And in every case in which the Senate may be convened in the recess
of Congress, each member thereof attending shall be entitled to the same
allowance; PROVIDED, That no Senator shall be entitled to more than one such
allowance for any one session of the Senate, nor more than at the rate of six
dollars per day from the end of any one session to the commencement of a
succeeding session: And in case any member shall on his journey to, or from
the session of that branch of which he is a member, be detained by sickness,
or be unable to attend after his arrival, he shall be entitled to the like daily,
compensation"—

And to substitute the following:—

"BE IT ENACTED BY THE SENATE AND HOUSE OF REPRESENTATIVES OF
THE UNITED STATES OF AMERICA, IN CONGRESS ASSEMBLED, That at every
session of Congress, and at every meeting of the Senate in the recess of Congress, prior to the fourth day of March, in the year one thousand seven hundred and ninety-five, each Senator shall be entitled to receive six dollars for
every day he shall attend the Senate, and shall also be allowed at the commencement and end of every such session and meeting, six dollars for every
twenty miles of the estimated distance, by the most usual road, from his place
of residence to the seat of Congress; and in case any member of the Senate
shall be detained by sickness on his journey to or from any such session or
meeting, or after his arrival shall be unable to attend the Senate, he shall be
entitled to the same daily allowance—PROVIDED ALWAYS, That no Senator
shall be allowed for travelling expenses a sum exceeding the rate of six dollars
a day, from the end of one such session or meeting, to the commencement of
another.

"AND BE IT FURTHER ENACTED, That at every session of Congress, and at
every meeting of the Senate, in the recess of Congress, after the aforesaid
fourth day of March, in the year one thousand seven hundred and ninety-five,
each Senator shall be entitled to receive eight dollars for every day he shall
attend the Senate, and shall also be allowed, at the commencement and end of
every such session and meeting, eight dollars for every twenty miles of the
estimated distance by the most usual road from his place of residence to the
seat of Congress, and in case any member of the Senate shall be detained by
sickness on his journey to or from any such session or meeting, or after his
arrival shall be unable to attend the Senate, he shall be entitled to the same
allowance of eight dollars a day—PROVIDED ALWAYS, That no Senator shall be
allowed for travelling expenses a sum exceeding the rate of eight dollars a
day from the end of one such session or meeting, to the commencement of
another.

"AND BE IT FURTHER ENACTED, That at every session of Congress, each

Representative shall be entitled to receive six dollars for every day he shall attend the House of Representatives, and shall also be allowed, at the commencement and end of every session, six dollars for every twenty miles of the estimated distance by the most usual road from his place of residence to the seat of Congress; and in case any Representative shall be detained by sickness on his journey to or from the session of Congress, or after his arrival shall be unable to attend the House of Representatives, he shall be entitled to the daily allowance aforesaid; And the Speaker of the House of Representatives, to defray the incidental expenses of his office, shall be entitled to receive, in addition to his compensation as a Representative, six dollars for every day he shall attend the House."

On motion, To postpone the Report for the purpose of taking up the following Resolve, to wit:—

RESOLVED, That there ought to be a discrimination between the compensation to be allowed to the Senators, and to the Members of the House of Representatives—

It passed in the Affirmative;

And on the question upon the Resolve, the Yeas and Nays being required by one fifth of the Senators present,

		Yea	Nay
Mr.	Bassett	Yea	
Mr.	Butler	Yea	
Mr.	Carroll		Nay
Mr.	Dalton	Yea	
Mr.	Ellsworth	Yea	
Mr.	Elmer		Nay
Mr.	Few	Yea	
Mr.	Gunn	Yea	
Mr.	Henry	Yea	
Mr.	Johnson	Yea	
Mr.	Izard	Yea	
Mr.	King	Yea	
Mr.	Lee	Yea	
Mr.	Maclay		Nay
Mr.	Morris	Yea	
Mr.	Paterson		Nay
Mr.	Read	Yea	
Mr.	Schuyler		Nay
Mr.	Wingate		Nay

Yeas 13
Nays 6

So it passed in the Affirmative.

The Senate resumed the consideration of the report of the Committee, And

On motion, To strike out therefrom, the clause providing for the compensation to the Representatives, "Six Dollars," and insert FIVE DOLLARS; The Yeas and Nays being required by one fifth of the Senators present,

Mr. Bassett		Nay
Mr. Butler		Nay
Mr. Carroll		Nay
Mr. Dalton		Nay
Mr. Ellsworth	Yea	
Mr. Elmer	Yea	
Mr. Few		Nay
Mr. Gunn		Nay
Mr. Henry		Nay
Mr. Johnson	Yea	
Mr. Izard		Nay
Mr. King		Nay
Mr. Lee		Nay
Mr. Maclay	Yea	
Mr. Morris		Nay
Mr. Paterson		Nay
Mr. Read		Nay
Mr. Schuyler	Yea	
Mr. Wingate	Yea	

Nays 13
Yeas 6

So it passed in the Negative.

On motion, To concur in the clause providing for the compensation to the Representatives, as reported by the Committee—

It passed in the Affirmative.

On motion, To allow twenty miles for a day's travel, in the clause providing for the compensation to the Senators, "Prior to the fourth day of March, one thousand seven hundred and ninety-five"—

It passed in the Affirmative.

On motion, To strike out of the report the words, "Prior to the fourth day of March, in the year one thousand seven hundred and ninety-five," in the same clause of the report—

It passed in the Negative.

On motion, To amend the Bill as it regards the compensation to the Senators, by striking out "Six Dollars" and inserting FIVE DOLLARS—

The Yeas and Nays being required by one fifth of the Senators present,

Mr. Bassett	Nay
Mr. Butler	Nay

Mr. Carroll		Nay
Mr. Dalton		Nay
Mr. Ellsworth		Nay
Mr. Elmer	Yea	
Mr. Few		Nay
Mr. Gunn		Nay
Mr. Henry		Nay
Mr. Johnson		Nay
Mr. Izard		Nay
Mr. King		Nay
Mr. Lee		Nay
Mr. Maclay	Yea	
Mr. Morris		Nay
Mr. Read		Nay
Mr. Schuyler	Yea	
Mr. Wingate	Yea	

Nays 14
Yeas 4

So it passed in the Negative.

On motion, To amend the second section of the report of the Committee, in which provision is made for the compensation to the Senate, after the year one thousand seven hundred and ninety-five, so as that "Seven" should be inserted instead of "Eight," in the four places in which "Eight" is mentioned—

It passed in the Affirmative—

And on the question upon the report, it was accepted as amended.

The Senate resumed the consideration of the Bill.

On motion, Upon the following clause, line 12th, to wit:—"That there shall be allowed to each Chaplain of Congress at the rate of five hundred dollars per annum, during the sessions of Congress"—To strike out the words, "At the rate of five"—And insert FOUR—And to strike out from line 13th, "During the sessions of Congress"—

It passed in the Affirmative.

In the clause of the Bill, beginning at line 13th, to wit:—"To the Secretary of the Senate and Clerk of the House of Representatives, at the rate of fifteen hundred dollars per annum, each, to commence from their respective appointments, and also a further allowance of two dollars per day to each, during the session of the branch for which he officiates"—

It was agreed to insert sixteen hundred to the Secretary of the Senate, in lieu of "Fifteen hundred"—Also,

To strike out "At the rate of"—

To strike out "Each"—And these words—"And also a further allowance of two dollars per day to each, during the session of that branch for which he officiates."

Line 17th, from this clause "To employ one principal Clerk, who shall be paid at the rate of three dollars"—it was agreed to strike out the words "At the rate of"—Also,

From this clause "And an engrossing Clerk, who shall be paid at the rate of two dollars per day"—it was agreed to strike out "At the rate of."

ORDERED, That the Bill have the THIRD reading on Monday next.[104]

The Senate proceeded to consider the Message from the House of Representatives of the twenty-eighth of August, proposing Amendments to the third and fifty-seventh Amendments of the Senate to a Bill, entitled, "An Act for registering and clearing of Vessels, regulating the Coasting Trade, and for other Purposes"—

RESOLVED, That the Senate do concur in the Amendments to the Amendments.

ORDERED, That the Secretary do carry a Message to the House of Representatives accordingly.[105]

The Vice President signed the Bill, entitled, "An Act to establish the Treasury Department." And it was delivered to the Committee of enrolment to lay before the President of the United States for his approbation.[106]

The Senate adjourned until 11 o'clock on Monday morning.

MONDAY, AUGUST 31, 1789

The SENATE assembled,
Present as on Friday.

The petition of Mathew Clarkson and others, public creditors,[107] praying that measures may be taken to fund the debt of the United States, was read—

ORDERED, That this petition lie for consideration.[108]

The Senate proceeded to the third reading of the Bill entitled, "An Act for allowing Compensation to the Members of the Senate and House of Representatives of the United States, and to the Officers of both Houses"—

On motion, To alter the clause in which provision is made, "For the incidental expenses of the Speaker's office," and insert THREE DOLLARS "For every day he shall attend the House," in the place of "Six dollars"—

It passed in the Negative.

---

[104] On August 31 this bill was read a third time, amended, and passed with amendments.

[105] On August 31 this bill, signed by the Speaker, was sent to the Senate for the Vice President's signature. It was then delivered to the committee on enrolled bills for presentation to the President.

[106] On September 1 the committee on enrolled bills reported that it had laid this bill before the President.

[107] The petition is in Petitions and Memorials: Various subjects, Senate Records, DNA.

[108] The Senate did not consider this petition, but the same petition was introduced in the House on August 28.

On motion, To alter the proviso in the first enacting clause reported by the Committee, to read as follows—"PROVIDED ALWAYS, That no Senator shall be allowed a sum exceeding the rate of six dollars a day, from the end of one such session or meeting, to the time of his taking a seat in another"—

It passed in the Affirmative.

On motion, To alter the proviso in the second enacting clause, reported by the Committee, to read as follows:

"PROVIDED ALWAYS, that no Senator shall be allowed a sum exceeding the rate of seven dollars a day, from the end of one such session or meeting, to the time of his taking a seat in another"—

It passed in the Affirmative.

On motion, To add the following proviso to the third enacting clause reported by the Committee, to wit: "PROVIDED ALWAYS, That no Representative shall be allowed a sum exceeding the rate of six dollars a day, from the end of one such session or meeting, to the time of his taking a seat in another"—

It passed in the Affirmative.

On motion, To reconsider the additional compensation agreed to for the Secretary of the Senate, and to concur with the House of Representatives in the compensation proposed in the Bill, as it came from that House, for the Secretary of the Senate, and for the Clerk of the House of Representatives, excepting the words, "At the rate of"—

It passed in the Affirmative.

On motion, To re-consider the compensation agreed to for the Chaplains of Congress, and to concur in the Bill as it came from the House of Representatives—

It passed in the Negative.

On motion, To reduce the compensation to the Serjeant at Arms, from four to three dollars per day—

It passed in the Negative.

On motion, To reduce the compensation to the Door-Keepers of the Senate and House of Representatives, from three to two dollars per day—

It passed in the Negative.

On motion, To strike out all those clauses that relate "To Door-Keepers and Assistant Door-Keepers"—

It passed in the Negative.

On the question upon the Bill, it was

RESOLVED, That the Senate do concur therein with the Amendments—

ORDERED, That the Secretary do carry a Message to the House of Representatives accordingly.[109]

The Bill, entitled, "An Act to provide for the safe keeping of the Acts,

---

[109] On September 1 this bill was returned to the House.

Records, and Seal of the United States, and for other Purposes," was read the FIRST time.

ORDERED, That this Bill have the SECOND reading on Tuesday next.[110]

RESOLVED, That the engrossed Bill, entitled, "An Act for the Punishment of certain Crimes against the United States," do pass.[111]

ORDERED, That the Secretary do carry the said Bill to the House of Representatives, and request their concurrence therein.[112]

A Message from the House of Representatives—

Mr. Beckley, their Clerk, brought to the Senate an enroled Bill, entitled, "An Act for registering and clearing of Vessels, regulating the Coasting Trade, and for other Purposes,"[113]—signed by the Speaker of the House of Representatives—

And he withdrew.

The enroled Bill was signed by the Vice-President, and delivered to the Committee for presentation.[114]

A Message from the House of Representatives—

Mr. Beckley, their Clerk, brought to the Senate a Bill, entitled, "An Act for establishing the Salaries of the Executive Officers of Government, with their Assistants and Clerks,"[115]—to which the concurrence of the Senate was requested—

And he withdrew.

ORDERED, That the last mentioned Bill be now read.

ORDERED, That this Bill be read a second time on Tuesday.[116]

The Senate adjourned to 11 o'clock to-morrow.

---

[110] On September 1 this bill was read a second time and the third reading was scheduled.

[111] This resolve has not been located.

[112] On September 1 the House received this bill and read it for the first time on September 2. On September 3 it was ordered to be committed to the committee of the whole which postponed consideration of the bill on September 14 and 15. On September 16 the House resolved that this bill should be postponed until the second session and it notified the Senate of this action on September 18.

[113] The inspected enrolled bill is in Enrolled Acts, RG 11, Senate Records, DNA. E–45696.

[114] On September 1 the committee on enrolled bills reported that this bill had been laid before the President on August 3.

[115] The annotated printed bill is in House Bills, Senate Records, DNA. E–45673.

[116] On September 1 this bill was read a second time and the third reading was assigned.

TUESDAY, September 1, 1789

The SENATE assembled,
Present as yesterday,
Except Mr. Few, absent with leave.

The Senate proceeded to the SECOND reading of the Bill, entitled, "An Act for establishing the Salaries of the Executive Officers of Government with their Assistants and Clerks."

ORDERED, That this Bill have the THIRD reading to-morrow.[1]

ORDERED, That the Secretary carry the Bill, entitled, "An Act for allowing Compensation to the Members of the Senate and House of Representatives of the United States, and to the Officers of both Houses"—to the House of Representatives, and request their concurrence in the Amendments.[2]

The Bill, entitled, "An Act to provide for the safe keeping of the Acts, Records, and Seal of the United States, and for other Purposes;" was read the SECOND time.

ORDERED, That this Bill have the THIRD reading to-morrow.[3]

Mr. Wingate, on behalf of the Committee of enrolment, reported, that they did yesterday lay before the President of the United States,

The Bill, entitled, "An Act for registering and clearing of Vessels, regulating the Coastal Trade, and for other Purposes;"[4]—And the Bill, entitled, "An Act to establish the Treasury Department;" for his Approbation.[5]

The Senate adjourned to 11 o'clock to-morrow.

WEDNESDAY, September 2, 1789

The SENATE assembled,
Present as yesterday.

The Bill, entitled, "An Act to provide for the safe keeping of the Acts, Records, and Seal of the United States, and for other Purposes," was read the THIRD time, and

ORDERED, That it be committed to

Mr. King
Mr. Paterson and
Mr. Read[6]

The THIRD reading of the Bill, entitled, "An Act for establishing the

---

[1] On September 2 the third reading of this bill was postponed.

[2] On September 2 the House agreed to all the Senate amendments except the first three. The House notified the Senate of this action on September 3.

[3] On September 2 this bill was read a third time and committed.

[4] On September 1 the President signed this bill and the Senate was notified on September 3.

[5] On September 2 the President signed this bill and on September 3 the Senate was notified of this action.

[6] On September 3 this committee reported and consideration of the report was postponed.

Salaries of the Executive Officers of Government, with their Assistants and Clerks;" was further postponed.[7]

The petition of Harman Stout, and others, in behalf of themselves and other Clerks in the Public Offices,[8] was read—

ORDERED, That the said petition lie for consideration.[9]

The Resolve of the House of Representatives of the 24th of August, one thousand seven hundred and eighty nine, "That certain Articles be proposed to the Legislatures of the several States, as Amendments to the Constitution of the United States"[10]—was taken into consideration—

And on motion, To amend this clause in the first Article, proposed by the House of Representatives, to wit:

"After the first enumeration required by the first Article of the Constitution, there shall be one Representative for every thirty thousand, until the number shall amount to one hundred"—by striking out "one" and inserting TWO, between the words "amount" and "hundred"—

The Yeas and Nays being required by one fifth of the Senators present,

Mr. Bassett		Nay
Mr. Butler		Nay
Mr. Carroll		Nay
Mr. Dalton	Yea	
Mr. Ellsworth		Nay
Mr. Elmer		Nay
Mr. Gunn	Yea	
Mr. Grayson	Yea	
Mr. Henry		Nay
Mr. Johnson		Nay
Mr. Izard		Nay
Mr. King	Yea	
Mr. Lee	Yea	
Mr. Morris		Nay
Mr. Paterson		Nay
Mr. Read		Nay
Mr. Schuyler	Yea	
Mr. Wingate		Nay

Nays 12
Yeas 6

So it passed in the Negative.

[7] On September 7 the Senate read this bill for the third time and passed it with nine amendments. The House was then notified of these actions.

[8] The petition is in Petitions and Memorials: Various subjects, Senate Records, DNA.

[9] This petition was not considered again in the First Congress.

[10] Drafts of resolves on amendments, proposed in response to the House resolve and differing somewhat in wording from the Journal, are in House Joint and Concurrent Resolutions, Senate Records, DNA.

On motion, To adopt the first Article, proposed by the Resolve of the House of Representatives, amended as follows, to strike out these words,—

"After which the proportion shall be so regulated by Congress, that there shall be not less than one hundred Representatives, nor less than one Representative for every forty thousand persons, until the number of Representatives shall amount to two hundred, after which the proportion shall be so regulated by Congress, that there shall not be less than two hundred Representatives, nor less than one Representative to every fifty thousand persons"—And to substitute the following clause after the words "One hundred," to wit:

"To which number one Representative shall be added for every subsequent increase of forty thousand, until the Representatives shall amount to two hundred, to which one Representative shall be added for every subsequent increase of sixty thousand persons."

It passed in the Affirmative.[11]

The Senate adjourned to 11 o'clock to-morrow.

THURSDAY, SEPTEMBER 3, 1789

The SENATE assembled,

Present as yesterday,

And resumed the consideration of the Resolve of the House of Representatives of the 24th of August, upon the proposed Amendments to the Constitution of the United States.

A Message from the House of Representatives—

Mr. Beckley, their Clerk, informed the Senate, that the President of the United States had affixed his signature to the Bill, entitled, "An Act for registering and clearing of Vessels, regulating the Coasting Trade, and for other Purposes"—And to the Bill, entitled, "An Act to establish the Treasury Department"—and had returned them to the House of Representatives—

He also brought up the Bill, entitled, "An Act for allowing Compensation to the Members of the Senate and House of Representatives of the United States, and to the Officers of both Houses"—And informed the Senate, that the House of Representatives had disagreed to the first, second, and third Amendments, and had agreed to all the others[12]—

He also brought up the Bill, entitled, "An Act to suspend part of an Act, entitled, an Act to regulate the Collection of the Duties imposed by Law on the Tonnage of Ships or Vessels, and on Goods, Wares, and Merchandizes imported into the United States"[13]—

---

[11] On September 3 these articles were considered again and the second and third articles were passed with amendments.

[12] On September 7 the Senate voted to adhere to its first amendment to this bill and recede from the second and third.

[13] This bill has not been located. On September 7 it was read for the first time and the second reading was scheduled.

And he withdrew.

The two last mentioned Bills were ordered to lie for consideration.

The Senate resumed the consideration of the Resolve of the House of Representatives on the Amendments to the Constitution of the United States.

On motion, To adopt the second Article proposed in the Resolve of the House of Representatives, amended as follows—

To strike out these words, "To the Members of Congress," and insert "For the Service of the Senate and House of Representatives of the United States,"

It passed in the Affirmative.

On motion, To amend Article third, and to strike out these words, "Religion or prohibiting the free Exercise thereof," and insert, "One Religious Sect or Society in preference to others,"

It passed in the Negative.

On motion, For reconsideration,

It passed in the Affirmative.

On motion, That Article the third be striken out,

It passed in the Negative.

On motion, To adopt the following, in lieu of the third Article,

"Congress shall not make any law, infringing the rights of conscience, or establishing any Religious Sect or Society,"

It passed in the Negative.

On motion, To amend the third Article, to read thus—

"Congress shall make no law establishing any particular denomination of religion in preference to another, or prohibiting the free exercise thereof, nor shall the rights of conscience be infringed"—

It passed in the Negative.

On the question upon the third Article as it came from the House of Representatives—

It passed in the Negative.

On motion, To adopt the third Article proposed in the Resolve of the House of Representatives, amended by striking out these words—

"Nor shall the rights of conscience be infringed"—

It passed in the Affirmative.

On the fourth Article it was moved to insert these words,—"To instruct their Representatives," after the words "Common good"—

And the Yeas and Nays being required by one fifth of the Senators present,

Mr. Bassett	Nay
Mr. Carroll	Nay
Mr. Dalton	Nay
Mr. Ellsworth	Nay
Mr. Elmer	Nay
Mr. Grayson	Yea

Mr. Gunn	Nay
Mr. Henry	Nay
Mr. Johnson	Nay
Mr. Izard	Nay
Mr. King	Nay
Mr. Lee	Yea
Mr. Morris	Nay
Mr. Paterson	Nay
Mr. Read	Nay
Mr. Wingate	Nay

Nays 14
Yeas 2
So it passed in the Negative.

On motion, To insert these words after "Press,"—"In as ample a manner as hath at any time been secured by the common law"—
It passed in the Negative.

On motion, To strike out the words "And consult for their common good and,"
It passed in the Negative.

And it was agreed, that the further consideration of this Article be postponed.[14]

Mr. King, in behalf of the Committee appointed on the Bill, entitled, "An act for allowing Compensation to the Members of the Senate and House of Representatives of the United States, and to the Officers of both Houses," reported Amendments:[15] The consideration of which was postponed until tomorrow.[16]

The Senate adjourned to 11 o'clock to-morrow.

---

[14] On September 4 these proposed amendments were considered again and articles five through eleven were passed, some of them with amendments.

[15] This committee is erroneously identified. The report was actually from the committee on the Records Bill ("An Act to provide for the safe keeping of the Acts, Records, and the Seal of the United States and for other purposes"). The report could not have been made on the Salaries-Legislative Bill, because this bill had already been passed with amendments and returned to the House. The House had notified the Senate of its actions on these amendments, but this message had not been committed. Two factors lead to the conclusion that the report is on the Records Bill. First, when the Records Bill is considered on September 7 the phrase, "And on the report of the Committee," is used. Elsewhere in the Journal, this phrase is found only when the committee has reported on a previous date. But the September 7 entry is the first mention of this committee report. Second, Mr. King was a member of the committees on both the Salaries-Legislative and the Records Bill, and the confusion might have been caused by this fact. The report has not been located. The bill, however, contains annotations which may correspond to amendments; it is located in House Bills, Senate Records, DNA.

[16] On September 7 this report was considered and the bill was passed with fourteen amendments (see note 20 below) and returned to the House for concurrence in the amendments.

FRIDAY, SEPTEMBER 4, 1789

The SENATE assembled,

Present as yesterday.

The petition of Thomas O'Hara and others, in behalf of themselves and other Clerks in the office of the Pay Master-General,[17] praying, that their compensation may be augmented, was read—

ORDERED, That this petition do lie on the table.[18]

The Senate proceeded in the consideration of the Resolve of the House of Representatives of the 24th of August, on "Articles to be proposed to the Legislatures of the several States, as Amendments to the Constitution of the United States."

On motion, To adopt the fourth Article proposed by the Resolve of the House of Representatives, to read as followeth,

"That Congress shall make no law, abridging the freedom of Speech, or of the Press, or the right of the People peaceably to assemble and consult for their common good, and to petition the Government for a redress of grievances,"

It passed in the Affirmative.

On motion, Upon the fifth Article, to subjoin the following proposition, to wit:

"That standing armies, in time of peace, being dangerous to Liberty, should be avoided as far as the circumstances and protection of the community will admit; and that in all cases the military should be under strict subordination to, and governed by the civil Power.—That no standing army or regular troops shall be raised in time of peace, without the consent of two thirds of the Members present in both Houses, and that no soldier shall be inlisted for any longer term than the continuance of the war."

And the Yeas and Nays being required by one fifth of the Senators present,

Mr. Butler	Yea	
Mr. Carroll		Nay
Mr. Dalton		Nay
Mr. Ellsworth		Nay
Mr. Elmer		Nay
Mr. Gunn	Yea	
Mr. Grayson	Yea	
Mr. Henry	Yea	
Mr. Johnson		Nay
Mr. King		Nay
Mr. Lee	Yea	
Mr. Paterson		Nay

[17] The petition is in Petitions and Memorials: Various subjects, Senate Records, DNA.

[18] This petition was not considered again in the First Congress.

Mr. Read		Nay
Mr. Schuyler		Nay
Mr. Wingate	Yea	

Nays 9
Yeas 6

So it passed in the Negative.

On motion, To adopt the fifth Article of the Amendments proposed by the House of Representatives, amended to read as followeth—

"A well regulated militia, being the best security of a free State, the right of the people to keep and bear arms, shall not be infringed"—

It passed in the Affirmative.

On motion, To adopt the sixth Article of Amendments proposed by the House of Representatives—

It passed in the Affirmative.

On motion, To adopt the seventh Article of Amendments proposed by the House of Representatives—

It passed in the Affirmative.

On motion, To adopt the eighth Article of Amendments proposed by the House of Representatives, striking out these words,—"Except in case of impeachment to more than one trial or one punishment," and substitute the following words—

"Be twice put in jeopardy of life or limb by any public prosecution"—

It passed in the Affirmative.

On motion, To adopt the ninth Article of Amendments proposed by the House of Representatives—

It passed in the Affirmative.

On motion, To adopt the tenth Article amended by striking out all the clauses in the Article, except the following:

"No person shall be held to answer for a capital, or otherwise infamous crime, unless on a presentment or indictment by a Grand Jury,"

It passed in the Affirmative.

On motion, To insert in lieu of the eleventh Article—

"The Supreme Judicial Federal Court, shall have no jurisdiction of causes between citizens of different States, unless the matter in dispute, whether it concerns the realty or personalty, be of the value of three thousand dollars, at the least: Nor shall the Federal Judicial Powers extend to any actions between citizens of different States, where the matter in dispute, whether it concerns the realty or personalty is not of the value of fifteen hundred dollars, at the least—And no part, triable by a Jury according to the course of the common law, shall be otherwise re-examinable, than according to the rules of common law"—

It passed in the Negative.

On motion, To adopt the eleventh Article amended to read as follows—

"No fact, triable by a Jury according to the course of common law, shall be otherwise re-examinable in any court of the United States, than according to the rules of common law"—

It passed in the Affirmative.[19]

The Senate adjourned until 11 o'clock on Monday morning.

MONDAY, SEPTEMBER 7, 1789

The SENATE assembled,
Present as on Friday.

Agreeably to the order of the day the Senate proceeded in the THIRD reading of the Bill, entitled, "An Act to provide for the safe keeping of the Acts, Records, and Seal of the United States, and for other Purposes"—And on the report of the Committee,

RESOLVED, To concur therein with fourteen Amendments:[20]

---

[19] On September 7 these proposed amendments were considered again and articles twelve, thirteen, fifteen, sixteen, and seventeen were passed, some of them with amendments.

[20] The smooth journal reads:

RESOLVED, to concur therein with the following Amendments:

A.	P.	L.	
1.	1.	5.	Strike out, "any law to the contrary notwithstanding"
2.		8.	After "Law," insert "Or take effect."
3.		11.	After "Law," insert "Or take effect."
4.		13.	After "Cause," strike out "Every law." and insert "Every such law, order, resolution, and vote."
5.		14.	After "Cause," strike out "Two fair" and insert "One printed Copy to be delivered to each Senator and Representative of the United States, and two printed."
6.		15. a 16.	After "Originals," strike out "Of all laws in proper cases."
7.		16.	Strike out "Shall."
8.		19.	Between the words "The" and "Seal" insert "Said."
9.		19. a 20.	Strike out "Of the United States."
10.		20.	Between the words "The" and "Seal" insert "Said."
11.			Strike out "Of the United States."
12.		23.	After "States," insert "Nor to any other instrument or act, without the special warrant of the President therefor."
13.	1.	28. a	Strike out the first part of the Clause to the words—"To wit" and insert "And be it further enacted, That there shall be paid
	2.	2.	to the Secretary for the use of the United States the following fees of office by the persons requiring the services to be performed, except when they are performed for any Officer of the United States, in a matter relating to the duties of his office, to wit:"
14.		4. a 5.	After "Twenty five cents," strike out the remaining part of the Clause.

ORDERED, That the Secretary do carry the Bill to the House of Representatives, and request their concurrence in the Amendments.[21]

The Senate proceeded in the THIRD reading of the Bill, entitled, "An Act for establishing the Salaries of the Executive Officers of Government, with their Assistants and Clerks"—And

RESOLVED, To concur therein with nine Amendments:[22]

ORDERED, That the Secretary do carry the Bill to the House of Representatives, and request their concurrence in the Amendments.[23]

The Bill, entitled, "An Act to suspend part of an Act, entitled, an Act to regulate the Collection of the Duties imposed by law on the Tonnage of Ships or Vessels, and on Goods, Wares, and Merchandizes imported into the United States," was read the FIRST time:

ORDERED, That this Bill be read the SECOND time to-morrow.[24]

The Senate proceeded to the consideration of the Resolve of the House of

---

[21] On September 8 the House concurred with these Senate amendments and notified the Senate.

[22] Annotations corresponding to the suggested amendments are noted on the printed bill and located in House Bills, Senate Records, DNA. The simple resolve is not included. The smooth journal reads:

RESOLVED, To concur therein with the following Amendments,

A.	P.	L.	
1.	1.	4. a 5.	After the words, "To the Secretary in the department of State, three thousand," insert "five hundred."
2.		6.	Strike out "Fifteen hundred," and insert "Twelve hundred and fifty."
		6. a 7.	Strike out "Sixteen hundred" and insert "Two thousand."
4.		8.	Strike out "Including the emoluments of the Superintendant of Indian Affairs" and insert, "For his Salary as such and for discharging the duties of Superintendant of Indian Affairs in the northern department."
5.		9.	Strike out "Five hundred."
6.		10.	Strike out "Fifteen," and insert "Seventeen."
7.		13.	After "Dollars," insert "To the principal Clerk of the Treasurer, six hundred Dollars."
8.		14.	Strike out "So many Clerks as in the opinion of the Secretary of the Treasury shall be necessary in either of the Departments aforesaid may be employed by the principal Officer thereof." And insert, "The Heads of the three Departments first above mentioned, shall appoint such Clerks therein respectively, as they shall find necessary."
9.		17.	Strike out "Four hundred and Fifty," and insert "Five hundred."

[23] On September 8 the House resolved to agree to some of these Senate amendments and disagree to others. The House notified the Senate of these resolutions and the Senate voted to recede from two of their amendments and insist on two others. They then notified the House of this action.

[24] On September 10 this bill was read a second time.

Representatives of the 2d of September, on their disagreement to the first, second, and third Amendments of the Senate to a Bill, entitled, "An Act for allowing Compensation to the Members of the Senate and House of Representatives of the United States, and to the Officers of both Houses"—

On motion, That the Senate do adhere to their first Amendment on the said Bill—

And the Yeas and Nays being required by one fifth of the Senators present,

Mr. Bassett	Yea	
Mr. Butler	Yea	
Mr. Carroll		Nay
Mr. Dalton	Yea	
Mr. Ellsworth	Yea	
Mr. Elmer		Nay
Mr. Gunn	Yea	
Mr. Henry	Yea	
Mr. Johnson	Yea	
Mr. Izard	Yea	
Mr. King	Yea	
Mr. Lee	Yea	
Mr. Morris	Yea	
Mr. Paterson		Nay
Mr. Read	Yea	
Mr. Schuyler		Nay
Mr. Wingate		Nay

Yeas 12
Nays 5

So it was,

Resolved, That the Senate do adhere to their first Amendment to the said Bill:

Resolved, That the Senate do recede from their second and third Amendments to the said Bill:

ORDERED, That the Secretary carry a Message to the House of Representatives accordingly.[25]

Proceeded in the THIRD reading of the Bill, entitled, "An Act for allowing a Compensation to the President and Vice President of the United States:"

And on the Report of the Committee,

RESOLVED, That the Senate do concur in the said Bill, with the following Amendment, to wit:

In the Compensation to the Vice President—

---

[25] On September 8 the House adhered to its disagreement to the Senate's first amendment and appointed a conference committee. On the same date the Senate was notified of this action and appointed a conference committee.

To strike out "Five thousand," and insert "Six thousand"[26]—

ORDERED, That the Secretary do carry the Bill to the House of Representatives, and request their concurrence in the Amendment.[27]

The Senate resumed the consideration of the Resolve of the House of Representatives of the 24th of August, on "Articles to be proposed to the Legislatures of the several States as Amendments to the Constitution of the United States."

On motion, To adopt the twelfth Article of the Amendments, proposed by the House of Representatives, amended by the addition of these words to the Article, to wit: "Where the consideration exceeds twenty dollars,"

It passed in the Affirmative.

On motion, To adopt the thirteenth Article of the Amendments proposed by the House of Representatives—

It passed in the Affirmative.

On motion, To adopt the fourteenth Article of the Amendments proposed by the House of Representatives—

It passed in the Negative.

In the consideration of the fifteenth Article, proposed by the House of Representatives—

On motion, To add the following to the proposed Amendments, to wit:

"That the general Government of the United States ought never to impose direct taxes but where the monies arising from the duties, impost, and excise, are insufficient for the public exigencies, nor then until Congress shall have made a requisition upon the States to assess, levy, and pay their respective proportions of such requisitions; and in case any State shall neglect or refuse to pay its proportion, pursuant to such requisition, then Congress may assess and levy such State's proportion, together with interest thereon at the rate of six per cent, per annum, from the time of payment prescribed by such requisition"—

It passed in the Negative.

On motion, To add the following to the proposed Amendments, to wit:

"That the third section of the sixth Article of the Constitution of the United States, ought to be amended by inserting the word OTHER between the words "No" and "Religious"—

It passed in the Negative.

On motion, To add the following Amendment to the Constitution of the United States, to wit:

"That Congress shall not exercise the powers vested in them by the fourth

[26] This resolve and the included amendment have not been located.

[27] On September 8 the House disagreed to this amendment and notified the Senate. The Senate then resolved to insist on its amendment and requested a conference committee.

Section of the first Article of the Constitution of the United States, but in cases where a State shall neglect or refuse to make regulations therein mentioned, or shall make regulations subversive of the Rights of the People, to a free and equal Representation in Congress, agreeably to the Constitution"—

It passed in the Negative.

On motion, To subjoin the following to the Amendments proposed by the House of Representatives, to wit:

"That Congress shall not erect any company of Merchants with exclusive advantages of Commerce"—

It passed in the Negative.

On motion, To subjoin the following to the Amendments proposed by the House of Representatives, to wit:

"That Congress shall at no time consent that any person holding an Office of trust or profit, under the United States, shall accept of a title of Nobility, or any other Title or Office, from any king, prince, or foreign State"—

It passed in the Negative.

On motion, To subjoin the following to the Amendments proposed by the House of Representatives, to wit:

"That no person, indebted to the United States, shall be entitled to a seat in either branch of the Legislature"[28]—

It passed in the Negative.

On motion, To adopt the fifteenth Article of Amendments to the Constitution of the United States, proposed by the House of Representatives—

It passed in the Affirmative.

On motion, To adopt the sixteenth Article of Amendments to the Constitution of the United States, proposed by the House of Representatives—

It passed in the Negative.

On motion, To amend the seventeenth Article, by inserting the word, EXPRESSLY, before the word "delegated"—

It passed in the Negative.

On motion, To adopt the seventeenth Article of Amendments to the Constitution of the United States, proposed by the House of Representatives, to read as follows,

"The powers not delegated to the United States by the Constitution, nor prohibited by it to the States, are reserved to the States respectively, or to the people."

It passed in the Affirmative.

On motion, To amend the preamble of the Resolve—

---

[28] The four preceding motions are in House Joint and Concurrent Resolutions, Senate Records, DNA.

A motion was made, To postpone the further consideration thereof until to-morrow—And,

It passed in the Affirmative.[29]

The Senate adjourned to 11 o'clock to-morrow.

TUESDAY, SEPTEMBER 8, 1789

The SENATE assembled,

Present as yesterday,

And proceeded in the consideration of the Resolve of the House of Representatives of the 24th of August, "On Articles to be proposed to the Legislatures of the several States, as Amendments to the Constitution of the United States."

On motion, To amend the Preamble to the Amendments proposed by the House of Representatives by preceding the same as follows, to wit:

"The Conventions of a number of the States having, at the time of their adopting the Constitution, expressed a desire, in order to prevent misconstruction or abuse of its powers, that further declaratory and restrictive clauses should be added; and as extending the grounds of public confidence in the Government, will best insure the beneficent ends of its institution"—

It passed in the Affirmative.

On motion, To amend the Preamble by striking out these words, lines 6th and 7th, "Deeming it necessary," and inserting instead thereof "Concurring"—

It passed in the Affirmative.

On motion, To add the following clause to the Articles of Amendment to the Constitution of the United States, proposed by the House of Representatives, to wit:

"That there are certain natural rights, of which men, when they form a social compact, cannot deprive or divest their posterity, among which are the enjoyment of life and liberty, with the means of acquiring, possessing, and protecting property, and pursuing and obtaining happiness and safety"—

It passed in the Negative.

On motion, To add the following clause to the Articles of Amendment to the Constitution of the United States, proposed by the House of Representatives, to wit:

"That all power is naturally vested in, and consequently derived from the people; that Magistrates, therefore, are their Trustees and Agents, and at all times amenable to them."

It passed in the Negative.

On motion, To add the following clause to the Articles of Amendment to the Constitution of the United States, proposed by the House of Representatives, to wit:

"That Government ought to be instituted for the common benefit, protec-

---

[29] On September 8 these proposed amendments were considered again and several motions were made on the articles. Most of these motions were defeated.

tion, and security of the people; and that the doctrine of non-resistence against arbitrary power and oppression, is absurd, slavish, and destructive of the good and happiness of mankind."

It passed in the Negative.

On motion, To add the following clause to the Articles of Amendment to the Constitution of the United States, proposed by the House of Representatives, to wit:

"That no man or set of men are entitled to exclusive or separate public emoluments or privileges from the community, but in consideration of public services, which not being descendible, neither ought the offices of Magistrate, Legislator, or Judge, or any other public Officer to be hereditary."

It passed in the Negative.

On motion, To add the following clause to the Articles of Amendment to the Constitution of the United States, proposed by the House of Representatives, to wit:—

"That the Legislative, Executive, and Judiciary Powers of Government should be separate and distinct, and that the members of the two first may be restrained from oppression by feeling and participating the public burthens, they should, at fixed periods, be reduced to a private station, return into the mass of the people, and the vacancies be supplied by certain and regular elections; in which all or any part of the former members to be eligible or ineligible, as the rules of the Constitution of Government, and the laws, shall direct"—

It passed in the Negative.

On motion, To add the following clause to the Articles of Amendment to the Constitution of the United States, proposed by the House of Representatives, to wit:

"That every freeman restrained of his liberty, is entitled to a remedy, to enquire into the lawfulness thereof and to remove the same, if unlawful, and that such remedy ought not to be denied nor delayed"—

It passed in the Negative.

On motion, To add the following clause to the Articles of Amendment to the Constitution of the United States, proposed by the House of Representatives, to wit:

"That every freeman ought to find a certain remedy by recourse to the laws, for all injuries and wrongs he may receive in his person, property, or character. He ought to obtain right and justice freely without sale, completely and without denial, promptly and without delay, and that all establishments or regulations contravening these rights, are oppressive and unjust"—

It passed in the Negative.

On motion, To add the following clause to the Articles of Amendment to the Constitution of the United States, proposed by the House of Representatives, to wit:

"That the members of the Senate and House of Representatives shall be

ineligible to, and incapable of holding any civil office under the authority of
the United States, during the time for which they shall respectively be
elected"—

It passed in the Negative.

On motion, To add the following clause to the Articles of Amendment to
the Constitution of the United States, proposed by the House of Representatives, to wit:

"That the journals of the proceedings of the Senate and House of Representatives shall be published, at least, once in every year, except such parts
thereof relating to treaties, alliances, or military operations, as in their judgment require secrecy"—

It passed in the Negative.

On motion, To add the following clause to the Articles of Amendment to
the Constitution of the United States, proposed by the House of Representatives, to wit:

"That a regular statement and account of the receipts and expenditures of
all public money shall be published, at least, once in every year"—

It passed in the Negative.

On motion, To add the following clause to the Articles of Amendment to
the Constitution of the United States, proposed by the House of Representatives, to wit:

"That no commercial Treaty shall be ratified without the concurrence of two
thirds of the whole number of the members of the Senate; and no Treaty,
ceding, contracting, restraining or suspending the territorial rights or claims
of the United States, or any of them or their, or any of their rights or claims
to fishing in the American Seas, or navigating the American Rivers, shall be
but in cases of the most urgent and extreme necessity; nor shall any such treaty
be ratified without the concurrence of three fourths of the whole number of
the members of both Houses respectively"—

It passed in the Negative.

On motion, To add the following clause to the Articles of Amendment to
the Constitution of the United States, proposed by the House of Representatives, to wit:

"That no navigation law, or law regulating commerce, shall be passed without the consent of two thirds of the members present in both Houses"—

It passed in the Negative.

On motion, To add the following clause to the Articles of Amendment to
the Constitution of the United States, proposed by the House of Representatives, to wit:

"That no standing army or regular troops shall be raised or kept up in time
of peace, without the consent of two thirds of the members present in both
Houses"—

It passed in the Negative.

On motion, To add the following clause to the Articles of Amendment to the Constitution of the United States, proposed by the House of Representatives, to wit:

"That no soldier shall be enlisted for any longer term than four years, except in time of war, and then for no longer term than the continuance of the war"—

It passed in the Negative.

On motion, To add the following clause to the Articles of Amendment to the Constitution of the United States, proposed by the House of Representatives, to wit:

"That each State respectively shall have the power to provide for organizing, arming, and disciplining its own militia, whensoever Congress shall omit or neglect to provide for the same. That the militia shall not be subject to martial law, except when in actual service in time of war, invasion or rebellion; and when not in the actual service of the United States, shall be subject only to such fines, penalties, and punishments as shall be directed or inflicted by the laws of its own State"—

It passed in the Negative.

On motion, To add the following clause to the Articles of Amendment to the Constitution of the United States, proposed by the House of Representatives, to wit:

"That the exclusive power of Legislation given to Congress over the Federal Town, and its adjacent district, and other places purchased or to be purchased by Congress of any of the States, shall extend only to such regulations as respect the police and good Government thereof"—

It passed in the Negative.

On motion, To add the following clause to the Articles of Amendment to the Constitution of the United States, proposed by the House of Representatives, to wit:

"That no person shall be capable of being President of the United States, for more than eight years in any term of sixteen years"—

It passed in the Negative.

On motion, To add the following clause to the Articles of Amendment to the Constitution of the United States, proposed by the House of Representatives, to wit:

"That the Judicial Power of the United States shall be vested in one Supreme Court, and in such Courts of Admiralty as Congress may from time to time ordain and establish in any of the different States; The Judicial Powers shall extend to all cases in law and equity arising under treaties made, or which shall be made under the authority of the United States; to all cases affecting Ambassadors, other foreign Ministers and Consuls; to all cases of Admiralty and Maritime Jurisdiction; to controversies to which the United States shall be a party; to controversies between two or more States; and be-

tween parties claiming lands under the grants of different States. In all cases
affecting Ambassadors, other foreign Ministers and Consuls, and those in
which a State shall be a party, the Supreme Court shall have original jurisdiction; in all other cases before mentioned the Supreme Court shall have appellate jurisdiction as to matters of law only, except in cases of equity, and of
Admiralty and Maritime Jurisdiction, in which the Supreme Court shall have
appellate Jurisdiction, both as to law and fact, with such exceptions, and under
such regulations as the Congress shall make. But the Judicial Power of the
United States shall extend to no case where the cause of action shall have
originated before the ratification of this Constitution; except in disputes between States about their Territory, disputes between persons claiming lands
under the grants of different States, and suits for debts due to the United
States"—

It passed in the Negative.

On motion, To add the following clause to the Articles of Amendment to
the Constitution of the United States, proposed by the House of Representatives, to wit:

"That Congress shall not alter, modify, or interfere in the times, places, or
manner of holding elections for Senators and Representatives, or either of
them, except when the Legislature of any State shall neglect, refuse, or be
disabled by invasion or rebellion, to prescribe the same"—

It passed in the Negative.

On motion, To add the following clause to the Articles of Amendment to
the Constitution of the United States, proposed by the House of Representatives, to wit:

"That some tribunal, other than the Senate, be provided for trying impeach-
ments of Senators"—

It passed in the Negative.

On motion, To add the following clause to the Articles of Amendment to
the Constitution of the United States, proposed by the House of Representatives, to wit:

"That the salary of a Judge shall not be increased or diminished during his
continuance in office, otherwise than by general regulations of salary, which
may take place on a revision of the subject at stated periods of not less than
seven years, to commence from the time such salaries shall be first ascertained
by Congress"—

It passed in the Negative.

ORDERED, That the further consideration of the Resolve of the House of
Representatives on the Articles of Amendment be postponed until to-morrow.[30]

A Message from the House of Representatives—

---

[30] On September 9 these articles were considered again and several amendments were
made. The Senate then passed the amended articles and notified the House.

Mr. Beckley, their Clerk, brought up the Bill, entitled, "An Act for allowing a Compensation to the President and Vice President of the United States," and informed the Senate, that the House of Representatives had disagreed to the Amendment thereon—

He also brought up the Bill, entitled, "An Act for establishing the Salaries of the Executive Officers of Government, with their Assistants and Clerks," and informed the Senate, that the House of Representatives had agreed to their FIRST, FOURTH, SEVENTH, EIGHTH, and NINTH Amendments, and had disagreed to all the rest—

Also, The Bill, entitled, "An Act for allowing Compensation to the members of the Senate and House of Representatives of the United States, and to the Officers of both Houses"—And he informed the Senate, that the House of Representatives requested a conference on the subject matter of the disagreement of the two Houses on the said Bill, and had appointed

> Mr. Sherman
> Mr. Tucker and
> Mr. Benson, managers on the part of the House of

Representatives—

He likewise informed the Senate, that the House of Representatives had concurred in their Amendments to the Bill, entitled, "An Act to provide for the safe keeping of the Acts, Records and Seal of the United States"[31]—

And he withdrew.

The Senate proceeded to consider the Resolve of the House of Representatives, and their disagreement to the Amendment of the Senate on the Bill, entitled, "An Act for allowing a Compensation to the President and Vice President of the United States"—and

RESOLVED, That the Senate do INSIST on their Amendment to the said Bill, and do request a conference on the subject matter of the disagreement, and that

> Mr. King
> Mr. Izard and
> Mr. Morris, be managers of the conference on the

part of the Senate.[32]

The Senate proceeded to consider the Resolve of the House of Representatives, of the eighth of September, and their disagreement to the Amendments of the Senate on the Bill, entitled, "An Act for establishing the Salaries of the Executive Officers of Government, with their Assistants and Clerks"—

RESOLVED, That the Senate do RECEDE from their SECOND and SIXTH Amendments, and do INSIST on their THIRD and FIFTH Amendments to the said Bill;

---

[31] On September 10 this bill, signed by the Speaker, was sent to the Senate for the Vice President's signature. It was then delivered to the President.

[32] On September 9 the House appointed a committee to meet with this committee and notified the Senate on September 10.

ORDERED, That the Secretary carry a message to the House of Representatives accordingly.[33]

The Senate proceeded to the consideration of the Resolve of the House of Representatives, of the eighth of September, desiring a conference on the subject matter of the FIRST Amendment proposed by the Senate, to the Bill, entitled, "An Act for allowing Compensation to the members of the Senate and House of Representatives of the United States, and to the officers of both Houses," And,

RESOLVED, That the Senate do agree to the proposed conference, and that

> Mr. King
>
> Mr. Izard and
>
> Mr. Morris, be managers thereof on the part of the

Senate.

ORDERED, That the Secretary do carry a Message to the House of Representatives accordingly.[34]

The Senate adjourned to 11 o'clock to-morrow.

WEDNESDAY, SEPTEMBER 9, 1789

The SENATE assembled,

Present as yesterday.

Proceeded in the consideration of the Resolve of the House of Representatives of the 24th of August, "On Articles to be proposed to the Legislatures of the several States as Amendments to the Constitution of the United States"— And

On motion, To amend Article the third, to read as follows:

"Congress shall make no law establishing articles of faith or a mode of worship, or prohibiting the free exercise of religion, or abridging the freedom of speech, or the press, or the right of the people peaceably to assemble, and petition to the Government for the redress of grievances"—

It passed in the Affirmative.

On motion, To strike out the fourth Article,

It passed in the Affirmative.

On motion, To amend Article the fifth, by inserting these words, "For the common defence," next to the words "Bear arms"—

It passed in the Negative.

---

[33] On September 9 the House receded from its disagreement to the two amendments insisted on by the Senate. On September 10 this bill, signed by the Speaker, was sent to the Senate for the Vice President's signature. It was then presented to the President.

[34] On September 10 the House voted to recede from its disagreement to the Senate's first amendment and to amend this amendment. On September 12 it notified the Senate of this action and the Senate concurred with the House amendment to its amendment.

On motion, To strike out of this Article, line the second, these words, "The best," and insert in lieu thereof "Necessary to the"

It passed in the Affirmative.

On motion, On Article the fifth, to strike out the word "Fifth," after "Article the," and insert "Fourth"—

And to amend the Article to read as follows,

"A well regulated militia being the security of a free State, the right of the people to keep and bear arms, shall not be infringed"—

It passed in the Affirmative.

On motion, To alter Article the sixth so as to stand Article the fifth, and Article the seventh so as to stand Article the sixth, and Article the eighth so as to stand Article the seventh—

It passed in the Affirmative.

On motion, That this last mentioned Article be amended to read as follows: "No person shall be held to answer for a capital or otherwise infamous crime, unless on a presentment or indictment of a Grand Jury, except in cases arising in the land or naval forces, or in the militia, when in actual service, in time of war or public danger, nor shall any person be subject to be put in jeopardy of life or limb, for the same offence, nor shall be compelled in any criminal case to be a witness against himself, nor be deprived of life, liberty or property, without due process of law: Nor shall private property be taken for public use without just compensation"—

It passed in the Affirmative.

On motion, To strike out from the ninth Article the word "Ninth," and insert "eighth"—

It passed in the Affirmative.

On motion, To strike out the tenth and the eleventh Articles—

It passed in the Affirmative.

On motion, To strike out of the twelfth Article the word "Twelfth," and insert "ninth"—

It passed in the Affirmative.

And on motion, To amend this Article, to read as follows:

"In suits at common law, where the value in controversy shall exceed twenty dollars, the right of trial by Jury shall be preserved, and no fact tried by a Jury, shall be otherwise re-examined in any Court of the United States, than according to the rules of the common law"—

It passed in the Affirmative.

On motion, To reconsider Article the tenth, and to restore these words, to wit:

"The trial of all crimes (except in cases of impeachment, and in cases arising in the land or naval forces, or in the militia, when in actual service in time of war or public danger) shall be by an impartial Jury of the vicinage, with the requisite of unanimity for conviction, the right of challenge, and other accustomed requisites"—

And the Yeas and Nays being required by one fifth of the Senators present,

	Yea	Nay
Mr. Bassett	Yea	
Mr. Carroll		Nay
Mr. Dalton	Yea	
Mr. Ellsworth		Nay
Mr. Grayson	Yea	
Mr. Gunn	Yea	
Mr. Henry	Yea	
Mr. Johnson		Nay
Mr. Izard		Nay
Mr. King		Nay
Mr. Lee	Yea	
Mr. Morris		Nay
Mr. Paterson	Yea	
Mr. Read		Nay
Mr. Schuyler	Yea	
Mr. Wingate		Nay

Yeas 8
Nays 8

So the question was lost.

On motion, To number the remaining Articles agreed to by the Senate, tenth, eleventh and twelfth, instead of the numbers affixed by the Resolve of the House of Representatives—

It passed in the Affirmative.

RESOLVED, That the Senate do concur in the Resolve of the House of Representatives, on "Articles to be proposed to the Legislatures of the States, as Amendments to the Constitution of the United States," with the Amendments,[35] two thirds of the Senators present concurring therein.

ORDERED, That the Secretary do carry a Message to the House of Representatives accordingly.[36]

The Senate adjourned to 11 o'clock to-morrow.

---

[35] Oliver Ellsworth's amendments to the amendments to the Constitution, dated September 9, 1789, are in House Joint and Concurrent Resolutions, Senate Records, DNA. An annotated printed copy of the amendments, as they were renumbered, is in the above citation.

[36] On September 10 the House received this message. On September 21 and 22, the House considered the Senate amendments. On the twenty-second, the House agreed to some of these amendments and disagreed to others. It then resolved that a conference committee be called and it notified the Senate of this action. On the same date the Senate acted on the House resolve and appointed a conference committee.

THURSDAY, September 10, 1789

The SENATE assembled,

Present as yesterday.

Mr. Wingate, in behalf of the Committee, reported, that they had examined the enroled Bill, entitled, "An Act to provide for the safe keeping of the Acts, Records and seal of the United States, and for other Purposes"[37]—Also, the Bill, entitled, "An Act for establishing the Salaries of the Executive Officers of Government, with their Assistants and Clerks,"[38] and that they were correct.

A Message from the House of Representatives—

Mr. Beckley, their Clerk, informed the Senate, that the House of Representatives had agreed to recede from their disagreement to the third and fifth Amendments proposed by the Senate to the Bill, entitled, "An Act for establishing the Salaries of the Executive Officers of Government, with their Assistants and Clerks"—

That the House of Representatives had agreed to the proposed conference on the subject matter of the Amendment to the Bill, entitled, "An Act for allowing Compensation to the President and Vice-President of the United States"—and had appointed

Mr. Baldwin

Mr. Livermore and

Mr. Goodhue, managers of the conference on the part of the House of Representatives[39]—

He also brought up a Resolve of the House of Representatives, "That until further provision be made by law, the general Post-Office of the United States shall be conducted according to the rules and regulations prescribed by the ordinances and resolutions of the late Congress, and that contracts be made for the conveyance of the mail in conformity thereto"[40]—and requested the concurrence of the Senate in the said Resolve:

He also brought up the enroled Bill, entitled, "An Act to provide for the safe keeping of the Acts, Records and Seal of the United States, and for other Purposes"—together with the enroled Bill, entitled, "An Act for establishing the Salaries of the Executive Officers of Government, with their Assistants and Clerks"—severally signed by the Speaker of the House of Representatives"—

And he withdrew.

The Vice-President affixed his signature to the above mentioned ENROLED

---

[37] The inspected enrolled bill is in Enrolled Acts, RG 11, DNA. E–45711.

[38] The inspected enrolled bill is in Enrolled Acts, RG 11, DNA. E–45692.

[39] On September 17 the House adhered to its disagreement to this amendment and notified the Senate.

[40] The House resolve is in Messages from the House, Senate Records, DNA.

Bills, and they were, by the Committee of enrolment, laid before the President of the United States for his approbation.[41]

The Resolve of the House of Representatives, for the regulation of the Post-Office, was read—

ORDERED, That it be committed to

> Mr. Butler
> Mr. Morris and
> Mr. Ellsworth

With an instruction to report a Bill upon the subject.[42]

The Senate proceeded in the SECOND reading of the Bill, entitled, "An Act, to suspend part of an Act, entitled, "An Act to regulate the Collection of the Duties imposed by Law on the Tonnage of Ships or Vessels, and on Goods, Wares and Merchandizes imported into the United States."

And on motion, That the Bill be postponed—

> It passed in the Affirmative.[43]

The Senate adjourned to 11 o'clock to-morrow.

FRIDAY, SEPTEMBER 11, 1789

> The SENATE assembled,
> Present as yesterday.

A Message from the House of Representatives—

Mr. Beckley, their Clerk, brought up the Bill, entitled, "An Act for suspending the Operation of part of an Act, entitled, 'An Act imposing Duties on Tonnage' "[44]—To which he requested the concurrence of the Senate.

He also informed the Senate, that the President of the United States had affixed his signature to the Bill, entitled, "An Act for establishing the Salaries of the Executive Officers of Government, with their Assistants and Clerks"— and had returned it to the House of Representatives—

And he withdrew.

ORDERED, That the Bill, entitled, "An Act for suspending the Operation of part of an Act, entitled, 'An Act imposing Duties on Tonnage,' " have the first reading at this time.

ORDERED, That the rules of the Senate be so far dispensed with, as that the Bill have a second reading at this time—

---

[41] On September 15 the Records Bill was signed by the President and the Senate was notified the next day. The Compensation Bill was signed by the President on September 11 and the Senate was notified on the same date.

[42] On September 11 this committee reported on this resolution and on a bill for establishing the Post Office. The resolution was defeated by the Senate and the bill was read for the first time.

[43] On September 11 this bill, together with the Tonnage [HR–24] Bill, was committed.

[44] The bill, as it passed the House, is in Engrossed House Bills, House Records, DNA.

ORDERED, That this Bill, together with the Bill, entitled, "An Act to suspend part of an Act, entitled, 'An Act to regulate the Collection of the Duties imposed by Law on the Tonnage of Ships or Vessels, and on Goods, Wares and Merchandizes imported into the United States,' " be committed to

Mr. Morris
Mr. Dalton and
Mr. Ellsworth[45]

Mr. Butler, in behalf of the Committee appointed on the tenth of September, on the Resolve of the House of Representatives, providing for the regulation of the Post-Office, reported not to concur in the Resolve, and a Bill upon the subject matter thereof—

And on the question of concurrence in the Resolve of the House of Representatives—

It passed in the Negative.

ORDERED, That the Bill, entitled, "An Act for the Temporary Establishment of the Post-Office," have the first reading at this time—

ORDERED, That this Bill have the SECOND reading to-morrow.[46]

The Senate adjourned to 11 o'clock to-morrow.

SATURDAY, SEPTEMBER 12, 1789

The SENATE assembled,
Present as yesterday.

A Message from the House of Representatives—

Mr. Beckley, their Clerk, informed the Senate, that the House of Representatives had receded from their disagreement to the first Amendment made by the Senate, to the Bill, entitled, "An Act for allowing Compensation to the members of the Senate and House of Representatives of the United States, and to the Officers of both Houses"—proposing the following Amendment to the Amendment of the Senate, to wit:

"And be it further enacted, That this Act shall continue in force until the fourth day of March, in the year one thousand seven hundred and ninety-six, and no longer."

To which Amendment to the Amendment he requested the concurrence of the Senate—

And he withdrew.

The Senate proceeded to consider the Amendment proposed by the House

---

[45] On September 12 this committee reported on both of these bills. The Collection [HR–23] Act was read a third time and passed with amendments after debate. The Tonnage [HR–24] Act was disagreed to by the Senate, and the House was notified of both of these actions.

[46] On September 14 this bill was read a second time and the third reading was scheduled.

of Representatives to the first Amendment of the Senate to the Bill last mentioned—And

RESOLVED, That the Senate do concur with the House of Representatives therein.[47]

ORDERED, That the Secretary do carry a Message to the House of Representatives accordingly.[48]

Mr. Morris, on behalf of the Committee appointed the eleventh of September, to consider the two Bills sent up from the House of Representatives for concurrence, reported an Amendment to the Bill, entitled, "An Act to suspend part of an Act, entitled an Act to regulate the Collection of the Duties imposed by Law on the Tonnage of Ships or Vessels, and on Goods, Wares and Merchandizes imported into the United States"—Which Report is as follows:[49]

"Be it further enacted, That all the privileges and advantages to which ships and vessels owned by citizens of the United States are by law entitled, shall be, until the fifteenth day of January next, extended to ships and vessels wholly owned by citizens of the States of North-Carolina and Rhode-Island and Providence Plantations: Provided, That the master of every such ship or vessel last mentioned, shall produce a register for the same, conformable to the laws of the State in which it shall have been obtained, shewing that the said ship or vessel is, and before the first day of September instant, was, owned as aforesaid; and make oath or affirmation before the Collector of the port in which the benefit of this act is claimed, that the ship or vessel for which such register is produced, is the same therein mentioned, and that he believes it is still wholly owned by the person or persons named in said register, and that he or they are citizens of one of the States aforesaid.

"And be it further enacted, That all rum, loaf sugar, and chocolate, manufactured or made in the States of North-Carolina, or Rhode-Island and Providence Plantations, and imported or brought into the United States, shall be deemed and taken to be subject to the like duties as goods of the like kinds, imported from any foreign State, Kingdom or Country are made subject to.

"And be it further enacted, That Rehoboth, in the State of Massachusetts, shall be a port of entry and delivery until the fifteenth day of January next, and that a Collector be appointed for the same."

The Senate agreed to postpone the report of the Committee, and proceed to the THIRD reading of the said Bill.

ORDERED, That sundry petitions of the citizens of the State of Rhode-Island and North-Carolina, praying for the relief proposed by this Bill, be read.

---

[47] The resolve and the House message with amendments are in House Joint and Concurrent Resolutions, Senate Records, DNA.

[48] On September 14 this bill, signed by the Speaker, was returned to the Senate for the Vice President's signature. It was then presented to the President.

[49] This committee report has not been located.

On motion, That "August" be stricken out of line the eighth of the Bill, and MAY inserted—

It passed in the Affirmative.

On motion, That the report of the Committee be accepted, as an Amendment to the Bill—

It passed in the Affirmative.

On motion, To amend the title of the Bill, by subjoining these words, "And for other Purposes"—

It passed in the Affirmative;

And upon the question on the Bill,

RESOLVED, That the Senate do concur therein with the Amendments.

On the other Bill referred to the Committee, entitled, "An Act for suspending the Operation of part of an Act, entitled, an Act imposing Duties on Tonnage"—They reported verbally,

Whereupon,

RESOLVED, That the Senate do not concur with the House of Representatives therein.[50]

ORDERED, That the Secretary carry a Message to the House of Representatives accordingly.[51]

The Senate adjourned until 11 o'clock on Monday morning.

M O N D A Y, SEPTEMBER 14, 1789

The SENATE assembled,

Present as on Saturday.

Agreeably to the order of the day the Senate proceeded in the SECOND reading of the Bill, entitled, "An Act for the Temporary Establishment of the Post-Office"—And

ORDERED, That this Bill have the THIRD reading to-morrow.[52]

A Message from the House of Representatives—

Mr. Beckley, their Clerk, informed the Senate, that the House of Representatives had concurred in the Amendments proposed by the Senate to a Bill, entitled, "An Act to suspend part of an Act, entitled, an Act to regulate the Collection of the Duties imposed by Law, on the Tonnage of Ships or Vessels, and on Goods, Wares, and Merchandizes imported into the United States."[53]

---

[50] The notation of nonconcurrence is in Engrossed House Bills, House Records, DNA.

[51] On September 14 the House concurred with the Senate amendments to the Collection [HR–23] Act and notified the Senate.

[52] On September 15 this bill was read a third time, engrossed, and passed. It was then sent to the House for concurrence.

[53] On September 15 this bill, signed by the Speaker, was brought to the Senate for the Vice President's signature. It was then given to the committee on enrolled bills for presentation to the President.

He also brought up an enroled Bill, entitled, "An Act for allowing Compensation to the Members of the Senate and House of Representatives of the United States, and to the Officers of both Houses,"[54] signed by the Speaker of the House of Representatives.—

And he withdrew.

The Vice President affixed his signature to the last mentioned enroled Bill, and it was delivered to the Committee of enrolment, to lay before the President of the United States for his approbation.[55]

Mr. Wingate, on behalf of the Committee of enrolment, reported, that they did lay before the President of the United States the enroled Bills, entitled, "An Act for establishing the Salaries of the Executive Officers of Government, with their Assistants and Clerks"—And a Bill, entitled, "An Act to provide for the safe keeping of the Acts, Records, and Seal of the United States, and for other Purposes."

The Senate adjourned to 11 o'clock to-morrow.

TUESDAY, September 15, 1789

The SENATE assembled,

Present as yesterday,

And proceeded in the THIRD reading of the Bill, entitled, "An Act for the Temporary Establishment of the Post-Office."

ORDERED, That this Bill be engrossed.

A Message from the House of Representatives—

Mr. Beckley, their Clerk, brought up the enroled Bill, entitled, "An Act to suspend part of an Act, entitled, an Act to regulate the Collection of the Duties imposed by Law on the Tonnage of Ships or Vessels, and on Goods, Wares, and Merchandizes imported into the United States, and for other Purposes,"[56] signed by the Speaker of the House of Representatives—

And he withdrew.

Whereupon, the Vice President affixed his signature to the Bill, and it was delivered to the Committee of enrolment, to be laid before the President of the United States for his approbation.[57]

RESOLVED, That the engrossed Bill, entitled, "An Act for the Temporary Establishment of the Post-Office," do pass.[58]

---

[54] The inspected enrolled bill is in Enrolled Acts, RG 11, DNA. E–45690.

[55] On September 16 the committee on enrolled bills reported that it had presented this bill to the President.

[56] The inspected enrolled bill is in Enrolled Acts, RG 11, DNA. E–45313.

[57] On September 16 the President signed this bill and the Senate was notified.

[58] The engrossed bill is in Engrossed Senate Bills and Resolutions, Senate Records, DNA. E–45625.

ORDERED, That the Secretary carry the last mentioned Bill to the House of Representatives, and request their concurrence therein.[59]

The Senate adjourned to 11 o'clock to-morrow.

WEDNESDAY, SEPTEMBER 16, 1789

The SENATE assembled,
Present as yesterday.

Mr. Wingate, on behalf of the Committee of enrolment, reported, that they yesterday laid before the President of the United States a Bill, entitled, "An Act for allowing Compensation to the Members of the Senate and House of Representatives of the United States, and to the Officers of both Houses"[60]— Also, a Bill, entitled, "An Act to suspend part of an Act, entitled, an Act to regulate the Collection of the Duties imposed by Law on the Tonnage of Ships or Vessels, and on Goods, Wares, and Merchandizes imported into the United States, and for other Purposes."

A Message from the President of the United States, by the Secretary at War, which he delivered to the Vice President—

And withdrew:

GENTLEMEN OF THE SENATE,

THE Governor of the Western Territory has made a statement to me of the reciprocal hostilities of the Wabash Indians, and the people inhabiting the frontiers bordering on the River Ohio, which I herewith lay before Congress.

The United States in Congress assembled, by their Acts of the 21st day of July, 1787, and of the 12th August, 1788, made a provisional arrangement for calling forth the militia of Virginia and Pennsylvania, in the proportions therein specified.

As the circumstances which occasioned the said[61] arrangement continue nearly the same, I think proper to suggest to your consideration the expediency of making some temporary provision for calling forth the militia of the United States for the purposes stated in the Constitution, which would embrace the cases apprehended by the Governor of the Western Territory.

GEO. WASHINGTON

September 16th, 1789[62]

---

[59] On September 16 the House read this bill for the first time. On September 17 the House read the bill for the second and third times and passed it. On September 18 this bill, signed by the Speaker, was returned to the Senate for the Vice President's signature. It was then given to the committee on enrolled bills for presentation to the President.

[60] The President signed this bill on September 23.

[61] In the smooth journal the word "said" is omitted.

[62] The message, with documents, is in President's Messages: Suggesting legislation, Senate Records, DNA.

ORDERED, That the Message from the President do lie for consideration.

A Message from the House of Representatives—

Mr. Beckley, their Clerk, informed the Senate, that the President of the United States had affixed his signature to a Bill, entitled, "An Act to provide for the safe keeping of the Acts, Records, and Seal of the United States, and for other Purposes"—Also to an Act to suspend part of an Act, entitled, "An Act to regulate the Collection of the Duties imposed by Law on the Tonnage of Ships or Vessels, and on Goods, Wares, and Merchandizes imported into the United States, and for other Purposes"—And had returned them to the House of Representatives.

The Senate adjourned to 11 o'clock to-morrow.

THURSDAY, SEPTEMBER 17, 1789

The SENATE assembled,
Present as yesterday.

Mr. Lee, in behalf of the Committee appointed to prepare a Bill for organizing the Judiciary of the United States, reported also a Bill, entitled, "An Act to regulate Processes in the Courts of the United States."[63]

ORDERED, That this Bill have the FIRST reading at this time.

ORDERED, That this Bill be read the SECOND time to-morrow.[64]

ORDERED, That the Message from the President of the United States of the 16th of September, be further postponed.

A Message from the House of Representatives—

Mr. Beckley, their Clerk, informed the Senate, that the House of Representatives adhered to their disagreement to the Amendment proposed by the Senate to a Bill, entitled, "An Act for allowing a Compensation to the President and Vice President of the United States"[65]—And that the House of Representatives had concurred in the Bill, entitled, "An Act for the Temporary Establishment of the Post-Office"—

He also informed the Senate, that the House of Representatives had concurred in the Bill, entitled, "An Act to establish the Judicial Courts of the United States," with Amendments:[66] To which Amendments the concurrence of the Senate was requested—

And he withdrew.

---

[63] A manuscript copy and fragments of a printed bill are in Senate Bills, Senate Records, DNA. An annotated printed copy is in the Broadside Collection, RBkRm, DLC. E–45677.

[64] On September 18 this bill was read for the second time.

[65] On September 21 the Senate receded from this amendment and notified the House.

[66] The concurrence and the amendments have not been located.

ORDERED, That the last mentioned Bill, together with the Amendments, be committed to   Mr. Ellsworth
                Mr. Butler and
                Mr. Paterson[67]

The Senate adjourned to 11 o'clock to-morrow.

FRIDAY, SEPTEMBER 18, 1789

The SENATE assembled,
Present as yesterday.

Mr. Wingate, on behalf of the Committee of enrolment, reported, that they had examined an enroled Bill, entitled, "An Act for the Temporary Establishment of the Post-Office,"[68] and had found it correct.

A Message from the House of Representatives—

Mr. Beckley, their Clerk, informed the Senate, that the House of Representatives had agreed to postpone the consideration of the Bill, entitled, "An Act for the Punishment of certain Crimes against the United States," which had PASSED the Senate and was sent to the House of Representatives for concurrence, until the next session of Congress[69]—

He also brought up a Resolve of the House of Representatives, making it "The duty of the Secretary of State to procure from time to time such of the statutes of the several States as may not be in his office:"[70] To which the concurrence of the Senate was requested—

He also brought up an enroled Bill, entitled, "An Act for the Temporary Establishment of the Post-Office," signed by the Speaker of the House of Representatives—

And he withdrew.

The Vice President affixed his signature to the last recited Bill, and it was delivered to the Committee of enrolment for presentation.[71]

The Senate proceeded to the SECOND reading of the Bill, entitled, "An Act to regulate Processes in the Courts of the United States:"

---

[67] On September 19 Mr. Ellsworth reported for this committee. The Senate resolved to agree to some of the House amendments and disagree to others. The House was notified of this action and the bill was returned to the House on this date.

[68] The inspected enrolled bill is in Enrolled Acts, RG 11, DNA. E–45699.

[69] On January 19, 1790, during the second session of Congress, a motion was made in the Senate to appoint a new committee to report "A Bill defining the crimes and offences that shall be cognizable under the authority of the United States, and their punishment." This motion was postponed.

[70] This resolve has not been located.

[71] On September 19 the committee on enrolled bills reported that it had presented this bill to the President.

ORDERED, That the further consideration thereof be postponed until to-morrow.[72]

The Resolve of the House of Representatives of the 18th[73] September, "im-powering the Secretary of State to procure, from time to time, such of the statutes of the several States as may not be in his office," was read—Where-upon,

RESOLVED, That the Senate do concur in the above Resolution sent up for concurrence by the House of Representatives.

The Senate adjourned to 11 o'clock to-morrow.

S A T U R D A Y, SEPTEMBER 19, 1789

The SENATE assembled,
Present as yesterday.

Mr. Wingate, on behalf of the Committee of enrolment, reported, that they had laid before the President of the United States for his approbation, an enroled Bill, entitled, "An Act for the Temporary Establishment of the Post-Office."[74]

Agreeably to the order of the day,

The Senate proceeded in the SECOND reading of the Bill, entitled, "An Act to regulate Processes in the Courts of the United States"—

ORDERED, That the rules be so far dispensed with as that the last recited Bill have the THIRD reading at this time—

ORDERED, That the Bill be engrossed.[75]

A Message from the House of Representatives—

Mr. Beckley, their Clerk, brought up a Bill, entitled, "An Act for amend-ing part of an Act, entitled, an Act to regulate the Collection of the Duties imposed by Law on the Tonnage of Ships or Vessels, and on Goods, Wares, and Merchandizes imported into the United States:"[76] To which the concur-rence of the Senate was requested—

And he withdrew.

ORDERED, That the last recited Bill now have the FIRST reading.

ORDERED, That the rules be so far dispensed with, as that this Bill have a SECOND reading at this time—

---

[72] On September 19 this bill was read for the third time and ordered to be engrossed. It was then carried to the House.

[73] The smooth journal inserts "of."

[74] On September 22 the President signed this bill and notified the Senate.

[75] The engrossed bill is in Engrossed Senate Bills and Resolutions, Senate Records, DNA.

[76] The bill, as it passed the House, is in Engrossed House Bills, House Records, DNA.

ORDERED, That this Bill have the THIRD reading on Monday next.[77]

Mr. Ellsworth, on behalf of the Committee appointed to consider the Amendments proposed by the House of Representatives to the Bill, entitled, "An Act to establish the Judicial Courts of the United States," reported:[78]

Whereupon,

RESOLVED, That the 9th, 16th, 41st and 52d Amendments be disagreed to, and that the rest be agreed to, with an Amendment to the 48th Amendment, so that the clause there proposed to be inserted shall read as follows:

"That in cases punishable with death, the trial shall be had in the county where the offence was committed, or where that cannot be done without great inconvenience, twelve petit Jurors, at least, shall be summoned from thence. And Jurors, in all cases, to serve in the Court of the United States, shall be designated by lot or otherwise, in each State respectively, according to the mode of forming Juries therein, now practised, so far as the laws of the same shall render such designation practicable by the Courts or Marshalls of the United States, and the Jurors."

ORDERED, That the Secretary do carry a Message to the House of Representatives accordingly:[79]

Also, That he carry the engrossed Bill, entitled, "An Act to regulate Processes in the Courts of the United States"—to the House of Representatives, and request concurrence therein.[80]

A Message from the House of Representatives—

Mr. Beckley, their Clerk, brought up the Bill, entitled, "An Act for allowing certain Compensation to the Judges of the Supreme and other Courts, and to the Attorney General of the United States,"[81] to which concurrence was requested—

And he withdrew.

ORDERED, That the last recited Bill have the FIRST reading at this time—

ORDERED, That the rules be so far dispensed with, as that this Bill be now read the SECOND time.[82]

The Senate adjourned until 11 o'clock on Monday morning.

---

[77] On September 26 this bill was read a third time and committed.

[78] The committee report is in Various Select Committee Reports, Senate Records, DNA. The resolve and amendments are in Senate Bills and in Engrossed Senate Bills and Resolutions, respectively, Senate Records, DNA.

[79] On September 19 this resolution was considered in the House. On September 21 the House voted to agree to the Senate resolution and the Senate was notified of this action.

[80] On September 19 this bill was read for the first and second times and committed to a committee of the whole by the House. The committee of the whole considered it on September 23; on September 24 it was amended, agreed to, and sent to the Senate. The Senate then agreed to all the amendments except the first and notified the House.

[81] This bill, as it passed the House, has not been located.

[82] On September 21 this bill was read a second time, amended, read a third time, and passed. The Senate then notified the House which concurred with all but one Senate amendment. The Senate then receded from this amendment.

MONDAY, September 21, 1789

The SENATE assembled,

Present as on Saturday.

A Message from the House of Representatives—

Mr. Beckley, their Clerk, brought up the Bill, entitled, "An Act to establish the Judicial Courts of the United States," and informed the Senate that the House of Representatives had receded from the 9th, 16th, 41st, and 52d Amendments, and had concurred in the Amendment of the Senate to the 48th Amendment proposed by the House of Representatives[83]—

And he withdrew.

The Senate proceeded in the SECOND reading of the Bill, entitled, "An Act for allowing certain Compensation to the Judges of the Supreme, and other Courts, and to the Attorney-General of the United States;"

And, on motion, To amend the clause providing for the salary of the Chief Justice, by striking out "Thirty-five hundred," and inserting FOUR THOUSAND—

It passed in the Affirmative.

On the question to amend the Bill, by inserting five hundred at the end of three thousand, in the salaries of the associate Justices of the Supreme Court—

The Yeas and Nays being requested by one fifth of the Senators present—

Mr. Bassett		Nay
Mr. Butler	Yea	
Mr. Carroll	Yea	
Mr. Dalton		Nay
Mr. Ellsworth		Nay
Mr. Grayson		Nay
Mr. Gunn	Yea	
Mr. Henry		Nay
Mr. Johnson		Nay
Mr. Izard	Yea	
Mr. King	Yea	
Mr. Lee		Nay
Mr. Maclay		Nay
Mr. Morris	Yea	
Mr. Paterson	Yea	
Mr. Read	Yea	
Mr. Schuyler	Yea	
Mr. Wingate		Nay

Yeas   9

Nays . . . .   9[84]

---

[83] The House resolve is in Engrossed Senate Bills and Resolutions, Senate Records, DNA. On September 22 this bill, signed by the Speaker, was brought to the Senate for the Vice President's signature. It was then sent to the President.

[84] The printed journal incorrectly gave the totals as 8 and 8.

The numbers being equal, the Vice President determined the question in the Affirmative.

ORDERED, That the rules be so far dispensed with, as that the Bill have a THIRD reading at this time.

On motion, That the clause providing for the salary of the Chief Justice be amended, so as to stand THREE THOUSAND EIGHT HUNDRED instead of "Four thousands dollars"—

It passed in the Negative.

On motion, That the clause providing for the salary of the Attorney-General, be amended by striking out "Fifteen hundred dollars," and inserting TWO THOUSAND—

It passed in the Affirmative.

RESOLVED, That the Senate do concur with the House of Representatives in the above recited Bill, with the Amendment[85]—

ORDERED, That the Secretary do carry this Bill to the House of Representatives, and request concurrence in the Amendments.

Mr. Morris, in behalf of the Senators from the State of Pennsylvania, introduced a Resolve of the General Assembly of that State, of March the 5th, 1789, making "A respectful offer to Congress of the use of any or all the public buildings in Philadelphia, the property of the State, &c. in case Congress should at any time incline to make choice of that city for the temporary residence of the Federal Government"[86]—which was read—

ORDERED, That it lie for consideration.

A Message from the House of Representatives—

Mr. Beckley, their Clerk, brought up a Resolve of the House of this date, to agree to the 2d, 4th, 8th, 12th, 13th, 16th, 18th, 19th, 25th, and 26th Amendments proposed by the Senate, "To Articles of Amendment to be proposed to the Legislatures of the several States, as Amendments to the Constitution of the United States," and to disagree to the 1st, 3d, 5th, 6th, 7th, 9th, 10th, 11th, 14th, 15th, 17th, 20th, 21st, 22d, 23d, and 24th Amendments: Two thirds of the members present concurring on each vote: And "That a conference be desired with the Senate on the subject matter of the Amendments disagreed to," and that   Mr. Madison

Mr. Sherman and

Mr. Vining be appointed managers of the same, on the part of the House of Representatives[87]—

And he withdrew.

RESOLVED, by the Senate and House of Representatives of the United States of America in Congress assembled, That it be recommended to the Legislatures

---

[85] The Senate resolve, with amendments in draft form, is in Senate Simple Resolutions and Motions, Senate Records, DNA.

[86] This resolve introduced by Mr. Morris has not been located.

[87] This House message and resolve have not been located.

of the several States, to pass laws, making it expressly the duty of the keepers of their gaols to receive and safe keep therein, all prisoners committed under the authority of the United States, until they shall be discharged by due course of the laws thereof, under the like penalties as in the case of prisoners committed under the authority of such States respectively:

The United States to pay for the use and keeping of such gaols, at the rate of fifty cents per month for each prisoner that shall, under their authority, be committed thereto, during the time such prisoners shall be therein confined; and also to support such of said prisoners as shall be committed for offences.[88]

ORDERED, That the Secretary do carry this Resolve to the House of Representatives, and request concurrence therein.

The Senate proceeded to consider the disagreement of the House of Representatives to their Amendment to the Bill, entitled, "An Act for allowing a Compensation to the President and Vice President of the United States"—And

RESOLVED, That the Senate do recede from their Amendment to the said Bill.

The Senate proceeded to consider the Message of the House of Representatives disagreeing to the Amendments made by the Senate "To Articles to be proposed to the Legislatures of the several States, as Amendments to the Constitution of the United States"—And

RESOLVED, That the Senate do recede from their third Amendment, and do insist on all the others.

RESOLVED, That the Senate do concur with the House of Representatives in a conference on the subject matter of disagreement on the said Articles of Amendment, and that   Mr. Ellsworth
                           Mr. Carroll and
                           Mr. Paterson be managers of the conference on the part of the Senate.

ORDERED, That the Secretary do carry the Bill, entitled, "An Act for allowing a Compensation to the President and Vice President of the United States,"[89] together with "The Articles to be proposed as Amendments to the Constitution of the United States," to the House of Representatives, and acquaint them with the proceedings of the Senate thereon.[90]

A Message from the House of Representatives—

Mr. Beckley, their Clerk, brought up the Resolve of the Senate of this day, making provision "For the safe keeping of the Prisoners committed under the

---

[88] The resolve and a draft resolve are in Senate Joint and Concurrent Resolutions, Senate Records, DNA.

[89] On September 22 this bill, signed by the Speaker, was brought to the Senate for the Vice President's signature. It was then sent to the President.

[90] On September 24 this committee reported and the report was ordered to lie for consideration.

Authority of the United States," concurred in by the House of Representatives[91]—

Also, the Bill, entitled, "An Act for allowing certain Compensation to the Judges of the Supreme and other Courts, and to the Attorney-General of the United States," and informed the Senate, that the House of Representatives had agreed to all the Amendments proposed to the said Bill, except the fourth, to which they had disagreed—

And he withdrew.

The Senate proceeded to consider the disagreement of the House of Representatives, to their fourth Amendment to the Bill last recited—And

RESOLVED, That the Senate do recede therefrom.

ORDERED, That the Secretary do carry a Message to the House of Representatives accordingly.[92]

The Senate adjourned to 11 o'clock to-morrow.

TUESDAY, SEPTEMBER 22, 1789

The SENATE assembled,

Present as yesterday.

Mr. Wingate, on behalf of the Committee of enrolment, reported, that they had examined the enroled Bill, entitled, "An Act to establish the Judicial Courts of the United States,"[93] and the enroled Resolve "For the safe keeping of Prisoners committed under the Authority of the United States,"[94] which they had found correct—

Also that they had examined the enroled Resolve, "That the Secretary of State procure the Statutes of the several States"[95]—The enroled Bill, entitled, "An Act for allowing a Compensation to the President and Vice President of the United States"[96]—And the Bill, entitled, "An Act for allowing certain Compensation to the Judges of the Supreme and other Courts, and to the Attorney-General of the United States,"[97] And had found them correct.

A Message from the House of Representatives—

Mr. Beckley, their Clerk, brought up the following enroled Bills and Resolves, signed by the Speaker of the House of Representatives, to wit:

The Bill, entitled, "An Act to establish the Judicial Courts of the United States;"

---

[91] On September 22 this resolution, signed by the Speaker, was sent to the Senate for the Vice President's signature. It was then presented to the President.

[92] On September 22 this bill, signed by the Speaker, was sent to the Senate for the Vice President's signature. This bill was then presented to the President.

[93] The inspected enrolled bill is in Enrolled Acts, RG 11, DNA. E–45707.

[94] The inspected enrolled resolve is in Enrolled Acts, RG 11, DNA. E–45721.

[95] The inspected enrolled resolve is in Enrolled Acts, RG 11, DNA. E–45722.

[96] The inspected enrolled bill is in Enrolled Acts, RG 11, DNA. E–45688.

[97] The inspected enrolled bill is in Enrolled Acts, RG 11, DNA. E–45689.

The Bill, entitled, "An Act for allowing certain Compensation to the Judges of the Supreme, and other Courts, and to the Attorney-General of the United States;"

The Bill, entitled, "An Act for allowing a Compensation to the President and Vice President of the United States;"

The Resolve, "That the Secretary of State do procure the Statutes of the several States;"

And, the Resolve "For the safe keeping of the Prisoners committed under the Authority of the United States"[98]—

Also, an Order of the House of Representatives for postponing the adjournment of Congress until the 26th of September;[99] for concurrence—

And he withdrew.

The Vice President affixed his signature to the enroled Bills and Resolves mentioned to be signed by the Speaker, and they were delivered to the Committee, and by them laid before the President of the United States for his approbation.[100]

A Message from the President of the United States—

Mr. Lear, his Secretary, brought in "The Act for the Temporary Establishment of the Post-Office"—And informed the Senate, that the President of the United States had approved of, and had affixed his signature thereto—

And he withdrew.

The Senate proceeded to consider the Order of the House of Representatives of this day, "Rescinding the Order to the Vice President and Speaker, of the 25th of August, to adjourn the respective Houses of Congress on the 22d, and empowering them to adjourn the same on the 26th instant"—And

RESOLVED, That the Senate do concur in the said Order.

ORDERED, That the Secretary do carry a Message to the House of Representatives accordingly[101]—

And that he do inform the House, that the President of the United States had approved of, and had affixed his signature to the "Act for the Temporary Establishment of the Post-Office."

ORDERED, That the Bill, entitled, "An Act to establish the Seat of Government of the United States,"[102] have the FIRST reading at this time—

ORDERED, That it be read a SECOND time to-morrow.[103]

The Senate adjourned to 11 o'clock to-morrow.

---

[98] At this point the smooth journal inserts: "Also, the Bill entitled An act to establish the seat of government, for concurrence."

[99] The House order is in Messages from the House, Senate Records, DNA.

[100] On September 23 the two resolves and the Salaries-Judiciary Bill were signed by the President. He signed the Judiciary Bill and the Compensation Bill on September 24.

[101] On September 26 the Senate resolved to postpone adjournment until the twenty-ninth and the House agreed.

[102] The bill, as it passed the House, is in Engrossed House Bills, House Records, DNA. E-45630.

[103] On September 23 this bill was read a second time and considered.

WEDNESDAY, September 23, 1789

The SENATE assembled,

Present as yesterday.

A Message from the House of Representatives—

Mr. Beckley, their Clerk, brought up the Bill, entitled, "An Act to recognize and adapt to the Constitution of the United States, the establishment of the Troops raised under the Resolves of the United States in Congress assembled, and for other Purposes therein mentioned;"[104] To which concurrence was requested—

He also informed the Senate, that the President of the United States had approved of, and affixed his signature to "An Act for allowing Compensation to the Members of the Senate and House of Representatives of the United States, and to the Officers of both Houses"—

To "An Act for allowing certain Compensation to the Judges of the Supreme and other Courts, and to the Attorney-General of the United States"—

To a Resolve, "That the Secretary of State do procure the Statutes of the several States:" And that he had returned them to the House of Representatives—

And he withdrew.

ORDERED, That the Bill brought up from the House of Representatives this morning, be now read the FIRST time.

ORDERED, That this Bill be read the SECOND time to-morrow.[105]

A Message from the President of the United States—

Mr. Lear, his Secretary, delivered to the Vice President, an enroled Resolve, "For the safe keeping of Prisoners committed under the Authority of the United States"—And informed the Senate, that the President of the United States had approved of, and affixed his signature thereto—

And he withdrew.

Agreeably to the order of the day, the Senate proceeded to the SECOND reading of the Bill, entitled, "An Act to establish the Seat of Government of the United States," and after progress[106]—

The Senate adjourned to 11 o'clock to-morrow.

THURSDAY, September 24, 1789

The SENATE assembled,

Present as yesterday.

Mr. Ellsworth, on behalf of the managers of the conference on "Articles to be proposed to the several States as Amendments to the Constitution of the United States," reported as follows:[107]

---

[104] This bill, as it passed the House, has not been located.

[105] On September 26 this bill was read for the second time and committed.

[106] On September 24 this bill was considered again and several amendments to it were defeated.

[107] The report is in House Joint and Concurrent Resolutions, Senate Records, DNA.

That it will be proper for the House of Representatives to agree to the said Amendments proposed by the Senate, with an Amendment to their fifth Amendment, so that the third Article shall read as follows: "Congress shall make no Law RESPECTING AN ESTABLISHMENT OF RELIGION, or prohibiting the free exercise thereof; or abridging the freedom of Speech, or of the Press; or the right of the People peaceably to assemble and petition the Government for a redress of Grievances;" And with an Amendment to the fourteenth Amendment proposed by the Senate, so that the eighth Article, as numbered in the Amendments proposed by the Senate, shall read as follows; "In all criminal prosecutions, the accused shall enjoy the right to a speedy and public trial BY AN IMPARTIAL JURY OF THE DISTRICT WHEREIN THE CRIME SHALL HAVE BEEN COMMITTED, AS THE DISTRICT SHALL HAVE BEEN PREVIOUSLY ASCERTAINED BY LAW, and to be informed of the nature and cause of the accusation, to be confronted with the witnesses against him, and to have compulsory process for obtaining witnesses in his favor, and to have the assistance of Counsel for his defence."

The managers were also of opinion, that it would be proper for both Houses to agree to amend the first Article, by striking out the word "Less" in the last line but one, and inserting in its place the word "More," and accordingly recommend that the said Article be reconsidered for that purpose.

ORDERED, That the Report lie for consideration.

A Message from the House of Representatives—

Mr. Beckley, their Clerk, brought up the Bill, entitled, "An Act to alter the Time for the next meeting of Congress"[108]—The Bill, entitled, "An Act to explain and amend an Act, entitled an Act for registering and clearing Vessels, regulating the Coasting Trade, and for other Purposes;"[109] and "A Resolve on the petition of Baron de Glaubeck"[110]—To which he requested the concurrence of the Senate—

And he withdrew.

ORDERED, That the Bill, entitled, "An Act to explain and amend an Act, entitled, an Act for registering and clearing Vessels, regulating the Coasting Trade, and for other Purposes," be now read the first time.

ORDERED, That this Bill be read the second time to-morrow.[111]

The Senate proceeded to consider the "Resolve of the House of Representatives, upon the petition of Baron de Glaubeck."

ORDERED, That this petition, together with the papers accompanying the same, be read.

On motion, That the opinion of the Senate be taken, whether the Baron de

---

[108] This bill, as it passed the House, has not been located. On September 25 the Senate read this bill for the second and third times and passed it.

[109] This bill, as it passed the House, has not been located.

[110] The House resolve is in Messages from the House, Senate Records, DNA.

[111] On September 26 this bill was read for the second time and committed.

Glaubeck is entitled to the pay of a Captain in the late army of the United States, from the 9th day of March, 1781, to the 24th day of August, 1782, as expressed in the Resolve of the House—

It passed in the Affirmative.

ORDERED, That the Resolve of the House of Representatives, and the papers accompanying the same, be committed to

Mr. Izard

Mr. Grayson and

Mr. Carroll with an instruction to bring in a Bill for the purposes expressed in the Resolve.

The Senate proceeded in a second reading of the Bill, entitled, "An Act to establish the Seat of Government of the United States."

On motion, To strike out these words—"In the State of Pennsylvania," after the word Susquehannah, line 4th; and the Yeas and Nays being required by one fifth of the Senators present—

Mr. Bassett	Yea	
Mr. Butler	Yea	
Mr. Carroll	Yea	
Mr. Dalton		Nay
Mr. Ellsworth		Nay
Mr. Grayson	Yea	
Mr. Gunn	Yea	
Mr. Henry	Yea	
Mr. Johnson		Nay
Mr. Izard	Yea	
Mr. King		Nay
Mr. Lee	Yea	
Mr. Maclay		Nay
Mr. Morris		Nay
Mr. Paterson		Nay
Mr. Read		Nay
Mr. Schuyler		Nay
Mr. Wingate		Nay

Nays 10
Yeas 8

So it passed in the Negative.

On motion, That these words—"At some convenient place on the banks of the river[112] Susquehannah, in the State of Pennsylvania," lines 3d and 4th, be stricken out—

It passed in the Negative.

---

[112] The smooth journal omits the word "river."

On motion, For reconsideration, on a suggestion that the question was not understood—

It passed in the Affirmative.

And on the main question—

The Yeas and Nays being required by one fifth of the Senators present—

Mr. Bassett	Yea	
Mr. Butler	Yea	
Mr. Carroll		Nay
Mr. Dalton	Yea	
Mr. Ellsworth	Yea	
Mr. Grayson	Yea	
Mr. Gunn	Yea	
Mr. Henry		Nay
Mr. Johnson		Nay
Mr. Izard		Nay
Mr. King		Nay
Mr. Lee	Yea	
Mr. Maclay		Nay
Mr. Morris	Yea	
Mr. Paterson	Yea	
Mr. Read	Yea	
Mr. Schuyler		Nay
Mr. Wingate	Yea	

Yeas 11
Nays 7

So it passed in the Affirmative.

On motion, To insert in the room of the word striken out, "At some convenient place on the northern banks of the river Potowmack"—

It passed in the Negative.

On motion, To restore these words—"At some convenient place on the banks of the river Susquehannah"—

A motion was made to postpone THIS, to insert the following motion to wit: To fill the blank with these words—"In the Counties of Philadelphia, Chester and Bucks, and State of Pennsylvania, including within it the town of Germantown, and such part of the northern liberties of the city of Philadelphia, as are not excepted by the Act of cession, passed by the Legislature of the said State"—

And the question of postponement passed in the Affirmative—

And on the main question—

The Yeas and Nays being required by one fifth of the Senators present—

Mr. Bassett	Yea	
Mr. Butler		Nay
Mr. Carroll		Nay

Mr. Dalton	Yea	
Mr. Ellsworth	Yea	
Mr. Grayson		Nay
Mr. Gunn		Nay
Mr. Henry		Nay
Mr. Johnson		Nay
Mr. Izard		Nay
Mr. King	Yea	
Mr. Lee		Nay
Mr. Maclay		Nay
Mr. Morris	Yea	
Mr. Paterson	Yea	
Mr. Read	Yea	
Mr. Schuyler	Yea	
Mr. Wingate	Yea	

Yeas 9
Nays 9

The numbers being equal, the Vice President determined the question in the Affirmative.[113]

A Message from the House of Representatives—

Mr. Beckley, their Clerk, brought up the Amendments to the "Articles to be proposed to the Legislatures of the several States, as Amendments to the Constitution of the United States;" and informed the Senate, that the House of Representatives had receded from their disagreement to the 1st, 3d, 5th, 6th, 7th, 9th, 10th, 11th, 14th, 15th, 17th, 20th, 21st, 22d, 23d, and 24th Amendments, insisted on by the Senate: Provided that the "Two Articles, which by the Amendments of the Senate are now proposed to be inserted as the third and eighth Articles," shall be amended to read as followeth:

Article the Third. "Congress shall make no Law respecting an establishment of Religion, or prohibiting the free exercise thereof; or abridging the freedom of Speech, or of the Press; or the right of the People peaceably to assemble, and petition the Government for a redress of Grievances."

Article the Eighth. "In all criminal prosecutions the accused shall enjoy the right to a speedy and public trial by an impartial Jury of the State and District, wherein the crime shall have been committed, which District shall have been previously ascertained by law, and to be informed of the nature and cause of the accusation, to be confronted with the witnesses against him, to have compulsory process for obtaining witnesses in his favor, and to have the assistance of Counsel for his defence."[114]

---

[113] On September 25 this bill was considered again and two amendments to it were passed.

[114] These two articles of amendment are in House Joint and Concurrent Resolutions, Senate Records, DNA.

And provided also, That the first Article be amended by striking out the word "Less," in the last place of the said first Article, and inserting in lieu thereof the word "More."[115]

He also informed the Senate, that the President of the United States had approved of, and had affixed his signature to, "An Act for allowing a Compensation to the President and Vice President of the United States;" and had returned it to the House of Representatives—

And he withdrew.

A Message from the President of the United States—

Mr. Lear, his Secretary, delivered to the Vice President, the Act, entitled, "An Act to establish the Judicial Courts of the United States," and informed him, that the President of the United States had approved of, and affixed his signature thereto—

And he withdrew.

ORDERED, That the Secretary do inform the House of Representatives, that the President of the United States had approved of, and affixed his signature to, "The Act to establish the Judicial Courts of the United States;" Also, to an enroled Resolve, "For the safe keeping of the Prisoners committed under the Authority of the United States," and had returned them to the Senate.

The Committee appointed to consider the Resolve of the House of Representatives, upon the petition of Baron de Glaubeck, reported a Bill.[116]

ORDERED, That this Bill have the FIRST reading at this time.

ORDERED, That this Bill be read the SECOND time to-morrow.[117]

The Senate adjourned until 11 o'clock to-morrow.

FRIDAY, SEPTEMBER 25, 1789

The SENATE assembled,

Present as yesterday.

Agreeably to the order of the day, the Senate proceeded in the SECOND reading of the Bill, entitled, "An Act to establish the Seat of Government of the United States:"

On motion, To strike out these words—"And that until the necessary buildings shall be erected therein, the Seat of Government shall continue at the City of New-York"—

And the Yeas and Nays being required by one fifth of the Senators present—

Mr. Bassett		Nay
Mr. Butler	Yea	
Mr. Carroll	Yea	

[115] On September 25 the Senate concurred with this House action and notified the House.

[116] A draft of this bill is in House Bills, Senate Records, DNA.

[117] On September 28 this bill was read for the second time.

Mr. Dalton		Nay
Mr. Ellsworth		Nay
Mr. Grayson	Yea	
Mr. Gunn	Yea	
Mr. Henry	Yea	
Mr. Johnson		Nay
Mr. Izard		Nay
Mr. King		Nay
Mr. Lee	Yea	
Mr. Maclay	Yea	
Mr. Morris		Nay
Mr. Paterson		Nay
Mr. Read		Nay
Mr. Schuyler		Nay
Mr. Wingate		Nay

Nays 11
Yeas 7

So it passed in the Negative.

On motion, To amend the second section, to read as follows:

"And be it further enacted, That the President of the United States be authorised to appoint three Commissioners, who are under his direction to locate a District, not exceeding ten miles square, in the said Counties, and including therein the said northern liberties, and town of Germantown, and to purchase such quantity of land within the same as may be necessary, and to accept grants of lands for the use of the United States, and to erect thereon, within four years, suitable buildings for the accommodation of the Congress, and of the Officers of the United States"—

It passed in the Affirmative.

On motion, To strike out the two last sections, and to substitute the following:

"Provided, That no powers herein vested in the President of the United States, shall be carried into effect, until the State of Pennsylvania, or individual Citizens of the same, shall give satisfactory security to the Secretary of the Treasury, to furnish and pay, as the same may be necessary, one hundred thousand dollars, to be employed in erecting the said buildings"[118]—

It passed in the Affirmative.

ORDERED, That this Bill be read the THIRD time to-morrow.[119]

A Message from the House of Representatives—

---

[118] Drafts of the preceding motions are in House Bills, Senate Records, DNA. A copy is in Engrossed House Bills, House Records, DNA.

[119] On September 26 this bill was read a third time and passed with amendments. It was then sent to the House for concurrence.

Mr. Beckley, their Clerk, informed the Senate, that the House of Representatives had passed a Resolve, requesting, "The President of the United States to transmit to the Executives of the several States, which have ratified the Constitution, copies of the Amendments proposed by Congress to be added thereto: And like copies to the Executives of the States of Rhode-Island and North-Carolina"[120]—

And that the House requested the concurrence of the Senate therein:[121]

Also, That the House of Representatives had concurred in the Bill which had PASSED the Senate, entitled, "An Act to regulate processes in the Courts of the United States," with Amendments; in which Amendments the House requested a concurrence of the Senate:[122]

He also informed the Senate, that the House of Representatives had passed a Bill, entitled, "An Act making appropriations for the service of the present year"[123]—

To which concurrence was also requested—

And he withdrew.

ORDERED, That the last mentioned Bill be now read the FIRST time,

ORDERED, That this Bill be read the SECOND time to-morrow.[124]

The Senate proceeded to consider the Message from the House of Representatives of the 24th, with Amendments to the Amendments of the Senate, to "Articles to be proposed to the Legislatures of the several States, as Amendments to the Constitution of the United States"—And

RESOLVED, That the Senate do concur in the Amendments proposed by the House of Representatives, to the Amendments of the Senate.

ORDERED, That the Secretary do carry a Message to the House of Representatives accordingly.[125]

A Message from the House of Representatives—

Mr. Beckley, their Clerk, informed the Senate, that the House of Representatives had passed a Resolve, appointing a joint Committee "To wait on the President of the United States, to request that he would recommend to the people of the United States, a day of public Thanksgiving and Prayer to be observed"[126]—

---

[120] The House resolve is in House Joint and Concurrent Resolutions, Senate Records, DNA.

[121] On September 26 this House resolution was considered by the Senate and concurred in.

[122] A copy of part of the message with amendments is in Engrossed Senate Bills and Resolutions, Senate Records, DNA.

[123] This bill has not been located.

[124] On September 26 this bill was read a second time and committed.

[125] These proposed amendments were then sent to the governors by the President.

[126] The House resolve, including the selection of the committee, is in House Joint and Concurrent Resolutions, Senate Records, DNA. On September 26 the Senate concurred with this resolution and appointed a committee to join the House committee.

Also, a Resolve, ascertaining "The time that John White, late Commissioner, and others, therein named, continued in office:"[127]

And, "An Act, providing for the payment of the invalid Pensioners of the United States"[128]—To all which the concurrence of the Senate was requested[129]—

And he withdrew.

The Senate proceeded to consider the Amendments of the House of Representatives, to the Bill, entitled, "An Act to regulate Processes in the Courts of the United States"—And

RESOLVED, That the Senate do concur in all the Amendments except the first, in which they do not concur.[130]

ORDERED, That the Secretary do carry a Message to the House of Representatives accordingly.[131]

The Senate proceeded in the SECOND reading of the Bill, entitled, "An Act to alter the Time for the next meeting of Congress."

ORDERED, That this Bill have the THIRD reading at this time.

RESOLVED, That the Senate do concur in the above mentioned Bill.

ORDERED, That the Secretary do carry a Message to the House of Representatives accordingly.[132]

The Senate adjourned to 10 o'clock to-morrow.

S A T U R D A Y, SEPTEMBER 26, 1789

The SENATE assembled,
Present as yesterday.

A Message from the President of the United States—

The Hon. Mr. Jay acquainted the Senate, that he was directed to lay before them the following communication, which he delivered to the Vice President—
And he withdrew.

United States, September 26, 1789

GENTLEMEN of the SENATE,

HAVING yesterday received a letter written in this month, by the Governor

---

[127] This resolve has not been located. On September 26 the Senate considered this resolution.

[128] This bill, as it passed the House, has not been located.

[129] On September 26 this bill was read for the first time and committed.

[130] The engrossed resolve, which includes the amendments, is with an extract of the House resolve in Engrossed Senate Bills and Resolutions, Senate Records, DNA.

[131] On September 25 the House adhered to its amendment and the Senate was notified of this on September 26. On this same date the Senate appointed a conference committee to consider this disagreement with a House committee, and the House appointed a similar committee.

[132] On September 28 this enrolled bill, signed by the Speaker, was sent to the Senate for the Vice President's signature. It was then presented to the President.

of Rhode-Island, at the request, and in behalf of the General Assembly of that State, addressed to the President, the Senate, and the House of Representatives of the Eleven United States of America, in Congress assembled, I take the earliest opportunity of laying a copy of it before you.

GEORGE WASHINGTON[133]

ORDERED, That the Message, together with the Letter therein referred to, lie for consideration.

RESOLVED, That the order of the 22d instant, directing the President of the Senate, and Speaker of the House of Representatives, to adjourn their respective Houses on this day, be rescinded, and instead thereof, that they be directed to close the present session by adjourning their respective Houses on the 29th instant.[134]

ORDERED, That the Secretary do carry this Resolve to the House of Representatives, and request their concurrence.

A Message from the House of Representatives—

Mr. Beckley, their Clerk, informed the Senate, that the House of Representatives had concurred in the above Resolve[135]—

And he withdrew.

The Senate proceeded to the second reading of the Bill, entitled, "An Act making Appropriations for the Service of the present Year."

ORDERED, That it be committed to

> Mr. Read
> Mr. Butler
> Mr. King
> Mr. Ellsworth and
> Mr. Morris[136]

A Message from the House of Representatives—

Mr. Beckley, their Clerk, informed the Senate, that the House of Representatives do insist on their Amendment to the Bill, entitled, "An Act to regulate Processes in the Courts of the United States"—

And he withdrew.

The Senate proceeded to the THIRD reading of the Bill, entitled, "An Act to establish the Seat of Government of the United States:"

---

[133] The message, with documents, is in President's messages: Suggesting legislation, Senate Records, DNA. The smooth journal reads: "G. WASHINGTON."

[134] The Senate resolve and the House resolve are in Senate Joint and Concurrent Resolutions, Senate Records, DNA.

[135] On September 26 the Senate appointed a committee to acquaint the President with the Congressional plans for adjournment.

[136] On September 28 this committee reported amendments to the bill. It was then passed with amendments and sent to the House. On the same date the House concurred with these amendments and the bill was signed by both the Speaker and the Vice President.

On motion, To postpone the further consideration hereof—

It passed in the Negative.

On the question, "Shall this Bill pass?"

The Yeas and Nays being required by one fifth of the Senators present—

Mr. Bassett	Yea	
Mr. Butler		Nay
Mr. Carroll		Nay
Mr. Dalton	Yea	
Mr. Ellsworth	Yea	
Mr. Grayson		Nay
Mr. Gunn		Nay
Mr. Henry		Nay
Mr. Johnson	Yea	
Mr. Izard		Nay
Mr. King	Yea	
Mr. Lee		Nay
Mr. Morris	Yea	
Mr. Paterson	Yea	
Mr. Read	Yea	
Mr. Schuyler	Yea	
Mr. Wingate	Yea	

Yeas 10

Nays 7

So it passed in the Affirmative.

ORDERED, That the Secretary do carry this Bill to the House of Representatives, and request their concurrence in the Amendments.[137]

The Senate proceeded to consider the Amendment insisted on by the House of Representatives, to the Bill, entitled, "An Act to regulate Processes in the Courts of the United States."

ORDERED, That a conference be proposed on the subject matter of disagreement—that   Mr. Ellsworth

Mr. King and

Mr. Read be Managers thereof on the part of the Senate, and that the Secretary do carry a Message to the House of Representatives accordingly, and request the appointment of Managers of the conference on their part.

A Message from the House of Representatives—

---

[137] The amendments and a statement of concurrence are in Engrossed House Bills, House Records, DNA. On September 26 the House received and considered this amended bill. On September 28 it agreed to the amended bill with another amendment and returned it to the Senate. The Senate voted to postpone consideration of this bill until the next session on the same date.

Mr. Beckley, their Clerk, informed the Senate, that the House had agreed to the proposed conference, and had appointed

Mr. White
Mr. Burke and
Mr. Jackson Managers on their part[138]—

And he withdrew.[139]

The Senate proceeded to the FIRST reading of the Bill, entitled, "An Act providing for the Payment of the Invalid Pensioners of the United States."

ORDERED, That this Bill be committed to

Mr. Read
Mr. Butler
Mr. King
Mr. Ellsworth and
Mr. Morris[140]

ORDERED, That   Mr. Wingate
Mr. Dalton and
Mr. Henry be the Committee to ascertain the attend-
ance and travelling expenses of the Members of the Senate.

The Senate proceeded to the SECOND reading of the Bill, entitled, "An Act to recognize and adapt to the Constitution of the United States, the Establishment of the Troops raised under the Resolves of the United States in Congress assembled, and for other Purposes therein mentioned."

ORDERED, That this Bill be committed to

Mr. Read
Mr. Butler
Mr. King
Mr. Ellsworth and
Mr. Morris[141]

The Senate proceeded to the THIRD reading of the Bill, entitled, "An Act for amending part of an Act, entitled, an Act to regulate the collection of the Duties imposed by Law on the Tonnage of Ships and Vessels, and on Goods, Wares, and Merchandizes, imported into the United States."

ORDERED, That this Bill be committed to

---

[138] A copy of the Senate order and of the message following it from the House is in Engrossed Senate Bills and Resolutions, Senate Records, DNA.

[139] The conference committee on this bill reported on September 28 and a resolution was made and accepted on the House amendments. The House voted to withdraw its adherence to the first amendment and agreed to the Senate resolution on the same date. This enrolled bill, signed by the Speaker, was then brought to the Senate for the Vice President's signature and sent to the President.

[140] On September 28 this committee reported and the bill was given second and third readings and passed. On the same date this enrolled bill was signed by both the Speaker and the Vice President and sent to the President.

[141] On September 28 this committee reported. The bill was then read for the third time, passed with amendments, and sent to the House for concurrence.

Mr. Read

Mr. Morris and

Mr. Dalton[142]

The Senate proceeded to the SECOND reading of the Bill, entitled, "An Act to explain and amend an Act, entitled, an Act for registering and clearing Vessels, regulating the Coasting Trade, and for other Purposes."

ORDERED, That this Bill be committed to

Mr. Read

Mr. Morris and

Mr. Dalton[143]

The Senate proceeded to consider the Resolve of the House of Representatives, of the 25th instant, to wit:

"In the House of Representatives of the United States

"September 25th, 1789

"RESOLVED, That a joint Committee of both Houses be appointed to wait on the President of the United States, to request that he would recommend to the People of the United States, a day of Public Thanksgiving and Prayer to be observed, by acknowledging with grateful hearts, the many and signal favors of ALMIGHTY GOD, especially by affording them an opportunity peaceably to establish a Constitution of Government for their safety and happiness.

"ORDERED, That Mr. Boudinot, Mr. Sherman, and Mr. Sylvester be appointed to the said Committee on the part of this House."

RESOLVED, That the Senate do concur in the above recited Resolution, and that   Mr. Johnson and

Mr. Izard, be the Committee on the part of the Senate.

ORDERED, That the Secretary do carry a Message to the House of Representatives accordingly.[144]

RESOLVED, That   Mr. Johnson and

Mr. Izard, be a Committee on the part of the Senate, together with such Committee as may be appointed on the part of the House of Representatives, to wait on the President of the United States, and acquaint him that Congress have agreed upon a recess on the 29th instant.[145]

---

[142] On September 28 this committee reported and the Senate voted not to pass this act.

[143] On September 28 this committee reported an amendment to the bill. The bill was then read a third time and passed with the amendment. On the same date the House agreed to this amendment and notified the Senate. The bill was then signed by both the Speaker and the Vice President and sent to the President.

[144] On September 28 the joint committee reported that it had laid this resolution before the President.

[145] The Senate resolve and the House resolve are in Senate Joint and Concurrent Resolutions, Senate Records, DNA.

ORDERED, That the Secretary do carry a Message to the House of Representatives, and request concurrence.[146]

The Senate proceeded to consider the Resolve of the House of Representatives of the 24th instant, to wit:

"In the HOUSE OF REPRESENTATIVES
"Thursday the 24th September, 1789

"RESOLVED, By the Senate and House of Representatives of the United States of America in Congress assembled, That the President of the United States be requested to transmit to the executives of the United States, which have ratified the Constitution, copies of the Amendments proposed by Congress, to be added thereto; and like copies to the executives of the States of Rhode-Island and North-Carolina."[147]

RESOLVED, That the Senate do concur in this Resolution.[148]

ORDERED, That the Secretary do carry a Message to the House of Representatives accordingly.

The Senate proceeded to consider the Resolve of the House of Representatives of the 25th instant, to wit:

"In the House of Representatives of the United States
"Friday, the 25th of September, 1789

"Upon the report of a Committee, to whom was referred, the memorial of John White, in behalf of himself, John Wright and Joshua Dawson—

"RESOLVED, That John White, late a Commissioner to settle the accounts between the United States, and the States of Pennsylvania, Delaware and Maryland, and his Clerks, John Wright and Joshua Dawson, be considered as in office until the Thirteenth of September, 1788, and be paid accordingly."

ORDERED, That the consideration hereof be postponed.[149]

The Senate adjourned until 11 o'clock on Monday morning.

MONDAY, SEPTEMBER 28, 1789

The SENATE assembled,
Present as on Saturday,
And proceeded to the SECOND reading of the Bill, entitled, "An Act to

---

[146] On September 28 the House concurred with this resolution and appointed a committee to join this committee.

[147] The smooth journal inserts the text of the amendments at this point. The printed journal runs them separately as the final page of the first session proceedings (see pages 208–10).

[148] The Senate and House resolves are in House Joint and Concurrent Resolutions, Senate Records, DNA.

[149] On September 29 the Senate amended and passed this resolve and returned it to the House. The Speaker, the Vice President, and the President signed this bill on the same date.

allow the Baron de Glaubeck the Pay of a Captain in the Army of the United States."

ORDERED, That this Bill have the THIRD reading to-morrow.[150]

A Message from the House of Representatives—

Mr. Beckley, their Clerk, informed the Senate, that the House had concurred in the appointment of a Committee on their part, "To wait on the President of the United States, and to acquaint him of the intended recess of Congress, on the 29th instant, and that

> Mr. Vining
> Mr. Lee and
> Mr. Gilman, were joined"[151]—

And he withdrew.

Mr. Read, on behalf of the Committee appointed on the Bill, entitled, "An Act to explain and amend an Act, entitled, an Act for registering and clearing of Vessels, regulating the Coasting Trade, and for other Purposes," reported the following Amendment, to wit:[152]

"And be it further enacted, That so much of an Act, entitled, 'An Act to regulate the Collection of the Duties imposed by Law on the Tonnage of Ships or Vessels, and on Goods, Wares and Merchandizes, imported into the United States,' as hath rated the rouble of Russia at one hundred cents, be, and the same is hereby repealed and made null and void."

ORDERED, That the report of the Committee be postponed to take up the Bill.

The Senate proceeded in the THIRD reading of the last recited Bill.

RESOLVED, That this Bill do pass, with the Amendment reported by the Committee.

ORDERED, That the Secretary do carry the Bill to the House of Representatives, and request concurrence in the Amendment.

Mr. Read, on behalf of the Committee appointed on the Bill, entitled, "An Act for amending Part of an Act, entitled, an Act to regulate the Collection of the Duties imposed by Law on the Tonnage of Ships or Vessels, and on Goods, Wares, and Merchandizes imported into the United States," reported non-concurrence[153]—

Whereupon,

RESOLVED, That this Bill do not pass.[154]

---

[150] On September 29 this bill was read a third time and passed. It was then sent to the House which passed it without amendment on the same day. Then the bill was signed by the Speaker, the Vice President, and the President.

[151] The concurrence and the appointment to committee are in Senate Joint and Concurrent Resolutions, Senate Records, DNA. This joint committee reported on September 28.

[152] The report is in Various Select Committee Reports, Senate Records, DNA.

[153] The report is in Various Select Committee Reports, Senate Records, DNA.

[154] A statement of nonconcurrence, included with the bill as it passed the House, is in Engrossed House Bills, House Records, DNA.

Mr. Read, on behalf of the Committee on the Bill, entitled, "An Act to recognize and adapt to the Constitution of the United States, the Establishment of the Troops raised under the Resolves of the United States in Congress assembled, and for other Purposes therein mentioned," reported Amendments.[155]

ORDERED, That the report be postponed to take up the Bill—

Proceeded in the THIRD reading of the Bill—

RESOLVED, That this Bill do pass, with the Amendments reported by the Committee.

ORDERED, That the Secretary do carry a Message to the House of Representatives, and request concurrence in the Amendments.[156]

Mr. Read, in behalf of the Committee appointed on the Bill, entitled, "An Act providing for the Payment of the Invalid Pensioners of the United States," reported concurrence.

ORDERED, That this Bill be now read the SECOND time.

ORDERED, That the rules be so far dispensed with as that this Bill have a THIRD reading at this time.

RESOLVED, That this Bill do pass.

ORDERED, That the Secretary do carry a Message to the House of Representatives accordingly.

The managers appointed on the part of the Senate, to confer on the subject of the disagreement of the two Houses, on the first Amendment proposed by the House of Representatives to the Bill, entitled, "An Act to regulate

---

[155] The report has not been located. The smooth journal reads:

reported the following Amendments, to wit:

1st   In Section 1. Line 4 next after the word "except" insert as follows, "as to the mode of appointing the Officers and also"

2nd   Strike out the whole of Section 2.

3rd   Strike out the whole of Section 4.

4th   In Section 5. Line 2nd and 3rd add the Letter /s/ to the words, "Oath—Affirmation."

5th   In same Section, last line, strike out the words "by him."

6th   Section 7th lines 2nd and 3rd strike out the words "first day of January which shall be in the year of our Lord one thousand seven hundred and ninety four" and insert instead thereof "End of the next session of Congress."

7th   Strike out the two last Sections 8 and 9—and insert the following between Sections 6. and 7. of the Bill—"AND BE IT FURTHER ENACTED, That for the purpose of protecting the inhabitants of the Frontiers of the United States from the hostile incursions of the Indians. The President is hereby authorised to call into service from time to time such part of the militia of the States respectively as he may judge necessary for the purposes aforesaid and that their pay and subsistence while in service be the same as the pay and subsistence of the Troops above mentioned."

[156] On September 28 the House agreed to all the Senate amendments to this bill except one and notified the Senate the next day. The Senate insisted on this amendment and the House receded from its disagreement. On the same day—September 29—this bill was signed by the Speaker, the Vice President, and the President.

Processes in the Courts of the United States," reported, that they could not agree on[157] a Report—

And on motion, To adopt the following resolution, to wit:

"That the Senate do agree to the first Amendment proposed by the House of Representatives, with an Amendment, by striking out after the word 'Issuing,' in the 3d and 4th lines of the first section, the following words, 'Out of any of the Courts of the United States of America, shall be in the name of the President of the United States of America, and if they issue'—

"And by inserting after the word 'Executions,' in the 2d line of the second section, the words, 'Except their style' "[158]—

It passed in the Negative.

On motion, That the Senate do recede from the first Amendment—

It passed in the Negative.

On motion, That the Senate do adhere to the first Amendment—

A motion was made to postpone THIS in order to reconsider the FIRST proposition, and

It passed in the Affirmative.

And on motion, To adopt the proposed Amendment to the first Amendment made by the House of Representatives on the Bill—

It passed in the Affirmative.

ORDERED, That the Secretary do carry a Message to the House of Representatives accordingly.

A Message from the House of Representatives—

Mr. Beckley, their Clerk, brought up the Bill, entitled, "An Act for establishing a permanent Seat of Government"—And informed the Senate, that the House had concurred in the Amendments thereto, with the following Amendment—"And provided that nothing herein contained shall be construed to affect the operation of the laws of Pennsylvania, within the district ceded and accepted, until Congress shall otherwise provide by law"[159]—

And he withdrew.

Mr. Read, on behalf of the Committee appointed to consider the Bill, entitled, "An Act making Appropriations for the Service of the present Year," reported Amendments.[160]

---

[157] "Upon" is substituted for "on" in smooth journal.

[158] The report and resolution are in Engrossed Senate Bills and Resolutions, Senate Records, DNA.

[159] The House amendment and concurrence are in Engrossed House Bills, House Records, DNA.

[160] The report has not been located. The smooth journal reads:

reported the following Amendments, to wit:

1 . . . In line 4th Strike out the words "the sum of," and insert in their stead "A sum not exceeding."

2 . . . In line 5th Strike out the words "eight thousand six hundred and seventy six

ORDERED, That the report of the Committee be postponed, and that this Bill have the THIRD reading at this time.

RESOLVED, That this Bill do pass with the Amendments reported by the Committee.

ORDERED, That the Secretary do carry the said Bill to the House of Representatives, and request concurrence in the Amendments.

A Message from the House of Representatives—

Mr. Beckley, their Clerk, informed the Senate, that the House of Representatives had agreed to the Amendment on the Amendment to a Bill, entitled, "An Act to regulate Processes in the Courts of the United States"[161]—

Also, to the Amendments on the Bill, entitled, "An Act to explain and amend an Act, entitled, an Act for registering and clearing Vessels, regulating the Coasting Trade, and for other Purposes"—

Also, in the Amendments proposed to the Bill, entitled, "An Act making Appropriations for the Service of the present Year"—

And he withdrew.

Mr. Wingate, on behalf of the Committee of enrolment reported, that they had examined the following enroled Bills, and had found them correct, to wit:

The Bill, entitled, "An Act making Appropriations for the Service of the present Year"[162]—

The Bill, entitled, "An Act providing for the Payment of the Invalid Pensioners of the United States"[163]—

The Bill, entitled, "An Act to explain and amend an Act, entitled, an Act

---

dollars and eleven cents towards" and insert in their stead "sixteen thousand dollars for."

3 . . . In line 6th next after the words "Civil List," insert the words "under the late and present Government," then in the same line strike out the words "the sum of" and insert in their stead "A sum not exceeding."

4 . . . In same line b, and in line 7. strike out the words "five hundred and three dollars and thirty two cents towards" and insert in their stead "Dollars for."

5 . . . In line 7. Strike out the words "the sum of," and in their stead insert "A sum not exceeding."

6 . . . In line 8th Strike out the words "Eighty nine thousand nine hundred and six dollars and thirty eight cents towards" and insert in their stead "Ninety thousand dollars for."

7 . . . In line 9. Strike out the words "the sum of" and insert in their stead "A sum not exceeding."

8 . . . In line 10. Strike out the words "and seventeen dollars and eighty one cents towards" and insert in their stead the words "Dollars for."

9 . . . Strike out the whole of the last enacting Clause as contained in lines 11, 12, and 13.

[161] A copy of the House resolve is in Engrossed Senate Bills and Resolutions, Senate Records, DNA.

[162] The inspected enrolled bill is in Enrolled Acts, RG 11, DNA. E–45701.

[163] The inspected enrolled bill is in Enrolled Acts, RG 11, DNA. A printed copy of the bill, including an explanation by Henry Knox, is in the Broadside Collection, RBkRm, DLC. E–22197, E–45704.

for registering and clearing Vessels, regulating the Coasting Trade, and for other Purposes"[164]—

The Bill, entitled, "An Act to alter the Time for the next Meeting of Congress"[165]—

And the Bill, entitled, "An Act to regulate Processes in the Courts of the United States."[166]

A Message from the House of Representatives—

Mr. Beckley, their Clerk, brought up the above recited enroled Bills, and acquainted the Senate, that they were signed by the Speaker of the House of Representatives—

And he withdrew.

Whereupon the Vice President affixed his signature to the aforesaid enroled Bills, and they were by the Committee laid before the President of the United States for his approbation.[167]

Mr. Johnson, on behalf of the Committee appointed on the 26th instant, reported, that they had waited on the President of the United States, and informed him of the intended recess of Congress on the 29th instant[168]—

Also, that the Committee appointed for the purpose, had laid before the President of the United States, the Resolve of the two Houses, "Requesting him to recommend a day of Thanksgiving and Prayer, to the People of the United States."

The Senate proceeded to the consideration of the Amendment proposed by the House of Representatives to the Amendment of the Senate, on the Bill, entitled, "An Act to establish the Seat of Government of the United States."

On motion, That the farther consideration of this Bill be postponed to the next session of Congress[169]—

It passed in the Affirmative.

The Senate adjourned to 10 o'clock to-morrow.

TUESDAY, September 29, 1789

The SENATE assembled,
Present as yesterday.

The Committee of enrolment reported, that they had laid before the President of the United States,

The Bill, entitled, "An Act making Appropriation for the Service of the present Year"—

---

[164] The inspected enrolled bill is in Enrolled Acts, RG 11, DNA. E–45709.
[165] The inspected enrolled bill is in Enrolled Acts, RG 11, DNA. E–45706.
[166] The inspected enrolled bill is in Enrolled Acts, RG 11, DNA. E–45714.
[167] On September 29 the President signed all these bills.
[168] On September 29 Congress adjourned.
[169] On May 31, 1790, a new Residence Bill was introduced in the Senate.

The Bill, entitled, "An Act providing for the Payment of the Invalid Pensioners of the United States"—

The Bill, entitled, "An Act to explain and amend an Act, entitled, an Act for registering and clearing Vessels, regulating the Coasting Trade, and for other Purposes"—

The Bill, entitled, "An Act to alter the Time for the next Meeting of Congress"—And,

The Bill, entitled, "An Act to regulate Processes in the Courts of the United States."

A Message from the President of the United States—

The Honorable Mr. Jay delivered the following communications to the Vice President—

And he withdrew.

United States, September 29, 1789

Gentlemen of the Senate

HIS most Christian Majesty, by a letter dated the 7th of June last, addressed to the President and members of the General Congress of the United States of North-America, announces the much lamented death of his Son, the Dauphin. The generous conduct of the French Monarch and nation towards this country, renders every event that may affect his or their prosperity interesting to us; and I shall take care to assure him of the sensibility with which the United States participate in the affliction which a loss so much to be regretted, must have occasioned both to him and to them.

GEO. WASHINGTON[170]

United States, September 29, 1789

Gentlemen of the Senate

HAVING been yesterday informed by a joint Committee of both Houses of Congress, that they had agreed to a recess to commence this day, and to continue until the first Monday of January next, I take the earliest opportunity of acquainting you that, considering how long and laborious this session has been, and the reasons which, I presume, have produced this Resolution, it does not appear to me expedient to recommend any measures to their consideration at present—or now to call your attention, Gentlemen, to any of those matters in my department, which require your advice and consent, and yet remain to be dispatched.

GEO. WASHINGTON[171]

---

[170] The message is in President's Messages: Suggesting legislation, Senate Records, DNA.
[171] The message is in President's Messages: Suggesting legislation, Senate Records, DNA.

A Message from the House of Representatives—

Mr. Beckley, their Clerk, informed the Senate, that the House had concurred in all the Amendments to the Bill, entitled, "An Act to recognize and adapt to the Constitution of the United States the Establishment of the Troops raised under the Resolves of the United States, in Congress assembled, and for other Purposes therein mentioned," except the 7th, to which they had disagreed—

And he withdrew.

A Message from the President of the United States—

Mr. Lear, his Secretary, informed the Senate, that the President of the United States had approved of and affixed his signature to the Bill, entitled, "An Act to regulate Processes in the Courts of the United States," and returned it to the Senate—

And he withdrew.

The Senate proceeded to consider their 7th Amendment, disagreed to by the House of Representatives, on the Bill, entitled, "An Act to recognize and adapt to the Constitution of the United States, the Establishment of the Troops raised under the Resolves of the United States in Congress assembled, and for other Purposes therein mentioned"—And

RESOLVED, To insist on the said 7th Amendment.

ORDERED, That the Secretary do acquaint the House of Representatives herewith.[172]

A Message from the House of Representatives—

Mr. Beckley, their Clerk, informed the Senate that the President of the United States had approved of, and affixed his signature to "An Act making Appropriations for the Service of the present Year"—

To "An Act providing for the Payment of the Invalid Pensioners of the United States"—

To "An Act to explain and amend an Act, entitled, an Act for registering and clearing Vessels, regulating the Coasting Trade, and for other Purposes"—

To "An Act to alter the Time of the next Meeting of Congress"—and had returned them to the House of Representatives:

And he withdrew.

The Senate proceeded to consider the Resolve of the House of Representatives, of the 25th instant, on the petition of John White, John Wright, and Joshua Dawson, postponed on the 26th.

RESOLVED, That the Senate do concur herein with the following Amendments in the two last lines, to wit:

To strike out "Thirteenth," and insert "Fourth:"

---

[172] The smooth journal inserts the following at this point: "ORDERED, That the Schedule of Compensation to the members amounting to twenty five thousand Nine hundred and ninety seven dollars, be sent to the Treasury."

To strike out "September 1788," and insert "February, 1789"—And to strike out the words "And be paid accordingly."

The Senate proceeded to the THIRD reading of the Bill, entitled, "An Act to allow the Baron de Glaubeck, the Pay of a Captain in the Army of the United States."

RESOLVED, That this Bill do pass.[173]

ORDERED, That the Secretary do carry the said Bill to the House of Representatives, and request their concurrence.

A Message from the House of Representatives—

Mr. Beckley, their Clerk, informed the Senate, that the House of Representatives had passed the following Resolve, to which the concurrence of the Senate was requested.

"In the House of Representatives of the United States

"Tuesday, the 29th September, 1789

"ORDERED, That it shall be the duty of the Secretary of the Senate, and Clerk of the House, at the end of each session, to send a printed copy of the Journals thereof respectively, to the Supreme Executives, and to each branch of the Legislature of every State"[174]—

He also informed the Senate, that the House of Representatives had receded from their disagreement to the 7th Amendment of the Senate to a Bill, entitled, "An Act to recognize and adapt to the Constitution of the United States, the Establishment of the Troops raised under the Resolves of the United States in Congress assembled, and for other Purposes therein mentioned"—And that the House had passed the Bill, entitled, "An Act to allow the Baron de Glaubeck, the Pay of a Captain in the Army of the United States"—

And he withdrew.

The Senate proceeded to consider the last recited order of the House of Representatives—

RESOLVED, That the Senate do concur therein.

ORDERED, That the Secretary do carry a Message to the House of Representatives accordingly.

The Committee of enrolment reported, that they had examined, and had found correct, the following enroled Bills and Resolve:

A Bill, entitled, "An Act to recognize and adapt to the Constitution of the United States, the Establishment of the Troops raised under the Resolves of the United States in Congress assembled, and for other Purposes therein mentioned"[175]—

---

[173] The engrossed resolve and the concurrence of the House are in Engrossed Senate Bills and Resolutions, Senate Records, DNA.

[174] This House message containing their resolve has not been located.

[175] The inspected enrolled bill is in Enrolled Acts, RG 11, DNA. E–45712.

A Resolve for continuing "John White, John Wright, and Joshua Dawson in office, until the 4th of February, 1789"[176]—

And a Bill, entitled, "An Act to allow the Baron de Glaubeck, the Pay of a Captain in the Army of the United States."[177]

A Message from the House of Representatives—

Mr. Beckley, their Clerk, brought up the last recited enroled Bills and Resolve, and informed the Senate, that the Speaker had affixed his signature thereto—

He also informed the Senate, that the House of Representatives had finished the business of the Session, and were ready to adjourn agreeably to the order of the two Houses of Congress—

And he withdrew.

Whereupon the Vice President affixed his signature to the last mentioned enroled Bills and Resolve, and they were delivered to the Committee to be laid before the President of the United States—

The Chairman of the Committee of enrolment reported, that they had laid the said Bills and Resolve before the President of the United States for his approbation.[178]

A Message from the President of the United States—

Mr. Lear, his Secretary, informed the Senate, that the President of the United States had approved of, and had affixed his signature to the Act, entitled, "An Act to allow the Baron de Glaubeck the Pay of a Captain in the Army of the United States," and had returned it to the Senate—

And he withdrew.

"The Act to recognize and adapt to the Constitution of the United States, the Establishment of the Troops raised under the Resolves of the United States in Congress assembled, and for other Purposes therein mentioned"—And

The Resolve, for continuing "John White, John Wright, and Joshua Dawson, in office, until the 4th of February, 1789," were by the President of the United States approved of, signed, and returned to the House of Representatives.

Agreeably to the Resolve of the two Houses of Congress, of the 26th instant, the Vice President did adjourn the Senate, to the first Monday in January next, "Then to meet at the City-Hall, in New-York."

Attest.

SAMUEL A. OTIS, Secretary[179]

---

[176] The inspected enrolled resolve is in Enrolled Acts, RG 11, DNA. E–45720.

[177] The inspected enrolled bill is in Enrolled Acts, RG 11, DNA. E–45705.

[178] The smooth journal inserts the following at this point: "ORDERED, that the Door-Keeper of the Senate be directed to take charge of the apartments of the Senate during the adjournment; That he lay in a sufficiency of Fuel, and have Stoves so placed as to give warmth to the Room."

[179] The smooth journal gives the signature as "Sam. A. Otis."

APPENDIX TO THE FIRST SESSION

*The Conventions of a Number of the States having, at the Time of their
adopting the Constitution, expressed a Desire, in order to prevent misconstruction or abuse of its Powers, that further declaratory and restrictive Clauses should be added: And as extending the Ground of public
Confidence in the Government, will best insure the beneficent Ends of its
Institution—*

RESOLVED, by the Senate and House of Representatives of the United
States of America in Congress assembled, two thirds of both Houses concurring, That the following Articles be proposed to the Legislatures of the
several States, as Amendments to the Constitution of the United States, all or
any of which Articles, when ratified by three fourths of the said Legislatures,
to be valid to all intents and purposes, as part of the said Constitution—Viz.

Articles in addition to, and amendment of, the Constitution of the United
States of America, proposed by Congress, and ratified by the Legislatures of
the several States, pursuant to the fifth Article of the original Constitution.

ARTICLE THE FIRST

After the first enumeration, required by the first Article of the Constitution,
there shall be one Representative for every thirty thousand, until the number
shall amount to one hundred; after which the proportion shall be so regulated
by Congress, that there shall be not less than one hundred Representatives, nor
less than one Representative for every forty thousand persons, until the number of Representatives shall amount to two hundred; after which the proportion shall be so regulated by Congress, that there shall not be less than two
hundred Representatives, nor more than one Representative for every fifty
thousand persons.

ARTICLE THE SECOND

No law, varying the compensation for the services of the Senators and Representatives, shall take effect, until an election of Representatives shall have
intervened.

ARTICLE THE THIRD

Congress shall make no law respecting an establishment of religion, or prohibiting the free exercise thereof, or abridging the freedom of speech, or of
the press, or the right of the people peaceably to assemble, and to petition the
Government for a redress of grievances.

ARTICLE THE FOURTH

A well regulated militia, being necessary to the security of a free State, the right of the people to keep and bear arms, shall not be infringed.

ARTICLE THE FIFTH

No soldier shall, in time of peace, be quartered in any house, without the consent of the owner, nor in time of war, but in a manner to be prescribed by law.

ARTICLE THE SIXTH

The right of the people to be secure in their persons, houses, papers, and effects, against unreasonable searches and seizures, shall not be violated, and no warrants shall issue, but upon probable cause, supported by oath or affirmation, and particularly describing the place to be searched, and the persons or things to be seized.

ARTICLE THE SEVENTH

No person shall be held to answer for a capital, or otherwise infamous crime, unless on a presentment or indictment of a Grand Jury, except in cases arising in the land or naval forces, or in the militia, when in actual service in time of war or public danger; nor shall any person be subject for the same offence to be twice put in jeopardy of life or limb; nor shall be compelled in any criminal case, to be a witness against himself, nor be deprived of life, liberty or property, without due process of law; nor shall private property be taken for public use without just compensation.

ARTICLE THE EIGHTH

In all criminal prosecutions the accused shall enjoy the right to a speedy and public trial by an impartial Jury of the State and District wherein the crime shall have been committed, which District shall have been previously ascertained by law; and to be informed of the nature and cause of the accusation, to be confronted with the witnesses against him, to have compulsory process for obtaining witnesses in his favor, and to have the assistance of counsel for his defence.

ARTICLE THE NINTH

In suits at common law, where the value in controversy shall exceed twenty dollars, the right of trial by Jury shall be preserved, and no fact, tried by a Jury, shall be otherwise re-examined in any court of the United States, than according to the rules of the common law.

ARTICLE the TENTH

Excessive bail shall not be required, nor excessive fines imposed, nor cruel and unusual punishments inflicted.

ARTICLE the ELEVENTH

The enumeration in the Constitution, of certain rights, shall not be construed to deny or disparage others retained by the people.

ARTICLE the TWELFTH

The powers not delegated to the United States by the Constitution, nor prohibited by it to the States, are reserved to the States respectively, or to the people.

FREDERICK AUGUSTUS MUHLENBERG,
SPEAKER OF THE HOUSE OF REPRESENTATIVES
JOHN ADAMS, VICE-PRESIDENT OF THE UNITED
STATES, AND PRESIDENT OF THE SENATE

Attest.

JOHN BECKLEY, *Clerk of the House of Representatives*
SAMUEL A. OTIS, *Secretary of the Senate*[1]

---

[1] The original is on display at the DNA. E–45717. This document appears in the smooth journal under the proceedings of September 26.

J O U R N A L

OF THE SECOND SESSION OF THE

SENATE OF THE UNITED STATES

TO WIT

NEW-HAMPSHIRE

MASSACHUSETTS

CONNECTICUT

NEW-YORK

NEW-JERSEY

PENNSYLVANIA

DELAWARE

MARYLAND

VIRGINIA

NORTH-CAROLINA

SOUTH-CAROLINA

GEORGIA

Being the TWELVE STATES that have respectively ratified the Constitution of Government for the UNITED STATES, proposed by the CONVENTION, held at Philadelphia, on the 17th of September, 1787.

M O N D A Y, JANUARY 4, 1790

THE following members of Senate assembled:[1]

From

New-Hampshire	The Honorable	{ John Langdon and Paine Wingate
Massachusetts	The Honorable	{ Caleb Strong and Tristram Dalton
Connecticut	The Honorable	William S. Johnson
New-York	The Honorable	{ Rufus King and Philip Schuyler
South-Carolina	The Honorable	{ Ralph Izard and Pierce Butler
Georgia	The Honorable	William Few

The number not being sufficient to constitute a quorum, they adjourned until to-morrow at 11 o'clock.

T U E S D A Y, JANUARY 5, 1790

The members of Senate present, as yesterday, and the Honorable John Henry, from the State of Maryland, attended.

The number not being sufficient to constitute a quorum, they adjourned until to-morrow at 11 o'clock.

W E D N E S D A Y, JANUARY 6, 1790

The SENATE assembled,
Present as yesterday,

And the Honorable William Maclay, from the State of Pennsylvania, attended.

ORDERED, That the Secretary inform the House of Representatives, that a quorum of the Senate have assembled, and are ready to proceed to business.[2]

---

[1] The smooth journal reads: "John Adams, Vice President of the United States & the following members of Senate assembled."

[2] Struck out with the marginal notation "A to B expunged by order/Attest Sam: A Otis Sec:" the following material was originally included in the rough journal.

And he accordingly delivered the Message.

A Letter from the President of the United States to the Vice President and President of the Senate was read as followeth, to wit:

"United States January 4th. 1790

"Sir,

"Whenever there shall be [a] sufficient number of the two Houses of Congress assem [led to (?) proceed (?) to] business I request to be informed of it. [*Several*

ORDERED, That   Mr. Strong and

                     Mr. Izard, be a Committee on the part of the Senate, with such Committee as the House of Representatives may appoint on their part, to inform the President of the United States, that a quorum of the two Houses is assembled, and will be ready in the Senate-Chamber, at such time as the President may appoint, to receive any communications he may be pleased to make.[3]

The Senate adjourned to 11 o'clock to-morrow.

THURSDAY, JANUARY 7, 1790

The SENATE assembled,

Present as yesterday,

And the Honorable Oliver Ellsworth, from the State of Connecticut,

And the Honorable William Paterson, from the State of New-Jersey, attended.

A message from the House of Representatives:

"Mr. PRESIDENT,

"A quorum of the House of Representatives have assembled, and are ready to proceed to business."

ORDERED, That the Secretary acquaint the House of Representatives, of the appointment of a Committee on the 6th January, to wait on the President of the United States, and inform him, that a quorum of both Houses of Congress had assembled, and are ready to receive any communications that he may be

---

words illegible] time and place it will be convenient for [*several words illegible*] in order to [*several words illegible*] some [*several words illegible*] at (?) the commencement of their sessio[n].

                                "I have the honor to be,
                                Sir
                                Your most humble servant
                                Go Washington

"The Vice President
   of the United States
      and
President of the Senate"

                Ordered, That Mr. Strong, and

                      Mr. Izard, be a Committee on the part of the Senate, with such Committee as the House of Representatives may appoint on their part, to take into consideration the President's Letter to the Vice-President, of the 4th January —and Report.

The message is in President's Messages: Suggesting legislation, Senate Records, DNA.

[3] This order is in Senate Joint and Concurrent Resolutions, Senate Records, DNA. On January 7 the House passed its own resolution for a joint committee to wait upon the President. On the same day Mr. Strong reported to the Senate for the joint committee.

pleased to make; and that he request the concurrence of the House of Representatives, in the appointment of a Committee on their part.

A message from the House of Representatives:

"Mr. PRESIDENT,

"The House of Representatives have appointed

Mr. Gilman

Mr. Ames and

Mr. Seney, a Committee on their part, to wait on the President of the United States."[4]

A message from the House of Representatives:

"Mr. PRESIDENT,

"The House of Representatives have resolved, That two Chaplains of different denominations be appointed to Congress for the present Session, one by each House, who shall interchange weekly."[5]

Mr. Strong on behalf of the joint Committee, reported to the Senate, that they had waited on the President of the United States, agreeably to the order of both Houses, and that he informed the Committee, that he would meet the two Houses in the Senate-Chamber, to-morrow at 11 o'clock.[6]

The Senate proceeded to consider the Resolve of the House of Representatives of this day, relative to the appointment of Chaplains,—and,

RESOLVED, That the Senate concur therein,—

And that,

The Right Reverend Doctor SAMUEL PROVOOST, be appointed for the present session, on the part of the Senate.[7]

ORDERED, That a message be sent to the House of Representatives accordingly.

The Senate adjourned to half past 10 o'clock to-morrow.

FRIDAY, JANUARY 8, 1790

The SENATE assembled,

Present as yesterday.

ORDERED, That the House of Representatives be informed, that the Senate are ready to meet them in the Senate-Chamber, to receive any communication

---

[4] The House message is in Senate Joint and Concurrent Resolutions, Senate Records, DNA.

[5] The House resolve is in House Joint and Concurrent Resolutions, Senate Records, DNA.

[6] On January 8 the President delivered his State of the Union address and the Senate appointed a committee to reply to this message.

[7] This Senate Resolve is in House Joint and Concurrent Resolutions, Senate Records, DNA.

the President of the United States may be pleased to make to the two Houses of Congress; and that the usual seats will be assigned them.

The House of Representatives having accordingly taken their seats, the President of the United States came into the Senate-Chamber, and addressed both Houses of Congress as followeth:

FELLOW CITIZENS of the SENATE, and
HOUSE of REPRESENTATIVES:

I EMBRACE with great satisfaction the opportunity, which now presents itself, of congratulating you on the present favorable prospects of our public affairs.—That recent accession of the important State of North-Carolina, to the Constitution of the United States (of which official information has been received)—the rising credit and respectability of our country,—the general and increasing good-will towards the Government of the Union,—and the concord, peace and plenty, with which we are blessed, are circumstances, auspicious, in an eminent degree to our national prosperity.

IN resuming your consultations for the general good, you cannot but derive encouragement from the reflection, that the measures of the last Session have been as satisfactory to your Constituents, as the novelty and difficulty of the work allowed you to hope.—Still further to realize their expectations, and to secure the blessings which a gracious Providence has placed within our reach, will in the course of the present important Session, call for the cool and deliberate exertion of your patriotism, firmness and wisdom.

AMONG the many interesting objects which will engage your attention, that of providing for the common defence will merit particular regard. To be prepared for War is one of the most effectual means of preserving Peace.

A FREE people ought not only to be armed but disciplined; to which end a uniform and well digested plan is requisite: And their safety and interest require that they should promote such manufactories, as tend to render them independent on others, for essential, particularly military supplies.

THE proper establishment of the Troops which may be deemed indispensable, will be entitled to mature consideration.—In the arrangements which may be made respecting it, it will be of importance to conciliate the comfortable support of the Officers and Soldiers with a due regard to economy.

THERE was reason to hope, that the pacific measures adopted with regard to certain hostile tribes of Indians, would have relieved the inhabitants of our Southern and Western frontiers from their depredations; but you will perceive from the information contained in the papers which I shall direct to be laid before you (comprehending a communication from the Commonwealth of Virginia) that we ought to be prepared to afford protection to those parts of the Union, and, if necessary, to punish aggressors.

THE interests of the United States require, that our intercourse with other nations should be facilitated by such provisions as will enable me to fulfil my duty in that respect, in the manner, which circumstances may render most conducive to the public good: And to this end, that the compensations to be made to the persons, who may be employed, should according to the nature of their appointments, be defined by law; and a competent fund designated for defraying the expences incident to the conduct of our Foreign affairs.

VARIOUS considerations also render it expedient, that the terms on which Foreigners may be admitted to the rights of Citizens, should be speedily ascertained by a uniform rule of naturalization.

UNIFORMITY in the Currency, Weights and Measures of the United States, is an object of great importance, and will, I am persuaded, be duly attended to.

THE advancement of Agriculture, Commerce and Manufactures, by all proper means, will not, I trust, need recommendation: But I cannot forbear intimating to you the expediency of giving effectual encouragement as well to the introduction of new and useful inventions from abroad, as to the exertions of skill and genius in producing them at home; and of facilitating the intercourse between the distant parts of our Country by a due attention to the Post-Office and Post Roads.

NOR am I less persuaded, that you will agree with me in opinion, that there is nothing which can better deserve your patronage, than the promotion of Science and Literature.—Knowledge is in every country, the surest basis of public happiness.—In one, in which the measures of Government receive their impression so immediately from the sense of the Community as in our's, it is proportionably essential.—To the security of a free Constitution it contributes in various ways: By convincing those who are entrusted with the public administration, that every valuable end of Government is best answered by the enlightened confidence of the people: And by teaching the people themselves to know and to value their own rights; to discern and provide against invasions of them; to distinguish between oppression and the necessary exercise of lawful authority; between burthens proceeding from a disregard to their convenience and those resulting from the inevitable exigencies of Society; to discriminate the spirit of liberty from that of licentiousness, cherishing the first, avoiding the last, and uniting a speedy but temperate vigilance against encroachments, with an inviolable respect to the laws.

WHETHER this desirable object will be best promoted by affording aids to Seminaries of Learning already established,—by the institution of a national University,—or by any other expedients, will be well worthy of a place in the deliberations of the Legislature.

GENTLEMEN of the HOUSE of REPRESENTATIVES,

I SAW with peculiar pleasure, at the close of the last Session, the resolution entered into by you, expressive of your opinion, that an adequate provision for the support of the public Credit is a matter of high importance to the national honor and prosperity. In this sentiment, I entirely concur.—And to a perfect confidence in your best endeavors to devise such a provision, as will be truly consistent with the end, I add an equal reliance on the chearful co-operation of the other branch of the Legislature.—It would be superfluous to specify inducements to a measure in which the character and permanent interests of the United States are so obviously and so deeply concerned; and which has received so explicit a sanction from your declaration.

GENTLEMEN of the SENATE, and
    HOUSE of REPRESENTATIVES,

I HAVE directed the proper Officers to lay before you respectively such papers and estimates as regard the affairs particularly recommended to your consideration, and necessary to convey to you that information of the State of the Union, which it is my duty to afford.

THE welfare of our Country is the great object to which our cares and efforts ought to be directed.—And I shall derive great satisfaction from a co-operation with you, in the pleasing though arduous task, of ensuring to our Fellow Citizens the blessings which they have a right to expect, from a free, efficient and equal Government.

G. WASHINGTON

UNITED STATES ⎫
January 8, 1790[8] ⎭

The President of the United States having retired, and the two Houses being separated,—

ORDERED, That   Mr. King
                   Mr. Izard and
                   Mr. Paterson, be a Committee, to prepare and report the draft of an Address to the President of the United States, in answer to his Speech delivered this day to both Houses of Congress, in the Senate-Chamber.[9]

ORDERED, That the Speech of the President of the United States, delivered this day, be printed for the use of the Senate.

The Senate adjourned to Monday next 11 o'clock.

MONDAY, JANUARY 11, 1790

The SENATE assembled,
Present as on Friday.

A message from the President of the United States, by Mr. Lear, his Secretary, was read as followeth:

---

[8] The speech is in President's Messages: Annual reports, Senate Records, DNA.
[9] On January 11 this committee reported and the draft was printed in the Journal.

UNITED STATES, January 11, 1790

GENTLEMEN of the SENATE,

I HAVE directed Mr. Lear, my private Secretary, to lay before you a copy of the adoption and ratification of the Constitution of the United States by the State of North-Carolina, together with the copy of a letter from his Excellency Samuel Johnston, President of the Convention of said State, to the President of the United States.

THE originals of the papers which are herewith transmitted to you, will be lodged in the office of the Secretary of State.

G. WASHINGTON[10]

ORDERED, That the Message from the President of the United States, with the papers accompanying the same, lie on the files of the Senate.

Mr. King, on behalf of the Committee, reported an address to the President of the United States, in answer to his speech to both Houses of Congress, which being amended, was adopted as followeth:

"To the PRESIDENT of the UNITED STATES

"SIR,

W E the Senate of the United States, return you our thanks for your speech delivered to both Houses of Congress. The accession of the State of North-Carolina to the Constitution of the United States, gives us much pleasure; and we offer you our congratulations on that event, which at the same time adds strength to our Union, and affords a proof that the more the Constitution has been considered, the more the goodness of it has appeared.—The information which we have received that the measures of the last session have been as satisfactory to our Constituents as we had reason to expect from the difficulty of the work in which we were engaged, will afford us much consolation, and encouragement in resuming our deliberations in the present session for the public good; and every exertion on our part shall be made to realize, and secure to our Country those blessings which a gracious Providence has placed within her reach.—We are persuaded that one of the most effectual means of preserving Peace, is to be prepared for War; and our attention shall be directed to the objects of common defence, and to the adoption of such plans as shall appear the most likely to prevent our dependence on other Countries for essential supplies.—In the arrangements to be made respecting the establishment of such Troops as may be deemed indispensable, we shall with pleasure provide for the comfortable support of the officers, and soldiers, with a due regard to economy.—We regret that the pacific measures adopted by Government with regard to certain hostile tribes of Indians, have not been attended

---

10 The ratification papers, including George Washington's letter and related documents, are in President's Messages: Suggesting legislation, Senate Records, DNA.

with the beneficial effects towards the inhabitants of our Southern and Western frontiers, which we had reason to hope; and we shall chearfully co-operate in providing the most effectual means for their protection; and if necessary, for the punishment of aggressors.—The uniformity of the currency, and of weights and measures, the introduction of new, and useful inventions from abroad, and the exertions of skill, and genius in producing them at home, the facilitating the communication between the distant parts of our country by means of the Post-Office, and Post Roads, a provision for the support of the department of foreign affairs, and a uniform rule of naturalization, by which Foreigners may be admitted to the rights of Citizens, are objects which shall receive such early attention as their respective importance requires.—Literature and Science are essential to the preservation of a free Constitution: The measures of Government should therefore be calculated to strengthen the confidence that is due to that important truth.—Agriculture, Commerce and Manufactures forming the basis of the wealth, and strength of our confederated Republic, must be the frequent subject of our deliberation; and shall be advanced by all proper means in our power.[11]—Public credit being an object of great importance, we shall chearfully co-operate in all proper measures for its support.—Proper attention shall be given to such papers and estimates as you may be pleased to lay before us.—Our cares and efforts shall be directed to the welfare of our Country; and we have the most perfect dependence upon your co-operating with us on all occasions in such measures as will insure to our fellow citizens, the blessings which they have a right to expect from a free, efficient, and equal government."[12]

The Senate adjourned to 11 o'clock to-morrow.

TUESDAY, JANUARY 12, 1790

The SENATE assembled,
Present as yesterday.

A message from the President of the United States, was received by the Secretary at War:[13]

---

[11] The rough journal includes the following canceled passage: "We are convinced that the continued prosperity of every Nation must depend upon the integrity, and justice of [its adminis]tration and are strongly impressed [by the necessity of (?)] making suitable provision for the support [of the public credit; (?)] and will with the greatest satisfaction [cooperate in the (?)] attainment of so admirable an object."

[12] The smooth journal inserts the following signature: "John Adams, Vice President of the United States and President of the Senate." This report is in Various Select Committee Reports, Senate Records, DNA. On January 12 it was ordered that the Vice President, accompanied by the entire Senate, deliver this address and a time was agreed upon by the President and the Senate.

[13] The reference to the Secretary at War is an error. Actually the document following is a covering letter from President Washington for a report prepared by the Secretary of War.

UNITED STATES, January 12, 1790

GENTLEMEN of the SENATE, and
HOUSE of REPRESENTATIVES,

I LAY before you a statement of the south western frontiers, and of the indian Department, which have been submitted to me by the Secretary for the Department of War.

I CONCEIVE that an unreserved, but CONFIDENTIAL communication of all the papers relative to the recent negociations with some of the Southern tribes of Indians, is indispensably requisite for the information of Congress. I am persuaded that they will effectually prevent either transcripts or publications of all such circumstances as might be injurious to the public interests.

G. WASHINGTON[14]

ORDERED, That the message from the President of the United States, together with the papers accompanying the same, lie for consideration.[15]

ORDERED, That the address to the President of the United States, in answer to his Speech, be presented by the Vice President, attended by the Senate, and that the Committee which reported the address, wait on the President, and desire to be informed at what time and place, he will receive the same.

Mr. King, in behalf of the Committee, reported, that it would be agreeable to the President to receive the address of the Senate, in answer to his Speech, on Thursday next at 11 o'clock, at his own House.[16]

The Senate adjourned to 11 o'clock to-morrow.

WEDNESDAY, JANUARY 13, 1790

The SENATE assembled,
Present as yesterday,

And,

The Honorable Jonathan Elmer, from the State of New-Jersey, attended.

The Honorable Benjamin Hawkins, from the State of North-Carolina, appeared, produced his credentials[17] and took his seat in the Senate.

The Vice President administered the oath to Mr. Hawkins.

The Senate adjourned to half past 10 o'clock to-morrow morning.

---

[14] This message and the statements from the Secretary of War are in President's Messages: Annual reports, Senate Records, DNA.

[15] On March 26 and 29 the House passed bills related to this message and notified the Senate. On the twenty-sixth, the Senate read the Military Establishment Bill the first time and scheduled the second reading. On March 29 the second bill was read a first time and the second reading was scheduled.

[16] On January 14 the Vice President delivered this address and the President replied.

[17] The credentials are in Election Records: Credentials of Senators, Senate Records, DNA.

THURSDAY, JANUARY 14, 1790

The SENATE assembled,
Present as yesterday.

Agreeably to the order of the 12th instant, the Senate waited on the President of the United States, at his own house, where, the Vice President in their name, delivered to the President of the United States, the address agreed to on the 11th instant,—

To which the President of the United States was pleased to make the following reply:

GENTLEMEN,

I THANK you for your address, and for the assurances which it contains, of attention to the several matters suggested by me to your consideration.

RELYING on the continuance of your exertions for the public good, I anticipate for our Country the salutary effects of upright and prudent Counsels.

G. WASHINGTON[18]

The Senate having returned to the Senate-Chamber, adjourned to 11 o'clock to-morrow.

FRIDAY, JANUARY 15, 1790

The SENATE assembled,
Present as yesterday.

The petition of William Montgomery and Abraham Owen,[19] relative to improvements on doctor Barker's mills, "And certain plans and specifications thereof, by James Rumsey," was read, and ordered to lie on file.[20]

ORDERED, That   Mr. Ellsworth
                   Mr. Hawkins and
                   Mr. Paterson, be a Committee to bring in a bill in addition to "An act to establish the judicial courts of the United States."[21]

The Senate adjourned to 11 o'clock on Monday morning.

MONDAY, JANUARY 18, 1790

The SENATE assembled,
Present as on the 15th;

And, the Honorable Richard Bassett, from the State of Delaware, attended.

A letter was read from Gerard Bancker, the treasurer of the State of New-

---

[18] This message is in President's Messages: Annual reports, Senate Records, DNA.

[19] This petition has not been located.

[20] On June 17 this petition was referred to the Secretary of State.

[21] On March 26 a petition from the citizens of New Hampshire was referred to this committee.

York, presenting on behalf of the Legislature, a copy of the revised laws of that State.[22]

ORDERED, That this letter lie for consideration.

A letter from Gaetan Drago di Domco.[23] proposing the plan of a truce between the United States and the regencies of Algiers and Tunis, was read,—

ORDERED, That this letter do lie on the files of the Senate.[24]

The Senate adjourned to 11 o'clock to-morrow morning.

T U E S D A Y, JANUARY 19, 1790

The SENATE assembled,

Present as yesterday.

On motion, That a Committee be appointed to report "A Bill defining the crimes and offences that shall be cognizable under the authority of the United States, and their punishment,"—

A motion was made for postponement,—and

It passed in the Affirmative.[25]

ORDERED, That   Mr. Strong

Mr. King

Mr. Johnson

Mr. Ellsworth and

Mr. Henry, be a Committee to report "A Bill to regulate processes in the courts of the United States."[26]

The Senate adjourned to 11 o'clock to-morrow.

W E D N E S D A Y, JANUARY 20, 1790

The SENATE assembled,

Present as yesterday.

On motion, To resume the consideration of the motion made yesterday, to wit:

"That a Committee be appointed to report a Bill, defining the crimes and offences that shall be cognizable under the authority of the United States, and their punishment,"—

A motion was made farther to postpone the consideration hereof,—and,

It passed in the Affirmative.[27]

---

[22] This letter is in Reports and Communications, Senate Records, DNA.

[23] The letter by Gaetan Drago de Dominico is printed on page 227, note 40 below.

[24] In the rough journal this phrase was corrected to read: "Ordered that this Letter lie for consideration." On January 26 this letter was read and sent to the House of Representatives.

[25] This motion was considered and again postponed on January 20.

[26] On April 23 this committee reported a bill which was then read for the first time.

[27] On January 26 the committee to prepare a bill on this matter was appointed. On the same day this committee reported a bill and it was read for the first time.

On motion, RESOLVED, That

> Mr. Ellsworth
>
> Mr. Maclay and
>
> Mr. Henry, be a Committee, to confer with such

Committee as may be appointed on the part of the House of Representatives, to consider and report, whether or not, the business began previous to the late adjournment of Congress, shall now be proceeded in, as if no adjournment had taken place.[28]

ORDERED, That a message be sent to the House of Representatives, acquainting them herewith, and requesting the appointment of a similar Committee on their part.[29]

The Senate adjourned to 11 o'clock to-morrow morning.

THURSDAY, JANUARY 21, 1790

The SENATE assembled,

Present as yesterday,

And, the Honorable Robert Morris, from the State of Pennsylvania, attended.

A message from the President of the United States, by the Secretary at War, was read:

UNITED STATES, January 21, 1790

GENTLEMEN of the SENATE, and

HOUSE of REPRESENTATIVES,

THE Secretary for the Department of War, has submitted to me certain principles to serve as a plan for the general arrangement of the Militia of the United States.

CONCEIVING the subject to be of the highest importance to the welfare of our Country, and liable to be placed in various points of view, I have directed him to lay the plan before Congress, for their information, in order that they may make such use thereof as they may judge proper.

G. WASHINGTON[30]

ORDERED, That the message from the President of the United States, lie for consideration.

ORDERED, That the Senate be supplied with News Papers as usual.

A message from the House of Representatives:

---

[28] This resolve is in Senate Joint and Concurrent Resolutions, Senate Records, DNA.

[29] On January 21 the House appointed a committee to confer with this Senate committee and notified the Senate.

[30] This message is in President's Messages: Transmitting reports from the Secretary of War, Senate Records, DNA. E–22988. The plan for Militia is in Reports of the Secretary of War, House Records, DNA. E–22987.

"Mr. PRESIDENT,

"The House of Representatives have agreed to the appointment of a Committee on their part, consisting of

> Mr. Sherman
> Mr. Thatcher
> Mr. Hartley
> Mr. White and
> Mr. Jackson, to confer with the Committee appointed

on the part of the Senate, to consider and report whether or not, the business begun previous to the late adjournment of Congress, shall now be proceeded in, as if no adjournment had taken place."[31]

The Senate adjourned to 11 o'clock to-morrow.

FRIDAY, JANUARY 22, 1790

The SENATE assembled,
Present as yesterday.

Mr. Ellsworth, on behalf of the Joint Committee of the two Houses, appointed to consider and report, "whether or not, the business begun previous to the late adjournment of Congress, shall now be proceeded in, as if no adjournment had taken place," reported.[32]

ORDERED, That the consideration of the Report be deferred until Monday next.[33]

The Senate adjourned to Monday next at 11 o'clock.

MONDAY, JANUARY 25, 1790

The SENATE assembled,
Present as on Friday.

Proceeded to consider the Report of the Joint Committee of the Senate and House of Representatives, appointed the 20th inst. to wit: "That the business unfinished between the two Houses at the late adjournment, ought to be regarded, as if it had not been passed upon by either,—"

And on motion, That the Report of the Committee be postponed,—
It passed in the Negative.

---

[31] The message is in Senate Joint and Concurrent Resolutions, Senate Records, DNA. On January 22 this committee reported and consideration of the report was postponed.

[32] The report in the form of a resolve is in Senate Joint and Concurrent Resolutions, Senate Records, DNA.

[33] On January 25 this report was considered and passed by resolution. A message was sent to the House requesting concurrence with this resolve.

And upon the question to agree to the Report of the Committee,—
The Yeas and Nays being required by one fifth of the Senators present,

Mr. Bassett	Nay	
Mr. Butler		Yea
Mr. Dalton		Yea
Mr. Ellsworth		Yea
Mr. Elmer	Nay	
Mr. Few		Yea
Mr. Hawkins		Yea
Mr. Henry		Yea
Mr. Johnson		Yea
Mr. Izard	Nay	
Mr. King		Yea
Mr. Langdon	Nay	
Mr. Maclay	Nay	
Mr. Morris	Nay	
Mr. Paterson	Nay	
Mr. Schuyler		Yea
Mr. Strong		Yea
Mr. Wingate	Nay	

Yeas—10
Nays—8

So it passed in the Affirmative:

And it was

RESOLVED, That the business unfinished between the two Houses at the late adjournment, ought to be regarded, as if it had not been passed upon by either.

ORDERED, That a message be sent to the House of Representatives requesting their concurrence in this Resolve.[34]

A message from the President of the United States, by his Secretary, was read:

UNITED STATES, January 25, 1790

GENTLEMEN of the SENATE, and
    HOUSE of REPRESENTATIVES,

I HAVE received from his Excellency John E. Howard, Governor of the State of Maryland, An act of the Legislature of Maryland, to ratify certain articles in addition to, and amendment of the Constitution of the United States of America, proposed by Congress to the Legislatures of the several States; and have directed my Secretary to lay a copy of the same before you, together with

---

[34] On this same date the House concurred with this Senate resolve and on January 26 the Clerk notified the Senate.

the copy of a letter accompanying the above Act, from his Excellency the Governor of Maryland, to the President of the United States.

THE originals will be deposited in the office of the Secretary of State.

G. WASHINGTON[35]

ORDERED, That the message from the President of the United States, together with the papers accompanying the same, lie for consideration.[36]

The Senate adjourned to 11 o'clock to-morrow morning.

TUESDAY, JANUARY 26, 1790

The SENATE assembled,
Present as yesterday.

ORDERED, That   Mr. Ellsworth
                    Mr. Johnson
                    Mr. Strong
                    Mr. Paterson and
                    Mr. Hawkins, be a Committee to report "A Bill defining the crimes and offences that shall be cognizable under the authority of the United States, and their punishment."

A message from the House of Representatives:

"Mr. PRESIDENT,

"The House of Representatives do agree with the Senate in their Resolution, that the business unfinished between the two Houses at the late adjournment, ought to be regarded as if it had not been passed upon by either."[37]

Mr. Ellsworth, on behalf of the Committee, reported "A Bill defining the crimes and offences that shall be cognizable under the authority of the United States, and their punishment."[38]

ORDERED, That this Bill have the FIRST reading at this time.[39]

ORDERED, That this Bill have the SECOND reading to-morrow.

The letter from Gaetan Drago di Domco. was read.[40]

---

[35] This message and related papers are in President's Messages: Suggesting legislation, Senate Records, DNA.

[36] The enclosures to this message appear in the Journal for June 14, 1790. No action was taken on the enclosures.

[37] The House message is in Senate Joint and Concurrent Resolutions, Senate Records, DNA.

[38] This manuscript bill is in Senate Bills, Senate Records, DNA.

[39] On January 27 this bill was read for the second time, considered, and postponed.

[40] The rough and smooth journals insert the text of the following document:

Right Honorable Gentlemen,

Always in hopes, that the Most Illustrious and most Honorable Congress, will deign to favor with some attention the humble attempts I have made bold to make in petitioning for the honor of the Thirteen United Provinces of America's Consulage,

—I have sufficient courage to flatter myself that it will not disapprove the liberty I now take to submit under the eyes of it's Sovereign Inspection the plan here annexed, which has been here conceived respecting a Truce with the Barbary Regencies of Algiers and Tunis in order to make the Flag of this Republick flourish which is at the eve of Subscribing to get an offer made in its' own name to the above Regencies who have too often signified their desire to enter into an Armistice provided the annual payment of a fixed sum, which can be deemed as nothing in comparison to the advantages that may result for its shipping.

This Republick has purchased from the English a 46 Gun frigate which jointly to another that is in agitation to be bought, and 4 Galleys, are to keep out cruising for the purpose of protecting its Commerce.

Should the most Illustrious and most Honorable Congress find nothing in it that merits its attention amongst the vast crowd of objects that worthily occupies it for the good of its happy subjects, it will not be a less proof of my ardent desire to become one of the number, and to demonstrate by the most earnest and studied service the sentiments of veneration and profound respect with which I have the honor to be

Right honorable Gentlemen,

Your most obedt. and most hum. servt.

Gaetan Drago di Domco.

Genoa, Sepr. 21, 1789
To the most Illustrious
and most honorable Congress

Project

The Owners and Masters of Genoese Vessels, offer themselves to pay to this most Serene Government £518,000 per annum, in order it should conclude a Truce with the Regencies of Algiers and Tunis for the obtaining a free Navigation for its Colors from the Barbary Cruisers.

Each Owner and Master of a Vessel of burthen more than 150 Salms, obliges himself to pay once a year £2.10 for each Salm, that his Vessel will be rated at, which according to the account on the other side of the number of Vessels being 358. Burthen 207,000 would amount to £518,000 which sum said Owners and Masters have no objection to pay in anticipation should it be required.

Account of Vessels that exist in the most Serene Republick of Genoas Dominion, of burthen above 150 Salms.

	Vessels No.	Salms	£
Genoa	13	16,500	40,750
Face	8	2,800	7,000
Sturla	40	42,000	105,000
Quinto e Nervi	36	8,500	21,250
Bogliasco	10	9,500	23,750
Sori	44	26,500	66,250
Recco & Camoglj	52	13,500	33,750
Portofino	6	3,600	9,000
Lavagna & Capi	16	11,200	28,000
Moneglia Deva & Framina	36	25,500	63,750
Bonasola	12	6,000	15,000
	Vessels No. 263	Salms 165,600	£414,000

Western Coast

	Vessels No.	Salms	£
St. Pier d'arena	4	2,000	5,000
Pra	2	1,700	4,250
Peglj	12	3,500	8,750
Savona Sportono Finale & Pietra	30	8,400	21,000
Allassio	15	4,500	11,250
Lengueglia	10	8,000	20,000
Cervo & Diano	8	5,500	13,750
Porto Maurizio e St. Remo	14	8,000	20,000
Total number of vessels	358	Salms 207,200	518,000

ORDERED, That the above letter, and the paper accompanying it, be sent to the House of Representatives.[41]

The Senate adjourned to 11 o'clock to-morrow.

WEDNESDAY, JANUARY 27, 1790

The SENATE assembled,
Present as yesterday.

Proceeded to the SECOND reading of the "Bill, defining the crimes and offences that shall be cognizable under the authority of the United States, and their punishment," and after progress,—

ORDERED, That the farther consideration hereof be postponed until to-morrow.[42]

A message from the House of Representatives:

"Mr. PRESIDENT,

"The House of Representatives have passed an Act, for giving effect to the several acts therein mentioned, in respect to the State of North-Carolina."[43]

ORDERED, That this Bill have the FIRST reading at this time.

ORDERED, That this Bill have the SECOND reading to-morrow.[44]

The Senate adjourned to 11 o'clock to-morrow.

THURSDAY, JANUARY 28, 1790

The SENATE assembled,
Present as yesterday.

Proceeded in the SECOND reading of the "Bill, defining the crimes and offences that shall be cognizable under the authority of the United States, and their punishment."

ORDERED, That the rules be so far dispensed with, as that this Bill have the THIRD reading at this time.

On motion, That the FOURTH SECTION be amended to read as followeth—

"That the court before whom any person shall be convicted of the crime of murder, for which he or she shall be sentenced to suffer death, may, at their discretion, add to the judgment, that the body of such offender shall be delivered to a Surgeon for dissection; and the Marshal who is to cause such sentence to be executed, shall accordingly deliver the body of such offender, after

---

[41] This letter was not considered again in the First Congress.

[42] On January 28 this bill was considered again, read a third time, amended, passed, and ordered to be sent to the House for concurrence.

[43] The bill has not been located.

[44] On January 28 this bill was read for the second time and committed.

execution done, to such Surgeon as the court shall direct for the purpose aforesaid: Provided, that such Surgeon, or some other person by him appointed for
the purpose, shall attend to receive, and take away the dead body at the time
of the execution of such offender,"[45]—

It passed in the Affirmative.

RESOLVED, That this Bill DO PASS as amended—That the title of the Bill be
"An Act for the punishment of certain crimes against the United States,"—
That it be engrossed and sent to the House of Representatives, for con-
currence.[46]

A message from the President of the United States, by his Secretary, was
read:

UNITED STATES, January 28, 1790

GENTLEMEN of the SENATE, and
    HOUSE of REPRESENTATIVES,

I HAVE directed my Secretary to lay before you the copy of an Act of the
Legislature of Rhode-Island and Providence Plantations, entitled, "An Act for
calling a convention, to take into consideration the Constitution proposed for
the United States, passed on the 17th day of September A. D. 1787, by the
general convention held at Philadelphia," together with the copy of a letter
accompanying said act, from his Excellency John Collins, Governor of the
State of Rhode-Island and Providence Plantations, to the President of the
United States.

THE originals of the foregoing act and letter, will be deposited in the office
of the Secretary of State.

G. WASHINGTON[47]

ORDERED, That the message, together with the papers accompanying it, lie
for consideration.

The Senate proceeded to the SECOND reading of the Bill, entitled, "An Act
for giving effect to the several acts therein mentioned, in respect to the State
of North-Carolina."

ORDERED, That this Bill be referred to a special Committee, to consist of

Mr. Hawkins
Mr. Ellsworth and
Mr. Butler

On motion,

ORDERED, That the letter from the Governor of Rhode-Island, of the 18th

---

[45] This amendment by Mr. Ellsworth is in Senate Bills, Senate Records, DNA.

[46] The engrossed bill is in Engrossed Senate Bills and Resolutions, Senate Records,
DNA. On January 29 this bill was sent to the House.

[47] The message, including the letter from the Governor of Rhode Island and the act,
are in President's Messages: Suggesting legislation, Senate Records, DNA.

of January instant, to the President of the United States, "Requesting a further suspension of the acts of Congress, subjecting the citizens of the State of Rhode-Island to the payment of foreign tonnage, and foreign duties, during the pleasure of Congress,"—and communicated with the President's message this day, be referred to the same Committee.[48]

The Senate adjourned to 11 o'clock to-morrow.

FRIDAY, JANUARY 29, 1790

The SENATE assembled,
Present as yesterday.

The Honorable Samuel Johnston, from the State of North-Carolina, appeared, produced his credentials,[49] and took his seat in the Senate.

The Vice President administered the oath to Mr. Johnston.

The engrossed Bill, entitled, "An Act for the punishment of certain crimes against the United States," was carried to the House of Representatives for concurrence.[50]

A letter from Samuel Meredith, Treasurer of the United States, to the Vice President, with his accounts to the first of January, 1790, were read.[51]

ORDERED, That the said letter and papers lie for consideration.

On motion, The Senators from the State of North-Carolina, proceeded to draw lots for their Classes, in conformity to the resolve of Senate of May the 14th, 1789: And two lots, No. 2 and 3, being by the Secretary rolled up and put into the box,—

Mr. Johnston drew LOT NO. 2:

whose seat in the Senate shall accordingly be vacated at the expiration of the FOURTH YEAR;

And Mr. Hawkins drew LOT NO. 3:

whose seat in the Senate shall accordingly be vacated at the expiration of the SIXTH YEAR.[52]

The Senate adjourned until 11 o'clock on Monday morning.

---

[48] On February 1 this committee reported and the bill was passed with thirteen amendments. The bill was then sent to the House for concurrence in the amendments.

[49] The credentials are in Election Records: Credentials of Senators, Senate Records, DNA.

[50] On January 29 the House received this bill and read it for the first time. The bill was read a second time on February 1 and ordered to be committed to the committee of the whole. From February 5–April 9 the committee of the whole considered and postponed this bill almost daily. On April 9 the bill was amended and the third reading was assigned. On April 10 the amended bill was read for a third time, passed, and sent to the Senate for concurrence.

[51] The letter from Samuel Meredith and the Treasury Reports for 1789–90 are in Reports from Executive Departments: Record books, Senate Records, DNA.

[52] The smooth journal inserts:

Which arranges the Classes in the following order—

Mr.	Dalton Ellsworth Elmer Maclay Read Carroll Grayson Schuyler	Mr.	Wingate Strong Paterson Bassett Lee Butler Few Johnston	Mr.	Langdon Johnson Morris Henry Izard Gunn King Hawkins

On June 25 the Senators from Rhode Island drew lots to determine their terms of office.

MONDAY, FEBRUARY 1, 1790

The SENATE assembled,
Present as on the 29th January.

Mr. Johnston and Mr. Hawkins laid before the Senate an exemplified copy of the act of the Legislature of North-Carolina, entitled, "An Act for the purpose of ceding to the United States of America, certain western lands therein described;"[1] which being read, was ordered to lie for consideration.

Mr. Hawkins, on behalf of the Committee, appointed the 28th of January, upon the Bill entitled, "An Act for giving effect to the several acts therein mentioned, in respect to the State of North-Carolina;" reported sundry amendments[2]—which were accepted.

ORDERED, That the rules be so far dispensed with, as that this Bill be now read the THIRD time.

RESOLVED, That the Senate do concur in this Bill, with thirteen amendments.[3]

---

[1] This bill from the state of North Carolina is in Deeds of Cession of Western Lands, Miscellany of the Continental and Confederation Congresses, 1774–89, RG 360, Records of the Continental Congress and the Constitutional Convention, DNA.

[2] The report is in Various Select Committee Reports, Senate Records, DNA. The amendments are printed in note 3 below.

[3] The smooth journal reads:
With the following amendments:

A.	P.	L.	
1.	1.	13.	Strike out *four* and insert "five."
2.		23.	Strike out *the* and insert "an."
3.		25.	Strike out *to the northern extremity of Black Bay* and insert "The other to be called the district of Cambden, and to comprehend North River, Pasquotank and Little Rivers, and all the waters, shores, bays, harbours, creeks and inlets from the junction of Currituck and Albemarle sounds to the northern extremity of Black Bay."
4.	2.	8.	Strike out *and the settlements called Daleys and Ryans*, and insert "Plymouth, Winsor, Skewarkey, Winton and Bennets-Creek."
5.		10.	After "Murpheysborough," strike out *and another*, and insert "one."
6.		11.	Strike out *one of the said settlements called Daleys and Ryans*, and insert "each of the ports of Plymouth, Winsor, Skewarkey, Winton and Bennets Creek."
7.		12.	Strike out *Daleys or Ryans* and insert "Plymouth, Winsor, Skewarkey, Winton and Bennets Creek."
8.		13.	After "Edenton," insert "That in the district of Cambden, Plankbridge on Sawyers Creek, shall be the Port of entry and delivery, and Nixinton, Indian town, New-biggen Creek, Currituck inlet and Pasquotank river bridge, ports of delivery, and there shall be a Collector at Plankbridge on Sawyers Creek, and a Surveyor at each of the ports of Nixinton, Indian town, Currituck inlet, Pasquotank river bridge, and New-biggen Creek."

ORDERED, That the Bill be carried to the House of Representatives for concurrence in the amendments.[4]

A message from the President of the United States, by his Secretary, was read:

UNITED STATES, February 1, 1790

GENTLEMEN of the SENATE, and
    HOUSE of REPRESENTATIVES,

I HAVE received from his Excellency Alexander Martin, Governor of the State of North-Carolina, an act of the General Assembly of that State, entitled, "An Act for the purpose of ceding to the United States of America, certain Western Lands therein described," and have directed my Secretary to lay a copy of the same before you, together with the copy of a letter accompanying said act from his Excellency Governor Martin, to the President of the United States.

THE originals of the foregoing act and letter, will be deposited in the office of the Secretary of State.

G. WASHINGTON[5]

ORDERED, That the communication made by the Senators from the State of North-Carolina, together with the President's message of this day, be committed to   Mr. Henry
                                  Mr. Izard

9.	2.	15.	Add the letter "S," to the word "Port," and after "Wilmington," insert "Newbern, Washington and Edenton."
10.		16.	To the word "Port," add the letter "s."
11.	3.	2.	Between the words "States" and "did," insert "and for other purposes."
12.			After the last Section, add the following:—"And be it further enacted, that the second and fourth Section of the Act, entitled 'An act to suspend part of an Act, entitled, An Act to regulate the collection of duties imposed by law, on the tonnage of Ships or Vessels, and on goods, wares and merchandizes imported into the United States, and for other purposes' passed the sixteenth day of September last, shall be, and hereby are declared to be revived, in respect to the Citizens of the State of Rhode Island and Providence plantations, and the same shall continue in force until the first day of April next and no longer."
13.			In the title of the Bill after the words "North Carolina" add "and other purposes."

[4] On February 1 the House concurred with the Senate amendments with an amendment, and the Clerk notified the Senate of this action on February 2. The Senate concurred with the House amendment with an amendment and returned the bill to the House on the same date.

[5] This message, including a copy of Governor Martin's letter, is in President's Messages: Suggesting legislation, Senate Records, DNA.

Mr. Ellsworth
Mr. Bassett and
Mr. Few[6]
The Senate adjourned to 11 o'clock to-morrow.

TUESDAY, FEBRUARY 2, 1790

The SENATE assembled,
Present as yesterday.
A message from the House of Representatives, was read as follows:

"IN THE HOUSE OF REPRESENTATIVES OF THE UNITED STATES
"February 1, 1790
"The House proceeded to consider the amendments proposed by the Senate, to the bill entitled, 'An Act for giving effect to the several acts therein mentioned in respect to the State of North-Carolina;'—whereupon

"RESOLVED, That this House doth agree to all the said amendments, with an amendment to the last amendment, as follows:

"Strike out from the word 'SECOND' to the end of the amendment, and in lieu thereof insert 'Section of the act, entitled, An Act to suspend part of an act, entitled, An Act to regulate the collection of duties imposed by law, on the tonnage of ships or vessels, and on goods, wares and merchandizes imported into the United States, and for other purposes, passed the sixteenth day of September last, shall with respect to the inhabitants and citizens of the State of Rhode-Island and Providence Plantations;' and also, 'That the fourth section of the said Act, shall continue in force, until the first day of April next, and no longer.' "[7]

Mr. Morris presented the petition of Francis Bailey,[8] upon his new invented method of making types; which was read.

ORDERED, That the petition be committed to
Mr. Morris
Mr. Izard and
Mr. Langdon[9]
The Senate proceeded to consider the message from the House of Representatives of this day,—and

RESOLVED, That they agree to the amendment proposed to the amendment of the Senate, with an amendment; by striking out what follows the word

---

[6] On February 17 this committee reported and consideration of the report was scheduled.

[7] This message has not been located.

[8] This petition is in Petitions and Memorials: Various subjects, Senate Records, DNA.

[9] On February 22 this committee reported and the petition was referred to the Secretary of the Treasury.

"PLANTATIONS," and inserting these words, "Be revived, and also, that the fourth section of the said act shall be revived, and both continue in force until the first day of April next, and no longer."

ORDERED, That a message be sent to the House of Representatives accordingly.[10]

The Senate adjourned to 11 o'clock to-morrow.

WEDNESDAY, FEBRUARY 3, 1790

The SENATE assembled,
Present as yesterday.

A message from the House of Representatives:

"Mr. PRESIDENT,

"Mr. Gilman and Mr. White are appointed a Committee for enroled Bills, on the part of the House of Representatives, agreeable to the joint rules of the two Houses."

The Senate proceeded to consider the message from the House of Representatives of this day,—and

ORDERED, That Mr. Wingate, be a Committee on their part for the purposes therein mentioned.

ORDERED, That a message be sent to the House of Representatives to inform them of the appointment.

The Senate adjourned to 11 o'clock to-morrow morning.

THURSDAY, FEBRUARY 4, 1790

The SENATE assembled,
Present as yesterday.

Mr. Wingate, on behalf of the Committee of Enrolment, reported, That they had examined the enroled Bill, entitled, "An Act for giving effect to the several acts therein mentioned, in respect to the State of North-Carolina,"[11] and found it correct.

A message from the House of Representatives:

"Mr. PRESIDENT,

"The Speaker having signed the enroled Bill, entitled, 'An Act for giving effect to the several acts therein mentioned, in respect to the State of North-Carolina,' I am directed to bring it to the Senate for the signature of the Vice President."

---

[10] On February 4 this bill was signed by both the Speaker and the Vice President and given to the committee on enrolled bills for delivery to the President.

[11] The inspected enrolled bill is in Enrolled Acts, RG 11, DNA. E–46035.

Whereupon the Vice President signed the Bill; it was then delivered to the Committee, to be laid before the President of the United States, for his approbation.[12]

The Senate adjourned to 11 o'clock to-morrow.

F R I D A Y, FEBRUARY 5, 1790

The SENATE assembled,
Present as yesterday.

Mr. Wingate, on behalf of the Committee on enroled Bills, reported, That he yesterday laid before the President of the United States, for his approbation, the Bill, entitled, "An Act for giving effect to the several acts therein mentioned, in respect to the State of North-Carolina, and other purposes."[13]

The Senate adjourned to 11 o'clock on Monday next.

M O N D A Y, FEBRUARY 8, 1790

The SENATE assembled,
Present as on the 5th.

The Memorial of the Hon. Robert Morris was read, as follows:

"To the PRESIDENT, the SENATE, and HOUSE of REPRESENTATIVES of the UNITED STATES of AMERICA

"The MEMORIAL of ROBERT MORRIS, late Superintendant of the Finances of the said United States,

"HUMBLY SHEWETH,

"THAT on the twentieth day of June, one thousand seven hundred and eighty five, and subsequent to your Memorialist's resignation of his office of Superintendant, the Congress passed a Resolution in the words following: 'Resolved, that three Commissioners be appointed to enquire into the receipts and expenditures of public monies during the administration of the late Superintendant of Finance, and to examine and adjust the accounts of the United States with that department during his administration, and to report a state thereof to Congress.' Which Resolution, to persons unacquainted with the nature of the office, and the mode of conducting the business of the department, gave occasion to the supposition, that your Memorialist had accounts both difficult and important to settle with the United States, in respect to his official transactions. That though your Memorialist foresaw the disagreeable consequences which might result to himself, from the diffusion of such an opinion, he notwithstanding, not only forbore any representation on the subject, but scrupulously avoided every species of interference direct or indirect,

---

[12] On February 5 this committee reported that it had delivered this bill to the President for his signature.

[13] On February 8 the President signed this bill and the Senate was notified.

lest it should be imagined, either that he was actuated by the desire of obtaining from Congress those marks of approbation, which had in repeated instances been bestowed on the servants of the public, or that he feared to meet the proposed investigation. Respect for the Sovereign of the United States, concurring with motives of delicacy, to forbid even the appearance of asking what, if merited, it was to be presumed would be conferred, (as being the proper reward of services, not of solicitation) and a firm confidence in the rectitude of his conduct, leaving your Memorialist no inducement to evade any enquiry into it which it might be thought fit to institute.

"That your Memorialist taking it for granted, that the reasons which had produced a determination to establish a mode of enquiry into the transactions of the most important office under the government, would have ensured a prosecution of the object, till it had been carried into effect, long remained in silent expectation of the appointment of Commissioners according to the Resolution which had been entered into for that purpose; but it has so happened, from what cause your Memorialist will not undertake to explain, that no further step has ever been taken in relation to it, and your Memorialist has remained exposed to the surmises, which the appearance of an intention to enquire into his conduct had a tendency to excite, without having been afforded an opportunity of obviating them.

"That the unsettled condition of certain accounts of a commercial nature, between the United States and the late house of Willing, Morris and Company and your Memorialist, prior to his appointment as Superintendant of the Finances, having been confounded with his transactions in that capacity, your Memorialist has in various ways, been subjected to injurious imputations on his official conduct; the only fruits of services which at the time they were rendered, he trusts he may without incurring the charge of presumption, affirm they were generally esteemed both important and meritorious, and were at least rendered with ardour and zeal; with unremitted attention, and unwearied application.

"That your Memorialist desirous of rescuing his reputation from the aspersions thrown upon it, came in the month of October 1788, to the city of New-York, as well for the purpose of urging the appointment of Commissioners to inspect his official transactions, as for that of procuring an adjustment of the accounts which existed previous to his administration: But the first object was frustrated by the want of a sufficient number of members to make a Congress, and the last was unavoidably delayed, by the preliminary investigations requisite on the part of the Commissioner named by the late Board of Treasury, towards a competent knowledge of the business.

"That in the month of February, 1789, your Memorialist returned to New-York for the same purposes, but the obstacles which he had before experienced, still operated, to put it out of his power to present the memorial which had been prepared by him in October, praying for an appointment of Commissioners. That he was therefore obliged to confine himself to measures for the settlement of his accounts respecting the transactions antecedent to his appointment as Superintendant, which he entered upon accordingly, with the Commissioner appointed by the Board of Treasury, and in which, as much progress as time and circumstances would permit was made, until the fourth of March last, when that Commissioner, conceiving his authority by the organization of the New Government, to have ceased, declined farther proceedings, and of course, your Memorialist was obliged to wait the establishment of the new Treasury Department, for the further prosecution of that settlement, which has been accordingly resumed, and he hopes will speedily be accomplished. But in as much as no mode of enquiry into his official conduct has hitherto been put into operation, and as doubts of its propriety have been raised by an act of the Government, your Memorialist conceives himself to have a claim upon the public justice, for some method of vindicating himself, which will be unequivocal and definitive. Wherefore, and encouraged by a consciousness of the integrity of his administration, your Memorialist is desirous, that a strict examination should be had into his conduct while in office, in order, that if he has been guilty of mal-administration, it may be detected and punished, if otherwise, that his innocence may be manifested, and acknowledged. Unwilling from this motive, that longer delay should attend the object of the Resolution which has been recited, your Memorialist humbly prays, that an appointment of Commissioners may take place, to carry the said Resolution into effect. And your Memorialist, as in duty bound, will pray, &c.

"ROBERT MORRIS

"NEW-YORK, February 8, 1790"[14]

ORDERED, That to-morrow be assigned to take this memorial into consideration.[15]

The Senate adjourned to 11 o'clock to-morrow.

TUESDAY, FEBRUARY 9, 1790

The SENATE assembled,
Present as yesterday.

Proceeded, agreeably to the order of the day, to take into consideration the memorial of Robert Morris, Esq;—and

ORDERED, That it be committed to
Mr. Izard
Mr. Henry and

---

[14] The letter enclosing the memorial is in Petitions and Memorials: Various subjects, Senate Records, DNA. The memorial is in Misc. Letters, M–177, roll 3, RG 59, General Records of the Department of State, DNA.

[15] On February 9 this memorial was considered and committed.

Mr. Ellsworth to consider and report what is proper to be done thereon.[16]

A message from the House of Representatives:

"Mr. PRESIDENT,

"The House of Representatives have passed a Bill, entitled, 'An Act providing for the actual enumeration of the inhabitants of the United States;'[17] to which they request the concurrence of the Senate.

"The President of the United States has approved of, and affixed his signature to, 'An Act for giving effect to the several acts therein mentioned, in respect to the State of North-Carolina;' and has returned it to the House of Representatives, where it originated."

ORDERED, That the Bill, entitled, "An Act providing for the actual enumeration of the inhabitants of the United States," be now read the FIRST time.

ORDERED, That this Bill have the SECOND reading on Friday next, and that in the mean time, it be printed for the use of the Senate.[18]

The Senate adjourned to 11 o'clock to-morrow.

WEDNESDAY, FEBRUARY 10, 1790

The SENATE assembled,
Present as yesterday.

Proceeded in the consideration of the executive business communicated from the President of the United States, in his message of the 9th instant.[19]

Mr. Izard, on behalf of the Committee appointed to take into consideration the memorial of the Hon. Robert Morris,—reported:[20]

ORDERED, That the consideration of the report be postponed until to-morrow.[21]

The Senate adjourned to 11 o'clock to-morrow.

THURSDAY, FEBRUARY 11, 1790

The SENATE assembled,
Present as yesterday.

Proceeded, agreeably to the order of the day, to consider the report of the

[16] On February 10 this committee reported and consideration of the report was postponed.

[17] An annotated printed copy of this bill is in House Bills, Senate Records, DNA. E–46052. A similar copy is in the Broadside Collection, RBkRm, DLC.

[18] On February 12 this bill was read a second time and committed.

[19] The letter from George Washington is in the George Washington Papers, series 2, vol. 25, reel 9, Manuscript Division, DLC.

[20] This committee report is in Various Select Committee Reports, Senate Records, DNA.

[21] On February 11 this report was accepted and a resolution was passed appointing a commission to investigate the finance accounts. The House was then notified.

Committee upon the memorial of the Hon. Robert Morris; and upon the question to accept the report—

It passed in the Affirmative:[22]

Whereupon,

RESOLVED, By the Senate and House of Representatives, that three Commissioners be appointed by the President of the United States, to enquire into the receipts and expenditures of public monies, during the administration of the late Superintendant of Finance; and to examine and adjust the accounts of the United States with that department, during his administration; and to report a state thereof to the President; and that five dollars per diem be allowed to each of the said Commissioners, while they shall be employed in that service.

ORDERED, That this resolve be sent to the House of Representatives for concurrence.

ORDERED, That Mr. Morris
Mr. Langdon
Mr. Butler
Mr. Dalton and
Mr. Ellsworth, be a Committee to report, (if they think it expedient) a plan for the regulation of the trade of the United States, with the countries and settlements of the European powers in America.[23]

The Senate adjourned to 11 o'clock to-morrow.

F R I D A Y, FEBRUARY 12, 1790

The SENATE assembled,
Present as yesterday.

Proceeded, agreeably to the order of the day, to the SECOND reading of the Bill, entitled, "An Act providing for the actual enumeration of the inhabitants of the United States."[24]

---

[22] The smooth journal inserts, in brackets:

[On motion, That the blank be filled with Six dollars—It passed in the Negative. On motion, That the blank should be filled with Five dollars.—

It passed in the Affirmative.]

[23] This committee did not report but there are notes, probably from the committee meeting, in the Pierce Butler Papers, PHi. On February 26 several members were added to this committee.

[24] At this point the smooth journal inserts in brackets:

[In Committee

A motion was made for a special Committee and agreed to.

A motion being made for the sense of the Senate to adopt the following amendment in the first clause of the bill, in lieu of that empowering the Marshals to take the enumeration, Vizt.:

"That the number of the inhabitants in the respective districts in the United States, shall, by one Commissioner in each to be appointed by the President of the United States,"

ORDERED, That the Bill be committed to

> Mr. Paterson
> Mr. Strong
> Mr. Ellsworth
> Mr. Hawkins and
> Mr. Johnson[25]

The Senate adjourned to Monday next, at 11 o'clock.

MONDAY, FEBRUARY 15, 1790[26]

The SENATE assembled,
Present as on the 12th February.

A letter from Benjamin Franklin, Esquire, to the Vice President, enclosing the copy of a letter from James Pemberton to the said Benjamin Franklin, Esquire, with a memorial, signed Benjamin Franklin, in behalf of a society, of which he is President; and an address, signed Nicholas Waln, in behalf of the yearly Meeting, of which he is clerk; together with an address, signed George Bowne, in behalf of the representatives of a society, of which he is clerk; were severally read.[27]

The Senate adjourned to 11 o'clock to-morrow.

TUESDAY, FEBRUARY 16, 1790

The SENATE assembled,
Present as yesterday.

Mr. Paterson, on behalf of the Committee appointed the 12th February, on the Bill, entitled, "An Act providing for the actual enumeration of the inhabitants of the United States;" reported sundry amendments,[28]—which were accepted, and

ORDERED, That the sixth Section be re-committed.[29]

The Senate adjourned to 11 o'clock to-morrow.

It passed in the Negative.

On motion, To expunge the second Schedule, requiring a description of the various occupations of the people—

It passed in the Affirmative.]

[25] On February 16 the committee reported some amendments to this bill which were accepted. Section 6 was recommitted.

[26] Certain proceedings of this date were entered in the Journal for June 14, 1790.

[27] The letters and the memorial are in Petitions and Memorials: Various subjects, DNA. The Senate did not consider this memorial or these addresses, but the House did. See Quakers: Petition of; and Pennsylvania Abolition Society: Petition of.

[28] A printed copy of the bill with annotations, which may correspond to amendments, is in House Bills, Senate Records, DNA. Another printed copy with annotations is in the Broadside Collection, RBkRm, DLC. The amendments are printed in note 35 below.

[29] On February 17 the committee reported on section 6. The report was accepted and the third reading was assigned.

WEDNESDAY, FEBRUARY 17, 1790

The SENATE assembled,

Present as yesterday.

Mr. Paterson, on behalf of the Committee to whom was referred the sixth Section of the Bill, entitled, "An Act providing for the actual enumeration of the inhabitants of the United States;" reported that no alteration is necessary,—

And the Report was accepted.

ORDERED, That this Bill have the THIRD reading to-morrow.[30]

Mr. Henry, on behalf of the Committee appointed February 1st, to whom was referred the communication by the Senators from the State of North-Carolina, of the act of their Legislature, entitled, "An Act for the purpose of ceding to the United States of America, certain western lands therein described;" together with the message from the President of the United States," of February 1st, on that subject,—reported:[31]

ORDERED, That to-morrow be assigned for the consideration of the report.[32]

The Senate adjourned to 11 o'clock to-morrow.

THURSDAY, FEBRUARY 18, 1790

The SENATE assembled,

Present as yesterday.

The representation of Mary Katherine Goddard, that she was superceded in the office of keeper of the Post-Office, in Baltimore;[33] was read.[34]

The Senate proceeded to the THIRD reading of the Bill, entitled, "An Act providing for the actual enumeration of the inhabitants of the United States."

RESOLVED, That this Bill DO PASS with twenty nine amendments.[35]

---

[30] On February 18 this bill was read a third time and passed with twenty-nine amendments. It was then returned to the House for concurrence.

[31] The report is in Various Select Committee Reports, Senate Records, DNA.

[32] On February 18 consideration of this report was postponed.

[33] The petition, the representation in favor of Miss Mary Katharine Goddard, and a responding letter from Mr. Samuel Osgood dated 1790 are in Petitions and Memorials: Applications for jobs, Senate Records, DNA.

[34] The Senate did not consider this petition, but the House did.

[35] The smooth journal reads:

With the following amendments:

A.	P.	L.	
1.			Strike out *actual* from the Title of the Bill.
2.	1.	4.	Strike out the words between "taken," and "omitting."
3.			Strike out *ages of.*
4.		6.	Strike out *above* and insert "of."
5.			After "sixteen," insert "years and upwards"
6.		9.	Strike out *A* (before County) and insert "one or more."
7.			After "Township," insert "Hundreds."
8.			Make the words "County, City, Town, Township or Parish," plural.

ORDERED, That the Bill be carried to the House of Representatives for concurrence in the amendments.[36]

On motion,

ORDERED, That the consideration of the report of the Committee to whom was referred the communication by the Senators from the State of North-Carolina, of the act of the Legislature of that State, entitled, "An Act for the purpose of ceding to the United States of America, certain western lands therein described;" together with the message from the President of the United States, of February 1st, on that subject; be postponed until Monday next.[37]

The Senate adjourned to 11 o'clock to-morrow.

FRIDAY, FEBRUARY 19, 1790

The SENATE assembled,
Present as yesterday.

On motion,—

The Senate adjourned until Monday next, at 11 o'clock.

9.		14.	After "enumeration." insert "and description."
10.		16.	Strike out *actual*
11.		18.	After "enumeration," insert "and description."
12.		20.	Strike out *actual*
13.		21. a 23.	Strike out all the words between "ability" and "The enumeration"
14.		25.	Strike out *six* and insert "nine."
15.		26.	Strike out *six* and insert "nine."
16.	2.	5.	Strike out (from the second column of the first Schedule) *above* and insert "of," and after "years"
17.		6.	insert "and upwars."
18.		5.	Strike out (in the fifth column of the first Schedule) *Free Blacks* and insert "all other free persons."
19.		8.	Strike out the second *Schedule*.
20.		22. a 25.	Strike out the Providing clause.
21.		31.	Strike out *June* and insert "September."
22.	3.	11.	Strike out *one* and insert "Two."
23.			Strike out *and fifty*.
24.		13.	Strike out *three* and insert "Four."
25.		14.	Strike out *one* and insert "Two."
26.			Strike out *and fifty*.
27.	4.	6.	Strike out *male*
28.		6. a 7.	Strike out *twenty one* and insert "Sixteen."
29.		9.	Insert "or her," between "his" and "knowledge."

[36] On February 19 the House received this message and considered it on the twenty-second. On that date they resolved to agree to all of the Senate amendments except five and notified the Senate. The Senate considered this resolution, receded from the five amendments that the House had disagreed to, and notified the House accordingly.

[37] On February 22 this report was considered, printed in the Journal, and accepted. It was then sent to the House for concurrence.

MONDAY, FEBRUARY 22, 1790

The SENATE assembled,

Present as on the 19th.

Mr. Morris, in behalf of the Committee to whom was referred the petition of Francis Bailey,—reported:[38] whereupon

ORDERED, That the said petition be referred to the Secretary of the Treasury, to report.[39]

Agreeably to the order of the day, the Senate proceeded to consider the report of the Committee appointed February 1st, to whom was referred the communication by the Senators from the State of North-Carolina, of the act of their Legislature, entitled, "An Act for the purpose of ceding to the United States of America, certain western lands therein described;" together with the Message from the President of the United States, of February 1st, on that subject,—to wit:

"That it will be expedient for Congress, in behalf of the United States, to accept the cession proposed by the said act, upon the conditions therein contained; and that when a deed shall be executed for the same, they express their acceptance thereof by a legislative act."—And,

RESOLVED, That the Senate do accept the report.

ORDERED, That it be sent to the House of Representatives, for their concurrence.[40]

A message from the House of Representatives:

"Mr. PRESIDENT,

"The House of Representatives agree to all the amendments proposed by the Senate to the Bill, entitled, 'An Act for the actual enumeration of the inhabitants of the United States;' except the 22d, 23d, 24th, 25th and 26th; to which they disagree."

The Senate proceeded to consider the above recited message from the House of Representatives;—and,

RESOLVED, That they do recede from their 22d, 23d, 24th, 25th and 26th amendments to the Bill therein mentioned.

ORDERED, That a message be sent to the House of Representatives accordingly.[41]

The Senate adjourned to 11 o'clock to-morrow.

---

[38] The report is in Various Select Committee Reports, Senate Records, DNA.

[39] On February 23 the Senate received the Secretary's report on this petition and the report was printed in the Journal. The report was ordered to lie for consideration.

[40] On February 23 the Senate appointed a committee to prepare a bill on this subject after the deed was executed.

[41] On February 25 this bill was signed by both the Speaker and the Vice President. It was then given to the committee on enrolled bills for delivery to the President.

TUESDAY, FEBRUARY 23, 1790

The SENATE assembled,
Present as yesterday.

ORDERED, That   Mr. Ellsworth
                       Mr. Strong and
                       Mr. Izard, be a Committee to bring in a Bill for
declaring the acceptance of certain lands ceded to the United States by the
Legislature of North-Carolina, as described in their act of cession, when a
deed thereof shall be executed.[42]

ORDERED, That   Mr. Hawkins
                       Mr. Langdon and
                       Mr. Few, be a Committee to prepare and report a
rule, determining in what cases a re-consideration of a vote of Senate shall be
admissible.[43]

The report of the Secretary of the Treasury, upon the petition of Francis
Bailey, was read as follows:

TREASURY DEPARTMENT
February 23d, 1790

PURSUANT to the above[44] order of the Senate of the United States, of the
22d of February instant, referring the petition of Francis Bailey, to the Secretary of the Treasury,—the said Secretary reports:

That he has received from the said Francis Bailey, a communication of the
invention to which he alludes in his petition:

That it appears to him difficult to decide, to what extent that invention will
afford the security against counterfeiting; which is the object of it:

That nevertheless, he is of opinion, it will be likely to add to the difficulty
of that pernicious practice, in a sufficient degree, to merit the countenance of
Government, by securing to the petitioner an exclusive right to the use of the
invention:

That with regard to the employment of the petitioner to print such papers
of a public nature, as may require precaution against counterfeit;—this, in the
judgment of the Secretary, ought to remain a matter of discretion to be regulated by the success of the experiment, and the convenience of the public.

All which is humbly submitted.

ALEXANDER HAMILTON
SECRETARY of the TREASURY

To the VICE PRESIDENT
of the UNITED STATES[45]

---

[42] On March 3 this committee reported a bill which was read for the first time.

[43] On February 24 this committee reported, and the report was ordered to lie for
consideration.

[44] The smooth journal omits the word "above."

[45] The report is in Reports from the Secretary of the Treasury, Senate Records, DNA.

ORDERED, That it lie for consideration.[46]

On motion, That a Committee be appointed to consider what measures may be necessary to be adopted relative to the inspection of exports from the United States; and if they think proper, to prepare a Bill on that subject.

ORDERED, That this motion lie for consideration.[47]

The Senate adjourned to 11 o'clock to-morrow.

W E D N E S D A Y, FEBRUARY 24, 1790

The SENATE assembled,
Present as yesterday.

On motion,—
ORDERED, That   Mr. Dalton
                       Mr. Morris
                       Mr. Izard
                       Mr. Langdon and
                       Mr. Johnston, be a Committee "to consider what measures may be necessary to be adopted relative to the inspection of exports from the United States; and if they think proper, to prepare a Bill on that subject."[48]

Mr. Hawkins, on behalf of the Committee appointed to prepare and report a rule determining in what cases, a re-consideration of a vote of Senate shall be admissible;—reported.[49]

ORDERED, That the report lie for consideration.[50]

The Senate adjourned to 11 o'clock to-morrow.

T H U R S D A Y, FEBRUARY 25, 1790

The SENATE assembled,
Present as yesterday.

Mr. Wingate, on behalf of the joint Committee on enrolled Bills, reported, that they had examined the Bill, entitled, "An Act providing for the enumeration of the inhabitants of the United States;"[51] and had found it correct.

The Senate proceeded to consider the report of the Committee appointed the 23d instant, "to prepare and report a rule determining in what cases a re-consideration of a vote of Senate shall be admissible;" which, being amended was accepted:

---

[46] On March 2 the House passed the Bailey Bill and notified the Senate which then read the bill for the first time.

[47] On February 24 a committee was appointed on this motion.

[48] On February 26 several Senators were added to this committee.

[49] The report has not been located.

[50] On February 25 this report was amended and accepted by resolution.

[51] The inspected enrolled bill is in Enrolled Acts, RG 11, DNA. E–46053.

Whereupon,—

RESOLVED,[52] That when a question has been once made and carried in the affirmative or negative, it shall be in order for any member of the majority, to move for a re-consideration of it.[53]

A message from the House of Representatives:

"Mr. PRESIDENT,

"The Speaker having signed an enrolled Bill, entitled, 'An Act providing for the enumeration of the inhabitants of the United States;' I am directed to bring it to the Senate, for the signature of the Vice President."

Whereupon, the Vice President signed the Bill, and it was delivered to the Committee, to be laid before the President of the United States, for his approbation.[54]

The Senate adjourned to 11 o'clock to-morrow.

FRIDAY, FEBRUARY 26, 1790

The SENATE assembled,
Present as yesterday.

ORDERED, That   Mr. Bassett
                       Mr. Few
                       Mr. Henry
                       Mr. King
                       Mr. Paterson and
                       Mr. Hawkins, be added to the Committee appointed
the 11th February, "to report (if they think it expedient) a plan for the regulation of the trade of the United States, with the countries and settlements of the European powers in America."[55]

ORDERED, That   Mr. Bassett
                       Mr. Few
                       Mr. Henry
                       Mr. King
                       Mr. Paterson and
                       Mr. Ellsworth, be added to the Committee appointed
the 24th February, to consider "what measures may be necessary to be adopted

---

[52] In the rough journal the words "Rule 21" are inserted preceeding the word "Resolved."

[53] The resolve has not been located.

[54] On March 1 the President signed this bill and the Senate was notified on March 2.

[55] On March 26 a petition from the citizens of New Hampshire was referred to this committee.

relative to the inspection of exports from the United States; and if they think proper, to prepare a Bill on that subject."[56]

The Senate adjourned to 11 o'clock on Monday next.

[56] This committee never reported, but a motion was made on this subject on March 3.

MONDAY, MARCH 1, 1790

The SENATE assembled,
Present as on the 26th of February.

On Motion,—
The Senate adjourned to 11 o'clock to-morrow.

TUESDAY, MARCH 2, 1790

The SENATE assembled,
Present as yesterday.

A message from the House of Representatives:

"Mr. PRESIDENT,

"The House of Representatives have passed a Bill, entitled, 'An Act to vest in Francis Bailey, the exclusive privilege of making, using, and vending to others, punches for stamping the matrices of types, and impressing marks on plates, or any other substance, to prevent[1] counterfeits, upon a principle by him invented, for a term of years,'—to which they desire the concurrence of the Senate.

"The President of the United States has affixed his signature to the Bill, entitled, 'An Act providing for the enumeration of the inhabitants of the United States;' and has returned it to the House of Representatives, where it originated."

ORDERED, That the Bill, entitled, "An Act to vest in Francis Bailey, the exclusive privilege of making, using, and vending to others, punches for stamping the matrices of types, and impressing marks on plates, or any other substance, to prevent counterfeits, upon a principle by him invented, for a term of years,"—have the FIRST reading at this time.

ORDERED, That this Bill have the SECOND reading to-morrow.[2]

The Senate adjourned to 11 o'clock to-morrow.

WEDNESDAY, MARCH 3, 1790

The SENATE assembled,
Present as yesterday.

Proceeded to the SECOND reading of the Bill, entitled, "An Act to vest in Francis Bailey, the exclusive privilege of making, using, and vending to others, punches for stamping the matrices of types, and impressing marks on plates, or any other substance, to prevent counterfeits, upon a principle by him invented, for a term of years."

---

[1] An annotated copy of the bill is in House Bills, Senate Records, DNA. The bill, as it passed the House, is also in Engrossed House Bills, House Records, DNA.

[2] On March 3 this bill was read a second time and committed.

ORDERED, That this Bill be committed to

Mr. Strong
Mr. Ellsworth
Mr. Hawkins
Mr. Few and
Mr. Henry[3]

Mr. Ellsworth, on behalf of the Committee appointed February 23d, reported a Bill "To accept a cession of the claims of the State of North-Carolina, to a certain district of western territory."[4]

ORDERED, That the rules be so far dispensed with, as that this Bill have the FIRST reading at this time.

ORDERED, That to-morrow be assigned for the SECOND reading of this[5] Bill.[6]

On motion, "That the Secretary of the Treasury direct the respective Collectors in the several ports of the United States, not to clear out any vessel having articles on board subject to inspection by the laws of the State, from which such vessel shall be about to depart, without having previously obtained such manifests, and other documents as are enjoined by the said laws."[7]

ORDERED, That the consideration hereof be deferred until to-morrow.[8]

The Senate adjourned to 11 o'clock to-morrow.

THURSDAY, MARCH 4, 1790

The SENATE assembled,
Present as yesterday.

Mr. Strong, on behalf of the Committee appointed the 3d of March, to take into consideration the Bill, entitled, "An Act to vest in Francis Bailey, the exclusive privilege of making, using, and vending to others, punches for stamping the matrices of types, and impressing marks on plates, or any other substance, to prevent counterfeits, upon a principle by him invented, for a term of years;" reported,—

That the consideration thereof be postponed until a "Bill to promote the progress of useful arts," shall be taken into consideration.

RESOLVED, That this report be accepted.[9]

---

[3] This committee appointment is in Senate Simple Resolutions and Motions, Senate Records, DNA. On March 4 this committee reported and the report was accepted. Consideration of the Bailey Bill was then postponed until consideration of the Patent Bill could be taken up.

[4] This bill is in Senate Bills, Senate Records, DNA.

[5] The smooth journal substitutes "the" for "this."

[6] On March 4 this bill was read a second time and the third reading was assigned.

[7] This motion, introduced by Mr. Izard, is in Senate Simple Resolutions and Motions, Senate Records, DNA.

[8] On March 4 this motion was considered and committed.

[9] On March 16 the Bailey Bill was referred to the Patent Bill Committee.

Agreeably to the order of the day, the Senate proceeded to the SECOND reading of the Bill, "To accept a cession of the claims of the State of North-Carolina, to a certain district of western territory."

ORDERED, That to-morrow be assigned for the THIRD reading of this Bill.[10]

The Senate proceeded to consider the motion made yesterday, and deferred to this morning; to wit:

"That the Secretary of the Treasury direct the respective Collectors in the several ports of the United States, not to clear out any vessel having articles on board, subject to inspection by the laws of the State, from which such vessel shall be about to depart, without having previously obtained such manifests and other documents, as are enjoined by the said laws."

ORDERED, That the motion[11] be committed to

Mr. Izard

Mr. Strong and

Mr. Bassett and that the Committee be instructed to report a Bill upon the subject matter of it, if a Bill shall appear to them necessary.[12]

A message from the House of Representatives:

"Mr. PRESIDENT,

"The House of Representatives have passed a Bill, entitled, 'An Act to establish a uniform rule of naturalization;'[13] to which they request the concurrence of the Senate."

ORDERED, That this Bill be now read the FIRST time.

ORDERED, That this Bill have the SECOND reading on Monday next; and that it be printed in the mean time for the use of the Senate.[14]

The Senate adjourned to 11 o'clock to-morrow.

F R I D A Y, MARCH 5, 1790

The SENATE assembled,

Present as yesterday.

Proceeded to the THIRD reading of the Bill, "To accept the cession of the claims of the State of North-Carolina, to a certain district of western territory."

ORDERED, That this Bill DO PASS,—that the title be "An Act to accept the cession of the claims of the State of North-Carolina, to a certain district of

---

[10] On March 5 this bill was read a third time, engrossed, and sent to the House for concurrence.

[11] The smooth journal substitutes "it" for "the motion."

[12] This order is in Senate Simple Resolutions and Motions, Senate Records, DNA. On March 5 this committee reported, and a resolution was passed on this subject and sent to the House.

[13] Two annotated printed copies are in House Bills, Senate Records, DNA. E–46022.

[14] On March 8 this bill was read a second time and considered.

western territory,"—that it be engrossed,[15] and sent to the House of Representatives, for their concurrence.[16]

Mr. Izard, on behalf of the Committee appointed the 4th of March,—reported:

Whereupon,

RESOLVED, by the Senate, and House of Representatives of the United States, in Congress assembled, That the respective Collectors in the several ports of the United States, be directed not to grant a clearance for any ship, or vessel having articles on board, subject to inspection by the laws of the State from which such ship or vessel shall be about to depart, without having previously obtained such manifests, and other documents as are enjoined by the said laws.[17]

ORDERED, That this resolve be sent to the House of Representatives, for their concurrence.[18]

The Senate adjourned to Monday next, at 11 o'clock.

MONDAY, MARCH 8, 1790

The SENATE assembled,
Present as on the 5th of March,—and
The Hon. George Read, from the State of Delaware, attended.
A message from the President of the United States:

UNITED STATES, March 8, 1790

GENTLEMEN of the SENATE, and
HOUSE of REPRESENTATIVES,

I HAVE received from his Excellency Joshua Clayton, President of the State of Delaware, the articles proposed by Congress to the Legislatures of the several States, as amendments to the Constitution of the United States; which articles were transmitted to him for the consideration of the Legislature of Delaware, and are now returned with the following resolutions annexed to them, viz.

---

[15] The engrossed act, in the form of a deed, is in Engrossed Senate Bills and Resolutions, Senate Records, DNA.

[16] On March 5 the House received this bill and presumably read it a first time. On March 8 it was read a second time and committed to the committee of the whole. On March 26 the committee of the whole considered this bill and added one amendment. On March 29 this bill was passed with one amendment and returned to the Senate for concurrence. On the same date the Senate concurred with the House amendment.

[17] This resolve is in Senate Simple Resolutions and Motions, Senate Records, DNA.

[18] On March 8 the House committed this resolve. The committee reported a bill which was read for the first time. On March 9 the bill was read a second time and committed to the committee of the whole. On March 26 the bill was considered in the committee of the whole, amended, and the third reading was assigned. On March 29 this bill was passed and the Senate was notified. The Senate then read the bill for the first time and assigned the second reading.

"The General Assembly of Delaware, having taken into their consideration the above amendments proposed by Congress to the respective Legislatures of the several States,—

"RESOLVED, That the first Article be postponed.

"RESOLVED, That the General Assembly do agree to the second, third, fourth, fifth, sixth, seventh, eighth, ninth, tenth, eleventh, and twelfth articles; and WE DO HEREBY ASSENT TO, RATIFY, AND CONFIRM, the same as part of the Constitution of the United States.

"In testimony whereof we have caused the great seal of the State to be hereunto affixed, this twenty-eighth day of January, in the year of our Lord one thousand seven hundred and ninety, and in the fourteenth year of the Independence of the Delaware State.

"Signed by order of Council,

GEORGE MITCHELL, Speaker

"Signed by order of the House of Assembly,

JEHU DAVIS, Speaker"

I HAVE directed a copy of the letter which accompanied the said articles, from his Excellency Joshua Clayton, to the President of the United States, to be laid before you.

THE before mentioned articles, and the original of the letter, will be lodged in the office of the Secretary of State.

G. WASHINGTON

(Copy)

"SIR,

"Agreeably to the directions of the General Assembly of this State, I do myself the honor to enclose your Excellency their ratification of the articles proposed by Congress to be added to the Constitution of the United States; and am, &c.

(Signed)   "JOSHUA CLAYTON

"DELAWARE

Feb. 19, 1790

His Excellency GEORGE WASHINGTON

President of the United States"

"UNITED STATES, March 8, 1790

"I hereby certify that the above letter is a true copy from the original.

"TOBIAS LEAR

Secretary to the President

of the United States"[19]

---

[19] This message, including documents, is in President's Messages: Suggesting legislation, Senate Records, DNA.

ORDERED, That the message from the President of the United States, of this day, with the papers accompanying it, lie for consideration.

A message from the House of Representatives:

"Mr. PRESIDENT,

"The House of Representatives have passed a Bill, entitled, 'An Act to provide for the remission or mitigation of fines, forfeitures, and penalties in certain cases;'[20]—to which they request the concurrence of the Senate."[21]

Agreeably to the order of the day, the Senate proceeded to the SECOND reading of the Bill, entitled, "An Act to establish an uniform rule of naturalization;"[22]—and after progress, deferred the farther consideration thereof until to-morrow.[23]

The Senate adjourned to 11 o'clock to-morrow.

TUESDAY, MARCH 9, 1790

The SENATE assembled,
Present as yesterday.

ORDERED, That the Bill, entitled, "An Act to provide for the remission or

---

[20] An annotated printed copy of this bill is in House Bills, Senate Records, DNA.

[21] On March 9 this bill was read a first time, and the second reading was scheduled.

[22] The smooth journal inserts the following in brackets:

[On motion, To strike out line 2, 3 "Other than an alien enemy."

It passed in the Affirmative.

On motion, To strike out from the word "assembled," line 2. to the words "United States." line 11 and insert "That any Alien being a free white person, who shall come into and reside within the limits and under the jurisdiction of the United States, shall be considered as a natural born Citizen of the United States, provided he shall in any common law Court of record give satisfactory proof to such Court that he is a person of good character, and shall taken the oath or affirmation prescribed by law to support the Constitution of the United States, which oath or affirmation such Court shall administer, and the Clerk of such Court shall enter the same into the records of the Court and give a Certificate thereof to the person having taken the same."

It passed in the Negative.

On motion, To strike out, line 3. 4. "who shall have resided within the limits and under the jurisdiction of the United States for the term of two years."

It passed in the Negative.

On motion, To strike out "Two," and insert "One," line 4.

It passed in the Negative.

On motion, To insert "natural born," between the words "as," and "Citizens," line 13.

It passed in the Negative.

On motion, To subjoin the following at the end of the enacting clause, line 15. "Provided that Aliens purchasing lands in the territories of the United States may lawfully hold and enjoy the same; although they may not have obtained the rights of Citizens in other respects."

A motion was carried for adjournment.]

[23] On March 9 this bill was considered and committed.

mitigation of fines, forfeitures, and penalties, in certain cases;" be now read the FIRST time.

ORDERED, That this Bill have the SECOND reading to-morrow.[24]

Agreeably to the order of the day, the Senate proceeded in the SECOND reading of the Bill, entitled, "An Act to establish an uniform rule of naturalization."

ORDERED, That the Bill be committed to

> Mr. Henry
> Mr. King
> Mr. Strong
> Mr. Ellsworth and
> Mr. Johnson[25]

The Senate adjourned to 11 o'clock to-morrow.

WEDNESDAY, MARCH 10, 1790

The SENATE assembled,
Present as yesterday.

Agreeably to the order of the day, the Senate proceeded to the SECOND reading of the Bill, entitled, "An Act to provide for the remission or mitigation of fines, forfeitures, and penalties, in certain cases."

ORDERED, That the consideration of this Bill be postponed until to-morrow.[26]

The Senate proceeded in the executive business communicated in the messages from the President of the United States, of the 9th and 18th of February last.

The Senate adjourned to 11 o'clock to-morrow.

THURSDAY, MARCH 11, 1790

The SENATE assembled,
Present as yesterday.

The memorial of David Olyphant, late director general of the hospital in the State of South-Carolina,[27] praying for an explanatory instruction to the Commissioner for settling the accounts in the hospital department, respecting his demands for past services,—was read, and

---

[24] On March 10 the second reading of this bill was begun and postponed.

[25] On March 12 this committee reported and consideration of the report was postponed.

[26] On March 11 the second reading of this bill was continued, and the bill was committed.

[27] This petition is in Petitions and Memorials: Various subjects, Senate Records, DNA.

ORDERED, To lie on the table.[28]

A message from the House of Representatives:

"Mr. PRESIDENT,

"The House of Representatives have passed a Bill, entitled, 'An Act to promote the progress of useful arts;'[29] also, a Bill, entitled, 'An Act for encreasing the salaries of clerks in the office of the Commissioners for settling accounts, between the United States and individual States;'[30] to which they request the concurrence of the Senate."

The Senate proceeded in the SECOND reading of the Bill, entitled, "An Act to provide for the remission or mitigation of fines, forfeitures, and penalties, in certain cases,"—and it was committed to

> Mr. Morris
> Mr. Izard
> Mr. Strong
> Mr. Henry and
> Mr. Langdon[31]

ORDERED, That the Bill, entitled, "An Act to promote the progress of useful arts;" have the FIRST reading at this time.

ORDERED, That this Bill be read a SECOND time on Monday next; and that in the mean time it be printed for the use of the Senate.[32]

ORDERED, That the Bill, entitled, "An Act for encreasing the salaries of clerks in the office of the Commissioners for settling accounts, between the United States and individual States,"—have the FIRST reading at this time.

ORDERED, That to-morrow be assigned for the SECOND reading of this Bill.[33]

The Senate adjourned to 11 o'clock to-morrow.

FRIDAY, MARCH 12, 1790

The SENATE assembled,
Present as yesterday.

Agreeably to the order of the day, the Senate proceeded to the SECOND reading of the Bill, entitled, "An Act for encreasing the salaries of clerks in the office of the Commissioners for settling accounts, between the United

---

[28] The Senate did not consider this petition, but the House did.

[29] The annotated printed bill is in House Bills, Senate Records, DNA. E–46067.

[30] The bill, as it passed the House, is in Engrossed House Bills, House Records, DNA.

[31] On March 15 this committee reported amendments to this bill which were postponed until the third reading.

[32] On March 15 this bill was read a second time and committed.

[33] On March 12 this bill was read a second time and postponed.

States and individual States,"—and the further consideration thereof was postponed.[34]

Mr. Henry, on behalf of the Committee appointed the 9th March, to consider the Bill, entitled, "An Act to establish an uniform rule of naturalization,"—reported;[35] and the consideration of the report was postponed.[36]

It being suggested that the Committees wanted time to perfect their reports,—

The Senate adjourned to Monday next, at 11 o'clock.

MONDAY, MARCH 15, 1790

The SENATE assembled,

Present as on the 12th of March,—and

The Honorable Mr. Carroll, from the State of Maryland, attended.

Mr. Morris, on behalf of the Committee appointed on the 11th inst. upon the Bill, entitled, "An Act to provide for the remission or mitigation of fines, forfeitures, and penalties, in certain cases,"—reported amendments;[37] which were postponed to the third reading of the Bill.

ORDERED, That to-morrow be assigned for the THIRD reading of this Bill.[38]

The Senate proceeded, agreeably to the order of the day, to the SECOND reading of the Bill, entitled, "An Act to promote the progress of useful arts."

ORDERED, That it be committed to

> Mr. Carroll
> Mr. Johnson
> Mr. Few
> Mr. Maclay and
> Mr. Paterson[39]

The Senate proceeded to consider the report of the Committee upon the Bill, entitled, "An Act to establish an uniform rule of naturalization;"[40] and after progress, went into the consideration of the executive business, postponed the 10th of March.

The Senate adjourned to 11 o'clock to-morrow.

---

[34] On March 30 this bill was read again and a motion to read it a third time was disagreed to.

[35] Annotations noted on two printed copies of the bill could be from this committee and are in House Bills, Senate Records, DNA.

[36] On March 15 this report was considered and postponed.

[37] Annotations on the printed bill and an attached suggested amendment could be from this committee and are in House Bills, Senate Records, DNA. The report has not been located.

[38] On March 16 the third reading of this bill was begun and consideration was postponed.

[39] On March 29 this committee reported. The report was accepted as amendments to the bill, and the third reading of the bill was scheduled.

[40] On March 16 this report was considered and postponed.

TUESDAY, MARCH 16, 1790

The SENATE assembled,

Present as yesterday, except Mr. Elmer, absent with leave.

The Senate proceeded to the THIRD reading of the Bill, entitled, "An Act to provide for the remission or mitigation of fines, forfeitures, and penalties, in certain cases;" and the report of the Committee being read,—after debate, the farther consideration of the Bill was postponed until to-morrow.[41]

The Senate proceeded in the consideration of the report of the Committee on the Bill, entitled, "An Act to establish an uniform rule of naturalization;" and the report of the Committee thereon being read,—

ORDERED, That the farther consideration hereof be postponed until to-morrow.[42]

ORDERED, That the Bill, entitled, "An Act to vest in Francis Bailey, the exclusive privilege of making, using, and vending to others, punches for stamping the matrices of types, and impressing marks on plates, or any other substance, to prevent counterfeits, upon a principle by him invented, for a term of years," be referred to the Committee appointed yesterday, to take into consideration the Bill, entitled, "An Act to promote the progress of useful arts."[43]

A message from the House of Representatives:

"Mr. PRESIDENT,

"The House of Representatives have passed a Bill, entitled, 'An Act making appropriations for the support of government for the year one thousand seven hundred and ninety;'[44] to which they request the concurrence of the Senate."

ORDERED, That this Bill have the FIRST reading at this time.

ORDERED, That this Bill have the SECOND reading to-morrow.[45]

A message from the President of the United States, by his Secretary, was read:

UNITED STATES, March 16, 1790

GENTLEMEN of the SENATE, and
HOUSE of REPRESENTATIVES,

I HAVE directed my Secretary to lay before you the copy of an Act, and the form of Ratification, of certain articles of amendment to the Constitution of the United States, by the Legislature of the State of Pennsylvania; together

---

[41] On March 17 this bill was considered and recommitted to a special committee.

[42] On March 17 this bill was read a second time and postponed.

[43] On March 29 this committee reported.

[44] This bill has not been located.

[45] On March 17 this bill was read a second time and consideration was postponed.

with the copy of a letter which accompanied the said Act, from the Speaker of the House of Assembly of Pennsylvania, to the President of the United States.

THE originals of the above, will be lodged in the office of the Secretary of State.

G. WASHINGTON

(Copy)

IN GENERAL ASSEMBLY,
STATE OF PENNSYLVANIA; to wit:

In pursuance of a resolution of the General Assembly of the State of Pennsylvania, (being the Legislature thereof) I do hereby certify, That the paper hereunto annexed, contains an exact and true exemplification of the Act whereof it purports to be a copy; by virtue whereof the several amendments therein mentioned, proposed to the Constitution of the United States, were, on the part of the Commonwealth of Pennsylvania, AGREED TO, RATIFIED and CONFIRMED.

Given under my hand, and the seal of the State, this eleventh day of March, in the year of our Lord one thousand seven hundred and ninety.

$\left(\begin{array}{c}\text{SEAL} \\ \text{appendant}\end{array}\right)$ (Signed)   RICHARD PETERS, Speaker

An ACT declaring the assent of this State, to certain amendments to the Constitution of the United States

SEC. 1. Whereas in pursuance of the fifth article of the Constitution of the United States, certain articles of amendment to the said Constitution have been proposed by the Congress of the United States, for the consideration of the Legislatures of the several States; and whereas this House being the Legislature of the State of Pennsylvania, having maturely deliberated thereupon, have resolved to adopt and ratify the articles hereafter enumerated, as part of the Constitution of the United States.

SEC. 2. Be it therefore enacted, and it is hereby enacted by the Representatives of the freemen of the Commonwealth of Pennsylvania, in General Assembly met, and by the authority of the same, That the following amendments to the Constitution of the United States, proposed by the Congress thereof, viz.—

[Here follow the third, fourth, fifth, sixth, seventh, eighth, ninth, tenth, eleventh and twelfth articles, which were proposed by Congress to the Legislatures of the several States, as amendments to the Constitution of the United States.]

—Be, and they are hereby ratified on behalf of this State, to become, when ratified by the Legislatures of three-fourths of the several States, part of the Constitution of the United States.

Signed by order of the House,
RICHARD PETERS, Speaker

Enacted into a law, at Philadelphia, on Wednesday the tenth day of March, in the year of our Lord one thousand seven hundred and ninety.

PETER ZACHARY LLOYD
Clerk of the General Assembly

I Mathew Irwin, Esq; master of the rolls for the State of Pennsylvania, do certify the preceding writing to be a true copy (or exemplification) of a certain law, remaining in my office.

Witness my hand and seal of office, the 11th March, 1790.

(Signed)   MATHEW IRWIN
M. R.

(SEAL)

UNITED STATES, March 16,   1790

I do certify the foregoing to be a true copy of the Act and form of Ratification, of certain articles of amendment to the Constitution of the United States, by the Legislature of the State of Pennsylvania, as transmitted to the President of the United States.

TOBIAS LEAR
Secretary to the President
of the United States

(Copy)

IN ASSEMBLY OF PENNSYLVANIA,
March 11th, 1790

SIR,

I HAVE the honor to transmit an exemplified copy of the Act declaring the assent of this State to certain amendments to the Constitution of the United States, that you may be pleased to lay it before Congress.

With the greatest respect,
I have the honor to be,
Your obedient servant,
(Signed)   RICHARD PETERS, Speaker

His Excellency the PRESIDENT }
   of the UNITED STATES   }

UNITED STATES, March 16, 1790

I certify the above to be a true copy from the original.

TOBIAS LEAR
Secretary to the President
of the United States[46]

---

[46] This message, including documents, is in President's Messages: Suggesting legislation, Senate Records, DNA.

The petition of James Mathers,[47] door-keeper to the Senate, for reasonable compensation for services in the recess;[48] was read.[49]

The Senate adjourned to 11 o'clock to-morrow.

WEDNESDAY, MARCH 17, 1790

The SENATE assembled,

Present as yesterday;

And proceeded to the SECOND reading of the Bill, entitled, "An Act making appropriations for the support of government, for the year one thousand seven hundred and ninety."

ORDERED, That the farther consideration of this Bill be deferred until to-morrow.[50]

The Senate proceeded in the THIRD reading of the Bill, entitled, "An Act to provide for the remission or mitigation of fines, forfeitures, and penalties, in certain cases;"—and the report of the Committee thereon being taken into consideration,—

ORDERED, That the rules be so far dispensed with, as that this Bill be again committed to a special Committee; to consist of

> Mr. Read
> Mr. Morris
> Mr. Strong
> Mr. Ellsworth and
> Mr. Bassett[51]

The Senate proceeded in the SECOND reading of the Bill, entitled, "An Act to establish an uniform rule of naturalization;" and the report of the Committee thereon being considered,—

ORDERED, That the farther consideration of this Bill be postponed until to-morrow.[52]

The Senate adjourned to 11 o'clock to-morrow.

THURSDAY, MARCH 18, 1790

The SENATE assembled,

Present as yesterday;

And proceeded in the SECOND reading of the Bill, entitled, "An Act to establish an uniform rule of naturalization."

---

[47] This petition is in Petitions and Memorials: Claims, Senate Records, DNA.

[48] The rough journal substitutes the phrase "taking care of the Senate Chamber & a." for the word "services."

[49] On March 18 this petition was referred to the committee on the Appropriations Bill.

[50] On March 18 this bill was considered again and committed.

[51] This order is in Various Select Committee Reports, Senate Records, DNA. On March 19 this committee reported and the bill was passed with one amendment. The House was then notified of this action and its concurrence was requested.

[52] On March 18 the second reading was concluded and the third reading was assigned.

ORDERED, That to-morrow be assigned for the THIRD reading of this Bill.[53]

The Senate proceeded in the SECOND reading of the Bill, entitled, "An Act, making appropriations for the support of government for the year one thousand seven hundred and ninety."

ORDERED, That it be committed to

> Mr. Few
> Mr. Johnston
> Mr. Butler
> Mr. Izard and
> Mr. Langdon

ORDERED, That the petition of James Mathers, door-keeper to the Senate, be committed to the above Committee, to report what is proper to be done thereon.[54]

The Senate adjourned to 11 o'clock to-morrow.

F R I D A Y, MARCH 19, 1790

The SENATE assembled,
Present as yesterday.

Mr. Read, on behalf of the Committee appointed March the 17th, to take into consideration the Bill, entitled, "An Act to provide for the remission or mitigation of fines, forfeitures, and penalties, in certain cases,"—reported;[55] which report was accepted as an amendment to the Bill.

RESOLVED, That this Bill DO PASS, with an amendment.[56]

---

[53] On March 19 this bill was passed with an amendment and sent to the House for concurrence in the amendment.

[54] On March 22 this committee reported on the Appropriations Bill and the James Mathers petition. This report was accepted as amendments to the bill. The bill was then read a third time and passed, and a message was sent to the House requesting concurrence in the amendments.

[55] The report is in Various Select Committee Reports, Senate Records, DNA.

[56] The smooth journal reads:

With the following amendment—
Strike out from lines 2 to 20 and insert
"That whenever any person who now is, or hereafter shall be, liable to a fine or penalty, or interested in any Vessel, Goods or other thing which may be subject to seizure and forfeiture, by force of the Laws of the United States, for collecting duties of Impost and Tonnage, and for regulating the coasting trade, shall prefer his petition to the judge of the district in which such fine, penalty or forfeiture may have accrued, truly and particularly setting forth the circumstances of his case, and shall pray that the same may be remitted, The said Judge shall enquire in a summary manner into the circumstances of the case, first causing reasonable notice to be given to the person or persons claiming such fine, penalty or forfeiture, and to the Attorney of the United States for such district, that each may have an opportunity of shewing cause against the mitigation or remission thereof; and shall cause the facts which shall appear upon such enquiry, to be stated and annexed to the petition, and direct their transmission to the Secretary of State, the Secretary of the Treasury, and the Attorney General, any two of whom, shall have power to mitigate or remit such fine, penalty or forfeiture, if in their opinion the same was incurred without wilful negligence or any intention

ORDERED, That a message be sent to the House of Representatives, to acquaint them herewith, and to request their concurrence in the amendment.[57]

The Senate proceeded, agreeably to the order of the day, to the THIRD reading of the Bill, entitled, "An Act to establish an uniform rule of naturalization."

RESOLVED, That this Bill DO PASS, with an amendment.[58]

ORDERED, That a message be sent to the House of Representatives, to acquaint them herewith, and to request their concurrence in the amendment.[59]

The Senate adjourned to Monday next, at 11 o'clock.

MONDAY, MARCH 22, 1790

The SENATE assembled,
Present as on the 19th March.

The petition of Nathaniel Tracy,[60] was read; praying that a law might be enacted for the relief of "unfortunate merchants, from embarrasments arising solely from inevitable mercantile misfortunes."

ORDERED, That this petition lie on the table.[61]

A message from the House of Representatives:

"Mr. PRESIDENT,

"The House of Representatives have agreed to the amendment proposed by the Senate, to the Bill, entitled, An Act to establish an uniform rule of naturalization."[62]

The petition of John Fitch, was read; praying that a clause, providing for

---

of fraud, and to direct the prosecution if any shall have been instituted for the recovery thereof to cease, upon such terms or conditions as they, or any two of them, may deem reasonable and just.

"PROVIDED, that nothing herein contained, shall be construed to affect the right or claim of any person, to that part of any fine, penalty or forfeiture, incurred by a breach of either of the Laws aforesaid, which such person may be entitled to by virtue of the said Laws, in cases where a prosecution has been commenced, or information has been given before the passing of this act."

[57] On March 24 the House considered this amendment, disagreed to it, and appointed a conference committee to meet with a Senate committee. On March 25 the Senate was notified of this action and appointed managers for the conference committee. The House was notified of this action.

[58] The smooth journal reads: "With the following amendment to wit: Line 2 and 3. To strike out *other than an alien enemy.*'"

[59] On March 22 the House concurred in this amendment and notified the Senate.

[60] This petition is in Petitions and Memorials: Various subjects, Senate Records, DNA. The smooth journal spells this name incorrectly as "Tracey."

[61] The rough journal reads: "For the relief of unfortunate ~~Bankrupts~~, was read, and Ordered, to lie on the table." "Merchants" was interlined as a substitution for "Bankrupts." This petition was not considered by the Senate but the House took some action on it.

[62] On March 25 this bill was signed by both the Speaker and the Vice President and given to the committee on enrolled bills for delivery to the President.

the trial by jury, might be inserted in a Bill before Congress, "To promote the progress of useful arts."

ORDERED, That this petition be referred to the Committee who have under consideration the last mentioned Bill.[63]

The Committee to whom was referred the Bill, entitled, "An Act making appropriations for the support of government, for the year one thousand seven hundred and ninety;" and to whom was referred the petition of James Mathers, —reported;[64] which report was accepted as amendments to the Bill.

The Senate proceeded in the SECOND reading of the Bill, entitled, "An Act making appropriations for the support of government, for the year one thousand seven hundred and ninety."

ORDERED, That the rules be so far dispensed with, as that this Bill have a THIRD reading at this time.

RESOLVED, That this Bill DO PASS, with three amendments.[65]

ORDERED, That a message be sent to the House of Representatives, to acquaint them herewith, and to request their concurrence in the amendments.[66]

The Senate adjourned to 11 o'clock to-morrow.

TUESDAY, MARCH 23, 1790

The SENATE assembled,
Present as yesterday.
A message from the House of Representatives:

"Mr. PRESIDENT,

"The House of Representatives have concurred in all the amendments proposed by the Senate to the Bill, entitled, 'An Act making appropriations for the support of government, for the year one thousand seven hundred and ninety;' except the last,—in which they concur with an amendment as follows:

---

[63] This petition and the order referring it to the committee are in Petitions and Memorials: Various subjects, Senate Records, DNA. On March 29 this committee reported.

[64] These reports have not been located. The rough journal inserts the lined out phrase: "To James Mathers and Gifford Dally each the sum of ninety six dollars."

[65] The smooth journal reads:

With the following amendments.

A.	P.	L.	
1.	1.	22.	Strike out *Fifty* and insert "Forty."
2.	2.	2.	Strike out *Fifty* and insert "Forty."
3.	2.	26.	Strike out *one hundred and ninety two dollars*, and insert "ninety six dollars to James Mathers" before the word "Gifford," and next the word "Dally" insert "each."

[66] On March 23 the House concurred with all these amendments with an amendment to the last one. The Senate's concurrence in the amendment was then requested. The Senate did not concur in the House amendment and insisted upon its own amendment. The House was notified of this action.

'To Gifford Dally, door-keeper to the House of Representatives, one hundred and ninety-two dollars; and to James Mathers, door-keeper to the Senate, ninety-six dollars.' "

The Senate proceeded to consider the amendment of the House of Representatives to the last amendment of the Senate, on the Bill, entitled, "An Act making appropriations for the support of government, for the year one thousand seven hundred and ninety,"—and,

RESOLVED, That the Senate do not agree to the amendment proposed by the House of Representatives, but that they do insist on their own amendment.

ORDERED, That a message be sent to the House of Representatives accordingly.[67]

The Senate adjourned to 11 o'clock to-morrow.

WEDNESDAY, MARCH 24, 1790

The SENATE assembled,
Present as yesterday.

A message from the House of Representatives:

"Mr. PRESIDENT,

"The House of Representatives recede from their amendment to the last amendment of the Senate, on the Bill, entitled, 'An Act making appropriations for the support of government, for the year one thousand seven hundred and ninety,'—and concur in the amendment of the Senate."[68]

The Senate, after finishing the executive business before them,—
Adjourned to 11 o'clock to-morrow.

THURSDAY, MARCH 25, 1790

The SENATE assembled,
Present as yesterday.

Mr. Wingate, on behalf of the Committee on enrolled Bills, reported, that they had examined the Bill, entitled, "An Act to establish an uniform rule of naturalization;"[69] and the Bill, entitled, "An Act making appropriations for the support of government, for the year one thousand seven hundred and ninety,"[70]—and had found them correct.

---

[67] On March 24 the House receded from its disagreement to the Senate amendment and notified the Senate.

[68] On March 25 this bill was signed by both the Speaker and the Vice President and given to the committee on enrolled bills for delivery to the President.

[69] The inspected enrolled bill is in Enrolled Acts, RG 11, DNA.

[70] The inspected enrolled bill is in Enrolled Acts, RG 11, DNA. E–46044.

A message from the House of Representatives:

"Mr. PRESIDENT,

"The House of Representatives disagree to the amendment of the Senate, upon the Bill, entitled, 'An Act to provide for the remission or mitigation of fines, forfeitures, and penalties, in certain cases,'—and request a conference on the subject matter of disagreement; and have appointed

> Mr. Ames
> Mr. Huntington and
> Mr. Jackson, managers of the conference on their part:

"The Speaker having affixed his signature to the Bill, entitled, 'An Act to establish an uniform rule of naturalization;' and to the Bill, entitled, 'An Act making appropriations for the support of government, for the year one thousand seven hundred and ninety,'—

"I am directed to bring them to the Senate, for the signature of the Vice President."

The Senate proceeded to appoint

> Mr. Strong
> Mr. Ellsworth and
> Mr. Read, managers of the conference requested on

the disagreeing votes of the Senate and House of Representatives, on the Bill, entitled, "An Act to provide for the remission or mitigation of fines, forfeitures, and penalties, in certain cases."

The Vice President affixed his signature to the enrolled Bill, entitled, "An Act making appropriations for the support of government, for the year one thousand seven hundred and ninety;" and to the Bill, entitled, "An Act to establish an uniform rule of naturalization:"—And they were delivered to the Committee on enrolled Bills, to be laid before the President of the United States, for his approbation.[71]

ORDERED, That a message be sent to the House of Representatives, to acquaint them, that the Senate had agreed to the proposed conference on the Bill, entitled, "An Act to provide for the remission or mitigation of fines, forfeitures, and penalties, in certain cases,"—and had appointed managers on their part.[72]

The Senate adjourned to 11 o'clock to-morrow.

---

[71] On March 26 this committee reported that it had delivered these bills to the President.

[72] The rough journal includes the following passage marked "not passed expunged": "Ordered, that the Secretary procure the latest edition of the Statutes at large and of Williams' digest for the use of the Senate." On April 5 this committee reported that it had not reached an agreement on the disputed amendment.

F R I D A Y, MARCH 26, 1790

The SENATE assembled,
Present as yesterday.

Mr. Wingate, on behalf of the Committee on enrolled Bills, reported, That they did yesterday, lay before the President of the United States, for his approbation, the Bill, entitled, "An Act making appropriations for the support of government, for the year one thousand seven hundred and ninety;" together with the Bill, entitled, "An Act to establish an uniform rule of naturalization."[73]

The petition of the merchants and traders of the town of Portsmouth, and State of New-Hampshire,[74] praying that a law might be enacted, "For the establishment of the foreign trade of the United States, upon principles of reciprocal benefit, becoming the dignity of a free and independent nation;" and also for an alteration in the law, to establish the Judicial Courts of the United States, "So far as that the District and Circuit Courts, for the State of New-Hampshire, may be held in the town of Portsmouth,"—was read.

ORDERED, That so much of this petition as respects the regulation of trade, be referred to the Committee appointed February 11th, to report, if they think it expedient, a plan for the regulation of the trade of the United States, with the countries and settlements of the European powers in America,[75]—

And that so much of the said petition as respects the places for holding the District and Circuit Courts in the State of New-Hampshire, be referred to the Committee appointed January 15th, 1790, to bring in a Bill in addition to "An Act to establish the Judicial Courts of the United States."[76]

The memorial of the officers of the late Navy of the United States,[77] praying that the same emoluments that were granted to the officers of the late Continental army, may be extended to them,—was read.

ORDERED, That this memorial lie on the table.

A message from the House of Representatives:

"Mr. PRESIDENT,

"The House of Representatives have had under consideration the confidential communications from the President of the United States, of the 12th January, to the Senate and House of Representatives, and have passed a Bill upon that subject;[78] to which they request the concurrence of the Senate."

---

[73] On March 26 the President signed both of these bills and the House notified the Senate on March 30.

[74] This petition is in Petitions and Memorials: Various subjects, Senate Records, DNA.

[75] On April 27 another member was appointed to this committee.

[76] On April 29 this committee reported a bill which was read for the first time.

[77] This memorial is in Petitions and Memorials: Various subjects, Senate Records, DNA.

[78] This printed bill is in the Broadside Collection, RBkRm, DLC. E–46036.

ORDERED, That the Bill, entitled, "An Act for regulating the military establishment of the United States," have the FIRST reading at this time.

ORDERED, That Monday next be assigned for the SECOND reading of this Bill; and that in the mean time, it be printed for the use of the Senate.[79]

The Senate adjourned to 11 o'clock on Monday next.

MONDAY, MARCH 29, 1790

The SENATE assembled,

Present as on the 26th March,—

Except Mr. Morris, absent with leave.

Mr. Carroll, on behalf of the Committee appointed March 15th, to consider the Bill, entitled, "An Act to promote the progress of useful arts;" and the Bill, entitled, "An Act to vest in Francis Bailey, the exclusive privilege of making, using, and vending to others, punches for stamping the matrices of types, and impressing marks on plates, or any other substance, to prevent counterfeits, upon a principle by him invented, for a term of years;" together with the petition of John Fitch, reported;[80] which report was accepted as amendments to the first mentioned Bill.

ORDERED, That the Bill, entitled, "An Act to promote the progress of useful arts," have the THIRD reading to-morrow.[81]

A message from the House of Representatives:

"Mr. PRESIDENT,

"The House of Representatives have passed another Bill upon the subject of the confidential communications made by the President of the United States,[82]—in which they request the concurrence of the Senate.

"They have also passed a Bill, entitled, 'An Act to prevent the exportation of goods not duly inspected according to the laws of the several States,'[83]—in which they request the concurrence of the Senate.

"The House of Representatives have considered the Bill, entitled, 'An Act to accept a cession of the claims of the State of North-Carolina, to a certain district of western territory;' and have concurred with the Senate therein, with an amendment,[84]—to which amendment they request the concurrence of the Senate."

---

[79] On March 29 this bill was read a second time.

[80] The annotated printed bill, with amendments which probably correspond to the report, is in House Bills, Senate Records, DNA. The report has not been located.

[81] On March 30 this bill was read a third time and passed with twelve amendments. The concurrence of the House was then requested.

[82] This bill has not been located.

[83] This bill has not been located.

[84] An attested extract from the House Journal with an amendment is in Engrossed Senate Bills and Resolutions, Senate Records, DNA.

The Senate proceeded to the FIRST reading of the Bill, entitled, "An Act providing for holding a treaty or treaties, to establish peace with certain Indian tribes."

ORDERED, That this Bill have a SECOND reading on Monday next.[85]

The Senate proceeded to the FIRST reading of the Bill, entitled, "An Act to prevent the exportation of goods not duly inspected according to the laws of the several States."

ORDERED, That this Bill have the SECOND reading to-morrow.[86]

The Senate proceeded to consider the amendment of the House of Representatives, to the Bill, entitled, "An Act to accept a cession of the claims of the State of North-Carolina, to a certain district of western territory."

RESOLVED, That they concur in the amendment of the House of Representatives, with an amendment.[87]

ORDERED, That a message be sent to the House of Representatives, accordingly.[88]

The Senate proceeded to the SECOND reading of the Bill, entitled, "An Act for regulating the military establishment of the United States."[89]

The Senate adjourned to 11 o'clock to-morrow.

TUESDAY, MARCH 30, 1790

The SENATE assembled,

Present as yesterday,—and

Proceeded in the SECOND reading of the Bill, entitled, "An Act for encreasing the salaries of clerks, in the office of the commissioners for settling ac-

---

[85] On April 5 this bill was read for the second time and postponed.

[86] On March 30 this bill was read a second time and the third reading was assigned.

[87] The resolve and amendment are in Engrossed Senate Bills and Resolutions, Senate Records, DNA. The smooth journal adds:

By striking out these words,—

"The Honorable Samuel Johnston and Benjamin Hawkins, Senators from the State of North Carolina, in the Congress of the United States of America, having pursuant to an act of the Legislature of the said State, of the   day of December, one thousand seven hundred and eighty nine, executed, and in the Senate, offered for acceptance, a Deed of Cession to the said United States of the claims of the said State of North Carolina, to a district of territory therein described, which Deed is in the words following; viz:"

And inserting instead thereof, these words,—

"A Deed of Cession having been executed, and in the Senate, offered for acceptance to the United States of the claims of the State of North Carolina, to a district of territory therein described; which Deed is in the words following, viz."

[88] On March 30 the House agreed to the amendment and notified the Senate.

[89] On March 30 the second reading of this bill was continued, and the bill was committed.

counts between the United States and individual States;" and on motion to assign a time for the THIRD reading of the Bill,—

It passed in the Negative.[90]

The Senate proceeded to the THIRD reading of the Bill, entitled, "An Act to promote the progress of useful arts,"—and

RESOLVED, That this Bill DO PASS, with twelve amendments.[91]

---

[90] Notation of Senate action is attached to the House Bill and is in Engrossed House Bills, House Records, DNA. This bill was not considered again in the First Congress.

[91] The smooth journal reads:

"With the following amendments.

A.	P.	L.	
1.	1.	2.	Strike out all the words between "State," and "which," and in-
		a	sert, "The Secretary for the Department of War, and the
		19.	Attorney General of the United States, setting forth, that he,

she, or they hath or have invented or discovered any useful Art, Manufacture, Engine, Machine or Device, or any improvement therein not before known or used, and praying that a Patent may be granted therefor, it shall and may be lawful to and for the said Secretary of State, the Secretary for the Department of War, and the Attorney General or any two of them, if they shall deem the invention or discovery sufficiently useful and important, to cause Letters patent to be made out in the name of the United States, to bear Test by the President of the United States, reciting the allegations and suggestions of the said petition and describing the said invention or discovery, clearly, truly and fully; and thereupon granting to such petitioner or petitioners, his, her or their Heirs, Administrators, or Assigns for any term not exceeding fourteen years, the sole and exclusive right and liberty of making, constructing, using and vending to others to be used the said invention or discovery."

2.	1.	21.	Strike out all the words between "him," and "cause," and insert
		a	"if he shall find the same conformable to this act, certify it to
		23.	be so, at the foot thereof, and present the Letters patent so

certified to the President who shall."

3.			Strike out the word *"great"*
4.	2.	2.	After the word "explanations," strike out the words included in

a parenthesis, and insert, "and Models (if the nature of the invention or discovery will admit of a Model)."

5.		4.	Strike out the word *"generally."*
6.		5.	After the word "particular," insert "and said Models so exact."
7.		6.	After the word "used," strike out the words *"within the United States."*
8.		12.	Strike out the whole of the Section, and insert,—"AND BE IT
		a	FURTHER ENACTED, That upon the application of any person
		29.	to the Secretary of State for a copy of any such specification,
&			and for permission to have similar model or models. It shall
	3.	1.	be the duty of the Secretary to give such copy and to permit
		a	the person so applying for a similar model or models to take
		3.	or make or cause the same to be taken or made at the expense

of such Applicant."

ORDERED, That a message be sent to the House of Representatives, to acquaint them herewith, and to request their concurrence in the amendments.[92]

A message from the House of Representatives:

"Mr. PRESIDENT,

"The House of Representatives have agreed to the amendment of the Senate, to their amendment to the Bill, entitled, 'An Act to accept a cession of the claims of the State of North-Carolina, to a certain district of western territory.' "[93]

9.	3.	23.	After the word "contrary," insert "or if it shall appear that the patentee, was not the first and true inventor or discoverer."
10.		24.	Between the Sections—insert "AND BE IT FURTHER ENACTED, That whenever the Grantee of such Patent shall neglect to offer for sale within the United States a sufficient number of any such manufacture, Engine, Machine, Art or Device, or any improvement therein or shall the same at a price beyond what may be judged an adequate compensation, the Supreme Court of the United States, or any two Justices thereof, out of Session, on complaint thereof made to them in writing, are hereby authorised to enquire, in a summary way, into the justness of the said complaint; and if the same be found to be true, to take sufficient Recognizance and Security of the Grantee, his Heirs, Administrators, or Assigns, conditioned, that he or they shall within such reasonable time as the said Court or Justices shall prescribe, offer for sale within the United States a sufficient number of such Manufacture, Engine, Machine, Art or Device, or improvement therein, at such reasonable prices as the said Court or Justices shall on due consideration affix; and if the Grantee, his Heirs, Administrators, or Assigns, shall neglect or refuse to give security as aforesaid, the said Court or Justices are hereby authorised to grant to the Complainant a full and ample Licence to make, construct, and vend such Manufacture, Engine, Art or Device, or improvement therein in such numbers, and for such Term as they shall judge proper, PROVIDED the Complainant shall give sufficient security to the Court or Justices aforesaid, to sell the same, at such reasonable prices as the said Court or Justices shall thereto affix, and if such complaint shall appear to be ill founded, the complainant shall be liable to pay all such costs as the Defendant shall be put to, in defending said complaint to be taxed and recovered as aforesaid."
11.	4.	10.	Strike out the words *"for making out the advertisement one Dollar"*
12.		13. a 15.	Strike out the words *"to each of the Referees to whom shall be referred any Petition, for examining the same and certifying their opinion, six dollars per day."*

[92] On April 3 the House considered these amendments and agreed to all of them except the tenth one. The Senate was notified on April 7 and resolved to recede from the tenth amendment. The House was then notified of this action.

[93] The House message attached to the Senate resolve is in Engrossed Senate Bills and Resolutions, Senate Records, DNA. On April 1 this bill was signed by both the Speaker and the Vice President and given to the committee on enrolled bills for delivery to the President.

The Senate proceeded to the SECOND reading of the Bill, entitled, "An Act to prevent the exportation of goods not duly inspected according to the laws of the several States,"—and

ORDERED, That to-morrow be assigned for the THIRD reading of this Bill.[94]

The Senate proceeded in the SECOND reading of the Bill, entitled, "An Act for regulating the military establishment of the United States."

ORDERED, That this Bill be committed to

> Mr. Few
> Mr. Ellsworth
> Mr. Butler
> Mr. Schuyler
> Mr. Carroll
> Mr. Langdon and
> Mr. Strong[95]

A message from the House of Representatives:

"Mr. PRESIDENT,

"I am directed to inform the Senate, that the President of the United States, did, on the 26th March, affix his signature to 'An Act making appropriations for the support of government, for the year one thousand seven hundred and ninety;' and to 'An Act to establish an uniform rule of naturalization.' "

The Senate adjourned to 11 o'clock to-morrow.

WEDNESDAY, MARCH 31, 1790

The SENATE assembled,
Present as yesterday,—and

Proceeded to the THIRD reading of the Bill, entitled, "An Act to prevent the exportation of goods not duly inspected according to the laws of the several States."

RESOLVED, That this Bill DO PASS.

ORDERED, That a message be sent to the House of Representatives, to acquaint them with the concurrence of the Senate in the above mentioned Bill.[96]

The Senate proceeded in the executive business communicated in the message from the President of the United States, of the 30th March.

The Senate adjourned to 11 o'clock to-morrow.

---

[94] On March 31 the Senate read this bill a third time, passed it, and notified the House of this concurrence.

[95] On April 6 this committee reported, and consideration of the report was postponed.

[96] On April 1 this bill was signed by both the Speaker and the Vice President and given to the committee on enrolled bills for delivery to the President.

THURSDAY, APRIL 1, 1790

The SENATE assembled,

Present as yesterday.

Mr. Wingate, on behalf of the joint Committee on enrolled bills, reported,
—That they had examined the Bill, entitled, "An Act to accept a cession of
the claims of the State of North-Carolina, to a certain district of western
territory;"[1] and the Bill, entitled, "An Act to prevent the exportation of goods
not duly inspected according to the laws of the several States,"[2]—and had
found them correct.

ORDERED, That   Mr. Ellsworth

                    Mr. Few and

                    Mr. Wingate, be a Committee to state the compen-
sation due to the members of the Senate, for the present session, to the 31st
March, inclusive.[3]

A message from the House of Representatives:

"Mr. PRESIDENT,

"The Committee on enrolled Bills, having examined the Bill, entitled,
'An Act to accept a cession of the claims of the State of North-Carolina, to a
certain district of western territory;' and the Bill, entitled, 'An Act to prevent
the exportation of goods not duly inspected according to the laws of the several States;' and found them correct; and the Speaker having affixed his signature thereto, I am directed to bring them to the Senate."

Whereupon the Vice President affixed his signature to the above mentioned
Bills, and they were delivered to the Committee, to be laid before the President of the United States, for his approbation.[4]

The Senate adjourned to Saturday next, at 11 o'clock.

SATURDAY, APRIL 3, 1790

The SENATE assembled,

Present as on the 1st April,—and,[5]

Mr. Elmer, from the State of New-Jersey, attended.

Mr. Wingate, on behalf of the joint Committee to examine enrolled Bills,

---

[1] The inspected enrolled bill is in Enrolled Acts, RG 11, DNA.

[2] The inspected enrolled bill is in Enrolled Acts, RG 11, DNA.

[3] Mr. Ellsworth's motion suggesting the committee is in Senate Simple Resolutions
and Motions, Senate Records, DNA. On April 3 this committee reported, and the report
was printed in the text and accepted.

[4] On April 3 this committee reported that it had laid these bills before the President.
The President signed the North Carolina Cession Act on April 3 and the Inspection Act
on April 2.

[5] The rough journal reads: "Present as ~~yesterday, & Except Mr. Paterson, absent with
leave.~~" "On the 1st April" was interlined as a substitution for the crossed-out words.

reported,—That they had on the 1st of April, presented to the President of the United States, for his approbation, the Bill, entitled, "An Act to accept a cession of the claims of the State of North-Carolina, to a certain district of western territory;" and the Bill, entitled, "An Act to prevent the exportation of goods not duly inspected according to the laws of the several States."

A message from the President of the United States:

"Mr. PRESIDENT,

"I am commanded to inform the Senate, that the President of the United States, did on the 2d of April, approve of and affix his signature to 'An Act to accept a cession of the claims of the State of North-Carolina, to a certain district of western territory.'

"I am also commanded to communicate to the Senate, a written message from the President of the United States."

The message and papers accompanying it, were read.

UNITED STATES, April 1, 1790

GENTLEMEN of the SENATE, and
    HOUSE of REPRESENTATIVES,

I HAVE directed my private Secretary to lay before you, a copy of the adoption, by the Legislature of South-Carolina, of the articles proposed by Congress to the Legislatures of the several States, as amendments to the Constitution of the United States; together with the copy of a letter from the Governor of the State of South-Carolina, to the President of the United States, which have lately come to my hands.—The originals of the foregoing, will be lodged in the office of the Secretary of State.

G. WASHINGTON

(Copy)

"CHARLESTON, January 28, 1790

"SIR,

"I have the honor to transmit you the entire adoption, by the Legislature of this State, of the amendments proposed to the Constitution of the United States.

"I am, with the most perfect esteem and respect,

Your most obedient servant,

(Signed)   CHARLES PINCKNEY

"To the PRESIDENT of the ⎫
    UNITED STATES"   ⎬

(Copy)

"In the HOUSE of REPRESENTATIVES
"January 18, 1790

"The House took into consideration the report of the Committee, to whom was referred the resolution of the Congress of the United States, of the 4th day of March, 1789, proposing amendments to the Constitution of the United States.

[Here follows a recital of the articles of amendment.[6]]

"Which being read through, was agreed to.

"Whereupon—

"RESOLVED, That this House do adopt the said several articles, and that they become a part of the Constitution of the United States.

"RESOLVED, That the resolution be sent to the Senate, for their concurrence.

"By order of the House,

JACOB READ
Speaker of the House of Representatives"

"In the SENATE
"January 19, 1790

"RESOLVED, That this House do concur with the House of Representatives, in the foregoing resolutions.

"By order of the Senate,

D. DE SAUSSURE
President of the Senate"[7]

ORDERED, That a message be sent to the House of Representatives, to inform them, that the President of the United States did, on the 2d April, approve of and affix his signature to "An Act to accept a cession of the claims of the State of North-Carolina, to a certain district of western territory."

Mr. Ellsworth, on behalf of the Committee appointed the 1st April, to state the compensation due to the members of the Senate, for the present session, reported,—

"That there is due to the Senators of the United States, for attendance in Congress, the present Session, to the 31st day of March inclusive, and expences of travel to Congress, as allowed by law, as follows, to wit:

To Mr. Bassett	496½ Dollars
Mr. Butler	796
Mr. Carroll	186
Mr. Dalton	612
Mr. Ellsworth	546½
Mr. Elmer	414
Mr. Few	833½
Mr. Henry	596½

---

[6] The rough journal originally included the articles of amendment, but they were canceled by Otis with the notations, "Articles not to be printed" and "NB expunged from A page 123 to B page 129 as superfluous. Sam: A Otis."

[7] This message, including documents, is in President's Messages: Suggesting legislation, Senate Records, DNA.

Mr. Hawkins ....615 ⎫	468
deduct certificate given ....147 ⎭	
Mr. Johnson	544
Mr. Johnston	534
Mr. King	522
Mr. Langdon	618
Mr. Maclay	585
Mr. Morris	430½
Mr. Paterson	514½
Mr. Read	195
Mr. Strong	575½
Mr. Schuyler	571½
Mr. Wingate	616½

10,655½ Dollars

Which report being accepted, the Vice President executed the following Certificate:

In SENATE of the UNITED STATES
NEW-YORK, the 3d day of April, 1790

I certify, that the sums affixed to the names of the Senators, are due to them respectively, according to law.

JOHN ADAMS
Vice President[8]

The Senate adjourned to 11 o'clock on Monday next.

MONDAY, APRIL 5, 1790

The SENATE assembled,
Present as on the 3d of April.

A message from the House of Representatives:

"Mr. PRESIDENT,

"The House of Representatives, agree to all the amendments of the Senate, to the Bill, entitled, 'An Act to promote the progress of useful arts,' except the tenth; to which they do not agree.

"The President of the United States, did on the 2d of April, approve of, and affixed his signature to 'An Act to prevent the exportation of goods not duly inspected according to the laws of the several States.' "

The Senate proceeded to consider the message from the House of Representatives, together with the Bill, entitled, "An Act to promote the progress

---

[8] This report is in the Office of the Financial Clerk of the Senate, Senate Records, DNA.

of useful arts;" and the disagreement of the House of Representatives, to their tenth amendment,—and

RESOLVED, That the Senate do recede from the said amendment.

ORDERED, That a message be sent to the House of Representatives, accordingly.[9]

Mr. Strong, on behalf of the managers appointed the 25th March, to confer with a Committee of the House of Representatives, on the amendment of the Senate, to the Bill, entitled, "An Act to provide for the remission or mitigation of fines, fortfeitures, and penalties, in certain cases," reported,[10]—

"That having conferred with the managers on the part of the House of Representatives, they could come to no agreement on the subject matter of the said amendments."

The Senate proceeded to the SECOND reading of the Bill, entitled, "An Act providing for holding a treaty or treaties, to establish peace with certain Indian tribes."

ORDERED, That the consideration hereof be postponed.[11]

A written message from the President of the United States, was communicated to the Senate, by his Secretary:

UNITED STATES, April 5, 1790

GENTLEMEN of the SENATE, and
    HOUSE of REPRESENTATIVES,

I HAVE directed my private Secretary to lay before you, copies of three acts of the Legislature of the State of New-York, which have been transmitted to me by the Governor thereof, viz.

"An Act declaring it to be the duty of the Sheriffs of the several counties within this State, to receive and safe keep such prisoners as shall be committed under the authority of the United States."

"An Act for vesting in the United States of America, the Light-House, and lands thereunto belonging, at Sandy-Hook;" and,

"An Act ratifying certain articles in addition to, and amendment of the Constitution of the United States of America, proposed by Congress."

A copy of a letter accompanying said Acts, from the Governor of the State of New-York, to the President of the United States, will at the same time be laid before you, and the originals deposited in the office of the Secretary of State.

G. WASHINGTON

---

[9] On April 8 this bill was signed by both the Speaker and the Vice President and given to the committee on enrolled bills for delivery to the President.

[10] On April 12 the House adhered to its disagreement to this Senate amendment and notified the Senate. On the same date the Senate considered this House action and postponed consideration.

[11] On May 4 this bill was again considered and postponed.

(Copy)

"NEW-YORK, 2d April, 1790

"SIR,

"I HAVE the honor of transmitting to your Excellency, herewith inclosed, exemplifications of three Acts of the Legislature of this State, passed at their present session,

"And to be, with the highest respect,
Your most obedient servant,
(Signed)   GEORGE CLINTON"

UNITED STATES, April 5, 1790

I hereby certify, that the foregoing is a true copy of the original letter from the Governor of the State of New-York, to the President of the United States.
(Signed)   TOBIAS LEAR
Secretary to the President
of the United States

"THE PEOPLE of the State of NEW-YORK, by the Grace of God, free and
        independent;
"To ALL to whom these presents shall come or may concern,—Greeting:

"KNOW YE, That We, having inspected the records remaining in our Secretary's-Office, do find there a certain Act of our Legislature, in the words and figures following: 'An Act ratifying certain articles in addition to, and amendment of, the Constitution of the United States of America, proposed by the Congress':—WHEREAS by the fifth article of the Constitution of the United States of America, it is provided that the Congress, whenever two thirds of both Houses shall deem it necessary, shall propose amendments to the said Constitution, which shall be valid, to all intents and purposes, as part of the said Constitution, when ratified by the Legislatures of three fourths of the several States, or by Conventions in three fourths thereof; as the one or the other mode of ratification may be proposed by the Congress. And whereas in the session of the Congress of the United States of America, begun and held at the city of New-York, on Wednesday the fourth of March, one thousand seven hundred and eighty nine, it was resolved by the Senate and House of Representatives of the United States of America in Congress assembled, two thirds of both Houses concurring, that the following articles be proposed to the Legislatures of the several States, as amendments to the Constitution of the United States; all or any of which articles, when ratified by three fourths of the said Legislatures, to be valid, to all intents and purposes, as part of the said Constitution, viz.—Articles in addition to, and amendment of the Constitution of the United States of America, proposed by Congress, and ratified by the Legislatures of the several States, pursuant to the fifth article of the original Constitution.

[Here follows the several articles.]

"And whereas the Legislature of this State, have considered the said articles, and do agree to the same, except the second article:—THEREFORE BE IT ENACTED by the People of the State of New-York, represented in Senate and Assembly, and it is hereby enacted by the authority of the same, that the said articles, except the second, shall be, and hereby are ratified by the Legislature of this State."

"STATE OF NEW-YORK
"In ASSEMBLY, February 22, 1790
"This Bill having been read the third time,—
"RESOLVED, That the Bill do pass.

"By order of the Assembly,
GULIAN VERPLANCK, Speaker"

"STATE OF NEW-YORK
"In SENATE, February 24, 1790
"This Bill having been read a third time,—
"RESOLVED, That the Bill do pass.

"By order of the Senate,
ISAAC ROOSEVELT
President, pro hac vice."

"COUNCIL OF REVISION
"February 27, 1790
"RESOLVED, That it does not appear improper to the Council, that this Bill, entitled, 'An Act ratifying certain articles in addition to, and amendment of the Constitution of the United States of America, proposed by the Congress,' should become a law of this State.

"GEORGE CLINTON"

"ALL WHICH WE HAVE caused to be exemplified by these presents: In TESTIMONY whereof, WE have caused these our letters to be made patent, and the[12] GREAT SEAL of our said State to be hereunto affixed: WITNESS our trusty and well-beloved GEORGE CLINTON, Esquire, Governor of our said State, General and Commander in Chief of all the Militia, and Admiral of the Navy of the same, at our City of New-York, the twenty-seventh day of March, in the year one thousand seven hundred and ninety, and in the fourteenth year of our Independence.

$\left(\begin{array}{c} \text{SEAL} \\ \text{appendant} \end{array}\right)$ (Signed)   "GEORGE CLINTON"

"Passed the Secretary's Office, the 27th March, 1790.

(Signed)   "LEWIS A. SCOTT, Secretary"

---

[12] The smooth journal substitutes "our" for "the."

UNITED STATES, April 5, 1790

I hereby certify, that the foregoing is a true copy of the exemplification of a certain act, transmitted to the President of the United States, by the Governor of the State of New-York.

TOBIAS LEAR
Secretary to the President
of the United States[13]

The Senate adjourned to 11 o'clock to-morrow.

TUESDAY, APRIL 6, 1790

The SENATE assembled,
Present as yesterday.

Mr. Few, reported from the Committee appointed the 30th March,[14] to take into consideration the Bill, entitled, "An Act for regulating the military establishment of the United States."

On motion, That the consideration of the report be postponed,—
It passed in the Affirmative.[15]

The Senate adjourned to 11 o'clock to-morrow.

WEDNESDAY, APRIL 7, 1790

The SENATE assembled,
Present as yesterday.

ORDERED, That   Mr. Ellsworth
Mr. Johnston and
Mr. Strong, be a Committee to bring in a Bill, for the government of the territory of the United States, south of the river Ohio.[16]

A message from the House of Representatives:

"Mr. PRESIDENT,

"The House of Representatives have passed a Bill, entitled, 'An Act further to suspend part of an Act, entitled, An Act to regulate the collection of the duties imposed by law on the tonnage of ships or vessels, and on goods, wares and merchandizes, imported into the United States;'[17] in which they request the concurrence of the Senate."

---

[13] This message, including documents, is in President's Messages: Suggesting legislation, Senate Records, DNA.

[14] A list of amendments, which probably came from the committee, is in House Bills, Senate Records, DNA. The report has not been located.

[15] On April 13 the Senate resumed the second reading of this bill and consideration was postponed.

[16] On April 9 this committee reported a bill which was read for the first time. The second reading was scheduled.

[17] This bill has not been located.

ORDERED, That this Bill have the FIRST reading at this time.

ORDERED, That to-morrow be assigned for the second reading of this Bill.[18]

The Senate adjourned to 11 o'clock to-morrow.

THURSDAY, APRIL 8, 1790

The SENATE assembled,

Present as yesterday.

Agreeably to the order of the day, the Senate proceeded in the SECOND reading of the Bill, entitled, "An Act further to suspend part of an Act, entitled, An Act to regulate the collection of the duties imposed by law on the tonnage of ships or vessels, and on goods, wares and merchandizes, imported into the United States."

ORDERED, That this Bill be committed to

> Mr. Langdon
>
> Mr. Ellsworth and
>
> Mr. Dalton[19]

A message from the House of Representatives:

"Mr. PRESIDENT,

"The Speaker having signed an enrolled Bill, I am directed to bring it to the Senate."

The Vice President affixed his signature to the Bill, entitled, "An Act to promote the progress of useful arts,"[20]—

And it was delivered to the Committee on enrolled Bills, to be laid before the President of the United States, for his approbation.[21]

The Senate adjourned to 11 o'clock to-morrow.

FRIDAY, APRIL 9, 1790

The SENATE assembled,

Present as yesterday.

Mr. Wingate, reported from the joint Committee on enrolled Bills, That they did yesterday lay before the President of the United States, for his approbation, the Bill, entitled, "An Act to promote the progress of useful arts."

Mr. Langdon, reported from the Committee appointed the 8th of April,[22] on the Bill, entitled, "An Act further to suspend part of an Act, entitled, An Act to regulate the collection of the duties imposed by law on the tonnage of

---

[18] On April 8 this bill was read a second time and committed.

[19] On April 9 this committee's report was accepted as an amendment to the bill, and the bill was read a third time and passed. The Senate then requested the House's concurrence in the amendments.

[20] The inspected enrolled bill is in Enrolled Acts, RG 11, DNA.

[21] On April 10 the President signed this bill and the Senate was notified on April 12.

[22] This report has not been located.

ships or vessels, and on goods, wares and merchandizes, imported into the United States;"—which report was accepted as an amendment to the Bill.

The Senate proceeded in the SECOND reading of the last mentioned Bill.

ORDERED, That the rules be so far dispensed with, as that this Bill have the THIRD reading at this time.

RESOLVED, That this Bill DO PASS with two amendments.[23]

ORDERED, That the Secretary do carry a message to the House of Representatives, and request their concurrence in the amendments to this Bill.[24]

Mr. Ellsworth, reported from the Committee appointed April 7th, "A Bill for the government of the territory of the United States, south of the river Ohio."[25]

ORDERED, That this Bill have the FIRST reading at this time.

ORDERED, That Monday next be assigned for the SECOND reading of this Bill.[26]

The Senate adjourned 'till 11 o'clock on Monday next.

M O N D A Y, APRIL 12, 1790

The SENATE assembled,

Present as on the 9th;—and

The Hon. Richard Henry Lee, from the State of Virginia, attended.

The Senate proceeded to the SECOND reading of the Bill, "For the government of the territory of the United States, south of the river Ohio;"—and

ORDERED, That it be printed for the use of the Senate.[27]

A message from the House of Representatives:

"Mr. PRESIDENT,

"The House of Representatives do adhere to their disagreement to the amendment proposed by the Senate to the Bill, entitled, 'An Act to provide for the remission or mitigation of fines, fortfeitures, and penalties, in certain cases;'

---

[23] The rough journal reads:

Resolved, that this bill do pass with the two *following* amendments

(Add the following Clause. And be it further enacted by the authority aforesaid that the landing places in Windsor and East Windsor in the State of Connecticut shall be ports of delivery and be included in the distrist of New London.

To add to the Title these words "and to amend the said act.")

A slip of paper pasted over this paragraph carries the following notation: "Mr. Bankson will omit to record the amendments in future. The minute books will be preserved and if ever recurrence is necessary it may be had to the first entry. April 21st 1790."

[24] On this date the House concurred in these amendments, and it notified the Senate on April 12.

[25] A printed copy of the bill is in the Broadside Collection, RBkRm, DLC. E–46040.

[26] At this point the rough journal originally included the sentence "Mr. Bassett had leave of absence" which was later lined out. On April 12 this bill was read a second time and ordered to be printed.

[27] On April 13 this bill was considered again, and the third reading was assigned.

"They do concur in the Bill, entitled, 'An Act for the punishment of certain crimes against the United States,' with sundry amendments,[28] to which they request the concurrence of the Senate;

"They also concur with the Senate in their amendments to the Bill, entitled, 'An Act further to suspend part of an Act, entitled, "An Act to regulate the collection of the duties imposed by law on the tonnage of ships or vessels, and on goods, wares, and merchandizes, imported into the United States" '[29]—

"I am directed to inform the Senate, that the President of the United States did, on the 10th of April, approve of, and affix his signature to 'An Act to promote the progress of useful arts.' "

The Senate proceeded to consider the adherence of the House of Representatives, to their amendment on the Bill, entitled, "An Act to provide for the remission or mitigation of fines, forfeitures, and penalties, in certain cases."

ORDERED, That the farther consideration hereof be postponed until tomorrow.[30]

The amendments of the House of Representatives, to the Bill, entitled, "An Act for the punishment of certain crimes against the United States," were read,—and

On motion,

ORDERED, That they lie until to-morrow, for consideration.[31]

The Senate adjourned to 11 o'clock to-morrow.

TUESDAY, APRIL 13, 1790

The SENATE assembled,
Present as yesterday;—and

The Honorable James Gunn, from the State of Georgia, attended.

Mr. Wingate, reported from the joint Committee on enrolled Bills, That they had examined the Bill, entitled, "An Act further to suspend part of an Act, entitled, 'An Act to regulate the collection of the duties imposed by law on the tonnage of ships or vessels, and on goods, wares, and merchandizes, imported into the United States, and to amend the said Act,' "[32] and had found it correct.

The Senate proceeded to consider the resolve of the House of Representatives, adhering to their disagreement to the amendment of the Senate, on the Bill, entitled, "An Act to provide for the remission or mitigation of fines, forfeitures, and penalties, in certain cases," and—

---

[28] An engrossed extract that includes a resolve with amendments is in Engrossed Senate Bills and Resolutions, Senate Records, DNA.

[29] On April 13 this bill was signed by both the Speaker and the Vice President and given to the committee on enrolled bills for delivery to the President.

[30] On April 13 the Senate adhered to its amendment.

[31] This amended bill was considered and postponed on April 8.

[32] The inspected enrolled bill is in Enrolled Acts, RG 11, DNA. E–22962.

RESOLVED, That the Senate do adhere to their amendment to the said Bill.

ORDERED, That the Secretary do carry a message to the House of Representatives, accordingly.[33]

The Senate proceeded to consider the amendments of the House of Representatives, to the Bill, entitled, "An Act for the punishment of certain crimes against the United States,"—and

On motion,

The farther consideration thereof was postponed until to-morrow.[34]

A message from the House of Representatives:

"Mr. PRESIDENT,

"The Speaker having signed an enrolled Bill, I am directed to bring it to the Senate."

The Vice President affixed his signature to the enrolled Bill, entitled, "An Act further to suspend part of an Act, entitled, 'An Act to regulate the collection of the duties imposed by law on the tonnage of ships or vessels, and on goods, wares and merchandizes, imported into the United States;' and to amend the said Act"—

And it was delivered to the Committee on enrolled Bills, to lay before the President of the United States, for his approbation.[35]

The Senate proceeded in the SECOND reading of the Bill, "For the government of the territory of the United States, south of the river Ohio."

ORDERED, That this Bill have the THIRD reading to-morrow.[36]

The Senate resumed the SECOND reading of the Bill, entitled, "An Act for regulating the military establishment of the United States;"

On motion, To postpone the further consideration thereof,[37]—

It passed in the Affirmative.[38]

The Senate adjourned to 11 o'clock to-morrow.

WEDNESDAY, APRIL 14, 1790

The SENATE assembled,

Present as yesterday;—

Except Mr. Bassett, absent with leave.

Mr. Wingate, reported from the joint Committee on enrolled Bills, That

---

[33] This bill was not considered again. See [HR–57] Mitigation of Forfeitures Bill.

[34] On April 14 these amendments were considered again and the Senate agreed to some and disagreed to others. The House was then notified of these actions.

[35] On April 14 this committee reported that it had laid the bill before the President.

[36] On April 14 this bill was read a third time, passed, and sent to the House for concurrence.

[37] The smooth journal reads "hereof" rather than "thereof."

[38] On April 15 the Senate resumed the second reading of this bill, and consideration was again postponed.

they had this day laid before the President of the United States, for his approbation, the Bill, entitled, "An Act further to suspend part of an Act, entitled,
'An Act to regulate the collection of the duties imposed by law on the tonnage
of ships or vessels, and on goods, wares and merchandizes, imported into the
United States;' and to amend the said Act."[39]

The Senate proceeded to the THIRD reading of the Bill, "For the government of the territory of the United States south of the river Ohio."

RESOLVED, That this Bill DO PASS; that the title of it be "An Act for the
government of the territory of the United States, south of the river Ohio;" that
it be engrossed,[40] and carried to the House of Representatives, for concurrence
therein.[41]

The Senate resumed the consideration of the amendments to the Bill, entitled, "An Act for the punishment of certain crimes against the United
States;"[42]

---

[39] On April 15 the President signed this bill and the Senate was notified on April 19.
[40] The engrossed bill is in Engrossed Senate Bills and Resolutions, Senate Records,
DNA. E–46040.
[41] On this date the House received this bill and read it a first time. It was read a
second time on April 15. On April 28 the bill was considered in the committee of the
whole, amended, and ordered to be read a third time. On April 29 it was read a third
time, passed with amendments, and sent to the Senate for concurrence.
[42] The rough journal adds:

(which are as follow:

Sect. 1st.	Line 7.	Strike out "by being hanged"
3.	3.	Strike out "by being hanged."
8.	3.	After "or" insert "if."
	5.	After "or" insert "if."
	8.	Strike out "by being hanged"
9.	5.	Strike out "by being hanged"
10.	2.	Strike out "Treason"
	7.	Strike out "by being hanged"
11.	1.	Strike out "Treason"
12.	9.	Strike out "shall be deemed and adjudged to be a pirate and."
14.	4.	After "payment" insert "or for sale"
	6.	Strike out "by being hanged"
16.	1.	Strike out "upon the land"
17.	5.	Strike out "is" and insert "are"
18.	5.	After the word "Dollars" insert "and shall stand in the pillory for one hour."
		In the same line strike out "forever"
	6 & 7.	Strike out "and shall stand in the pillory for one hour."
19.	1.	Strike out "information" and insert "presentment."
	2.	Strike out "the substance of."
20.	1.	Strike out "information" and insert "presentment."
	3.	Strike out "the substance of."
23.	4.	Strike out "by being hanged."
25.	4.	Strike out "or Vice President when he shall act as President."

Whereupon—

RESOLVED, That they do agree to the amendments proposed in the 1st, 3d, 8th, 9th, 10th, 11th, 12th, 14th, 16th, 17th, 18th, 23d, 25th and 27th sections—

To the proposed amendments in

Section 19	Line 1
20	1
26	9 and 10th

and in the additional clause proposed to the Bill—

That they do disagree to the amendments in

Section 19	Line 2
20	3
26	2

And that they do agree to the amendments in section 28, with an amendment.[43]

ORDERED, That the Secretary do carry a message to the House of Representatives, accordingly.[44]

The Senate adjourned to 11 o'clock to-morrow.

26.	2.	Strike out "or soliciting."
	9 & 10.	Strike out "for the time being."
27.	4.	Strike out "seven" and insert "three"
28.	1 & 2.	Strike out "or any other capital Crimes aforesaid."
	2.	After "witness" insert "on whose testimony."
	2 & 3.	Strike out "to be produced on the trial for proving."
	3.	After "Indictment" insert "was found"
	4.	Strike out "two," and insert "ten"
28.	4.	after the word "same" insert, "and in other Capital offences the prisoner shall have such Copy and list three days at least before the trial."
	7.	Strike out "and so many."
		To the end of the bill
		add
		"And be it further enacted that the manner of inflicting the punishment of death shall be by hanging the person convicted by the Neck until dead.")

[43] The engrossed Senate resolve, with an amendment, is in Engrossed Senate Bills and Resolutions, Senate Records, DNA. The rough journal adds the following sentence: "(to wit strike out all the words after the word Treason in the first line to the word (same) inclusive in the fourth line and insert the following words 'shall have a Copy of the Indictment and a list of the Jury and Witnesses to be produced on the trial for proving the said indictment, mentioning the Names and places of abode of such Witnesses and Jurors delivered unto him at least three entire days before he shall be tried for the same and in other capital offences shall have such Copy of the Indictment and List of the Jury two entire days at least before the trial.')"

[44] On April 15 the House received this message and reconsidered its amendments on April 19. It resolved to agree to the Senate's resolutions on these amendments and notified the Senate of this agreement.

THURSDAY, April 15, 1790

The SENATE assembled,
Present as yesterday.

The Senate resumed the SECOND reading of the Bill, entitled, "An Act to regulate the military establishment of the United States;" and after progress, the farther consideration thereof was postponed.[45]

The Senate adjourned to 11 o'clock to-morrow.

FRIDAY, April 16, 1790

The SENATE assembled,
Present as yesterday;—and

Mr. Morris from the State of Pennsylvania, attended.

The Senate proceeded in the SECOND reading of the Bill, entitled, "An Act for regulating the military establishment of the United States."[46]

---

[45] On April 16 this bill was considered again and recommitted.

[46] The rough journal adds:

(And on Motion to strike out "one thousand six hundred and eighty:" (in line 2d) The Yeas and Nays being required by one fifth of the Senators present

Mr. Butler	. . . . Nay	
Carroll	. . . . Nay	
Dalton	. . . .	Ayea
Ellsworth	. . . . . Nay	
Elmer	. . . .	Ayea
Few	. . . . Nay	
Gunn	. . . .	Ayea
Hawkins	. . . .	Ayea
Henry	. . . .	Ayea
Johnson	. . . . . . Nay	
Johnston	. . . . . Nay	
Izard	. . . . Nay	
King	. . . . Nay	
Mr. Langdon	. . . .	Ayea
Lee	. . . .	Ayea
Maclay	. . . .	Ayea
Paterson	. . . .	Ayea
Read	. . . . Nay	
Strong	. . . .	Ayea
Wingate	. . . .	Ayea
Yeas	 11	
Nays	 9	

The entire paragraph of votes is surrounded by a wavy line to indicate intended deletion (see note 48 below). The rough journal then continues:

It passed in the affirmative and the words were striken out.

On Motion that the blank be filled with "One thousand two hundred."

It passed in the affirmative.)

On motion, That the Bill be re-committed—
It passed in the affirmative.[47]
The Senate adjourned until 11 o'clock on Monday next.

MONDAY, APRIL 19, 1790

The SENATE assembled,
Present as on the 16th.[48]
A message from the House of Representatives:

"Mr. PRESIDENT,

"The House of Representatives have receded from such of their amendments to the Bill, entitled, 'An Act for the punishment of certain crimes
against the United States,' as were disagreed to by the Senate; and do concur
with the Senate in the amendment to their amendment on the said Bill[49]—

"The President of the United States did, on the 15th instant, approve of,
and affix his signature to 'An Act, further to suspend part of an Act, entitled,
"An Act to regulate the collection of the duties imposed by law on the tonnage of ships or vessels, and on goods, wares, and merchandizes, imported
into the United States;" and to amend the said Act.' "

The Senate adjourned to 11 o'clock to-morrow.

TUESDAY, APRIL 20, 1790

The SENATE assembled,
Present as yesterday.
Mr. Few, reported from the Committee appointed March the 30th, to take
under consideration the Bill, entitled, "An Act for regulating the military

---

[47] On April 20 this committee reported, and the report was accepted as an amendment to the bill. The third reading of the bill was scheduled.

[48] At this point the rough journal includes the following canceled paragraphs:

On Motion to expunge the yeas and Nays from the Journal of April 16th. on
suggestion that the Senate were in Committee when they were required, and there not
being one fifth of the Senators present who insisted on retaining them on the
Journals.

It passed in the affirmative.

[49] This message, in the form of an attested journal extract, is in Engrossed Senate
Bills and Resolutions, Senate Records, DNA. On April 22 the joint committee on
enrolled bills reported that it had found this bill to be correct. On the same date it was
signed by both the Speaker of the House and the Vice President and sent to the committees on enrolled bills for delivery to the President.

establishment of the United States"—which report being considered, was adopted as amendments to the Bill.

ORDERED, That this Bill have the THIRD reading to-morrow.[50]

The Senate adjourned to 11 o'clock to-morrow.

WEDNESDAY, APRIL 21, 1790

The SENATE assembled,
Present as yesterday.

Agreeably to the order of the day, the Senate proceeded to the THIRD reading of the Bill, entitled, "An Act for regulating the military establishment of the United States."[51]

RESOLVED, That this Bill DO PASS, with amendments.[52]

---

[50] On April 21 this bill was read a third time and passed with amendments. The House was then notified.

[51] The rough journal has the following inserted between the lines:

On motion to restore the 17th Section
It passed in the Negative.

[52] The rough journal includes the amendments as follows:

Sec. 1.	line 2.	Strike out *"six"* and insert "two"
	3.	Strike out *"eighty"* and insert "sixteen"
3.		Strike out from the word "into" in the second line to the word "Musicians" included in the 6th line—and insert—"One Regiment of infantry to consist of three Battalions, and one Battalion of Artillery. The Regiment of infantry to be composed of one Lieutenant Colonel Commandant, three Majors, three Adjutants, three Quarter Masters, One Paymaster, one Surgeon, two Surgeons Mates and twelve Companies each of which shall consist of one Captain, one Lieutenant, one Ensign, four serjeants, four Corporals, sixty six privates and two Musicians."
	9.	Between "sixty" and "privates" insert "six"
4.		From the word "two" in 2nd line strike out the remainder of the Section, and insert "Inspectors as to him shall seem meet to inspect the said Troops who shall also muster the same, and each of whom shall receive the like pay and subsistence as a Captain and be allowed ten dollars per Month for forage."
5.	2.	Strike out *"seventy five"* and insert "sixty."
	3.	Strike out *"fifty"* and insert "forty."
		Strike out *"five."*
		Strike out *"five."*
	4.	Strike out *"six"* and insert "two"
		Strike out *"twenty"* and insert "eighteen"
		Strike out *"forty five"* and insert "thirty"
	5.	Strike out "thirty" and insert "eighteen"
	6.	Strike out *"Regiment"* and insert "Battalion."
6.	2.	Strike out *"Quarter Masters and Pay Masters aforesaid"* and at the end of the Section add "and Quarter Masters and Paymasters so appointed each five dollars per Month."

ORDERED, That a message be sent to the House of Representatives, requesting their concurrence in the amendments.[53]

A message from the House of Representatives:

"Mr. PRESIDENT,

"The House of Representatives have passed a Bill, entitled, 'An Act for the relief of a certain description of officers therein mentioned;'[54] in which they request the concurrence of the Senate."

The Senate proceeded to the FIRST reading of the Bill, entitled, "An Act for the relief of a certain description of officers therein mentioned."

ORDERED, That this Bill have the SECOND reading to-morrow.[55]

The Senate adjourned to 11 o'clock to-morrow.

7.		Strike out all except the first line, and insert "For their daily subsistence the following number of Rations of provisions to wit Lieutenant Colonel Commandant six, A Major four, a Captain three, a Lieutenant two, an Ensign two, a Surgeon three, a Surgeons Mate two, or Money in lieu thereof at the option of the Said Officers at the contract price at the ports respectively where the Rations shall becom due.
8.	3.	Strike out "*eighteen dollars*" and insert "twelve"
		Strike out "*fifteen dollars.*"
		Strike out from "Majors" to the end of the Section, and insert "and Surgeon each ten dollars, Surgeons Mates each six dollars"
10.	3.	Strike out "*baked*" and "*equivalent thereto*"
		After "Rum" insert "Brandy" and after "Whiskey" insert "or the value thereof at the contract price where the same shall become due"
11.		Strike out the whole Section.
12.	3.	Strike the Letter "*s*" from the word "Rates"
15.	6.	Strike from the word "Nine" to the word "That" in the 9th line—and insert—"*and who shall decline to reinlist under* the establishment made by this Act shall be discharged whenever the President of the United States shall direct the same, provided further."
		Strike out in the last line of the Section—"*one hundred and eighty*" and insert "two hundred and sixteen."
16.	1.	After "*purpose of*" insert "aiding the Troops now in service or to be raised by this act in"
	2.	Strike out "from the hostile incursions of the Indians."
	5.	After the word "mentioned" strike out the remainder of the Section and insert "and shall be subject to the Rules and articles of war."
17.		Strike out the whole of the Section.

[53] On April 22 the House concurred in these amendments with an amendment and notified the Senate on April 23. The Senate then receded from its own amendment to concur with the House amendment and notified the House.

[54] The bill is in Engrossed House Bills, House Records, DNA.

[55] On April 22 this bill was read a second time and committed.

THURSDAY, April 22, 1790

The SENATE assembled,
Present as yesterday.

Mr. Wingate, reported from the joint Committee on enrolled Bills, That they had examined the Bill, entitled, "An Act for the punishment of certain crimes against the United States,"[56] and had found it correct.

Agreeably to the order of the day, the Senate proceeded to the SECOND reading of the Bill, entitled, "An Act for the relief of a certain description of officers therein mentioned."

ORDERED, That this Bill be committed to

Mr. Schuyler
Mr. Hawkins and
Mr. Ellsworth[57]

A message from the House of Representatives:

"Mr. PRESIDENT,

"The Speaker having signed an enrolled Bill, I am directed to bring it to the Senate."

The Vice President affixed his signature to the Bill, entitled, "An Act for the punishment of certain crimes against the United States;" and it was delivered to the Committee on enrolled Bills, to be laid before the President of the United States.[58]

The Senate adjourned to 11 o'clock to-morrow.

FRIDAY, April 23, 1790

The SENATE assembled,
Present as yesterday.

Mr. Strong, from the Committee, appointed January 19th, reported a Bill, "To continue in force an Act, passed at the last session of Congress, 'To regulate processes in the courts of the United States;' "[59]—which was read the FIRST time.

ORDERED, That this Bill have the SECOND reading on Monday next.[60]

A message from the House of Representatives:

---

[56] The inspected enrolled bill is in Enrolled Acts, RG 11, DNA. E-46041.

[57] On April 23 this committee reported and a motion for a third reading was disagreed to.

[58] On April 29 the joint committee on enrolled bills reported that it had delivered this bill to the President.

[59] This bill is in Senate Bills, Senate Records, DNA.

[60] On April 26 this bill was read for the second time and the third reading was assigned.

"Mr. PRESIDENT,

"The House of Representatives agree to the amendments of the Senate, to the Bill, entitled, 'An Act for regulating the military establishment of the United States,'—with an amendment to the 8th amendment of the 5th section, by inserting the words 'TWENTY-FOUR,' instead of 'EIGHTEEN,' proposed by the Senate to be inserted."

The Senate proceeded to consider the above message from the House of Representatives,—and

RESOLVED, That they do recede from their amendment to the Bill,[61] entitled, "An Act for regulating the military establishment of the United States," so far as to concur with the House of Representatives in their amendment to the amendment.

ORDERED, That a message be carried to the House of Representatives accordingly.[62]

Mr. Schuyler, reported from the Committee appointed yesterday, to take into consideration the Bill, entitled, "An Act for the relief of a certain description of officers therein mentioned:"[63]

And on the question, shall this Bill have a THIRD reading?—

It passed in the Negative.[64]

The Senate adjourned to Monday next, at 11 o'clock.

MONDAY, APRIL 26, 1790

The SENATE assembled,
Present as on the 23d April;—and

The Hon. John Walker, from the State of Virginia, produced his credentials,[65] and took his seat in Senate.

The Vice President administered the oath, required by law, to Mr. Walker.

The petition of Messrs. Bertier, and Co. merchants, of the city of Philadelphia,[66] was read, stating, That certain goods consigned to them on board of the ship Van Staphorst, Captain Atkinson, were seized by one of the Inspec-

---

[61] The rough journal reads: "Resolved, that they do recede from their own amendment Line 5. 'Section 5,' of the Bill . . ."

[62] On April 28 this bill was signed by both the Speaker and the Vice President and given to the committee on enrolled bills for delivery to the President.

[63] The smooth journal places the word "reported" at the end rather than at the beginning of this phrase. The rough journal also places the word "reported" at the end of the phrase and follows it with these words, which were later lined out: "that the bill be rejected. which report was accepted and."

[64] This bill was not considered again.

[65] The credentials are in Election Records: Credentials of Senators, Senate Records, DNA.

[66] This petition is in Petitions and Memorials: Claims, Senate Records, DNA. A copy of a bill of lading and protest is attached.

tors of the port of Baltimore, in consequence of a mistake committed by the mate of the said ship, although without any intention of fraud; and praying, that Congress would make such provision for their relief, in an Act, said to be under the consideration of Congress, as in their wisdom shall seem just.

Agreeably to the order of the day, the Senate proceeded to the SECOND reading of the Bill, "To continue in force an Act passed at the last session of Congress, entitled, 'An Act to regulate processes in the courts of the United States.' "

ORDERED, That this Bill have the THIRD reading to-morrow.[67]

The Senate adjourned to 11 o'clock to-morrow.

TUESDAY, APRIL 27, 1790

The SENATE assembled,
Present as yesterday.

Agreeably to the order of the day, the Senate proceeded to the THIRD reading of the Bill "To continue in force an Act, passed at the last session of Congress, entitled, 'An Act to regulate processes in the courts of the United States;' "—and

RESOLVED, That this Bill DO PASS; that the title of it be "An Act to continue in force an Act passed at the last session of Congress, entitled, 'An Act to regulate processes in the courts of the United States;' " that the Bill be engrossed,[68] and carried to the House of Representatives, for concurrence therein.[69]

On motion,

ORDERED, That Mr. Lee be added to the Committee, appointed 11th February, "To report a plan for the regulation of the trade of the United States, with the countries and settlements of the European powers in America," and to whom also was referred the petition of the merchants of New-Hampshire.[70]

The Senate adjourned to 11 o'clock to-morrow.

WEDNESDAY, APRIL 28, 1790

The SENATE assembled,
Present as yesterday.

On motion,
ORDERED, That   Mr. Carroll

---

[67] On April 27 this bill was read a third time, passed, and sent to the House for concurrence.

[68] This resolve is in Engrossed Senate Bills and Resolutions, Senate Records, DNA.

[69] On April 27 this bill was received by the House and read a first time. On April 28 it was read for the second time; on the following day, it was read again and passed. On April 30 the Senate was notified of this action.

[70] This committee never reported, but on April 30 the House passed a bill on this subject and sent it to the Senate.

Mr. Ellsworth

Mr. Morris

Mr. Izard and

Mr. Butler, be a Committee to consider what provisions will be proper for Congress to make, in the present session, respecting the State of Rhode-Island.[71]

A message from the House of Representatives, by Mr. Beckley, their clerk:

"Mr. PRESIDENT,

"I am directed to bring to the Senate, an enrolled Bill, which has been signed by the Speaker of the House of Representatives,"—

And he withdrew.

The Vice President affixed his signature to the enrolled Bill, entitled, "An Act for regulating the military establishment of the United States;"[72] and it was delivered to the Committee on enrolled Bills, to be laid before the President of the United States, for his approbation.[73]

The Senate proceeded to consider the executive business before them; after which,

They adjourned to 11 o'clock to-morrow.

THURSDAY, APRIL 29, 1790

The SENATE assembled,

Present as yesterday.

Mr. Wingate reported from the Committee on enrolled Bills, That they had this day laid before the President of the United States, for his approbation, the enrolled Bill, entitled, "An Act for the punishment of certain crimes against the United States;" together with the enrolled Bill, entitled, "An Act for regulating the military establishment of the United States."[74]

Mr. Ellsworth, from the Committee appointed 15th January, to bring in a Bill in addition to an Act to establish the judicial courts of the United States, and to whom was referred the petition of the merchants of New-Hampshire, reported a Bill "For giving effect to the Act therein mentioned, in respect to the State of North-Carolina; and to amend the said Act."[75]

ORDERED, That this Bill be now read the FIRST time.

---

[71] A draft of this order is in Senate Simple Resolutions and Bills, Senate Records, DNA. On May 5 this committee reported, and a date was assigned for consideration of the report.

[72] The inspected enrolled bill is in Enrolled Acts, RG 11, DNA. E–22954.

[73] On April 29 this committee reported that it had delivered this bill to the President.

[74] On April 30 the President signed both of these bills.

[75] This bill is in Senate Bills, Senate Records, DNA.

ORDERED, That this Bill be read the SECOND time to-morrow.[76]

On motion, "That the doors of the Senate Chamber shall be open when the Senate is sitting in their legislative capacity; to the end that such of the citizens of the United States as may chuse to hear the debates of this House, may have a opportunity of so doing:"[77]

A motion was made, that the consideration hereof be postponed until to-morrow, and—

It passed in the Affirmative.[78]

ORDERED, That Mr. Strong be added to the Committee appointed the 28th April, "To consider what provisions will be proper for Congress to make, in the present session, respecting the State of Rhode-Island," instead of Mr. Butler, excused at his own desire, his colleague being on the Committee.

The Senate proceeded in the executive business before them; after which,

They adjourned to 11 o'clock to-morrow.

F R I D A Y, APRIL 30, 1790

The SENATE assembled,
Present as yesterday.

Agreeably to the order of the day, the Senate proceeded to the SECOND reading of the Bill "For giving effect to the Act therein mentioned, in respect to the State of North-Carolina; and to amend the said Act."

ORDERED, That this Bill have the THIRD reading on Monday next.[79]

A message from the President of the United States, by Mr. Nelson:

"Mr. PRESIDENT,

"The President of the United States has this day approved of, and affixed his signature to the Act, entitled, 'An Act for the punishment of certain crimes against the United States,' "—

And he withdrew.

A message from the House of Representatives, by Mr. Beckley, their clerk:

"Mr. PRESIDENT,

"The House of Representatives have passed a Bill, entitled, 'An Act supplemental to the Act for establishing the salaries of the executive officers of government, with their assistants and clerks'[80]—

"A Bill, entitled, 'An Act for the encouragement of learning, by securing

---

[76] On April 30 this bill was read a second time and the third reading was scheduled.
[77] This motion is in Senate Simple Resolutions and Motions, Senate Records, DNA.
[78] On April 30 this motion was considered and defeated.
[79] On May 3 this bill was read a third time, passed, and sent to the House for concurrence.
[80] A printed copy of this bill is in the Broadside Collection, RBkRm, DLC. E–46057.

the copies of maps, charts, books and other writings, to the authors and proprietors of such copies, during the times therein mentioned'[81]—

"A Bill, entitled, 'An Act providing the means of intercourse between the United States and foreign nations,'[82]—and

"A Bill, entitled, 'An Act to provide for mitigating or remitting the forfeitures and penalties accruing under the revenue laws, in certain cases therein mentioned;'[83] to which they request the concurrence of the Senate,—

"The House of Representatives have also concurred in the Bill, entitled, 'An Act to continue in force an Act passed at the last session of Congress, entitled, "An Act to regulate processes in the courts of the United States;" '[84] and in the Bill, entitled, 'An Act for the government of the territory of the United States south of the river Ohio,' with amendments; to which amendments they request the concurrence of the Senate,[85]—

"I am farther directed to inform the Senate that the House of Representatives have appointed   Mr. Sherman

Mr. Smith (South-Carolina) and

Mr. Vining, a Committee to confer with any Committee to be appointed by the Senate, to consider and report whether any, and what further regulations are necessary for conducting the business between the two Houses; to which they request the concurrence of the Senate,"—

And he withdrew.

The Bill, entitled, "An Act supplemental to the Act for establishing the salaries of the executive officers of government, with their assistants and clerks," was read the FIRST time.

ORDERED, That this Bill have the SECOND reading on Monday next.[86]

The Bill, entitled, "An Act for the encouragement of learning, by securing the copies of maps, charts, books and other writings, to the authors and proprietors of such copies, during the times therein mentioned," was read the FIRST time.

ORDERED, That this Bill have the SECOND reading on Monday next.[87]

The Bill, entitled, "An Act providing the means of intercourse between the United States and foreign nations," was read the FIRST time.

---

[81] An annotated printed copy of this bill is in House Bills, Senate Records, DNA. E–46037.

[82] A clear printed copy of this bill is in the Broadside Collection, RBkRm, DLC. E–46054.

[83] A clear printed copy of this bill is in the Broadside Collection, RBkRm, DLC. E–46068.

[84] On May 10 this bill was signed by both the Speaker and the Vice President and given to the committee on enrolled bills for delivery to the President.

[85] On May 4 the Senate considered and disagreed to the House amendments to this bill, and notified the House.

[86] On May 3 this bill was read a second time and committed.

[87] On May 4 this bill was read a second time and committed.

ORDERED, That this Bill have the SECOND reading on Monday next.[88]

The Bill, entitled, "An Act to provide for mitigating or remitting the forfeitures and penalties accruing under the revenue laws, in certain cases therein mentioned," was read the FIRST time.

ORDERED, That this Bill have the SECOND reading on Monday next.[89]

The Senate proceeded, agreeably to the order of the day, to consider the motion made yesterday, to wit; "That the doors of the Senate Chamber shall be open when the Senate is sitting in their legislative capacity, to the end that such of the citizens of the United States as may chuse to hear the debates of this House, may have an opportunity of so doing;" and the question being taken—

It passed in the Negative.

The Senate proceeded to consider the resolve of the House of Representatives, appointing a Committee on their part, "to confer with any Committee appointed by the Senate, to consider and report whether any, and what further regulations are necessary for conducting the business between the two Houses," —and

RESOLVED, That the Senate concur therein, and that

> Mr. Lee
> Mr. Izard and
> Mr. Strong, be the Committee on the part of the

Senate.

ORDERED, That the Secretary do acquaint the House of Representatives herewith.[90]

The Senate adjourned to Monday next, at 11 o'clock.

---

[88] On May 3 this bill was read a second time and committed.

[89] On May 3 this bill was read a second time and consideration was postponed.

[90] On June 8 this committee reported and consideration of the report was postponed.

MONDAY, MAY 3, 1790

The SENATE assembled,

Present as on the 30th April.

The order of the day being called for, the Senate proceeded to the SECOND reading of the Bill, entitled, "An Act supplemental to the Act for establishing the salaries of the executive officers of government, with their assistants and clerks."

ORDERED, That this Bill be committed to

> Mr. Few
> Mr. Izard and
> Mr. Ellsworth, to consider and report what is proper

to be done thereon.[1]

The Senate proceeded to the SECOND reading of the Bill, entitled, "An Act providing the means of intercourse between the United States and foreign nations."

ORDERED, That this Bill be committed to

> Mr. Strong
> Mr. Ellsworth
> Mr. Carroll
> Mr. Maclay and
> Mr. Few[2]

A message from the House of Representatives, by Mr. Beckley, their clerk:

"Mr. PRESIDENT,

"The House of Representatives have passed a Bill, entitled, 'An Act to allow compensation to John Ely, for his attendance as a physician and surgeon on the prisoners of the United States;'[3] and a Bill, entitled, 'An Act to prescribe the mode in which the public acts, records, and judicial proceedings in each State shall be authenticated, so as to take effect in every other State;'[4] in which they request the concurrence of the Senate,—

"The House of Representatives have also appointed Mr. Benson, Mr. Clymer, Mr. Huntington, Mr. Moore and Mr. Carroll, a Committee to join with a Committee to be appointed by the Senate, to consider and report their opinion on the question, 'When, according to the Constitution, the terms for which the President, Vice President, Senators and Representatives have been respectively chosen, shall be deemed to have commenced?' and also to con-

---

[1] On May 28 this committee reported. The bill was read a third time and passed, and the House was notified.

[2] On May 7 this committee reported and consideration of the report was postponed.

[3] Two copies of this bill, one printed, are in House Bills, Senate Records, DNA. E–46060.

[4] A printed copy of this bill is in the Broadside Collection, RBkRm, DLC. E–46064.

sider of and report their opinion on such other matters as they shall conceive
have relation to this question; and request the concurrence of the Senate in
the appointment of a Committee on their part,—

"I am directed to acquaint the Senate, that the President of the United
States did, on the 30th of April, approve of, and affix his signature to the Act,
entitled, 'An Act for regulating the military establishment of the United
States,' "—

And he withdrew.

The Senate proceeded to the consideration of the resolve of the House of
Representatives, appointing a Committee to confer on the question recited in
their message of this day.

RESOLVED, That the Senate do concur therein, and that

Mr. Ellsworth

Mr. King and

Mr. Morris, be appointed to confer on the part of

the Senate.

ORDERED, That the Secretary acquaint the House of Representatives herewith.[5]

The Senate proceeded to the THIRD reading of the Bill, "For giving effect
to the Act therein mentioned, in respect to the State of North-Carolina, and
to amend the said Act."

RESOLVED, That this Bill DO PASS; that the title of it be "An Act for giving
effect to the Act therein mentioned, in respect to the State of North-Carolina,
and to amend the said Act;" that it be engrossed,[6] and carried to the House of
Representatives, for concurrence therein.[7]

The Senate proceeded to the FIRST reading of the Bill, entitled, "An Act to
prescribe the mode in which the public acts, records, and judicial proceedings
in each State shall be authenticated, so as to take effect in every other State."

ORDERED, That this Bill be read a SECOND time to-morrow.[8]

The Senate proceeded to the FIRST reading of the Bill, entitled, "An Act to
allow compensation to John Ely, for his attendance as a physician and surgeon
on the prisoners of the United States."

---

[5] On May 13 this committee reported and consideration of the report was postponed.

[6] The engrossed bill is in Engrossed Senate Bills and Resolutions, Senate Records,
DNA.

[7] On May 4 this bill was received by the House and read a first time. On the fifth, it
was read a second time and ordered to be committed to the committee of the whole. On
May 7 it was considered in the committee of the whole and amended, and the third
reading was scheduled. The House read it again on May 10 and passed it with amendments. The Senate was then notified. On the same date the Senate postponed consideration of the House amendments.

[8] On May 4 this bill was read a second time, and the third reading was scheduled.

ORDERED, That this Bill have the SECOND reading to-morrow.[9]

Agreeably to the order of the day, the Senate proceeded to the SECOND reading of the Bill, entitled, "An Act to provide for mitigating or remitting the forfeitures and penalties accruing under the revenue laws, in certain cases therein mentioned;" and after progress[10]—

Adjourned to 11 o'clock to-morrow.

TUESDAY, MAY 4, 1790

The SENATE assembled,
Present as yesterday.

Agreeably to the order of the day, the Senate resumed the consideration of the amendments to the Bill, entitled, "An Act for the government of the territory of the United States south of the river Ohio."

RESOLVED, That the Senate do not agree to the proposed amendments.[11]

ORDERED, That a message be sent to the House of Representatives, to acquaint them therewith.[12]

The Senate proceeded to the THIRD reading of the Bill, entitled, "An Act to provide for mitigating or remitting the forfeitures and penalties accruing under the revenue laws, in certain cases therein mentioned."

RESOLVED, That they concur therein, with amendments.[13]

ORDERED, That the Secretary acquaint the House of Representatives therewith, and request their concurrence in the amendments.[14]

The Senate proceeded to the SECOND reading of the Bill, entitled, "An Act to allow compensation to John Ely, for his attendance as a physician and surgeon on the prisoners of the United States."

ORDERED, That it be committed to

Mr. Maclay

---

[9] On May 4 this bill was read a second time and committed.

[10] On May 4 this bill was read a third time and passed with amendments. The concurrence of the House was requested.

[11] The engrossed Senate resolve is in Engrossed Senate Bills and Resolutions, Senate Records, DNA.

[12] On May 5 the House receded from its amendments to this bill, and the Senate was notified of this action on May 6.

[13] The rough journal reads:

"RESOLVED, that they do concur therein with ~~the following~~ three amendments.

A.	P.	L.	
1.		12.	Strike out "*any one of the Justices of the Supreme Court.*" and insert "The Secretary of the Treasury."
2.		14.	Strike out "*by accident or*"
3.		19.	Strike out "*at the option of the parties.*"
		20.	

[14] On May 5 the House concurred in these amendments and the Senate was notified on the sixth.

Mr. Wingate and

Mr. Elmer[15]

The Senate proceeded to the SECOND reading of the Bill, entitled, "An Act to prescribe the mode in which the public records and judicial proceedings in each State shall be authenticated, so as to take effect in every other State."

ORDERED, That this Bill have the THIRD reading to-morrow.[16]

The Senate resumed the SECOND reading of the Bill, entitled, "An Act providing for holding a treaty or treaties, to establish peace with certain Indian tribes."

ORDERED, That the consideration hereof be further postponed.[17]

The Senate proceeded to the SECOND reading of the Bill, entitled, "An Act for the encouragement of learning, by securing the copies of maps, charts, books and other writings, to the authors and proprietors of such copies, during the times therein mentioned."

ORDERED, That it be committed to

Mr. Read

Mr. Paterson and

Mr. Johnson[18]

A message from the House of Representatives, by Mr. Beckley, their clerk:

"Mr. PRESIDENT,

"The House of Representatives have passed a Bill, entitled, 'An Act to authorize the issuing of certificates to a certain description of invalid officers;'[19] in which they request the concurrence of the Senate,"—

And he withdrew.

ORDERED, That the Bill last mentioned, be now read the FIRST time.

ORDERED, That this Bill have the SECOND reading to-morrow.[20]

The Senate adjourned to 11 o'clock to-morrow.

WEDNESDAY, MAY 5, 1790

The SENATE assembled,

Present as yesterday;—and

Proceeded to the THIRD reading of the Bill, entitled, "An Act to prescribe the mode in which the public acts, records, and judicial proceedings in each State shall be authenticated, so as to take effect in every other State."

---

[15] The names of these committeemen are noted at the bottom of the printed copy of the bill which is in House Bills, Senate Records, DNA. On May 11 this committee reported, and a motion for a third reading of the bill was disagreed to.

[16] On May 5 this bill was read a third time and passed, and the House was notified.

[17] On July 9 this bill was considered again and committed.

[18] On May 12 this committee reported and consideration of the report was postponed.

[19] This bill, as it passed the House, is in Engrossed House Bills, House Records, DNA.

[20] On May 5 this bill was read a second time and committed.

RESOLVED, That this Bill DO PASS.

ORDERED, That a message be sent to the House of Representatives, to acquaint them of the concurrence of the Senate in the last mentioned Bill.[21]

The Senate proceeded to the SECOND reading of the Bill, entitled, "An Act to authorize the issuing of certificates to a certain description of invalid officers."

ORDERED, That it be committed to

> Mr. Schuyler
> Mr. Hawkins and
> Mr. Ellsworth[22]

Mr. Carroll reported from the Committee appointed the 28th of April, "To consider what provisions will be proper for Congress to make in the present session, respecting the State of Rhode-Island."[23]

ORDERED, That Monday next, be assigned to take this report into consideration.[24]

The following letter was read; which, with a volume of the work therein mentioned, was laid on the table, by Mr. Morris:

"To the honorable the SENATORS of the United States, in Congress assembled

"Thomas Dobson begs leave to present, in succession as they are published, the volumes of the American edition of the Encyclopedia, which he is now printing and publishing; and at the same time to solicit the patronage and encouragement of gentlemen, in an undertaking of such magnitude and utility.[25]

"PHILADELPHIA, 1st May, 1790"

The Senate adjourned to 11 o'clock to-morrow.

THURSDAY, MAY 6, 1790

The SENATE assembled,
Present as yesterday.

A message from the House of Representatives by Mr. Beckley their clerk:

---

[21] On May 10 this bill was signed by both the Speaker and the Vice President and given to the committee on enrolled bills for delivery to the President.

[22] On July 7 this committee reported and the bill was read a third time. The Senate voted not to concur in this bill.

[23] This report is in Various Select Committee Reports, Senate Records, DNA. The rough journal canceled the phrase in quotation marks, but it was later restored with the comment "(restore what is stricken out above)." Below this remark the following paragraph was canceled: "That all commercial intercourse between the United States and the State of Rhode Island, from and after the   day of   next should be prohibited under suitable penalties; and that a bill should be brought in for that purpose."

[24] On May 10 this report was considered and postponed.

[25] This letter is in Reports and Communications, Senate Records, DNA.

"Mr. PRESIDENT,

"The House of Representatives recede from their amendments to the Bill, entitled, 'An Act for the government of the territory of the United States south of the river Ohio,'[26] and agree to the amendments of the Senate to the Bill, entitled, 'An Act to provide for mitigating or remitting the forfeitures and penalties accruing under the revenue laws, in certain cases therein mentioned,' "[27]—

And he withdrew.[28]

The Senate adjourned to 11 o'clock to-morrow.

FRIDAY, MAY 7, 1790

The SENATE assembled,
Present as yesterday,—except
Mr. Paterson, absent with leave.

Mr. Strong reported from the Committee appointed May the 3d,[29] on the Bill, entitled, "An Act providing the means of intercourse between the United States and foreign nations."

ORDERED, That the consideration of the report be postponed until Monday next.[30]

The Senate adjourned to 11 o'clock on Monday next.

MONDAY, MAY 10, 1790

The SENATE assembled,
Present as on the 7th of May.

Mr. Wingate reported from the joint Committee on enrolled Bills, That they had examined the enrolled Bill, entitled, "An Act to prescribe the mode in which the public records and judicial proceedings in each State shall be authenticated, so as to take effect in every other State,"[31]—the enrolled Bill, entitled, "An Act to provide for mitigating or remitting the forfeitures and penalties accruing under the revenue laws, in certain cases therein mentioned,"[32]—the enrolled Bill, entitled, "An Act to continue in force an Act

---

[26] On May 10 this bill was signed by both the Speaker and Vice President and given to the committee on enrolled bills for delivery to the President.

[27] On May 10 this bill was signed by both the Speaker and the Vice President and given to the committee on enrolled bills for delivery to the President.

[28] The rough journal inserted, but then canceled, the following: "Mr. Paterson had leave of absence for ten days."

[29] This report has not been located.

[30] On May 10 this committee report was considered and recommitted.

[31] The inspected enrolled bill is in Enrolled Acts, RG 11, DNA. E–22968.

[32] The inspected enrolled bill is in Enrolled Acts, RG 11, DNA.

passed at the last session of Congress, entitled, 'An Act to regulate processes in the courts of the United States,' "[33]—and the enrolled Bill, entitled, 'An Act for the government of the territory of the United States south of the river Ohio,' "[34] and had found them correct.[35]

The Senate proceeded to consider the report of the Committee appointed on the Bill, entitled, "An Act providing the means of intercourse between the United States and foreign nations,"—whereupon

ORDERED, That this Bill be re-committed.[36]

A message from the House of Representatives by Mr. Beckley their clerk:

"Mr. PRESIDENT,

"The House of Representatives have passed the Bill sent from the Senate, entitled, 'An Act for giving effect to the Act therein mentioned, in respect to the State of North-Carolina, and to amend the said Act,' with amendments,[37] in which they desire the concurrence of the Senate,—

"I am directed to bring to the Senate several enrolled Bills, which have been signed by the Speaker of the House of Representatives,"—

And he withdrew.

Whereupon the Vice President affixed his signature to the following enrolled Bills, to wit; "An Act to prescribe the mode in which the public acts, records, and judicial proceedings in each State shall be authenticated, so as to take effect in every other State;" "An Act to provide for mitigating or remitting the forfeitures and penalties accruing under the revenue laws, in certain cases therein mentioned;" "An Act to continue in force an Act passed at the last session of Congress, entitled, 'An Act to regulate processes in the courts of the United States;' " and "An Act for the government of the territory of the United States south of the river Ohio," and they were delivered to the Committee on enrolled Bills, to be laid before the President of the United States, for his approbation.[38]

The Senate proceeded to consider the report of the Committee appointed the 28th of April, "To consider what provisions will be proper for Congress to make in the present session, respecting the State of Rhode-Island,"—and

---

[33] The inspected enrolled bill is in Enrolled Acts, RG 11, DNA.

[34] The inspected enrolled bill is in Enrolled Acts, RG 11, DNA. E–46039.

[35] The rough journal contains the following canceled paragraph: "The report of the Committee appointed the 28th of April 'to consider what provisions will be proper for Congress to make in the present Session respecting the State of Rhode Island' being the order of the day was farther postponed."

[36] On May 25 this committee reported again, and its report was accepted as an amendment to the bill. The third reading was then assigned.

[37] The House amendments, in the form of a Journal extract, are in Engrossed Senate Bills and Resolutions, Senate Records, DNA.

[38] On May 26 the President signed all these bills.

ORDERED, That the consideration hereof be postponed until to-morrow.[39]

A message from the House of Representatives by Mr. Beckley their clerk:

"Mr. PRESIDENT,

"The House of Representatives have passed a Bill, entitled, 'An Act for finally adjusting and satisfying the claims of Frederick William de Steuben,'[40] to which they desire the concurrence of the Senate,"—

And he withdrew.

The Senate proceeded to consider the amendments of the House of Representatives, to the Bill, entitled, "An Act for giving effect to the Act therein mentioned, in respect to the State of North-Carolina, and to amend the said Act."

ORDERED, That the further consideration hereof be postponed until to-morrow.[41]

The Bill, entitled, "An Act for finally adjusting and satisfying the claims of Frederick William de Steuben," was read the FIRST time.

ORDERED, That this Bill have the SECOND reading to-morrow.[42]

The Senate adjourned to 11 o'clock to-morrow.

TUESDAY, MAY 11, 1790

The SENATE assembled,
Present as yesterday.

The Senate resumed the SECOND reading of the Bill, entitled, "An Act for finally adjusting and satisfying the claims of Frederick William de Steuben."

ORDERED, That it be committed to

> Mr. Maclay
> Mr. Strong
> Mr. Izard
> Mr. Ellsworth and
> Mr. Johnston[43]

The Senate proceeded to consider the amendments proposed by the House of Representatives, to the Bill, entitled, "An Act for giving effect to the Act therein mentioned, in respect to the State of North-Carolina, and to amend the said act."

RESOLVED, That the Senate disagree to the amendment section 3d, line 8th,—

---

[39] On May 11 a resolution was passed on this committee report, and the committee was requested to prepare a bill on this subject.

[40] This bill has not been located.

[41] On May 11 the Senate considered the House amendments and agreed to some while disagreeing to others. The House was notified of these actions.

[42] On May 11 this bill was read a second time and committed.

[43] On May 24 this committee reported and consideration of the report was postponed.

That they disagree to the propostion to "strike out the last section" of the Bill; but that they agree in the amendments proposed by the House of Representatives, so far, as to subjoin these clauses to the Bill, to wit;—

"And be it further enacted, That the stated District Court for the district of Pennsylvania, shall hereafter be held solely at the city of Philadelphia,—

"And be it further enacted, That from and after the first day of January next, there shall be held annually, three sessions of the District Court, for the district of Kentucky, and no more; to commence on the second Mondays in each of the months of April, August and November; any law to the contrary notwithstanding."[44]

ORDERED, That a message be sent to the House of Representatives accordingly.[45]

The Senate proceeded to consider the report of the Committee appointed the 28th of April, "To consider what provisions will be proper for Congress to make in the present session, respecting the State of Rhode-Island,"—whereupon

RESOLVED, That all commercial intercourse between the United States and the State of Rhode-Island, from and after the first day of July next, be prohibited under suitable penalties; and that the President of the United States be authorized to demand of the State of Rhode-Island,   dollars, to be paid into the Treasury of the United States, by the   day of next; which shall be credited to the said State, in account with the United States,—and that a Bill or Bills be brought in for those purposes.[46]

ORDERED, That the Committee who brought in the above report, prepare and report a Bill accordingly.[47]

The Senate adjourned to 11 o'clock to-morrow.

WEDNESDAY, MAY 12, 1790

The SENATE assembled,
Present as yesterday.

Mr. Maclay reported from the Committee appointed the 4th of May, to consider the Bill, entitled, "An Act to allow compensation to John Ely, for his attendance as a physician and surgeon on the prisoners of the United States,"—whereupon

RESOLVED, That the Bill do not have the THIRD reading.

---

[44] The attested Senate resolve is in Engrossed Senate Bills and Resolutions, Senate Records, DNA.

[45] On May 12 the House reconsidered its amendments to this bill and requested a conference on it. On the same date the Senate agreed to a conference and appointed managers.

[46] This resolve has not been located.

[47] On May 13 this committee reported a bill which was read a first time and scheduled for a second reading.

A message from the House of Representatives by Mr. Beckley their clerk:

"Mr. PRESIDENT,

"The House of Representatives have proceeded to re-consider such of their amendments to the Bill sent from the Senate, entitled, 'An Act for giving effect to the Act therein mentioned, in respect to the State of North-Carolina, and to amend the said Act,' as were disagreed to by the Senate, and have

"RESOLVED, That a conference be desired with the Senate, on the subject matter of the said amendments, and that

>Mr. White
>Mr. Steele
>Mr. Foster
>Mr. Livermore and
>Mr. Williamson, be appointed managers at the same,

on the part of the House of Representatives."[48]

The Senate proceeded to consider the last recited message, and

RESOLVED, That they concur in the proposed conference, and that

>Mr. Johnston
>Mr. Langdon
>Mr. Hawkins
>Mr. King and
>Mr. Butler be managers thereof, on the part of the

Senate.[49]

ORDERED, That a message be sent to the House of Representatives, accordingly.[50]

Mr. Read reported from the Committee appointed May the 4th,[51] on the Bill, entitled, "An Act for the encouragement of learning, by securing the copies of maps, charts, books and other writings, to the authors and proprietors of such copies, during the times therein mentioned,"—the consideration of which report was postponed.[52]

The Senate adjourned to 11 o'clock to-morrow.

---

[48] The House resolve is in Engrossed Senate Bills and Resolutions, Senate Records, DNA.

[49] This resolve and the committee appointments are in Engrossed Senate Bills and Resolutions, Senate Records, DNA.

[50] On May 14 this committee reported to the House, and on May 18 the House resolved to recede from its first amendment and adhere to the second. The Senate was notified, and on the same date the Senate agreed to the first House amendment with an amendment but adhered to its disagreement to the second amendment.

[51] The annotation on the printed bill may correspond to the actions taken by the committee. The bill is in House Bills, Senate Records, DNA. The report has not been located.

[52] On May 13 this report was agreed to as amendments to the bill, and the third reading of the bill was assigned.

THURSDAY, May 13, 1790

The SENATE assembled,
Present as yesterday.

The Senate proceeded to consider the report of the Committee on the Bill, entitled, "An Act for the encouragement of learning, by securing the copies of maps, charts, books and other writings, to the authors and proprietors of such copies, during the times therein mentioned,"—which report was agreed to as amendments to the Bill.

ORDERED, That to-morrow be assigned for the THIRD reading of this Bill.[53]

Mr. Morris from the Committee appointed the 28th of April, "To consider what provisions will be proper for Congress to make in the present-session, respecting the State of Rhode-Island," reported a Bill on that subject,[54] which was read the FIRST time.

ORDERED, That this Bill have the SECOND reading to-morrow.[55]

Mr. Ellsworth reported from the Committee appointed May the 3d,[56] "To consider and report their opinion on the question, when, according to the Constitution, the terms for which the President, Vice President, Senators and Representatives, have been respectively chosen, shall be deemed to have commenced? and also to consider of, and report their opinion on such other matters as they shall conceive have relation to this question."

ORDERED, That this report lie for consideration.[57]

The Senate adjourned to 11 o'clock to-morrow.

FRIDAY, May 14, 1790

The SENATE assembled,
Present as yesterday;—and
Mr. Bassett, from the State of Delaware, attended.

Agreeably to the order of the day, the Senate proceeded to the THIRD reading of the Bill, entitled, "An Act for the encouragement of learning, by securing the copies of maps, charts, books and other writings, to the authors and proprietors of such copies, during the times therein mentioned."

---

[53] On May 14 this bill was read a third time, passed with amendments, and sent to the House for concurrence.

[54] Two annotated copies of the bill, one printed, are in Senate Bills, Senate Records, DNA. Two printed copies of the bill, one clear and one annotated, are in the Broadside Collection, RBkRm, DLC. E–46066.

[55] On May 14 this bill was read a second time and the third reading was scheduled.

[56] This report has not been located.

[57] On May 14 this report was printed in the Journal and agreed to by the Senate. The House was then notified.

RESOLVED, That this Bill DO PASS, with amendments.[58]

ORDERED, That a message be sent to the House of Representatives, to request their concurrence in the amendments.[59]

The Senate proceeded to consider the report of the joint Committee, appointed the 28th of April, which is as follows:

The Committee of Senate, to joint with a Committee appointed by the House of Representatives, to consider and report their opinion on the question, when, according to the Constitution, the terms for which the President, Vice President, Senators and Representatives, have been respectively chosen, shall be deemed to have commenced? and also to consider of, and report their opinion on such other matters as they should conceive to have relation to this question,

Report as the opinion of the said joint Committees—

That the terms for which the President, Vice President, Senators and Representatives of the United States, were respectively chosen, did, according to the Constitution, commence on the 4th day of March, 1789; and so the Senators of the first class, and the Representatives, will not, according to the Constitution, be entitled by virtue of the same election by which they hold seats in the present Congress, to seats in the next Congress, which will be assembled after the 3d day of March 1791; and further, that whenever a vacancy shall happen in the Senate or House of Representatives, and an election to fill such vacancy, the person elected, will not, according to the Constitution, be entitled by virtue of such election, to hold a seat beyond the time for which the Senator or Representative in whose stead such person shall have been elected, would, if the vacancy had not happened, have been entitled to hold a seat,—

That it will be advisable for the Congress to pass a Law or Laws for determining, agreeable to the provision in the first section of the 2d article of the Constitution, the time when the electors shall, in the year which will terminate on the 3d day of March 1793, and so in every fourth year thereafter, be chosen, and the day on which they shall give their votes: For declaring what officer shall, in case of vacancy, both in the office of President and Vice President, act as President: For assigning a public office where the lists, mentioned

---

[58] The rough journal includes the text of these amendments as follows:

Strike out the words "*other writing*" in the several parts of the Bill—and insert "Books"

Sect. 1.	Line 21.	Strike out "*after*" and insert "before"
2.	1.	Strike out "whatsoever"—
	17.	Strike out "*two*" Years and insert "one" Year—
3.	12.	between "Charts" and "Books" insert "and"—
	13.	Strike out "*and other writings*"—

In the rough journal, these amendments precede the last sentence of this day's proceedings, with a notation that they should be placed at this point.

[59] On May 17 the House agreed to these amendments and notified the Senate on May 18.

in the 2d paragraph of the 1st section of the 2d article of the Constitution, shall, in case of vacancy in the office of President of the Senate, or his absence from the seat of government, be in the mean time deposited: And for directing the mode in which such lists shall be transmitted,—

Whereupon,

RESOLVED, That the Senate do agree to this report.

ORDERED, That a message be sent to the House of Representatives, to acquaint them herewith.[60]

The Senate proceeded to the SECOND reading of the Bill, "To prevent bringing goods, wares and merchandizes from the State of Rhode-Island and Providence Plantations, into the United States; and to authorize a demand of money from the said State,"—

And on the question, to assign a time for the THIRD reading of this Bill, the yeas and nays being required by one fifth of the Senators present,

Mr. Bassett	Yea	
Mr. Butler		Nay
Mr. Carroll	Yea	
Mr. Dalton	Yea	
Mr. Ellsworth	Yea	
Mr. Elmer		Nay
Mr. Gunn		Nay
Mr. Henry		Nay
Mr. Johnson	Yea	
Mr. Johnston	Yea	
Mr. Izard	Yea	
Mr. King	Yea	
Mr. Langdon	Yea	
Mr. Maclay		Nay
Mr. Morris	Yea	
Mr. Read	Yea	
Mr. Schuyler	Yea	
Mr. Strong	Yea	
Mr. Walker		Nay
Mr. Wingate		Nay

Yeas—13

Nays—7

So it was

ORDERED, That this Bill have the THIRD reading on Monday next.[61]

The Senate adjourned to 11 o'clock on Monday next.

---

[60] On May 19 the House notified the Senate that it had agreed to this report and appointed a committee to bring in a bill on the last paragraph.

[61] On May 17 this bill was read a third time and recommitted.

MONDAY, May 17, 1790

The SENATE assembled,
Present as on the 14th.

The Senate proceeded to the THIRD reading of the Bill, "To prevent bringing goods, wares and merchandizes, from the State of Rhode-Island and Providence Plantations, into the United States; and to authorize a demand of money from the said State:"

And on motion—

ORDERED, That this Bill be re-committed.[62]

The Senate adjourned to 11 o'clock to-morrow.

TUESDAY, May 18, 1790

The SENATE assembled,
Present as yesterday.

A message from the House of Representatives by Mr. Beckley their clerk:

"Mr. PRESIDENT,

"The House of Representatives have agreed to all the amendments proposed by the Senate, to the Bill, entitled, 'An Act for the encouragement of learning, by securing the copies of maps, charts, books and other writings, to the authors and proprietors of such copies, during the times therein mentioned,'[63]—

"They do recede from their first amendment to the Bill, entitled, 'An Act for giving effect to the Act therein mentioned, in respect to the State of North-Carolina, and to amend the said Act;' and in lieu thereof propose to strike out, in the last line of the third section, the words 'and Hillsborough alternately, beginning at the first:' But they do insist on their second amendment to the said Bill,[64]—

He also communicated the following resolves of the House of Representatives, in which the concurrence of the Senate was requested,"—

And he withdrew.

"CONGRESS OF THE UNITED STATES
"IN THE HOUSE OF REPRESENTATIVES
"May 17, 1790

"RESOLVED, That the President of the United States be requested to cause to be forthwith transmitted to the executives of the States of Virginia, North-

---

[62] On May 18 this committee's report was agreed to as amendments to the bill, and the bill was passed and sent to the House for concurrence.

[63] On May 25 this bill was signed by both the Speaker and the Vice President and given to the committee on enrolled bills for delivery to the President.

[64] This House message is in Engrossed Senate Bills and Resolutions, Senate Records, DNA.

Carolina and South-Carolina, a complete list of the officers, non-commissioned officers and privates, of the lines of those States respectively, who are entitled to receive arrears of pay due for services in the years 1782 and 1783, annexing the particular sum that is due to each individual; with a request to the executives of the said States, to make known to the claimants, in the most effectual manner, that the said arrears are ready to be discharged on proper application.

"RESOLVED, That the President of the United States be requested to cause the Secretary of the Treasury to take the necessary steps for paying, within the said States respectively, the money appropriated by Congress on the twenty-ninth day of September 1789, for the discharging the arrears of pay due to the troops of the lines of the said States respectively.

"RESOLVED, That the Secretary of the Treasury in cases where the payment has not been made to the original claimant in person, or to his representative, be directed to take order for making the payment to the original claimant, or to such person or persons only as shall produce a power of attorney, duly attested by two Justices of the Peace of the county in which such person or persons reside, authorizing him or them to receive a certain specified sum."[65]

Mr. Carroll, from the Committee appointed April the 28th, "To consider what provisions will be proper for Congress to make in the present session, respecting the State of Rhode-Island," and to whom it was referred to bring in a Bill on that subject, reported several additional clauses to the Bill "To prevent bringing goods, wares and merchandizes, from the State of Rhode-Island and Providence Plantations, into the United States; and to authorize a demand of money from the said State:"[66] Which report was agreed to as amendments to the Bill.

The Senate proceeded to the THIRD reading of the Bill, "To prevent bringing goods, wares and merchandizes, from the State of Rhode-Island and Providence Plantations, into the United States; and to authorize a demand of money from the said State,"—

And on the question, shall this Bill pass? the yeas and nays being required by one fifth of the Senators present,

Mr. Bassett	Yea	
Mr. Butler		Nay
Mr. Carroll	Yea	
Mr. Dalton	Yea	
Mr. Ellsworth	Yea	
Mr. Elmer		Nay

[65] These House resolves have not been located.

[66] Two annotated bills, one printed, are in Senate Bills, Senate Records, DNA. There is also an annotated printed copy of the bill in the Broadside Collection, RBkRm, DLC. The report has not been located.

Mr. Hawkins		Nay
Mr. Henry		Nay
Mr. Johnson	Yea	
Mr. Johnston	Yea	
Mr. Izard	Yea	
Mr. King	Yea	
Mr. Langdon	Yea	
Mr. Lee		Nay
Mr. Maclay		Nay
Mr. Morris	Yea	
Mr. Read	Yea	
Mr. Schuyler	Yea	
Mr. Strong	Yea	
Mr. Walker		Nay
Mr. Wingate		Nay

Yeas—13
Nays—8

So it was

RESOLVED, That this Bill DO PASS; that the title of it be "An Act to prevent bringing goods, wares and merchandizes, from the State of Rhode-Island and Providence Plantations, into the United States, and to authorize a demand of money from the said State;" That it be engrossed and carried to the House of Representatives, for concurrence therein.[67]

Mr. Johnston reported from the managers of the conference,[68] on the amendments proposed by the House of Representatives to the Bill, entitled, "An Act for giving effect to the Act therein mentioned, in respect to the State of North-Carolina, and to amend the said Act," "That it is proper the Circuit Courts in the district of North-Carolina, be held at Newbern only, and not at Newbern and Hillsborough alternately, as the Bill now provides. And that the District Court for New-Hampshire, be held at Portsmouth only, agreeably to the provision made in the Bill as it passed in the Senate,"—

And the report was agreed to.

The Senate proceeded to consider the message from the House of Representatives of this day, communicating their resolve of the 17th of May, on their amendments to the Bill, entitled, "An Act for giving effect to the Act therein mentioned, in respect to the State of North-Carolina, and to amend the said Act,"—

---

[67] On May 19 the House read this bill for the first time, and it was read a second time and committed on May 20. On June 1 the committee of the whole was released from any further consideration of this bill due to the ratification of the Constitution by Rhode Island.

[68] This report is in Joint Committee Reports, Senate Records, DNA.

Whereupon,

RESOLVED, That the Senate do agree to the first amendment of the House of Representatives on the said Bill, by striking out these words section 3d, line 8th, after the word Newbern, "and Hillsborough alternately, beginning at the first;"

RESOLVED, That the Senate do adhere to their disagreement to the second amendment of the House of Representatives, in which they propose to strike out the last section of the Bill.[69]

ORDERED, That a message be carried to the House of Representatives accordingly.[70]

The Senate proceeded to consider the resolve of the House of Representatives of the 17th of May, "Respecting certain arrearages of pay due to the non-commissioned officers and soldiers of the late Virginia, North-Carolina and South-Carolina lines of the army."

ORDERED, That the further consideration hereof be postponed.[71]

The Senate adjourned to 11 o'clock to-morrow.

WEDNESDAY, MAY 19, 1790

The SENATE assembled,
Present as yesterday.

Proceeded to the consideration of the resolve of the House of Representatives of the 17th of May, "Respecting certain arrearages of pay due to the non-commissioned officers and soldiers of the late Virginia, North-Carolina and South-Carolina lines of the army."

ORDERED, That the resolve be committed to

> Mr. Ellsworth
> Mr. Lee
> Mr. Johnston
> Mr. Izard and
> Mr. King[72]

A message from the House of Representatives by Mr. Beckley their clerk:

"Mr. PRESIDENT,

"The House of Representatives have agreed to the report of the joint Committee appointed to consider and report their opinion on the question, When,

---

[69] The resolves, in the form of an extract from the Journal, are in Engrossed Senate Bills and Resolutions, Senate Records, DNA.

[70] On May 20 the House adhered to its second amendment to this bill and appointed a committee to bring in a new bill. This bill was presented and read the first time on May 21. On May 24 it was read a third time, passed, and sent to the Senate. On the same date the Senate read the bill a first time and scheduled the second reading.

[71] On May 19 this resolution was considered and committed.

[72] On May 20 the report of this committee was considered and postponed.

according to the Constitution, the terms for which the President, Vice President, Senators and Representatives, have been respectively chosen, shall be deemed to have commenced?—and have appointed a Committee to report a Bill pursuant to the last paragraph of the said report"—

And he withdrew.

The Senate adjourned to 11 o'clock to-morrow.

THURSDAY, MAY 20, 1790

The SENATE assembled,
Present as yesterday.

A message from the House of Representatives by Mr. Beckley their clerk:

"Mr. PRESIDENT,

"The House of Representatives do adhere to their second amendment to the Bill, entitled, 'An Act for giving effect to the Act therein mentioned, in respect to the State of North-Carolina, and to amend the said Act' "[73]—

And he withdrew.

Mr. Ellsworth reported from the Committee appointed the 19th of May,[74] on the resolve of the House of Representatives, "Respecting certain arrearages of pay due to the non-commissioned officers and soldiers of the late Virginia, North-Carolina and South-Carolina lines of the army;" which being considered—

ORDERED, That the further consideration hereof be postponed until to-morrow.[75]

The Senate adjourned to 11 o'clock to-morrow.

FRIDAY, MAY 21, 1790

The SENATE assembled,
Present as yesterday.

Proceeded to the consideration of the report of the Committee appointed the 19th of May, on the resolve of the House of Representatives, "Respecting certain arrearages of pay due to the non-commissioned officers and soldiers of the late Virginia, North-Carolina and South-Carolina lines of the army," which was as follows:

"In the first resolve, page 1st, line 7th, insert 'and,' before 'North-Carolina,' and expunge 'and South-Carolina.' "

---

[73] The message is in Engrossed Senate Bills and Resolutions, Senate Records, DNA.
[74] This report is in Various Select Committee Reports, Senate Records, DNA.
[75] On May 21 this report was considered, and several amendments to the resolutions were agreed to and printed in the Journal. The Senate then agreed to the amended resolutions and notified the House.

Subjoin the following at the end of the last resolution,—

"Except where certificates or warrants have been issued under authority of the United States for any of the said arrears of pay, and the same shall be produced by the claimant or claimants. Except also where powers of attorney otherwise attested or expressed than as aforesaid, drawn before the passing of these resolutions, shall be presented, and no circumstances shall appear, before, or within four months after demand made by virtue of them, of the commissioner or agent that shall be entrusted to pay out the monies aforesaid, rendering it probable, in the opinion of such commissioner or agent, that the said powers of attorney are forged, or have been obtained by fraud."

On motion, To adopt the report, so far as it respects the first resolution of the House of Representatives, and to agree to the resolution thus amended,—

It passed in the Affirmative.[76]

On motion, To agree to the second resolution of the House of Representatives,—

It passed in the Affirmative.

On motion, To agree to the third resolution of the House of Representatives, subjoining the first exception reported by the Committee, to wit: "Except where certificates or warrants have been issued under authority of the United States for any of the said arrears of pay, and the same shall be produced by the claimant or claimants;" The yeas and and nays being required by one fifth of the Senators present,

Mr. Bassett		Yea
Mr. Butler		Yea
Mr. Carroll		Yea
Mr. Dalton	Nay	
Mr. Ellsworth	Nay	
Mr. Few		Yea
Mr. Gunn		Yea
Mr. Hawkins		Yea
Mr. Henry		Yea
Mr. Johnson	Nay	
Mr. Johnston		Yea
Mr. Izard	Nay	
Mr. King	Nay	
Mr. Langdon	Nay	
Mr. Lee		Yea
Mr. Maclay		Yea
Mr. Morris	Nay	
Mr. Read		Yea

[76] At this point the rough journal included the last vote on this date and the two preceding motions.

Mr. Schuyler	Nay	
Mr. Strong	Nay	
Mr. Walker		Yea
Mr. Wingate		Yea

Yeas—13

Nays—9

So it passed in the Affirmative.

On motion, To strike out the word "four," before the word "months," in the second exception reported by the Committee,—

It passed in the Affirmative.

On motion, To agree to the second exception reported by the Committee thus amended; the yeas and nays being required by one fifth of the Senators present,

Mr. Bassett		Nay
Mr. Butler	Yea	
Mr. Carroll		Nay
Mr. Dalton	Yea	
Mr. Ellsworth	Yea	
Mr. Few		Nay
Mr. Gunn		Nay
Mr. Hawkins		Nay
Mr. Henry		Nay
Mr. Johnson	Yea	
Mr. Johnston		Nay
Mr. Izard	Yea	
Mr. King	Yea	
Mr. Langdon	Yea	
Mr. Lee		Nay
Mr. Maclay		Nay
Mr. Morris	Yea	
Mr. Read	Yea	
Mr. Schuyler	Yea	
Mr. Strong	Yea	
Mr. Walker		Nay
Mr. Wingate		Nay

Yeas—11

Nays—11

The numbers being equal, the question was by the Vice President, determined in the Negative.

RESOLVED, That the Senate concur in the resolutions of the House of Representatives of the 17th of May, with the amendments agreed to.[77]

---

[77] The House resolves, with Senate amendments, are in the Executive Papers, Vi-Ar.

ORDERED, That the Secretary acquaint the House of Representatives herewith, and request their concurrence in the amendments.[78]

The Senate adjourned to 11 o'clock on Monday next.

MONDAY, MAY 24, 1790

The SENATE assembled,
Present as on the 21st.

Mr. Maclay reported from the Committee appointed May the 11th,[79] on the Bill, entitled, "An Act for finally adjusting and satisfying the claims of Frederick William de Steuben."

ORDERED, That this report lie for consideration until to-morrow.[80]

A message from the House of Representatives by Mr. Beckley their clerk:

"Mr. PRESIDENT,

"The House of Representatives have agreed to all the amendments to the Resolve 'respecting certain arrearages of pay due to the non-commissioned officers and soldiers of the late Virginia, North-Carolina and South-Carolina lines'[81]—

"The House of Representatives have passed a Bill, entitled, 'An Act for the relief of Thomas Jenkins and company.'[82] A Bill, entitled, 'An Act for giving effect to an Act, entitled, "An Act to establish the Judicial Courts of the United States, within the State of North-Carolina;" '[83] to which they request the concurrence of the Senate,"—

And he withdrew.

The Bill, entitled, "An Act for the relief of Thomas Jenkins, and company," was read the FIRST time.

ORDERED, That this Bill have the SECOND reading to-morrow.[84]

The Bill, entitled, "An Act for giving effect to an Act, entitled, 'An Act to establish the Judicial Courts of the United States, within the State of North-Carolina,' " was read the FIRST time.

ORDERED, That this Bill have the SECOND reading to-morrow.[85]

---

[78] On May 24 the Senate amendments to these resolutions were agreed to by the House, and the Senate was notified.

[79] This report is in Various Select Committee Reports, Senate Records, DNA.

[80] On May 25 this report was considered and postponed.

[81] On May 25 these resolves were signed by both the Speaker and the Vice President and given to the committee on enrolled bills for delivery to the President.

[82] This bill has not been located.

[83] This bill has not been located.

[84] On May 27 this bill was read a second time and the third reading was scheduled.

[85] On May 27 this bill was read a second time and the third reading was scheduled.

The petition of John Calhorda, and others, merchants of the State of North-Carolina,[86] was read, stating, "That notwithstanding the duties upon certain merchandizes, where the same was chargeable with duties under the impost law of Congress, were paid previously to the exportation of the said merchandize for the State of North-Carolina, yet, upon the arrival of the same at the port of Wilmington, the duties laid by Act of Assembly of said State, were exacted from your petitioners, in the same manner as before the impost law of the United States took place," and praying relief—

ORDERED, That this petition lie for consideration.[87]

On motion, That it be

RESOLVED, That Congress shall meet and hold their next session in the city of Philadelphia,[88]—

ORDERED, That the consideration hereof be postponed until to-morrow.[89]

The Senate adjourned to 11 o'clock to-morrow.

TUESDAY, MAY 25, 1790

The SENATE assembled,
Present as yesterday.

Mr. Strong from the Committee appointed May the 3d,[90] on the Bill, entitled, "An Act providing the means of intercourse between the United States and foreign nations," reported, to strike out from the word "always," in the 6th line, to the word "also," in the 12th line inclusive;[91]

Which report was accepted as an amendment to the Bill.

ORDERED, That this Bill be read the THIRD time to-morrow.[92]

---

[86] This petition is in Petitions and Memorials: Claims, Senate Records, DNA.

[87] This petition was not considered in the Senate. The House referred it to the Secretary of the Treasury.

[88] This resolve by Mr. Morris is in Senate Simple Resolutions and Motions, Senate Records, DNA.

[89] On May 26 this resolution was considered and postponed.

[90] This report has not been located.

[91] The rough journal phrases this paragraph as follows:

Mr. Strong reported from the Committee appointed May the 3rd. on the Bill entitled "An Act providing the means of intercourse between the United States and foreign nations"

~~That the Committee find the usual allowance to a foreign Minister plenipotentiary from the United States is nine thousand to a Charge des affaires is four thousand five hundred dollars, That in that respect the Bill stands well. That To strike out of the Bill all that is contained between~~ reported, to "strike out from the word 'always' in the 6th line to the word—'also' in the 12th line inclusive—'be ~~stricken out'~~ "—

[92] On May 26 the Senate passed this Bill with an amendment and notified the House.

A message from the House of Representatives by Mr. Beckley their clerk:

"Mr. PRESIDENT,[93]

"The Speaker of the House of Representatives, having signed an enrolled Bill, and an enrolled Resolve, I am directed to bring them to the Senate,"—

And he withdrew.

Mr. Wingate reported from the Committee on enrolled Bills, That they had this day laid before the President of the United States, for his approbation, an enrolled Bill, entitled, "An Act to prescribe the mode in which the public acts, records, and judicial proceedings in each State shall be authenticated, so as to take effect in every other State,"—an enrolled Bill, entitled, "An Act to provide for mitigating or remitting the forfeitures and penalties accruing under the revenue laws, in certain cases therein mentioned,"—an enrolled Bill, entitled, "An Act to continue in force an Act passed at the last session of Congress, entitled, 'An Act to regulate processes in the courts of the United States,' "—and an enrolled Bill, entitled, "An Act for the government of the territory of the United States south of the river Ohio,"—

He farther reported,

That they had examined the enrolled Bill, entitled, "An Act for the encouragement of learning, by securing the copies of maps, charts, and books, to the authors and proprietors of such copies, during the times therein mentioned,"[94] —and the enrolled Resolve "respecting certain arrearages of pay due to the non-commissioned officers and soldiers of the late Virginia and North-Carolina lines,"[95] and had found them correct.

The Senate proceeded to consider the report of the Committee on the Bill, entitled, "An Act for finally adjusting and satisfying the claims of Frederick William de Steuben;" which is as follows:

In the second line, strike out from the word "order" inclusive, to the end of the Bill, and insert "consideration of the eminent services of the Baron de Steuben rendered to the United States during the late war, there be paid to him an annuity of one thousand dollars, to commence on the first day of January last; to be paid in quarterly payments, at the Treasury of the United States,"—

And after debate,

[93] At this point the rough journal contains the following canceled paragraph: "The House of Representatives have agreed to a gramatical amendment to the enroled Bill entitled 'An Act for the encouragement of Learning by securing the Copies of Maps, Charts and Books to the Authors and proprietors of such Copies during the times therein mentioned,' by inserting Section 3nd [sic], Line 2nd. The words 'or have'— after 'hath.' "

[94] The inspected enrolled bill is in Enrolled Acts, RG 11, DNA. E–46038.

[95] The inspected enrolled bill is in Enrolled Acts, RG 11, DNA. E–22985.

The further consideration hereof was postponed until to-morrow.[96]

The Vice President affixed his signature to the enrolled Bill, entitled, "An Act for the encouragement of learning, by securing the copies of maps, charts, and books, to the authors and proprietors of such copies, during the times therein mentioned,"—and to an enrolled Resolve, "respecting certain arrearages of pay due to the non-commissioned officers and soldiers of the late Virginia and North-Carolina lines," and they were delivered to the Committee on enrolled Bills, to be laid before the President of the United States, for his approbation.[97]

The Senate adjourned to 11 o'clock to-morrow.

WEDNESDAY, MAY 26, 1790

The SENATE assembled,
Present as yesterday,—and
Mr. Paterson from the State of New-Jersey, attended.

The Senate proceeded to the THIRD reading of the Bill, entitled, "An Act providing the means of intercourse between the United States and foreign nations."

RESOLVED, That the Senate concur therein, with an amendment.[98]

ORDERED, That the Secretary acquaint the House of Representatives herewith, and request their concurrence in the amendment.[99]

A message from the President of the United States, by Mr. Lear his Secretary:

"Mr. PRESIDENT,

"The President of the United States has this day approved of, and affixed his signature to 'An Act for the government of the territory of the United States south of the river Ohio,'—and to 'An Act to continue in force an Act

---

[96] At this point the rough journal contains the following canceled lines: "The Senate agreed to the grammatical amendment proposed by the H of R to the enroled Bill, entitled, 'An Act for the encouragement of Learning by securing the Copies of Maps, Charts and Books to the Authors and proprietors of such Copies during the times therein mentioned.' by inserting the words 'or have' Section 3rd. Line 2nd, after the word 'hath.' Ordered that the Secretary acquaint the House of Representatives herewith." On May 26 this report was disagreed to, and one motion on the bill was accepted while another was defeated. The third reading was scheduled.

[97] On May 28 this committee reported that it had delivered this bill and the resolution to the President.

[98] The rough journal reads:

Resolved that the Senate do concur herein with the following amendment.

Strike out from the word "always" in the fifth line to the word "also" in the twelfth line inclusive.

[99] On May 27 the House disagreed to the Senate amendment and the Senate was notified on May 28. On the same date the Senate decided to insist upon its amendment and notified the House.

passed at the last session of Congress, entitled, "An Act to regulate processes in the courts of the United States," ' "—

And he withdrew.

ORDERED, That the Secretary acquaint the House of Representatives herewith.

The Senate proceeded to the consideration of the report of the Committee on the Bill, entitled, "An Act for finally adjusting[100] the claims of Frederick William de Steuben,"—

And on the question to agree to the report of the Committee, the yeas and nays being required by one fifth of the Senators present,

Mr. Bassett		Nay
Mr. Butler		Nay
Mr. Carroll		Nay
Mr. Dalton		Nay
Mr. Ellsworth	Yea	
Mr. Elmer	Yea	
Mr. Few	Yea	
Mr. Gunn		Nay
Mr. Hawkins	Yea	
Mr. Henry		Nay
Mr. Johnson		Nay
Mr. Johnston	Yea	
Mr. Izard		Nay
Mr. King		Nay
Mr. Langdon	Yea	
Mr. Lee		Nay
Mr. Maclay		Nay
Mr. Morris		Nay
Mr. Paterson		Nay
Mr. Read		Nay
Mr. Schuyler		Nay
Mr. Strong	Yea	
Mr. Walker		Nay
Mr. Wingate	Yea	

Nays, 16——Yeas, 8

So it passed in the Negative.[101]

---

[100] The smooth journal adds the words "and satisfying."

[101] The rough journal contains the following canceled paragraphs at this point:

On Motion that "Frederick Wm." be stricken out as often as it occurs in this Bill, and "Baron" be inserted in its stead.

It passed in the affirmative.

On motion, That the opinion of the Senate be taken, Whether two thousand dollars, line 7th, shall stand in the Bill? The yeas and nays being required by one fifth of the Senators present,

Mr. Bassett		Yea
Mr. Butler		Yea
Mr. Carroll		Yea
Mr. Dalton	Nay	
Mr. Ellsworth	Nay	
Mr. Elmer	Nay	
Mr. Few	Nay	
Mr. Gunn		Yea
Mr. Hawkins	Nay	
Mr. Henry		Yea
Mr. Johnson	Nay	
Mr. Johnston	Nay	
Mr. Izard		Yea
Mr. King		Yea
Mr. Langdon	Nay	
Mr. Lee		Yea
Mr. Maclay	Nay	
Mr. Morris		Yea
Mr. Paterson	Nay	
Mr. Read		Yea
Mr. Schuyler		Yea
Mr. Strong	Nay	
Mr. Walker		Yea
Mr. Wingate	Nay	

Yeas—12

Nays—12

The yeas and nays being equal, the Vice President determined the question in the Affirmative.

On motion, That these words "the sum of seven thousand dollars, in addition to the monies already received by him, and also," be stricken out of the Bill; the yeas and nays being required by one fifth of the Senators present,

Mr. Bassett		Nay
Mr. Butler	Yea	
Mr. Carroll		Nay
Mr. Dalton	Yea	
Mr. Ellsworth	Yea	
Mr. Elmer	Yea	
Mr. Few	Yea	

Mr. Gunn		Nay
Mr. Hawkins	Yea	
Mr. Henry		Nay
Mr. Johnson	Yea	
Mr. Johnston		Nay
Mr. Izard		Nay
Mr. King		Nay
Mr. Langdon	Yea	
Mr. Lee		Nay
Mr. Maclay	Yea	
Mr. Morris		Nay
Mr. Paterson	Yea	
Mr. Read		Nay
Mr. Schuyler		Nay
Mr. Strong	Yea	
Mr. Walker		Nay
Mr. Wingate	Yea	

Yeas—12

Nays—12

The numbers being equal, the Vice President determined the question in the Negative.

ORDERED, That to-morrow be assigned for the THIRD reading of this Bill.[102]

The Senate proceeded to consider the motion made the 24th of May, to wit, "That it be resolved, that Congress shall meet and hold their next session in the city of Philadelphia;" and after debate—

ORDERED, That the further consideration hereof be postponed until Thursday the 3d of June next.[103]

The Senate adjourned to 11 o'clock to-morrow.

THURSDAY, MAY 27, 1790

The SENATE assembled,

Present as yesterday.

Proceeded to the SECOND reading of the Bill, entitled, "An Act for the relief of Thomas Jenkins, and company."

ORDERED, That this Bill have the THIRD reading to-morrow.[104]

The Senate proceeded to the SECOND reading of the Bill, entitled, "An Act

---

[102] On May 27 this bill was read a third time and passed with amendments. The concurrence of the House was then requested.

[103] On May 28 this resolution was withdrawn.

[104] On May 28 this bill was read a third time and committed.

for giving effect to an Act, entitled, 'An Act to establish the Judicial Courts of the United States, within the State of North-Carolina.' "

ORDERED, That this Bill have the THIRD reading to-morrow.[105]

The petition of John Frederick Amelung, of the State of Maryland,[106] was read, stating the difficulties he labours under in establishing the glass manufacture, and soliciting "the aid of the government of the United States, in this important undertaking."

ORDERED, That this petition lie on the table.[107]

The Senate proceeded to the THIRD reading of the Bill, entitled, "An Act for finally adjusting and satisfying the claims of Frederick William de Steuben."

On motion, To strike out "two thousand dollars annuity," proposed in the Bill, and insert "one thousand dollars," in lieu thereof—

It passed in the Negative.

On motion, To strike out "seven thousand," line 6th—

It passed in the Affirmative.

On motion, To insert "five thousand," in lieu of "seven thousand,"—

It passed in the Negative.

On motion, To insert "four thousand five hundred," in the place of "seven thousand,"—

It passed in the Negative.

On motion, To insert "four thousand," in the place of "seven thousand,"—

It passed in the Negative.

On motion, To strike out these words, "the sum of   dollars, in addition to the monies already received by him, and also"—

It passed in the Affirmative.

On motion, To strike out, line 4th, "as well as for the commutation or half-pay promised by the Resolutions of Congress,"—

It passed in the Affirmative.

On motion, To insert, line 7th, "five hundred," after the words "two thousand,"—

The yeas and nays being required by one fifth of the Senators present,

Mr. Bassett	Yea	
Mr. Butler	Yea	
Mr. Carroll	Yea	
Mr. Dalton		Nay

---

[105] On May 28 this bill was read a third time and passed. The House was then notified.

[106] This petition is in Petitions and Memorials: Various subjects, Senate Records, DNA.

[107] This petition was not considered by the Senate, but the House referred it to the Secretary of the Treasury.

Mr. Ellsworth		Nay
Mr. Elmer		Nay
Mr. Few		Nay
Mr. Gunn	Yea	
Mr. Hawkins		Nay
Mr. Henry	Yea	
Mr. Johnson		Nay
Mr. Johnston		Nay
Mr. Izard	Yea	
Mr. King	Yea	
Mr. Langdon		Nay
Mr. Lee	Yea	
Mr. Maclay		Nay
Mr. Morris	Yea	
Mr. Paterson		Nay
Mr. Read	Yea	
Mr. Schuyler	Yea	
Mr. Strong		Nay
Mr. Walker	Yea	
Mr. Wingate		Nay

Yeas—12

Nays—12

The yeas and nays being equal, the Vice President determined the question in the affirmative.

Whereupon,

RESOLVED, That this Bill DO PASS with the amendments.

ORDERED, That the Secretary acquaint the House of Representatives herewith, and request their concurrence in the amendments.[108]

A message from the House of Representatives by Mr. Beckley their clerk:

"Mr. PRESIDENT,

"I am directed to inform the Senate, that the President of the United States did, on the 26th of May, approve of, and affix his signature to 'An Act to prescribe the mode in which the public acts, records, and judicial proceedings in each State shall be authenticated, so as to take effect in every other State,'— and 'An Act to provide for mitigating or remitting the forfeitures and penalties accruing under the revenue laws, in certain cases therein mentioned,' "—

And he withdrew.

The Senate adjourned to 11 o'clock to-morrow.

---

[108] On May 28 the House concurred in the Senate amendments and it notified the Senate on May 31.

FRIDAY, MAY 28, 1790

The SENATE assembled,
Present as yesterday.

Proceeded to the THIRD reading of the Bill, entitled, "An Act for the relief of Thomas Jenkins and company;" and on motion—

ORDERED, That it be committed to

> Mr. Dalton
> Mr. Butler and
> Mr. Langdon[109]

A message from the House of Representatives by Mr. Beckley their clerk:

"Mr. PRESIDENT,

"The House of Representatives disagree to the amendment proposed by the Senate to the Bill, entitled, 'An Act providing the means of intercourse between the United States and foreign nations,' "—

And he withdrew.

Mr. Few from the Committee appointed May the 3d, on the Bill, entitled, "An Act supplemental to the Act for establishing the salaries of the executive officers of government, with their assistants and clerks," reported;[110] whereupon—

The Senate proceeded to the THIRD reading of the Bill.

RESOLVED, That this Bill DO PASS.

ORDERED, That the Secretary acquaint the House of Representatives herewith.[111]

The Senate proceeded to the THIRD reading of the Bill, entitled, "An Act for giving effect to an Act, entitled, 'An Act to establish the Judicial Courts of the United States, within the State of North-Carolina.' "

RESOLVED, That this Bill DO PASS.

ORDERED, That the Secretary acquaint the House of Representatives herewith.[112]

The motion made the 24th of May, to wit, "That Congress shall meet and hold their next session in the City of Philadelphia," was withdrawn.[113]

Mr. Wingate from the Committee on enrolled Bills, reported, That they did on the 28th of April, lay before the President of the United States, the

---

[109] On June 1 this committee reported and the bill passed. The House was then notified.

[110] This report has not been located.

[111] On June 1 the committee on enrolled bills reported that it found this bill to be correct.

[112] On June 1 the committee on enrolled bills reported that it had found this bill to be correct.

[113] On June 1 the Senate received a House resolution to hold the next session in Philadelphia.

enrolled Bill, entitled, "An Act for the encouragement of learning, by securing the copies of maps, charts, and books, to the authors and proprietors of such copies, during the times therein mentioned,"—and the enrolled Resolve "respecting certain arrearages of pay due to the non-commissioned officers and soldiers of the late Virginia and North-Carolina lines."[114]

The Senate proceeded to consider the message from the House of Representatives of this day, and the amendment of the Senate disagreed to, on the Bill, entitled, "An Act providing the means of intercourse between the United States and foreign nations;" whereupon—

RESOLVED, That the Senate do INSIST on their amendment to the said Bill.

ORDERED, That the Secretary acquaint the House of Representatives herewith.[115]

The Senate adjourned to 11 o'clock on Monday next.

MONDAY, MAY 31, 1790

The SENATE assembled,
Present as on the 28th.

A message from the House of Representatives by Mr. Beckley their clerk:

"Mr. PRESIDENT,

"The House of Representatives have agreed to the amendments of the Senate to the Bill, entitled, 'An Act for finally adjusting and satisfying the claims of Frederick William de Steuben,'[116]—

"They do insist on their disagreement to the amendment of the Senate, on the Bill, entitled, 'An Act providing the means of intercourse between the United States and foreign nations,' "—

And he withdrew.

The Senate proceeded to the consideration of the message from the House of Representatives on the Bill, entitled, "An Act providing the means of intercourse between the United States and foreign nations," and *their* amendment disagreed to by the House of Representatives; whereupon—

RESOLVED, That the Senate do still insist on *their* amendment, and request a conference with such Committee as may be appointed by the House of Representatives, on the subject matter of disagreement, and that

---

[114] The President signed the Copyright Act on May 31, and the Senate was notified on June 1. The Compensation List Resolutions were signed by the President on June 4, and the Senate was notified on the seventh.

[115] On May 28 the House insisted on its disagreement to this amendment and notified the Senate on May 31. On the same date the Senate resolved to set up a conference committee on the amendment and notified the House.

[116] On June 1 the committee on enrolled bills reported that it had found this bill to be correct.

Mr. King

Mr. Izard and

Mr. Read, be managers of the conference on the part of the Senate.

ORDERED, That the Secretary acquaint the House of Representatives herewith, and request their concurrence in the appointment of a Committee on *their* part.[117]

Mr. Butler having moved for leave to bring in a Bill to determine "the permanent seat of Congress, and the government of the United States;"[118] leave was accordingly given, and the Bill being presented,—

ORDERED, That this Bill have the FIRST reading at this time.

ORDERED, That this Bill have the SECOND reading to-morrow.[119]

The Senate adjourned to 11 o'clock to-morrow.

---

[117] On June 1 the House agreed to this resolution and appointed a conference committee.

[118] This bill is in Senate Bills, Senate Records, DNA.

[119] On June 1 this bill was read a second time and postponed.

TUESDAY, JUNE 1, 1790

The SENATE assembled,

Present as yesterday.

Mr. Wingate from the Committee on enrolled Bills, reported, That they had examined the enrolled Bill, entitled, "An Act for finally adjusting and satisfying the claims of Frederick William de Steuben,"[1]—the enrolled Bill, entitled, "An Act for giving effect to an Act, entitled, 'An Act to establish the Judicial Courts of the United States, within the State of North-Carolina,' "[2]— and the enrolled Bill, entitled, "An Act supplemental to the Act for establishing the salaries of the executive officers of government, with their assistants and clerks,"[3] and had found them correct.[4]

Mr. Dalton reported from the Committee appointed the 28th of May,[5] on the Bill, entitled, "An Act for the relief of Thomas Jenkins and company;" whereupon—

RESOLVED, That this Bill DO PASS.

ORDERED, That the Secretary acquaint the House of Representatives herewith.[6]

The Senate proceeded to the SECOND reading of the Bill to determine "the permanent Seat of Congress, and the government of the United States;" and after debate—

ORDERED, That the further consideration hereof be postponed until tomorrow.[7]

A written message from the President of the United States, by Mr. Lear his Secretary, was read as follows:

UNITED STATES, June 1, 1790

GENTLEMEN of the SENATE, and
    HOUSE of REPRESENTATIVES,

HAVING received official information of the accession of the State of Rhode-Island and Providence Plantations, to the Constitution of the United States, I take the earliest opportunity of communicating the same to you, with my congratulations on this happy event, which unites under the general government all the States which were originally confederated; and have directed my Secre-

---

[1] The inspected enrolled bill is in Enrolled Acts, RG 11, DNA. E–46033.

[2] The inspected enrolled bill is in Enrolled Acts, RG 11, DNA.

[3] The inspected enrolled bill is in Enrolled Acts, RG 11, DNA. E–46056.

[4] On June 2 all of these bills were signed by both the Speaker and the Vice President and given to the committee on enrolled bills for delivery to the President.

[5] This report has not been located.

[6] On June 4 the committee on enrolled bills reported that it had found this bill to be correct.

[7] On June 2 this bill was considered again and committed. A House resolution on the next session of Congress was also committed to this committee.

tary to lay before you a copy of the letter from the President of the Convention of the State of Rhode-Island, to the President of the United States.

G. WASHINGTON

(Copy)

"STATE OF RHODE-ISLAND
"NEWPORT, May 29, 1790

"SIR,

"I have the pleasing satisfaction of informing your Excellency, that the Constitution of the United States of America, was this day ratified and adopted by the Convention of the people of this State, agreeable to the recommendation of the General Convention assembled at Philadelphia, and the consequent resolution of Congress thereon.

"The lower House of the General Assembly of this State, at their session the former part of this month, past a resolution requesting his Excellency the Governor, in case the Constitution should be adopted by the Convention, to call the Assembly together by warrant, as soon after the adoption as might be, for the special purpose of electing the Senators, and taking measures for a representation of this State in Congress; I can therefore assure your Excellency that in the course of a few days, not to exceed sixteen, the Legislature will be assembled, either by special warrant or pursuant to their adjournment on the second Monday of June, when I have not the least doubt the Senators will be immediately appointed, and the State represented in Congress agreeable to the Constitution, as soon as the elections can be accomplished.

"The ratification of the Constitution will be made out and forwarded by way of the Post-Office, with all possible expedition.

"Colonel William Barton, who was a member of the Convention, will have the honor of delivering this letter.

"With the highest sentiments of esteem and respect,
I have the honor of being your Excellency's
Most obedient Servant,
(Signed)   DANIEL OWEN, President"

"The President of the United States"

A true Copy
TOBIAS LEAR
Secretary to the President
of the United States[8]

ORDERED, That the message and paper accompanying the same, be filed.

A message from the House of Representatives by Mr. Beckley their clerk:

---

[8] This message and documents are in President's Messages: Suggesting legislation, Senate Records, DNA.

"Mr. PRESIDENT,

"The President of the United States did, on the 31st of May, approve of, and affix his signature to 'An Act for the encouragement of learning, by securing the copies of maps, charts and books, to the authors and proprietors of such copies, during the times therein mentioned,'—

"They have agreed to the conference proposed by the Senate, on the Bill, entitled, 'An Act providing the means of intercourse between the United States and foreign nations,' and have appointed

Mr. Gerry

Mr. White and

Mr. Williamson, managers thereof on their part,"[9]—

He also communicated the following Resolve of the House of Representatives,—

And he withdrew.

"CONGRESS OF THE UNITED STATES

"IN THE HOUSE OF REPRESENTATIVES

"Monday the 31st of May, 1790

"RESOLVED, That Congress shall meet and hold their next session at the city of Philadelphia."[10]

ORDERED, That the consideration of the last recited resolve, be postponed until to-morrow.[11]

The Senate adjourned to 11 o'clock to-morrow.

WEDNESDAY, JUNE 2, 1790

The SENATE assembled,

Present as yesterday.

A message from the House of Representatives by Mr. Beckley their clerk:

"Mr. PRESIDENT,

"I am directed to bring to the Senate several enrolled Bills, which have been signed by the Speaker of the House of Representatives,"—

He also communicated the following Resolve of the House of Representatives,—

And he withdrew.

---

[9] On June 23 this joint committee reported. The report was printed in the Journal and accepted. The House was then notified.

[10] This resolve has not been located.

[11] On June 2 this resolve was committed to the committee on the Residence Bill.

"CONGRESS OF THE UNITED STATES
"IN THE HOUSE OF REPRESENTATIVES
"Tuesday the 1st of June, 1790

"RESOLVED, That all Treaties made, or which shall be made and promulged under the authority of the United States, shall, from time to time, be published and annexed to their code of Laws, by the Secretary of State."[12]

The Senate proceeded to the SECOND reading of the Bill to determine "the permanent Seat of Congress, and the government of the United States."

ORDERED, That this Bill be committed to

Mr. Butler
Mr. Johnston
Mr. Henry
Mr. Lee and
Mr. Dalton

On motion,

ORDERED, That the resolve of the House of Representatives of the 31st of May, to wit, "That Congress shall meet and hold their next session at the city of Philadelphia," be referred to the same Committee.[13]

The Senate proceeded to consider the Resolve of the House of Representatives of June the first, providing that "all Treaties made, or which shall be made and promulged under the authority of the United States, shall, from time to time, be published and annexed to their code of Laws, by the Secretary of State," and—

RESOLVED, That the Senate concur in this resolution.[14]

ORDERED, That the Secretary acquaint the House of Representatives with the concurrence.

A message from the House of Representatives by Mr. Beckley their clerk:

"Mr. PRESIDENT,

"The House of Representatives have passed a Bill, entitled, 'An Act making provision for the debt of the United States;'[15] in which they request the concurrence of the Senate,"—

And he withdrew.

ORDERED, That the Bill, entitled, "An Act making provision for the debt of the United States," have the FIRST reading at this time.

ORDERED, That this Bill pass to the SECOND reading.[16]

---

[12] This resolve has not been located.

[13] On June 4 a motion to add a member to this committee was defeated.

[14] On June 10 this resolve was signed by both the Speaker and the Vice President and given to the committee on enrolled bills for delivery to the President.

[15] One clear and two annotated printed versions of this bill are in the Broadside Collection, RBkRm, DLC. E-46049.

[16] On June 3 this bill was read a second time and consideration of it was postponed.

The Vice President affixed his signature to the enrolled Bill, entitled, "An Act for finally adjusting and satisfying the claims of Frederick William de Steuben,"—to an enrolled Bill, entitled, "An Act for giving effect to an Act, entitled, 'An Act to establish the Judicial Courts of the United States, within the State of North-Carolina,' "—and to an enrolled Bill, entitled, "An Act supplemental to the Act for establishing the salaries of the executive officers of government, with their assistants and clerks;" and they were delivered to the Committee on enrolled Bills, to be laid before the President of the United States for his approbation.[17]

RESOLVED, That the Senate will attend the funeral of Col. Bland, late a member of the House of Representatives of the United States, at 5 o'clock this afternoon.[18]

The Senate adjourned to 11 o'clock to-morrow.

THURSDAY, JUNE 3, 1790

The SENATE assembled,
Present as yesterday.

Mr. Wingate from the Committee on enrolled Bills, reported, That they did this day lay before the President of the United States, the enrolled Bill, entitled, "An Act for finally adjusting and satisfying the claims of Frederick William de Steuben,"—the enrolled Bill, entitled, "An Act for giving effect to an Act, entitled, 'An Act to establish the Judicial Courts of the United States, within the State of North-Carolina,' "—and the enrolled Bill, entitled, "An Act supplemental to the Act for establishing the salaries of the executive officers of government, with their assistants and clerks,"[19]—

He further reported, That the Committee had examined an enrolled Bill, entitled, "An Act for the relief of Thomas Jenkins and company,"[20] and had found it correct.[21]

The Senate proceeded to the SECOND reading of the Bill, entitled, "An Act making provision for the debt of the United States."

ORDERED, That the further consideration hereof be postponed until Monday next.[22]

The Senate adjourned to 11 o'clock to-morrow.

---

[17] On June 3 this committee reported that it had laid these bills before the President.
[18] This resolve has not been located.
[19] The President signed these three bills on June 4, and the Senate was notified on June 7.
[20] The inspected enrolled bill is in Enrolled Acts, RG 11, DNA.
[21] On June 4 this bill was signed by both the Speaker and the Vice President and given to the committee on enrolled bills for delivery to the President.
[22] On June 7 this bill was considered again.

FRIDAY, JUNE 4, 1790

The SENATE assembled,
Present as yesterday.

A message from the House of Representatives by Mr. Beckley their clerk:

"Mr. PRESIDENT,

"The House of Representatives have passed a Bill, entitled, 'An Act to satisfy the claims of John McCord, against the United States;'[23] and a Bill, entitled, 'An Act for giving effect to the several Acts therein mentioned in respect to the State of Rhode-Island and Providence Plantations,'[24] in which they desire the concurrence of the Senate,—

"The Speaker of the House of Representatives having signed an enrolled Bill, I am directed to bring it to the Senate,"—

And he withdrew.

The Senate proceeded to the FIRST reading of the Bill, entitled, "An Act to satisfy the claims of John McCord, against the United States."

ORDERED, That this Bill pass to the SECOND reading.[25]

The Senate proceeded to the FIRST reading of the Bill, entitled, "An Act for giving effect to the several Acts therein mentioned, in respect to the State of Rhode-Island and Providence Plantations."

ORDERED, That this Bill pass to the SECOND reading.[26]

The Vice President affixed his signature to the enrolled Bill, entitled, "An Act for the relief of Thomas Jenkins and company;" and it was delivered to the Committee on enrolled Bills, to be laid before the President of the United States.[27]

On motion, To appoint an additional member to the Committee on the Bill to determine "the permanent seat of Congress, and the government of the United States," Mr. Johnston being detained by sickness,—

It passed in the Negative.[28]

The Senate adjourned to 11 o'clock on Monday next.

MONDAY, JUNE 7, 1790

The SENATE assembled,
Present as on the 4th of June.

Agreeably to the order of the day, proceeded to the SECOND reading of the

---

[23] This bill has not been located.

[24] This bill has not been located.

[25] On June 7 this bill was read a second time and committed.

[26] On June 7 this bill was read a second time.

[27] On June 14 this committee reported that it had delivered this bill to the President. The President signed this bill on the same day.

[28] On June 7 this committee reported on the bill and consideration of the report was postponed.

Bill, entitled, "An Act to satisfy the claims of John McCord, against the United States."

ORDERED, That this Bill, together with the papers accompanying the same, be committed to   Mr. Morris

  Mr. Maclay and

  Mr. Elmer[29]

Agreeably to the order of the day, the Senate proceeded to the SECOND reading of the Bill, entitled, "An Act for giving effect to the several Acts therein mentioned, in respect to the State of Rhode-Island and Providence Plantations."

ORDERED, That this Bill pass to the THIRD reading.[30]

A message from the House of Representatives by Mr. Beckley their clerk:

"Mr. PRESIDENT,

"I am directed to inform the Senate, that the President of the United States did, on the 4th of June 1790, approve of and affix his signature to 'An Act for finally adjusting and satisfying the claims of Frederick William de Steuben,'—to 'An Act for giving effect to an Act, entitled, "An Act to establish the Judicial Courts of the United States, within the State of North-Carolina," ' —and to 'An Act, supplemental to the Act for establishing the Salaries of the executive officers of government, with their assistants and clerks;' and that he did, on the 7th of June, approve of and affix his signature to the Resolve 'respecting certain arrearages of pay due to the non-commissioned officers and soldiers of the late Virginia and North-Carolina lines,' "—

And he withdrew.

Mr. Butler reported from the Committee appointed June the 2d,[31] on the Bill to determine "the permanent Seat of Congress, and the government of the United States."

ORDERED, That the report be postponed until to-morrow, for consideration.[32]

Agreeable to the order of the day, the Senate proceeded to the SECOND reading of the Bill, entitled, "An Act making provision for the debt of the United States," and after progress,[33]

The Senate adjourned to 11 o'clock to-morrow.

---

[29] On June 18 this committee reported, and the report was accepted as an amendment to the bill which then passed to a third reading.

[30] On June 9 the Senate passed this bill with an amendment, and the House concurred in the amendment.

[31] This report is in Various Select Committee Reports, Senate Records, DNA.

[32] On June 8 the committee report was rejected and several motions on the bill were defeated. On the same day the House resolution to hold the next session of Congress in Philadelphia was defeated.

[33] On June 9 this bill was considered again.

TUESDAY, JUNE 8, 1790

The SENATE assembled,

Present as yesterday.

Mr. Lee from the joint Committee appointed the 30th of May, "To consider and report whether any, and what further regulations are necessary for conducting the business between the two Houses," reported.[34]

ORDERED, That the report lie for consideration.[35]

A message from the House Representatives by Mr. Beckley their clerk:

"Mr. PRESIDENT,

"The House of Representatives have passed a Bill, entitled, 'An Act for giving effect to an Act, entitled, "An Act to establish the Judicial Courts of the United States, within the State of Rhode-Island and Providence Plantations," '[36] in which they request the concurrence of the Senate,"[37]—

He also communicated the following resolve of the House of Representatives; in which the concurrence of the Senate was desired,—

And he withdrew.

"IN THE HOUSE OF REPRESENTATIVES
"OF THE UNITED STATES
"Tuesday the 8th of June, 1790

"On motion,

"RESOLVED, That a Committee be appointed, to join with a Committee of the Senate, to be appointed for the purpose to consider of and report when it will be convenient and proper that an adjournment of the present session of Congress should take place; and to consider and report such business now before Congress necessary to be finished before the adjournment, and such as may be conveniently postponed; and also to consider and report such matters not now before Congress, but which it will be necessary should be considered and determined by Congress before an adjournment—

"And a Committee was appointed of Mr. Wadsworth, Mr. Carroll and Mr. Hartley."[38]

The last recited resolve of the House of Representatives was read.[39]

---

[34] A sentence which is initialed by Richard Henry Lee and may be a part of this report is in the Office of the Financial Clerk of the Senate, Senate Records, DNA. The complete report has not been located.

[35] On June 10 the Senate agreed to this report with amendments and notified the House.

[36] This bill has not been located.

[37] On June 10 this bill was read for the first time.

[38] A copy of the resolve is in Messages from the House, Senate Records, DNA.

[39] On June 21 the Senate agreed to this resolution and appointed a committee to meet with the House committee.

On motion, That the consideration of the "Bill to determine the permanent Seat of Congress, and the government of the United States," be postponed, in order to take up the resolution from the House of Representatives for declaring the place where the next session of Congress shall be held[40]—

A motion was made to postpone THIS motion until to-morrow, and,

It passed in the Negative:

Whereupon the Senate proceeded to the consideration of the resolve of the House of Representatives, to wit, "That Congress shall meet, and hold their next session at the city of Philadelphia,"—

And on motion to concur therein, the yeas and nays being required by one fifth of the Senators present,

Mr. Bassett		Yea
Mr. Butler	Nay	
Mr. Carroll		Yea
Mr. Dalton	Nay	
Mr. Ellsworth	Nay	
Mr. Elmer		Yea
Mr. Few	Nay	
Mr. Gunn	Nay	
Mr. Hawkins	Nay	
Mr. Henry		Yea
Mr. Johnson	Nay	
Mr. Johnston	Nay	
Mr. Izard	Nay	
Mr. King	Nay	
Mr. Langdon		Yea
Mr. Lee		Yea
Mr. Maclay		Yea
Mr. Morris		Yea
Mr. Paterson	Nay	
Mr. Read		Yea
Mr. Schuyler	Nay	
Mr. Strong	Nay	
Mr. Walker		Yea
Mr. Wingate		Yea

Nays—13
Yeas—11

So it was

RESOLVED, That the Senate do not concur in the resolution proposed by the House of Representatives.

---

[40] This motion is in Senate Simple Resolutions and Motions, Senate Records, DNA.

ORDERED, That the Secretary acquaint the House of Representatives herewith.[41]

The Senate resumed the consideration of the report of the Committee on the Bill to determine "the permanent seat of Congress, and the government of the United States," which is as follows:

1st. That in their opinion, taking a combination of circumstances into consideration, the present session is a proper time for fixing on the permanent residence of Congress, and the government of the United States; and after due consideration, recommend that it be placed on the eastern or northeastern bank of the Patomack—

Your Committee further recommend, that such sums of money as may be offered by the States, for the carrying this Bill into effect, may be accepted of; then the Bill will read thus, "And to accept of grants of money or land." Your Committee were of opinion that Congress can best determine the time to be allowed for compleating the buildings—

With respect to the temporary residence of Congress, your Committee, after weighing all circumstances, consider the ground of choice to be so narrowed as to be fully in the view of Senate,—

Your Committee recommend that the Senate should agree with all the other parts of the Bill.

Whereupon a motion was made, That the opinion of the Senate be taken, whether it be expedient at this time to determine upon any place for the permanent seat of government of the United States? The yeas and nays being required by one fifth of the Senators present,

Mr. Bassett		Nay
Mr. Butler	Yea	
Mr. Carroll		Nay
Mr. Dalton	Yea	
Mr. Ellsworth		Nay
Mr. Elmer		Nay
Mr. Few	Yea	
Mr. Gunn	Yea	
Mr. Hawkins	Yea	
Mr. Henry		Nay
Mr. Johnson	Yea	
Mr. Johnston	Yea	
Mr. Izard	Yea	
Mr. King	Yea	
Mr. Langdon		Nay
Mr. Lee		Nay

[41] On June 14 the Senate received a House resolve to hold the next session in Baltimore, and consideration of this resolution was postponed.

Mr.	Maclay		Nay
Mr.	Morris		Nay
Mr.	Paterson	Yea	
Mr.	Read		Nay
Mr.	Schuyler	Yea	
Mr.	Strong	Yea	
Mr.	Walker		Nay
Mr.	Wingate		Nay

Yeas—12

Nays—12

The number of votes being equal, the question was by the Vice President determined in the Negative.

On motion,

ORDERED, That the consideration of the Bill to determine "the permanent Seat of Congress, and the government of the United States," be resumed; the report of the Committee being rejected.

On motion, To fill up the blank in the first paragraph of the Bill with these words, "the easterly bank of the Patomack," the yeas and nays being required by one fifth of the Senators present,

Mr.	Bassett		Nay
Mr.	Butler	Yea	
Mr.	Carroll		Nay
Mr.	Dalton		Nay
Mr.	Ellsworth		Nay
Mr.	Elmer		Nay
Mr.	Few	Yea	
Mr.	Gunn	Yea	
Mr.	Hawkins	Yea	
Mr.	Henry		Nay
Mr.	Johnson	Yea	
Mr.	Johnston	Yea	
Mr.	Izard	Yea	
Mr.	King	Yea	
Mr.	Langdon		Nay
Mr.	Lee		Nay
Mr.	Maclay		Nay
Mr.	Morris		Nay
Mr.	Paterson		Nay
Mr.	Read		Nay
Mr.	Schuyler	Yea	
Mr.	Strong		Nay

Mr. Walker	Nay
Mr. Wingate	Nay

Nays—15

Yeas—9

So it passed in the Negative.

On motion, To postpone the further consideration of this Bill for a fortnight—

It passed in the Negative.

On motion, To fill up the blank in the first paragraph of the Bill with the word "Baltimore," the yeas and nays being required by one fifth of the Senators present,

Mr. Bassett		Nay
Mr. Butler	Yea	
Mr. Carroll		Nay
Mr. Dalton		Nay
Mr. Ellsworth		Nay
Mr. Elmer		Nay
Mr. Few	Yea	
Mr. Gunn	Yea	
Mr. Hawkins	Yea	
Mr. Henry		Nay
Mr. Johnson	Yea	
Mr. Johnston	Yea	
Mr. Izard	Yea	
Mr. King		Nay
Mr. Langdon		Nay
Mr. Lee		Nay
Mr. Maclay		Nay
Mr. Morris		Nay
Mr. Paterson		Nay
Mr. Read		Nay
Mr. Schuyler		Nay
Mr. Strong		Nay
Mr. Walker		Nay
Mr. Wingate		Nay

Nays—17

Yeas—7

So it passed in the Negative.

On motion, To postpone the Bill generally—

It passed in the Negative.

On motion, To postpone the Bill 'till the next session of Congress—
It passed in the Negative.

On motion, To reject the first enacting clause of the Bill, to wit, "Be it enacted by the Senate, and House of Representatives of the United States of America, in Congress assembled, That a district of territory not exceeding ten miles square, to be located as hereafter directed, at   and the same is hereby accepted as the permanent seat of Congress, and the government of the United States,"—
It passed in the Negative.

On motion, To adjourn—
It passed in the Negative.

On motion, To fill up the blank in the first enacting clause of the Bill with the words "Wilmington, in the State of Delaware,"—
It passed in the Negative.

A motion was made that the first enacting clause of the Bill be agreed to;[42] which was superseded by a motion to adjourn.—Whereupon,[43]

The Senate adjourned to 11 o'clock to-morrow.

WEDNESDAY, JUNE 9, 1790

The SENATE assembled,
Present as yesterday.

ORDERED, That the Bill, entitled, "An Act for giving effect to the several Acts therein mentioned, in respect to the State of Rhode-Island and Providence Plantations," have the THIRD reading at this time.

RESOLVED, That this Bill DO PASS, with an amendment.[44]

ORDERED, That the Secretary acquaint the House of Representatives herewith, and desire their concurrence in the amendment.

A message from the House of Representatives by Mr. Beckley their clerk:

"Mr. PRESIDENT,

"The House of Representatives agree to the amendment of the Senate on the Bill, entitled, 'An Act for giving effect to the several Acts therein mentioned, in respect to the State of Rhode-Island and Providence Plantations,' "[45]—

And he withdrew.

---

[42] In the rough journal this clause was originally entered as "A Motion was made, that the first enacting clause of the Bill be rejected," but the word "rejected" is lined out and the words "agreed to" inserted above the line.

[43] On June 25 a motion to resume consideration of this bill was defeated.

[44] The rough journal reads: "Resolved, that this Bill do pass with the following Amendment, to wit: Strike out the whole of the Third Section—"

[45] On June 10 this bill was signed by both the Speaker and the Vice President and given to the committee on enrolled bills for delivery to the President.

The Senate proceeded in the SECOND reading of the Bill, entitled, "An Act making provision for the debt of the United States," and after progress,[46]

Adjourned to 10 o'clock to-morrow.

THURSDAY, JUNE 10, 1790

The SENATE assembled,

Present as yesterday.

Mr. Wingate from the joint Committee on enrolled Bills, reported, That they had examined the enrolled Bill, entitled, "An Act for giving effect to the several Acts therein mentioned, in respect to the State of Rhode-Island and Providence Plantations."[47]—and an enrolled Resolve "that all Treaties made, or which shall be made and promulged, shall be published and annexed to the laws of the United States."[48]

A message from the House of Representatives by Mr. Beckley their clerk:

"Mr. PRESIDENT,

"I am directed to bring to the Senate an enrolled Bill and an enrolled Resolve, which are signed by the Speaker of the House of Representatives"—

And he withdrew.

The Vice President affixed his signature to the enrolled Bill, entitled, "An Act for giving effect to the several Acts therein mentioned, in respect to the State of Rhode-Island and Providence Plantations"—and to an enrolled Resolve "That all Treaties made, or which shall be made and promulged, shall be published and annexed to the laws of the United States;" and they were delivered to the Committee, to be laid before the President of the United States for his approbation.[49]

The Bill, entitled, "An Act for giving effect to an Act, entitled, 'An Act to establish the Judicial Courts of the United States, within the State of Rhode-Island and Providence Plantations,' " was read the FIRST time.

ORDERED, That this Bill pass to the SECOND reading.[50]

Mr. Lee from the Committee appointed to confer with a Committee of the House of Representatives, to consider and report whether any, and what further regulations are necessary for conducting the business between the two Houses, reported[51]—

Whereupon,

---

[46] On June 10 this bill was considered again.

[47] The inspected enrolled bill is in Enrolled Acts, RG 11, DNA. E–22957.

[48] The inspected enrolled resolve is in Enrolled Acts, RG 11, DNA.

[49] On June 14 the President signed this bill and resolve, and the Senate was notified.

[50] On June 11 this bill was read a second time and passed to the third reading.

[51] An annotated copy of the report is in Joint Committee Reports, Senate Records, DNA.

RESOLVED, That the Senate agree to the report amended to read as follows:

1st. That when a Bill or Resolution which shall have passed in one House shall be rejected in the other, notice thereof shall be given to the House in which the same shall have passed.

2d. When a Bill or Resolution which has been passed in one House shall be rejected in the other, it shall not be brought in during the same session, without a notice of ten days, and leave of two thirds of that House in which it shall be renewed.

3d. Each House shall transmit to the other all papers on which any Bill or Resolution shall be founded.

4th. After each House shall have adhered to their disagreement, a Bill or Resolution shall be lost.

ORDERED, That the Secretary acquaint the House of Representatives that the Senate agree to the report of the joint Committee, thus amended.

The consideration of the resolve of the House of Representatives of the 8th of June, appointing a Committee to join a Committee that may be appointed on the part of the Senate, "to consider and report when it will be convenient and proper that an adjournment of the present session of Congress should take place," was further postponed.

The Senate proceeded in the SECOND reading of the Bill, entitled, "An Act making provision for the debt of the United States," and after progress,[52]

Adjourned to 11 o'clock to-morrow.

FRIDAY, JUNE 11, 1790

The SENATE assembled,
Present as yesterday.

The petition of John Wagner, and others, tanners of the city of Philadelphia,[53] was read, stating, "That they labour under some inconveniences arising from the construction of the Act of Congress, entitled, 'An Act for laying a duty on goods, wares, and mechandizes imported into the United States,' " and praying for the interposition of government.

ORDERED, That this petition lie on the table.

A message from the President of the United States by Mr. Lear, his Secretary, was read as follows:

UNITED STATES, June the 11th, 1790

GENTLEMEN of the SENATE, and
HOUSE of REPRESENTATIVES,

I HAVE directed my Secretary to lay before you a copy of the ratification of

---

[52] On June 11 this bill was considered again and committed.
[53] This petition is in Petitions and Memorials: Various subjects, Senate Records, DNA.

the Amendments to the Constitution of the United States, by the State of North-Carolina; together with an extract from a letter accompanying said ratification, from the Governor of the State of North-Carolina, to the President of the United States.

G. WASHINGTON

Extract of a letter from his Excellency Alexander Martin, Governor of the State of North-Carolina, to the President of the United States

"ROCKINGHAM, May the 25th, 1790

"SIR,

"I do myself the honor to transmit you herewith inclosed, an Act of the General Assembly of this State, passed at their last session, entitled, 'An Act to ratify the amendments to the Constitution of the United States.' "
(Copy)

"STATE OF NORTH-CAROLINA

"His Excellency ALEXANDER MARTIN, Esquire, Governor, Captain-General and Commander in Chief in and over the said State

"To all to whom these presents shall come:

"IT is certified, That the Honorable James Glasgow, Esquire, who hath attested the annexed copy of an Act of the General Assembly of this State, was at the time thereof, and now is Secretary of the said State, and that full faith and credit are due to his official acts.

"Given under my hand and the Great Seal of the State, at Danbury, the fourteenth day of February, Anno Dom. 1790, and the fourteenth year of our Independence.

(Signed) "ALEXANDER MARTIN"
"By his Excellency's command,

(Signed) THOMAS ROGERS, P. Sec."

$\left(\begin{array}{c} \text{SEAL} \\ \text{appendant} \end{array} \right)$

"An Act to ratify the Amendments to the Constitution of the United States

"WHEREAS the Senate and House of Representatives of the United States of America, in Congress assembled, on the fourth day of March, did resolve, two thirds of both Houses concurring, that the following articles be proposed to the Legislatures of the several States, as amendments to the Constitution of the United States; all or any of which articles, when ratified by three fourths of the said Legislatures, to be valid to all intents and purposes, as part of the said Constitution.

[Here follow the several articles of amendment verbatim, as proposed by Congress to the Legislatures of the several States.]

"Be it therefore enacted by the General Assembly of the State of North-Carolina, and it is hereby enacted by the authority of the same, that the said Amendments, agreeable to the fifth article of the original Constitution, be held and ratified on the part of this State, as articles in addition to, and amendment of the Constitution of the United States of America.

"Read three times, and ratified in General Assembly, this 22d day of December, A. D. 1789.

(Signed)   "CHARLES JOHNSON, S. S.
S. CABARRUS, S. H. C."

"STATE OF NORTH-CAROLINA

"I James Glasgow, Secretary of the said State, do hereby certify the foregoing to be a true copy of the original Act of the Assembly, filed in the Secretary's Office.

"In testimony whereof, I have hereto set my hand this tenth day of February, 1790.

(Signed)   J. GLASGOW"

UNITED STATES, June the[54] 11th, 1790

I do certify the preceding to be a true copy of the transcript of the Act transmitted to the President of the United States, by his Excellency Governor Martin.

TOBIAS LEAR
Secretary to the President
of the United States[55]

ORDERED, That the message and papers from the President of the United States be filed.

The Senate proceeded in the SECOND reading of the Bill, entitled, "An Act making provision for the debt of the United States."

ORDERED, That it be committed to

Mr. Lee
Mr. Ellsworth
Mr. Maclay
Mr. King and
Mr. Paterson[56]

The Senate proceeded in the SECOND reading of the Bill, entitled, "An Act for giving effect to an Act, entitled, 'An Act to establish the Judicial Courts of the United States, within the State of Rhode-Island and Providence Plantations.'"

---

[54] The smooth journal omits "the."

[55] This message and documents are in President's Messages: Suggesting legislation, Senate Records, DNA.

[56] On June 15 this committee reported and consideration of the report was postponed.

ORDERED, That this Bill pass to the THIRD reading.[57]

Mr. Ellsworth notified the Senate, that on Monday next he should bring in a Bill making "provision for the debts of the respective States, by the United States."[58]

The Senate adjourned to 11 o'clock on Monday next.

MONDAY, JUNE 14, 1790

The SENATE assembled,
Present as on the 11th.

A written message from the President of the United States by Mr. Lear, his Secretary, was read on the 15th of February last, as follows:[59]

UNITED STATES, February 15, 1790

GENTLEMEN of the SENATE, and
    HOUSE of REPRESENTATIVES,

I HAVE directed my Secretary to lay before you the copy of a Vote of the Legislature of the State of New-Hampshire, to accept the articles proposed in addition to, and amendment of the Constitution of the United States of America, except the second article. At the same time will be delivered to you the copy of a letter from his Excellency the President of the State of New-Hampshire, to the President of the United States.

THE originals of the above mentioned vote and letter, will be lodged in the office of the Secretary of State.

G. WASHINGTON

(Copy)

"STATE OF NEW-HAMPSHIRE
"IN THE HOUSE OF REPRESENTATIVES
"January the 25th, 1790

"Upon reading and maturely considering the proposed amendments to the federal Constitution—

"Voted to accept the whole of said amendments, except the second article, which was rejected.

"Sent up for concurrence.

(Signed)   THOMAS BARTLETT, Speaker"

---

[57] On June 14 this bill was read a third time, passed with an amendment, and sent to the House for concurrence.

[58] In the rough journal the original wording was "a Bill to provide for the assumption of the State Debts of the respective States in the Union," but these words were lined out and the phrasing as it appears in the printed journal above was substituted. On June 14 Mr. Ellsworth introduced a resolution, rather than a bill, on this subject.

[59] The rough and smooth manuscript journals, as well as the printed journal, include these documents at this place. They were omitted from the February 15 proceedings.

"In Senate, the same day read and concurred.

(Signed)   J. PEARSON, Secy."

"A true copy   Attest.   J. PEARSON, Secy."

I certify the above to be a true copy of the copy transmitted to the President of the United States.

TOBIAS LEAR
Secretary to the President
of the United States

(Copy)

"DURHAM, in New-Hampshire, January 29, 1790

"SIR,

"I have the honor to inclose you, for the information of Congress, a Vote of the Assembly of this State, to accept all the articles of amendments to the Constitution of the United States, except the second, which was rejected.

"I have the honor to be, &c.

(Signed)   JOHN SULLIVAN"

"The PRESIDENT of the United States"

I do certify the foregoing to be a true copy of the letter to the President of the United States, from his Excellency John Sullivan.

TOBIAS LEAR
Secretary to the President
of the United States[60]

The papers referred to in the President's message of the 25th of January, 1790, are as follow:[61]

(Copy)

"An Act to ratify certain articles in addition to, and amendment of the Constitution of the United States of America, proposed by Congress to the Legislatures of the several States

"WHEREAS it is provided by the fifth article of the Constitution of the United States of America, That Congress, whenever two thirds of both Houses shall deem it necessary, shall propose amendments to the said Constitution; or on the application of the Legislatures of two thirds of the several States, shall call a convention for proposing amendments; which, in either case, shall be valid to all intents and purposes as part of the said Constitution, when ratified by the Legislatures of three fourths of the several States, or by conventions in

---

[60] This message and documents are in President's Messages: Suggesting legislation, Senate Records, DNA.

[61] The rough and smooth manuscript journals, as well as the printed journal, include these documents at this place. They had been omitted from the January 25 proceedings.

three fourths thereof, as the one or the other modes of ratification may be proposed by the Congress.

"And whereas at a session of the United States begun and held at the city of New-York, on Wednesday the fourth day of March, in the year of our Lord one thousand seven hundred and eighty-nine, it was resolved by the Senate and House of Representatives of the said United States, in Congress assembled, two thirds of both Houses concurring, that the following articles be proposed to the Legislatures of the several States, as amendments to the Constitution of the United States; all or any of which articles, when ratified by three fourths of the said Legislatures, to be valid to all intents and purposes as part of the said Constitution, viz.

[Here follow the several articles of amendment.]

"Be it enacted by the General Assembly of Maryland, that the aforesaid articles, and each of them be, and they are hereby confirmed and ratified.

"By the House of Delegates, December 17, 1789

"Read and assented to.   By order,

(Signed)   W. HARWOOD, Cl."

"By the Senate, December 19, 1789

"Read and assented to.   By order,

(Signed)   HY. RIDGELY, Cl.

(Signed)   J. E. HOWARD"

$\left(\begin{array}{c}\text{SEAL} \\ \text{appendant}\end{array}\right)$

"I hereby certify that the above is a true copy from the original engrossed Act, as passed by the Legislature of the State of Maryland.

(Signed)   T. JOHNSON, jun. Cl. Council"

"MARYLAND, ss—In testimony that Thomas Johnson, junior, is clerk of the executive council for the State of Maryland, I have hereto affixed the Great Seal of the said State. Witness my hand this fifteenth day of January, Anno Domini 1790.

(Signed)   SAMUEL HARVEY HOWARD
Reg. Cor. Can."

I certify the foregoing to be a true copy of the Act transmitted to the President of the United States, by J. E. Howard, Governor of the State of Maryland.

TOBIAS LEAR
Secretary to the President
of the United States

(Copy)

"ANNAPOLIS, January 15, 1790

"Sir,

"I have the honor to inclose a copy of an Act of the Legislature of Maryland, to ratify certain articles in addition to, and amendments of the Constitution of the United States of America, proposed by Congress to the Legislatures of the several States.

"I have the honor to be, &c.
(Signed)   J. E. HOWARD"

"To his Excellency the PRESIDENT
of the United States"

I do certify the foregoing to be a true copy from the original letter from J. E. Howard, Governor of the State of Maryland, to the President of the United States.

TOBIAS LEAR
Secretary to the President
of the United States[62]

The petition of the Reverend Joseph Willard and others, in behalf of the congregational clergy of the commonwealth of Massachusetts was read,[63] stating, "That as printers in some of the States are now undertaking to publish editions of the Holy Bible, a work which in its nature requires a most critical and faithful inspection, and which in other Christian countries is performed under the direction of the supreme authority," and praying[64] "Congress to take this interesting subject into their consideration, and direct to such measures as in their wisdom may be thought proper, to secure the public from impositions by inaccurate editions of the holy scriptures."

ORDERED, That this petition lie for consideration.

The following written message from the House of Representatives, was communicated by Mr. Beckley their clerk—

And he withdrew.

"IN THE HOUSE OF REPRESENTATIVES
"OF THE UNITED STATES
"Friday the 11th of June, 1790

"RESOLVED, That when the two Houses shall adjourn to close the present session, the President of the Senate, and Speaker of the House of Representatives, do adjourn their respective Houses to meet and hold their next session at the town of Baltimore."[65]

---

[62] This message and documents are in President's Messages: Suggesting legislation, Senate Records, DNA.

[63] This petition is in Petitions and Memorials: Various subjects, Senate Records, DNA.

[64] In the rough journal the quotation from the petition was originally uninterrupted, and the phrasing read "therefore most humbly beg your Congress. . . ." The Secretary apparently decided to abridge this since the phrase is lined out and the words "and praying" are interlined.

[65] This House resolve is in Messages from the House, Senate Records, DNA.

Mr. Wingate from the joint Committee on enrolled Bills, reported, That they had on the 11th of June, laid before the President of the United States, an enrolled Bill, entitled, "An Act for giving effect to the several Acts therein mentioned, in respect to the State of Rhode-Island and Providence Plantations,"—and an enrolled Bill, entitled, "An Act for the relief of Thomas Jenkins and company,"—together with an enrolled Resolve, "That all Treaties made, or which shall be made and promulged, shall be published and annexed to the laws of the United States."

Agreeable[66] to the order of the day, the Senate proceeded to the THIRD reading of the Bill, entitled, "An Act for giving effect to an Act, entitled, 'An Act to establish the Judicial Courts of the United States, within the State of Rhode-Island and Providence Plantations.' "

RESOLVED, That this Bill DO PASS with the following amendment—

In the last paragraph, strike out the words "one thousand dollars," and insert "eight hundred dollars."

ORDERED, That the Secretary acquaint the House of Representatives herewith, and desire their concurrence in the amendment.[67]

Mr. Ellsworth instead of the Bill proposed on the 11th, submitted the following motion: That it be

"RESOLVED, That provision shall be made the next session of Congress, for loaning to the United States a sum not exceeding twenty two millions of dollars, in the certificates issued by the respective States for services or supplies towards the prosecution of the late war. The certificates which shall be loaned, to stand charged to the respective States by whom they were issued, until a liquidation of their accounts with the United States can be compleated."[68]

ORDERED, That this motion lie on the table.

A motion was then made, that to-morrow be assigned to take it into consideration, and,

It passed in the Negative.[69]

The Resolve of the House of Representatives of June the 11th, "That when the two Houses shall adjourn to close the present session, the President of the Senate, and Speaker of the House of Representatives, do adjourn their respective Houses to meet and hold their next session at the town of Baltimore," being read—

On motion, That the consideration hereof should be postponed to this day fortnight, the yeas and nays were required by one fifth of the Senators present,

---

[66] The smooth journal substitutes "Agreeably" for "Agreeable."

[67] On June 14 the House concurred in the amendment and the Senate was notified on June 15.

[68] This motion is in Senate Simple Resolutions and Motions, Senate Records, DNA.

[69] On July 2 this motion was committed.

Mr. Bassett		Nay
Mr. Butler	Yea	
Mr. Carroll		Nay
Mr. Dalton	Yea	
Mr. Ellsworth	Yea	
Mr. Elmer		Nay
Mr. Few	Yea	
Mr. Gunn	Yea	
Mr. Hawkins	Yea	
Mr. Henry		Nay
Mr. Johnson	Yea	
Mr. Johnston	Yea	
Mr. Izard	Yea	
Mr. King	Yea	
Mr. Langdon		Nay
Mr. Lee		Nay
Mr. Maclay		Nay
Mr. Morris		Nay
Mr. Paterson	Yea	
Mr. Read		Nay
Mr. Schuyler	Yea	
Mr. Strong	Yea	
Mr. Walker		Nay
Mr. Wingate		Nay

Yeas—13

Nays—11

So it passed in the Affirmative.[70]

A message from the House of Representatives by Mr. Beckley their clerk:

"Mr. PRESIDENT,

"The President of the United States did, on the 14th of June 1790, approve of, and affix his signature to 'An Act for giving effect to the several Acts therein mentioned, in respect to the State of Rhode-Island and Providence Plantations'—to 'An Act for the relief of Thomas Jenkins, and company'— and to a Resolve 'That all Treaties made, or which shall be made and promulged, shall be published and annexed to the laws of the United States' "—

And he withdrew.

The Senate adjourned to 11 o'clock to-morrow.

---

[70] On June 28 consideration of this resolve was again postponed.

TUESDAY, JUNE 15, 1790

The SENATE assembled,

Present as yesterday.[71]

A message from the House of Representatives by Mr. Beckley their clerk:

"Mr. PRESIDENT,

"The House of Representatives have passed a Bill, entitled, 'An Act for the relief of Nathaniel Twining,'[72] in which they request the concurrence of the Senate—

"They have agreed to the amendment of the Senate upon the Bill, entitled, 'An Act for giving effect to an Act, entitled, "An Act to establish the Judicial Courts of the United States, within the State of Rhode-Island and Providence Plantations" ' "[73]—

And he withdrew.

Mr. Lee, on behalf of the Committee appointed June the 11th, on the Bill, entitled, "An Act making provision for the debt of the United States," reported[74]—and the consideration of the report was postponed until to-morrow.[75]

ORDERED, That the Bill, entitled, "An Act for the relief of Nathaniel Twining," be now read the FIRST time.

ORDERED, That this Bill pass to the SECOND reading.[76]

The Senate adjourned to 11 o'clock to-morrow.

WEDNESDAY, JUNE 16, 1790

The SENATE assembled,

Present as yesterday.

Mr. Wingate from the Committee on enrolled Bills, reported, That they had examined the Bill, entitled, "An Act for giving effect to an Act, entitled, 'An Act to establish the Judicial Courts of the United States, within the State of Rhode-Island and Providence Plantations,' "[77] and had found it correct.

The Senate proceeded to the SECOND reading of the Bill, entitled, "An Act for the relief of Nathaniel Twining."

ORDERED, That it be committed to

---

[71] The smooth journal reads "Present as on the 14th of June."

[72] This bill has not been located.

[73] On June 16 this bill was signed by both the Speaker and the Vice President and given to the committee on enrolled bills for delivery to the President.

[74] The report is in Various Select Committee Reports, Senate Records, DNA.

[75] On June 16 this report was considered and postponed.

[76] On June 16 this bill was read a second time and committed.

[77] The inspected enrolled bill is in Enrolled Acts, RG 11, DNA.

Mr. Langdon
Mr. Wingate and
Mr. Maclay[78]

The Senate proceeded to the consideration of the report of the Committee on the Bill, entitled, "An Act making provision for the debt of the United States," and after debate postponed the further consideration thereof until to-morrow.[79]

A message from the House of Representatives by Mr. Beckley their clerk:

"Mr. PRESIDENT,

"I am directed to bring to the Senate an enrolled Bill which has been signed by the Speaker of the House of Representatives"—

And he withdrew.

The Vice President affixed his signature to the enrolled Bill, entitled, "An Act for giving effect to an Act, entitled, 'An Act to establish the Judicial Courts of the United States, within the State of Rhode-Island and Providence Plantations,'" and it was delivered to the Committee, to be laid before the President of the United States.[80]

A written message from the President of the United States, was communicated by Mr. Lear his Secretary—

And he withdrew.

UNITED STATES, June 16, 1790

GENTLEMEN of the SENATE, and
HOUSE of REPRESENTATIVES,

THE ratification of the Constitution of the United States of America, by the State of Rhode-Island and Providence Plantations, was received by me last night; together with a letter to the President of the United States, from the President of the convention. I have directed my Secretary to lay before you a copy of each.

G. WASHINGTON

(Copy)

"RHODE-ISLAND

"NEWPORT, June 9, 1790

"SIR,

"I had on the 29th ult. the satisfaction of addressing you after the ratification of the Constitution of the United States of America, by the convention of this State; I have now the honor of inclosing the ratification, as then agreed

---

[78] On June 17 the petition of Nathaniel Twining was committed to this committee.
[79] On June 17 this report was considered and postponed.
[80] On June 22 this committee reported that it had delivered this bill to the President.

upon by the convention of the people of this State: The Legislature is now in session in this town; an appointment of Senators will undoubtedly take place in the present week, and from what appears to be the sense of the Legislature, it may be expected that the gentlemen who may be appointed will immediately proceed to take their seats in the Senate of the United States.

"I have the honor to be, &c.

(Signed)   DANIEL OWEN, President"

"PRESIDENT of the United States"

A true copy   TOBIAS LEAR
Secretary to the President
of the United States

[The Constitution of the United States of America, precedes the following ratification.]

(SEAL)

"RATIFICATION of the Constitution, by the convention of the State of Rhode-Island and Providence Plantations

"WE the delegates of the People of the State of Rhode-Island, and Providence Plantations, duly elected and met in convention, having maturely considered the Constitution for the United States of America, agreed to on the seventeenth day of September, in the year one thousand seven hundred and eighty-seven, by the convention then assembled at Philadelphia, in the commonwealth of Pennsylvania (a copy whereof precedes these presents) and having also seriously and deliberately considered the present situation of this State, do declare and make known—

"1st. That there are certain natural rights, of which men, when they form a social compact, cannot deprive or divest their posterity, among which are the enjoyment of life and liberty, with the means of acquiring, possessing and protecting property, and pursuing and obtaining happiness and safety.

"2d. That all power is naturally vested in, and consequently derived from the People; that magistrates are therefore their trustees and agents, and at all times amenable to them.

"3d. That the powers of government may be reassumed by the People whensoever it shall become necessary to their happiness: That the rights of the States respectively, to nominate all state officers, and every other power, jurisdiction and right, which is not by the said Constitution clearly delegated to the Congress of the United States, or to the departments of the government thereof, remain to the People of the several States, or their respective State Governments to whom they may have granted the same, and that those clauses in the said Constitution, which declare, that Congress shall not have or exercise certain powers, do not imply that Congress is entitled to any powers not given by the said Constitution, but such clauses are to be construed as exceptions to certain specified powers, or as inserted merely for greater caution.

"4th. That religion, or the duty which we owe to our Creator, and the manner of discharging it, can be directed only by reason and conviction, and not by force or violence, and therefore all men have an equal, natural and unalienable right to the free exercise of religion, according to the dictates of conscience, and that no particular religious sect or society ought to be favored, or established by law in preference to others.

"5th. That the legislative, executive and judiciary powers of government, should be separate and distinct, and that the members of the two first may be restrained from oppression by feeling and participating the public burthens, they should at fixed periods be reduced to a private station, return into the mass of the people, and the vacancies be supplied by certain and regular elections, in which all, or any part of the former members to be eligible or ineligible, as the rules of the Constitution of government and the laws shall direct.

"6th. That elections of Representatives in legislature ought to be free and frequent, and all men having sufficient evidence of permanent common interest with, and attachment to the community, ought to have the right of suffrage, and no aid, charge, tax or fee can be set, rated or levied upon the people without their own consent, or that of their representatives so elected; nor can they be bound by any law to which they have not in like manner assented for the public good.

"7th. That all power of suspending laws, or the execution of laws, by any authority, without the consent of the representatives of the People in the Legislature, is injurious to their rights, and ought not to be exercised.

"8th. That in all capital and criminal prosecutions, a man hath a right to demand the cause and nature of his accusation, to be confronted with the accusers and witnesses, to call for evidence, and be allowed counsel in his favour, and to a fair and speedy trial by an impartial jury of his vicinage, without whose unanimous consent he cannot be found guilty (except in the government of the land and naval forces) nor can he be compelled to give evidence against himself.

"9th. That no freeman ought to be taken, imprisoned, or disseized of his freehold, liberties, privileges or franchises, or outlawed, or exiled, or in any manner destroyed or deprived of his life, liberty or property, but by the trial by jury, or by the law of the land.

"10th. That every freeman restrained of his liberty, is entitled to a remedy to inquire into the lawfulness thereof, and to remove the same if unlawful, and that such remedy ought not to be denied or delayed.

"11th. That in controversies respecting property, and in suits between man and man, the ancient trial by jury, as hath been exercised by us and our ancestors, from the time whereof the memory of man is not to the contrary, is one of the greatest securities to the rights of the people, and ought to remain sacred and inviolable.

"12th. That every freeman ought to obtain right and justice freely, and without sale, completely and without denial, promptly and without delay; and that all establishments or regulations contravening these rights are oppressive and unjust.

"13th. That excessive bail ought not to be required, nor excessive fines imposed, nor cruel or unusual punishments inflicted.

"14th. That every person has a right to be secure from all unreasonable searches and seizures of his person, his papers or his property, and therefore that all warrants to search suspected places, or seize any person, his papers, or his property, without information upon oath or affirmation, of sufficient cause, are grievous and oppressive; and that all general warrants (or such in which the place or person suspected, are not particularly designated) are dangerous, and ought not to be granted.

"15th. That the people have a right peaceably to assemble together, to consult for their common good, or to instruct their representatives; and that every person has a right to petition or apply to the Legislature for redress of grievances.

"16th. That the people have a right to freedom of speech, and of writing and publishing their sentiments; that freedom of the press is one of the greatest bulwarks of liberty, and ought not to be violated.

"17th. That the people have a right to keep and bear arms; that a well regulated militia, including the body of the people capable of bearing arms, is the proper, natural and safe defence of a free state; that the militia shall not be subject to martial law, except in time of war, rebellion or insurrection; that standing armies in time of peace, are dangerous to liberty, and ought not to be kept up, except in cases of necessity; and that at all times the military should be under strict subordination to the civil power; that in time of peace no soldier ought to be quartered in any house, without the consent of the owner, and in time of war, only by the civil magistrate, in such manner as the law directs.

"18th. That any person religiously scrupulous of bearing arms, ought to be exempted, upon payment of an equivalent to employ another to bear arms in his stead.—

"Under these impressions, and declaring that the rights aforesaid cannot be abridged or violated, and that the explanations aforesaid are consistent with the said Constitution, and in confidence that the amendments hereafter mentioned, will receive an early and mature consideration, and conformably to the fifth article of said Constitution, speedily become a part thereof; we the said delegates, in the name and in the behalf of the people of the State of Rhode-Island and Providence Plantations, do by these presents, assent to and ratify the said Constitution: In full confidence nevertheless, that until the amendments hereafter proposed and undermentioned, shall be agreed to and ratified, pursuant to the aforesaid fifth article: The militia of this State will not be continued in service out of this State, for a longer term than six weeks, without the consent of the Legislature thereof: That the Congress will not make or alter any regulation in this State, respecting the times, places and manner of holding elections for Senators or[81] Representatives, unless the Legislature of this State shall neglect or refuse to make laws or regulations for the purpose, or from any circumstance be incapable of making the same,—and that in those cases such power will only be exercised until the Legislature of this State shall make provision in the premises: That the Congress will not lay direct taxes within this State, but where the monies arising from the impost, tonnage and excise shall be insufficient for the public exigencies, nor until Congress shall have first made a requisition upon this State to assess, levy and pay the amount of such requisition made agreeable to the census fixed in the said Constitution, in such way and manner as the Legislature of this State shall judge best; and that Congress will not lay any capitation or poll tax.

"Done in convention at Newport, in the county of Newport, in the State of Rhode-Island and Providence Plantations, the twenty-ninth day of May, in the year of our Lord one thousand seven hundred and ninety, and in the fourteenth year of the independence of the United States of America.

"By order of the convention,

(Signed)   DANIEL OWEN, President"

"Attest.

DANIEL UPDIKE, Secretary"

"And the convention do, in the name and behalf of the people of the State of Rhode-Island and Providence Plantations, enjoin it upon their Senators and Representative or Representatives, which may be elected to represent this State in Congress, to exert all their influence, and use all reasonable means to obtain a ratification of the following amendments to the said Constitution, in the manner prescribed therein, and in all laws to be passed by the Congress in the mean time, to conform to the spirit of the said amendments, as far as the Constitution will admit.

---

[81] The smooth journal substitutes "and" for "or."

AMENDMENTS

"1st. The United States shall guarantee to each State its sovereignty, freedom and independence, and every power, jurisdiction and right, which is not by this Constitution expressly delegated to the United States.

"2d. That Congress shall not alter, modify or interfere in the times, places or manner of holding elections for Senators and Representatives, or either of them, except when the Legislature of any State shall neglect, refuse, or be disabled by invasion or rebellion, to prescribe the same; or in case when the provision made by the States is so imperfect, as that no consequent election is had, and then only until the Legislature of such State shall make provision in the premises.

"3d. It is declared by the convention, that the judicial power of the United States, in cases in which a State may be a party, does not extend to criminal prosecutions, or to authorize any suit by any person against a State; but to remove all doubts or controversies respecting the same, that it be especially expressed as a part of the Constitution of the United States, that Congress shall not directly or indirectly, either by themselves or through the judiciary, interfere with any one of the States in the redemption of paper money already emitted, and now in circulation, or in liquidating or discharging the public securities of any one State: That each and every State shall have the exclusive right of making such laws and regulations for the before-mentioned purpose, as they shall think proper.

"4th. That no amendments to the Constitution of the United States hereafter to be made, pursuant to the fifth article, shall take effect, or become a part of the Constitution of the United States, after the year one thousand seven hundred and ninety-three, without the consent of eleven of the States heretofore united under one confederation.

"5th. That the judicial powers of the United States shall extend to no possible case, where the cause of action shall have originated before the ratification of this Constitution, except in disputes between States about their territory—disputes between persons claiming lands under grants of different States, and debts due to the United States.

"6th. That no person shall be compelled to do military duty otherwise than by voluntary enlistment, except in cases of general invasion; any thing in the second paragraph of the sixth article of the Constitution, or any law made under the Constitution to the contrary notwithstanding.

"7th. That no capitation or poll tax shall ever be laid by Congress.

"8th. In cases of direct taxes, Congress shall first make requisitions on the several States to assess, levy and pay their respective proportions of such requisitions, in such way and manner as the Legislatures of the several States shall judge best; and in case any State shall neglect or refuse to pay its proportion, pursuant to such requisition, then Congress may assess and levy such State's proportion, together with interest, at the rate of six per cent. per annum, from the time prescribed in such requisition.

"9th. That Congress shall lay no direct taxes, without the consent of the Legislatures of three fourths of the States in the Union.

"10th. That the Journals of the proceedings of the Senate and House of Representatives, shall be published as soon as conveniently may be, at least once in every year, except such parts thereof relating to treaties, alliances or military operations, as in their judgment require secrecy.

"11th. That regular statements of the receipts and expenditures of all public monies, shall be published at least once a year.

"12th. As standing armies in time of peace are dangerous to liberty, and ought not to be kept up except in cases of necessity; and as at all times the military should be under strict subordination to the civil power, that therefore no standing army or regular troops shall be raised or kept up in time of peace.

"13th. That no monies be borrowed on the credit of the United States, without the assent of two thirds of the Senators and Representatives present in each House.

"14th. That the Congress shall not declare war, without the concurrence of two thirds of the Senators and Representatives present in each House.

"15th. That the words 'without the consent of Congress,' in the seventh clause in the ninth section of the first article of the Constitution, be expunged.

"16th. That no Judge of the Supreme Court of the United States, shall hold any other office under the United States, or any of them; nor shall any officer appointed by Congress, or by the President and Senate of the United States, be permitted to hold any office under the appointment of any of the States.

"17th. As a traffic tending to establish or continue the slavery of any part of the human species, is disgraceful to the cause of liberty and humanity, that Congress shall, as soon as may be, promote and establish such laws and regulations as may effectually prevent the importation of slaves of every description, into the United States.

"18th. That the State Legislatures have power to recall, when they think it expedient, their federal Senators, and to send others in their stead.

"19th. That Congress have power to establish a uniform rule of inhabitancy or settlement of the poor of the different States, throughout the United States.

"20th. That Congress erect no company with exclusive advantages of commerce.

"21st. That when two Members shall move or call for the ayes or nays on any question, they shall be entered on the journals of the Houses respectively.

"Done in convention at Newport, in the county of Newport, in the State of

Rhode-Island and Providence Plantations, the twenty-ninth day of May, in the year of our Lord one thousand seven hundred and ninety, and the fourteenth year of the independence of the United States of America.

"By order of the Convention,

(Signed)   DANIEL OWEN, President"

"Attest.

DANIEL UPDIKE, Secretary"

A true copy   TOBIAS LEAR

Secretary to the President

of the United States[82]

The Senate adjourned to 11 o'clock to-morrow.

THURSDAY, JUNE 17, 1790

The SENATE assembled,

Present as yesterday.

ORDERED, That the Secretary transmit the petition of William Montgomery and Abraham Owen to the Secretary of State.

A message from the House of Representatives by Mr. Beckley their clerk:

"Mr. PRESIDENT,

"The House of Representatives have passed a Bill, entitled, 'An Act to authorize the purchase of a tract of land for the use of the United States,'[83] to which the concurrence of the Senate is desired—

And he withdrew.

ORDERED, That this Bill have the FIRST reading at this time.

ORDERED, That this Bill pass to the SECOND reading.[84]

ORDERED, That the petition of Nathaniel Twining, be committed to the Committee appointed the 16th of June, on the Bill, entitled, "An Act for the relief of Nathaniel Twining."[85]

The Senate resumed the consideration of the report of the Committee on the Bill, entitled, "An Act making provision for the debt of the United States," and after debate, postponed the further consideration thereof until to-morrow.[86]

The Senate adjourned to 11 o'clock to-morrow.

---

[82] This message and documents are in President's Messages: Suggesting legislation, Senate Records, DNA.

[83] This bill has not been located.

[84] On June 18 this bill was read and committed, along with a petition from Stephen Moore.

[85] On June 23 this committee reported, and the report was ordered to lie for consideration.

[86] On June 18 this report was considered and postponed.

FRIDAY, JUNE 18, 1790

The SENATE assembled,
Present as yesterday.

The petition of Stephen Moore,[87] was read, stating, "That the United States occupy a tract of land on which are erected the fortifications and arsenal at West-Point," the property of the petitioner, and requesting compensation; together with sundry papers accompanying the petition.

Agreeably to the order of the day, the Senate proceeded to the SECOND reading of the Bill, entitled, "An Act to authorize the purchase of a tract of land for the use of the United States."

ORDERED, That this Bill, together with the petition of Stephen Moore, and the papers communicated with his petition, be committed to

Mr. Izard
Mr. Gunn and
Mr. Langdon[88]

Mr. Morris from the Committee appointed June the 7th, to consider the Bill, entitled, "An Act to satisfy the claims of John McCord, against the United States," reported,[89] and it was agreed to amend the Bill accordingly.

ORDERED, That this Bill pass to the THIRD reading.[90]

The Senate resumed the consideration of the report of the Committee appointed the 11th of June, on the Bill, entitled, "An Act making provision for the debt of the United States," and after debate, the consideration thereof was further postponed.[91]

The Senate adjourned to 11 o'clock on Monday next.

MONDAY, JUNE 21, 1790

The SENATE assembled,
Present as on the 18th.

Agreeable to the order of the day, the Senate proceeded to the THIRD reading of the Bill, entitled, "An Act to satisfy the claims of John McCord, against the United States."

---

[87] This petition has not been located.

[88] On June 25 this committee reported, and the bill was amended and passed to the third reading.

[89] This report is in Various Select Committee Reports, Senate Records, DNA.

[90] On June 21 this bill was read a third time, passed with an amendment, and sent to the House for concurrence.

[91] On June 21 this report was considered and one amendment to the bill was passed. Further consideration of the bill was postponed.

RESOLVED, That this Bill DO PASS with an amendment.[92]

ORDERED, That the Secretary carry this Bill to the House of Representatives and desire their concurrence in the amendment.[93]

The Senate proceeded to the consideration of the Resolve of the House of Representatives of June the 8th, proposing a joint Committee for the purposes therein mentioned, and

RESOLVED, That they do agree to the appointment of a Committee, and that

Mr. Strong

Mr. Bassett and

Mr. Walker, be the Committee on the part of the

Senate.

ORDERED, That the Secretary acquaint the House of Representatives herewith.[94]

A message from the House of Representatives by Mr. Beckley the clerk:

"Mr. PRESIDENT,

"The House of Representatives have passed a Bill, entitled, 'An Act to establish the Post-Office and Post-Roads within the United States,' "[95] in which the concurrence of the Senate is desired[96]—

And he withdrew.

The Senate resumed the consideration of the report of the Committee on the Bill, entitled, "An Act making provision for the debt of the United States," and

On motion, to agree to the following paragraph of the report, to wit:

"In the 4th section 2d line, strike out from the word 'entitled,' to the word 'or,' at the end of the next paragraph inclusive; also strike out from the word 'sum,' in the 5th line of the next paragraph, to the proviso at the end of the section; and then the Bill will read—'That for any sum which shall be subscribed to the said loan by any person or persons, or body politic, the subscriber or subscribers shall be entitled to a certificate, purporting that the United States owe to the holder or holders thereof, his, her or their assigns,

---

[92] The rough journal reads: "Resolved that this Bill do pass with [an *inserted above the line*] Amendment. / Strike out 'One Thousand dollars'—and insert as follows Line 3rd & 4th: 'Eight hundred nine dollars seventy one Cents, being the amount of his account against the United States, as settled and admitted by the Auditor and Comptroller of the Treasury in a Bill of Exchange dated the 5th of August A.D. 1776 drawn in Canada for supplies by General William Thomson, General William Irvine and other officers in favor of William Pagan, on Messrs. Meredith and Clymer of Philadelphia. And the further sum of five hundred dollars.'—"

[93] On June 22 the House concurred in the amendment and the Senate was notified on June 23.

[94] On June 28 this committee reported and consideration of the report was postponed.

[95] Two annotated printed copies of this bill are in House Bills, Senate Records, DNA.

[96] On June 22 this bill was read the first time and passed to the second reading.

the whole of the sum by him, her or them subscribed; bearing an interest of four per cent. per annum, payable quarter yearly, and subject to redemption by payments not exceeding in one year, on account both of principal and interest, the proportion of six dollars upon a hundred of the same sum: Provided always, That it shall not be understood, that the United States shall be bound or obliged to redeem in the proportion aforesaid, but it shall be understood only that they have a right so to do'—

"The design of this amendment of your Committee is to discharge the alternatives proposed in the Bill, and to fund the domestic debt of the United States at an interest of four per cent. per annum." To this clause the yeas and nays were required by one fifth of the Senators present,

Mr. Bassett		Yea
Mr. Butler	Nay	
Mr. Carroll		Yea
Mr. Dalton		Yea
Mr. Ellsworth		Yea
Mr. Few		Yea
Mr. Gunn	Nay	
Mr. Hawkins		Yea
Mr. Henry		Yea
Mr. Johnson	Nay	
Mr. Johnston		Yea
Mr. Izard	Nay	
Mr. King	Nay	
Mr. Langdon	Nay	
Mr. Lee		Yea
Mr. Maclay		Yea
Mr. Morris	Nay	
Mr. Paterson	Nay	
Mr. Read		Yea
Mr. Schuyler	Nay	
Mr. Strong		Yea
Mr. Walker	Nay	
Mr. Wingate		Yea

Yeas—13

Nays—10

So it passed in the Affirmative.

ORDERED, That the further consideration of the report be postponed.[97]

The Senate adjourned to 11 o'clock to-morrow.

---

[97] On June 22 the committee report was accepted as an amendment to the bill and the bill passed to the third reading.

TUESDAY, JUNE 22, 1790

The SENATE assembled,
Present as yesterday.

Proceeded to the FIRST reading of the Bill, entitled, "An Act to establish the Post-Office and Post-Roads within the United States."

ORDERED, That this Bill pass to the SECOND reading.[98]

Mr. Wingate from the Committee on enrolled Bills, reported, that they did this day, lay before the President of the United States, an enrolled Bill, entitled, "An Act for giving effect to an Act, entitled, 'An Act to establish the Judicial Courts of the United States, within the State of Rhode-Island and Providence Plantations.' "[99]

The Senate resumed the consideration of the report of the Committee on the Bill, entitled, "An Act making provision for the debt of the United States," which being amended, was accepted as amendment to the Bill.

ORDERED, That this Bill pass to the THIRD reading.[100]

The Senate adjourned to 11 o'clock to-morrow.

WEDNESDAY, JUNE 23, 1790

The SENATE assembled,
Present as yesterday.

Mr. Langdon from the Committee on the Bill, entitled, "An Act for the relief of Nathaniel Twining," reported.[101]

ORDERED, That the report lie for consideration.[102]

The petition of Sarah, widow of the late Earl of Stirling,[103] was read, stating, "That her late husband was a Major-General in the late war, and that he died in the service of the United States, on the 14th day of January 1783.

"That by the act of Congress of the 24th of August 1780, your petitioner is entitled to seven years half pay of her late husband, but that she has never received any part thereof; she therefore prays that Congress may take such measures in the premises as in their wisdom shall appear proper, to secure to her the benefit intended by the act above mentioned."

ORDERED, That this petition lie on the table.[104]

---

[98] On June 23 this bill was read a second time.

[99] On June 23 the President signed this bill and the Senate was notified.

[100] On June 23 the third reading of this bill was postponed.

[101] This report is in Various Select Committee Reports, Senate Records, DNA.

[102] On June 24 this committee report was printed in the Journal and rejected. The bill then passed to the third reading.

[103] This petition is in Petitions and Memorials: Claims, Senate Records, DNA.

[104] On August 6 the House passed a bill which resulted from the petition. On the same day the Senate read the bill for the first and second times and committed it.

A message from the House of Representatives by Mr. Beckley their clerk:

"Mr. PRESIDENT,

"The House of Representatives have concurred in the amendments to the Bill, entitled, 'An Act to satisfy the claims of John McCord, against the United States'[105]—

"They have passed a Bill, entitled, 'An Act to provide more effectually for the settlement of the accounts between the United States and the individual States,'[106] in which they request the concurrence of the Senate"—

And he withdrew.

ORDERED, That the Bill, entitled, "An Act to provide more effectually for the settlement of the accounts between the United States and the individual States," have the FIRST reading at this time.

ORDERED, That this Bill pass to the SECOND reading.[107]

The order of the day being the THIRD reading of the Bill, entitled, "An Act making provision for the debt of the United States"—

On motion, The THIRD reading was postponed.[108]

Mr. King reported from the managers appointed May the 31st,[109] to confer with those appointed by the House of Representatives, on the disagreeing votes of the two Houses on the subject matter of amendments to the Bill, entitled, "An Act providing the means of intercourse between the United States and foreign nations"—

"That the word 'thirty,' line 3d of the Bill, be struck out, and the word 'forty' inserted; that the Senate do recede from their amendment on the Bill, and that all the words proposed to be struck out of the Bill by the Senate, except the three last words, be expunged, and the following words be inserted in their stead—'That exclusive of an outfit, which shall in no case exceed the amount of one year's full salary to the person to whom the same may be allowed, the President of the United States shall not allow to any Minister Plenipotentiary, a greater sum than at the rate of nine thousand dollars per annum, as a compensation for all his personal services and other expences; nor a greater sum for the same than four thousand five hundred dollars per annum to a Charge des Affairs, nor a greater sum for the same than one thousand three hundred and fifty dollars per annum to any of their Secretaries' "—

And the report was agreed to.

---

[105] On June 29 this bill was signed by both the Speaker and the Vice President and given to the committee on enrolled bills for delivery to the President.

[106] Two annotated printed copies of this bill are in House Bills, Senate Records, DNA. A third printed copy is in the Broadside Collection, RBkRm, DLC. E–46028.

[107] On June 25 the second reading of this bill was postponed.

[108] On July 15 this bill and a motion on a loan for the United States were committed to a special committee.

[109] This report is in Joint Committee Reports, Senate Records, DNA.

ORDERED, That the Secretary carry a message to the House of Representatives accordingly.[110]

The Senate proceeded to the SECOND reading of the Bill, entitled, "An Act to establish the Post-Office and Post-Roads within the United States."

ORDERED, That the further consideration thereof be postponed.[111]

A message from the House of Representatives by Mr. Beckley their clerk:

"Mr. PRESIDENT,

"The House of Representatives have passed a Bill, entitled, 'An Act to regulate trade and intercourse with the Indian tribes,'[112] in which they desire the concurrence of the Senate—

"The President of the United States did on the 23d of June, approve of, and affix his signature to 'An Act for giving effect to an Act, entitled, "An Act to establish the Judicial Courts of the United States, within the State of Rhode-Island and Providence Plantations" ' "[113]—

And he withdrew.

ORDERED, That the Bill, entitled, "An Act to regulate trade and intercourse with the Indian tribes," be now read the FIRST time.

ORDERED, That this Bill pass to the SECOND reading.[114]

The Senate adjourned to 11 o'clock to-morrow.

THURSDAY, JUNE 24, 1790

The SENATE assembled,
Present as yesterday.

Proceeded in the SECOND reading of the Bill, entitled, "An Act to establish the Post-Office and Post-Roads within the United States."

ORDERED, That it be committed to

> Mr. Johnston
> Mr. Langdon
> Mr. Carroll
> Mr. Strong and
> Mr. Maclay[115]

ORDERED, That the SECOND reading of the Bill, entitled, "An Act to regu-

---

[110] On June 25 the House received this message and agreed to the Senate amendment with amendments. The Senate was then notified. On the same date the Senate concurred in the House amendments and notified the House.

[111] On June 23 consideration of this bill was continued and it was committed.

[112] An annotated printed copy of this bill is in House Bills, Senate Records, DNA. E–46015.

[113] The statement of the President's action is in Committee on Enrolled Bills, Senate Records, DNA.

[114] On June 24 the second reading of this bill was postponed.

[115] One June 30 this committee reported and consideration of the report was postponed.

late trade and intercourse with the Indian tribes," be postponed for consideration.[116]

ORDERED, That the SECOND reading of the Bill, entitled, "An Act to provide more effectually for the settlement of the accounts between the United States and the individual States," be postponed for consideration.

A message from the House of Representatives by Mr. Beckley their clerk:

"Mr. PRESIDENT,

"The House of Representatives have passed a Bill, entitled, 'An Act imposing duties on the tonnage of ships or vessels,'[117] in which they request the concurrence of the Senate"—

And he withdrew.

The Senate proceeded to the consideration of the report of the Committee on the Bill, entitled, "An Act for the relief of Nathaniel Twining," which is as follows:

"That they have heard Mr. Twining on the subject, and examined the documents relative to his contract for transporting the mail between Charlestown[118] and Savannah, for the year 1787, and taken into consideration his repeated failures in the course of that year, the forfeitures remitted, and the allowance already made him; it is therefore the opinion of the Committee that the forfeiture incurred by the said Twining, in neglect to transport the mail agreeably to contract, from the month of September 1787, to the first of January 1788, should not be remitted, and that the said Bill be disagreed to by the Senate;" And on the question to agree to the report of the Committee—

It passed in the Negative.

ORDERED, That this Bill pass to the THIRD reading.[119]

The Senate proceeded to the FIRST reading of the Bill, entitled, "An Act imposing duties on the tonnage of ships or vessels."

ORDERED, That this Bill pass to the SECOND reading.[120]

The Senate adjourned to 11 o'clock to-morrow.

FRIDAY, JUNE 25, 1790

The SENATE assembled,
Present as yesterday.

ORDERED, That the SECOND reading of the Bill, entitled, "An Act imposing duties on the tonnage of ships or vessels," be postponed until Monday next.[121]

---

[116] On June 25 the second reading of this bill was again postponed.

[117] This printed bill is in the Broadside Collection, RBkRm, DLC. E–22964.

[118] The smooth journal uses the form "Charleston."

[119] On June 25 this bill was read a third time and passed. The House was then notified.

[120] On June 25 the second reading of this bill was postponed.

[121] On June 29 this bill was read a second time and committed.

ORDERED, That the SECOND reading of the Bill, entitled, "An Act to regulate trade and intercourse with the Indian tribes," be postponed until Monday next.[122]

Mr. Izard from the Committee appointed the 18th of June, to take into consideration the Bill, entitled, "An Act to authorize the purchase of a tract of land for the use of the United States," reported the Bill without amendment—

Whereupon,

The Senate proceeded in the SECOND reading of the Bill, and on motion to adopt the following clause thereof, to wit: "That it shall be lawful for the President of the United States, and he is hereby authorized to cause to be purchased for the use of the United States, the whole or such part of that tract of land situate in the State of New-York, commonly called West-Point, as shall be by him judged requisite for the purpose of such fortifications and garrisons as may be necessary for the defence of the same," the yeas and nays were required by one fifth of the Senators present:

Mr. Bassett	Nay	
Mr. Butler		Yea
Mr. Carroll		Yea
Mr. Dalton		Yea
Mr. Elmer	Nay	
Mr. Few		Yea
Mr. Gunn		Yea
Mr. Henry		Yea
Mr. Johnson		Yea
Mr. Johnston		Yea
Mr. Izard		Yea
Mr. King		Yea
Mr. Langdon	Nay	
Mr. Lee		Yea
Mr. Maclay	Nay	
Mr. Morris	Nay	
Mr. Paterson		Yea
Mr. Schuyler		Yea
Mr. Strong	Nay	
Mr. Walker		Yea
Mr. Wingate	Nay	

Yeas—14
Nays—7

So it passed in the Affirmative.

---

[122] On July 2 this bill was read a second time and committed.

ORDERED, That this Bill pass to the THIRD reading.[123]

ORDERED, That the SECOND reading of the Bill, entitled, "An Act to provide more effectually for the settlement of the accounts between the United States and the individual States," be postponed until Monday next.[124]

The Senate proceeded to the THIRD reading of the Bill, entitled, "An Act for the relief of Nathaniel Twining."

RESOLVED, That this Bill DO PASS.

ORDERED, That the Secretary acquaint the House of Representatives herewith.[125]

The Hon. Joseph Stanton, jun. and the Hon. Theodore Foster, from the State of Rhode-Island and Providence Plantations, appeared, produced their credentials,[126] and took their seats in Senate; and the oaths required by law were administered to them.

On motion, To resume the SECOND reading of the Bill, "To determine the permanent Seat of Congress, and the government of the United States"—

A motion was made to postpone the consideration thereof until Monday next, and

It passed in the Affirmative.[127]

A message from the House of Representatives by Mr. Beckley their clerk:

"Mr. PRESIDENT,

"The House of Representatives have passed a Bill, entitled, 'An Act to satisfy the claim of the representatives of David Gould, deceased, against the United States,'[128] in which they desire the concurrence of the Senate—

"They have also agreed to the amendments of the Senate to the Bill, entitled, 'An Act providing the means of intercourse between the United States and foreign nations,' with amendments;[129] to which amendments they desire the concurrence of the Senate"—

And he withdrew.

The Senate took into consideration the message from the House of Representatives, and their resolution communicated this day; which is as follows:

"RESOLVED, That this House do agree to the amendments proposed by the Senate to the Bill, entitled, 'An Act providing the means of intercourse be-

---

[123] On June 28 this bill was read a third time and passed, and the House was notified.

[124] On June 30 this bill was read a second time and consideration was postponed.

[125] On June 29 this bill was signed by both the Speaker and the Vice President and given to the committee on enrolled bills for delivery to the President.

[126] These credentials are in Election Records: Credentials of Senators, Senate Records, DNA.

[127] On June 28 the second reading of this bill was continued. Several amendments to the bill were considered and some were passed.

[128] This bill has not been located.

[129] The resolve and amendments that follow have not been located.

tween the United States and foreign nations,' with the following amendments, to wit:

"Line 9th, strike out the word 'person,' and in lieu thereof insert 'the Minister Plenipotentiary, or Charge des Affairs.

"Line 19th, strike out 'any of their Secretaries,' and in lieu thereof insert 'the Secretary of any Minister Plenipotentiary' "—

Whereupon,

RESOLVED, That the Senate do agree to the amendments of the House of Representatives, to their amendments to the said Bill.

ORDERED, That the Secretary acquaint the House of Representatives therewith.[130]

A letter was read from the Treasurer of the United States, inclosing a statement of his accounts to the 31st of March 1790.[131]

ORDERED, That these accounts be committed to

> Mr. Butler
> Mr. Morris and
> Mr. Wingate[132]

The Bill, entitled, "An Act to satisfy the claim of the representatives of David Gould, deceased, against the United States," was read the FIRST time.

ORDERED, That this Bill pass to the SECOND reading.[133]

On motion, the Senators from the State of Rhode-Island and Providence Plantations, proceeded to draw lots for their classes, in conformity to the resolve of the 14th of May 1789; and three lots, No. 1, 2, and 3, being by the Secretary rolled up and put into the box—

> Mr. Stanton drew LOT NO. 2:

whose seat shall accordingly be vacated in the Senate, at the expiration of the FOURTH YEAR.

> And Mr. Foster drew LOT NO. 1:

whose seat shall accordingly be vacated in the Senate, at the expiration of the SECOND YEAR.

The Senate adjourned to Monday next at 11 o'clock.

M O N D A Y, JUNE 28, 1790

The SENATE assembled,
Present as on the 25th.

Mr. Strong reported from the joint Committee appointed June the[134]

---

[130] This bill was signed by both the Speaker and the Vice President on June 29 and given to the committee on enrolled bills for delivery to the President.

[131] The letter and statements from the Treasurer of the United States are in Accounts and Receipts of the Treasurer of the United States, Records of the Executive Departments, vol. 1, House Records, DNA.

[132] Undated notes, probably from the committee, are in the Pierce Butler Papers, PHi. The committee did not report.

[133] On June 29 this bill was read a second time and committed.

[134] The smooth journal omits the word "the."

21st,[135] "To consider of and report when it will be convenient and proper that an adjournment of the present session of Congress should take place."

ORDERED, That the report lie for consideration.[136]

Agreeably to the order of the day, the Senate proceeded to the THIRD reading of the Bill, entitled, "An Act to authorize the purchase of a tract of land for the use of the United States"—

And on the question, Shall this Bill pass? The yeas and nays were required by one fifth of the Senators present:

Mr. Bassett		Nay
Mr. Butler	Yea	
Mr. Carroll	Yea	
Mr. Dalton	Yea	
Mr. Ellsworth		Nay
Mr. Elmer		Nay
Mr. Few	Yea	
Mr. Foster	Yea	
Mr. Hawkins	Yea	
Mr. Henry	Yea	
Mr. Johnson	Yea	
Mr. Johnston	Yea	
Mr. Izard	Yea	
Mr. King	Yea	
Mr. Langdon		Nay
Mr. Lee	Yea	
Mr. Maclay		Nay
Mr. Morris		Nay
Mr. Paterson	Yea	
Mr. Read		Nay
Mr. Schuyler	Yea	
Mr. Stanton		Nay
Mr. Strong		Nay
Mr. Walker	Yea	
Mr. Wingate		Nay

Yeas—15

Nays—10

So it was,

RESOLVED, That this Bill DO PASS.

ORDERED, That the Secretary carry this Bill to the House of Representatives, and inform them of the concurrence of the Senate therein.[137]

[135] This report and a draft copy are in Joint Committee Reports, Senate Records, DNA.

[136] On July 16 the House passed a resolution to adjourn on July 27 and notified the Senate. This resolve was read and laid for consideration.

[137] On July 2 this bill was signed by both the Speaker and the Vice President and given to the committee on enrolled bills for delivery to the President.

A message from the House of Representatives by Mr. Beckley their clerk:

"Mr. PRESIDENT,

"The House of Representatives have passed a Bill, entitled, 'An Act for the government and regulation of seamen in the merchants service,'[138] in which they request the concurrence of the Senate"—

And he withdrew.

ORDERED, That the last mentioned Bill have the FIRST reading at this time.

ORDERED, That this Bill pass to the SECOND reading.[139]

The Senate proceeded to the consideration of the resolve of the House of Representatives of the 11th of June, "That when the two Houses shall adjourn to close the present session, the President of the Senate, and Speaker of the House of Representatives, do adjourn their respective Houses to meet and hold their next session at the town of Baltimore," and,

On motion, To postpone the consideration thereof, to take up the "Bill to determine the permanent Seat of Congress and the government of the United States"—

It passed in the Affirmative.[140]

Agreeably to the order of the day, the Senate resumed the SECOND reading of the Bill last mentioned.[141]

On motion,

ORDERED, That the consideration of the Bill be postponed, and that the representation of John O'Donnell, in behalf of himself and others, citizens of Baltimore town,[142] stating that town to be exceedingly commodious and eligible for the permanent seat of government of the United States;—and the representation of Robert Peters, in behalf of himself and other freeholders and other inhabitants, of George Town,[143] to the same purpose, be severally read.

The consideration of the Bill was resumed, and the first enacting clause being read as follows, "Be it enacted by the Senate and House of Representatives of the United States of America, in Congress assembled, that a district of territory not exceeding ten miles square, to be located as hereafter directed, at   and the same is hereby accepted as the permanent seat of Congress and the government of the United States"—

---

[138] This printed bill is in the Broadside Collection, RBkRm, DLC. E–46018.

[139] On July 1 this bill was read a second time and committed.

[140] A provision for the temporary seat of government eventually became part of the Residence Bill.

[141] The smooth journal reads: "the last mentioned Bill."

[142] This petition (Representation) has not been located.

[143] This petition (Representation) may be the same as an earlier one, dated December 7, 1789, from the citizens of Georgetown and Alexandria. It is located in the Broadside Collection, RBkRm, DLC.

A motion was made to fill up the blank with the word "Baltimore," and the yeas and nays were required by one fifth of the Senators present:

Mr. Bassett		Nay
Mr. Butler	Yea	
Mr. Carroll		Nay
Mr. Dalton		Nay
Mr. Ellsworth	Yea	
Mr. Elmer		Nay
Mr. Few	Yea	
Mr. Foster	Yea	
Mr. Hawkins		Nay
Mr. Henry		Nay
Mr. Johnson	Yea	
Mr. Johnston	Yea	
Mr. Izard	Yea	
Mr. King	Yea	
Mr. Langdon		Nay
Mr. Lee		Nay
Mr. Maclay		Nay
Mr. Morris		Nay
Mr. Paterson		Nay
Mr. Read		Nay
Mr. Schuyler	Yea	
Mr. Stanton	Yea	
Mr. Strong		Nay
Mr. Walker		Nay
Mr. Wingate		Nay

Nays—15
Yeas—10

So it passed in the Negative.

On motion, after the word "DIRECTED," in the fifth line of the Bill, to strike out to the end of the clause, and insert, "on the river Potomack, at some place between the mouths of the eastern branch and Connogochegue, be, and the same is hereby accepted for the permanent seat of the government of the United States; provided nevertheless that the operation of the laws of the State within such district shall not be affected by this acceptance, until the time fixed for the removal of the government thereto, and until Congress shall otherwise by law provide,"[144] the yeas and nays were required by one fifth of the Senators present:

Mr. Bassett	Yea

---

[144] This motion is in Senate Bills, Senate Records, DNA.

Mr. Butler	Yea	
Mr. Carroll	Yea	
Mr. Dalton		Nay
Mr. Ellsworth		Nay
Mr. Elmer	Yea	
Mr. Few	Yea	
Mr. Foster	Yea	
Mr. Hawkins	Yea	
Mr. Henry	Yea	
Mr. Johnson		Nay
Mr. Johnston	Yea	
Mr. Izard	Yea	
Mr. King		Nay
Mr. Langdon	Yea	
Mr. Lee	Yea	
Mr. Maclay	Yea	
Mr. Morris	Yea	
Mr. Paterson		Nay
Mr. Read	Yea	
Mr. Schuyler		Nay
Mr. Stanton		Nay
Mr. Strong		Nay
Mr. Walker	Yea	
Mr. Wingate		Nay

Yeas—16
Nays—9

So it passed in the Affirmative.

On motion that the Bill be amended to read as follows, "after the word 'authorized,' in the second clause, strike out to the end of the said clause, and insert—'to appoint, and by supplying vacancies happening from refusals to act or other causes, to keep in appointment as long as may be necessary, three Commissioners, who, or any two of whom, shall under the direction of the President survey, and by proper metes and bounds define and limit a district of territory, under the limitations above mentioned; and the district so defined, limited, and located, shall be deemed the district accepted by this act for the permanent seat of the government of the United States;' "—and the motion was agreed to.

On motion to subjoin to the amendment last agreed to, as follows, "And be it enacted, that the said Commissioners, or any two of them, shall have power to purchase or accept such quantity of land on the eastern side of the said river within the said district, as the President shall deem proper for the use of the United States; and according to such plans as the President shall approve, the said Commissioners, or any two of them shall, prior to the first Monday in December, in the year one thousand eight hundred, provide suitable buildings for the accommodation of Congress, and of the President, and for the public offices of the government of the United States"[145]—

A motion was made to amend the amendment, so as that it should read, "prior to the first Monday in December, one thousand seven hundred and ninety four;" and the yeas and nays were required on this amendment to the proposed amendment, by one fifth of the Senators present:

Mr. Bassett		Nay
Mr. Butler	Yea	
Mr. Carroll		Nay
Mr. Dalton		Nay
Mr. Ellsworth		Nay
Mr. Elmer		Nay
Mr. Few	Yea	
Mr. Foster	Yea	
Mr. Hawkins		Nay
Mr. Henry		Nay
Mr. Johnson	Yea	
Mr. Johnston	Yea	
Mr. Izard	Yea	
Mr. King	Yea	
Mr. Langdon		Nay
Mr. Lee		Nay
Mr. Maclay		Nay
Mr. Morris		Nay
Mr. Paterson		Nay
Mr. Read		Nay
Mr. Schuyler	Yea	
Mr. Stanton	Yea	
Mr. Strong		Nay
Mr. Walker		Nay
Mr. Wingate		Nay

Nays—16

Yeas—9

So it passed in the Negative.

A motion was then made to amend the proposed amendment, so as that it should read, "prior to the first Monday in December, one thousand seven hundred and ninety-eight"—

And it passed in the Negative.

---

[145] These two motions are in Senate Bills, Senate Records, DNA.

And on motion to agree to the proposed amendment to the Bill, the yeas and nays were required by one fifth of the Senators present:

Mr. Bassett		Nay
Mr. Butler	Yea	
Mr. Carroll		Nay
Mr. Dalton		Nay
Mr. Ellsworth		Nay
Mr. Elmer		Nay
Mr. Few	Yea	
Mr. Foster		Nay
Mr. Hawkins		Nay
Mr. Henry		Nay
Mr. Johnson	Yea	
Mr. Johnston	Yea	
Mr. Izard	Yea	
Mr. King	Yea	
Mr. Langdon		Nay
Mr. Lee		Nay
Mr. Maclay		Nay
Mr. Morris		Nay
Mr. Paterson		Nay
Mr. Read		Nay
Mr. Schuyler	Yea	
Mr. Stanton	Yea	
Mr. Strong		Nay
Mr. Walker		Nay
Mr. Wingate		Nay

Nays—17

Yeas—8

So it passed in the Negative.[146]

On motion to strike out the third, fourth, and fifth enacting clauses in the Bill, and insert the following—"And be it enacted, that for defraying the expence of such purchases and buildings, the President of the United States be authorized and requested to accept grants of money, and cause to be borrowed a sum not exceeding one hundred thousand dollars, at an interest not exceeding six per cent; for payment of which, and repayment of the principal within twenty years, so much of the duties on imposts and tonnage as may be

[146] The rough journal originally carried this sentence as printed, but it was later altered to read: "And on motion to agree to the proposed amendment—it passed in the affirmative." In addition, this phrasing occurs in the smooth journal. The rough journal also adds a sentence, which was later canceled: "And the clause proposed to be subjoined, as an amendment to the Bill, was agreed to."

sufficient, is hereby pledged and appropriated,"[147] the yeas and nays were required by one fifth of the Senators present:

Mr. Bassett	Yea	
Mr. Bulter	Yea	
Mr. Carroll	Yea	
Mr. Dalton		Nay
Mr. Ellsworth		Nay
Mr. Elmer		Nay
Mr. Few	Yea	
Mr. Foster		Nay
Mr. Hawkins	Yea	
Mr. Henry	Yea	
Mr. Johnson		Nay
Mr. Johnston	Yea	
Mr. Izard	Yea	
Mr. King		Nay
Mr. Langdon	Yea	
Mr. Lee	Yea	
Mr. Maclay	Yea	
Mr. Morris	Yea	
Mr. Paterson		Nay
Mr. Read	Yea	
Mr. Schuyler		Nay
Mr. Stanton	Yea	
Mr. Strong		Nay
Mr. Walker	Yea	
Mr. Wingate		Nay

Yeas—15
Nays—10

So it passed in the Affirmative.

On motion to subjoin the following to the clause last agreed to—"And be it enacted, that on the said first Monday in December, in the year one thousand eight hundred, the seat of the government of the United States shall, by virtue of this act, be transferred to the district and place aforesaid; and all offices attached to the said seat of government shall accordingly be removed thereto by their respective holders, and shall after the said day cease to be exercised elsewhere; and the necessary expence of such removal, shall be defrayed out of the duties on imposts and tonnage, of which a sufficient sum is hereby appropriated,"[148] the yeas and nays were required by one fifth of the Senators present:

[147] This motion is in Senate Bills, Senate Records, DNA.
[148] A draft of this motion is in Senate Bills, Senate Records, DNA.

Mr. Bassett	Yea	
Mr. Butler	Yea	
Mr. Carroll	Yea	
Mr. Dalton		Nay
Mr. Ellsworth		Nay
Mr. Elmer		Nay
Mr. Few		Nay
Mr. Foster		Nay
Mr. Hawkins	Yea	
Mr. Henry	Yea	
Mr. Johnson		Nay
Mr. Johnston	Yea	
Mr. Izard	Yea	
Mr. King		Nay
Mr. Langdon	Yea	
Mr. Lee	Yea	
Mr. Maclay	Yea	
Mr. Morris	Yea	
Mr. Paterson		Nay
Mr. Read	Yea	
Mr. Schuyler		Nay
Mr. Stanton		Nay
Mr. Strong		Nay
Mr. Walker	Yea	
Mr. Wingate		Nay

Yeas—13

Nays—12

So it passed in the Affirmative.

On motion to fill up the first blank in the last paragraph of the Bill, to wit, "And be it further enacted by the authority aforesaid, that the temporary residence of Congress shall be and continue in the   till the year and no longer," with these words, "city of New-York," the yeas and nays were required by one fifth of the Senators present:

Mr. Bassett		Nay
Mr. Butler	Yea	
Mr. Carroll		Nay
Mr. Dalton	Yea	
Mr. Ellsworth	Yea	
Mr. Elmer		Nay
Mr. Few	Yea	
Mr. Foster	Yea	

Mr. Hawkins		Nay
Mr. Henry		Nay
Mr. Johnson	Yea	
Mr. Johnston	Yea	
Mr. Izard	Yea	
Mr. King	Yea	
Mr. Langdon		Nay
Mr. Lee		Nay
Mr. Maclay		Nay
Mr. Morris		Nay
Mr. Paterson	Yea	
Mr. Read		Nay
Mr. Schuyler	Yea	
Mr. Stanton	Yea	
Mr. Strong	Yea	
Mr. Walker		Nay
Mr. Wingate		Nay

Yeas—13

Nays—12

So it passed in the Affirmative.[149]

The Senate adjourned to 11 o'clock to-morrow.

TUESDAY, JUNE 29, 1790

The SENATE assembled,

Present as yesterday.

Mr. Wingate from the Committee on enrolled Bills, reported, That they had examined the enrolled Bill, entitled, "An Act providing the means of intercourse between the United States and foreign nations,"[150] the enrolled Bill, entitled, "An Act for the relief of Nathaniel Twining,"[151] and the enrolled Bill, entitled, "An Act to satisfy the claims of John McCord, against the United States,"[152] and had found them correct.

The Senate proceeded in the SECOND reading of the Bill, entitled, "An Act to satisfy the claim of the representatives of David Gould, deceased, against the United States."

ORDERED, That this Bill be committed to

---

[149] On June 29 the second reading of this bill was continued, and several amendments to it were proposed. Only one of the amendments was passed.

[150] The inspected enrolled bill is in Enrolled Acts, RG 11, DNA. E–46055.

[151] The inspected enrolled bill is in Enrolled Acts, RG 11, DNA.

[152] The inspected enrolled bill is in Enrolled Acts, RG 11, DNA. E–46074.

Mr. Wingate
Mr. Elmer and
Mr. Maclay[153]

A message from the House of Representatives by Mr. Beckley their clerk:

"Mr. PRESIDENT,

"The House of Representatives have passed a Bill, entitled, 'An Act for giving effect to an Act, entitled, "An Act providing for the enumeration of the inhabitants of the United States," in respect to the State of Rhode-Island and Providence Plantations'[154]—

"The Speaker of the House of Representatives has signed several enrolled Bills, which I am directed to bring to the Senate"—

And he withdrew.

The Vice President affixed his signature to the enrolled Bill, entitled, "An Act providing the means of intercourse between the United States and foreign nations," to the enrolled Bill, entitled, "An Act for the relief of Nathaniel Twining," and to the enrolled Bill, entitled, "An Act to satisfy the claims of John McCord against the United States," and they were delivered to the Committee on enrolled Bills, to be laid before the President of the United States.[155]

ORDERED, That the Bill, entitled, "An Act for giving effect to an Act, entitled, 'An Act providing for the enumeration of the inhabitants of the United States,' in respect to the State of Rhode-Island and Providence Plantations," be now read the FIRST time.

ORDERED, That this Bill pass to the SECOND reading.[156]

The Senate proceeded in the SECOND reading of the Bill, entitled, "An Act imposing duties on the tonnage of ships or vessels."

ORDERED, That this Bill be committed to

Mr. Read
Mr. Dalton and
Mr. Morris[157]

The Senate resumed the SECOND reading of the Bill, "to determine the permanent Seat of Congress, and the government of the United States."

On motion to fill up the blank in the last paragraph of the Bill, with the words "one thousand eight hundred," the yeas and nays were required by one fifth of the Senators present:

---

[153] On July 5 this committee reported and the report was laid for consideration.

[154] This bill has not been located.

[155] On June 30 this committee reported that it had delivered these bills to the President.

[156] On June 30 this bill was read a second time.

[157] This order is in Senate Joint and Concurrent Resolutions, Senate Records, DNA. On July 12 this committee reported, and the bill was read a third time and passed without amendments.

Mr. Bassett		Yea
Mr. Butler	Nay	
Mr. Carroll		Yea
Mr. Dalton	Nay	
Mr. Ellsworth		Yea
Mr. Elmer	Nay	
Mr. Few	Nay	
Mr. Foster		Yea
Mr. Gunn	Nay	
Mr. Henry	Nay	
Mr. Johnson		Yea
Mr. Johnston		Yea
Mr. Izard		Yea
Mr. King		Yea
Mr. Langdon		Yea
Mr. Lee		Yea
Mr. Maclay	Nay	
Mr. Morris	Nay	
Mr. Paterson		Yea
Mr. Read	Nay	
Mr. Schuyler		Yea
Mr. Stanton		Yea
Mr. Strong	Nay	
Mr. Walker	Nay	
Mr. Wingate	Nay	

Yeas—13

Nays—12

So it passed in the Affirmative.

On motion to agree to the last clause of the Bill, amended to read as follows, "Be it further enacted by the authority aforesaid, that the temporary residence of Congress shall be and continue in the city of New-York till the year one thousand eight hundred, and no longer," the yeas and nays were required by one fifth of the Senators present:

Mr. Bassett		Nay
Mr. Butler		Nay
Mr. Carroll		Nay
Mr. Dalton		Nay
Mr. Ellsworth	Yea	
Mr. Elmer		Nay
Mr. Few		Nay
Mr. Foster	Yea	

Mr. Gunn		Nay
Mr. Henry		Nay
Mr. Johnson	Yea	
Mr. Johnston	Yea	
Mr. Izard	Yea	
Mr. King	Yea	
Mr. Langdon		Nay
Mr. Lee		Nay
Mr. Maclay		Nay
Mr. Morris		Nay
Mr. Paterson	Yea	
Mr. Read		Nay
Mr. Schuyler	Yea	
Mr. Stanton	Yea	
Mr. Strong		Nay
Mr. Walker		Nay
Mr. Wingate		Nay

Nays—16
Yeas—9

So it was passed in the Negative.

A motion was made to subjoin the following paragraph to the Bill, in lieu of that last struck out, to wit, "And be it enacted, that prior to the first Monday in December next, all offices attached to the seat of the government of the United States, shall be removed to, and until the said first Monday in December, in the year one thousand eight hundred, shall remain at the city of Philadelphia, in the State of Pennsylvania; at which place the two Houses do hereby resolve that the session of Congress next ensuing the present, shall be held"[158] —and,

A motion was made to amend the motion as follows, "And be it enacted, that Congress shall continue to hold their sessions in the city of New-York, until the first Monday in December, in the year one thousand seven hundred and ninety-four; and from and after the said first Monday in December, one thousand seven hundred and ninety-four, Congress shall hold their sessions in the city of Philadelphia, and shall continue there to hold the same until the first Monday of December, one thousand eight hundred"[159]—Upon this amendment to the motion, the yeas and nays were required by one fifth of the Senators present:

Mr. Bassett		Nay
Mr. Butler	Yea	
Mr. Carroll		Nay

---

[158] This motion is in Senate Bills, Senate Records, DNA.
[159] This motion is in Senate Bills, Senate Records, DNA.

Mr. Dalton	Yea	
Mr. Ellsworth	Yea	
Mr. Elmer		Nay
Mr. Few	Yea	
Mr. Foster	Yea	
Mr. Gunn		Nay
Mr. Hawkins		Nay
Mr. Henry		Nay
Mr. Johnson	Yea	
Mr. Johnston	Yea	
Mr. Izard	Yea	
Mr. King	Yea	
Mr. Langdon		Nay
Mr. Lee		Nay
Mr. Maclay		Nay
Mr. Morris		Nay
Mr. Paterson	Yea	
Mr. Read		Nay
Mr. Schuyler	Yea	
Mr. Stanton	Yea	
Mr. Strong	Yea	
Mr. Walker		Nay
Mr. Wingate		Nay

Yeas—13

Nays—13

The numbers being equal, the Vice President determined the question in the negative.

A motion was then made to amend the motion as follows, "And be it enacted, that Congress shall continue to hold their sessions in the city of New-York, until the first Monday in December, in the year one thousand seven hundred and ninety-four; and from and after the said first Monday of December, one thousand seven hundred and ninety-four, Congress shall hold their sessions in the town of Baltimore, and shall continue there to hold the same until the first Monday of December, one thousand eight hundred"[160]—Upon this amendment to the motion, the yeas and nays were required by one fifth of the Senators present:

Mr. Bassett		Nay
Mr. Butler	Yea	
Mr. Carroll		Nay
Mr. Dalton		Nay

[160] This motion is in Senate Simple Resolutions and Motions, Senate Records, DNA.

Mr. Ellsworth	Yea	
Mr. Elmer		Nay
Mr. Few	Yea	
Mr. Foster	Yea	
Mr. Gunn		Nay
Mr. Hawkins		Nay
Mr. Henry		Nay
Mr. Johnson	Yea	
Mr. Johnston	Yea	
Mr. Izard	Yea	
Mr. King	Yea	
Mr. Langdon		Nay
Mr. Lee		Nay
Mr. Maclay		Nay
Mr. Morris		Nay
Mr. Paterson		Nay
Mr. Read		Nay
Mr. Schuyler	Yea	
Mr. Stanton	Yea	
Mr. Strong		Nay
Mr. Walker		Nay
Mr. Wingate		Nay

Nays—16

Yeas—10

So it passed in the Negative.

A motion was then made to amend the motion as follows, "And be it enacted by the authority aforesaid, that Congress shall continue to hold their sessions in the city of New-York, till the first Monday of December, one thousand seven hundred and ninety-two; and from and after that period to adjourn to the city of Philadelphia, where Congress shall hold their sessions till the first Monday in December, one thousand eight hundred, and no longer"[161]— Upon this amendment to the motion, the yeas and nays were required by one fifth of the Senators present:

Mr. Bassett		Nay
Mr. Butler	Yea	
Mr. Carroll		Nay
Mr. Dalton	Yea	
Mr. Ellsworth	Yea	
Mr. Elmer		Nay
Mr. Few	Yea	

---

[161] This motion is in Senate Bills, Senate Records, DNA.

Mr. Foster	Yea	
Mr. Gunn		Nay
Mr. Hawkins		Nay
Mr. Henry		Nay
Mr. Johnson	Yea	
Mr. Johnston	Yea	
Mr. Izard	Yea	
Mr. King	Yea	
Mr. Langdon		Nay
Mr. Lee		Nay
Mr. Maclay		Nay
Mr. Morris		Nay
Mr. Paterson	Yea	
Mr. Read		Nay
Mr. Schuyler	Yea	
Mr. Stanton	Yea	
Mr. Strong	Yea	
Mr. Walker		Nay
Mr. Wingate		Nay

Yeas—13

Nays—13

The numbers being equal, the question was by the Vice President determined in the Negative.

On the question to agree to the original motion, the yeas and nays were required by one fifth of the Senators present:

Mr. Bassett		Yea
Mr. Butler	Nay	
Mr. Carroll		Yea
Mr. Dalton	Nay	
Mr. Ellsworth	Nay	
Mr. Elmer		Yea
Mr. Few	Nay	
Mr. Foster	Nay	
Mr. Gunn		Yea
Mr. Hawkins		Yea
Mr. Henry		Yea
Mr. Johnson	Nay	
Mr. Johnston	Nay	
Mr. Izard	Nay	
Mr. King	Nay	
Mr. Langdon		Yea

Mr. Lee		Yea
Mr. Maclay		Yea
Mr. Morris		Yea
Mr. Paterson	Nay	
Mr. Read		Yea
Mr. Schuyler	Nay	
Mr. Stanton	Nay	
Mr. Strong	Nay	
Mr. Walker		Yea
Mr. Wingate		Yea

Yeas—13

Nays—13

The numbers being equal, the question was by the Vice President determined in the Negative.

On motion that this Bill do pass to the THIRD reading, the further consideration thereof was postponed, by a motion for adjournment.[162]

The Senate adjourned to 11 o'clock to-morrow.

WEDNESDAY, JUNE 30, 1790

The SENATE assembled,

Present as yesterday.

Mr. Wingate from the Committee on enrolled Bills, reported, That they had this day laid before the President of the United States, for his approbation, the enrolled Bill, entitled, "An Act providing the means of intercourse between the United States and foreign nations," the enrolled Bill, entitled, "An Act for the relief of Nathaniel Twining," and the enrolled Bill, entitled, "An Act to satisfy the claims of John McCord, against the United States."[163]

The following written message from the President of the United States, was communicated by his private Secretary—

And he withdrew.

UNITED STATES, June 30, 1790

GENTLEMEN of the SENATE, and

HOUSE of REPRESENTATIVES,

AN act of the Legislature of the State of Rhode-Island and Providence Plantations, for ratifying certain articles as amendments to the Constitution of the United States, was yesterday put into my hands; and I have directed my Secretary to lay a copy of the same before you.

G. WASHINGTON

---

[162] On June 30 the second reading of this bill was continued, and several amendments to it were considered. Some of the amendments were adopted, while others failed to pass. The bill then passed to the third reading.

[163] The President signed all of these bills on July 1, and the Senate was notified on the same date.

(Copy)
"STATE OF RHODE-ISLAND AND PROVIDENCE PLANATATIONS
"In GENERAL ASSEMBLY, June session, A. D. 1790
"An Act for ratifying certain articles as amendments to the Constitution of
the United States of America, and which were proposed by the Congress
of the said States, at their session in March A. D. 1789, to the Legisla-
tures of the several States, pursuant to the fifth article of the aforesaid
Constitution—

"BE it enacted by this General Assembly, and by the authority thereof it is
hereby enacted, that the following articles proposed by the Congress of the
United States of America, at their session in March A. D. 1789, to the Legislatures of the several States, for ratification, as amendments to the Constitution
of the said United States, pursuant to the fifth article of the said Constitution,
be, and the same are hereby fully assented to and ratified on the part of this
State; to wit:

[Here follow all the articles, except the second.]

"It is ordered, that his Excellency the Governor be, and he is hereby requested to transmit to the President of the said United States, under the seal
of this State, a copy of this act to be communicated to the Senate and House of
Representatives of the Congress of the said United States.

"A true copy duly examined,
(Signed)   Witness, HENRY WARD, Secretary"

⟨SEAL⟩

"By his Excellency ARTHUR FENNER, Esquire, Governor, Captain General
and Commander in Chief of, and over the State of Rhode-Island and
Providence Plantations:

"BE it known that Henry Ward, Esquire, who hath under his hand certified
the annexed paper, purporting an act of the General Assembly of the said
State, to be a true copy, is Secretary of the said State, duly elected and engaged
according to law; wherefore unto his certificate of that matter, full faith is to
be rendered.

"Given under my hand and the seal of the said State, at Providence, this
fifteenth day of June A. D. 1790, and in the fourteenth year of Independence.
(Signed)   ARTHUR FENNER"

"By his Excellency's command,
HENRY WARD, Secretary"[164]

---

[164] This message and documents are in President's Messages: Suggesting legislation,
Senate Records, DNA. In the rough journal this certificate was originally copied immediately after Washington's letter, but a note indicated that it ought to be inserted at
this place.

ORDERED, That the message from the President of the United States, and papers therewith communicated, lie on the files of Senate.

The Senate resumed the SECOND reading of the Bill, "to determine the permanent Seat of Congress, and the government of the United States."

On motion to re-consider the last paragraph of the Bill, which was yesterday struck out—

It passed in the Affirmative.[165]

On motion to amend the paragraph to read as follows, "And be it enacted, that prior to the first Monday in December next, all offices attached to the seat of the government of the United States, shall be removed to, and until the said first Monday in December, in the year one thousand eight hundred, shall remain at the city of Philadelphia, in the State of Pennsylvania; at which place the session of Congress next ensuing the present, shall be held"—

A motion was made to amend the motion to read as follows, "And be it enacted, that Congress shall continue to hold their sessions in the city of New-York, until the first Monday in December, in the year one thousand seven hundred and ninety-four; and from and after the said first Monday of December, one thousand seven hundred and ninety-four, Congress shall hold their sessions in the city of Philadelphia, and shall continue there to hold the same until the first Monday of December, one thousand eight hundred:"

And on the question thus to amend the amendment proposed to the Bill—

It passed in the Negative.

A motion was then made to amend the motion to read as follows, "And be it enacted, that Congress shall continue to hold their sessions in the city of New-York, until the first Monday in December, one thousand seven hundred and ninety-two; and from and after the said first Monday of December, one thousand seven hundred and ninety-two, Congress shall hold their sessions in the city of. Philadelphia, and shall continue there to hold the same until the first Monday of December, one thousand eight hundred:"

And on the question thus to amend the amendment proposed to the Bill—

It passed in the Negative.

On the question to agree to the original motion, the yeas and nays were[166] required by one fifth of the Senators present:

Mr. Bassett	Yea
Mr. Butler	Yea
Mr. Carroll	Yea
Mr. Dalton	Nay

---

[165] The rough journal reads: "The S resumed the second reading of the bill/ On Motion by one of the Majority, to reconsider the last Paragraph of the bill 'to determine the permanent Seat of Congress and the Government of the United States.' which was expunged yesterday./ It passed in the affirmative."

[166] In the smooth journal the word "being" is substituted for "were."

Mr. Ellsworth	Nay	
Mr. Elmer		Yea
Mr. Few	Nay	
Mr. Foster	Nay	
Mr. Gunn		Yea
Mr. Hawkins		Yea
Mr. Henry		Yea
Mr. Johnson	Nay	
Mr. Johnston	Nay	
Mr. Izard	Nay	
Mr. King	Nay	
Mr. Langdon		Yea
Mr. Lee		Yea
Mr. Maclay		Yea
Mr. Morris		Yea
Mr. Paterson	Nay	
Mr. Read		Yea
Mr. Schuyler	Nay	
Mr. Stanton	Nay	
Mr. Strong	Nay	
Mr. Walker		Yea
Mr. Wingate		Yea

Yeas—14

Nays—12

So it passed in the Affirmative.

On motion to re-consider[167] the following clause of the Bill, agreed to yesterday, to wit: "And cause to be borrowed a sum not exceeding one hundred thousand dollars, at an interest not exceeding six per cent. for payment of which, and repayment of the principal within twenty years, so much of the duties on impost and tonnage as may be sufficient, is hereby pledged and appropriated"—

It passed in the Affirmative.

And on motion to expunge this whole paragraph, the yeas and nays were required by one fifth of the Senators present:

Mr. Bassett		Yea
Mr. Butler	Nay	
Mr. Carroll		Yea
Mr. Dalton		Yea
Mr. Ellsworth		Yea

---

[167] At this point the rough journal at first inserted but then lined out the phrase "by one of the majority."

Mr. Elmer		Yea
Mr. Few	Nay	
Mr. Foster		Yea
Mr. Gunn	Nay	
Mr. Hawkins	Nay	
Mr. Henry		Yea
Mr. Johnson		Yea
Mr. Johnston	Nay	
Mr. Izard	Nay	
Mr. King		Yea
Mr. Langdon		Yea
Mr. Lee		Yea
Mr. Maclay		Yea
Mr. Morris		Yea
Mr. Paterson		Yea
Mr. Read		Yea
Mr. Schuyler		Yea
Mr. Stanton	Nay	
Mr. Strong		Yea
Mr. Walker		Yea
Mr. Wingate		Yea

Yeas—19

Nays—7

So it passed in the Affirmative.

On the question, Shall this Bill pass to the THIRD reading? The yeas and nays were required by one fifth of the Senators present:

Mr. Bassett		Yea
Mr. Butler		Yea
Mr. Carroll		Yea
Mr. Dalton	Nay	
Mr. Ellsworth	Nay	
Mr. Elmer		Yea
Mr. Few		Yea
Mr. Foster	Nay	
Mr. Gunn		Yea
Mr. Hawkins		Yea
Mr. Henry		Yea
Mr. Johnson	Nay	
Mr. Johnston		Yea
Mr. Izard	Nay	
Mr. King	Nay	

Mr. Langdon		Yea
Mr. Lee		Yea
Mr. Maclay		Yea
Mr. Morris		Yea
Mr. Paterson	Nay	
Mr. Read		Yea
Mr. Schuyler	Nay	
Mr. Stanton	Nay	
Mr. Strong	Nay	
Mr. Walker		Yea
Mr. Wingate		Yea

Yeas—16

Nays—10

So it passed in the Affirmative.

ORDERED, That this Bill be engrossed.[168]

The Senate proceeded to the SECOND reading of the Bill, entitled, "An Act for giving effect to an Act, entitled, 'An Act providing for the enumeration of the inhabitants of the United States,' in respect to the State of Rhode-Island and Providence Plantations."

ORDERED, That this Bill pass to a THIRD reading.[169]

Mr. Johnson from the Committee appointed June the 24th, to take into consideration the Bill, entitled, "An Act to establish the Post-Office and Post-Roads within the United States," reported amendments;[170] which were read.

ORDERED, That the report lie until to-morrow for consideration.[171]

The Senate proceeded to the SECOND reading of the Bill, entitled, "An Act to provide more effectually for the settlement of the accounts between the United States and the individual States," and after progress, the further consideration thereof was postponed until to-morrow.[172]

The Senate adjourned to 11 o'clock to-morrow.

---

[168] On July 1 this bill was read a third time, and several amendments to it were rejected. The bill was then passed and sent to the House for concurrence.

[169] On July 1 this bill was read a third time and passed.

[170] A draft of this committee report is in Various Select Committee Reports, Senate Records, DNA. An undated fragment of postal duties is in Other Records: Various papers, Senate Records, DNA. The amendments are printed on pages 399–401, note 24 below.

[171] On July 2 this committee report was considered and postponed.

[172] On July 1 this bill was considered again and committed.

THURSDAY, JULY 1, 1790

The SENATE assembled,
Present as yesterday.

The Senate proceeded to the THIRD reading of the Bill, entitled, "An Act for giving effect to an Act, entitled, 'An Act providing for the enumeration of the inhabitants of the United States,' in respect to the State of Rhode-Island and Providence Plantations."

RESOLVED, That this Bill DO PASS.

ORDERED, That the Secretary acquaint the House of Representatives of the concurrence of the Senate in this Bill.[1]

The Senate proceeded in the SECOND reading of the Bill, entitled, "An Act for the government and regulation of seamen in the merchants service."

ORDERED, That this Bill[2] be committed to

> Mr. Dalton
> Mr. Morris and
> Mr. Langdon[3]

The Senate proceeded in the SECOND reading of the Bill, entitled, "An Act to provide more effectually for the settlement of the accounts between the United States and the individual States."

ORDERED, That this Bill be committed to

> Mr. King
> Mr. Strong
> Mr. Read
> Mr. Ellsworth and
> Mr. Hawkins[4]

A message from the House of Representatives by Mr. Beckley their clerk:

"Mr. PRESIDENT,

"The House of Representatives have passed the Bill, entitled, 'An Act further to provide for the payment of the invalid pensioners of the United States,'[5] to which they desire the concurrence of the Senate[6]—

"I am directed to inform the Senate, that the President of the United States has this day approved of, and affixed his signature to the following Acts, to wit: 'An Act providing the means of intercourse between the United States

---

[1] On July 2 this bill was signed by both the Speaker and the Vice President and given to the committee on enrolled bills for delivery to the President.

[2] The smooth journal substitutes "it" for "this bill."

[3] On July 7 this committee reported and the bill was amended accordingly.

[4] On July 3 this committee reported amendments to the bill and consideration of the report was postponed.

[5] This bill has not been located.

[6] On July 2 this bill was read for the first time.

and foreign nations,' 'An Act for the relief of Nathaniel Twining,' and, 'An Act to satisfy the claims of John McCord, against the United States' "—

And he withdrew.

Agreeably to the order of the day, the Senate proceeded to the THIRD reading of the engrossed Bill, "to determine the permanent Seat of Congress, and the government of the United States:"

On motion to strike out these words in the first enacting clause, "between the mouths of the eastern branch and Connogochegue," and insert, "within thirty miles of Hancock-Town"[7]—

It passed in the Negative.

On motion to strike out these words from the fifth enacting clause of the Bill, "the first Monday of December next," and insert, "the first Monday in May next," the yeas and nays were required by one fifth of the Senators present:

Mr.	Bassett		Nay
Mr.	Butler	Yea	
Mr.	Carroll		Nay
Mr.	Dalton	Yea	
Mr.	Ellsworth	Yea	
Mr.	Elmer		Nay
Mr.	Few	Yea	
Mr.	Foster	Yea	
Mr.	Gunn		Nay
Mr.	Hawkins		Nay
Mr.	Henry		Nay
Mr.	Johnson	Yea	
Mr.	Johnston	Yea	
Mr.	Izard	Yea	
Mr.	King	Yea	
Mr.	Langdon		Nay
Mr.	Lee		Nay
Mr.	Maclay		Nay
Mr.	Morris		Nay
Mr.	Paterson	Yea	
Mr.	Read		Nay
Mr.	Schuyler	Yea	
Mr.	Stanton	Yea	
Mr.	Strong	Yea	

---

[7] A draft of this motion is in Senate Bills, Senate Records, DNA.

| Mr. Walker | Nay |
| Mr. Wingate | Nay |

Yeas—13

Nays—13

The numbers being equal, the Vice President determined the question in the Negative.

A motion was made to restore the following clause, which it was agreed yesterday should be struck out; to wit, "And cause to be borrowed a sum not exceeding one hundred thousand dollars, at an interest not exceeding six per cent. for payment of which, and repayment of the principal within twenty years, so much of the duties on impost and tonnage as may be sufficient, is hereby pledged and appropriated"—

And it passed in the Negative.

On the question, Shall this Bill pass? The yeas and nays were required by one fifth of the Senators present:

Mr. Bassett		Yea
Mr. Butler		Yea
Mr. Carroll		Yea
Mr. Dalton	Nay	
Mr. Ellsworth	Nay	
Mr. Elmer		Yea
Mr. Few	Nay	
Mr. Foster	Nay	
Mr. Gunn		Yea
Mr. Hawkins		Yea
Mr. Henry		Yea
Mr. Johnson	Nay	
Mr. Johnston		Yea
Mr. Izard	Nay	
Mr. King	Nay	
Mr. Langdon		Yea
Mr. Lee		Yea
Mr. Maclay		Yea
Mr. Morris		Yea
Mr. Paterson	Nay	
Mr. Read		Yea
Mr. Schuyler	Nay	
Mr. Stanton	Nay	
Mr. Strong	Nay	

Mr. Walker   Yea
Mr. Wingate   Nay
            Yeas—14
            Nays—12

So it was,

RESOLVED, That this Bill DO PASS, and that the title of it be "An Act for establishing the temporary and permanent seat of the government of the United States."[8]

ORDERED, That the Secretary carry this Bill to the House of Representatives, and desire their concurrence therein.[9]

The Senate adjourned to 11 o'clock to-morrow.

FRIDAY, JULY 2, 1790

The SENATE assembled,
Present as yesterday.

The petition of John Fitch,[10] was read, stating sundry improvements which he has made "in applying steam to the purposes of propelling boats or vessels through the water," and requesting "a law in his favor, independant of the general one now in force."

ORDERED, That this petition lie on the table.

Mr. Wingate from the Committee on enrolled Bills, reported, That they had examined the Bill, entitled, "An Act to authorize the purchase of a tract of land for the use of the United States,"[11] and the Bill, entitled, "An Act for giving effect to an Act, entitled, 'An Act providing for the enumeration of the inhabitants of the United States,' in respect to the State of Rhode-Island and Providence Plantations,"[12] and had found them correct.

The Bill, entitled, "An Act further to provide for the payment of the invalid pensioners of the United States," was read the FIRST time.

ORDERED, That this Bill pass to the SECOND reading.[13]

ORDERED, That the motion made June the 14th, "That provision shall be

---

[8] The notation of passage is written on the engrossed bill and is in Engrossed Senate Bills and Resolutions, Senate Records, DNA.

[9] On July 2 the House received this bill, read it the first and second times, and committed it to the committee of the whole. It was considered in the committee of the whole on July 6, 7, and 8. On July 9 the bill was read a third time and passed. On July 12 the Senate was notified of this action, and on the same day the bill was signed by both the Speaker and the Vice President.

[10] This petition is in Petitions and Memorials: Various subjects, Senate Records, DNA.

[11] The inspected enrolled bill is in Enrolled Acts, RG 11, DNA. E–46062.

[12] The inspected enrolled bill is in Enrolled Acts, RG 11, DNA. E–46034.

[13] On July 6 this bill was read a second time.

made the next session of Congress, for loaning to the United States a sum not exceeding twenty-two millions of dollars," be committed to

Mr. Carroll
Mr. Lee
Mr. Strong
Mr. Ellsworth and
Mr. Paterson, to report what is proper to be done thereon.[14]

A message from the House of Representatives by Mr. Beckley their clerk:

"Mr. PRESIDENT,

"The Speaker of the House of Representatives, having signed several enrolled Bills, I am directed to bring them to the Senate"—

And he withdrew.

The Senate proceeded in the SECOND reading of the Bill, entitled, "An Act to regulate trade and intercourse with the Indian tribes,"

ORDERED, That this Bill be committed to

Mr. Hawkins
Mr. Few and
Mr. Schuyler[15]

The Vice President affixed his signature to the enrolled Bill, entitled, "An Act to authorize the purchase of a tract of land for the use of the United States," and to the enrolled Bill, entitled, "An Act for giving effect to an Act, entitled, 'An Act providing for the enumeration of the inhabitants of the United States,' in respect to the State of Rhode-Island and Providence Plantations;" and they were delivered to the Committee to be laid before the President of the United States, for his approbation.[16]

The Senate proceeded in the consideration of the report of the Committee on the Bill, entitled, "An Act to establish the Post-Office and Post-Roads within the United States," and after progress,[17]

Adjourned to 11 o'clock to-morrow.

SATURDAY, JULY 3, 1790

The SENATE assembled,
Present as yesterday.

Agreeably to the order of the day, the Senate proceeded to the consideration

---

[14] On July 12 the report of this committee was read and ordered to be printed for consideration.

[15] On July 8 this committee's report was accepted as amendments to the bill, and the bill passed to the third reading.

[16] On July 5 the President signed both of these bills. The Senate was notified on July 8.

[17] On July 3 this report was considered and the bill was amended.

of the report of the Committee appointed June the 24th, on the Bill, entitled, "An Act to establish the Post-Office and Post-Roads within the United States," and it was agreed to amend the Bill accordingly.

ORDERED, That this Bill pass to the THIRD reading.[18]

Mr. King from the Committee appointed July the first, on the Bill, entitled, "An Act to provide more effectually for the settlement of the accounts between the United States and the individual States," reported amendments.[19]

ORDERED, That the consideration of the report be postponed.[20]

The Senate adjourned to Monday next at 11 o'clock.

MONDAY, JULY 5, 1790

The SENATE assembled,
Present as on the 3d of July.

Agreeably to the order of the day, the Senate proceeded to the THIRD reading of the Bill, entitled, "An Act to establish the Post-Office and Post-Roads within the United States."

On motion to restore the first and second paragraphs, ordered to be expunged—

It passed in the Negative.

ORDERED, That the further consideration of this Bill be postponed.[21]

Mr. Wingate reported from the Committee on the Bill,[22] entitled, "An Act to satisfy the claim of the representatives of David Gould, deceased, against the United States."

ORDERED, That the report lie for consideration.[23]

The Senate adjourned to 11 o'clock to-morrow.

TUESDAY, JULY 6, 1790

The SENATE assembled,
Present as yesterday.

Agreeably to the order of the day, the Senate proceeded to the THIRD reading of the Bill, entitled, "An Act to establish the Post-Office and Post-Roads within the United States."

RESOLVED, That this Bill DO PASS with amendments.[24]

---

[18] On July 5 this bill was read a third time, considered, and postponed.

[19] This report is in Various Select Committee Reports, Senate Records, DNA.

[20] On July 6 the amendments in this report were agreed to, and the bill passed to the third reading.

[21] On July 6 this bill was passed with amendments and the House was notified.

[22] This report has not been located.

[23] On July 6 the Senate voted not to concur with this bill and notified the House.

[24] The rough journal includes the amendments as follows:

Sections 1st & 2nd: Line 1 a 27.

Strike out the whole of Sections 1st and 2nd except the enacting Style and insert.

"That it shall be the duty of the Post Master General with the consent of the President of the United States to establish a Post Road from Wiscasset in the district of Maine to Augusta or Savannah in the State of Georgia and to establish other Roads as Post Roads and alter or discontinue the same as the convenience of the People of the United States or the Improvement of the Revenue arising by the Post Office may require—"

Section 3rd. Line 4th.

Strike out "by contract" and Line 5th after the word—"States—" insert—"by Stage Carriages or Horses as he may judge most expedient—"

Section 4th Lines 7 & 8

Strike out the words "respectively, the Contractors for carrying the Mail, and their Servants or agents to whom the care of the Mail may be entrusted."

Line 9th.   Strike out the word "*shall.*"

     12th.   Strike out the word "or" before the word—"procure"—and after the word "procure" insert these words "permit or Suffer."

     18th.   At the end of the Section insert "And the Contractors for carrying the Mail and their Agents or Servants to whom the care of the Mail shall be entrusted shall before their discharging the said trust, take and subscribe the following Oath or Affirmation and cause a Certificate thereof to be filed as aforesaid 'I do swear (or affirm as the case may be) that I will faithfully execute and perform all the duties required of me, and abstain from everything forbidden by the act entitled "An Act to establish the Post Office and Post roads within the United States" '—"

Section 5th. Line 2nd.

Strike out the words—"by Contract or otherwise—" Lines 4 & 5. Strike out the words "suffer ten days imprisonment and shall moreover—"

Section 6th. Line 4th.

At the end of the Section add these words "And the Letters to be delivered at any other Post Office shall be sealed up together and the Seal shall not be broken until they are so delivered."

Section 7th. Line 2nd.

Strike out "*sixteen*" and insert "fifteen."

Section 8th. Line 1st.

After the word "that"—insert—"from and after the last day of September next—"

Lines 3rd. and 4th.

Strike out the words "of lawful money of the United States—"

Section 9th. Line 6th.

Strike out the word—"*six*" and insert "eight"
Strike out the word "*twelve*" & insert "sixteen."
Line 7th.   Strike out the word "eighteen" and insert "twenty four."

Section 11th. Line 2.

After the word "established"—insert "other than from a district in the same or in an adjoining State."

Line 4th.   After the word—"Care"—insert "or within his power—"

     5th.   After the word "Consignee:" insert "or person concerned in any Merchandize or Lading in such Ship or Vessel."

Section 13th. Line 1 a 7.

Strike out the whole of the Section.

Section 15th. Line 7th.

After the word "packets—" insert—"by any private friend or—"

Section 20th. Lines 3rd. and 4th.

Strike out the words "that have been and remained in their"—and insert "then remaining in their—"

Line 4th   After the word "Offices" strike out "*three months—*"

Section 21st. Line 4 a 7.

ORDERED, That the Secretary carry this Bill to the House of Representatives, and desire their concurrence in the amendments.[25]

The Senate proceeded to consider the report of the Committee on the Bill, entitled, "An Act to provide more effectually for the settlement of the accounts between the United States and the individual States," and agreed to amend the Bill accordingly.

ORDERED, That this Bill pass to the THIRD reading.[26]

The Senate proceeded to the consideration of the report of the Committee on the Bill, entitled, "An Act to satisfy the claim of the representatives of David Gould, deceased, against the United States:"

Whereupon,

Strike out from the words "to or from"—to the word "ended" inclusive and insert "Which during any Session of Congress and twenty days before and twenty days after such Session shall be sent to any place within the United States and signed on the outside thereof by any Member of the Senate or House of Representatives and whereof the whole Superscription shall be of the hand writing of such Member, provided that the Letters sent by any Member as aforesaid in any one Mail shall not exceed two ounces in Weight, and all Letters from any place within the United States not exceeding the weight of two ounces each directed to any Member of the Senate or House of Representatives during any Session of Congress and twenty days before and after such Session—"

Line 10 a 17.   Strike out from the word "All"—to the word "Act"—inclusive—

Section 23rd. Line 1 a 5.

After the word "enacted" Strike out the whole Section and insert—"That it shall and may be lawful for the Post Master General for the time being to authorize any Person whatsoever to send and receive News Papers by the Post under such uniform Regulations as he may think proper to establish and with such abatement of Postage as may be necessary for the easy conveyance of information to the Citizens of the United States—"

Section 24th. Line 1 a 7.

Strike out the whole Section.

Section 28th. Line 6th.

Strike out the word "three"—and insert "six"—

Section 31st. Line 1 a 4.

Strike out the whole Section.

Section 32nd. Line 3rd.

Before the word "Militia"—insert "Serving on Juries and from."

Section 3rd. is to be numbered Section 2d. and the following Section in succession to No. 11 inclusive—

Section 14 to stand Section 12, and the following sections numbered in succession to No. 20 inclusive, Section 23 to stand Section 21. No. 25 of the Bill to stand No. 22 and the following Sections numbered in succession to 27 inclusive. No. 32 to be numbered 28—

The smooth journal inserts the following marginal notation: "(For the Amendments on this Bill see Original Minutes Page 453)."

[25] On July 7 the House received this message and considered it on the eighth. On July 10 the House agreed to some of the Senate amendments and disagreed to others, and the Senate was notified on July 12. On the same date the Senate insisted on its amendments and appointed a conference committee. The House's concurrence was then requested.

[26] On July 7 this bill was read a third time and committed.

RESOLVED, That they do not concur in the said Bill.

ORDERED, That the Secretary acquaint the House of Representatives therewith.

The Senate proceeded to the SECOND reading of the Bill, entitled, "An Act further to provide for the payment of the invalid pensioners of the United States."

ORDERED, That this Bill pass to the THIRD reading.[27]

The Senate adjourned to 11 o'clock to-morrow.

WEDNESDAY, JULY 7, 1790

The SENATE assembled,
Present as yesterday.

The Senate proceeded to the THIRD reading of the Bill, entitled, "An Act further to provide for the payment of the invalid pensioners of the United States."

RESOLVED, That this Bill DO PASS with an amendment.[28]

ORDERED, That the Secretary acquaint the House of Representatives therewith, and request their concurrence in the amendment.[29]

The Senate proceeded to the THIRD reading of the Bill, entitled, "An Act to provide more effectually for the settlement of the accounts between the United States and the individual States."

ORDERED, That this Bill be committed to

Mr. Morris

Mr. Schuyler

Mr. King

Mr. Lee and

Mr. Ellsworth[30]

Mr. Dalton from the Committee appointed on the Bill, entitled, "An Act for the government and regulation of seamen in the merchants service," re-

---

[27] On July 7 this bill was read a third time and passed with an amendment.

[28] The rough journal gives the wording of the amendment thus: "Line 5. Between the words 'are' and 'declared'—insert 'or shall be'—" The smooth journal inserts the following marginal notation: "(for the Amendment see Original Minutes Page 462)."

[29] The rough journal originally carried this sentence as it appears in the printed journal, but corrected it to read: "Ordered that the Secretary carry this bill to the House of Representatives and desire their concurrence in the amendment." On July 9 the House agreed to this amendment, and the Senate was notified on July 12. On the twelfth, the bill was signed by both the Speaker and the Vice President and given to the committee on enrolled bills for delivery to the President.

[30] On July 8 this committee reported, and the report was accepted as an amendment to the bill.

ported,[31] which, being read, it was agreed that the Bill should be amended accordingly.

ORDERED, That this Bill pass to the THIRD reading.[32]

Mr. Schuyler from the Committee appointed May the 4th, on the Bill, entitled, "An Act to authorize the issuing of certificates to a certain description of invalid officers," reported:[33]

Whereupon,

ORDERED, That this Bill pass to the THIRD reading.

The Senate proceeded to the THIRD reading of the Bill last mentioned—and RESOLVED, That they do not concur therein.[34]

The Senate adjourned to 11 o'clock to-morrow.

THURSDAY, JULY 8, 1790

The SENATE assembled,
Present as yesterday.

The Senate proceeded to the THIRD reading of the Bill, entitled, "An Act for the government and regulation of seamen in the merchants service."

RESOLVED, That this Bill DO PASS with amendments.[35]

---

[31] The amendments reported are in Various Select Committee Reports, Senate Records, DNA.

[32] On July 8 this bill was read for the third time and passed with amendments.

[33] This report has not been located.

[34] This resolve, attached to the House Bill, is in Engrossed House Bills, House Records, DNA.

[35] The rough journal includes the amendments as follows:

Section 1st. Line 5th.
Strike out the word *"another"*—and insert "any other than adjoining"
In the same line strike out the words *"by Sea"*
Line 16 a 18.
Strike out from the word "and—" line 16th. to the words "United States" line 18th. inclusive.
Section 2nd. Line 11th.
Strike out the words *"when the Voyage shall be ended—"*
Section 4th. Line 6th.
Strike out the word *"three"* and insert "one"
Section 8th. Line 5th.
Strike out the words *"from the same Apothecary—"*
In the same line strike out the words *"signed by him and"*—
Line 6 a 7.
Strike out all the words from "certified" to "year" inclusive.
Section 9th. Line 5th.
Strike out the words *"be thought necessary"* and insert "or Passengers be put on board."

The smooth journal inserts the following marginal notation: "(For the Amendments See Original Minutes Page 465)."

ORDERED, That the Secretary carry this Bill to the House of Representatives, and desire their concurrence in the amendments.[36]

A message from the House of Representatives by Mr. Beckley their clerk:

"Mr. PRESIDENT,

"I am directed to inform the Senate, that the President of the United States has notified the House of Representatives, that he did on the 5th of July, approve and affix his signature to 'An Act for giving effect to an Act, entitled, "An Act providing for the enumeration of the inhabitants of the United States," in respect to the State of Rhode-Island and Providence Plantations,' and to 'An Act to authorize the purchase of a tract of land for the use of the United States' "—

And he withdrew.

Mr. Morris reported from the Committee appointed July the 7th,[37] on the Bill, entitled, "An Act to provide more effectually for the settlement of the accounts between the United States and the individual States;" and it was agreed to amend the Bill accordingly.

ORDERED, That this Bill pass to the THIRD reading.[38]

Mr. Hawkins reported from the Committee appointed July the 2d,[39] on the Bill, entitled, "An Act to regulate trade and intercourse with the Indian tribes;" and it was agreed to amend the Bill accordingly.

ORDERED, That this Bill pass to the THIRD reading.[40]

The Senate adjourned to 11 o'clock to-morrow.

FRIDAY, JULY 9, 1790

The SENATE assembled,
Present as yesterday.

Agreeably to the order of the day, proceeded to the THIRD reading of the Bill, entitled, "An Act to regulate trade and intercourse with the Indian tribes."

RESOLVED, That this Bill DO PASS with amendments.[41]

---

[36] On July 10 the House agreed to all of the Senate amendments except the third. The Senate was notified on July 12. On the same date the Senate receded from its third amendment and notified the House.

[37] Proposed amendments, noted with printed copies of the bill, are in House Bills, Senate Records, DNA. The committee report has not been located.

[38] On July 9 this bill was passed with amendments and sent to the House for concurrence.

[39] This report is in Various Select Committee Reports, Senate Records, DNA.

[40] On July 9 this bill was passed with amendments and the House was notified.

[41] This resolve and the amendments are in Senate Joint and Concurrent Resolutions, Senate Records, DNA. The rough journal carries the amendments as follows:

Section 1st. Line 8th.

ORDERED, That the Secretary carry this Bill to the House of Representatives, and desire their concurrence in the amendments.[42]

The Senate proceeded to the THIRD reading of the Bill, entitled, "An Act to provide more effectually for the settlement of the accounts between the United States and the individual States."

RESOLVED, That this Bill DO PASS with amendments.[43]

Strike out the words *"three thousand"* and insert "one thousand"
Line 15th.
At the end of the Section add these words "Provided nevertheless that the President may make such order respecting the tribes surrounded in their Settlements by the Citizens of the United States as to secure an intercourse without license if he may deem it proper."
See omission below [*note at foot of page*]. The Senate concurred, striking out also the whole of Section 4th, but the entry was omitted in copy
Section 5th. Line 1st.
Strike out the word *"further"*—
In the same line after the word "enacted" insert these words—"and declared"—
The smooth journal inserts the following marginal notation: "For the Amendnt. See Original Minutes Page 469—"

[42] On July 10 the House concurred in these amendments, but on July 12 a mistake was discovered in the Senate message and the House disagreed to one Senate amendment. On the same day the Senate insisted upon this amendment. The letter correcting the mistake is in Other Records: Various papers, Senate Records, DNA.

[43] The rough journal includes the amendments as follows:
Sections 1st. 2nd. & 3rd. Line 2 a. 13.
Strike out all the words from "that" to "enacted"—inclusive.
Section 3rd. Line 14th.
Strike out the words *"said Commissioners"* and insert—"Board of Commissioners established for the settlement of accounts between the United States and individual States—"
After Section 4th. insert
"And be it further enacted, that the Commissioners shall debit each State with all advances which have been or may be made to it by the United States, and with the interest thereon to the last day of the year one thousand seven hundred and eighty nine and shall credit each State for its disbursements and advances on the principles contained in the third Section of this Act with interest to the day aforesaid, and having struck the balance due to each State shall find the aggregate of all the balances, which aggregate shall be apportioned between the States agreeably to the rule hereinafter given, and the difference between such apportionments and the respective balances shall be carried in a new account to the debit or credit of the States respectively as the case may be—"
Section 5th. Line 2nd.
Strike out these words *"expences of the war—"* and insert "aggregate of the balances first above mentioned—"
Line 4th.
Strike out all that follows the word "made—"
Section 6th. Line 1 a 5th.
Strike out the whole Section.
Section 8th. Line 2nd.
Strike out the word *"three"* and insert "two"—
And the Sections numbered conformable to the amendments.
The smooth journal inserts the following marginal notation: "For the Amendments See Original Minutes Page 470."

ORDERED, That the Secretary carry this Bill to the House of Representatives, and desire their concurrence in the amendments.[44]

The Senate proceeded in the SECOND reading of the Bill, entitled, "An Act providing for holding a treaty or treaties to establish peace with certain Indian tribes."

ORDERED, That this Bill be committed to

> Mr. Schuyler
> Mr. Gunn and
> Mr. Langdon[45]

The Senate adjourned to 11 o'clock on Monday next.

MONDAY, JULY 12, 1790

The SENATE assembled,
Present as on the 9th of July.

Mr. Carroll reported from the Committee appointed July the 2d,[46] on the motion, "That provision shall be made the next session of Congress, for loaning to the United States, a sum not exceeding twenty-two millions of dollars, in certificates issued by the respective States, for services or supplies towards the prosecution of the late war," which report was read, and

ORDERED, That the said report be printed for the consideration of the Senate.[47]

A message from the House of Representatives by Mr. Beckley their clerk:

"Mr. PRESIDENT,

"The House of Representatives have agreed to the amendment of the Senate to the Bill, entitled, 'An Act further to provide for the payment of the invalid pensioners of the United States'—

"They disagree to the first and second amendments of the Senate to the Bill, entitled, 'An Act to establish the Post-Office and Post-Roads within the United States;' they disagree to the first amendment in the 11th section, and to the several amendments in the 13th, 23d, 24th and 31st sections, and agree to all the other amendments proposed by the Senate to the said Bill—

"They disagree to the third amendment of the Senate to the Bill, entitled,

---

[44] The House considered these amendments on July 10 and 13. On July 14 the House disagreed to the Senate amendments and appointed a conference committee on this bill. The Senate was notified of this action and appointed a conference committee on July 14.

[45] On July 16 this committee reported and the report was accepted as an amendment to the bill.

[46] Three copies of this report, one in manuscript form, a clear printed one, and an annotated printed one, are in Various Select Committee Reports, Senate Records, DNA. E–46029.

[47] On July 13 this report, which included several new resolutions, was considered and printed in the Journal. On the same day an amendment to the report was defeated, along with several motions to postpone consideration of the report.

'An Act for the government and regulation of seamen in the merchants service,' and they agree to all the other amendments proposed by the Senate—

"They have also passed the Bill sent from the Senate for concurrence, entitled, 'An Act for establishing the temporary and permanent seat of the government of the United States' "—

And he withdrew.

Mr. Wingate from the Committee on enrolled Bills, reported, That they had examined the enrolled Bill, entitled, "An Act for establishing the temporary and permanent seat of the government of the United States,"[48] and the enrolled Bill, entitled, "An Act further to provide for the payment of the invalid pensioners of the United States,"[49] and had found them correct.

A message from the House of Representatives by Mr. Beckley their clerk:

"Mr. PRESIDENT,

"The House of Representatives agree to all the amendments proposed by the Senate to the Bill, entitled, 'An Act to regulate trade and intercourse with the Indian tribes,' except the third, to which they disagree[50]—

"The Speaker of the House of Representatives having signed several enrolled Bills, I am directed to bring them to the Senate, for the signature of the Vice President"—

And he withdrew.

The Vice President signed the enrolled Bill, entitled, "An Act for establishing the temporary and permanent seat of the government of the United States," and the enrolled Bill, entitled, "An Act further to provide for the payment of the invalid pensioners of the United States," and they were delivered to the Committee to be laid before the President of the United States, for his approbation.[51]

The Senate proceeded to the consideration of their amendments disagreed to by the House of Representatives, to the Bill, entitled, "An Act to establish the Post-Office and Post-Roads within the United States," and

RESOLVED, That they insist on their amendments disagreed to by the House of Representatives, that a conference be desired with such managers as the House of Representatives may appoint, on the disagreeing votes of the two Houses, and that   Mr. Ellsworth

---

[48] The inspected enrolled bill is in Enrolled Acts, RG 11, DNA.

[49] The inspected enrolled bill is in Enrolled Acts, RG 11, DNA.

[50] Following the Senate resolve passing [HR–65] Indian Trade Bill, there is a statement indicating that the House agreed to the amendments. This statement, located in Senate Joint and Concurrent Resolutions, Senate Records, DNA, probably preceded the discovery of a mistake in the Senate message. The House then disagreed to one amendment.

[51] On July 13 this committee reported that it had laid these bills before the President on July 12.

Mr. King and

Mr. Strong be managers at the conference, on the part of the Senate.

ORDERED, That the Secretary acquaint the House of Representatives with this resolution, and request the appointment of managers at the conference on their part.[52]

The Senate proceeded to consider their amendment, disagreed to by the House of Representatives, on the Bill, entitled, "An Act for the government and regulation of seamen in the merchants service."

RESOLVED, That they recede from their amendment to this Bill.

ORDERED, That the Secretary acquaint the House of Representatives with this resolution.[53]

The Senate proceeded to consider their third amendment disagreed to by the House of Representatives, on the Bill, entitled, "An Act to regulate trade and intercourse with the Indian tribes," and

RESOLVED, That they insist on their amendment to the said Bill.

ORDERED, That the Secretary acquaint the House of Representatives with this resolution.[54]

Mr. Read from the Committee appointed the 29th of June, on the Bill, entitled, "An Act imposing duties on the tonnage of ships or vessels," reported the Bill without amendment:[55]

Whereupon,

ORDERED, That this Bill be now read the THIRD time.

RESOLVED, That this Bill DO PASS.

ORDERED, That the Secretary acquaint the House of Representatives of the concurrence of the Senate in this Bill.[56]

The Senate adjourned to 11 o'clock to-morrow.

TUESDAY, JULY 13, 1790

The SENATE assembled,
Present as yesterday.

Mr. Wingate from the joint Committee on enrolled Bills, reported, That

---

[52] On July 13 the House appointed members to this conference committee. On July 22 the committee reported to the House, and the House receded from its disagreement to some amendments but insisted upon its disagreement to others. The Senate was notified on July 23.

[53] On July 17 this bill was signed by both the Speaker and the Vice President and given to the committee on enrolled bills for delivery to the President.

[54] On July 13 the House insisted upon its disagreement to this amendment and requested a conference.

[55] A one-sentence report is in Senate Joint and Concurrent Resolutions, Senate Records, DNA.

[56] On July 17 this bill was signed by both the Speaker and the Vice President and given to the committee on enrolled bills for delivery to the President.

they did on the 12th of July, lay before the President of the United States for his approbation, the enrolled Bill, entitled, "An Act for establishing the temporary and permanent seat of the government of the United States," and the enrolled Bill, entitled, "An Act further to provide for the payment of the invalid pensioners of the United States."[57]

A message from the House of Representatives by Mr. Beckley their clerk:

"Mr. PRESIDENT,

"The House of Representatives have agreed to the proposed conference, on the Bill, entitled, 'An Act to establish the Post-Office and Post-Roads within the United States,' and have appointed managers on their part—

"They insist on their disagreement to the third amendment proposed by the Senate, to the Bill, entitled, 'An Act to regulate trade and intercourse with the Indian tribes,' and desire a conference thereon, and having appointed managers on their part, request the concurrence of the Senate in their appointment of managers at the proposed conference"[58]—

And he withdrew.

The Senate proceeded to consider the report of the Committee appointed July the 2d, on the motion, "That provision shall be made the next session of Congress, for loaning to the United States, a sum not exceeding twenty-two millions of dollars," which report is in the words following:

WHEREAS a provision for the debt of the respective States by the United States, would be greatly conducive to an orderly, economical and effectual arrangement of the public finances—would tend to an equal distribution of burthens among the citizens of the several States—would promote more general justice to the different classes of public creditors, and would serve to give stability to public credit: And whereas the said debts having been essentially contracted in the prosecution of the late war, it is just that such provision should be made.

RESOLVED, That a loan be proposed, to the amount of twenty-one million of dollars, and that subscriptions to the said loan be received at the same times and places, by the same persons, and upon the same terms as in respect to the loan which may be proposed concerning the domestic debt of the United States, subject to the exceptions and qualifications hereafter mentioned.—And that the sums which shall be subscribed to the said loan, shall be payable in the principal and interest of the certificates or notes, which, prior to the first day of January last, were issued by the respective States, as acknowledgments or evidences of debts by them respectively owing, and which shall appear by oath or affirmation (as the case may be) to have been the property of an indi-

---

[57] The President signed both of these bills on July 16, and the Senate was notified.
[58] On July 14 the Senate agreed to this conference and appointed its managers.

vidual or individuals, or body politic, other than a State, on the said first day of January last.—Provided, that no greater sum shall be received in the certificates of any State, than as follows—That is to say,

	Dollars
In those of New-Hampshire	300,000
In those of Massachusetts	4,000,000
In those of Rhode-Island and Providence Plantations	200,000
In those of Connecticut	1,600,000
In those of New-York	1,200,000
In those of New-Jersey	800,000
In those of Pennsylvania	2,200,000
In those of Delaware	200,000
In those of Maryland	800,000
In those of Virginia	3,200,000
In those of North-Carolina	2,200,000
In those of South-Carolina	4,000,000
In those of Georgia	300,000
	21,000,000

And provided that no such certificate shall be received which from the tenor thereof or from any public record, act or document, shall appear or can be ascertained to have been issued for any purpose other than compensations and expenditures for services or supplies towards the prosecution of the late war, and the defence of the United States, or of some part thereof during the same.

RESOLVED, That the interest upon the certificates which shall be received in payment of the sums subscribed towards the said loan, shall be computed to the last day of the year one thousand seven hundred and ninety-one inclusively; and the interest upon the stock which shall be created by virtue of the said loan, shall commence or begin to accrue on the first day of the year one thousand seven hundred and ninety-two, and shall be payable quarter yearly, at the same time, and in like manner as the interest on the stock to be created by the virtue of the loan that may be proposed in the domestic debt of the United States.

RESOLVED, That if the whole of the sum allowed to be subscribed in the debt or certificates of any State, as aforesaid, shall not be subscribed within the time for that purpose limited, such State shall be entitled to receive, and shall receive from the United States, at the rate of four per centum per annum, upon so much of the said sum as shall not have been so subscribed, in trust for the non subscribing creditors of such State; to be paid in like manner as the interest on the stock which may be created by virtue of the said loan, and to continue until there shall be a settlement of accounts between the United States and the individual States; and in case a balance shall then appear in favor of such State, until provision shall be made for the said balance.

But as certain States have respectively issued their own certificates, in exchange for those of the United States, whereby it might happen that interest might be twice payable on the same sums:

RESOLVED, That the payment of interest, whether to States or to individuals, in respect to the debt of any State, by which such exchange shall have been made, shall be suspended, until it shall appear to the satisfaction of the Secretary of the Treasury, that certificates issued for that purpose, by such State, have been re-exchanged or redeemed, or until those which shall not have been re-exchanged or redeemed, shall be surrendered to the United States.

And it is further,

RESOLVED, That the faith of the United States be, and the same is hereby pledged to make like provision for the payment of interest on the amount of the stock arising from subscriptions to the said loan, with the provision which shall be made touching the loan that may be proposed in the domestic debt of the United States; and so much of the debt of each State as shall be subscribed to the said loan, shall be a charge against such State, in account with the United States.[59]

It was agreed that the preamble should be postponed.

A motion was made to amend the first paragraph of the report as follows:

After the word "persons," in the third[60] line, strike out "and upon the same terms as in respect to the loans which may be proposed concerning the domestic debt of the United States," and insert after the word "mentioned," in the 5th[61] line, as follows: "And the subscribers shall receive certificates for the principal and interest of the sum so subscribed, one of which certificates shall purport, that the United States owe to the holder or holders thereof, his, her or their assigns, a sum equal to two thirds of the said sum so subscribed, bearing an interest of six per centum per annum, payable quarter yearly, and subject to redemption by payments, not exceeding in one year, on account both of principal and interest, the proportion of eight dollars upon a hundred of the sum mentioned in such certificate; and to another certificate, purporting that the United States owe to the holder or holders thereof, his, her or their assigns, a sum equal to twenty-six dollars and eighty-eight cents on every hundred dollars of the sum so subscribed, which, after the year one thousand eight hundred, shall bear an interest of six per centum per annum, payable quarter yearly, and subject to redemption by payments, not exceeding in one year, on account both of principal and interest, the proportion of eight dollars

---

[59] The text of this document was bound into the rough journal and the pages were numbered "482 A, 482 B, 482 C, and 482 D." The original heading of the document, "Congress of the United States/ In Senate July 14th 1790," is lined out, and the back of the last page, which originally served as a wrapper for the document, is endorsed "Resolve/Assumption."

[60] In the rough journal the word "Third" is canceled, and "5th." is interlined.

[61] In the rough journal the word "fifth" is canceled, and "10th" is interlined.

upon a hundred of the sum mentioned in such certificate: Provided always, that it shall not be understood, that the United States shall be bound or obliged to redeem in the proportion aforesaid, but it shall be understood only that they have a right so to do."[62]

On motion to postpone the amendment, to take the opinion of the Senate, Whether the debts of the individual States shall be assumed by the United States?

The motion for postponement passed in the Negative.

On motion to postpone the report of the Committee, to take up the Bill, entitled, "An Act making provision for the debt of the United States"—

It passed in the Negative.

On motion to agree to the original amendment, proposed to the report of the Committee—

It passed in the Negative.

On motion,

RESOLVED, That the rule prescribed for the SECOND reading of Bills, be adopted in considering this report of the Committee.[63]

On motion to strike out the words, "twenty-one millions of dollars," in the first paragraph of the report, and that it stand a blank—

It passed in the Negative.[64]

The Senate adjourned to 11 o'clock to-morrow.

WEDNESDAY, JULY 14, 1790

The SENATE assembled,
Present as yesterday.

Proceeded to consider the resolve of the House of Representatives of the 13th of July, proposing a conference on the third amendment of the Senate to the Bill, entitled, "An Act to regulate trade and intercourse with the Indian tribes"—and

RESOLVED, That the Senate agree to the proposed conference, and that

Mr. Schuyler
Mr. Ellsworth and
Mr. Strong be managers thereof on the part of the Senate.

---

[62] This motion is in Senate Simple Resolutions and Motions, Senate Records, DNA.

[63] This paragraph is on a slip pasted into the rough journal as a substitute for the following: "Resolved, that the Report of the Committee be considered agreeably to the rule by which Bills are considered in their/Second reading as if in/in [sic] Committee of the whole House—"

[64] On July 14 the preamble and four of the resolutions in this report were agreed to, and a motion to commit this report and the Funding Bill [HR–63] to a special committee was defeated.

ORDERED, That the Secretary communicate this vote of Senate to the House of Representatives.[65]

A message from the House of Representatives by Mr. Beckley their clerk:

"Mr. PRESIDENT,

"The House of Representatives have disagreed to all the amendments of the Senate, to the Bill, entitled, 'An Act to provide more effectually for the settlement of the accounts between the United States and the individual States,' they propose a conference on the amendments, and having appointed managers on their part, desire the concurrence of the Senate in their appointment of managers at the proposed conference"—

And he withdrew.

The Senate took into consideration the resolve of the House of Representatives of this day, proposing a conference on the Bill, entitled, "An Act to provide more effectually for the settlement of the accounts between the United States and the individual States."

RESOLVED, That the Senate agree to the conference, and that

   Mr. Ellsworth

   Mr. King and

   Mr. Lee be managers thereof, on the part of the Senate.

ORDERED, That the Secretary communicate this vote of Senate to the House of Representatives.[66]

The Senate resumed the consideration of the report of the Committee appointed July the 2d, on the motion, "That provision shall be made the next session of Congress, for loaning to the United States a sum, not exceeding twenty-two millions of dollars."

On motion to agree to the following paragraph of the report:

"RESOLVED, That a loan be proposed, to the amount of twenty-one millions of dollars, and that subscriptions to the said loan be received at the same times and places, by the same persons, and upon the same terms, as in respect to the loans which may be proposed concerning the domestic debt of the United States, subject to the exceptions and qualifications hereafter mentioned." The yeas and nays were required by one fifth of the Senators present:

Mr. Bassett	Nay
Mr. Butler	Yea
Mr. Carroll	Yea
Mr. Dalton	Yea
Mr. Ellsworth	Yea

[65] On July 19 this committee reported in the House which then receded from its disagreement to the amendment and notified the Senate.

[66] On July 21 this committee reported and the report was laid for consideration.

Mr. Elmer	Yea	
Mr. Few		Nay
Mr. Foster		Nay
Mr. Hawkins		Nay
Mr. Henry		Nay
Mr. Johnson	Yea	
Mr. Johnston		Nay
Mr. Izard	Yea	
Mr. King	Yea	
Mr. Langdon	Yea	
Mr. Lee		Nay
Mr. Maclay		Nay
Mr. Morris	Yea	
Mr. Paterson	Yea	
Mr. Read	Yea	
Mr. Schuyler	Yea	
Mr. Stanton		Nay
Mr. Strong	Yea	
Mr. Walker		Nay
Mr. Wingate		Nay

Yeas—14

Nays—11

So it passed in the Affirmative.

On motion, the paragraph of the report following the above, from the words, "and the sums," to the words "January last" inclusive, was agreed to.

A motion was made to add to the paragraph last agreed to, after the words "January last," "and in bills of the new emission money due from the States respectively,"—and

It passed in the Negative.

On motion, it was agreed to adopt the clauses of the report in course to the end of the schedule.

On motion to expunge the last paragraph of the first resolve reported, to wit: from the words "and provided," to the word "same," inclusive—

It passed in the Negative.

On the question to agree to this paragraph—

It passed in the Affirmative.

On motion, it was agreed to adopt the second resolution, to the reported words "United States," inclusive.

On motion to amend the third resolution, by striking out these reported words, "at the rate of four per centum per annum," and insert, "an interest per centum per annum, at the same rate as shall be allowed to the domestic creditors of the United States"—

It passed in the Negative.[67]

On motion to adopt the third resolution as follows:

"RESOLVED, That if the whole of the sum allowed to be subscribed in the debt or certificates of any State, as aforesaid, shall not be subscribed within the time for that purpose limited, such State shall be entitled to receive, and shall receive from the United States, at the rate of four per centum per annum, upon so much of the said sum as shall not have been so subscribed, in trust for the non-subscribing creditors of such State; to be paid in like manner as the interest on the stock which may be created by virtue of the said loan, and to continue until there shall be a settlement of accounts between the United States and the individual States; and in case a balance shall then appear in favor of such State, until provision shall be made for the said balance."

The yeas and nays were required by one fifth of the Senators present:

Mr. Bassett	Yea	
Mr. Butler		Nay
Mr. Carroll	Yea	
Mr. Dalton		Nay
Mr. Ellsworth	Yea	
Mr. Elmer		Nay
Mr. Few	Yea	
Mr. Foster		Nay
Mr. Gunn	Yea	
Mr. Hawkins	Yea	
Mr. Henry	Yea	
Mr. Johnson	Yea	
Mr. Johnston	Yea	
Mr. Izard	Yea	
Mr. King		Nay
Mr. Langdon		Nay
Mr. Lee	Yea	
Mr. Maclay	Yea	
Mr. Morris		Nay
Mr. Paterson		Nay
Mr. Read	Yea	
Mr. Schuyler		Nay
Mr. Stanton	Yea	
Mr. Strong		Nay

[67] This motion is in Senate Simple Resolutions and Motions, Senate Records, DNA.

Mr. Walker   Yea
Mr. Wingate   Nay
             Yeas—15
             Nays—11
        So it passed in the Affirmative.

On motion, the clauses of the report were agreed to, from the words "But as certain States," to the words "United States," in the fourth resolution.

On motion to expunge these words in the last resolution, to wit: "from subscriptions to the said loan," and insert the following words in their place, "under this act"—

        It passed in the Negative.

And on motion, the last resolution reported by the Committee was agreed to.

On motion to agree to the preamble of the report, the yeas and nays were required by one fifth of the Senators present:

Mr. Bassett   Nay
Mr. Butler   Yea
Mr. Carroll   Yea
Mr. Dalton   Yea
Mr. Ellsworth   Yea
Mr. Elmer   Yea
Mr. Few   Yea
Mr. Foster   Yea
Mr. Gunn   Nay
Mr. Hawkins   Nay
Mr. Henry   Nay
Mr. Johnson   Yea
Mr. Johnston   Nay
Mr. Izard   Yea
Mr. King   Yea
Mr. Langdon   Yea
Mr. Lee   Nay
Mr. Maclay   Nay
Mr. Morris   Yea
Mr. Paterson   Yea
Mr. Read   Yea
Mr. Schuyler   Yea
Mr. Stanton   Nay
Mr. Strong   Yea
Mr. Walker   Nay

Mr. Wingate   Nay
    Yeas—16
    Nays—10

So it passed in the Affirmative.

On motion, that this report, together with the Bill, entitled, "An Act making provision for the debt of the United States," be referred to a special Committee, the yeas and nays were required by one fifth of the Senators present:

Mr. Bassett		Nay
Mr. Butler	Yea	
Mr. Carroll		Nay
Mr. Dalton	Yea	
Mr. Ellsworth		Nay
Mr. Elmer		Nay
Mr. Few		Nay
Mr. Foster		Nay
Mr. Gunn	Yea	
Mr. Hawkins		Nay
Mr. Henry		Nay
Mr. Johnson	Yea	
Mr. Johnston		Nay
Mr. Izard	Yea	
Mr. King	Yea	
Mr. Langdon		Nay
Mr. Lee		Nay
Mr. Maclay		Nay
Mr. Morris	Yea	
Mr. Paterson	Yea	
Mr. Read		Nay
Mr. Schuyler	Yea	
Mr. Stanton		Nay
Mr. Strong	Yea	
Mr. Walker		Nay
Mr. Wingate		Nay

    Nays—16
    Yeas—10

So it passed in the Negative.

ORDERED, That the report of the Committee pass to another reading.[68]

The Senate adjourned to 11 o'clock to-morrow.

---

[68] On July 15 this report was read again and, along with the Funding Bill [HR–63], was committed to a special committee.

THURSDAY, JULY 15, 1790

The SENATE assembled,
Present as yesterday.

The report of the Committee on the motion "That provision shall be made the next session of Congress, for loaning to the United States a sum not exceeding twenty-two millions of dollars," was again read, and together with the Bill, entitled, "An Act making provision for the debt of the United States," was committed to   Mr. Butler
                                            Mr. Morris
                                            Mr. Read
                                            Mr. Ellsworth
                                            Mr. King
                                            Mr. Lee and
                                            Mr. Strong[69]

The Senate adjourned to 11 o'clock to-morrow.

FRIDAY, JULY 16, 1790

The SENATE assembled,
Present as yesterday.

A message from the President of the United States by his Secretary:

"Mr. PRESIDENT,

"The President of the United States has on this day approved of, and affixed his signature to the 'Act for establishing the temporary and permanent seat of the government of the United States' "—

And he withdrew.

A message from the House of Representatives by Mr. Beckley their clerk:

"Mr. PRESIDENT,

"The House of Representatives have passed a Bill, entitled, 'An Act to amend the Act for the establishment and support of light-houses, beacons, buoys and public piers,'[70] and a

"RESOLVE, 'That in the opinion of this House the business now depending before the two Houses, may be finished by Tuesday the 27th instant, and that

---

[69] On July 16 this committee reported and the report, with the exception of the recommendation that the resolutions on loans for the United States should be included in the Funding Bill, was accepted. This report, the report on the motion on a loan for the United States, and the Funding Bill were then recommitted so that the bill could be conformed to the principles in the reports.

[70] This bill has not been located.

it will be convenient and proper that an adjournment of the present session of Congress, should take place on that day;'[71] in which Bill and Resolve they desire the concurrence of the Senate—

"The President of the United States has notified the House of Representatives, that he has this day approved of, and affixed his signature to the 'Act further to provide for the payment of the invalid pensioners of the United States' "[72]—

And he withdrew.

ORDERED, That the Bill, entitled, "An Act to amend the Act for the establishment and support of light-houses, beacons, buoys, and public piers," be now read the FIRST time.

ORDERED, That this Bill pass to the SECOND reading.[73]

The resolve of the House of Representatives of this day, that Congress do adjourn on Tuesday the 27th instant, was read.

ORDERED, That it lie for consideration.[74]

Mr. Schuyler reported from the Committee appointed July the 9th,[75] on the Bill, entitled, "An Act providing for holding a treaty or treaties to establish peace with certain Indian tribes," which report was read, and it was agreed that the Bill should be amended accordingly.

ORDERED, That this Bill pass to the THIRD reading.[76]

Mr. Butler from the Committee appointed July the 15th, on the Bill, entitled, "An Act making provision for the debt of the United States," and to whom was committed the report of the Committee on the motion "That provision shall be made the next session of Congress, for loaning to the United States a sum not exceeding twenty-two millions of dollars," reported as follows:[77]

"That having maturely considered all circumstances, they are of opinion that the principal of the domestic debt should be funded agreeable to the third alternative in the report of the Secretary of the Treasury; and that the interest which may be due thereon, including indents, be funded at the rate of three per cent. per annum, and that whatever sum the Legislature may think proper

---

[71] This resolve is in Messages from the House, Senate Records, DNA.

[72] This message is in Committee on Enrolled Bills, Senate Records, DNA.

[73] On July 17 this bill was read for the second time.

[74] On August 6 the House passed another resolution on adjournment and notified the Senate. The resolution was then read and laid for consideration.

[75] This report is in Various Select Committee Reports, Senate Records, DNA.

[76] On July 17 this bill was read a third time and passed with an amendment. The concurrence of the House was then requested.

[77] This report, initialed by Pierce Butler, is in Various Select Committee Reports, Senate Records, DNA. The order that followed it is included. A draft of the report is in the Pierce Butler Papers, PHi.

to assume of the States debts, be funded at the proportion of two thirds thereof, agreeable to the third alternative in the Secretary's report, and the other third at three per cent. per annum.

"Your Committee further recommend, that the resolutions for the assumption, be added to the funding Bill, and the whole made one system"—

And it was agreed to adopt this report, except the last clause—and on the question to agree to the last clause, to wit: "Your Committee further recommend, that the resolutions for the assumption, be added to the funding Bill, and the whole made one system," the yeas and nays were required by one fifth of the Senators present:

Mr. Bassett		Nay
Mr. Butler	Yea	
Mr. Carroll	Yea	
Mr. Dalton	Yea	
Mr. Ellsworth	Yea	
Mr. Elmer	Yea	
Mr. Few	Yea	
Mr. Foster		Nay
Mr. Gunn		Nay
Mr. Hawkins		Nay
Mr. Henry		Nay
Mr. Johnson	Yea	
Mr. Johnston		Nay
Mr. Izard	Yea	
Mr. King	Yea	
Mr. Langdon	Yea	
Mr. Lee		Nay
Mr. Maclay		Nay
Mr. Morris	Yea	
Mr. Paterson	Yea	
Mr. Read	Yea	
Mr. Schuyler	Yea	
Mr. Stanton		Nay
Mr. Strong	Yea	
Mr. Walker		Nay
Mr. Wingate		Nay

Yeas—15
Nays—11

It passed in the Affirmative, and the report was agreed to.

ORDERED, That the report committed July the 15th, the report now agreed to, together with the Bill, entitled, "An Act making provision for the debt of the United States," be re-committed, with an instruction to the Committee to conform the Bill to the principles of the reports.[78]

The Senate adjourned to 11 o'clock to-morrow.

SATURDAY, JULY 17, 1790

The SENATE assembled,
Present as yesterday.

The petition of Donald Campbell was read,[79] praying for compensation for services and supplies during the late war.

ORDERED, That it be committed to

Mr. Wingate
Mr. Maclay and
Mr. Elmer[80]

The Senate proceeded to the THIRD reading of the Bill, entitled, "An Act providing for holding a treaty or treaties to establish peace with certain Indian tribes."

RESOLVED, That this Bill DO PASS with an amendment.[81]

ORDERED, That the Secretary communicate this amendment to the House of Representatives, and desire their concurrence therein.[82]

The Senate proceeded to the SECOND reading of the Bill, entitled, "An Act to amend the Act for the establishment and support of light-houses, beacons, buoys and public piers."

ORDERED, That this Bill pass to the THIRD reading.[83]

Mr. Wingate from the Committee on enrolled Bills, reported, That they had examined the Bill, entitled, "An Act for the government and regulation of seamen in the merchants service,"[84] and the Bill, entitled, "An Act imposing duties on the tonnage of ships or vessels,"[85] and had found them correct.

Mr. Butler from the Committee to whom was re-committed the Bill, en-

---

[78] On July 17 this committee reported amendments to the Funding Bill to make it conform to the reports and the bill was ordered to be printed.

[79] The petition, with enclosures and the order committing it, is in Petitions and Memorials: Claims, Senate Records, DNA.

[80] On July 27 this committee reported, and the report was tabled.

[81] The rough journal includes the text of the amendment as follows: "Line 6th. After the word 'treaties,' insert 'And for promoting a friendly intercourse and preserving peace.'" The smooth journal inserts the following marginal notation: "(For the Amendment See Original Minutes Page 510)."

[82] On July 17 the House concurred in this amendment, and the Senate was notified on July 19.

[83] On July 19 this bill was read a third time and passed.

[84] The inspected enrolled bill is in Enrolled Acts, RG 11, DNA. E–23849.

[85] The inspected enrolled bill is in Enrolled Acts, RG 11, DNA. E–22963.

titled, "An Act making provision for the debt of the United States," reported the Bill,[86] amended upon the principles agreed on yesterday.

ORDERED, That the Bill as amended by the Committee, be printed for the consideration of the Senate.[87]

A message from the House of Representatives by Mr. Beckley their clerk:

"Mr. PRESIDENT,

"The Speaker of the House of Representatives having signed several enrolled Bills, I am directed to bring them to the Senate, for the signature of the Vice President"—

And he withdrew.

Whereupon the Vice President signed the enrolled Bill, entitled, "An Act imposing duties on the tonnage of ships or vessels," and the enrolled Bill, entitled, "An Act for the government and regulation of seamen in the merchants service," and they were delivered to the Committee to be laid before the President of the United States, for his approbation.[88]

The Senate adjourned to 11 o'clock on Monday next.

MONDAY, JULY 19, 1790

The SENATE assembled,
Present as on the 17th.

The petition of John F. Amelung was read,[89] praying for "a grant of a certain number of acres of land in that extensive tract which the State of Carolina has ceded to the United States, free of taxes for   years, to build two or three glass-houses upon."

ORDERED, That this petition lie on the table.

The Senate proceeded to the THIRD reading of the Bill, entitled, "An Act to amend the Act for the establishment and support of light-houses, beacons, buoys and public piers."

RESOLVED, That this Bill DO PASS.

ORDERED, That the Secretary acquaint the House of Representatives therewith.[90]

A message from the House of Representatives by Mr. Beckley their clerk:

---

[86] The annotated printed bill is in House Bills, Senate Records, DNA. E–46047, fourteen sections.

[87] On July 19 the amendments in the committee report were agreed to, and the third reading of the bill was begun. Several amendments were proposed and voted upon. Consideration was then postponed.

[88] On July 20 the President signed these bills, and the Senate was notified.

[89] This petition is in Petitions and Memorials: Various subjects, Senate Records, DNA.

[90] On July 20 this bill was signed by both the Speaker and the Vice President and given to the committee on enrolled bills for delivery to the President.

"Mr. PRESIDENT,

"The House of Representatives have passed a Bill, entitled, 'An Act to provide more effectually for the collection of the duties imposed by law on goods, wares and merchandize imported into the United States, and on the tonnage of ships or vessels,'[91] and a resolve, providing for the salaries of the clerks in the office of the commissioner of army accounts,[92] to which they desire the concurrence of the Senate—

"They have agreed to the amendment proposed by the Senate, to the Bill, entitled, 'An Act providing for holding a treaty or treaties to establish peace with certain Indian tribes'[93]—

"They have passed a Bill, entitled, 'An Act making further provision for the payment of the debts of the United States,'[94] to which they desire the concurrence of the Senate—

"And they have agreed to the third amendment of the Senate, to the Bill, entitled, 'An Act to regulate trade and intercourse with the Indian tribes' "[95]—

And he withdrew.

The Senate proceeded to consider the report of the Committee, to whom was re-committed the Bill, entitled, "An Act making provision for the debt of the United States," and the report thereon, which report being read, it was agreed to amend the Bill accordingly.

The Senate proceeded in the THIRD reading of the Bill, entitled, "An Act making provision for the debt of the United States," and agreed to sundry amendments.[96]

---

[91] This bill has not been located. A sixty-eight page printed copy of a bill entitled "A Bill to regulate the collection of duties on imposts and tonnage," located in American Imprints, 1790, Folio, United States Laws and Statutes, RBkRm, DLC, has been incorrectly cited as a document dating from 1790. This date is impossible because the text refers to the states of Kentucky and Tennessee which were not admitted to the union until 1792 and 1796, respectively. Unfortunately this tentative citation was also used in Shipton and Mooney's *National Index of American Imprints through 1800, The Short-Title Evans*, and thus will be classified as a 1790 document in the microprint edition. On July 20 this bill was committed before the first reading.

[92] This resolve has not been located. On July 20 this resolve was read.

[93] On July 20 this bill was signed by both the Speaker and the Vice President and given to the committee on enrolled bills for delivery to the President.

[94] A printed copy of this bill, as it passed the House, is in House Bills, Senate Records, DNA. E-46027. On July 20 this bill was read a second time.

[95] On July 20 this bill was signed by both the Speaker and the Vice President and given to the committee on enrolled bills for delivery to the President.

[96] Attached to the printed bill, located in House Bills, Senate Records, DNA, is a list of all the amendments that were passed during the third reading of the bill. The rough journal reads: "The Senate proceeded in the/Third reading/of the bill entitled 'An Act making Provision for the Debt of the United States'—and agreed—Section 3d./line 7. to Strike out 'September' and insert 'October'—[line] 8. to strike out 'August' and insert 'September'—Line 10th to strike out *'said'* & after 'December' to insert [*conclusion lacking*] and Line 23. To strike out 'Those which shall be issued for' & 'insert and in.' "

On motion further to amend the Bill, section third, and provide for funding of the bills of credit issued by the authority of the United States, at the
rate of forty for one, the yeas and nays were required by one fifth of the Senators present:

Mr. Bassett		Nay
Mr. Butler		Nay
Mr. Carroll		Nay
Mr. Dalton	Yea	
Mr. Ellsworth		Nay
Mr. Elmer		Nay
Mr. Few		Nay
Mr. Foster	Yea	
Mr. Gunn		Nay
Mr. Hawkins		Nay
Mr. Henry		Nay
Mr. Johnston		Nay
Mr. Izard		Nay
Mr. King	Yea	
Mr. Langdon	Yea	
Mr. Lee		Nay
Mr. Maclay		Nay
Mr. Morris	Yea	
Mr. Paterson	Yea	
Mr. Read		Nay
Mr. Schuyler	Yea	
Mr. Stanton		Nay
Mr. Strong	Yea	
Mr. Walker		Nay
Mr. Wingate	Yea	

Nays—16
Yeas—9

So it passed in the Negative.

On motion to amend the Bill, so as that the above mentioned bills of credit
be funded at the rate of seventy-five for one—

It passed in the Negative.

And it was agreed, line 23d, to strike out "seventy-five," and fund the said
bills of credit at the rate of one hundred for one; and to strike out from the
original Bill the proviso in the third section.[97]

---

[97] The rough journal reads: "to strike out from the original bill that following
Proviso 'Provided that the interest which shall have been paid on Certificates of either of
the above descriptions by any State, and endorsed thereon by the Officers of such State,
shall not be computed and funded as aforesaid. And certificates shall be issued for the
amount of interest which shall appear to have been paid by such State, in the like
manner as if indents had been originally given for the same'—"

It was agreed to strike out the whole of section fourth, and insert section fourth and fifth amended.[98]

On motion to amend section fourth of the amendment, to read as follows: "And be it further enacted, That for the whole or any part of any sum subscribed to the said loan by any person or persons, or body politic, which shall be paid in the principal of the said domestic debt, the subscriber or subscribers shall be entitled to a certificate purporting that the United States owe to the holder or holders thereof, his, her or their assigns, a sum to be expressed therein equal to the sum so paid, bearing an interest of six per centum per annum, payable quarter yearly, and subject to redemption by payments, not exceeding in one year, on account both of principal and interest, the proportion of seven dollars upon a hundred of the sum mentioned in such certificate: Provided always, that it shall not be understood, that the United States shall be bound or obliged to redeem in the proportion aforesaid, but it shall be understood only that they have a right so to do," the yeas and nays were required by one fifth of the Senators present:

Mr. Bassett		Nay
Mr. Butler		Nay
Mr. Carroll		Nay
Mr. Dalton		Nay
Mr. Ellsworth		Nay
Mr. Elmer		Nay
Mr. Few		Nay
Mr. Foster		Nay
Mr. Gunn	Yea	
Mr. Hawkins		Nay

[98] The rough journal adds the following to section fourth amended:

a. "two thirds of" is inserted between "equal to" and "the sum" in line 6.

b. "& to another Certificate purporting that the United States owe to the holder or holders thereof, his, her or their Assigns a sum to be expressed therein equal to the proportion of 26 Dolls. & 88 Cents upon a 100 of the sum so paid which after the year 1800 shall bear an interest of 6 per Centum per Annum payable quarter yearly & subject to redemption by payments not exceeding in one year on account both of Principal & Interest the proportion of 7 dolls. upon a 100 of the sum mentioned in such Certificate;" is inserted between "such certificate" and "Provided" lines 9–10.

The rough journal also contains section fifth amended as follows:

Sect 5. And be it further enacted, that for the whole or any part of any sum subscribed to the said Loan by any person or Persons or body politic which shall be paid in the interest of the said domestic Debt computed to the said last day of December next, or in the said Certificates issued in payment of interest commonly called Indents of interest, the subscriber or subscribers shall be entitled to a Certificate purporting that the United States owe to the holder or holders thereof his, her or their Assigns a sum to be specified therein equal to that by him, her or them so paid bearing an interest of three per Centum per Annum payable quarter yearly & subject to redemption by payment of the sum specified therein whenever provision shall be made by law for that purpose.

Mr. Henry		Nay
Mr. Johnston		Nay
Mr. Izard		Nay
Mr. King	Yea	
Mr. Langdon		Nay
Mr. Lee		Nay
Mr. Maclay		Nay
Mr. Morris	Yea	
Mr. Paterson	Yea	
Mr. Read		Nay
Mr. Schuyler	Yea	
Mr. Stanton		Nay
Mr. Strong		Nay
Mr. Walker	Yea	
Mr. Wingate		Nay

Nays—19
Yeas—6

So it passed in the Negative.

On motion to amend the first clause of the amendment agreed to, section fourth, to read thus: "And be it further enacted, That for the whole or any part of any sum subscribed to the said loan by any person or persons, or body politic, which shall be paid in the principal and interest of the said domestic debt," so as to enable the subscribers to the loan to pay their subscription in *interest*, as well as *principal*, the yeas and nays were required by one fifth of the Senators present:

Mr. Bassett		Nay
Mr. Butler		Nay
Mr. Carroll		Nay
Mr. Dalton		Nay
Mr. Ellsworth		Nay
Mr. Elmer		Nay
Mr. Few	Yea	
Mr. Foster		Nay
Mr. Gunn		Nay
Mr. Hawkins	Yea	
Mr. Henry		Nay
Mr. Johnston		Nay
Mr. Izard		Nay
Mr. King	Yea	
Mr. Langdon	Yea	
Mr. Lee		Nay
Mr. Maclay		Nay

Mr. Morris	Yea	
Mr. Paterson	Yea	
Mr. Read		Nay
Mr. Schuyler	Yea	
Mr. Stanton		Nay
Mr. Strong		Nay
Mr. Walker	Yea	
Mr. Wingate		Nay

Nays—17

Yeas—8

So it passed in the Negative.

On motion to amend the amendment agreed to, so that the fourth section may provide that the second certificate given the subscriber, should entitle him to "a sum to be expressed therein, equal to the proportion of thirty-three and one third dollars, instead of twenty-six dollars and eighty-eight cents, upon one hundred of the sum so paid, which after the year 1800 shall bear an interest of six per cent." the yeas and nays were required by one fifth of the Senators present:

Mr. Bassett		Nay
Mr. Butler	Yea	
Mr. Carroll		Nay
Mr. Dalton		Nay
Mr. Ellsworth		Nay
Mr. Elmer	Yea	
Mr. Few		Nay
Mr. Foster		Nay
Mr. Hawkins		Nay
Mr. Henry	Yea	
Mr. Johnston		Nay
Mr. Izard		Nay
Mr. King	Yea	
Mr. Langdon	Yea	
Mr. Lee		Nay
Mr. Maclay		Nay
Mr. Morris	Yea	
Mr. Paterson	Yea	
Mr. Read		Nay
Mr. Schuyler	Yea	
Mr. Stanton		Nay
Mr. Strong		Nay
Mr. Walker	Yea	
Mr. Wingate		Nay

Nays—15
Yeas—9

So it passed in the Negative.

On motion to amend section fourth of the amendment agreed to, as follows: "And be it further enacted, That for the whole or any part of any sum subscribed to the said loan by any person or persons, or body politic, which shall be paid in the principal of the said domestic debt, the subscriber or subscribers shall be entitled to a certificate purporting that the United States owe to the holder or holders thereof, his, her or their assigns, the whole of the sum by him, her or them subscribed, bearing an interest of four per centum per annum, payable quarter yearly, and subject to redemption by payments, not exceeding in one year, on account both of principal and interest, the proportion of six dollars upon a hundred of the said sum: Provided, that it shall not be understood, that the United States shall be bound or obliged to redeem in the proportion aforesaid, but it shall be understood only that they have a right so to do," the yeas and nays were required by one fifth of the Senators present:

Mr. Bassett		Yea
Mr. Butler	Nay	
Mr. Carroll	Nay	
Mr. Dalton	Nay	
Mr. Ellsworth	Nay	
Mr. Elmer	Nay	
Mr. Few		Yea
Mr. Foster		Yea
Mr. Gunn	Nay	
Mr. Hawkins		Yea
Mr. Henry	Nay	
Mr. Johnston		Yea
Mr. Izard	Nay	
Mr. King	Nay	
Mr. Langdon	Nay	
Mr. Lee	Nay	
Mr. Maclay		Yea
Mr. Morris	Nay	
Mr. Paterson	Nay	
Mr. Read	Nay	
Mr. Schuyler	Nay	
Mr. Stanton		Yea
Mr. Strong	Nay	
Mr. Walker	Nay	
Mr. Wingate		Yea

Nays—17

Yeas—8

So it passed in the Negative.

On motion to amend the last clause of the last amendment agreed to, to wit, of section fifth, so as to entitle the subscriber, for any sum subscribed to the said loan, and which shall be paid in the *interest* of the domestic debt, to a certificate for such sum subscribed, bearing an interest of six per cent. the yeas and nays were required by one fifth of the Senators present:

Mr. Bassett		Nay
Mr. Butler		Nay
Mr. Carroll		Nay
Mr. Dalton		Nay
Mr. Ellsworth		Nay
Mr. Elmer		Nay
Mr. Few		Nay
Mr. Foster		Nay
Mr. Gunn		Nay
Mr. Hawkins		Nay
Mr. Henry		Nay
Mr. Johnston		Nay
Mr. Izard		Nay
Mr. King	Yea	
Mr. Langdon		Nay
Mr. Lee		Nay
Mr. Maclay		Nay
Mr. Morris	Yea	
Mr. Paterson	Yea	
Mr. Read		Nay
Mr. Schuyler	Yea	
Mr. Stanton		Nay
Mr. Strong		Nay
Mr. Walker	Yea	
Mr. Wingate		Nay

Nays—20

Yeas—5

So it passed in the Negative.

On motion to amend the last clause of the last amendment agreed to, to wit, of section fifth, so as to entitle the subscribers, for any sum subscribed to the said loan, and which shall be paid in the *interest* of the domestic debt, to a certificate for the sum subscribed, bearing an interest of four per cent. the yeas and nays were required by one fifth of the Senators present:

Mr. Bassett		Nay
Mr. Butler		Nay
Mr. Carroll		Nay
Mr. Dalton		Nay
Mr. Ellsworth		Nay
Mr. Elmer	Yea	
Mr. Few		Nay
Mr. Foster		Nay
Mr. Gunn		Nay
Mr. Hawkins		Nay
Mr. Henry	Yea	
Mr. Johnston		Nay
Mr. Izard		Nay
Mr. King	Yea	
Mr. Langdon	Yea	
Mr. Lee		Nay
Mr. Maclay		Nay
Mr. Morris	Yea	
Mr. Paterson	Yea	
Mr. Read		Nay
Mr. Schuyler	Yea	
Mr. Stanton		Nay
Mr. Strong		Nay
Mr. Walker	Yea	
Mr. Wingate		Nay

Nays—17

Yeas—8

So it passed in the Negative.

Sundry other amendments being agreed to[99]—

---

[99] The rough journal describes these amendments thus:

It was agreed Section 5th. of the Original Bill, line 5 & 6, to strike out these words "As well for land as stock, to record such as shall be issued for land."

Section 7th Line 6 of Original bill. It was agreed to strike out "of" and insert "for"—

On Motion to strike out these words from Section 7th. Original bill. "But if the interest for any one quarter shall not be demanded before the expiration of a third quarter, the same shall be afterwards demandable only at the Treasury"

It passed in the Negative.

It was agreed to expunge Section 8, of the original bill, and in

Section 10th of the Original bill, line 6th. to expunge the word "*four*" and insert the words "and interest—" and in the same section, Line 7th after the word "amounts" to insert "equal to that payable to subscribing creditors."

It was agreed to insert—Section 11th of the Original bill, between lines 5 & 6,

"The commissioner for the State of Rhode Island & Providence Plantations 600 Dollars."

ORDERED, That the further consideration of this Bill be postponed until to-morrow.[100]

The Senate adjourned to 11 o'clock to-morrow.

TUESDAY, JULY 20, 1790

The SENATE assembled,
Present as yesterday.

Mr. Wingate from the Committee on enrolled Bills, reported, That they had examined the enrolled Bill, entitled, "An Act to amend the Act for the establishment and support of light-houses, beacons, buoys and public piers,"[101] and the enrolled Bill, entitled, "An Act providing for holding a treaty or treaties to establish peace with certain Indian tribes,"[102] and to the enrolled Bill, entitled, "An Act to regulate trade and intercourse with the Indian tribes,"[103] and had found them correct.

The Senate agreed to dispense with the rules, so far as that the Bill, entitled, "An Act to provide more effectually for the collection of the duties imposed by law on goods, wares and merchandize imported into the United States, and on the tonnage of ships or vessels," be referred to

> Mr. Morris
> Mr. Langdon
> Mr. Dalton
> Mr. Foster and
> Mr. Henry, prior to the FIRST reading, to consider

and report thereon.[104]

A message from the House of Representatives by Mr. Beckley their clerk:

"Mr. PRESIDENT,

"The House of Representatives have passed a Bill, entitled, 'An Act to enable the officers and soldiers of the Virginia line, on continental establishment, to obtain titles to certain lands lying north-west of the river Ohio, between the little Miami and Sciota.'[105]—

"The Speaker of the House of Representatives having signed several enrolled Bills, I am directed to bring them to the Senate, for the signature of the Vice President—

"The President of the United States has notified the House of Representa-

---

[100] On July 20 the third reading of this bill was continued, and one amendment to it was defeated while several others were passed. Consideration was then postponed.

[101] The inspected enrolled bill is in Enrolled Acts, RG 11, DNA. E–22967.

[102] The inspected enrolled bill is in Enrolled Acts, RG 11, DNA. E–22966.

[103] The inspected enrolled bill is in Enrolled Acts, RG 11, DNA. E–22971.

[104] On July 22 this committee reported, and the bill was read a second time and considered. On the same day the House sent the Senate some papers related to this bill.

[105] This bill has not been located.

tives, that he has approved of, and affixed his signature to 'An Act imposing duties on the tonnage of ships or vessels,' and to 'An Act for the government and regulation of seamen in the merchants service' "—

And he withdrew.

The Vice President signed the enrolled Bill, entitled, "An Act to amend the Act for the establishment and support of light-houses, beacons, buoys and public piers," the enrolled Bill, entitled, "An Act providing for holding a treaty or treaties to establish peace with certain Indian tribes," and to the enrolled Bill, entitled, "An Act to regulate trade and intercourse with the Indian tribes," and they were delivered to the Committee on enrolled Bills, to be laid before the President of the United States, for his approbation.[106]

The Senate proceeded in the THIRD reading of the Bill, entitled, "An Act making provision for the debt of the United States."[107]

On motion to strike out the following sections reported by the Committee:

"Sect. 13. And whereas a provision for the debts of the respective States, by the United States, would be greatly conducive to an orderly, economical and effectual arrangement of the public finances:[108]

"Be it therefore further enacted, That a loan be proposed to the amount of twenty-one million and five hundred thousand dollars, and that subscriptions to the said loan be received at the same times and places, and by the same persons, as in respect to the loan herein before proposed concerning the domestic debt of the United States. And that the sums which shall be subscribed to the said loan, shall be payable in the principal and interest of the certificates or notes, which, prior to the first day of January last, were issued by the respective States, as acknowledgements or evidences of debts by them respectively owing: Provided, That no greater sum shall be received in the certificates of any State than as follows; that is to say,

	Dollars
In those of New-Hampshire	300,000
In those of Massachusetts	4,000,000

---

[106] On July 21 this committee reported that it had delivered these bills to the President on July 20.

[107] In the rough journal five sheets endorsed "Congress of the United States / In Senate July the 1st. 1790" are bound into the volume. The text which follows in the printed journal above, including the roll-call vote, appears on these sheets with markings indicating where it should be inserted in the Journal.

[108] The text of the bill in the rough journal includes the following canceled phrases at this point: *"would tend to an equal distribution of the burthens among the Citizens of the several States—would promote more general justice to the different classes of public creditors, and would serve to give stability to public credit: whereas the said debts having been essentially contracted in the prosecution of the late war, it is just that such provision should be made."* A marginal notation reading "Between Section 10 & 11th insert" has been lined out, and another reading "End of the Bill—add" has been written below it.

In those of Rhode-Island and Providence Plantations	200,000
In those of Connecticut	1,600,000
In those of New-York	1,200,000
In those of New-Jersey	800,000
In those of Pennsylvania	2,200,000
In those of Delaware	200,000
In those of Maryland	800,000
In those of Virginia	3,500,000
In those of North-Carolina	2,400,000
In those of South-Carolina	4,000,000
In those of Georgia	300,000
	21,500,000

"And provided that no such certificate shall be received, which, from the tenor thereof, or from any public record, act or document, shall appear, or can be ascertained to have been issued for any purpose other than compensations and expenditures for services or supplies towards the prosecution of the late war, and the defence of the United States, or of some part thereof during the same.

"Sect. 14. And be it further enacted, That for two thirds of any sum subscribed to the said loan by any person or persons, or body politic, which shall be paid in the principal and interest of the certificates or notes issued as aforesaid by the respective States, the subscriber or subscribers shall be entitled to a certificate, purporting that the United States owe to the holder or holders thereof, or his, her or their assigns, a sum to be expressed therein, equal to two thirds of the aforesaid two thirds, bearing an interest of six per centum per annum, payable quarter yearly, and subject to redemption by payments, not exceeding in one year, on account both of principal and interest, the proportion of seven dollars upon a hundred of the sum mentioned in such certificate, and to another certificate, purporting that the United States owe to the holder or holders thereof, his, her or their assigns, a sum to be expressed therein, equal to the proportion of twenty-six dollars and eighty-eight cents upon a hundred of the said two thirds of such sum so subscribed, which, after the year one thousand eight hundred, shall bear an interest of six per centum per annum, payable quarter yearly, and subject to redemption by payments, not exceeding in one year, on account both of principal and interest, the proportion of seven dollars upon a hundred of the sum mentioned in such certificate; and that for the remaining third of any sum so subscribed, the subscriber or subscribers shall be entitled to a certificate, purporting that the United States owe to the holder or holders thereof, his, her or their assigns, a sum to be expressed therein, equal to the said remaining third, bearing an interest of three per centum per annum, payable quarter yearly, and subject to redemption by payment of the sum specified therein whenever provision shall be made by law for that purpose.

"Sect. 15. And be it further enacted, that the interest upon the certificates which shall be received in payment of the sums subscribed towards the said loan, shall be computed to the last day of the year one thousand seven hundred and ninety-one, inclusively; and the interest upon the stock which shall be created by virtue of the said loan, shall commence or begin to accrue on the first day of the year one thousand seven hundred and ninety-two, and shall be payable quarter yearly, at the same time, and in like manner as the interest on the stock to be created by virtue of the loan above proposed in the domestic debt of the United States.

"Sect. 16. And be it further enacted, That if the whole sum allowed to be subscribed in the debt or certificates of any State, as aforesaid, shall not be subscribed within the time for that purpose limited, such State shall be entitled to receive, and shall receive from the United States, at the rate of four per centum per annum, upon so much of the said sum as shall not have been so subscribed, in trust for the non-subscribing creditors of such State, who are holders of certificates or notes issued on account of services or supplies towards the prosecution of the late war, and the defence of the United States, or of some part thereof, to be paid in like manner as the interest on the stock which may be created by virtue of the said loan, and to continue until there shall be a settlement of accounts between the United States and the individual States; and in case a balance shall then appear in favor of such State, until provision shall be made for the said balance.

"Sect. 17. But as certain States have respectively issued their own certificates, in exchange for those of the United States, whereby it might happen, that interest might be twice payable on the same sums:

"Be it further enacted, That the payment of interest, whether to States or to individuals, in respect to the debt of any State, by which such exchange shall have been made, shall be suspended, until it shall appear to the satisfaction of the Secretary of the Treasury, that certificates issued for that purpose by such State, have been re-exchanged or redeemed, or until those which shall not have been re-exchanged or redeemed, shall be surrendered to the United States.

"Sect. 18. And be it further enacted, That so much of the debt of each State as shall be subscribed to the said loan, shall be charged against such State, in account with the United States"—

The yeas and nays were required by one fifth of the Senators present:

Mr. Bassett		Yea
Mr. Butler	Nay	
Mr. Carroll	Nay	
Mr. Dalton	Nay	

Mr. Ellsworth	Nay	
Mr. Elmer	Nay	
Mr. Few		Yea
Mr. Foster		Yea
Mr. Gunn		Yea
Mr. Hawkins		Yea
Mr. Henry		Yea
Mr. Johnson	Nay	
Mr. Johnston		Yea
Mr. Izard	Nay	
Mr. King	Nay	
Mr. Langdon	Nay	
Mr. Lee		Yea
Mr. Maclay		Yea
Mr. Morris	Nay	
Mr. Paterson	Nay	
Mr. Read	Nay	
Mr. Schuyler	Nay	
Mr. Stanton		Yea
Mr. Strong	Nay	
Mr. Walker		Yea
Mr. Wingate		Yea

Nays—14

Yeas—12

So it passed in the Negative.

Sundry other amendments being agreed to[109]—

---

[109] The rough journal substitutes the following for this line:

On Motion it being agreed to subjoin the following Sections as amendments to the bill to wit:

A Motion was made to strike out 300,000 dollars out of Section 13th. of the Amendment agreed to next following the word "Hampshire" and insert "400,000 dollars."

It passed in the Negative.

On Motion in the same Section after the words "In those of New York" to strike out "1,200,000" and insert "1,400,000—"

It passed in the Negative.

On Motion to expunge the 16th Section agreed to as an Amendment to the bill.

It passed in the Negative.

It was agreed to amend Section the 16th. line 4th. & strike out "*at the rate of*" and insert "and Interest" and

After the word "subscribed" in the 6th. line to insert "Equal to that which would have accrued on the deficiency had the same been subscribed."

It was agreed to amend Section 10th. after "1794" by striking out "an interest" & inserting "a rate."

In the 4th. line after the word "next" to amend the amendment to read thus: "equal to the interest payable to subscribing Creditors—"

ORDERED, That the further consideration of this Bill be postponed.[110]

The Senate proceeded to the FIRST reading of the Bill, entitled, "An Act making further provision for the payment of the debts of the United States."

ORDERED, That this Bill pass to a SECOND reading.[111]

The Senate proceeded to the FIRST reading of the Bill, entitled, "An Act to enable the officers and soldiers of the Virginia line, on continental establish-

---

On Motion to insert Section 16th. between the words "limited" and "such" these words "The Commissioner to be appointed for"

It passed in the Negative.

On Motion to add this proviso to Section 16th. "Provided always that each State which shall receive any Interest in trust as aforesaid shall report to the Secretary of the Treasury (annually) the expenditure of such Interest."

It passed in the Negative.

Section 12th. of Amendment. It was agreed to insert after "bound" these words "except certificates issued by the Commissioners of army accounts in the State of North Carolina in the year 1786."

Section 18th. of the Amendment after the word "Loan" it was agreed to insert "and the Monies (if any) that shall be advanced to the same pursuant to this Act."

And it was agreed to add the following as Sections 19, 20, and 21 to the bill to wit:

Sec. 19. *And be it further enacted,* That the monies arising under the revenue laws, which have been, or during the present session of Congress, may be passed or so much thereof, as may be necessary, shall be, and are hereby pledged and appropriated for the payment of the interest on the stock which shall be created by the loans aforesaid, pursuant to the provisions of this act, first paying that which shall arise on the stock created by virtue of the said first mentioned loan, to continue so pledged and appropriated, until the final redemption of the said stock, any law to the contrary notwithstanding, subject nevertheless to such reservations and priorities, as may be requisite to satisfy the appropriations heretofore made, and which during the present session of Congress may be made by law, including the sums herein before reserved and appropriated; and to the end, that the said monies may be inviolably applied in conformity to this act, and may never be diverted to any other purpose, an account shall be kept of the receipts and disposition thereof, separate and distinct from the product of any other duties, imposts, excises and taxes whatsoever, except such as may be hereafter laid, to make good any deficiency which may be found in the product thereof towards satisfying the interest aforesaid.

Sec. 20. *And be it further enacted,* That the faith of the United States be, and the same is hereby pledged to provide and appropriate hereafter such additional and permanent funds as may be requisite towards supplying any such deficiency, and making full provision for the payment of the interest which shall accrue on the stock to be created by virtue of the loans aforesaid, in conformity to the terms thereof respectively, and according to the tenor of the certificates to be granted for the same pursuant to this act.

Sec. 21. *And be it further enacted,* That the proceeds of the sales which shall be made of lands in the Western Territory, now belonging, or that may hereafter belong to the United States, shall be, and are hereby appropriated towards sinking or discharging the debts, for the payment whereof the United States now are, or by virtue of this act may be holden, and shall be applied solely to that use until the said debts shall be fully satisfied.

[110] On July 21 the third reading of this bill was continued and it was passed with amendments. The bill was then returned to the House for concurrence in the amendments.

[111] On July 21 this bill was read a second time and committed.

ment, to obtain titles to certain lands lying north-west of the river Ohio, between the little Miami and Sciota."

ORDERED, That this Bill pass to a SECOND reading.[112]

The "Resolve providing for the salaries of the clerks in the office of the Commissioner of army accounts" was read, and

ORDERED, To lie for consideration.[113]

The Senate adjourned to 11 o'clock to-morrow.

WEDNESDAY, JULY 21, 1790

The SENATE assembled,

Present as yesterday.

Mr. Wingate from the Committee on enrolled Bills, reported, That they did yesterday lay before the President of the United States, for his approbation, the enrolled Bill, entitled, "An Act to amend the Act for the establishment and support of light-houses, beacons, buoys and public piers," the enrolled Bill, entitled, "An Act providing for holding a treaty or treaties to establish peace with certain Indian tribes," and the enrolled Bill, entitled, "An Act to regulate trade and intercourse with the Indian tribes."[114]

The Senate proceeded to the SECOND reading of the Bill, entitled, "An Act making further provision for the payment of the debts of the United States."

ORDERED, That this Bill be committed to

> Mr. Lee
> Mr. Izard
> Mr. Morris
> Mr. Ellsworth and
> Mr. Few[115]

Proceeded to the SECOND reading of the Bill, entitled, "An Act to enable the officers and soldiers of the Virginia line, on continental establishment, to obtain titles to certain lands lying north-west of the river Ohio, between the little Miami and Sciota."

ORDERED, That this Bill be committed to

> Mr. Lee
> Mr. Strong and
> Mr. Ellsworth[116]

A message from the House of Representatives by Mr. Beckley their clerk:

"Mr. PRESIDENT,

"The House of Representatives have passed a Bill, entitled, 'An Act con-

---

[112] On July 21 this bill was read a second time and committed.
[113] On July 21 this resolve was considered and committed.
[114] The President signed these bills on July 22.
[115] On August 2 this committee reported.
[116] On July 22 this committee reported.

cerning consuls and vice consuls of the United States, in foreign parts,'[117] in which they request the concurrence of the Senate"—

And he withdrew.

ORDERED, That the Bill, entitled, "An Act concerning consuls and vice consuls of the United States, in foreign parts," be now read the FIRST time.

ORDERED, That this Bill pass to the SECOND reading.[118]

The Senate proceeded in the THIRD reading of the Bill, entitled, "An Act making provision for the debt of the United States."

On the question, Shall this Bill pass as amended? the yeas and nays were required by one fifth of the Senators present:

Mr. Bassett		Nay
Mr. Butler	Yea	
Mr. Carroll	Yea	
Mr. Dalton	Yea	
Mr. Ellsworth	Yea	
Mr. Elmer	Yea	
Mr. Few		Nay
Mr. Foster		Nay
Mr. Gunn		Nay
Mr. Hawkins		Nay
Mr. Henry		Nay
Mr. Johnson	Yea	
Mr. Johnston		Nay
Mr. Izard	Yea	
Mr. King	Yea	
Mr. Langdon	Yea	
Mr. Lee		Nay
Mr. Maclay		Nay
Mr. Morris	Yea	
Mr. Paterson	Yea	
Mr. Read	Yea	
Mr. Schuyler	Yea	
Mr. Stanton		Nay
Mr. Strong	Yea	
Mr. Walker		Nay
Mr. Wingate		Nay

Yeas—14

Nays—12

So it was,

---

[117] This bill, as it passed the House, is in Engrossed House Bills, House Records, DNA.

[118] On July 26 this bill was read the second time and committed.

RESOLVED, That this Bill DO PASS as amended.[119]

ORDERED, That the Secretary acquaint the House of Representatives therewith, and desire their concurrence in the amendments.[120]

The Senate proceeded to consider the resolve of the House of Representatives, "providing for the salaries of the clerks in the office of the Commissioner of army accounts."

ORDERED, That it be committed to

> Mr. Wingate
> Mr. Maclay and
> Mr. Elmer[121]

Mr. Ellsworth reported from the managers on the conference on the amendments of the Senate,[122] to the Bill, entitled, "An Act to provide more effectually for the settlement of the accounts between the United States and the individual States."

ORDERED, That the report lie for consideration.[123]

The Senate adjourned to 11 o'clock to-morrow.

THURSDAY, JULY 22, 1790

The SENATE assembled,
Present as yesterday.

Mr. Morris reported from the Committee appointed July the 20th,[124] on the Bill, entitled, "An Act to provide more effectually for the collection of the duties imposed by law on goods, wares and merchandize imported into the United States, and on the tonnage of ships or vessels."

ORDERED, That the rule be dispensed with, and that this Bill be considered as in the SECOND reading; in which, having made progress, the further consideration of it was postponed until to-morrow.

A message from the House of Representatives by Mr. Beckley their clerk:

"Mr. PRESIDENT,

"The House of Representatives have resolved, That they do insist on their disagreement to some, and recede therefrom to other amendments proposed by the Senate to the Bill, entitled, 'An Act to provide more effectually for the

---

[119] This resolve and the amendments are in House Bills, Senate Records, DNA.

[120] On July 21 and 22 the House considered the Senate amendments to the Funding Bill. On July 24 and 26, resolutions, agreeing to some of the amendments and amending the rest, were passed by the House. On July 27 the Senate was notified of this action. On the same day the Senate considered the House resolutions and ordered them to be printed.

[121] On July 23 this committee reported.

[122] This report is in Joint Committee Reports, Senate Records, DNA.

[123] On July 22 the House notified the Senate that it had receded from its disagreement to some of the Senate amendments to this bill and adhered to its disagreement to others.

[124] This report has not been located.

settlement of the accounts between the United States and the individual States'[125]—

"The President of the United States has notified the House of Representatives, that he did on the 22d of July, approve of, and affix his signature to 'An Act to regulate trade and intercourse with the Indian tribes,' to 'An Act providing for holding a treaty or treaties to establish peace with certain Indian tribes,' and to 'An Act to amend the Act for the establishment and support of light-houses, beacons, buoys and public piers'—

"I am directed to bring to the Senate sundry papers respecting the Bill, entitled, 'An Act to provide more effectually for the collection of the duties imposed by law on goods, wares and merchandize imported into the United States, and on the tonnage of ships or vessels' "[126]—

And he withdrew.

Mr. Lee from the Committee appointed July the 21st, on the Bill, entitled, "An Act to enable the officers and soldiers of the Virginia line, on continental establishment, to obtain titles to certain lands lying north-west of the river Ohio, between the Little Miami and Sciota," reported the Bill without amendment.[127]

The Senate adjourned to 11 o'clock to-morrow.

FRIDAY, JULY 23, 1790

The SENATE assembled,
Present as yesterday.

Proceeded to consider the resolve of the House of Representatives on the report of the managers of the conference on the disagreeing votes of the two Houses, in the amendments of the Senate to the Bill, entitled, "An Act to provide more effectually for the settlement of the accounts between the United States and the individual States."

RESOLVED, That the Senate recede from so much of their amendment, section 1st, as to agree to the amendment of the House of Representatives on the amendment as follows: After the word "assembled," section 1st, line 2d, "that a board, to consist of three Commissioners, be, and hereby is established to settle the accounts between the United States and the individual States; and the determination of a majority of the said Commissioners on the claims submitted to them, shall be final and conclusive; and they shall have power to employ such number of clerks as they may[128] find necessary"[129]—

---

[125] This resolve is in Messages from the House, Senate Records, DNA. On July 23 the Senate receded from the amendments that the House disagreed to.

[126] On July 23 this bill was considered again and recommitted.

[127] On July 24 this bill was read a second time.

[128] In the smooth journal "shall" is substituted for "may."

[129] This amendment is in House Bills, Senate Records, DNA. The complete resolve has not been located.

That they recede from their first amendment, so far as to restore section 2d, of the Bill—

That they recede from their amendments to the 3d section, and

From their sixth amendment, and agree to restore the 6th section.

ORDERED, That the Secretary acquaint the House of Representatives therewith.[130]

A message from the House of Representatives by Mr. Beckley their clerk:

"Mr. PRESIDENT,

"The House of Representatives do adhere to and insist on some, and recede from other amendments of the Senate to the Bill, entitled, 'An Act to establish the Post-Office and Post-Roads within the United States' "[131]—

And he withdrew.

Mr. Wingate reported from the Committee appointed July the 21st,[132] on the "Resolve, providing for the salaries of the clerks in the office of the Commissioner of army accounts."[133]

The Senate proceeded in the SECOND reading of the Bill, entitled, "An Act to provide more effectually for the collection of the duties imposed by law on goods, wares and merchandize imported into the United States, and on the tonnage of ships or vessels."

ORDERED, That this Bill be re-committed, for the purpose of making some further amendments.[134]

The Senate adjourned to 11 o'clock to-morrow.

SATURDAY, JULY 24, 1790

The SENATE assembled,

Present as yesterday.

A message from the House of Representatives by Mr. Beckley their clerk:

"Mr. PRESIDENT,

"The House of Representatives have agreed to a resolution for defraying the expence of seals for the Supreme and Circuit Courts of the United States;[135] to which they desire the concurrence of the Senate"—

And he withdrew.

---

[130] On July 26 this bill was signed by both the Speaker and the Vice President and given to the committee on enrolled bills for delivery to the President.

[131] This resolve is in Messages from the House, Senate Records, DNA. On July 24 the conference committee reported to the Senate, and the Senate adhered to some of its amendments and receded from others.

[132] This report is in Various Select Committee Reports, Senate Records, DNA.

[133] On July 24 the Senate concurred in the House resolve and notified the House.

[134] On July 26 some amendments to this bill were approved and the third reading was begun.

[135] This resolve is in House Joint and Concurrent Resolutions, Senate Records, DNA.

The Senate proceeded to consider the above resolution of the House of Representatives, and

RESOLVED, That they concur therein, with an amendment as follows: Line 7th, strike out "AND," and insert between the words "circuit" and "courts," the words "and district."[136]

ORDERED, That the Secretary acquaint the House of Representatives therewith, and request their concurrence in the amendment.[137]

Mr. Ellsworth reported from the managers on the Bill,[138] entitled, "An Act to establish the Post-Office and Post-Roads within the United States;" whereupon the Senate proceeded to consider the resolve of the House of Representatives of the 22d of July, adhering to some, insisting on some, and agreeing to other amendments of the Senate to the said Bill—

RESOLVED, That the Senate adhere to their amendment section 1st and 2d, line 1st to 27th; and recede from their amendments in the 24th and 31st sections, with the exceptions proposed by the House of Representatives—and

That they agree to the amendment proposed by the House of Representatives, in the 23d section, with an amendment.[139]

ORDERED, That the Secretary carry a message to the House of Representatives accordingly.[140]

The Senate proceeded in the SECOND reading of the Bill, entitled, "An Act to enable the officers and soldiers of the Virginia line, on continental establishment, to obtain titles to certain lands lying north-west of the river Ohio, between the Little Miami and Sciota."

ORDERED, That the further consideration thereof be postponed.[141]

The Senate proceeded to the consideration of the report of the Committee on the resolution of the House of Representatives, of the 17th of July, to wit: "That the clerks in the office of the Commissioner of army accounts, are entitled to receive for their services a sum not exceeding five hundred dollars; to be paid in the same manner and at the same rate as the salary allowed to the clerks in the department of Treasury; and that the Auditor and Comptroller be authorized to adjust the accounts of the clerks in the said office, upon the

---

[136] This resolve has not been located.

[137] On July 26 the House notified the Senate that it concurred in the amendment.

[138] This report is in Joint Committee Reports, Senate Records, DNA.

[139] The rough journal adds: "(to wit, insert at the end of the said proposed amendment these words—'Provided the same be sent without cover and in such Manner as that they may be examined; and if any other Matter or Thing be found inclosed in such Papers, the whole Shall be subject to the payment of like Postage as other Packets are made subject to the Payment of by this Act.')"

[140] On July 28 a new bill, "A Bill to continue in force for a limited time, an act, entitled 'an Act for the temporary establishment of the Post Office' " was introduced and read the first and second times in the House. On July 29 the House passed this bill and sent it to the Senate which read it for the first and second times on the same date.

[141] On July 27 this bill was considered again.

same principles as those of the Treasury department, agreeably to the appropriation by law"—and,

RESOLVED, That they concur in the said resolution.

ORDERED, That the Secretary communicate their concurrence to the House of Representatives.[142]

ORDERED, That the consideration of the Bill, entitled, "An Act to provide more effectually for the collection of the duties imposed by law on goods, wares and merchandize imported into the United States, and on the tonnage of ships or vessels," be further postponed.[143]

The Senate adjourned to Monday next, at 11 o'clock.

MONDAY, JULY 26, 1790

The SENATE assembled,

Present as on the 24th, except

Mr. Maclay absent with leave for the remainder of the session.

Mr. Wingate from the Committee on enrolled Bills, reported, That they had examined the enrolled Bill, entitled, "An Act to provide more effectually for the settlement of the accounts between the United States and the individual States,"[144] and had found it correct.

A message from the House of Representatives by Mr. Beckley their clerk:

"Mr. PRESIDENT,

"The Speaker of the House of Representatives having signed an enrolled Bill, I am directed to bring it to the Senate for the signature of the Vice President—

"The House of Representatives agree to the amendment proposed by the Senate, to the resolve for defraying the expence of seals for the Supreme and Circuit Courts of the United States"[145]—

And he withdrew.

The Vice President signed the enrolled Bill, entitled, "An Act to provide more effectually for the settlement of the accounts between the United States and the individual States," and it was delivered to the Committee on enrolled Bills, to be laid before the President of the United States, for his approbation.[146]

The Senate proceeded in the SECOND reading of the Bill, entitled, "An Act

---

[142] On July 27 this resolution was signed by both the Speaker and Vice President and was given to the committee on enrolled bills for delivery to the President.

[143] On July 26 this bill was considered again and amended.

[144] The inspected enrolled bill is in Enrolled Acts, RG 11, DNA. E–22969.

[145] On July 27 both the Speaker and the Vice President signed this resolve and it was given to the committee on enrolled bills for delivery to the President.

[146] On July 28 this committee reported that it had laid this bill before the President.

concerning Consuls and Vice-Consuls of the United States, in foreign parts," and it was referred to   Mr. Morris

Mr. King and

Mr. Langdon, to consider and report thereon.[147]

The Senate resumed the SECOND reading of the Bill, entitled, "An Act to provide more effectually for the collection of the duties imposed by law on goods, wares and merchandize imported into the United States, and on the tonnage of ships or vessels," and having agreed to sundry amendments—

ORDERED, That the rule be dispensed with so far as that this Bill have the THIRD reading at this time; in which, having made progress, the further consideration thereof was postponed.[148]

The Senate adjourned to 11 o'clock to-morrow.

TUESDAY, JULY 27, 1790

The SENATE assembled,

Present as yesterday.

Mr. Wingate from the Committee on enrolled Bills, reported, that they did yesterday examine the enrolled "Resolve, respecting the salaries of the clerks in the office of the Commissioner of army accounts,"[149] and the enrolled "Resolve, for defraying the expence of seals for the Supreme, Circuit and District Courts of the United States,"[150] and found them correct."

A message from the House of Representatives by Mr. Beckley their clerk:

"Mr. PRESIDENT,

"The House of Representatives have agreed to some amendments of the Senate to the Bill, entitled, 'An Act making provision for the debt of the United States,' and have agreed to others with amendments; in which amendments to the amendments,[151] they desire the concurrence of the Senate—

"The Speaker of the House of Representatives having signed two enrolled Resolves, I am directed to bring them to the Senate for the signature of the Vice President"—

And he withdrew.

The Vice President signed the enrolled "Resolve respecting the salaries of the clerks in the office of the Commissioner of army accounts," and the enrolled "Resolve for defraying the expence of seals for the Supreme, Circuit

---

[147] On August 2 this committee reported and consideration of the bill was postponed until the next session.

[148] On July 27 this bill was passed with amendments and the bill was returned to the House for concurrence.

[149] The inspected enrolled resolve is in Enrolled Acts, RG 11, DNA. E–46075.

[150] The inspected enrolled resolve is in Enrolled Acts, RG 11, DNA.

[151] The amendments, in printed and manuscript forms, are in House Bills, Senate Records, DNA, and in Other Records: Yeas and nays, Senate Records, DNA.

and District Courts of the United States," and they were delivered to the Committee, to be laid before the President of the United States, for his approbation.[152]

Mr. Wingate from the Committee on the petition of Donald Campbell, reported.[153]

ORDERED, That the report lie on the table.[154]

The Senate proceeded to consider the resolution of the House of Representatives, upon the amendments proposed by the Senate, to the Bill, entitled, "An Act making provision for the debt of the United States."

ORDERED, That the resolution be printed for the use of the Senate.[155]

The Senate resumed the THIRD reading of the Bill, entitled, "An Act to provide more effectually for the collection of the duties imposed by law on goods, wares and merchandize imported into the United States, and on the tonnage of ships or vessels,"—and

RESOLVED, That this Bill DO PASS with amendments.[156]

---

[152] On July 28 the committee on enrolled bills notified the Senate that it had delivered this bill to the President.

[153] This report is in Various Select Committee Reports, Senate Records, DNA.

[154] On August 3 this report was considered and the petition was dismissed.

[155] On July 28 the House resolutions were considered at length. The amendments, with the exception of numbers three, five, nine, and eleven, were agreed to and the House was notified of these actions.

[156] Some draft amendments are in House Bills, Senate Records, DNA. The rough journal reads: "Resolved that the Bill pass with the following Amendments." The amendments, on five sheets headed "Congress of the United States, / In Senate July the 27th. 1790," are bound into the journal at this point and read as follows:

Sect. 1st. Page 2nd. line 9th.
After "Sandwich" add "Falmouth"—
Sect. 1st. Page 2. Line 13th.
Strike out *"To"* and insert "In—"
Sect. 1st. Same Page 2 Line 14th.
Strike out the words *"shall be annexed Falmouth as a port of delivery only and"*
Sect. 1st. Page 4th. Lines 1st & 2nd.
Strike out the words "excepting the *Town of Falmouth"*
Sect. 1 Page 4 Line 4th.
Strike out the words *"and the Town of Falmouth."*
Sect. 1 Same Page 4 Line 23rd
Strike out *"Kinnimicut"* and insert "James Town."
Sect. 1st Page 12th. Line 16th
Strike out *"Port Washington"* and insert "any port of entry connected with the waters of the said Inlet."
Sect. 4. Page 15. Line 5th
Strike out the word *"and."*
Sect 4th Page 15th Line 8th
After the word "Manifest"—insert "and if bound to the District of South Quay shall before he pass by the Port of Edenton and immediately after his arrival deposit with the Collector of the Port of Edenton a like manifest"—
Section 16th Line 1st
Strike out *"Twelve"* and insert "Twenty four"—

Section 16th Line 13th

After "her" add these Words "Unless the whole of such Information required on the second report as aforesaid shall have been given at the time of making the first report in which Case it shall not be necessary to make a further report."

Section 20th Lines 5th & 6th

Strike out the words "and shall make entry thereof with the said *Collector*"

Insert after Section 22nd

"And whereas by the letter of the Act entitled 'An Act for laying a duty on goods, wares and Merchandizes imported into the United States' articles of the growth or manufacture of the United States exported to foreign countries and brought back to the United States are subject to duty on their importation into the said States, And whereas it was not the intention of Congress that they should be so subject to Duty.

"Be it therefore further enacted, that in every case in which a duty may have been heretofore paid on goods, wares or merchandizes of the growth or manufacture of the United States exported to a foreign Country and brought back to the said States, the amount thereof shall be repaid to the person or persons by whom the same shall have been paid or to his, her or their representatives and that in every case in which such duty may have accrued but may not have been paid the same be remitted and that no such duty shall hereafter be demanded, provided that the regulations hereinafter prescribed for ascertaining the identity of such goods, wares or merchandize be observed and complied with, and that as well in respect to those heretofore imported, as far as may be practicable, as to those hereafter to be imported."

Section 29th. Line 17th.

After the word "affixed" add "except by special Licence from the Chief Officer of the Port—"

Section 35th. Line 7th.

After "by—" insert—"Number"

Section 38th. Line 5th.

Instead of "Real Plate" say "Real of Plate"—

Section 50th. Line 8th.

After "Wilmington" insert "in the State of Delaware"

Sect. 51. Page 41st. Line 11th.

Strike out "hundred" and insert "one Cent per Ton"—

Section 51 Page 41 Line 24 a 28.

Expunge from the word "but" to "compensation" inclusive

Section 52nd. Line 10th.

Strike out "*Dighton*" and insert "and"

Same line

Strike out "*and New Bedford*"

Line 13th.

Strike out "*Middletown*"

Same line

After "Stonington" insert "East Greenwich."

Sect. 60th. Page 45 and 46.

Strike out the 60th. Section and insert in lieu thereof the following "And be it further enacted, That there shall be to each of the said Boats or Cutters, One Master and not more than three Mates, first, second, and third, four Mariners and two Boys, and that the compensations and allowances to the said Officers, Mariners and Boys respectively shall be to the Master Thirty Dollars per Month, and the subsistence of a Captain in the Army of the United States, to a first Mate Twenty dollars per Month, to a Second Mate Sixteen dollars per Month, to a third Mate fourteen Dollars per Month and to every Mate the subsistence of a Lieutenant in the said Army. To each Mariner eight Dollars per Month, to each Boy four Dollars per Month and to each Mariner and Boy the same Ration of Provisions which is or shall be allowed to a Soldier in the said Army. The said allowances for subsistence to be paid in Provisions or Money at the Contract prices at the option of the Secretary of the Treasury."

ORDERED, That the Secretary carry this Bill to the House of Representatives, and desire their concurrence in the amendments.[157]

The Senate resumed the SECOND reading of the Bill, entitled, "An Act to enable the officers and soldiers of the Virginia line, on continental establishment, to obtain titles to certain lands lying north-west of the river Ohio, between the Little Miami and Sciota," and after debate the further consideration thereof was postponed.[158]

The Senate adjourned to 11 o'clock to-morrow.

WEDNESDAY, JULY 28, 1790

The SENATE assembled,
Present as yesterday.

Mr. Wingate from the Committee on enrolled Bills, reported, That they did yesterday lay before the President of the United States, for his approbation, the enrolled Bill, entitled, "An Act to provide more effectually for the settle-

---

Section 61st. Line 1st.
After the word "said" add "Boats or."

Section 67th. Line 4th.
Strike out *"Districts of Louisville and Passamaquoddy,"* and insert "District of Louisville."

After the 69th. Section add the following Clause
"And be it further enacted, that the Master or Person having the charge or Command of a Ship or Vessel bound to a foreign Port or Place shall deliver to the Collector of the district from which such Ship or Vessel shall be about to depart a Manifest of the Cargo on board the same, and shall make Oath or Affirmation to the Truth thereof whereupon the said Collector shall grant a Clearance for the said Ship or Vessell and her Cargo but without specifying the Particulars thereof unless required by the said Master or Person having said charge or command. And if any Ship or Vessel bound to a foreign Port or Place shall depart on her Voyage to such foreign Port or Place without such clearance the said Master or Person having the said Charge or command shall forfeit and pay the sum of two Hundred Dollars for such offence."

To the end of the Bill add
"And whereas by the Act intitled 'An Act to regulate the collection of the duties imposed by law on the tonnage of Ships or Vessels and on Goods, Wares and Merchandizes imported into the United States' it was declared that the Ruble of Russia should be rated at one hundred Cents and by the Act intitled 'An Act to explain and amend an Act intitled "An Act for regestering and clearing Vessels regulating the Coasting trade and for other purposes"' that part of the said first mentioned Act, which so rated the Ruble of Russia was repealed and made null and void. And whereas it is doubted whether the said repeal can operate with respect to duties incurred prior thereto as was intended by Congress.

"Therefore Be it enacted and declared that the said repeal shall be deemed to operate in respect to all duties which may have arisen or accrued prior thereto."

"The Sections to be numbered in succession conformably to the amendments."
The smooth journal inserts the following marginal notation: "(For Amendments See Original Minutes Page 568)."

[157] On July 28 the House agreed to the Senate amendments and notified the Senate.
[158] On July 28 this bill was considered again and recommitted.

ment of the accounts between the United States and the individual States,"[159] the enrolled "Resolve for defraying the expence of seals for the Supreme, Circuit and District Courts of the United States," and the enrolled "Resolve respecting the salaries of the clerks in the office of the Commissioner of army accounts."[160]

The Senate resumed the SECOND reading of the Bill, entitled, "An Act to enable the officers and soldiers of the Virginia line, on continental establishment, to obtain titles to certain lands lying north-west of the river Ohio, between the Little Miami and Sciota."

ORDERED, That it be re-committed.[161]

A message from the House of Representatives by Mr. Beckley their clerk:

"Mr. PRESIDENT,

"The House of Representatives have agreed to all the amendments of the Senate to the Bill, entitled, 'An Act to provide more effectually for the collection of the duties imposed by law on goods, wares and merchandize imported into the United States, and on the tonnage of ships or vessels'[162]—

"They have passed the Bill, entitled, 'An Act for the relief of disabled soldiers and seamen lately in the service of the United States, and of certain other persons,'[163] the Bill, entitled, 'An Act for the relief of John Stewart and John Davidson,'[164] and the Resolution 'for allowing to Francis Mentges, certain extra expences incurred in the public service;'[165] in which Bills and Resolution they desire the concurrence of the Senate"—

And he withdrew.

The Senate proceeded to consider the Resolution of the House of Representatives, of the 24th and 26th of July, and their amendments to the amendments of the Senate, to the Bill, entitled, "An Act making provision for the debt of the United States"—and

RESOLVED, That they agree to the first amendment, to wit: Line 12th, strike out "SEVEN," and insert "eight"[166]—

---

[159] On August 5 the President signed this bill and notified the Congress.

[160] On August 2 the President signed these resolves, and the Senate was notified on August 4.

[161] On August 3 this bill was read the third time, passed with amendments, and returned to the House for concurrence.

[162] On August 2 this bill was signed by both the Speaker and the Vice President and given to the committee on enrolled bills for delivery to the President.

[163] This bill has not been located. On July 29 this bill was read the first and second times and committed.

[164] This bill has not been located. On July 29 this bill was read the first and second times and committed.

[165] This resolve is in House Joint and Concurrent Resolutions, Senate Records, DNA. On July 29 this resolve was read and committed.

[166] This resolve has not been located.

This reserves to the United States the power to redeem, at their option, of the sum borrowed, at the rate of eight per cent. per annum.

On motion to agree to the second amendment, to wit: Line 17th, strike out "TWENTY-SIX DOLLARS AND EIGHTY-EIGHT CENTS," and insert "thirty-three dollars and one third of a dollar"—

This will entitle the subscriber to a second certificate for thirty-three and one third dollars of the sum subscribed, instead of twenty-six dollars and eighty-eight cents on every hundred; his second or deferred certificate to bear an interest of six per cent. after the year 1800—The yeas and nays were required by one fifth of the Senators present:

Mr. Bassett		Nay
Mr. Butler	Yea	
Mr. Carroll		Nay
Mr. Dalton	Yea	
Mr. Ellsworth		Nay
Mr. Elmer	Yea	
Mr. Few		Nay
Mr. Foster		Nay
Mr. Gunn	Yea	
Mr. Hawkins		Nay
Mr. Henry	Yea	
Mr. Johnston		Nay
Mr. Izard	Yea	
Mr. King	Yea	
Mr. Langdon	Yea	
Mr. Lee		Nay
Mr. Morris	Yea	
Mr. Paterson	Yea	
Mr. Read		Nay
Mr. Schuyler	Yea	
Mr. Stanton		Nay
Mr. Strong		Nay
Mr. Walker	Yea	
Mr. Wingate		Nay

Yeas, 12.   Nays, 12.[167]

The numbers being equal, the Vice President determined the question in the Affirmative.

On motion to disagree to the third amendment, to wit: Line 19th, strike out "EIGHT HUNDRED,"

And insert "seven hundred and ninety-seven"—

---

[167] Record of the vote is in Other Records: Yeas and nays, Senate Records, DNA.

This provides that the subscriber shall be entitled to an interest of six percent. on his deferred certificate, after the year 1797, instead of 1800—The yeas and nays were required by one fifth of the Senators present:

Mr. Bassett		Yea
Mr. Butler	Nay	
Mr. Carroll		Yea
Mr. Dalton	Nay	
Mr. Ellsworth		Yea
Mr. Elmer	Nay	
Mr. Few		Yea
Mr. Foster		Yea
Mr. Gunn	Nay	
Mr. Hawkins		Yea
Mr. Henry	Nay	
Mr. Johnston		Yea
Mr. Izard	Nay	
Mr. King	Nay	
Mr. Langdon	Nay	
Mr. Lee		Yea
Mr. Morris	Nay	
Mr. Paterson	Nay	
Mr. Read		Yea
Mr. Schuyler	Nay	
Mr. Stanton		Yea
Mr. Strong		Yea
Mr. Walker	Nay	
Mr. Wingate		Yea

Yeas, 12.   Nays, 12.[168]

The numbers being equal, the Vice President determined the question in favor of the amendment.

The fourth amendment to the amendments, "line 23d, strike out 'SEVEN,' and insert 'eight,' " was agreed to.

This provides that the United States may redeem by annual payments on account of principal and interest, at the rate of eight per cent. instead of seven per cent. per annum.

On the question to agree to the fifth amendment, to wit:

"Line 40th, strike out 'THREE,' and insert 'four' "—

This provides that the subscriber shall be entitled to an interest of four, instead of three per cent. for such part of their subscription as they may pay in the arrears of interest, including indents—

---

[168] Record of the vote is in Other Records: Yeas and nays, Senate Records, DNA.

The yeas and nays were required by one fifth of the Senators present:

Mr. Bassett		Nay
Mr. Butler		Nay
Mr. Carroll		Nay
Mr. Dalton	Yea	
Mr. Ellsworth		Nay
Mr. Elmer		Nay
Mr. Few		Nay
Mr. Foster		Nay
Mr. Gunn		Nay
Mr. Hawkins		Nay
Mr. Henry	Yea	
Mr. Johnston		Nay
Mr. Izard		Nay
Mr. King	Yea	
Mr. Langdon	Yea	
Mr. Lee		Nay
Mr. Morris	Yea	
Mr. Paterson	Yea	
Mr. Read		Nay
Mr. Schuyler	Yea	
Mr. Stanton		Nay
Mr. Strong		Nay
Mr. Walker	Yea	
Mr. Wingate		Nay

Nays—16

Yeas—8[169]

It passed in the Negative.

The sixth amendment to the amendments, was agreed to as follows:

"Provided also, and be it further enacted, that if the total amount of the sums which shall be subscribed to the said loan, in the debt of any State within the time limited for receiving subscriptions thereto, shall exceed the sum by this act allowed to be subscribed within such State, the certificates and credits granted to the respective subscribers, shall bear such proportion to the sums by them respectively subscribed, as the total amount of the said sums shall bear to the whole sum so allowed to be subscribed in the debt of such State within the same: And every subscriber to the said loan, shall, at the time of subscribing, deposit with the Commissioner, the certificates or notes to be loaned by him."

The seventh amendment to the amendments, was agreed to, to wit:

---

[169] Record of the vote is in Other Records: Yeas and nays, Senate Records. DNA.

"To the second clause or section, line 13th, strike out 'SEVEN,' and insert 'eight' "—

This applies to the assumed debt, and provides that the United States may redeem by annual payments, on account of principal and interest, at the rate of eight per cent. instead of seven per cent. per annum.

On motion to agree to the eight amendment, to wit: "Lines 18th and 19th, strike out 'TWENTY-SIX DOLLARS AND EIGHTY-EIGHT CENTS,' and insert 'thirty-three dollars and one third of a dollar' "—

This applies to the assumed part of the debt, and will entitle the subscriber to a second certificate for thirty-three dollars and one third of a dollar, per cent. instead of twenty-six dollars and eighty-eight cents, on every hundred; the said second certificate to be on interest at six per cent. after the year 1800—

The yeas and nays were required by one fifth of the Senators present:

Mr. Bassett		Nay
Mr. Butler	Yea	
Mr. Carroll		Nay
Mr. Dalton	Yea	
Mr. Ellsworth		Nay
Mr. Elmer	Yea	
Mr. Few		Nay
Mr. Foster		Nay
Mr. Gunn		Nay
Mr. Hawkins		Nay
Mr. Henry	Yea	
Mr. Johnston	Yea	
Mr. Izard	Yea	
Mr. King	Yea	
Mr. Langdon	Yea	
Mr. Lee		Nay
Mr. Morris	Yea	
Mr. Paterson	Yea	
Mr. Read		Nay
Mr. Schuyler	Yea	
Mr. Stanton		Nay
Mr. Strong	Yea	
Mr. Walker	Yea	
Mr. Wingate		Nay

Yeas—13
Nays—11[170]
It passed in the Affirmative.

---

[170] Record of the vote is in Other Records: Yeas and nays, Senate Records, DNA.

On motion to agree to the ninth amendment to the amendments, to wit:
"Line 21st, strike out 'EIGHT HUNDRED,' and insert 'seven hundred and ninety-seven' "—

This provides, as it applies to the assumed debts, that the subscriber shall
be entitled to an interest of six per cent. on the deferred part of the sum
subscribed, after the year 1797, instead of 1800—

The yeas and nays were required by one fifth of the Senators present:

Mr. Bassett		Nay
Mr. Butler	Yea	
Mr. Carroll		Nay
Mr. Dalton	Yea	
Mr. Ellsworth		Nay
Mr. Elmer	Yea	
Mr. Few		Nay
Mr. Foster		Nay
Mr. Gunn		Nay
Mr. Hawkins		Nay
Mr. Henry	Yea	
Mr. Johnston		Nay
Mr. Izard	Yea	
Mr. King	Yea	
Mr. Langdon	Yea	
Mr. Lee		Nay
Mr. Morris	Yea	
Mr. Paterson	Yea	
Mr. Read		Nay
Mr. Schuyler	Yea	
Mr. Stanton		Nay
Mr. Strong	Yea	
Mr. Walker		Nay
Mr. Wingate		Nay

Nays—13
Yeas—11[171]

It passed in the Negative.

On motion to re-consider the third amendment to the amendments of the
Senate, the yeas and nays were required by one fifth of the Senators present:

Mr. Bassett		Yea
Mr. Butler	Nay	
Mr. Carroll		Yea
Mr. Dalton		Yea

[171] Record of the vote is in Other Records: Yeas and nays, Senate Records, DNA.

Mr. Ellsworth		Yea
Mr. Elmer		Yea
Mr. Few		Yea
Mr. Foster		Yea
Mr. Gunn	Nay	
Mr. Hawkins		Yea
Mr. Henry	Nay	
Mr. Johnston		Yea
Mr. Izard		Yea
Mr. King	Nay	
Mr. Langdon	Nay	
Mr. Lee		Yea
Mr. Morris	Nay	
Mr. Paterson		Yea
Mr. Read		Yea
Mr. Schuyler	Nay	
Mr. Stanton		Yea
Mr. Strong	Yea	
Mr. Walker		Nay
Mr. Wingate	Yea	

Yeas—16

Nays—8[172]

It passed in the Affirmative.

On the question to agree to the third amendment of the House of Representatives on the amendments of the Senate, the yeas and nays were required by one fifth of the Senators present:

Mr. Bassett		Nay
Mr. Butler	Yea	
Mr. Carroll		Nay
Mr. Dalton		Nay
Mr. Ellsworth		Nay
Mr. Elmer		Nay
Mr. Few		Nay
Mr. Foster		Nay
Mr. Gunn	Yea	
Mr. Hawkins		Nay
Mr. Henry	Yea	
Mr. Johnston		Nay
Mr. Izard		Nay
Mr. King	Yea	
Mr. Langdon	Yea	

---

[172] Record of the vote is in Other Records: Yeas and nays, Senate Records, DNA.

Mr. Lee		Nay
Mr. Morris	Yea	
Mr. Paterson		Nay
Mr. Read		Nay
Mr. Schuyler	Yea	
Mr. Stanton		Nay
Mr. Strong		Nay
Mr. Walker	Yea	
Mr. Wingate		Nay

Nays—16
Yeas—8[173]

It passed in the Negative.

On motion to agree to the tenth amendment to the amendments, to wit: "Line 25th, strike out 'SEVEN,' and insert 'eight' "—

This applies to the assumed part of the debt, as the amendment seventh applies to the domestic debt—

The yeas and nays were required by one fifth of the Senators present:

Mr. Bassett		Nay
Mr. Butler	Yea	
Mr. Carroll		Nay
Mr. Dalton	Yea	
Mr. Ellsworth		Nay
Mr. Elmer	Yea	
Mr. Few		Nay
Mr. Foster		Nay
Mr. Gunn		Nay
Mr. Hawkins		Nay
Mr. Henry	Yea	
Mr. Johnston		Nay
Mr. Izard	Yea	
Mr. King	Yea	
Mr. Langdon	Yea	
Mr. Lee		Nay
Mr. Morris	Yea	
Mr. Paterson	Yea	
Mr. Read		Nay
Mr. Schuyler	Yea	
Mr. Stanton		Nay
Mr. Strong	Yea	
Mr. Walker	Yea	
Mr. Wingate		Nay

[173] Record of the vote is in Other Records: Yeas and nays, Senate Records, DNA.

Yeas—12

Nays—12[174]

The numbers being equal, the question was by the Vice President, determined in the Affirmative.

On motion to agree to amendment eleventh, on the amendments of the Senate, to wit:

"Line 31st, strike out 'THREE,' and insert 'four' "—

This provides, as it applies to the assumed debts, that the subscriber shall be entitled to an interest of four per cent. instead of three per cent. for one third of the sum by him subscribed[175]—

The yeas and nays were required by one fifth of the Senators present:

Mr. Bassett		Nay
Mr. Butler		Nay
Mr. Carroll		Nay
Mr. Dalton	Yea	
Mr. Ellsworth		Nay
Mr. Elmer		Nay
Mr. Few		Nay
Mr. Foster		Nay
Mr. Gunn		Nay
Mr. Hawkins		Nay
Mr. Henry	Yea	
Mr. Johnston		Nay
Mr. Izard		Nay
Mr. King	Yea	
Mr. Langdon	Yea	
Mr. Lee		Nay
Mr. Morris	Yea	
Mr. Paterson	Yea	
Mr. Read		Nay
Mr. Schuyler	Yea	
Mr. Stanton		Nay
Mr. Strong		Nay
Mr. Walker	Yea	
Mr. Wingate		Nay

Nays—16

Yeas—8[176]

It passed in the Negative.

---

[174] Record of the vote is in Other Records: Yeas and nays, Senate Records, DNA.

[175] The rough journal adds the following canceled passage: "to wit: on his second or deferred Certificate."

[176] Record of the vote is in Other Records: Yeas and nays, Senate Records, DNA.

ORDERED, That the Secretary communicate to the House of Representatives the proceedings of the Senate upon their amendments to the amendments of the Senate, on the Bill last mentioned.[177]

The Senate adjourned to 11 o'clock to-morrow.

THURSDAY, JULY 29, 1790

The SENATE assembled,

Present as yesterday.

ORDERED, That the Bill, entitled, "An Act for the relief of John Stewart and John Davidson," be now read the FIRST time.

ORDERED, That this Bill pass to the SECOND reading.

The Senate proceeded to the FIRST reading of the Bill, entitled, "An Act for the relief of disabled soldiers and seamen, lately in the service of the United States, and of certain other persons."

ORDERED, That this Bill pass to the SECOND reading.

The Resolve "for allowing to Francis Mentges certain extra expences incurred in the public service," was read and committed to

> Mr. Wingate
> Mr. Elmer and
> Mr. Stanton, to consider and report what is proper to

be done thereon.[178]

A message from the House of Representatives by Mr. Beckley their clerk:

"Mr. PRESIDENT,

"The House of Representatives have receded from such of their amendments to the amendments of the Senate as were disagreed to on the Bill, entitled, 'An Act making provision for the debt of the United States'[179]—

"They have passed the Bill, entitled, 'An Act to continue in force for a limited time, an Act, entitled, "An Act for the temporary establishment of the post-office," '[180] and the Bill, entitled, 'An Act to compensate Thomas Barclay for various public services,'[181] in which they desire the concurrence of the Senate"—

And he withdrew.

ORDERED, That the Bill, entitled, "An Act to continue in force for a limited

---

[177] On July 29 the House receded from its third, fifth, ninth, and eleventh amendments to the Senate amendments to the Funding Bill.

[178] On August 3 this committee reported.

[179] On August 2 this bill was signed by both the Speaker and the Vice President and given to the committee on enrolled bills for delivery to the President.

[180] This bill has not been located.

[181] This bill has not been located.

time, an Act, entitled, 'An Act for the temporary establishment of the post-office,' " be now read the FIRST time.

It was agreed that the rule should be so far dispensed with as that this Bill have the SECOND reading at this time.

ORDERED, That this Bill pass to the THIRD reading.[182]

The Senate proceeded to the FIRST reading of the Bill, entitled, "An Act to compensate Thomas Barclay for various public services."

ORDERED, That this Bill pass to the SECOND reading.[183]

The Senate agreed to dispense with the rule, so far as that the Bill, entitled, "An Act for the relief of disabled soldiers and seamen lately in the service of the United States, and of certain other persons," be now read the SECOND time.

ORDERED, That this Bill be committed to
> Mr. Schuyler
> Mr. Gunn and
> Mr. Bassett[184]

The Senate agreed to dispense with the rule so far as that the Bill, entitled, "An Act for the relief of John Stewart and John Davidson," be now read the SECOND time.

ORDERED, That this Bill be committed to
> Mr. Dalton
> Mr. Foster and
> Mr. Henry[185]

The Senate adjourned to 11 o'clock to-morrow.

FRIDAY, JULY 30, 1790

The SENATE assembled,
Present as yesterday.

Mr. Dalton from the Committee, reported the Bill, entitled, "An Act for the relief of John Stewart and John Davidson," without amendment—whereupon,

The Senate proceeded to the THIRD reading of this Bill.

RESOLVED, That this Bill DO PASS.

ORDERED, That the Secretary acquaint the House of Representatives with the concurrence of the Senate in this Bill.[186]

---

[182] On July 30 the Senate read this bill a third time, passed it, and notified the House.

[183] On July 30 this bill was read a second time and committed.

[184] On August 2 the petition of Jacob Weed was referred to this committee. On the same day the committee reported on the bill and the petition. The petition was referred to the Secretary of the Treasury.

[185] On July 30 this committee reported and the bill was read a third time and passed.

[186] On August 2 this bill was signed by both the Speaker and the Vice President and given to the committee on enrolled bills for delivery to the President.

The Senate proceeded to the THIRD reading of the Bill, entitled, "An Act to continue in force for a limited time, an Act, entitled, 'An Act for the temporary establishment of the post-office.' "

RESOLVED, That this Bill DO PASS.

ORDERED, That the Secretary acquaint the House of Representatives with the concurrence of the Senate in this Bill.[187]

The Senate proceeded to the SECOND reading of the Bill, entitled, "An Act to compensate Thomas Barclay for various public services."

ORDERED, That it be committed to

> Mr. King
> Mr. Morris and
> Mr. Langdon[188]

The Senate adjourned to Monday next at 11 o'clock.

---

[187] On August 2 this bill was signed by both the Speaker and the Vice President and given to the committee on enrolled bills for delivery to the President.

[188] On August 3 this committee reported several amendments to the bill.

MONDAY, August 2, 1790

The SENATE assembled,
Present as on the 30th of July.

Mr. Wingate from the Committee on enrolled Bills, reported, That they had examined the enrolled Bill, entitled, "An Act to provide more effectually for the collection of the duties imposed by law on goods, wares and merchandize imported into the United States, and on the tonnage of ships or vessels,"[1] the enrolled Bill, entitled, "An Act for the relief of John Stewart and John Davidson,"[2] the enrolled Bill, entitled, "An Act to continue in force for a limited time, an Act, entitled 'An Act for the temporary establishment of the post-office,' "[3] and the enrolled Bill, entitled, "An Act making provision for the debt of the United States,"[4] and had found them correct.

The petition of Jacob Weed was read,[5] stating that he was employed during the late war in the department of the Commissary General of Issues, and praying that his accounts may be settled, the resolution of Congress passed the 23d day of July, 1787, notwithstanding.

ORDERED, That this petition be committed to the Committee to whom was referred the Bill, entitled, "An Act for the relief of disabled soldiers and seamen lately in the service of the United States, and of certain other persons."

A message from the House of Representatives by Mr. Beckley their clerk:

"Mr. PRESIDENT,

"The Speaker of the House of Representatives having signed several enrolled Bills, I am directed to bring them to the Senate for the signature of the Vice President"—

And he withdrew.

The Vice President signed the enrolled Bill, entitled, "An Act to provide more effectually for the collection of the duties imposed by law on goods, wares and merchandize imported into the United States, and on the tonnage of ships or vessels," the enrolled Bill, entitled, "An Act for the relief of John Stewart and John Davidson," the enrolled Bill, entitled, "An Act to continue in force for a limited time, an Act, intitled, 'An Act for the temporary establishment of the post-office,' " and the enrolled Bill, entitled, "An Act making provision for the debt of the United States," and they were delivered to the Committee on enrolled Bills, to be laid before the President of the United States, for his approbation.[6]

---

[1] The inspected enrolled bill is in Enrolled Acts, RG 11, DNA. E–22970.
[2] The inspected enrolled bill is in Enrolled Acts, RG 11, DNA.
[3] The inspected enrolled bill is in Enrolled Acts, RG 11, DNA. E–46063.
[4] The inspected enrolled bill is in Enrolled Acts, RG 11, DNA. E–46048.
[5] This petition is in Petitions and Memorials: Various subjects, Senate Records, DNA.
[6] On August 3 this committee reported that it had delivered these bills to the President.

A letter from the Treasurer of the United States was read, enclosing his quarterly accounts made up to the 30th of June, 1790.[7]

ORDERED, That this letter and the enclosures lie for consideration.

Mr. Schuyler reported from the Committee,[8] to whom was referred the Bill, entitled, "An Act for the relief of disabled soldiers and seamen lately in the service of the United States, and of certain other persons," and it was agreed to amend the Bill accordingly.

ORDERED, That this Bill pass to the THIRD reading.

Mr. Schuyler further reported from the same Committee, on the petition of Jacob Weed[9]—whereupon,

ORDERED, That this petition be referred to the Secretary of the Treasury, to consider and report thereon.[10]

Mr. Lee from the Committee to whom was referred the Bill, entitled, "An Act making further provision for the payment of the debts of the United States," reported sundry amendments.[11]

ORDERED, That the Bill as proposed by the Committee to be amended, be printed for the consideration of the Senate.[12]

Mr. King reported from the Committee on the Bill, entitled, "An Act concerning Consuls and Vice Consuls of the United States, in foreign parts"—whereupon,

ORDERED, That the further consideration of this Bill be postponed until the next session.[13]

The Senate adjourned to 11 o'clock to-morrow.

TUESDAY, AUGUST 3, 1790

The SENATE assembled,
Present as yesterday.

Mr. Wingate from the Committee on enrolled Bills, reported, that they did on the 2d instant, lay before the President of the United States, the enrolled Bill, entitled, "An Act to provide more effectually for the collection of the duties imposed by law on goods, wares and merchandize imported into the United States, and on the tonnage of ships or vessels," the enrolled Bill, entitled, "An Act for the relief of John Stewart and John Davidson," the en-

---

[7] The letter, with the accounts, is in Accounts and Receipts of the Treasurer of the United States, Records of the Executive Departments, vol. 1, House Records, DNA.

[8] This report is in Various Select Committee Reports, Senate Records, DNA.

[9] This report is in Various Select Committee Reports, Senate Records, DNA.

[10] On August 5 this bill was considered.

[11] This report is in Various Select Committee Reports, Senate Records, DNA.

[12] On August 3 this committee report was considered.

[13] The notation of the postponement is in Engrossed House Bills, House Records, DNA.

rolled Bill, entitled, "An Act to continue in force for a limited time, an Act, entitled, 'An Act for the temporary establishment of the post-office,' " and the enrolled Bill, entitled, "An Act making provision for the debt of the United States"[14]—

He further reported from the Committee appointed July the 29th,[15] for allowing to Francis Mentges certain extra expences incurred in the public service—

Which last report was ordered to lie for consideration.[16]

The Senate proceeded in the SECOND reading of the Bill, entitled, "An Act to enable the officers and soldiers of the Virginia line, on continental establishment, to obtain titles to certain lands lying north-west of the river Ohio, between the Little Miami and Sciota," and agreed to expunge the second, third and fourth sections.

ORDERED, That this Bill, as amended, pass to the THIRD reading.[17]

Mr. King from the Committee appointed July the 30th, on the Bill, entitled, "An Act to compensate Thomas Barclay for various public services," reported sundry amendments;[18] and the report was ordered to lie for consideration.[19]

The Senate proceeded to consider the report of the Committee on the Bill, entitled, "An Act making further provision for the payment of the debts of the United States," and agreed that it be the order of the day for to-morrow.[20]

The Senate proceeded to the consideration of the report of the Committee on the petition of Donald Campbell—whereupon,

ORDERED, That this petition be dismissed.

The Senate adjourned to 11 o'clock to-morrow.

WEDNESDAY, AUGUST 4, 1790

The SENATE assembled,
Present as yesterday.

A message from the House of Representatives by Mr. Beckley their clerk:

---

[14] On August 4 the President signed all these bills and the Senate was notified.

[15] This report is in Various Select Committee Reports, Senate Records, DNA. It is also printed on page 473, note 43 below.

[16] On August 6 this report was considered and the Senate resolved not to concur in the resolve.

[17] On August 7 this bill was read the third time and several amendments to it were proposed. Consideration was then postponed.

[18] This report is in Various Select Committee Reports, Senate Records, DNA.

[19] On August 4 this report was considered and the bill was amended according to the report. The bill was then read the third time.

[20] On August 4 this report was printed in the Journal and several motions on it were defeated. It was agreed to as amendments to the bill.

"Mr. PRESIDENT,

"The House of Representatives have passed the Bill, entitled, 'An Act declaring the assent of Congress to certain Acts of the States of Maryland, Georgia and Rhode-Island and Providence Plantations,'[21] in which they desire the concurrence of the Senate[22]—

"I am directed to inform the Senate, that the President of the United States has notified the House of Representatives, that he did on the 2d day of August 1790, approve of and affix his signature to a 'Resolve making allowance for the service of the clerks employed in the office of the Commissioner of army accounts,' and to a 'Resolve to defray the expence of procuring seals for the Supreme, Circuit and District Courts of the United States,' and—

"That on the 4th day of August 1790, he did approve of and sign 'An Act making provision for the debt of the United States,' 'An Act to provide more effectually for the collection of the duties imposed by law on goods, wares and merchandize imported into the United States, and on the tonnage of ships or vessels,' 'An Act to continue in force for a limited time, an Act, entitled, "An Act for the temporary establishment of the post-office," ' and 'An Act for the relief of John Stewart and John Davidson' "[23]—

And he withdrew.

The Senate proceeded to consider the report of the Committee on the Bill, entitled, "An Act making further provision for the payment of the debts of the United States;" and which report is that the Bill be amended to read as follows:

"WHEREAS by an Act, entitled, 'An Act for laying a duty on goods, wares and merchandizes imported into the United States,' divers duties were laid on goods, wares and merchandize so imported, for the discharge of the debts of the United States, and the encouragement and protection of manufactures: And whereas the support of government and the discharge of the said debts, render it necessary to increase the said duties:

"SEC. 1. *Be it enacted by the Senate and House of Representatives of the United States of America, in Congress assembled,* That from and after the last day of December next, the duties specified and laid in and by the act aforesaid, shall cease and determine; and that upon all goods, wares and merchandize (not herein particularly excepted) which after the said day shall be brought into the United States, from any foreign port or place, there shall be levied, collected and paid, the several and respective duties following, that is to say:

Madeira wine of the quality of London particular....... per gallon	35 cents
Other Madeira wine................................. per gallon	30 cents

---

[21] This bill has not been located.

[22] On August 5 this bill was read the first time.

[23] This message is in Committee on Enrolled Bills, Senate Records, DNA.

Sherry wine..	per gallon	25 cents
Other wines.......................................	per gallon	20 cents

Distilled spirits:

If more than ten per cent. below proof according to Dycas's hydrometer,	per gallon	12 cents
If under five and not more than ten per cent. below proof, according to the same hydrometer,	per gallon	12½ cents
If of proof and not more than five per cent. below proof, according to the same hydrometer,	per gallon	13 cents
If above proof but not exceeding twenty per cent. according to the same hydrometer,	per gallon	15 cents
If of more than twenty and not more than forty per cent. above proof, according to the same hydrometer,	per gallon	20 cents
If of more than forty per cent. above proof, according to the same hydrometer,	per gallon	25 cents
Molasses..	per gallon	3 cents
Beer, ale and porter, in casks.......................	per gallon	5 cents
Beer, ale and porter, in bottles......................	per dozen	20 cents

Teas from China and India, in ships or vessels of the United States:

Bohea..	per lb.	10 cents
Souchong and other black teas......................	per lb.	18 cents
Hyson..	per lb.	32 cents
Other green teas..................................	per lb.	20 cents

Teas from Europe, in ships or vessels of the United States:

Bohea..	per lb.	12 cents
Souchong and other black teas......................	per lb.	21 cents
Hyson..	per lb.	40 cents
Other green teas..................................	per lb.	24 cents

Teas from any other place, or in any other ships or vessels:

Bohea..	per lb.	15 cents
Souchong and other black teas......................	per lb.	27 cents
Hyson..	per lb.	50 cents
Other green teas..................................	per lb.	30 cents
Coffee..	per lb.	4 cents
Cocoa..	per lb.	1 cent
Loaf sugar..	per lb.	5 cents
Brown sugar......................................	per lb.	1½ cent
Other sugar.......................................	per lb.	2½ cents
Candles of tallow..................................	per lb.	2 cents
Candles of wax or spermaceti.......................	per lb.	6 cents
Cheese..	per lb.	4 cents
Soap..	per lb.	2 cents
Pepper..	per lb.	6 cents
Pimento...	per lb.	4 cents
Manufactured tobacco..............................	per lb.	6 cents
Snuff...	per lb.	10 cents
Indigo..	per lb.	25 cents
Cotton..	per lb.	3 cents
Nails and spikes...................................	per lb.	1 cent

Bar and other lead	per lb.	1 cent
Steel unwrought	per 112 lbs.	75 cents
Hemp	per 112 lbs.	60 cents
Cables	per 112 lbs.	150 cents
Tarred cordage	per 112 lbs.	150 cents
Untarred cordage and yarn	per 112 lbs.	180 cents
Twine and packthread	per 112 lbs.	400 cents
Salt	per bushel	12 cents
Malt	per bushel	10 cents
Coal	per bushel	3 cents
Boots	per pair	50 cents
Shoes, slippers and goloshoes, made of leather	per pair	7 cents
Shoes and slippers, made of silk or stuff	per pair	10 cents
Wool and cotton cards	per dozen	50 cents
Playing cards	per pack	10 cents

Coaches, chariots, phaetons, chaises, chairs, solos, or other carriages, or parts of carriages,

$15\frac{1}{2}$ per centum ad valorem

All goods, wares and merchandize (except teas) from China or India, in ships or vessels not of the United States,

All China ware,

Looking-Glasses, window and other glass, and all manufactures of glass (black quart bottles excepted)

$12\frac{1}{2}$ per centum ad valorem

Marble, slate, and other stones, bricks, tiles, tables, mortars, and other utensils of marble or slate, and generally all stone and earthen ware,

Blank books,

Writing paper and wrapping paper, paper hangings, pasteboards, parchment and vellum,

Pictures and prints,

Painters colours, including lamp-black, except those commonly used in dying,

Gold, silver and plated ware,

Gold and silver lace,

Jewellery and paste work,

Clocks and watches,

Shoe and knee buckles,

10 per centum ad valorem

Grocery (except the articles before enumerated, namely, cinnamon, cloves, mace, nutmegs, ginger, anniseed, currants, dates, figs, plums, prunes, raisins, sugar candy, oranges, lemons, limes, and generally all fruits and comfits, olives, capers and pickles of every sort),

Oil,

Gun-powder,

Mustard in flour.

Cabinet wares,

Buttons,

Saddles,

Gloves of leather,

Hats of beaver, felt, wool, or a mixture of any of them,

Millinery ready made,
Castings of iron, and slit and rolled iron,
Leather tanned or tawed, and all manufactures of which leather
   is the article of chief value, except such as are herein otherwise
   rated,
Canes, walking-sticks and whips,
Cloathing ready made,
Brushes,
Anchors,
All wares of tin, pewter or copper, all or any of them.

} $7\frac{1}{2}$ per centum ad valorem

Medicinal drugs, except those commonly used in dying,
Carpets and carpeting,
All velvets, velverets, sattins, and other wrought silks, cambricks, muslins, muslinets, lawns, laces, gauzes, chintzes and
   colored callicoes and nankeens.

} $5\frac{1}{2}$ per centum ad valorem

"All other goods, wares and merchandize, except bullion, tin in pigs, tin in plates, old pewter, brass, teutenague, iron and brass wire, copper in plates, saltpetre, plaster of Paris, wool, dying woods, and dying drugs, raw hides and skins, furrs of every kind, the sea stores of ships or vessels, the cloaths, books, houshold furniture, and the tools or implements of the trade or profession of persons who come to reside in the United States, philosophical apparatus specially imported for any seminary of learning, all goods intended to be re-exported to a foreign port or place in the same ship or vessel in which they shall be imported, and generally all articles of the growth, product or manufactures of the United States, five per centum, ad valorem.

"SEC. 2. *And be it further enacted*, That an addition of ten per centum shall be made to the several rates of duties above specified and imposed, in respect to all goods, wares and merchandize which after the said last day of December next shall be imported in ships or vessels not of the United States, except in the cases in which an additional duty is herein before specially laid on any goods, wares or merchandize which shall be imported in such ships or vessels.

"SEC. 3. *And be it further enacted*, That all duties which shall be paid or secured to be paid by virtue of this act, shall be returned or discharged in respect to all such goods, wares or merchandize whereupon they shall have been so paid, or secured to be paid, as within twelve calendar months after payment made or security given, shall be exported to any foreign port or place, except one per centum on the amount of the said duties, which shall be retained as an indemnification for whatever expence may have accrued concerning the same.

"SEC. 4. *And be it further enacted*, That there shall be allowed and paid on dried and pickled fish of the fisheries of the United States, and on other provisions salted within the said States, which after the said last day of December next shall be exported therefrom to any foreign port or place, in lieu of a drawback of the duty on the salt which shall have been expended thereupon, according to the following rates, viz.

Dried fish, per quintal .... 9 cents

Pickled fish, and other salted provisions, per barrel .... 9 cents

"SEC. 5. *And be it further enacted,* That where duties by this act are imposed, or drawbacks allowed on any specific quantity of goods, wares and merchandize, the same shall be deemed to apply in proportion to any quantity less than such specific quantity.

"SEC. 6. *And be it further enacted,* That all duties which by virtue of the act, entitled, "An Act for laying a duty on goods, wares and merchandizes imported into the United States," accrued between the time specified in the said act for the commencement of the said duties, and the respective times when the collectors entered upon the duties of their respective offices in the several districts, be, and they are hereby remitted and discharged; and that in any case in which they may have been paid to the United States, restitution thereof shall be made.

"SEC. 7. *And be it further enacted,* That the several duties imposed by this act shall continue to be collected and paid until the debts and purposes for which they are pledged and appropriated, shall be fully discharged: *Provided,* That nothing herein contained shall be construed to prevent the Legislature of the United States from substituting other duties or taxes of equal value, to any or all of the said duties and imposts."[24]

On motion to amend the report, so as that a duty of 6 cents, may be collected on every pound of cotton imported, instead of 3 cents—

It passed in the Negative.

On motion to amend the report, so as that a duty may be collected on every 112 lb. of imported cables and tarred cordage, of 120 instead of 150 cents—

It passed in the Negative.

On motion to amend the report, so as that a duty may be collected on every bushel of imported salt, of 8 instead of 12 cents—

It passed in the Negative.

On motion to amend the report, so as that the drawback on every quintal of dried fish, should be 10 instead of 9 cents; and on every barrel of pickled fish and other salted provisions, 10 instead of 9 cents—

It passed in the Negative.

---

[24] A printed copy of this bill is in House Bills, Senate Records, DNA. A printed copy of this bill is also bound into the rough journal with two manuscript corrections: in the first paragraph of the first page, "manufacturers" is changed to "manufactures"; and in the second paragraph of the third page, "plaister of Paris" is changed to "plaster of Paris." A note to the copyist reads: "The Bill verbatim as printed with the Amendments."

And it was agreed to amend the Bill as reported by the Committee.

ORDERED, That this Bill as amended, pass to the THIRD reading.[25]

The Senate adjourned to 11 o'clock to-morrow.

THURSDAY, AUGUST 5, 1790

The SENATE assembled,

Present as yesterday.

The Bill, entitled, "An Act declaring the assent of Congress to certain Acts of the States of Maryland, Georgia and Rhode-Island and Providence Plantations," was read the FIRST time.

ORDERED, That this Bill pass to the SECOND reading.[26]

A message from the House of Representatives by Mr. Beckley their clerk:

"Mr. PRESIDENT,

"The President of the United States has notified the House of Representatives, that he did on the 5th of August, approve of and affix his signature to the 'Act to provide more effectually for the settlement of the accounts between the United States and the individual States'—

"The House of Representatives have passed the Bill, entitled, 'An Act for adding two Commissioners to the board established for settling the accounts between the United States and the individual States,'[27] in which they desire the concurrence of the Senate"—

And he withdrew.

Agreeably to the order of the day, the Senate proceeded to the THIRD reading of the Bill, entitled, "An Act making further provision for the payment of the debt of the United States."

On motion to reduce the impost duty on every 112 lb. of imported hemp, from 60 to 50 cents—

It passed in the Negative.

On motion, it was agreed to re-consider the question, and that the duty on hemp should stand at 54 cents, instead of 60 cents, for every 112 lb. imported.

It was agreed to amend the Bill, so as that the impost duty on cables and tarred cordage, for every 112 lb. should stand at 100 instead of 150 cents, and

On untarred cordage and yarn, for every 112 lb. 150 instead of 180 cents.

On twine and packthread, for every 112 lb. 300 instead of 400 cents.

---

[25] On August 5 this bill was read the third time and several amendments to it were passed. It was then passed as amended and returned to the House for concurrence in the amendments.

[26] On August 6 this bill was read a second time and committed.

[27] The bill, as it passed the House, is in Engrossed House Bills, House Records, DNA.

It was agreed that this clause of the amended Bill, to wit: "all goods, wares and merchandizes (except teas) from China or India, in ships or vessels not of the United States," should be amended and transposed, so as to succeed the word "nankeens," the last of the enumerated articles, as follows: "all goods, wares and merchandize imported directly from China or India, in ships or vessels not of the United States (teas excepted) 12½ per centum, ad valorem."

It was agreed to amend the following clause, and that on "all wares of tin, pewter or copper, all or any of them; medicinal drugs, (except those commonly used in dying) carpets and carpeting, all velvets, velverets, sattins and other wrought silks, cambricks, muslins, muslinets, lawns, laces, gauzes, chintzes and colored callicoes and nankeens," an impost duty of 7½ instead of 5½ per centum ad valorem, be collected.

It was agreed that the word "undressed," be inserted between the words "skins" and "furrs," in the last clause of the first section.

In the fifth section of the amendments, it was agreed to insert between the words "quantity" and "less," the words "greater or."

It was agreed that the drawback on every quintal of dried fish exported, be 10 instead of 9 cents; and on every barrel of pickled fish, and other salted provisions exported, 10 instead of 9 cents.[28]

RESOLVED, That this Bill DO PASS as amended.

ORDERED, That the Secretary carry this Bill to the House of Representatives, and desire their concurrence in the amendments.[29]

The Senate proceeded to the FIRST reading of the Bill, entitled, "An Act for adding two Commissioners to the board established for settling the accounts between the United States and the individual States,"—

And the question whether it shall pass to the SECOND reading? was postponed.[30]

The Bill, entitled, "An Act for the relief of disabled soldiers and seamen, lately in the service of the United States, and of certain other persons," was taken into consideration, and it was agreed further to postpone the THIRD reading.[31]

The Senate took into consideration the report of the Committee on the Bill, entitled, "An Act to compensate Thomas Barclay for various public services," which report is as follows:

Line 3, strike out the word "from," and insert the word "between."

Line 4, strike out the words "one until," and insert the words "and the."

---

[28] The amended printed copy of this bill is in House Bills, Senate Records, DNA.

[29] On August 6 the House concurred in the Senate amendments to this bill with amendments and notified the Senate. On the same day the Senate concurred in the House amendments.

[30] On August 6 the Senate voted not to have this bill pass to the second reading.

[31] On August 6 the Senate considered the committee report on this bill and agreed to amend the bill accordingly. The bill was then read a third time and passed.

Same line, strike out the word "seven," and insert the word "eight"—so that the Bill read thus, between the year 1780, and the year 1788.

Strike out line 6th to line the 9th, these words, "as appointed by the late Congress to that office: On all goods purchased and shipped by him in Holland for the United States, a commission of 2½ per cent. on the value of all the supplies of goods for the United States repacked and shipped by him in France and Holland, a commission of 1 per cent." and insert in their place these words, "in lieu of all commissions for business done on account of the United States, according to the resolution of Congress of the third day of November, 1780."

Line 10th, between the word "years," and the words "a salary," insert "in addition to his actual expences for office rent, clerks, stationary and postage."

Same line, strike out "four," and insert "three."

Same line, strike out "fifteen hundred," and insert "two thousand."

Line 11th, between the words "Morocco," and "the," insert these words, "in addition to his actual expences in conducting the same."

Line 12th, strike out the word "two," and insert "four."

Same line, strike out "which several allowances shall be exclusive of the account of the private expences incurred by the said Thomas Barclay, whilst employed as commissioner and agent aforesaid."

And it was agreed to amend the Bill as reported by the Committee.

ORDERED, That this Bill as amended, pass to the THIRD reading.[32]

The Senate adjourned to 11 o'clock to-morrow.

FRIDAY, AUGUST 6, 1790

The SENATE assembled,
Present as yesterday.

A message from the House of Representatives by Mr. Beckley their clerk:

"Mr. PRESIDENT,

"The House of Representatives have passed a Bill, entitled, 'An Act authorizing the Secretary of the Treasury to finish the light-house on Portland Head, in the district of Maine,'[33] and the Bill, entitled, 'An Act making an appropriation for discharging the claim of Sarah Alexander, the widow of the late Major General Lord Stirling, who died in the service of the United States,'[34] and the Resolve, 'that the President of the Senate and Speaker of the House of Representatives, be authorized to close the present session, by adjourning their respective Houses on Tuesday next, to meet again on the first

---

[32] On August 6 this bill was read a third time, passed as amended, and returned to the House for concurrence.

[33] This bill has not been located.

[34] This bill has not been located.

Monday of December next,'[35] in which Bills and Resolve they desire the concurrence of the Senate"—

And he withdrew.

The Resolve of the House of Representatives, proposing an adjournment of the two Houses on Tuesday next, was read, and ordered to lie on the table.[36]

The Bill, entitled, "An Act authorizing the Secretary of the Treasury to finish the light-house on Portland Head, in the district of Maine," was read the FIRST time.

ORDERED, That this Bill pass to the SECOND reading.[37]

The Bill, entitled, "An Act making an appropriation for discharging the claim of Sarah Alexander, the widow of the late Major General Lord Stirling, who died in the service of the United States," was read the FIRST time.

ORDERED, That this Bill pass to the SECOND reading.

The Senate proceeded to the consideration of the Bill, entitled, "An Act for adding two Commissioners to the board established for settling the accounts between the United States and the individual States,"—and the question, Shall this Bill pass to the SECOND reading?

It passed in the Negative.[38]

The Senate proceeded to the THIRD reading of the Bill, entitled, "An Act to enable the officers and soldiers of the Virginia line on continental establishment, to obtain titles to certain lands lying north-west of the river Ohio, between the Little Miami and Sciota," and

A motion was made, that the following paragraphs should be adopted in lieu of the three sections stricken out, to wit:

"And whereas the agents for such of the troops of the State of Virginia, who served on the continental establishment in the army of the United States, during the late war, have reported to the executive of the said State, that there is not a sufficiency of good land on the south-easterly side of the river Ohio, and within the limits assigned by the laws of the said State, to satisfy the said troops for the bounty lands due to them in conformity to the said laws: To the intent therefore that the difference between what has already been located for the said troops, on the south-easterly side of the said river, and the aggregate of what is due to the whole of the said troops, may be located on the north-westerly side of the said river, and between the Sciota and Little Miami rivers, as stipulated by the said State,

"SEC. 2. *Be it further enacted*, That the Secretary of the department of war,

---

[35] This bill has not been located.

[36] On August 7 the Senate agreed to this House resolution, and the House was notified.

[37] On August 7 this bill was read the second and third times and passed.

[38] The notation that the bill did not pass to a second reading is in Engrossed House Bills, House Records, DNA. This bill was not considered again.

shall make return to the executive of the State of Virginia, of the names of such of the officers, non-commissioned officers and privates of the line of the said State, who served in the army of the United States on the continental establishment during the late war, and who in conformity to the laws of the said State, are entitled to bounty lands; and shall also in such return, state the aggregate amount in acres due to the said line by the laws aforesaid.

"SEC. 3. *And be it further enacted*, That it shall and may be lawful for the said agents to locate to and for the use of the said troops, between the rivers Sciota and Little Miami, such a number of acres of good land as shall, together with the number already located between the said two rivers and the number already located on the south-easterly side of the river Ohio, be equal to the aggregate amount, so to be returned as aforesaid by the Secretary for the department of war.

"SEC. 4. *Be it further enacted*, That the said agents, as soon as may be after the locations, surveys and allotments are made and completed, shall enter in regular order, in a book to be by them provided for that purpose, the bounds of each location and survey between the said two rivers, annexing the name of the officer, non-commissioned officer or private originally entitled to each; which entries being certified by the said agents or the majority of them, to be true entries, the book containing the same shall be filed in the office of the Secretary of State.

"SEC. 5. *And be it further enacted*, That it shall be lawful for the President of the United States, to cause letters patent to be made out in such words and form as he shall devise and direct, granting to such person so originally entitled to bounty lands, to his use, and to the use of his heirs or assigns, or his or their legal representative or representatives, his, her or their heirs or assigns, the lands designated in the said entries: *Provided always*, That before the seal of the United States shall be affixed to such letters patent, the Secretary for the department of war, shall have indorsed thereon that the grantee therein named was originally entitled to such bounty lands, and that he has examined the bounds thereof with the book of entries filed in the office of the Secretary of State, and finds the same truly inserted; and every such letters patent shall be countersigned by the Secretary of State, and a minute of the date thereof, and of the name of the grantee, shall be entered of record in his office, in a book to be specially provided for the purpose.

"SEC. 6. *And be it further enacted*, That it shall be the duty of the Secretary of State, as soon as may be after the letters patent shall be so completed and entered of record, to transmit the same to the executive of the State of Virginia, to be by him delivered to each grantee; or in case of his death, or that the right of the grantee shall have been legally transferred before such delivery, then to his legal representative or representatives, or to one of them.

"SEC. 7. *And be it further enacted*, That no fees shall be charged for such letters patent and record, to the grantees their heirs or assigns, or to his or their legal representative or representatives."[39]

ORDERED, That the further consideration of this Bill be postponed, and that the proposed amendment be printed for consideration.[40]

It was agreed so far to dispense with the rule as that the Bill, entitled, "An Act declaring the assent of Congress to certain Acts of the States of Maryland, Georgia and Rhode-Island and Providence Plantations," be now read the SECOND time.

ORDERED, That this Bill be committed to
          Mr. Foster
          Mr. Gunn and
          Mr. Henry, to consider and report thereon.[41]

The Senate proceeded to the THIRD reading of the Bill, entitled, "An Act to compensate Thomas Barclay for various public services."

RESOLVED, That this Bill DO PASS as amended.

ORDERED, That the Secretary carry this Bill to the House of Representatives, and desire their concurrence in the amendments.[42]

The Senate proceeded to consider the report of the Committee on the Resolve "for allowing to Francis Mentges certain extra expences incurred in the public service"[43]—whereupon,

---

[39] The above seven sections have not been located. The committee report from the second commitment of this bill has not been located.

[40] On August 7 the committee on this bill reported amendments to the bill. The report was amended and the bill was passed with the amended committee report as amendments.

[41] The attested order is in the Theodore Foster Papers, RHi. On August 9 this committee reported an amendment to the bill which was agreed to. The bill was then read the third time and passed with the amendment. On the same day the House agreed to the amendment.

[42] This bill was not mentioned again in either Journal after it was returned to the House. It apparently did not pass.

[43] The rough journal adds:

which report is as follows:

That on an application to Congress for the like extra allowance, the late board of Treasury reported, April 18th. 1787, stating his claims & the reasons why they ought not to be admitted—

That in conformity to said report, Congress resolved August 20th. 1788, that the Memorial of Frances Mentges, late a Lieutenant Colonel in the Pennsylvania Line be dismissed, the Prayer there of being inadmissible—

That Colo. Mentges appears to have produced no new Circumstance in favor of his claim excepting a Letter from the late Commander in Chief of the American Army, which is dated about ten Months previous to the passing of the said Resolution, but is said, by accident, not to have been produced in Congress; In which Letter the Commander in Chief admits the facts as undoubted, that Colo. Mentges was employed in the superintendance of the hospital in Williamsburg, & so far as he can recollect from memory, during the time from Novr. 5th. 1781 to the latter part of the

RESOLVED, That the Senate do not concur in the said Resolution.[44]

A written message from the President of the United States, was by his Secretary communicated to the Vice President—

And he withdrew.

UNITED STATES, August 6, 1790

GENTLEMEN of the SENATE, and
    HOUSE of REPRESENTATIVES,

I HAVE directed my Secretary to lay before you a copy of an exemplified copy of a law to ratify, on the part of the State of New-Jersey, certain amendments to the Constitution of the United States, together with a copy of a letter which accompanied said ratification, from the Honorable Elisha Lawrence, Esq; Vice President of the State of New-Jersey, to the President of the United States.

G. WASHINGTON

(Copy)

"BURLINGTON, August 4, 1790

"Sir,

"I have the honor to transmit an exemplified copy of a law of the State of New-Jersey, ratifying certain amendments to the Constitution of the United States.

"I have the honor to be,
Your most obedient humble Servant,
(Signed)   ELISHA LAWRENCE

"The PRESIDENT of the United States"

(Copy)

(SEAL)

"STATE OF NEW-JERSEY

"The Honorable ELISHA LAWRENCE, Esq; Vice President, Captain General and Commander in Chief, in and over the State of New-Jersey, and territories thereunto belonging, Chancellor and Ordinary in the same

---

following Spring, And adds, that he should suppose Colo. Mentges had acted under written orders, which orders are said to be mislaid & not to be found—

The Committee further report, that Colo. Mentges exhibits no account of actual, extra expences while on this extra service, & admits that he has none, but expects a per diem allowance—

That in 1784 he applied to Congress & obtained an extra allowance as inspector of Contracts for the Southern Army of 110 Dollars per Month, in addition to his pay as an Officer in the Line during the time he executed that Office; but does not appear to have solicited of Congress any allowance for superintending the Hospital until 1787, When his claim was refused—

[44] This resolve is in House Joint and Concurrent Resolutions, Senate Records, DNA.

"To all to whom these presents shall come, greeting:

"These are to certify that Bowes Reed, Esquire, whose name subscribed to the annexed certificate, certifying the annexed law to be a true copy taken from the original, enrolled in his office, is, and was at the time of signing thereof, Secretary of the State of New-Jersey, and that full faith and credit is and ought to be due to his attestation as such.

"In testimony whereof I have hereunto subscribed my name, and caused the Great Seal of the State of New-Jersey, to be hereunto affixed, at the city of Burlington, the third day of August, in the year of our Lord one thousand seven hundred and ninety, and of our independence the fifteenth.

(Signed)   "ELISHA LAWRENCE

"By his Honor's command,
(Signed)   BOWES REED"

(Copy)

"STATE OF NEW-JERSEY

"An Act to ratify, on the part of this State, certain amendments to the Constitution of the United States

"WHEREAS the Congress of the United States, begun and held at the city of New-York on Wednesday the fourth day of March one thousand seven hundred and eighty-nine, resolved, two thirds of both Houses concurring, that sundry articles be proposed to the Legislatures of the several States, as amendments to the Constitution of the United States; all or any of which articles, when ratified by three fourths of the said Legislatures, to be valid to all intents and purposes, as part of the said Constitution. And whereas the President of the United States did in pursuance of a resolve of the Senate and House of Representatives of the United States of America, in Congress assembled, transmit to the Governor of this State the amendments proposed by Congress, which were by him laid before the Legislature, for their consideration,—wherefore,

"I. Be it enacted by the Council and General Assembly of this State, and by the authority of the same it is hereby enacted, that the following articles proposed by Congress in addition to and amendment of the Constitution of the United States, to wit:

[Here follow verbatim, the first, third, fourth, fifth, sixth, seventh, eight, ninth, tenth, eleventh and twelfth articles of the said amendments proposed by Congress to the Legislatures of the several States.]

be, and the same are hereby ratified and adopted by the State of New-Jersey."

"Council Chamber, November 20, 1789—

"This Bill having been three times read in council, resolved that the same do pass.

"By order of the House,
(Signed)   WIL. LIVINGSTON, President"

"House of Assembly, November 18, 1789—

"This Bill having been three times read in this House, resolved that the same do pass.

"By order of the House,

(Signed)   JOHN BEATTY, Speaker"

"City of Burlington, State of New-Jersey,

August 3d, A. D. 1790

"These are to certify that the annexed law is a true copy taken from the original, enrolled in my office.

(Signed)   "BOWES REED, Secretary"[45]

ORDERED, That the message and enclosures be filed.

The Senate proceeded to consider the report of the Committee on the Bill, entitled, "An Act for the relief of disabled soldiers and seamen, lately in the service of the United States, and of certain other persons," which report is as follows:

"That they have examined the vouchers, documents or cases of the several persons for whom provision is intended by the Bill, as having been disabled whilst in the service of the United States; and it appears to your Committee, that if they had respectively applied to the Commissioners appointed by the several States, in conformity to the acts of the late Congress, they would have received certificates to entitle them to be placed on the list of pensioners: That in general, for want of information or through ignorance, they did not apply within the time assigned by the act of the 11th of June 1788, within which applications were to be made; that in the opinion of your Committee they are nevertheless equitably entitled to the intended relief.

"That the relief intended for the other persons in the Bill, appears to your Committee just and proper.

"That your Committee are of opinion that similiar relief should be extended to the several other persons who were disabled in the service of the United States, as appears from the documents delivered with this report, and therefore propose the following amendments to the Bill:

"Sec. 1, line 2d, to strike out 'James,' and insert 'Joseph.'

"Line 3d, strike out 'AND,' and after 'Steele,' insert 'Joseph Shuttlief and Daniel Culver.'

"Line 6th, after the word 'discharge,' insert 'that Edward Scott, a disabled soldier, be allowed a pension at the rate of three dollars per month, from the date of his discharge. That David Weaver and George Schell, disabled soldiers, be each allowed a pension at the rate of two dollars per month, from

---

[45] The message, including copies of the above statements, is in President's Messages: Suggesting legislation, Senate Records, DNA.

the date of their respective discharges. That Seth Boardman, a disabled soldier, be allowed a pension at the rate of three dollars and one third of a dollar per month, from the 17th day of March 1786. That Severenus Koch, a disabled captain of colonel Jacob Klock's regiment of New-York militia, be allowed a pension at the rate of five dollars per month, from the 20th day of August 1777. That John Younglove, a disabled major of colonel Lewis Van Woort's regiment of New-York militia, be allowed a pension at the rate of six dollars per month, from the 30th day of July 1781. That William White, a disabled private of colonel Williams's regiment of New-York militia, be allowed a pension at the rate of three dollars and one third of a dollar per month, from the first day of April 1786. That Jacob Newkirk, a disabled soldier of colonel John Harper's regiment of New-York State troops, be allowed a pension at the rate of three dollars per month, from the 22d day of October 1780' "—

And it was agreed to amend the Bill accordingly; and that the 5th section of the Bill be struck out.

ORDERED, That this Bill pass to the THIRD reading.

RESOLVED, That this Bill DO PASS as amended.

ORDERED, That the Secretary carry this Bill to the House of Representatives, and desire their concurrence in the amendments.[46]

It was agreed by unanimous consent, that the Bill, entitled, "An Act making an appropriation for discharging the claim of Sarah Alexander, the widow of the late Major General Lord Stirling, who died in the service of the United States," be now read the SECOND time.

ORDERED, That this Bill be committed to

　　　　Mr. Schuyler
　　　　Mr. Butler and
　　　　Mr. Izard[47]

The Senate adjourned to 11 o'clock to-morrow.

SATURDAY, AUGUST 7, 1790

The SENATE assembled,

Present as yesterday,

And proceeded to the SECOND reading of the Bill, entitled, "An Act authorizing the Secretary of the Treasury to finish the light-house on Portland Head, in the district of Maine."

It was agreed by unanimous consent, that this Bill be now read the THIRD time.

RESOLVED, That this Bill DO PASS.

---

[46] On August 9 the House concurred in the Senate amendments to this bill and notified the Senate.

[47] On August 6 this committee reported amendments which were accepted and the bill was passed. The House was notified of this action.

ORDERED, That the Secretary acquaint the House of Representatives with the concurrence of the Senate in this Bill.[48]

The Senate proceeded to consider the report of the Committee on the THIRD reading of the Bill, entitled, "An Act to enable the officers and soldiers of the Virginia line on continental establishment, to obtain titles to certain lands lying north-west of the river Ohio, between the Little Miami and Sciota;" which report was amended as follows:

After the word "Ohio," 4th line, insert "according to the act of cession from the said State, to the United States"[49]—

And it was agreed to amend the Bill in conformity to the report.

RESOLVED, That this Bill DO PASS as amended.

ORDERED, That the Secretary carry this Bill to the House of Representatives, and desire their concurrence in the amendments.[50]

A message from the House of Representatives by Mr. Beckley their clerk:

"Mr. PRESIDENT,

"The House of Representatives have agreed to the amendments of the Senate, to the Bill, entitled, 'An Act making further provision for the payment of the debts of the United States,' with amendments,[51] to which they desire the concurrence of the Senate"—

And he withdrew.

The Senate proceeded to consider the amendments of the House of Representatives, to their amendments on the Bill, entitled, "An Act making further provision for the payment of the debts of the United States"—and

RESOLVED, That they concur therein.

ORDERED, That the Secretary acquaint the House of Representatives therewith.[52]

Mr. Schuyler from the Committee on the Bill, entitled, "An Act making an appropriation for discharging the claim of Sarah Alexander, the widow of the late Major General Lord Stirling, who died in the service of the United States," reported amendments,[53] to wit:

---

[48] On August 9 this bill was signed by both the Speaker and the Vice President and given to the committee on enrolled bills for delivery to the President.

[49] These amendments have not been located.

[50] The House concurred in these amendments on August 7. On August 9 this bill was signed by both the Speaker and the Vice President and given to the committee on enrolled bills for delivery to the President.

[51] These amendments have not been located.

[52] On August 9 this bill was signed by both the Speaker and the Vice President and given to the committee on enrolled bills for delivery to the President.

[53] This report is in Various Select Committee Reports, Senate Records, DNA.

"Strike out of the section all subsequent to the word 'that,' in the second line, and substitute as follows—'The Register of the Treasury shall, and is hereby required to grant unto Sarah the widow of the late Major General Earl of Stirling, who died in the service of the United States, a certificate to entitle her to a sum equal to an annuity for seven years half pay of a Major General; to commence as from the 14th day of January 1783, in conformity to the act of the late Congress, passed on the 24th day of August 1780; the amount for which the said certificate is to be granted, to be ascertained by the Secretary of the Treasury, and on similar principles as other debts of the United States are liquidated and certified.'

"And be it further enacted, that the said Register shall grant unto Francis Eleanor Laurens, the orphan daughter of the late Lieutenant Colonel John Laurens, who was killed whilst in the service of the United States, a certificate to entitle her to a sum equal to an annuity for seven years half pay of a Lieutenant Colonel; to commence as from the 25th day of August 1782, according to the act of the late Congress, of the 24th day of August 1780; the amount for which the said certificate is to be granted to be ascertained by the Secretary of the Treasury in manner aforesaid.

"And whereas no provision hath heretofore been made for discharging the arrears of pensions due to officers, non-commissioned officers and soldiers, who were wounded and disabled whilst in the service of the United States—therefore be it further enacted, that each of the officers, non-commissioned officers and soldiers who were so wounded and disabled, and who is now placed in the books in the office of the Secretary of the department of war, as a pensioner, or to be so placed in conformity to any law of this Congress, shall receive from the Register of the Treasury, (who is hereby required to grant the same) a certificate, to be liquidated and settled in such manner as the Secretary of the Treasury shall direct, for a sum equal to the pension annually due to him; to commence from the time he became entitled thereto, or from the time to which the same had been paid, as the case may be; which shall be ascertained and certified by the said Secretary for the department of war, and which annuity shall be liquidated to the 4th day of March 1789; from which day the United States have assumed the payment of the pensions certified by the several States: And in case of the death of any person so entitled, the certificate shall pass to his heirs or legal representative or representatives.

"And be it further enacted, that the widow or orphan of each officer, non-commissioned officer or soldier, who was killed or died whilst in the service of the United States, and who is now placed on the books in the office of the said Secretary as entitled to a pension by virtue of any act of the said late Congress, or any law of this Congress, and for whom provision has not been made by any State, and to whom any arrears of such pension are due, and which have arisen prior to the said 4th day of March 1789, shall receive a certificate therefore in like manner and on the same principles as certificates are by this act directed to be given to officers, non-commissioned officers and soldiers who were wounded or disabled as aforesaid—

"Expunge from the title all after the word 'act,' and substitute 'for the relief of the persons therein mentioned or described' "—

And it was agreed to amend the Bill agreeably to the report of the Committee.

ORDERED, That this Bill be now read the THIRD time.

RESOLVED, That this Bill DO PASS.

ORDERED, That the Secretary desire the concurrence of the House of Representatives in the amendments to this Bill.[54]

The Bill for altering the times of holding the courts in South Carolina and Georgia, was read the FIRST time.[55]

It was agreed by unanimous consent that this Bill be now read the SECOND time.

ORDERED, That it pass to the THIRD reading.[56]

On motion to take up the Resolution of the House of Representatives, of the 6th of August, to wit: "That the President of the Senate and Speaker of the House of Representatives, be authorized to close the present session, by adjourning their respective Houses on Tuesday next, to meet again on the first Monday of December next"—

A motion was made to postpone the consideration thereof, to take up the following motion—"That leave be given to bring in a Bill to repeal the fifth section of an act, entitled, 'An Act for establishing the temporary and permanent seat of the government of the United States,' "—which passed in the negative, and the consideration of the Resolution of the House of Representatives was resumed—and

RESOLVED, That the Senate do concur in the Resolution of the House of Representatives.

ORDERED, That the Secretary acquaint the House of Representatives therewith.[57]

The Senate adjourned to 11 o'clock on Monday next.

---

[54] On August 9 the House concurred in the Senate amendments to this bill and notified the Senate.

[55] This bill is in Senate Bills, Senate Records, DNA.

[56] On August 9 the Senate read the bill a third time and passed it. It was then sent to the House which read it three times and passed it with an amendment on the same day. The Senate immediately concurred in the amendment.

[57] On August 9 the House passed a resolution appointing a committee to confer with a Senate committee on adjournment. On the same day the Senate received this resolution and read it, and it was laid for consideration.

MONDAY, AUGUST 9, 1790

The SENATE assembled,
Present as on the 7th, except

Mr. Bassett   Mr. Langdon and
Mr. Elmer   Mr. Strong, absent with leave

Mr. Wingate reported from the Committee on enrolled Bills, that they had examined the enrolled Bill, entitled, "An Act making further provision for the payment of the debts of the United States,"[58] the enrolled Bill, entitled, "An Act to enable the officers and soldiers of the Virginia line on continental establishment, to obtain titles to certain lands lying north-west of the river Ohio, between the Little Miami and Sciota,"[59] and the enrolled Bill, entitled, "An Act authorizing the Secretary of the Treasury to finish the light-house on Portland Head, in the district of Maine,"[60] and had found them correct.

A message from the House of Representatives by Mr. Beckley their clerk:

"Mr. PRESIDENT,

"The Speaker of the House of Representatives having signed several enrolled Bills, I am directed to bring them to the Senate, for the signature of the Vice President—

"The House of Representatives have 'Resolved that Mr. Gilman, Mr. White and Mr. Smith (of South-Carolina) be a Committee to join with such Committee as the Senate shall appoint, to wait on the President of the United States, and notify him of the proposed recess of Congress;'[61] they have also passed a Bill, entitled, 'An Act for the relief of Adam Caldwell,'[62] in which Bill and Resolution, they desire the concurrence of the Senate, and the appointment of a Committee on their part—

"They have concurred in the amendments of the Senate on the Bill, entitled, 'An Act to enable the officers and soldiers of the Virginia line on continental establishment, to obtain titles to certain lands lying north-west of the River Ohio, between the Little Miami and Sciota;' they have concurred in the amendments of the Senate on the Bill, entitled, 'An Act making an appropriation for discharging the claim of Sarah Alexander, the widow of the late Major General Lord Stirling, who died in the service of the United States,'[63] and in the amendments of the Senate on the Bill, entitled, 'An Act for the relief of dis-

---

[58] The inspected enrolled bill is in Enrolled Acts, RG 11, DNA. E–22965.

[59] The inspected enrolled bill is in Enrolled Acts, RG 11, DNA. E–46065.

[60] The inspected enrolled bill is in Enrolled Acts, RG 11, DNA. E–22955.

[61] This resolve has not been located.

[62] The bill, as it passed the House, is in Engrossed House Bills, House Records, DNA.

[63] On August 10 this bill (referred to as "An Act for the relief of the persons therein mentioned or described") was signed by both the Speaker and the Vice President. On the same day the committee on enrolled bills delivered this bill to the President.

abled soldiers and seamen, lately in the service of the United States, and of certain other persons' "[64]—

And he withdrew.

The Vice President signed the enrolled Bill, entitled, "An Act making further provision for the payment of the debts of the United States," the enrolled Bill, entitled, "An Act to enable the officers and soldiers of the Virginia line on continental establishment, to obtain titles to certain lands lying north-west of the river Ohio, between the Little Miami and Sciota;" and the enrolled Bill, entitled, "An Act authorizing the Secretary of the Treasury to finish the lighthouse on Portland Head, in the district of Maine," and they were delivered to the Committee on enrolled Bills, to lay before the President of the United States, for his approbation.[65]

Mr. Foster from the Committee appointed to consider the Bill, entitled, "An Act declaring the assent of Congress to certain Acts of the States of Maryland, Georgia and Rhode-Island and Providence Plantations," reported the following amendment:[66]

Strike out the words "for the term of three years from the passing of this act," and in their place insert these words, "until the tenth day of January next."

It was agreed by unanimous consent that this Bill be now read the THIRD time.

RESOLVED, That this Bill DO PASS as amended.

ORDERED, That the Secretary carry this Bill to the House of Representatives, and desire their concurrence in the amendment.

The Resolution of the House of Representatives "that Mr. Gilman, Mr. White and Mr. Smith (of South-Carolina) be a Committee to join with such Committee as the Senate shall appoint, to wait on the President of the United States, and notify him of the proposed recess of Congress," was read, and ordered to lie for consideration.[67]

The Bill for altering the times of holding the courts in South-Carolina and Georgia, was read the THIRD time.

RESOLVED, That this Bill DO PASS, and that the title of it be "An Act to

---

[64] On August 10 this bill was signed by both the Speaker and the Vice President and given to the committee on enrolled bills for delivery to the President.

[65] On August 10 the President signed all these bills.

[66] This report has not been located.

[67] On August 10 the Senate resolved to set August 12 as the date for adjournment and notified the House. On the same day the Senate agreed to the House resolution appointing a committee on adjournment. A committee was appointed to meet with the House committee and the House was notified. On the same day the House agreed to the Senate resolution to adjourn on August 12.

alter the times for holding the Circuit Courts of the United States in the districts of South-Carolina and Georgia."[68]

ORDERED, That the Secretary carry this Bill to the House of Representatives, and desire their concurrence in the amendments.

The Senate proceeded to the FIRST reading of the Bill, entitled, "An Act for the relief of Adam Caldwell."

ORDERED, That this Bill lie for consideration.[69]

A message from the House of Representatives by Mr. Beckley their clerk:

"Mr. PRESIDENT,

"The House of Representatives agree to the amendment of the Senate, to the Bill, entitled, 'An Act declaring the assent of Congress to certain acts of the States of Maryland, Georgia and Rhode-Island and Providence Plantations'[70]—

"They have concurred in the Bill, entitled, 'An Act to alter the times for holding the Circuit Courts of the United States in the districts of South-Carolina and Georgia,' with amendments,[71] in which amendments they desire the concurrence of the Senate—

"They have 'Resolved that all surveys of lands in the western territory made under the direction of the late geographer Thomas Hutchins, be returned to and perfected by the Secretary of the Treasury' "[72]—

"The House of Representatives have also passed a Bill, entitled, 'An Act making provision for the reduction of the public debt;'[73] in which Bill and Resolution they desire the concurrence of the Senate"—

And he withdrew.

The Senate proceeded to consider the amendments of the House of Representatives to the Bill, entitled, "An Act to alter the times for holding the Circuit Courts of the United States in the districts of South-Carolina and Georgia" —and

RESOLVED, That they concur therein.[74]

ORDERED, That the Secretary acquaint the House of Representatives therewith.[75]

---

[68] The bill, as it passed the Senate, is in Engrossed Senate Bills and Resolutions, Senate Records, DNA.

[69] On August 11 this bill was read a second time and postponed until the next session.

[70] On August 10 this bill was signed by both the Speaker and the Vice President and given to the committee on enrolled bills for delivery to the President.

[71] The amendments are in Engrossed Senate Bills and Resolutions, Senate Records, DNA.

[72] This resolve has not been located.

[73] An annotated printed copy of this bill is in House Bills, Senate Records, DNA.

[74] This resolve is in Engrossed Senate Bills and Resolutions, Senate Records, DNA.

[75] On August 10 this bill was signed by both the Speaker and the Vice President and delivered to the President.

The Bill, entitled, "An Act making provision for the reduction of the public debt," was read the FIRST time.

ORDERED, That this Bill pass to the SECOND reading, and that it be printed for consideration.[76]

The Senate proceeded to consider the Resolution of the House of Representatives of this day, "that all surveys of lands in the western territory made under the direction of the late geographer Thomas Hutchins, agreeable to contracts for part of the said lands made with the late board of Treasury, be returned to, and perfected by the Secretary of the Treasury, so as to complete the said contracts; and that the said Secretary be, and is hereby authorized to direct the making and completing any other surveys that remain to be made, so as to comply on the part of the United States with the several contracts aforesaid, in conformity to the terms thereof,"—and

RESOLVED, That they concur therein.

ORDERED, That the Secretary acquaint the House of Representatives therewith.[77]

ORDERED, That the consideration of the Resolution of the House of Representatives, proposing a joint Committee to wait on the President of the United States, to notify him of the proposed recess of Congress, be postponed.

The Senate adjourned to 11 o'clock to-morrow.

TUESDAY, AUGUST 10, 1790

The SENATE assembled,
Present as yesterday.

Mr. Wingate reported from the Committee on enrolled Bills, that they did yesterday lay before the President of the United States for his approbation, the enrolled Bill, entitled, "An Act making further provision for the payment of the debts of the United States," the enrolled Bill, entitled, "An Act to enable the officers and soldiers of the Virginia line on continental establishment, to obtain titles to certain lands lying north-west of the river Ohio, between the Little Miami and Sciota," and the enrolled Bill, entitled, "An Act authorizing the Secretary of the Treasury to finish the light-house on Portland Head, in the district of Maine." That they have this day examined the enrolled Bill, entitled, "An Act to alter the times for holding the Circuit Courts of the United States, in the districts of South-Carolina and Georgia, and providing that the District Court of Pennsylvania, shall in future be held at the city of

---

[76] On August 10 this bill was read for the second time, amended, read a third time, and passed with amendments. It was then returned to the House for concurrence in the amendments.

[77] On August 11 this resolve was signed by both the Speaker and the Vice President.

Philadelphia only,"[78] the enrolled Bill, entitled, "An Act for the relief of disabled soldiers and seamen lately in the service of the United States, and of certain other persons,"[79] the enrolled Bill, entitled, "An Act declaring the assent of Congress to certain acts of the States of Maryland, Georgia and Rhode-Island and Providence Plantations,"[80] and the enrolled Bill, entitled, "An Act for the relief of the persons therein mentioned or described,"[81] and had found them correct.

A message from the House of Representatives by Mr. Beckley their clerk:

"Mr. PRESIDENT,

"The President of the United States has notified the House of Representatives, that he hath on this day approved of and affixed his signature to 'An Act making further provision for the payment of the debts of the United States,' to 'An Act to enable the officers and soldiers of the Virginia line on continental establishment, to obtain titles to certain lands lying north-west of the river Ohio, between the Little Miami and Sciota,' and to 'An Act authorizing the Secretary of the Treasury to finish the light-house on Portland Head, in the District of Maine'[82]—

"The House of Representatives have passed the Bill, entitled, 'An Act making certain appropriations therein mentioned,'[83] in which they desire the concurrence of the Senate—

"The Speaker of the House of Representatives having signed several enrolled Bills,[84] I am directed to bring them to the Senate for the signature of the Vice President"—

And he withdrew.

The Vice President signed the enrolled Bill, entitled, "An Act to alter the times for holding the Circuit Courts of the United States, in the districts of South-Carolina and Georgia, and providing that the District Court of Pennsylvania, shall in future be held at the city of Philadelphia only," the enrolled Bill, entitled, "An Act for the relief of disabled soldiers and seamen lately in the service of the United States, and of certain other persons," the enrolled Bill, entitled, "An Act declaring the assent of Congress to certain acts of the States of Maryland, Georgia, and Rhode-Island and Providence Plantations," and the enrolled Bill, entitled, "An Act for the relief of the persons therein

---

[78] The inspected enrolled bill is in Enrolled Acts, RG 11, DNA. E–46061.

[79] The inspected enrolled bill is in Enrolled Acts, RG 11, DNA. E–46042.

[80] The inspected enrolled bill is in Enrolled Acts, RG 11, DNA.

[81] The inspected enrolled bill is in Enrolled Acts, RG 11, DNA.

[82] This message is in Committee on Enrolled Bills, Senate Records, DNA.

[83] This bill has not been located.

[84] A list of the following inspected enrolled bills is in Committee on Enrolled Bills, Senate Records, DNA.

mentioned or described," and they were delivered to the Committee on enrolled Bills, to be laid before the President of the United States for his approbation.

The Senate proceeded to the SECOND reading of the Bill, entitled, "An Act making provision for the reduction of the public debt."

On motion that the consideration thereof be postponed—

It passed in the Negative.

It was agreed to expunge these words in the preamble, line 3d, "to the present session"—

And these words, line 4th and 5th, "by counteracting the purchase thereof by foreigners below its true value, will at the same time."

And section 2d, line 2, to strike out the words "five Commissioners, who shall be"—

On motion to expunge these words, section 2d, line 6th, "openly and"—

It passed in the Negative.

On motion to insert these words, section 2d, line 10, after "reservations," "and not less than five hundred thousand dollars"—

It passed in the Negative.

It was agreed to expunge these words, section 2d, line 12th, "of the product, after the said last day of December next"—

To insert at the end of section 2d, these words, "and the tonnage of ships or vessels, after the last day of December next"—

To expunge section 3d, line 4th, the word "Commissioners," and insert "five persons, or any three of them"—

To expunge lines 6 and 7, the words "by them"—

To amend the proviso to read as follows: "Provided, that out of the interest arising on the debt to be purchased in manner aforesaid, there shall be appropriated and applied a sum not exceeding the rate of eight per centum per annum, on account both of principal and interest, towards the re-payment of the two millions of dollars so to be borrowed."[85]

It was agreed by unanimous consent, that this Bill as amended, should be read the THIRD time.

RESOLVED, That this Bill DO PASS as amended.

ORDERED, That the Secretary desire the concurrence of the House of Representatives in the amendments to this Bill.[86]

On motion,

RESOLVED, That the Resolution of the 7th instant, authorizing the President of the Senate, and the Speaker of the House of Representatives, to adjourn

---

[85] A printed copy of this bill, with amendments written in, is in House Bills, Senate Records, DNA.

[86] On August 11 the House concurred in all of these amendments. On the same day this bill was signed by both the Speaker and the Vice President.

their respective Houses on this day, be repealed, and instead thereof that they be authorized and directed to adjourn their respective Houses on the 12th instant, to meet again on the first Monday of December next.

ORDERED, That the Secretary carry this Resolution to the House of Representatives, and desire their concurrence therein.[87]

The Senate resumed the consideration of the Resolution of the House of Representatives of the 9th of August, appointing a Committee to wait on the President of the United States, and notify him of the proposed recess of Congress—and

RESOLVED, That they concur therein, and that

> Mr. Izard and
>
> Mr. Johnston, be the Committee on the part of the

Senate.

ORDERED, That the Secretary acquaint the House of Representatives with the concurrence of the Senate in the Resolution above mentioned.

The Bill, entitled, "An Act making certain appropriations therein mentioned," was read the FIRST time.

ORDERED, That this Bill pass to the SECOND reading.[88]

A message from the House of Representatives by Mr. Beckley their clerk:

"Mr. PRESIDENT,

"The House of Representatives agree to the Resolution of Senate, to defer the adjournment of the two Houses of Congress to Thursday the 12th instant"[89]—

And he withdrew.

The Committee on enrolled Bills, did this day lay before the President of the United States, for his approbation, the enrolled Bill, entitled, "An Act to alter the times for holding the Circuit Courts of the United States, in the districts of South-Carolina and Georgia, and providing that the District Court of Pennsylvania, shall in future be held at the city of Philadelphia only," the enrolled Bill, entitled, "An Act for the relief of disabled soldiers and seamen lately in the service of the United States, and of certain other persons," the enrolled Bill, entitled, "An Act declaring the assent of Congress to certain acts of the States of Maryland, Georgia, and Rhode-Island and Providence

---

[87] The resolution by Mr. Rufus King and the Senate order are in Senate Simple Resolutions and Motions, Senate Records, DNA. The resolve is in Senate Joint and Concurrent Resolutions, Senate Records, DNA.

[88] On August 11 this bill was read a second time, amended, read a third time, and passed. It was then sent to the House which agreed to the amendments. On the same day the bill was signed by both the Speaker and the Vice President.

[89] The House message, attached to the Senate resolve, is in Senate Joint and Concurrent Resolutions, Senate Records, DNA. On August 11 the joint committee on adjournment reported that it had notified the President of the adjournment date.

Plantations," and the enrolled Bill, entitled, "An Act for the relief of the persons therein mentioned or described."[90]

The Senate adjourned to 10 o'clock to-morrow.

WEDNESDAY, AUGUST 11, 1790

The SENATE assembled,
Present as yesterday, except
Mr. Wingate.

Mr. Izard from the Committee of both Houses appointed to notify the President of the United States of the intended adjournment of Congress, reported, that they had waited on the President of the United States, and informed him, that the two Houses of Congress had agreed to adjourn on Thursday the 12th instant.[91]

A message from the House of Representatives by Mr. Beckley their clerk:

"Mr. PRESIDENT,

"The House of Representatives agree to all the amendments of the Senate to the Bill, entitled, 'An Act making provision for the reduction of the public debt' "—

And he withdrew.

A message from the President of the United States by his Secretary:

"Mr. PRESIDENT,

"The President of the United States has this day approved of and affixed his signature to 'An Act to alter the times for holding the Circuit Courts of the United States in the districts of South-Carolina and Georgia, and providing that the District Court of Pennsylvania, shall in future be held in the city of Philadelphia only.' "

On motion,

ORDERED, That Mr. Foster be appointed on the part of the Senate on the joint Committee to examine enrolled Bills.

ORDERED, That the Secretary acquaint the House of Representatives therewith.

The Senate proceeded to the SECOND reading of the Bill, entitled, "An Act making certain appropriations therein mentioned."

On motion it was agreed to amend the Bill by the insertion of the following

---

[90] On August 11 the President signed all these bills, and the Senate was notified on the next day.

[91] On August 12 Congress adjourned.

clause after the word "captivity," in the 7th line, "the sum of forty thousand dollars, towards discharging certain debts contracted by colonel Timothy Pickering, late Quarter-master General; and which sum was included in the amount of a warrant drawn in his favour by the late Superintendant of the Finances of the United States, and which warrant was not discharged."[92]

It was agreed by unanimous consent that this Bill as amended, pass to the THIRD reading.

RESOLVED, That this Bill DO PASS as amended.

ORDERED, That the Secretary desire the concurrence of the House of Representatives in the amendment to this Bill.

The Senate proceeded to the SECOND reading of the Bill, entitled, "An Act for the relief of Adam Caldwell,"—and

RESOLVED, That it be postponed to the next session of Congress.[93]

Mr. Foster reported from the Committee on enrolled Bills, that they had this day examined the enrolled Bill, entitled, "An Act making certain appropriations therein mentioned,"[94] the enrolled Bill, entitled, "An Act making provision for the reduction of the public debt,"[95] and the enrolled "Resolve respecting surveys of lands under the direction of the late geographer Thomas Hutchins,"[96] and had found them truly enrolled.

A message from the House of Representatives by Mr. Beckley their clerk:

"Mr. PRESIDENT,

"The House of Representatives agree to the amendment of the Senate to the Bill, entitled, 'An Act making certain appropriations therein mentioned'—

"The Speaker having signed several enrolled Bills, and an enrolled Resolve, I am directed to bring them to the Senate, for the signature of the Vice President"—

And he withdrew.

Whereupon the Vice President signed the enrolled Bill, entitled, "An Act making provision for the reduction of the public debt," the enrolled Bill, entitled, "An Act making certain appropriations therein mentioned," and the enrolled "Resolve respecting surveys of lands under the direction of the late geographer Thomas Hutchins," and they were delivered to the Committee on enrolled Bills, to be laid before the President of the United States.[97]

The Senate adjourned to 9 o'clock to-morrow morning.

---

[92] This amendment is in House Bills, Senate Records, DNA.
[93] This simple resolution is in Engrossed House Bills, House Records, DNA.
[94] The inspected enrolled bill is in Enrolled Acts, RG 11, DNA. E–46045.
[95] The inspected enrolled bill is in Enrolled Acts, RG 11, DNA. E–46050.
[96] The inspected enrolled resolve is in Enrolled Acts, RG 11, DNA. E–46074.
[97] On August 12 the President signed both of these bills and the resolve.

THURSDAY, AUGUST 12, 1790

The SENATE assembled,
Present as yesterday.

Mr. Foster from the Committee on enrolled Bills, reported that they did yesterday lay before the President of the United States for his approbation, the enrolled Bill, entitled, "An Act making provision for the reduction of the public debt," the enrolled Bill, entitled, "An Act making certain appropriations therein mentioned," and the enrolled "Resolve respecting surveys of lands under the direction of the late geographer Thomas Hutchins."

A message from the House of Representatives by Mr. Beckley their clerk:

"Mr. PRESIDENT,

"The President of the United States, has notified the House of Representatives, that he did on the 11th instant, approve of and affix his signature to 'An Act declaring the assent of Congress to certain acts of the States of Maryland, Georgia and Rhode-Island and Providence Plantations,' to 'An Act for the relief of disabled soldiers and seamen lately in the service of the United States, and of certain other persons,' and to 'An Act for the relief of the persons therein mentioned or described;' and that he has this day, approved of and affixed his signature to 'An Act making provision for the reduction of the public debt,' to 'An Act making certain appropriations therein mentioned,' and to a 'Resolve respecting surveys of lands made under the direction of the late geographer Thomas Hutchins'[98]—

"I am directed to inform the Senate that the House of Representatives having finished the business before them, are about to adjourn, agreeably to the vote of the two Houses of Congress on Tuesday last"—

And he withdrew.

On motion,

RESOLVED UNANIMOUSLY, That the thanks of the Senate be given to the Corporation of the City of New-York, for the elegant and convenient accommodations provided for Congress; and that a copy of this Resolve be enclosed in the following letter from the Vice President.

NEW-YORK, August 12, 1790

SIR,

IT is with great pleasure, that, in obedience to an order of the Senate of the United States, I have the honor to enclose their Resolution of this date, which was unanimously agreed to; and in behalf of the Senate, I request that you will be pleased to communicate the same to the Corporation of this city, and at the same time signify to them, that it is the wish of the Senate, that the

---

[98] This message is in Committee on Enrolled Bills, Senate Records, DNA.

Corporation will permit such articles of furniture, &c. now in the City-Hall, as have been provided by Congress, to remain for the use of that building.

> I am, SIR, your most obedient
>> Humble servant,
>>> JOHN ADAMS
>>> VICE PRESIDENT of the United States,
>>> and PRESIDENT of the SENATE

To the MAYOR of the
  City of New-York[99]

ORDERED, That the Secretary acquaint the House of Representatives, that the Senate having finished the legislative business before them, are about to adjourn, agreeably to the vote of both Houses of Congress of the 10th inst.—

And the Vice President adjourned the Senate accordingly, to meet on the first Monday in December next.

> Attest. SAMUEL A. OTIS, Secretary

---

[99] A copy of this resolve and this letter are in Senate Simple Resolutions and Motions, Senate Records, DNA.

J O U R N A L

OF THE THIRD SESSION OF THE

SENATE OF THE UNITED STATES

TO WIT

NEW-HAMPSHIRE

MASSACHUSETTS

RHODE-ISLAND

CONNECTICUT

NEW-YORK

NEW-JERSEY

PENNSYLVANIA

DELAWARE

MARYLAND

VIRGINIA

NORTH-CAROLINA

SOUTH-CAROLINA

GEORGIA

Being the THIRTEEN STATES that have respectively ratified the Constitution of Government for the UNITED STATES, proposed by the CONVENTION held at Philadelphia, on the 17th of Sept. 1787.

M O N D A Y, December 6, 1790

The Senate assembled—present,
JOHN ADAMS, Vice President of the United States, and
President of the Senate
From

NEW-HAMPSHIRE	The Honorable	⎰ John Langdon and ⎱ Paine Wingate
MASSACHUSETTS	The Honorable	Tristram Dalton
CONNECTICUT	The Honorable	Oliver Ellsworth
NEW-YORK	The Honorable	Rufus King
PENNSYLVANIA	The Honorable	⎰ William Maclay and ⎱ Robert Morris
DELAWARE	The Honorable	Richard Bassett
NORTH-CAROLINA	The Honorable	⎰ Samuel Johnston and ⎱ Benjamin Hawkins
SOUTH-CAROLINA	The Honorable	⎰ Pierce Butler and ⎱ Ralph Izard
GEORGIA	The Honorable	William Few

The Honorable Philemon Dickinson, from the State of New-Jersey, produced his credentials[1] and took his seat in the Senate, in the place of his Excellency Governor Paterson, resigned.

The Honorable James Monroe, appointed by the Legislature of the State of Virginia, in the place of the Honorable John Walker, who was appointed by the executive of the said State in the room of the Honorable William Grayson, deceased, produced his credentials[2] and took his seat in the Senate.

The Vice President administered the oath required by law, to Mr. Dickinson and Mr. Monroe, respectively.

A letter was read from his Excellency William Paterson,[3] Governor of the State of New-Jersey,[4] communicating the resignation of his appointment to be a Senator of the United States.

ORDERED, That the Secretary inform the House of Representatives, that a quorum of the Senate is assembled and ready to proceed to business.

The Senate adjourned to 11 o'clock to-morrow.

---

[1] The credentials are in Election Records: Credentials of Senators, Senate Records, DNA.

[2] The credentials are in Election Records: Credentials of Senators, Senate Records, DNA.

[3] This letter has not been located.

[4] The rough journal here includes the canceled phrase "to the Vice President."

T U E S D A Y, December 7, 1790

The Senate assembled—present as yesterday.

A message from the House of Representatives by Mr. Beckley their clerk:

"Mr. President,

"I am directed to inform the Senate that a quorum of the House of Representatives is assembled,[5] and ready to proceed to business,"—

And he withdrew.

The petition of James Alexander was read,[6] praying that he might be appointed Serjeant at Arms, Door-keeper or Messenger.

Ordered, That this petition lie on the table.

Resolved, That

> Mr. Langdon and
>
> Mr. Morris, be a Committee on the part of the Senate,

with such Committee as the House of Representatives may appoint on their part, to inform the President of the United States, that a quorum of the two Houses is assembled, and will be ready in the Senate Chamber at such time as the President of the United States may appoint, to receive any communications he may be pleased to make.[7]

Ordered, That the Secretary desire the concurrence of the House of Representatives, in this resolution.

A message from the House of Representatives by Mr. Beckley their clerk:

"Mr. President,

"The House of Representatives have resolved that a Committee be appointed, jointly, with such Committee as the Senate shall appoint, to wait on the President of the United States, and notify him that a quorum of both Houses is assembled,"[8]—

And he withdrew.

The resolution of the House of Representatives was read.

A message from the House of Representatives by Mr. Beckley their Clerk:

"Mr. President,

"I am directed to inform the Senate, that the House of Representatives have

---

[5] The rough journal originally included and then canceled the word "are."

[6] This petition has not been located.

[7] This resolve has not been located.

[8] This resolve is in House Joint and Concurrent Resolutions, Senate Records, DNA. The rough journal includes the following canceled passage: "and a Committee was appointed of

Mr. Boudinot
Mr. Lawrence &
Mr. Smith
          of South Carolina"

disagreed to the resolution of the Senate, of this day, appointing a joint Committee to wait on the President of the United States,"—

And he withdrew.

The Senate proceeded to consider the resolution of the House of Representatives of this day, appointing a Committee "jointly with such Committee as the Senate shall appoint to wait on the President of the United States," and

RESOLVED, That they do concur in the said resolution, and that

Mr. Langdon and

Mr. Morris, be the Committee on the part of the

Senate.[9]

ORDERED, That the Secretary acquaint the House of Representatives of the concurrence of the Senate in this resolution.

Mr. Langdon, from the joint Committee appointed to wait on the President of the United States, agreeably to the resolution of the two Houses of this day, reported—

That they had executed the business, and that the President of the United States proposed to-morrow at 12 o'clock to meet the two Houses of Congress in the Senate Chamber.[10]

The Senate adjourned to 11 o'clock to-morrow.

WEDNESDAY, DECEMBER 8, 1790

The SENATE assembled—present as yesterday, and

The Honorable Jonathan Elmer, from the State of New-Jersey,

The Honorable Caleb Strong, from the State of Massachusetts, and

The Honorable George Read, from the State of Delaware,—attended.

A letter from Messrs. Evan Thomas and Andrew Geyer, in behalf of the Commissioners of the city and county of Philadelphia, was, by Mr. Morris, presented and read,[11] offering "the county Court House in Philadelphia, to the Representatives of the Union, for their accommodation during their residence in the city of Philadelphia."[12]

ORDERED, That the Secretary inform the House of Representatives, that the Senate are ready to meet them in the Senate Chamber, to receive any communications the President of the United States may be pleased to make to the two Houses of Congress; and that the usual seats will be assigned them.

The House of Representatives having accordingly taken their seats, the

---

[9] This resolve is in House Joint and Concurrent Resolutions, Senate Records, DNA.

[10] On December 8 the President addressed the Congress. On the same day a committee was appointed to draft a reply to the President's message.

[11] This letter is in Reports and Communications, Senate Records, DNA.

[12] On December 9 the Senate replied to this letter.

President of the United States came into the Senate Chamber, and addressed both Houses of Congress, as followeth:

"FELLOW CITIZENS of the SENATE, and
        HOUSE of REPRESENTATIVES,
    IN meeting you again I feel much satisfaction in being able to repeat my congratulations on the favorable prospects which continue to distinguish our public affairs. The abundant fruits of another year have blessed our Country with plenty, and with the means of a flourishing Commerce. The progress of public Credit is witnessed by a considerable rise of American stock abroad as well as at home; and the revenues allotted for this and other national purposes, have been productive beyond the calculations by which they were regulated. This latter circumstance is the more pleasing as it is not only a proof of the fertility of our resources, but as it assures us of a further increase of the national respectability and Credit; and let me add, as it bears an honorable testimony to the patriotism and integrity of the mercantile and marine part of our Citizens. The punctuality of the former in discharging their engagements has been exemplary.

    "In conforming to the powers vested in me by Acts of the last session, a Loan of three millions of florins, towards which some provisional measures had previously taken place, has been compleated in Holland. As well the celerity with which it has been filled, as the nature of the terms, (considering the more than ordinary demand for borrowing, created by the situation of Europe) give a reasonable hope that the further execution of those powers may proceed with advantage and success. The Secretary of the Treasury has my directions to communicate such further particulars as may be requisite for more precise information.[13]

    "Since your last sessions I have received communications by which it appears that the district of Kentucky, at present a part of Virginia, has concurred in certain propositions contained in a law of that State; in consequence of which the District is to become a distinct member of the Union in case the requisite sanction of Congress be added;—for this sanction application is now made. I shall cause the papers on this very important transaction to be laid before you. The liberality and harmony with which it has been conducted, will be found to do great honor to both the parties; and the sentiments of warm attachment to the Union and its present government, expressed by our fellow Citizens of Kentucky, cannot fail to add an affectionate concern for their particular welfare to the great national impressions under which you will decide on the case submitted to you.[14]

---

[13] On February 25 the Secretary of the Treasury sent the Senate a report on this loan.
[14] On December 9 the President sent the communications from Kentucky to the Senate.

"It has been heretofore known to Congress that frequent incursions have been made on our frontier settlements by certain banditti of Indians from the North West side of the Ohio. These, with some of the Tribes dwelling on and near the Wabash, have of late been particularly active in their depredations; and being emboldened by the impunity of their crimes, and aided by such parts of the neighbouring Tribes, as could be seduced to join in their hostilities, or afford them a retreat for their prisoners and plunder, they have, instead of listening to the humane invitations and overtures made on the part of the United States renewed their violences with fresh alacrity and greater effect. The lives of a number of valuable citizens have thus been sacrificed, and some of them under circumstances peculiarly shocking; whilst others have been carried into a deplorable captivity.

"These aggravated provocations rendered it essential to the safety of the Western settlements, that the aggressors should be made sensible that the government of the Union is not less capable of punishing their crimes, than it is disposed to respect their rights and reward their attachments. As this object could not be effected by defensive measures, it became necessary to put in force, the Act which empowers the President to call out the Militia, for the protection of the frontiers; and I have accordingly authorized an expedition, in which the regular Troops in that quarter are combined with such draughts of Militia, as were deemed sufficient: the event of the measure is yet unknown to me. The Secretary of War is directed to lay before you a statement of the information on which it is founded, as well as an estimate of the expence with which it will be attended.

"The disturbed situation of Europe, and particularly the critical posture of the great maritime powers, whilst it ought to make us the more thankful for the general peace and security enjoyed by the United States, reminds us at the same time, of the circumspection with which it becomes us to preserve these blessings. It requires also, that we should not overlook the tendency of a war, and even of preparations for a war, among the nations most concerned in active commerce with this country, to abridge the means, and thereby at least enhance the price of transporting its valuable productions to their proper markets. I recommend it to your serious reflections how far and in what mode, it may be expedient to guard against embarrassments from these contingencies, by such encouragements to our own navigation as will render our Commerce and Agriculture less dependant on foreign bottoms, which may fail us in the very moments most interesting to both of these great objects. Our Fisheries and the transportation of our own produce, offer us abundant means for guarding ourselves against this evil.

"Your attention seems to be not less due to that particular branch of our Trade which belongs to the Mediterranean. So many circumstances unite in rendering the present state of it distressful to us, that you will not think any deliberations misemployed, which may lead to its relief and protection.[15]

"The Laws you have already passed for the establishment of a Judiciary System have opened the doors of Justice to all descriptions of persons. You will consider in your wisdom whether improvements in that System may yet be made; and particularly whether an uniform Process of Execution, on Sentences issuing from the Federal Courts, be not desirable through all the States.

"The patronage of our Commerce, of our Merchants and Seamen, has called for the appointment of Consuls in foreign countries. It seems expedient to regulate by law the exercise of that jurisdiction and those functions which are permitted them, either by express convention, or by a friendly indulgence, in the places of their residence. The Consular Convention too with His Most Christian Majesty has stipulated in certain cases, the aid of the National Authority to his Consuls established here. Some legislative provision is requisite to carry these stipulations into full effect.[16]

"The establishment of the Militia, of a Mint, of Standards of Weights and Measures, of the Post-Office and Post-Roads, are subjects which (I presume) you will resume of course, and which are abundantly urged by their own importance.[17]

"GENTLEMEN of the HOUSE of REPRESENTATIVES,

"THE sufficiency of the revenues you have established for the objects to which they are appropriated, leaves no doubt that the residuary provisions will be commensurate to the other objects for which the public faith stands now pledged. Allow me moreover to hope that it will be a favorite policy with you not merely to secure a payment of the interest of the debt funded, but as far, and as fast as the growing resources of the country will permit, to exonerate it of the principal itself. The appropriation you have made of the Western Lands, explains your dispositions on this subject, and I am persuaded the sooner that valuable fund can be made to contribute along with other means, to the actual reduction of the public debt, the more salutary will the measure be to every Public Interest, as well as the more satisfactory to our constituents.

"GENTLEMEN of the SENATE and HOUSE of REPRESENTATIVES,

"IN pursuing the various and weighty business of the present session, I indulge the fullest persuasion that your consultations will be equally marked with wisdom, and animated by the love of your country. In whatever belongs to my duty, you shall have all the co-operation which an undiminished zeal for

---

[15] On December 15 a committee was appointed to consider Mediterranean trade.

[16] On December 16 a committee was appointed to consider this subject.

[17] On February 7 a report of the Secretary of the Treasury on the establishment of a mint was sent to the Senate and committed. On February 12 the House sent the Military Establishment Bill to the Senate.

its welfare can inspire. It will be happy for us both, and our best reward, if by a successful administration of our respective trusts, we can make the established government more and more instrumental in promoting the good of our fellow citizens, and more and more the object of their attachment and confidence.

"G. WASHINGTON

"UNITED STATES
December the 8th, 1790"[18]

The President of the United States having retired, and the two Houses being separated,

ORDERED, That   Mr. Ellsworth
                 Mr. King and
                 Mr. Izard, be a Committee to prepare and report the draft of an address to the President of the United States, in answer to his speech delivered this day to both Houses of Congress, in the Senate Chamber.

ORDERED, That the speech of the President of the United States, delivered this day, be printed for the use of the Senate.[19]

The Senate adjourned to 11 o'clock to-morrow.

THURSDAY, DECEMBER 9, 1790

The SENATE assembled—present as yesterday.

ORDERED, That the following letter be[20] addressed to the Commissioners of the city and county of Philadelphia, in reply to their letter of the 6th of December, addressed to the Senate and House of Representatives of the United States.

GENTLEMEN,

THE Senate have considered the letter that you were pleased to address to the Senate and the House of Representatives, on the 6th instant, and they entertain a proper sense of the respect shewn to the General Government of the United States, by providing so commodious a building as the Commissioners of the city and county of Philadelphia have appropriated for the ac-

---

[18] This speech is in President's Messages: Annual reports, Senate Records, DNA.

[19] On December 10 the committee to prepare a reply to the President's address reported. The report was amended and adopted, and the committee was instructed to confer with the President about a time for him to receive the Senate's message.

[20] The rough journal includes the canceled phrase "by the Vice President."

commodation of the Representatives of the Union, during their residence in
this city.[21]

> I have the honor to be,
> Your most humble servant,
> JOHN ADAMS,
> Vice President of the United States,
> and President of the Senate

To the Commissioners of the city }
  and county of Philadelphia[22]   }

A message from the House of Representatives by Mr. Beckley their clerk:

"Mr. PRESIDENT,

"The House of Representatives have resolved that two Chaplains of different denominations be appointed to Congress, for the present session; one by
each House, who shall interchange weekly,"[23]—

And he withdrew.

Whereupon the Senate proceeded to consider the resolution of the House of
Representatives of this day, for the appointment of two Chaplains,—and

RESOLVED, That they do concur therein, and that the Right Rev. Dr.
WILLIAM WHITE,[24] be appointed on the part of the Senate.[25]

ORDERED, That the Secretary communicate the concurrence of the Senate in
this resolution, to the House of Representatives; together with their proceedings thereon.[26]

A message from the President of the United States by Mr. Lear his Secretary, who communicated sundry papers referred to in the President's speech to
both Houses of Congress on the 8th instant,—

And he withdrew.

(Copy)   "DANVILLE, October 4th, 1790
"SIR,

"BY order of Convention, I now enclose to you a copy of the resolutions of
Convention, respecting the separation of the district of Kentucky from the
State of Virginia; and, their address to the President and Congress of the
United States.

---

[21] In the rough journal the phrase "in this city" was altered to read "in the city of
Philadelphia."

[22] This letter has not been located.

[23] This resolve has not been located.

[24] The rough journal originally read: "the Right Reverend Bishop White D.D."; this
was then corrected to read as it appears in the printed journal above.

[25] This resolve has not been located.

[26] On December 10 the House notified the Senate that it had appointed Doctor Blair
as Chaplain.

"I have the honor to be, &c.

(Signed)   GEORGE MUTER

President of the Convention

"The PRESIDENT of   ⎫
   the United States" ⎭

(Copy)   "District of KENTUCKY: To wit—

"In Convention, July 28th, 1790

"RESOLVED, That it is expedient for, and the will of the good people of the district of Kentucky, that the same be erected into an independent State, on the terms and conditions specified in an Act of the Virginia Assembly, passed the 18th day of December 1789, entitled, 'An Act concerning the erection of the district of Kentucky into an independent State.'

"RESOLVED, That we the Representatives of the people of Kentucky, duly elected in pursuance of an Act of the Legislature of Virginia, passed the 18th day of December 1789, entitled, 'An Act concerning the erection of the district of Kentucky into an independent State,' and now met in Convention; having with full powers maturely investigated the expediency of the proposed separation on the terms and conditions specified in the above recited act; do by these presents, and in behalf of the people of Kentucky, accept the terms and conditions, and do declare, that on the first day of June 1792, the said district of Kentucky shall become a State separate from and independent of the government of Virginia, and that the said articles become a solemn compact, binding on the said people."

To the PRESIDENT and the Honorable the CONGRESS of the UNITED STATES of AMERICA

The Memorial of the Representatives of the people of Kentucky, in Convention assembled, pursuant to an Act of the Legislature of Virginia, passed the 18th December 1789, entitled, "An Act concerning the erection of the district of Kentucky into an independent State,"

HUMBLY SHEWETH,

THAT the inhabitants of this county are warmly devoted to the American Union, and as firmly attached to the present happy establishment of the Federal Government, as any of the citizens of the United States.

That migrating from thence, they have with great hazard and difficulty, effected their present settlements. The hope of increasing numbers could alone have supported the early adventurers under those arduous exertions. They have the satisfaction to find that hope verified. At this day, the population and strength of this country, render it fully able, in the opinion of your memorialists, to form and support an efficient domestic government.

The inconveniencies resulting from its local situation, as a part of Virginia, at first but little felt, have for some time been objects of their most serious attention; which occasioned application to the Legislature of Virginia for redress.

Here your memorialists would acknowledge with peculiar pleasure, the benevolence of Virginia in permitting them to remove the evils arising from that source, by assuming upon themselves a State of independence.

This they have thought expedient to do, on the terms and conditions stipulated in the above recited Act; and fixed on the first day of June 1792, as the period when the said independence shall commence.

It now remains with the President and the Congress of the United States, to sanction these proceedings, by an Act of their honorable Legislature, prior to the first day of November 1791, for the purpose of receiving into the Federal Union, the people of Kentucky, by the name of THE STATE OF KENTUCKY.

Should this determination of your memorialists meet the approbation of the General Government, they have to call a Convention to form a Constitution, subsequent to the Act of Congress and prior to the day fixed for the independence of this country.

When your memorialists reflect on the present comprehensive system of Federal Government, and when they also recollect the determination of a former Congress on this subject, they are left without a doubt that the object of their wishes will be accomplished.

And your memorialists as in duty bound, shall forever pray.

(Signed)   GEORGE MUTER, PR.
(Attest)   THOMAS TODD, Clk. C.[27]

A letter from the Secretary at War was communicated to the Vice President, enclosing sundry papers referred to in the President's speech to both Houses of Congress, on the 8th instant, which being read,[28] were ordered to lie for consideration.

The Senate adjourned to 11 o'clock to-morrow.

FRIDAY, DECEMBER 10, 1790

The SENATE assembled—present as yesterday.

A letter from Monsieur BENIERE, President of the Commonalty of Paris,[29]

---

[27] This message, containing the resolves and the memorial, is in Petitions and Memorials: Various subjects, Senate Records, DNA. A bill from the Kentucky General Assembly regarding statehood, dated December 15, 1788, is probably a forerunner of the above memorial; it is in Vi-Ar. On December 14 a committee was appointed to consider these communications from Kentucky.

[28] This letter and enclosed documents relating to Indian Affairs are in Reports from the Secretary of War, Senate Records, DNA.

[29] In Other Records: Various papers, Senate Records, DNA, there is a slip in the

addressed to the PRESIDENT and Members of CONGRESS of the United States, with twenty-six copies of a Civic EULOGY on BENJAMIN FRANKLIN pronounced the 21st of July 1790, in the name of the Commonalty of Paris by Monsieur L'ABBE FAUCHET,[30] was delivered to the Senate by Mr. Lear, Secretary to the President of the United States—

And he withdrew.

Read and

ORDERED, That the letter and copies of the Eulogy be sent to the House of Representatives.

A message from the House of Representatives by Mr. Beckley their clerk:

"Mr. PRESIDENT,

"The House of Representatives, have on their part, appointed the Reverend Doctor BLAIR,[31] one of the Chaplains to the present Congress,"—

And he withdrew.

Mr. Ellsworth, from the Committee appointed to prepare and report the draft of an address to the President of the United States, reported accordingly,[32] and the report being amended, was adopted as followeth:

To the PRESIDENT of the UNITED STATES of AMERICA

W E receive, Sir, with particular satisfaction, the communications contained in your speech, which confirm to us the progressive state of the public credit, and afford, at the[33] time, a new proof of the solidity of the foundation on which it rests; and we cheerfully join in the acknowledgment which is due to the probity and patriotism of the mercantile and marine part of our fellow-citizens, whose enlightened attachment to the principles of good government, is not less conspicuous in this, than it has been in other important respects.

In confidence that every constitutional preliminary has been observed, we assure you of our disposition to concur, in giving the requisite sanction, to the admission of Kentucky as a distinct member of the Union; in doing which, we

---

handwriting of John Adams, endorsed: "French/Titles./Jany/1791." The note reads: "Monsieur Beniere (Doctor in Theology of the House and Society of the Sorbonne, honorary Canon of the Metropolitan Church of Rouen, Pastor of the Parish of St. Peter of Chaillot, one of the Electors of Paris, a supplementary Deputy of the National Assembly and) President of the Commonalty of Paris." The entire passage in parentheses is canceled. It may be conjectured that Samuel Otis requested Adams's assistance in preparing the journal entry referring to Beniere and decided to use only the last of several titles suggested by Adams.

[30] The eulogy by L'Abbe Fauchet, written in French, and titled *Eloge Civique De Benjamin Franklin*, is in the RBkRm, DLC. An English translation is printed in *The Private Life of the Late Benjamin Frankiln, LL.D.*, originally written by Franklin. It is also located in the RBkRm, DLC.

[31] In the rough journal there is a note in Otis's hand over the word "Blair" reading "(see for his C name)."

[32] This report is in Various Select Committee Reports, Senate Records, DNA.

[33] The smooth journal inserts the word "same."

shall anticipate the happy effects to be expected from the sentiments of attachment towards the Union, and its present government, which have been expressed by the patriotic inhabitants of that district.

While we regret, that the continuance, and increase of the hostilities and
depredations which have distressed our north-western frontiers, should have
rendered offensive measures necessary, we feel an entire confidence in the sufficiency of the motives which have produced them, and in the wisdom of the
dispositions which have been concerted, in pursuance of the powers vested in
you; and whatever may have been the event, we shall cheerfully concur in the
provisions which the expedition that has been undertaken may require on the
part of the Legislature, and in any other, which the future peace and safety of
our frontier settlements may call for.

The critical posture of the European powers will engage a due portion of
our attention, and we shall be ready to adopt any measures which a prudent
circumspection may suggest, for the preservation of the blessings of peace.
The navigation and the fisheries of the United States, are objects too interesting, not to inspire a disposition to promote them, by all the means which shall
appear to us consistent with their natural progress and permanent prosperity.

Impressed with the importance of a free intercourse with the Mediterranean,
we shall not think any deliberations misemployed, which may conduce to the
adoption of proper measures for removing the impediments that obstruct it.

The improvement of the judiciary system, and the other important objects,
to which you have pointed our attention, will not fail to engage the consideration they respectively merit.

In the course of our deliberations, upon every subject, we shall rely upon
that co-operation which an undiminished zeal, and incessant anxiety for the
public welfare on your part, so thoroughly ensure; and as it is our anxious
desire, so it shall be our constant endeavour, to render the established government more and more instrumental in promoting the good of our fellow-
citizens, and more and more the object of their attachment and confidence.

ORDERED, That the address to the President of the United States, in answer
to his speech, be presented by the Vice President, attended by the Senate, and
that the Committee which reported the address, wait on the President and desire to be informed, at what time and place he will receive the same.[34]

The Senate adjourned to Monday, 11 o'clock.

MONDAY, DECEMBER 13, 1790

The SENATE assembled—present as on the 10th, and
The Honorable William S. Johnson, from the State of Connecticut, and—

---

[34] On December 13 this committee reported, and the Senate delivered its reply to the
President. The President replied to this Senate address given by the Vice President.

The Honorable Philip Schuyler, from the State of New-York, attended.

Mr. Ellsworth, from the Committee appointed on the 10th to wait on the President of the United States, reported—

That it would be agreeable to the President to receive the address of the Senate, in answer to his speech to both Houses of Congress, on Monday next, at 12 o'clock:

Whereupon, The Senate waited on the President of the United States at his own house, and the Vice President in their name, communicated to him the address agreed to on the 10th instant—to which, the President of the United States was pleased to make the following reply—

GENTLEMEN,

THESE assurances of favorable attention to the subjects I have recommended, and of entire confidence in my views, make the impression on me which I ought to feel. I thank you for them both, and shall continue to rely much for the success of all our measures for the public good, on the aid they will receive from the wisdom and integrity of your councils.

G. WASHINGTON[35]

The Senate returned to the Senate-Chamber.

On motion,

ORDERED, That the Secretary furnish the members of Senate, from such printers as they may respectively direct, each, three newspapers, to be left from time to time during the session, at their several places of abode.

The Senate adjourned to 11 o'clock to-morrow.

TUESDAY, DECEMBER 14, 1790

The SENATE assembled—present as yesterday.

A written message from the President of the United States, was by his Secretary, delivered to the Vice President,—

And he withdrew.

UNITED STATES, December 14th, 1790

GENTLEMEN of the SENATE and
    HOUSE of REPRESENTATIVES,

HAVING informed Congress of the expedition which had been directed against certain Indians north-west of the Ohio, I embrace the earliest opportunity of laying before you the official communications which have been received upon that subject.

G. WASHINGTON[36]

---

[35] This message is in President's Messages: Annual reports, Senate Records, DNA.

[36] This message and copies of the official communications are in President's Messages: Transmitting reports from the Secretary of War, Senate Records, DNA.

The message and communications referred to, being read, were ordered to lie for consideration.

On motion,[37]

ORDERED, That   Mr. Schuyler

Mr. Monroe and

Mr. Johnson, be a Committee to consider and report on the papers referred to in the President's speech, relative to the district of Kentucky.[38]

The Senate adjourned to 11 o'clock to-morrow.

WEDNESDAY, DECEMBER 15, 1790

The SENATE assembled—present as yesterday, and

The Honorable Joseph Stanton, junior, from the State of Rhode-Island, attended.

ORDERED, That   Mr. Langdon

Mr. Morris

Mr. King

Mr. Strong and

Mr. Ellsworth, be a Committee to consider that part of the President's speech which relates to the commerce of the Mediterranean.[39]

The petition of Ann Roberts, widow of Colonel Owen Roberts, of South-Carolina,[40] mortally wounded at the attack made on the British lines at Stono Ferry, 20th June, 1779, was read, praying that she may be allowed the "seven years half-pay of a Colonel, as the widow of the aforesaid Colonel Roberts; agreeably to an Act of Congress of 20th August, 1780."

ORDERED, That this petition lie on the table.[41]

The petition of Samuel Prioleau, junior, was read, praying for compensation for certain buildings pulled down in the town of Charleston, South-Carolina,[42] by order of General Lincoln, the materials whereof were converted to the defence of that town during the late war.

ORDERED, That the petition lie on the table.

The Senate adjourned to 11 o'clock to-morrow.

---

[37] Philip Schuyler's motion to commit the Kentucky papers is in Senate Simple Resolutions and Motions, Senate Records, DNA.

[38] On January 3 this committee reported and the report was accepted. The committee was then instructed to prepare a bill to admit Kentucky to the Union.

[39] This vote for committee is in Other Records: Yeas and nays, Senate Records, DNA. On December 30 the President sent a report on the American prisoners in Algiers to the Senate. This report was committed to the committee on Mediterranean trade.

[40] This petition has not been located. In the rough journal the phrase "of South-Carolina" follows the name "Ann Roberts."

[41] The Senate did not consider this petition but the House did.

[42] This petition has not been located.

THURSDAY, DECEMBER 16, 1790

The SENATE assembled—present as yesterday.

ORDERED, That   Mr. Schuyler

                Mr. Hawkins and

                Mr. Ellsworth, be a Committee to prepare and bring in a Bill supplementary to the Act, entitled, "An Act making further provision for the payment of the debts of the United States."

Mr. Schuyler, from the above-mentioned Committee reported a Bill,[43] which was read the FIRST time.

ORDERED, That this Bill pass to the SECOND reading.[44]

ORDERED, That   Mr. Ellsworth

                Mr. Hawkins and

                Mr. Schuyler, be a Committee[45] to take into consideration and report on that part of the President's speech which relates to the appointment of Consuls.[46]

The Senate adjourned to 11 o'clock to-morrow.

FRIDAY, DECEMBER 17, 1790

The SENATE assembled—present as yesterday, and

The Honorable Theodore Foster, from the State of Rhode-Island, attended.

Agreeably to the order of the day, the Senate proceeded to the SECOND reading of the Bill, "supplementary to the Act, entitled, 'An Act making further provision for the payment of the debts of the United States.'"

Agreed by unanimous consent, so far to dispense with the rule, as that this Bill now pass to the THIRD reading.

RESOLVED, That this Bill DO PASS, that it be entitled, "An Act supplementary to an Act, entitled, 'An Act making further provision for the payment of the debts of the United States,'" that it be engrossed[47] and carried to the House of Representatives for concurrence therein.[48]

The Senate adjourned to Monday, 11 o'clock.

---

[43] A draft of this bill is in Senate Bills, Senate Records, DNA.

[44] On December 17 this bill was read the second and third times, passed, and sent to the House for concurrence.

[45] The vote for this committee is in Other Records: Yeas and nays, Senate Records, DNA.

[46] On January 7 this committee reported a bill which was read a first time and passed to the second reading.

[47] This engrossed bill, with a notation of passage, is in Engrossed Senate Bills and Resolutions, Senate Records, DNA.

[48] On December 17 the House read this bill for the first time. On December 20 it was read a second time; it was read the third time, passed, and returned to the Senate on the twenty-first. On the same day a motion was made on the subject of this bill, and consideration of the motion was postponed.

MONDAY, December 20, 1790

The SENATE assembled—present as on the 17th.

A message from the House of Representatives by Mr. Beckley their Clerk:

"Mr. PRESIDENT,

"The House of Representatives have passed a Bill, entitled, 'An Act to continue an Act, entitled, "An Act declaring the assent of Congress to certain Acts of the States of Maryland, Georgia, and Rhode-Island and Providence Plantations," '[49] in which they desire the concurrence of the Senate,"—

And he withdrew.

ORDERED, That this Bill be read the FIRST time.

ORDERED, That this Bill pass to the SECOND reading.[50]

The memorial and remonstrance of the Public Creditors who are citizens of the Commonwealth of Pennsylvania,[51] praying for the revision of "An Act making provision for the debt of the United States," was, by Mr. Morris, presented and read.

ORDERED, That this memorial lie on the table.[52]

The Senate adjourned to 11 o'clock to-morrow.

TUESDAY, December 21, 1790

The SENATE assembled—present as yesterday.

Agreeably to the order of the day, proceeded in the SECOND reading of the Bill, entitled, "An Act to continue an Act, entitled, 'An Act declaring the assent of Congress to certain Acts of the States of Maryland, Georgia, and Rhode-Island and Providence Plantations.' "

ORDERED, That this Bill be committed to

> Mr. Hawkins
> Mr. Langdon and
> Mr. Read[53]

The Vice President, from the Commissioners appointed by the Law passed the last session of Congress, "making provision for the reduction of the public debt," communicated the following report:

---

[49] An annotated copy of this bill is in House Bills, Senate Records, DNA.

[50] On December 21 this bill was read a second time and committed.

[51] This petition is in Petitions and Memorials: Various subjects, Senate Records, DNA. At this point the rough journal includes the canceled phrase "by their Committee duly appointed, instructed and authorized."

[52] On December 23, during consideration of the Ways and Means Bill, the Senate voted not to grant this petition.

[53] On December 28 this committee reported an amendment to the bill which was agreed to. The bill was then recommitted.

"PHILADELPHIA, December 21st, 1790

"The Vice President of the United States and President of the Senate, the
    Chief Justice, the Secretary of State, the Secretary of the Treasury and the
    Attorney-General,

"Respectfully report to the CONGRESS of the UNITED STATES of AMERICA—

"THAT pursuant to the Act, entitled, 'An Act making provision for the reduction of the public debt,' they, on the 26th day of August last, convened at
the city of New-York and entered upon the execution of the trust thereby
reposed in them.

"That in conformity to a resolution agreed upon by them, on the 27th, and
approved by the President of the United States, on the 28th of the said month,
they have caused purchases of the said debt to be made, through the agency
of Samuel Meredith, Treasurer of the United States, which on the 6th day of
December instant, amounted to two hundred and seventy-eight thousand, six
hundred and eighty-seven dollars and thirty cents, and for which there have
been paid one hundred and fifty thousand and two hundred and thirty-nine
dollars and twenty-four cents in specie; as will more particularly appear by a
return of the said Samuel Meredith, confirmed by an authenticated copy of his
account settled at the Treasury of the United States, which are herewith submitted, and prayed to be received as part of this report, and in which are
specified the places where, the times when, the prices at which, and the persons of whom the said purchases have been made.

"Signed by order of the Board,
JOHN ADAMS"

"TREASURY DEPARTMENT, Auditor's Office
"December 20th, 1790

"I have examined and adjusted an account between the United States and
Samuel Meredith, Esquire, Agent to the Trustees named in the Act of Congress passed on the 12th day of August 1790, for reducing the domestic debt;
for purchases of said debt made before the 7th day of December 1790, and
find—that the said Samuel Meredith, Esquire, is debited in the books of the
Treasury for this sum advanced to him on account of said agency.

Dollars
200,000

"I also find that the following purchases have been made by said Agent:
    In certificates of registered debt, issued by the Register of the
Treasury, exclusive of interest since the first day of January 1788,
purchased at thirteen shillings on the pound,   54,494.99

    In certificates purchased at twelve shillings and ten pence on
the pound,   1,500

In said certificates purchased at twelve shillings and six pence
on the pound,   87,434.95
In funded six per cent stock on the books of the Treasury, purchased at fourteen shillings on the pound,   60,688.54
In funded three per cent stock on the books of the Treasury,
purchased at seven shillings and two pence two farthings on the
pound,   10,484.14
In deferred six per cent stock on the books of the Treasury,
purchased at six shillings in the pound,   13,262.49
In indents of interest issued by direction of the late Board of
Treasury, purchased at seven shillings and four pence on the
pound,   299
In said indents of interest purchased at seven shillings and
two pence on the pound,   19,988.12
In warrants drawn on the Treasury for said indents purchased
at seven shillings and four pence on the pound,   800.30
In said warrants purchased at seven shillings and two pence
on the pound,   3,462.16
In arrearages of interest on certificates, calculated to the first
day of January 1788, for which payment was made, as for in-
dents at seven shillings and two pence on the pound,   455.23

    Amounting to   *Dollars*   252,869.92

On the certificates of registered debt before mentioned amounting in the whole to 143,429.94 dollars, interest was due from
January 1st 1788, in addition to the sums before stated, which
interest calculated to the first day of January 1791, would amount
to   25,817.38
The amount of the domestic debt extinguished by the pur-
chases of the said Agent, including interest thereon to January
1st 1791, is therefore   *Dollars*   278,687.30

For which purchases, the said Agent has paid in specie, at the
rates before mentioned, agreeably to a particular statement of his
accounts herewith transmitted, the sum of   150,239.24
Leaving a balance in his hands in specie, for which he is to
be debited in a future settlement of his accounts, the sum of   49,760.76

                                                    Dollars   200,000

"The statement on which this report is founded, and the indents and warrants for indents before-mentioned, are herewith transmitted for the decision
of the Comptroller of the Treasury thereon.

                    (Signed)   "OLIVER WOLCOTT, jun. Aud.

"To NICHOLAS EVELEIGH, Esq.; Comp.   ⎫
  of the Treasury of the United States" ⎬

                        Admitted and certified,
                (Signed)   NICHOLAS EVELEIGH, Compt.

               TREASURY DEPARTMENT, Register's-Office
                        December 21st, 1790

The foregoing statement of Samuel Meredith, Agent to the Trustees named in the Act passed on the 12th day of August 1790, for the reduction of the public debt, his account of monies received and purchases made under the said Act, to the sixth instant inclusively, is a true copy of the original transmitted to me by the Comptroller of the Treasury, to be entered in the Treasury books, the said original being filed on record in this office.

              (Signed)   JOSEPH NOURSE, Reg.[54]

ORDERED, That this report lie for consideration.

A message from the House of Representatives by Mr. Beckley their clerk:

"Mr. PRESIDENT,

"The House of Representatives have passed the Bill sent from the Senate, entitled, 'An Act supplementary to an Act, entitled, "An Act making further provision for the payment of the debts of the United States," ' "—

And he withdrew.

A motion being made that it be "Resolved, as the opinion of the Senate, that any deviation from the principles of the system contained in the Act, entitled, 'An Act making provision for the debt of the United States,' would be dangerous and inexpedient"—it was agreed that the consideration hereof be postponed 'till Thursday next.[55]

The Senate adjourned to 11 o'clock to-morrow.

---

[54] This report and the Treasury report are in Reports and Communications, Senate Records, DNA.

[55] This motion and the resolution following it are in Senate Simple Resolutions and Motions, Senate Records, DNA. The rough journal originally recorded this motion in two paragraphs. The first paragraph which was later canceled read as follows:

The system adopted during the last session of Congress relative to a provision for the public debt having so far enhanced the value of the same as to afford an assurance of public confidence, and of the satisfaction of the generality of the public creditors, and there being reason to rely that when such additional measures shall have been taken, as are still requisite in pursuance thereof, the said System will prove still further satisfactory and adequate to the firm establishment of public credit, (in which measures the Senate will chearfully concur), and there being good ground to believe, that many alienations, and purchases of the said debt and numerous contracts respecting the same, have been made in contemplation of the said system, and that the interests of many individuals, who have relied on the stability of the measures of the government, wou'd be injuriously affected by a change, and as any attempt toward such change, might tend to unsettle the public mind, and to create doubt and appre-

WEDNESDAY, December 22, 1790

The SENATE assembled—present as yesterday.

ORDERED, That Mr. Foster be of the joint Committee on the part of the Senate, with such as the House of Representatives may appoint on their part, to examine enrolled Bills.[56]

ORDERED, That the Secretary desire the concurrence of the House of Representatives in the appointment of a joint Committee, for enrolled Bills, on their part.

A message from the House of Representatives by Mr. Beckley their clerk:

"Mr. PRESIDENT,

"The House of Representatives have agreed to the appointment of a joint Committee on their part, for enrolled Bills,"[57]—

And he withdrew.

The Senate adjourned to 11 o'clock to-morrow.

THURSDAY, December 23, 1790

The SENATE assembled—present as yesterday.

A message from the House of Representatives by Mr. Beckley their clerk:

"Mr. PRESIDENT,

"I am directed to acquaint the Senate, that the House of Representatives has received a report from the Secretary of State, respecting Coins, Weights and Measures;[58] and also a report from the Secretary of the Treasury, containing a plan for a national Bank;[59] and to bring the said reports to the Senate,"[60]—

And he withdrew.

ORDERED, That these communications from the House of Representatives lie for consideration.

Agreeably to the order of the day, the Senate proceeded to consider the motion made on the 21st instant—That it be

---

hensions which might disturb the present favourable progress of public credit— therefore. . .

On December 23 this resolution was postponed in order to consider a new resolution which was passed by a roll-call vote.

[56] The Senate order is in Senate Joint and Concurrent Resolutions, Senate Records, DNA.

[57] The House order appointing committeemen is in Senate Joint and Concurrent Resolutions, Senate Records, DNA.

[58] The report of the Secretary of State is in A Record of the Reports of the Secretary of State, vol. 1, House Records, DNA. E–23910. On December 28 a committee was appointed to consider this report.

[59] The report of the Secretary of the Treasury is in Reports of Alexander Hamilton, House Records, DNA.

[60] This message is in Messages from the House, Senate Records, DNA.

"RESOLVED, As the opinion of the Senate, that any deviation from the principles of the system contained in the Act, entitled, 'An Act making provision for the debt of the United States,' would be dangerous and inexpedient"—

On motion to postpone this resolution, and substitute the following—

"RESOLVED, That it would be inexpedient to alter the system for funding the public debt established during the last session of Congress, and that the petition of Thomas McKean and others, styling themselves a Committee of the Public Creditors of the Commonwealth of Pennsylvania, cannot be granted,"[61]—

It passed in the Affirmative.

And on the main question, the yeas and nays being required by one fifth of the Senators present, were—

Mr. Bassett	Yea	
Mr. Butler	Yea	
Mr. Dalton	Yea	
Mr. Dickinson	Yea	
Mr. Ellsworth	Yea	
Mr. Elmer	Yea	
Mr. Few	Yea	
Mr. Foster	Yea	
Mr. Hawkins	Yea	
Mr. Johnson	Yea	
Mr. Johnston	Yea	
Mr. Izard	Yea	
Mr. King	Yea	
Mr. Langdon	Yea	
Mr. Maclay	Yea	
Mr. Morris		Nay
Mr. Read	Yea	
Mr. Schuyler	Yea	
Mr. Stanton	Yea	
Mr. Strong	Yea	
Mr. Wingate	Yea	

Yeas—20
Nays—1[62]

So it was—

RESOLVED, That it would be inexpedient to alter the system for funding the

---

[61] This resolve is in Senate Simple Resolutions and Motions, Senate Records, DNA. There is also a document labeled "Mr. Ellsworth's motion, which was withdrawn." Except for slight word variations, it is the same as the resolution in the printed journal above.

[62] This vote is in Other Records: Yeas and nays, Senate Records, DNA.

public debt established during the last session of Congress, and that the petition of Thomas McKean and others, styling themselves a Committee of the Public Creditors of the Commonwealth of Pennsylvania, cannot be granted.[63]

On motion,

ORDERED, That   Mr. Strong
                     Mr. Morris
                     Mr. Schuyler
                     Mr. Butler and
                     Mr. Ellsworth, be a Committee[64] to take into consideration the report of the Secretary of the Treasury upon the plan of a national Bank, and to prepare a Bill upon that subject.[65]

The Senate adjourned to 11 o'clock to-morrow.

FRIDAY, DECEMBER 24, 1790

The SENATE assembled—present as yesterday.

Mr. Foster, from the Committee on enrolled Bills, reported, That they had examined the enrolled Bill, entitled, "An Act supplementary to an Act, entitled, 'An Act making further provision for the payment of the debts of the United States,' "[66] and found it correct.

A message from the House of Representatives by Mr. Beckley their clerk:

"Mr. PRESIDENT,

"The Speaker having signed an enrolled Bill, I am directed to bring it to the Senate,—

"I am also directed to bring to the Senate, a message from the President of the United States, addressed to both Houses of Congress, with sundry papers referred to therein,"—

And he withdrew.

The message from the President of the United States was read, as follows:

UNITED STATES, December 23d, 1790

GENTLEMEN of the SENATE and
      HOUSE of REPRESENTATIVES,

IT appearing by the report of the Secretary of the Government north-west of the Ohio, that there are certain cases respecting grants of land within that territory, which require the interference of the Legislature of the United

---

[63] On December 24 the Ways and Means Bill was signed by both the Speaker and the Vice President and given to the committee on enrolled bills for delivery to the President.

[64] This vote for a committee is in Other Records: Yeas and nays, Senate Records, DNA.

[65] On January 3 this committee reported a bill which was read the first time and passed to the second reading.

[66] The inspected enrolled bill is in Enrolled Acts, RG 11, DNA. E–23867, E–46059.

States,—I have directed a copy of said report and the papers therein referred to, to be laid before you; together with a copy of the report of the Secretary of State upon the same subject.

G. WASHINGTON[67]

The papers referred to in the above recited message were read, and—

ORDERED, That the message and papers accompanying it, lie for consideration.[68]

The Vice President signed the enrolled Bill, entitled, "An Act supplementary to an Act, entitled, 'An Act making further provision for the payment of the debts of the United States,'" and it was delivered to the Committee of enrollment to be laid before the President of the United States.[69]

The Senate adjourned to Monday, 11 o'clock.

M O N D A Y, DECEMBER 27, 1790

The SENATE assembled—present as on the 24th.

Mr. Foster, from the Committee on enrolled Bills, reported, That they did on the 24th instant, lay before the President of the United States, the enrolled Bill, entitled, "An Act supplementary to an Act entitled, 'An Act making further provision for the payment of the debts of the United States.'"

A message from the President of the United States by Mr. Lear his Secretary:

"Mr. PRESIDENT,

"I am directed to communicate to the Senate, that the President of the United States, has this day approved and signed an Act, entitled, 'An Act supplementary to the Act, entitled, "An Act making further provision for the payment of the debts of the United States," ' "[70]—

And he withdrew.

ORDERED, That the Secretary communicate the message of the President of the United States, to the House of Representatives.

The Senate adjourned to 11 o'clock to-morrow.

T U E S D A Y, DECEMBER 28, 1790

The SENATE assembled—present as yesterday.

ORDERED, That   Mr. Izard
                   Mr. Monroe
                   Mr. Morris

---

[67] This message, including documents, is in President's Messages: Transmitting reports from the Secretary of State, Senate Records, DNA.

[68] On December 31 a committee was appointed to consider the papers sent by the President.

[69] On December 27 the President signed this bill and the Senate was notified.

[70] This message is in Committee on Enrolled Bills, Senate Records, DNA.

Mr. Langdon and

Mr. Schuyler, be a Committee[71] to take into consideration the report of the Secretary of State, on the uniformity of Weights, Coins and Measures, and report what is proper to be done thereon.[72]

Mr. Hawkins, from the Committee appointed to take into consideration the Bill, entitled, "An Act to continue an Act, entitled, 'An Act declaring the assent of Congress to certain Acts of the States of Maryland, Georgia, and Rhode-Island and Providence Planations,' " reported an amendment,[73] which report was agreed to.

ORDERED, That this Bill be re-committed for further amendments,[74] and that   Mr. Morris and

Mr. Schuyler, be added to the Committee.[75]

The Senate adjourned to 11 o'clock to-morrow.

W E D N E S D A Y, DECEMBER 29, 1790

The SENATE assembled—present as yesterday.

The memorial of the College of Physicians of the city of Philadelphia,[76] praying, that "such heavy duties may be imposed upon all distilled spirits, as shall be effectual to restrain their intemperate use in our country," was presented by Mr. Morris, and read.

ORDERED, That this memorial lie on the table.

The Senate adjourned to 11 o'clock to-morrow.

T H U R S D A Y, DECEMBER 30, 1790

The SENATE assembled—present as yesterday.

A written message from the President of the United States, was communicated by Mr. Lear his Secretary,—

And he withdrew.

---

[71] This vote for committee is in Other Records: Yeas and nays, Senate Records, DNA.

[72] On January 18 the Secretary of State sent a postscript to his report to the Senate. This postscript was laid for consideration.

[73] The bill notes some amendments, one of which may have resulted from this report. It is located in House Bills, Senate Records, DNA.

[74] In the rough journal the following canceled passage originally stood in place of the phrase "for further amendments": "for the purpose of bringing in a Clause providing that the monies to be raised by this act be collected under the authority of the United States & paid over to the Commissrs appointed by the several States for whose benefit the money shall be collected."

[75] The vote for committee is in Other Records: Yeas and nays, Senate Records, DNA. On January 5 this committee reported additional amendments to the bill, which were postponed in order to consider a resolution on the bill. The resolution was defeated, and the committee's amendments were agreed to. The bill then passed to the third reading.

[76] This petition is in Petitions and Memorials: Various subjects, Senate Records, DNA.

UNITED STATES, December 30th, 1790

GENTLEMEN of the SENATE and
    HOUSE of REPRESENTATIVES,

I LAY before you a report of the Secretary of State on the subject of the citizens of the United States in captivity at Algiers, that you may provide on their behalf what to you shall seem most expedient.

G. WASHINGTON[77]

The message and papers communicated were read, and—

ORDERED, That they be referred to the Committee appointed on the 15th instant, to consider that part of the President's speech which relates to the commerce of the Mediterranean.[78]

The Senate adjourned to 11 o'clock to-morrow.

FRIDAY, DECEMBER 31, 1790

The SENATE assembled—present as yesterday.

ORDERED, That   Mr. Strong
                    Mr. Ellsworth and
                    Mr. Maclay, be a Committee[79] to take into consideration the message from the President of the United States, of the 23d instant, respecting cases of grants of lands in the Western Territory north-west of the river Ohio, with the papers therein referred to, and report what is proper to be done thereon.[80]

The petition of Col. Henry Laurens,[81] was by Mr. Butler presented and read, praying compensation for ten thousand bushels of rough rice, supplied the late continental army, as set forth in his petition. Also—

The petition of Col. Henry Laurens,[82] praying that interest may be allowed on the compensation granted to his son, the late Col. Henry Laurens,[83] deceased, whilst acting as special Minister at the Court of France.

ORDERED, That these petitions lie on the table until Monday next.[84]

The Senate adjourned to Monday next, at 11 o'clock.

---

[77] The President's message, the report from the Secretary of State, and letters regarding captives in Algiers are in Papers Pertaining to Citizens of the United States Held Prisoners in Algiers, Foreign Relations, Senate Records, DNA.

[78] On January 3 a confidential report on Mediterranean trade from the Secretary of State was brought to the Senate. The report was read and laid for consideration.

[79] The vote for committee is in Other Records: Yeas and nays, Senate Records, DNA.

[80] On January 6 this committee reported and was instructed to bring a bill on the subject.

[81] This petition is in Petitions and Memorials: Claims, Senate Records, DNA.

[82] This petition is in Petitions and Memorials: Claims, Senate Records, DNA.

[83] This name is an error. The Journal should have read "Lieutenant Colonel John Laurens."

[84] On January 3 both of these petitions were considered and tabled.

MONDAY, January 3, 1791

The SENATE assembled—present as on the 31st of December.

A message from the House of Representatives by Mr. Beckley their clerk:

"Mr. PRESIDENT,

"The House of Representatives have passed a Bill, entitled, 'An Act to provide for the unlading of ships and vessels in cases of obstruction by ice,'[1] in which they desire the concurrence of the Senate—

"I am also directed to bring to the Senate the report and confidential communication from the Secretary of State, respecting the trade of the United States in the Mediterranean,"[2]—

And he withdrew.

The above mentioned Bill was read the FIRST time.

ORDERED, That this Bill pass to the SECOND reading.[3]

The report of the Secretary of State respecting the trade of the Mediterranean, was read, and—

ORDERED, That it lie for consideration.[4]

The petition of Col. Henry Laurens, that compensation may be allowed him for a quantity of rice supplied the troops of the United States; also his petition that interest may be allowed on the compensation granted to his son, the late Col. Henry Laurens,[5] deceased, were severally taken into consideration, and—

ORDERED, That they lie on the table.[6]

A written message from the President of the United States, was communicated by Mr. Lear his Secretary,—

And he withdrew.

UNITED STATES, January 3d, 1791

GENTLEMEN of the SENATE and
    HOUSE of REPRESENTATIVES,

I LAY before you a copy of an exemplified copy of an Act passed by the Legislature of the State of New-Jersey, for vesting in the United States of America, the jurisdiction of a lot of land at Sandy-Hook, in the county of Monmouth; and a copy of the letter which accompanied said Act, from the Governor of the State of New-Jersey, to the President of the United States.

G. WASHINGTON

---

[1] This bill has not been located.

[2] This report, including letters from captives in Algiers and from Thomas Jefferson, is in Reports and Communications from the Secretary of State, Senate Records, DNA.

[3] On January 4 this bill was read a second time and passed to the third reading.

[4] On January 6 the committee on Mediterranean trade reported, and consideration of the report was postponed.

[5] The Journal should have read "Lieutenant Colonel John Laurens."

[6] The House also considered these petitions.

(Copy)   "NEW-BRUNSWICK, 30th December 1790
"SIR,

"I HAVE the honor to transmit an exemplified copy of a Statute passed by the Legislature of this State at their last session.

"I am, Sir, &c.

(Signed)   "WILLIAM PATERSON

"The PRESIDENT of }
  the United States" }

(Copy)

NEW-JERSEY

[SEAL] WILLIAM PATERSON, Esquire, Governor, Captain General, and Commander in Chief, in and over the State of New-Jersey, and Territories thereunto belonging, Chancellor and Ordinary in the same,—

To all to whom these Presents shall come:

KNOW YE, That among the Statutes enrolled in the Secretary's office at Burlington, it is thus contained,—

"STATE OF NEW-JERSEY

"An ACT for vesting in the United States of America, the jurisdiction of a
lot of land at Sandy-Hook, in the county of Monmouth

"BE it enacted by the Council and General Assembly of this State, and it is hereby enacted by the Authority of the same, That the jurisdiction of this State in and over a lot of land situate at the point of Sandy-Hook, in the county of Monmouth, containing four acres, on which a light-house and other buildings are erected, shall be, and the same is hereby ceded to, and vested in the United States of America, forever hereafter."

"House of Assembly, November 15th, 1790

"This Bill having been three times read in this House,
"RESOLVED, That the same do pass.

"By order of the House,

"JONATHAN DAYTON, Speaker"

"Council Chamber, November 16th, 1790

"This Bill having been three times read in Council,
"RESOLVED, That the same do pass.

"By order of the House,

"WILLIAM PATERSON, President"

All which by the tenor of these presents I have caused to be exemplified:—
In testimony whereof I have hereunto subscribed my name, and caused the

great seal of the State to be affixed, at New-Brunswick, the thirtieth day of December, in the year of our Lord one thousand seven hundred and ninety.

(Signed)   WILLIAM PATERSON[7]

ORDERED, That the above recited message and papers communicated therewith, lie for consideration.

Mr. Strong, from the Committee appointed to consider the report of the Secretary of the Treasury upon the plan of a national Bank, reported a Bill,[8] which was read the FIRST time.

ORDERED, That this Bill pass to the SECOND reading, and that one hundred and fifty copies thereof be printed.[9]

Mr. Schuyler, from the Committee appointed on that part of the speech of the President of the United States, which referred[10] to the district of Kentucky, reported[11]—

"That it appears to the Committee that the General Assembly of the Commonwealth of Virginia, did (upon the application of the inhabitants residing in the district of Kentucky, part of the Commonwealth of Virginia, to be separated therefrom, to the intent that the said district might become an independent State, and a member of the Union of the United States of America) by Act of the Legislature passed on the eighteenth day of December 1789, entitled, 'An Act concerning the erection of the district of Kentucky into an independent State,' assent to the independence of the said district, on certain conditions stipulated and contained in the said Act, a printed copy whereof is herewith submitted,—

"That is appears from the papers referred to the consideration of the Committee, that a Convention of Deputies from the several counties in the said district, was held in conformity to the said Act, which in the name and in behalf of the people whom they represented, declared it as the will of the said people to be erected into an independent State, on the terms and conditions specified in the said Act of the Commonwealth of Virginia,—

"That by the memorial of the said Convention, to Congress, bearing date the 28th of July 1790, praying to be received into the Federal Union, by the name of the State of Kentucky, it is declared that the people of the said district 'are as warmly devoted to the American Union, and as firmly attached to the present happy establishment of the Federal Government, as any of the citizens of the United States,'—

---

[7] The message from the President is in the George Washington Papers, series 2, vol. 25, reel 9, Manuscript Division, DLC.

[8] A manuscript copy of the bill is in Senate Bills, Senate Records, DNA. Two printed copies of this bill, one clear and the other annotated, are in the Broadside Collection, RBkRm, DLC.

[9] On January 6 this bill was read a second time and consideration of it was postponed.

[10] The rough journal substitutes the word "relates" for "referred."

[11] This report is in Various Select Committee Reports, Senate Records, DNA.

"That from such information as the Committee have been able to procure, the inhabitants resident in the said district are sufficiently numerous for all the purposes of an independent State,—

"That from these facts the Committee have concluded that it would be proper for Congress to consent that the said district should become an independent State, and admitted as a member of the United States of America, and that a Bill should be prepared for that purpose."—

And this report was accepted; whereupon—

ORDERED, That the Committee which made the report, be instructed to prepare a Bill accordingly.[12]

The Senate adjourned to 11 o'clock to-morrow.

TUESDAY, JANUARY 4, 1791

The SENATE assembled—present as yesterday.

A message from the House of Representatives by Mr. Beckley their clerk:

"Mr. PRESIDENT,

"The House of Representatives have passed a Bill, entitled, 'An Act for the relief of Shubael Swain,'[13] in which they desire the concurrence of the Senate,"—

And he withdrew.

The petition of Shubael Swain was read,[14] praying for the remission of a fine incurred for the breach of the revenue laws; for reasons mentioned in the petition.

ORDERED, That the Bill, entitled, "An Act for the relief of Shubael Swain," be now read the FIRST time.

ORDERED, That this Bill pass to the SECOND reading.[15]

Agreeably to the order of the day, the Bill, entitled, "An Act to provide for the unlading of ships or vessels in cases of obstruction by ice," was read the SECOND time.

ORDERED, That this Bill pass to the THIRD reading.[16]

The Committee to whom was referred that part of the speech of the Presi-

---

[12] On January 4 this committee reported a bill which was read for the first time.

[13] This bill is in Engrossed House Bills, House Records, DNA.

[14] This petition is in Petitions and Memorials: Various subjects, Senate Records, DNA.

[15] On January 5 this bill was read a second time and committed.

[16] On January 5 the Senate read this bill a third time, passed it, and notified the House.

dent of the United States, which relates to the district of Kentucky, agreeably to order reported a Bill;[17] which was read the FIRST time, and—

ORDERED, That this Bill pass to the SECOND reading.[18]

The following letter was communicated from the Treasurer of the United States:

TREASURY of the UNITED STATES
January 3d, 1791

SIR,

MY accounts having lain a considerable time in the offices for settlement, and being now passed, permit me through you to lay them before the Honorable the Senate, and to assure you that

I am, &c.

(Signed)   SAMUEL MEREDITH,

Treasurer of the United States

The VICE PRESIDENT
of the United States[19] }

ORDERED, That this letter and the accounts therein referred to, lie on the table.

The Senate adjourned to 11 o'clock to-morrow.

WEDNESDAY, JANUARY 5, 1791

The SENATE assembled—present as yesterday.

The Senate proceeded to the THIRD reading of the Bill, entitled, "An Act to provide for the unlading of ships or vessels, in cases of obstruction by ice," and—

RESOLVED, That this Bill DO PASS.

ORDERED, That the Secretary communicate to the House of Representatives, the concurrence of the Senate in this Bill.[20]

Agreeably to the order of the day, the Senate proceeded to the SECOND reading of the Bill, providing that the district of Kentucky should become an independent State, and be admitted as a member of the United States of America; and—

---

[17] Three manuscript copies of this bill are in Senate Bills, Senate Records, DNA.

[18] On January 5 this bill was read a second time and consideration of it was postponed.

[19] The letter, the Treasury report, and the Treasurer's accounts are in Transcribed Reports and Communications from the Executive Departments, Record Books, Senate Records, DNA.

[20] The Speaker signed this bill on January 6; the Vice President and the President signed it on January 7.

ORDERED, That the further consideration hereof be postponed, and that in the mean time the Bill be printed for the consideration of Congress.[21]

The Senate proceeded to the SECOND reading of the Bill, entitled, "An Act for the relief of Shubael Swain," and—

ORDERED, That it be committed to

> Mr. Morris
> Mr. Langdon and
> Mr. Hawkins[22]

Mr. Hawkins, from the Committee appointed to take into consideration the Bill, entitled, "An Act to continue an Act, entitled, 'An Act declaring the assent of Congress to certain Acts of the States of Maryland, Georgia, and Rhode-Island and Providence Plantations,'" reported amendments,[23]—

On motion to postpone the consideration of the amendments, to take up the following resolution reported by the Committee, to wit:

"That it be resolved that the President of the United States be requested to direct an enquiry as to the extent of the obstructions in the river Savannah, and in that leading to the town of Providence in the State of Rhode-Island and Providence Planations; the progress that has been made in their removal, together with a state of facts relative to the objects for which the said Acts were passed by the respective States previous to the adoption of the present Constitution of the United States, and by which a duty of tonnage is laid on the ships and vessels navigating the said rivers,"—

It passed in the Negative.

The Senate proceeded in the SECOND reading of the Bill, and agreed thereto, with the following amendments reported by the Committee,—to limit the operation thereof to the States of Georgia and Rhode-Island, by inserting these words, line 5th, after the word "force"—

"So far as the same respects the States of Georgia and Rhode-Island and Providence Plantations."

To limit the duration of the Act to one year, by striking out, in the same line, *five*, and inserting "one;" and to make the word *years*, in the same line, singular.

To insert in the title of the Bill, after the word "Plantations,"

"So far as the same respects the States of Georgia and Rhode-Island and Providence Plantations."

---

[21] A printed copy of this bill is in the Broadside Collection, RBkRm, DLC. E–46031. On January 7 the second reading of this bill was continued and consideration of it was postponed.

[22] This vote for committee is in Other Records: Yeas and nays, Senate Records, DNA. On January 6 this committee reported, and the bill was read the third time and disagreed to.

[23] This report is in Various Select Committee Reports, Senate Records, DNA.

ORDERED, That this Bill as amended, pass to the THIRD reading.[24]

The Senate adjourned to 11 o'clock to-morrow.

THURSDAY, JANUARY 6, 1791

The SENATE assembled—present as yesterday.

Mr. Strong from the Committee appointed to take into consideration the message from the President of the United States, of the 23d December last, respecting cases of grants of lands in the western territory north-west of the Ohio, reported that a Bill be brought in for the purposes mentioned in the report;[25] whereupon—

ORDERED, That the same Committee be instructed to prepare and report a Bill accordingly.[26]

Agreeably to the order of the day, the Senate proceeded to the THIRD reading of the Bill, entitled, "An Act to continue an Act, entitled, 'An Act declaring the assent of Congress to certain Acts of the States of Maryland, Georgia, and Rhode-Island and Providence Plantations,' " and—

RESOLVED, That this Bill DO PASS with the amendments.

ORDERED, That the Secretary desire the concurrence of the House of Representatives, in the amendments.[27]

The Bill "to incorporate the subscribers to the bank of———" was read the SECOND time, and the consideration thereof was postponed to Monday next.[28]

Mr. Morris, from the Committee appointed to take into consideration the Bill, entitled, "An Act for the relief of Shubael Swain," reported;[29] whereupon—

The Senate proceeded to the THIRD reading of the Bill, and—

RESOLVED, That this Bill DO NOT PASS.[30]

Mr. Foster, from the joint Committee on enrolled Bills, reported, That they had examined the enrolled Bill, entitled, "An Act to provide for the unlading of ships or vessels, in cases of obstruction by ice,"[31] and had found it correct.

Mr. Langdon, from the Committee to whom was referred that part of the

---

[24] On January 6 this bill was read a third time, passed, and returned to the House for concurrence in the amendments.

[25] This report is in Various Select Committee Reports, Senate Records, DNA.

[26] This order is in Various Select Committee Reports, Senate Records, DNA. On January 7 this committee reported a bill which was read for the first time.

[27] On January 7 the House agreed to these Senate amendments.

[28] On January 10 this bill was again considered.

[29] This report has not been located.

[30] This resolve, noted on the House Bill, is in Engrossed House Bills, House Records, DNA. On February 25 Shubael Swain petitioned Congress again and the petition was tabled. On the same day the rejected bill was printed in the Journal.

[31] The inspected enrolled bill is in Enrolled Acts, RG 11, DNA. E-23877, E-46329.

President's speech which relates to the trade of the Mediterranean; together with the President's message of the 30th of December, and the papers accompanying the same; made report.[32]

ORDERED, That the consideration of the report be postponed until to-morrow.[33]

The Senate adjourned to 11 o'clock to-morrow.

FRIDAY, JANUARY 7, 1791

The SENATE assembled—present as yesterday.

Agreeably to the order of the day, proceeded to the consideration of the report of the Committee to whom was referred that part of the speech of the President of the United States which relates to the trade of the Mediterranean; together with the President's message of the 30th of December, and the papers accompanying the same, and—

ORDERED, That the report lie on the table.[34]

Mr. Strong, from the Committee to whom was referred the message of the President of the United States, of the 23d of December ult. reported "a Bill for granting lands to the inhabitants and settlers at Vincennes and the Il-ionois[35] country, in the territory north-west of the Ohio, and for confirming them in their possessions;"[36] which Bill was read the FIRST time.

ORDERED, That this Bill pass to the SECOND reading.[37]

A message from the House of Representatives by Mr. Beckley their clerk:

"Mr. PRESIDENT,

"The House of Representatives have concurred in the amendments of the Senate to the Bill, entitled, 'An Act to continue an Act, entitled, "An Act declaring the assent of Congress to certain Acts of the States of Maryland, Georgia, and Rhode-Island and Providence Plantations," '[38]—

"The Speaker having signed an enrolled Bill, I am directed to bring it to the Senate,"—

And he withdrew.

The Vice President signed the enrolled Bill, entitled, "An Act to provide for the unlading of ships or vessels, in cases of obstruction by ice," and it was

---

[32] This report is in Various Select Committee Reports, Senate Records, DNA.

[33] On January 7 this report was considered and tabled.

[34] On January 21 this report was recommitted, along with a letter from the Secretary of State concerning American prisoners in Algiers.

[35] The smooth journal uses the spelling "Ielionois."

[36] This bill is in Senate Bills, Senate Records, DNA.

[37] On January 10 this bill was read a second time and passed to the third reading.

[38] This extract from the House Journal is in Messages from the House, Senate Records, DNA. On January 10 this bill was signed by the Speaker, the Vice President, and the President.

delivered to the Committee on enrolled Bills, to be laid before the President of the United States.

Mr. Ellsworth, from the Committee appointed to take into consideration that part of the speech of the President of the United States, which relates to the appointment of Consuls in foreign countries, reported a Bill;[39] which was read the FIRST time.

ORDERED, That this Bill pass to the SECOND reading, and that in the mean time it be printed for the consideration of Congress.[40]

The Senate proceeded in the SECOND reading of the Bill, providing "that the district of Kentucky should become an independent State, and be admitted as a member of the United States of America;" and after progress, the further consideration of the Bill was postponed until Tuesday next.[41]

Mr. Foster, from the Committee on enrolled Bills, reported, That they had on this day laid before the President of the United States, the enrolled Bill, entitled, "An Act to provide for the unlading of ships or vessels, in cases of obstruction by ice."[42]

The Senate adjourned to Monday next, at 11 o'clock.

MONDAY, JANUARY 10, 1791

The SENATE assembled—present as on the 7th, and

The Honorable John Henry, from the State of Maryland, attended.

The Senate proceeded in the SECOND reading of the Bill "to incorporate the subscribers to the bank of————;" and after progress, the further consideration thereof was postponed.[43]

Agreeably to the order of the day, the Senate proceeded to the SECOND reading of the "Bill for granting lands to the inhabitants and settlers at Vincennes and the Ilionois country, in the territory north-west of the Ohio, and for confirming them in their possessions;" and—

ORDERED, That this Bill pass to the THIRD reading.[44]

Mr. Foster, from the Committee on enrolled Bills, reported,[45] That they had examined the enrolled Bill, entitled, "An Act to continue an Act, entitled, 'An Act declaring the assent of Congress to certain Acts of the States of Mary-

---

[39] A manuscript copy of this bill is in Senate Bills, Senate Records, DNA. A printed copy is in the Broadside Collection, RBkRm, DLC. E–46308.

[40] On January 12 this bill was read a second time and recommitted.

[41] On January 12 this bill was read a third time, passed, engrossed, and sent to the House for concurrence.

[42] On this same date the President signed this bill and on January 10 the Senate was notified.

[43] On January 11 this bill was considered again.

[44] On January 11 this bill was read a third time, passed, and sent to the House for concurrence.

[45] This report is in Committee on Enrolled Bills, Senate Records, DNA.

land, Georgia, and Rhode-Island and Providence Plantations, so far as the same respects the States of Georgia and Rhode-Island:' "[46] and found it correct.

A message from the House of Representatives by Mr. Beckley their clerk:

"Mr. PRESIDENT,

"The Speaker of the House of Representatives having signed an enrolled Bill, I am directed to bring it to the Senate,—

"The President of the United States has notified the House of Representatives, that he did on the 7th instant, approve and fix his signature to 'An Act to provide for unlading of ships or vessels, in cases of obstruction by ice,' "[47]—

And he withdrew.

Whereupon the Vice President signed the enrolled Bill, entitled, "An Act to continue an Act, entitled, 'An Act declaring the assent of Congress to certain Acts of the States of Maryland, Georgia, and Rhode-Island and Providence Plantations, so far as the same respects the States of Georgia and Rhode-Island;' " and it was delivered to the Committee on enrolled Bills, to be laid before the President of the United States.[48]

The Senate adjourned to 11 o'clock to-morrow.

TUESDAY, JANUARY 11, 1791

The SENATE assembled—present as yesterday.

Agreeably to the order of the day, the Senate proceeded to the THIRD reading of the Bill "for granting lands to the inhabitants and settlers at Vincennes and the Ilionois[49] country, in the territory north-west of the Ohio, and for confirming them in their possessions;" and—

RESOLVED, That this Bill DO PASS; that the title thereof be "An Act for granting lands to the inhabitants and settlers at Vincennes and the Ilionois country, in the territory north-west of the Ohio, and confirming them in their possessions;" and that this Bill be engrossed and sent to the House of Representatives for their concurrence.[50]

---

[46] The inspected enrolled bill is in Enrolled Acts, RG 11, DNA. E–23870.

[47] This message is in Committee on Enrolled Bills, Senate Records, DNA.

[48] On January 11 the House notified the Senate that the President had signed this bill on January 10.

[49] The smooth journal uses the spelling "Illinois."

[50] The bill, as it passed the Senate, is in Engrossed Senate Bills and Resolutions, Senate Records, DNA. On January 11 the House read this bill the first time, and on the next day it was read the second time and committed to the committee of the whole. On February 26 the committee of the whole discharged this bill and a committee was appointed to consider it. On March 2 this committee reported amendments to the bill which were agreed to by the House. On the same day the bill was read the third time, passed, and returned to the Senate for concurrence in the amendments. The Senate committed the amendments.

Mr. Foster, from the Committee on enrolled Bills, reported,[51] That they did yesterday, lay before the President of the United States, the enrolled Bill, entitled, "An Act to continue an Act, entitled, 'An Act declaring the assent of Congress to certain Acts of the States of Maryland, Georgia, and Rhode-Island and Providence Plantations, so far as the same respects the States of Georgia and Rhode-Island.' "

A message from the House of Representatives by Mr. Beckley their clerk:

"Mr. PRESIDENT,

"The President of the United States has notified the House of Representatives, that he did on the 10th, approve and affix his signature to the Act, entitled, 'An Act to continue an Act, entitled, "An Act declaring the assent of Congress to certain Acts of the States of Maryland, Georgia, and Rhode-Island and Providence Plantations, so far as the same respects the States of Georgia and Rhode-Island," ' "[52]

And he withdrew.

The Senate proceeded in the SECOND reading of the "Bill to incorporate the subscribers to the bank of————;" and after progress[53]—

Adjourned to 11 o'clock to-morrow.

WEDNESDAY, JANUARY 12, 1791

The SENATE assembled—present as yesterday.

Agreeably to the order of the day, the Senate proceeded in the SECOND reading of "the Bill to incorporate the subscribers to the bank of————;" and on motion, it was agreed to postpone the further consideration thereof until to-morrow.[54]

The Senate proceeded to the THIRD reading of the Bill "providing that the district of Kentucky should become an independent State, and be admitted as a member of the United States of America" and—

RESOLVED, That this Bill DO PASS; that the title thereof be "An Act providing that the district of Kentucky should become an independent State, and be admitted as a member of the United States of America;"[55] that the Bill be

---

[51] This report is in Committee on Enrolled Bills, Senate Records, DNA.

[52] This message is in Committee on Enrolled Bills, Senate Records, DNA.

[53] On January 12 this bill was considered again.

[54] On January 13 the Senate passed an amendment to this bill, and a motion was made on the bill.

[55] The title of the bill is incorrect here. See note in text of proceedings for January 28, page 542 below.

engrossed,[56] and that the Secretary carry it to the House of Representatives, and desire their concurrence.[57]

The Senate proceeded in the SECOND reading of the "Bill concerning Consuls and Vice Consuls;" and after progress—

ORDERED, That it be re-committed to

Mr. Ellsworth

Mr. Morris

Mr. Schuyler

Mr. Hawkins and

Mr. King[58]

The Senate adjourned to 11 o'clock to-morrow.

THURSDAY, JANUARY 13, 1791

The SENATE assembled—present as yesterday.

Several Resolutions,[59] and a Memorial of the Legislature of the Commonwealth of Virginia,[60] calling the attention of Congress to "An Act making provision for the debt of the United States," were by Mr. Monroe, communicated to the Senate; which being read—

ORDERED, That they lie on the table.

The Senate proceeded in the SECOND reading of "the Bill to incorporate the subscribers to the bank of———;" and agreed to fill the blank in the title, with these words "the United States of America."

On motion to limit the term of incorporation to seven years—

A motion was made to extend the term of incorporation to March the 4th 1815; and on this the yeas and nays being required by one fifth of the Senators present, were—

Mr. Bassett	Yea	
Mr. Butler		Nay
Mr. Dickinson	Yea	
Mr. Ellsworth	Yea	
Mr. Elmer	Yea	

---

[56] The engrossed bill and the resolve are in Engrossed Senate Bills and Resolutions, Senate Records, DNA.

[57] On January 12 the House read this bill the first time, and it was read a second time and committed to the committee of the whole the following day. The committee of the whole considered the bill on January 28; the House passed the bill on the same day and notified the Senate. On the same day a correction in the title of the bill was also made.

[58] This vote for committee is in Other Records: Yeas and nays, Senate Records, DNA. On January 26 this committee reported amendments to this bill which were agreed to during the second reading. The bill then passed to the third reading.

[59] These resolutions are included in George Washington's message of January 17, 1791, located in President's Messages: Suggesting legislation, Senate Records, DNA.

[60] The memorial is included in George Washington's message of January 17, 1791, located in President's Messages: Suggesting legislation, Senate Records, DNA.

Mr. Few		Nay
Mr. Foster		Nay
Mr. Hawkins		Nay
Mr. Henry		Nay
Mr. Johnson	Yea	
Mr. Johnston		Nay
Mr. Izard		Nay
Mr. King	Yea	
Mr. Langdon	Yea	
Mr. Maclay		Nay
Mr. Monroe		Nay
Mr. Morris	Yea	
Mr. Read	Yea	
Mr. Schuyler	Yea	
Mr. Strong	Yea	
Mr. Wingate		Nay

Yeas—11
Nays—10[61]

So it passed in the Affirmative.

A motion was made to subjoin to the last clause agreed to, as follows,—
"Provided nevertheless that nothing herein contained shall be construed to
exclude the right of amending the same, on giving twelve months notice, from
and after the first of January 1800;"[62] and after debate the further consideration hereof was postponed.[63]

The Senate adjourned to 11 o'clock to-morrow.

FRIDAY, JANUARY 14, 1791

The SENATE assembled—present as yesterday.

Proceeded in the SECOND reading of the "Bill to incorporate the subscribers
to the bank of————;" and the question being taken on the motion made
yesterday and postponed, to wit:—

"Provided nevertheless that nothing herein contained shall be construed to
exclude the right of amending the same, on giving twelve months notice, from
and after the first of January 1800"—

It passed in the Negative.

On motion, it was agreed to re-consider the term of incorporation agreed

---

[61] This vote is in Other Records: Yeas and nays, Senate Records, DNA.

[62] This motion, introduced by Pierce Butler, is in Senate Simple Resolutions and
Motions, Senate Records, DNA.

[63] On January 14 the Senate defeated this motion and agreed to reconsider the term
of incorporation of the bank.

to yesterday, and limit it to the 4th day of March 1811; and having made further progress in the Bill[64]—

The Senate adjourned to Monday next at 11 o'clock.

MONDAY, JANUARY 17, 1791

The SENATE assembled—present as on the 14th, and

The Honorable James Gunn, from the State of Georgia, attended.

The Senate proceeded in the SECOND reading of the "Bill to incorporate the subscribers to the Bank of———;" and after progress, the further consideration hereof was postponed.[65]

A written message from the President of the United States, was communicated by Mr. Lear his Secretary,—

And he withdrew.

UNITED STATES, January 17th, 1791

GENTLEMEN of the SENATE and
    HOUSE of REPRESENTATIVES,

I LAY before you an official statement of the appropriation of ten thousand dollars, granted to defray the contingent expences of Government, by an Act of the 26th March 1790.

A copy of two resolutions of the Legislature of Virginia, and a petition of sundry officers, and assignees of officers and soldiers of the Virginia line on continental establishment, on the subject of bounty lands allotted to them on the north-west side of the Ohio; and—

A copy of an Act of the Legislature of Maryland, to empower the Wardens of the port of Baltimore, to levy and collect the duty therein mentioned.

G. WASHINGTON[66]

ORDERED, That the message lie for consideration.[67]

The Senate adjourned to 11 o'clock to-morrow.

TUESDAY, JANUARY 18, 1791

The SENATE assembled—present as yesterday.

A letter was read from the Secretary of State,[68] enclosing "a postscript to the report on measures, weights and coins, now before Senate," and—

---

[64] On January 17 this bill was considered again.

[65] On January 18 this bill was considered and recommitted. On the same day this committee reported amendments to the bill which were agreed to.

[66] This message and documents are in President's Messages: Suggesting legislation, Senate Records, DNA. The statement of appropriation is printed in the Appendix, page 714 below.

[67] On January 18 the papers that the President sent were read and laid for consideration.

[68] This letter, signed by Thomas Jefferson, is in Reports and Communications from the Secretary of State, Senate Records, DNA.

ORDERED, That the letter and enclosure lie for consideration.[69]

The papers referred to in the message of the President of the United States, of the 17th instant, were read, and—

ORDERED, To lie for consideration.[70]

The Senate proceeded in the SECOND reading of the "Bill to incorporate the subscribers to the bank of————;" and ordered that it be re-committed for further amendments.

Mr. Strong, from the Committee to whom was referred the last mentioned Bill, reported sundry amendments;[71] which being agreed to—

The Senate proceeded in the SECOND reading of the Bill, and having amended the same, the further consideration hereof was postponed.[72]

The Senate adjourned to 11 o'clock to-morrow.

WEDNESDAY, JANUARY 19, 1791

The SENATE assembled—present as yesterday.

A resolution of the Directors of the library of Philadelphia,[73] was communicated to the Senate, and read, providing "that the President, and Members of the Senate and House of Representatives of the United States, shall have free use of the books in the library in as full and ample manner as if they were members of the company."

The memorial of the Surgeons and Surgeons-mates in the medical department,[74] during a very considerable part of the late war, praying allowance for depreciation, was by Mr. Morris, communicated to the Senate; which being read, was—

ORDERED, To lie on the table.[75]

The Senate proceeded in the SECOND reading of the "Bill to incorporate the subscribers to the bank of————;"

On motion to expunge the 12th section, to wit, "And be it further enacted, that no other bank shall be established by any future law of the United States, during the continuance of the Corporation hereby created; for which the faith of the United States is hereby pledged,"—

It passed in the Negative.

---

[69] On March 1 the committee on the Secretary of State's report on weights and measures reported, and the report was adopted.

[70] On January 31 a committee was appointed to consider the papers from Virginia.

[71] The committee report is in Senate Bills, Senate Records, DNA. An annotated printed bill is in the Broadside Collection, RBkRm, DLC.

[72] On January 19 this bill was considered again, and an amendment to it was defeated. The bill then passed to the third reading.

[73] This resolution is in Reports and Communications, Senate Records, DNA.

[74] This petition is in Petitions and Memorials: Claims, Senate Records, DNA.

[75] The Senate did not consider this petition. The House referred it to the Secretary of War.

ORDERED, That this Bill pass to the THIRD reading.[76]
The Senate adjourned to 11 o'clock to-morrow.

T H U R S D A Y, JANUARY 20, 1791

The SENATE assembled—present as yesterday,

And proceeded to the THIRD reading of the "Bill to incorporate the subscribers to the bank of————;" and,

"On motion to re-consider the term of incorporation, and limit it to the year 1801, instead of 1811,"—the yeas and nays were required by one fifth of the Senators present.

Mr. Bassett	Nay	
Mr. Butler		Yea
Mr. Dalton	Nay	
Mr. Dickinson	Nay	
Mr. Ellsworth	Nay	
Mr. Elmer	Nay	
Mr. Few		Yea
Mr. Foster	Nay	
Mr. Gunn		Yea
Mr. Hawkins		Yea
Mr. Johnson	Nay	
Mr. Izard		Yea
Mr. King	Nay	
Mr. Langdon	Nay	
Mr. Maclay	Nay	
Mr. Monroe		Yea
Mr. Morris	Nay	
Mr. Read	Nay	
Mr. Schuyler	Nay	
Mr. Stanton	Nay	
Mr. Strong	Nay	
Mr. Wingate	Nay	

Nays—16

Yeas—6[77]

So it passed in the Negative.

On motion to expunge the 12th section, to wit, "And be it further enacted, that no other bank shall be established by any future law of the United States, during the continuance of the Corporation hereby created; for which the faith

---

[76] On January 20 two amendments to this bill were defeated, and the bill was passed and sent to the House for concurrence.

[77] This vote is in Other Records: Yeas and nays, Senate Records, DNA.

of the United States is hereby pledged,"—the yeas and nays were required by one fifth of the Senators present.

Mr. Bassett	Nay	
Mr. Butler		Yea
Mr. Dalton	Nay	
Mr. Dickinson	Nay	
Mr. Ellsworth	Nay	
Mr. Elmer	Nay	
Mr. Few		Yea
Mr. Foster	Nay	
Mr. Gunn	Nay	
Mr. Hawkins		Yea
Mr. Johnson	Nay	
Mr. Johnston	Nay	
Mr. Izard		Yea
Mr. King	Nay	
Mr. Langdon	Nay	
Mr. Maclay	Nay	
Mr. Monroe		Yea
Mr. Morris	Nay	
Mr. Read	Nay	
Mr. Schuyler	Nay	
Mr. Stanton	Nay	
Mr. Strong	Nay	
Mr. Wingate	Nay	

Nays—18

Yeas—5[78]

And it passed in the Negative.

RESOLVED, That this Bill DO PASS; that the title of it be "An Act to incorporate the subscribers to the bank of the United States;" that it be engrossed,[79] and that the Secretary carry it to the House of Representatives for concurrence.[80]

A motion was made, "That the Secretary furnish any member of the Senate with such extracts from the executive Journal, as he may direct."[81]

---

[78] The vote is in Other Records: Yeas and nays, Senate Records, DNA.

[79] The engrossed bill and the resolve are in Engrossed Senate Bills and Resolutions, Senate Records, DNA.

[80] On January 21 the House read this bill the first and second times and committed it to the committee of the whole. On January 31 the committee of the whole considered the bill and reported on it. On February 1 the bill was read the third time, and it was debated on February 2, 3, 4, 5, and 7. It was passed on February 8, and the Senate was notified.

[81] This motion is in Senate Simple Resolutions and Motions, Senate Records, DNA.

ORDERED; That the consideration of this motion be postponed until to-morrow.[82]

The Senate adjourned to 11 o'clock to-morrow.

FRIDAY, JANUARY 21, 1791

The SENATE assembled—present as yesterday, and
The Honorable Charles Carroll, from the State of Maryland, attended.

A letter from the Secretary of State was communicated, with sundry enclosures relative to the American Prisoners in Algiers;[83] which being read—

ORDERED, That they be referred to the Committee who had under consideration that part of the message from the President of the United States, which refers to the trade of the Mediterranean; and that their report of the sixth of January, be re-committed.[84]

A message from the House of Representatives by Mr. Beckley their clerk:

"Mr. PRESIDENT,

"The House of Representatives have 'Ordered, That a Committee be appointed, to join a Committee of the Senate, to consider and report what time will be proper for the commencement of the next Congress; to the end that timely notice may be given to the members who are to serve for the ensuing two years,' "[85]—

And he withdrew.

The order of the House of Representatives was read, and agreed to, and—

ORDERED, That   Mr. Strong
                  Mr. Izard and
                  Mr. Ellsworth, be of the joint Committee on the part of the Senate;[86] and that the Secretary communicate this appointment, to the House of Representatives.[87]

The memorial of the merchants of Philadelphia,[88] trading to India and

---

[82] On January 21 this motion was considered, amended, and committed.

[83] This letter and copies of several enclosures are in Papers Pertaining to Citizens of the United States Held Prisoners in Algiers, Foreign Relations, Senate Records, DNA.

[84] This order is in Various Select Committee Reports, Senate Records, DNA. On January 31 this committee reported and the report was laid for consideration.

[85] Two versions of this House order, one included with the Senate response and one alone, are in Messages from the House, Senate Records, DNA, and in Joint Committee Reports, Senate Records, DNA.

[86] This vote for committee is in Other Records: Yeas and nays, Senate Records, DNA. The order which included the results of the vote is in Joint Committee Reports, Senate Records, DNA.

[87] On January 25 this committee reported.

[88] This petition is in Petitions and Memorials: Various subjects, Senate Records, DNA.

China, praying "such encouragement and protection as in their wisdom Congress shall deem expedient," was by Mr. Morris, presented and read, and—

ORDERED, That it lie for consideration.[89]

The Senate resumed the consideration of the motion made yesterday; to wit, "That the Secretary furnish any member of Senate with such extracts from the executive Journal, as he may direct;" and it was agreed to amend the motion to read as follows:

"RESOLVED, That the Secretary do furnish the members of Senate, when required, with extracts of such parts of the executive Journal as are not, by a vote of the Senate, considered secret;"[90] and it was agreed that the motion be committed to

Mr. Ellsworth
Mr. Gunn and
Mr. King[91]

ORDERED, That the Secretary do furnish Mr. Gunn with an attested copy of sundry extracts from the records of Senate, when acting in their executive capacity.

The Senate adjourned to Monday next, at 11 o'clock.

MONDAY, JANUARY 24, 1791

The SENATE assembled—present as on the 21st.

A written message from the President of the United States, was communicated by Mr. Lear, his Secretary,—

And he withdrew.

UNITED STATES, January 24th, 1791

GENTLEMEN of the SENATE and
HOUSE of REPRESENTATIVES,

I LAY before you a statement relative to the Frontiers of the United States, which has been submitted to me by the Secretary for the department of war.—

I rely upon your wisdom to make such arrangements as may be essential for the preservation of good order, and the effectual protection of the Frontiers.

G. WASHINGTON[92]

ORDERED, That the Secretary communicate the message and papers accompanying it, to the House of Representatives.

Another written message from the President of the United States, was communicated by his Secretary; which is as follows:

---

[89] The Senate did not consider this petition but the House did.

[90] The resolution is in Senate Simple Resolutions and Motions, Senate Records, DNA.

[91] The vote for committee is in Other Records: Yeas and nays, Senate Records, DNA. This committee did not report.

[92] This message and related documents are in President's Messages: Transmittting reports from the Secretary of War, Senate Records, DNA.

UNITED STATES, January 24th, 1791

GENTLEMEN of the SENATE and
    HOUSE of REPRESENTATIVES,

IN execution of the powers with which Congress were pleased to invest me by their Act, entitled, "An Act for establishing the temporary and permanent seat of government of the United States;" and on mature consideration of the advantages and disadvantages of the several positions within the limits prescribed by the said Act, I have by a proclamation bearing date this day, (a copy of which is herewith transmitted) directed Commissioners, appointed in pursuance of the Act, to survey and limit a part of the territory of ten miles square, on both sides of the river Powtomac, so as to comprehend Georgetown, in Maryland, and extend to the eastern branch.—

I have not, by this first act, given to the said territory the whole extent of which it is susceptible in the direction of the river; because I thought it important that Congress should have an opportunity of considering whether by an amendatory law they would authorize the location of the residue, at the lower end of the present, so as to comprehend the eastern branch itself, and some of the country on its lower side, in the State of Maryland, and the town of Alexandria in Virginia: If however they are of opinion, that the federal territory should be bounded by the water edge of the eastern branch, the location of the residue will be to be made at the upper end of what is now directed.—

I have thought best to await a survey of the territory, before it is decided on what particular spot on the north-eastern side of the river, the public buildings shall be erected.

G. WASHINGTON[93]

ORDERED, That this message lie for consideration.[94]

The Senate adjourned to 11 o'clock to-morrow.

TUESDAY, JANUARY 25, 1791

The SENATE assembled—present as yesterday.

Mr. Strong reported from the joint Committee appointed on the 21st instant,[95] "to consider and report what time will be proper for the commencement of the next Congress."

ORDERED, That the report lie for consideration.[96]

The Senate adjourned to 11 o'clock to-morrow.

---

[93] The letter from the President is in the George Washington Papers, series 4, reel 100, Manuscript Division, DLC.

[94] On February 16 Charles Carroll announced his intention to bring in a bill amendatory to the Residence Act and pursuant to this message.

[95] This report is in Joint Committee Reports, Senate Records, DNA.

[96] On January 31 the House notified the Senate that it had agreed to this report by resolve. This resolution was then read by the Senate and consideration of it was postponed.

W E D N E S D A Y, JANUARY 26, 1791

The SENATE assembled—present as yesterday.

The petition of Albert Roux, late a captain in the second continental regiment of South-Carolina,[97] praying compensation for services; was read, and—

ORDERED, That it be referred to the Secretary at War to report thereon to the Senate.

A written message from the President of the United States, was communicated by Mr. Lear, his Secretary,—

And he withdrew.

UNITED STATES, January 26th, 1791

GENTLEMEN of the SENATE and
    HOUSE of REPRESENTATIVES,

I LAY before you the copy of a letter from the President of the National Assembly of France, to the President of the United States; and of a decree of that Assembly, which was transmitted with the above mentioned letter.

G. WASHINGTON[98]

The message and papers were read.[99]

Mr. Ellsworth, from the Committee to whom was referred the Bill "concerning Consuls and Vice-Consuls," reported amendments;[100] which report was agreed to; whereupon—

The Senate proceeded in the SECOND reading of the Bill, which was amended conformably to the report, and—

ORDERED, That this Bill pass to the THIRD reading.[101]

The Senate adjourned to 11 o'clock to-morrow.

T H U R S D A Y, JANUARY 27, 1791

The SENATE assembled—present as yesterday.

Agreeably to the order of the day the Senate proceeded to the THIRD reading of the Bill "concerning Consuls and Vice-Consuls," and—

RESOLVED, That this Bill DO PASS; that the title thereof be "An Act con-

---

[97] This petition is in Petitions and Memorials: Claims, Senate Records, DNA.

[98] This message enclosing documents is in President's Messages: Suggesting legislation, Senate Records, DNA.

[99] This decree was a tribute to the memory of Benjamin Franklin. On February 22 the Senate passed and sent to the House for concurrence a resolution thanking the National Assembly of France for this tribute.

[100] This committee report is in Various Select Committee Reports, Senate Records, DNA.

[101] On January 27 this bill was read a third time, passed, and sent to the House for concurrence.

cerning Consuls and Vice-Consuls;" that it be engrossed,[102] and that the Secretary carry it to the House of Representatives and desire concurrence therein.[103]

A written message from the President of the United States, was communicated by Mr. Lear, his Secretary,—

And he withdrew.

UNITED STATES, January 27th, 1791

GENTLEMEN of the SENATE and
    HOUSE of REPRESENTATIVES,

IN order that you may be fully informed of the situation of the Frontiers, and the prospects of hostility in that quarter, I lay before you the intelligence of some recent depredations, received since my message to you upon this subject of the 24th instant.

G. WASHINGTON[104]

The message and papers therein referred to, were read, and—

ORDERED, That the Secretary communicate them to the House of Representatives.

The Senate adjourned to 11 o'clock to-morrow.

FRIDAY, JANUARY 28, 1791

The SENATE assembled—present as yesterday.

The petition of a number of the inhabitants of the county of Lancaster,[105] was read, praying that the Bill laying an excise on spirituous liquors, pending before Congress, may not pass, for reasons therein expressed.

ORDERED, That the petition lie on the table.

A message from the House of Representatives by Mr. Beckley their clerk:

"Mr. PRESIDENT,

"The House of Representatives have passed a Bill, entitled, 'An Act repealing after the last day of June next, the duties heretofore laid upon distilled spirits imported from abroad, and laying others in their stead; and also upon

---

[102] This engrossed resolve and a fragment of the bill are in Engrossed Senate Bills and Resolutions, Senate Records, DNA. E–46321.

[103] On January 28 the House read this bill the first and second times. Consideration was then postponed several times until March 2 when the bill was considered in the committee of the whole, amended, agreed to, and returned to the Senate for concurrence in the amendments. On the same day the Senate disagreed to the House amendments and notified the House which adhered to its amendments.

[104] This message and enclosed documents are in President's Messages: Transmitting reports from the Secretary of War, Senate Records, DNA.

[105] This petition is in Petitions and Memorials: Various subjects, Senate Records, DNA.

spirits distilled within the United States, and for appropriating the same;'[106] in which they desire the concurrence of the Senate,"—

And he withdrew.

ORDERED, That this Bill have the FIRST reading at this time.

ORDERED, That this Bill pass to the SECOND reading; and that in the mean time it be printed for the use of the Senate.[107]

A message from the House of Representatives by Mr. Beckley their clerk:

"Mr. PRESIDENT,

"The House of Representatives have passed the Bill, entitled, 'An Act declaring the consent of Congress that a new State be formed within the jurisdiction of the Commonwealth of Virginia, and admitted into this union by the name of the State of Kentucky,' "—

And he withdrew.

☞ The title of this Bill was wrong copied in the resolution of Senate of January 12th, on the third reading of the Bill, page 530,[108] the above being the *amended title*, as agreed to in Senate.[109]

The Senate adjourned to Monday next, at 11 o'clock.

MONDAY, JANUARY 31, 1791

The SENATE assembled—present as on the 28th.

Mr. Foster, from the Committee on enrolled Bills, reported, That they had examined the enrolled Bill, entitled, "An Act declaring the consent of Congress that a new State be formed within the jurisdiction of the Commonwealth of Virginia, and admitted into this union by the name of the State of Kentucky;"[110] and found it correct.

A message from the House of Representatives by Mr. Beckley their clerk:

"Mr. PRESIDENT,

"The House of Representatives have passed a Bill, entitled, 'An Act declaring the consent of Congress to a certain Act of the State of Maryland;'[111] in which they desire the concurrence of the Senate.—

"The House of Representatives have agreed to the report of the Committee

---

[106] This bill is in American Imprints, 1791, Folio, United States Laws and Statutes, RBkRm, DLC.

[107] On January 31 this bill was read a second time and consideration of it was postponed.

[108] The page number has been corrected to correspond to the pagination of this edition.

[109] On January 31 this bill was signed by both the Speaker and the Vice President and given to the committee on enrolled bills for delivery to the President.

[110] The inspected enrolled bill is in Enrolled Acts, RG 11, DNA. E–23850.

[111] This bill has not been located.

appointed on their part to confer with the Committee on the part of the Senate, respecting the time for the commencement of the next session of Congress.[112]—

"The Speaker of the House of Representatives having signed an enrolled Bill, I am directed to bring it to the Senate,"—

And he withdrew.

The Vice President signed the enrolled Bill, entitled, "An Act declaring the consent of Congress that a new State be formed within the jurisdiction of the Commonwealth of Virginia, and admitted into this union by the name of the State of Kentucky;" and it was delivered to the Committee on enrolled Bills, to be laid before the President of the United States, for his approbation.[113]

The resolution of the House of Representatives, agreeing to the report of the Committee appointed to confer with the Committee of the Senate, on the time for the commencement of the next session of Congress, was read, and the consideration thereof was postponed.[114]

The Bill, entitled, "An Act declaring the consent of Congress to a certain Act of the State of Maryland," was read the FIRST time, and—

ORDERED, That this Bill pass to the SECOND reading.[115]

The Senate proceeded to the SECOND reading of the Bill, entitled, "An Act repealing after the last day of June next, the duties heretofore laid upon distilled spirits imported from abroad, and laying others in their stead; and also upon spirits distilled within the United States, and for appropriating the same."

ORDERED, That the further consideration hereof be postponed until Wednesday next.[116]

On motion,

ORDERED, That   Mr. Monroe
Mr. Schuyler and
Mr. Read, be a Committee[117] to take into consideration the extract of a letter from governor Randolph, of Virginia, communicated by message from the President of the United States; together with the resolutions of the Commonwealth of Virginia, relative to the bounty lands to

---

[112] This resolution of the House, in the form of an extract from the Journal, is in Messages from the House, Senate Records, DNA.

[113] On February 4 the President signed the bill and notified the Senate.

[114] On February 12 this resolution and committee report were considered and postponed.

[115] On February 1 this bill was read a second time and passed to the third reading.

[116] On February 2 this bill was considered again and committed.

[117] This vote for committee is in Other Records: Yeas and nays, Senate Records, DNA.

the officers and soldiers of the Virginia line on continental establishment; and to report what is proper to be done thereon.[118]

Mr. Langdon, from the Committee to whom was referred that part of the message of the President of the United States, which relates to the commerce of the Mediterranean, together with the message of the President of the United States of 30th December; made report.[119]

ORDERED, That this report lie for consideration.[120]

The Senate adjourned to 11 o'clock to-morrow.

---

[118] On February 14 more papers were given to this committee for consideration.

[119] This report is in Various Select Committee Reports, Senate Records, DNA.

[120] On February 1 Mr. Langdon reported for this committee in an Executive session of the Senate. The report was printed in the Executive Journal, amended, approved, and then reprinted as amended. On the same date the committee reported a second time and that report was recommitted. On February 22 the President sent a message to the Senate in Executive session on the procedures for releasing the captives in Algiers and the message was printed in the Executive Journal. On March 1 the committee on Mediterranean trade reported on the President's message, and a resolution on the Algerian captives was passed. On the same day Mr. Langdon reported a bill called "An Act making appropriations for the purposes therein mentioned" [Moroccan Treaty Bill] to the Senate in legislative session. This bill was then read the first and second times.

TUESDAY, FEBRUARY 1, 1791

The SENATE assembled—present as yesterday.

The Bill, entitled, "An Act declaring the consent of Congress to a certain Act of the State of Maryland," was read the SECOND time, and—

ORDERED, That this Bill pass to the THIRD reading.[1]

The Senate took into consideration the executive business before them, and after progress therein—

Adjourned to 11 o'clock to-morrow.

WEDNESDAY, FEBRUARY 2, 1791

The SENATE assembled—present as yesterday.

A message from the House of Representatives by Mr. Beckley their clerk:

"Mr. PRESIDENT,

"The House of Representatives have passed the Bill, entitled, 'An Act making appropriations for the support of government during the year one thousand seven hundred and ninety-one, and for other purposes,' "[2]—

And he withdrew.

The Bill from the House of Representatives was read the FIRST time.

ORDERED, That this Bill pass to the SECOND reading.[3]

The Senate proceeded to the THIRD reading of the Bill, entitled, "An Act declaring the consent of Congress to a certain Act of the State of Maryland," and—

RESOLVED, That this Bill DO PASS, and that the Secretary acquaint the House of Representatives with the concurrence of the Senate therein.[4]

The Senate proceeded in the SECOND reading of the Bill, entitled, "An Act repealing after the last day of June next, the duties heretofore laid upon distilled spirits imported from abroad, and laying others in their stead; and also upon spirits distilled within the United States, and for appropriating the same;" and after debate—

ORDERED, That this Bill be committed to

> Mr. Morris
> Mr. Ellsworth
> Mr. Langdon

---

[1] On February 2 this bill was read a third time and passed. The House was notified of this action.

[2] This bill has not been located.

[3] On February 3 this bill was read a second time and committed. The petition of James Mathers was referred to this committee.

[4] On February 8 this bill was signed by both the Speaker and the Vice President.

Mr. Schuyler and
Mr. Strong[5]
The Senate adjourned to 11 o'clock to-morrow.

THURSDAY, FEBRUARY 3, 1791

The SENATE assembled—present as yesterday.

The petition of John Jones,[6] for compensation for certain stores destroyed during the late war, was read, and—

ORDERED, To lie on the table.[7]

The Senate proceeded in the SECOND reading of the Bill, entitled, "An Act making appropriations for the support of government during the year one thousand seven hundred and ninety-one, and for other purposes."

ORDERED, That it be committed to

Mr. Dalton
Mr. Carroll and
Mr. Bassett[8]

The petition of James Mathers,[9] for allowance for services during the recess, was read, and—

ORDERED, That the petition be referred to the Committee above mentioned.[10]

Mr. Foster, from the Committee on enrolled Bills, reported, That they did yesterday lay before the President of the United States, the Bill, entitled, "An Act declaring the consent of Congress that a new State be formed within the jurisdiction of the Commonwealth of Virginia, and admitted into this union by the name of the State of Kentucky."

The Senate adjourned to 11 o'clock to-morrow.

FRIDAY, FEBRUARY 4, 1791

The SENATE assembled—present as yesterday.

A message from the House of Representatives by Mr. Beckley their clerk:

---

[5] This vote for committee is in Other Records: Yeas and nays, Senate Records, DNA. On February 7 this committee reported amendments to the bill which were read and printed.

[6] This petition is in Petitions and Memorials: Claims, Senate Records, DNA.

[7] The Senate did not consider this petition. The House referred it to the Secretary of the Treasury.

[8] This vote for committee is in Other Records: Yeas and nays, Senate Records, DNA.

[9] The petition is in Petitions and Memorials: Claims, Senate Records, DNA.

[10] On February 5 this committee reported amendments to the Appropriations Bill. It also reported on the petition of James Mathers. Both reports were laid for consideration.

"Mr. PRESIDENT,

"I am directed to bring to the Senate a report of the Secretary of State,[11] made to the House of Representatives,"—

And he withdrew.

The report and papers therein referred to, were read, and—

ORDERED, That they lie until to-morrow.[12]

A message from the President of the United States, by Mr. Lear, his Secretary:

"Mr. PRESIDENT,

"I am commanded to inform the Senate, that the President of the United States has this day approved and signed an Act, entitled, 'An Act declaring the consent of Congress that a new State be formed within the jurisdiction of the Commonwealth of Virginia, and admitted into this union by the name of the State of Kentucky,' "—

And he withdrew.

The Senate adjourned to 11 o'clock to-morrow.

S A T U R D A Y, FEBRUARY 5, 1791

The SENATE assembled—present as yesterday.

Mr. Dalton, from the Committee appointed to consider and report on the Bill sent from the House of Representatives, entitled, "An Act making appropriations for the support of government during the year one thousand seven hundred and ninety-one, and for other purposes," reported sundry amendments.[13]

ORDERED, That this report lie until Monday next, for consideration.—

He also reported, from the same Committee, on the petition of James Mathers,[14] and—

ORDERED, That the report lie for consideration until Monday next.[15]

ORDERED, That two hundred copies of the report of the Secretary of State, on the subject of the cod and whale fisheries, made to the House of Repre-

---

[11] This report and several papers are in Reports and Communications from the Secretary of State, Senate Records, DNA. E–23911, E–23912.

[12] On February 5, 200 copies of this report were ordered to be printed.

[13] This report is in Various Select Committee Reports, Senate Records, DNA.

[14] This report is in Various Select Committee Reports, Senate Records, DNA.

[15] On February 7 the committee report on the Appropriations Bill was disagreed to, and the bill was passed to the third reading. The report of the committee on the petition of James Mathers was agreed to.

sentatives,and on the fourth instant communicated by message to the Senate, be printed for the use of the Members of Congress.[16]

The Senate adjourned to Monday next, at 11 o'clock.

MONDAY, FEBRUARY 7, 1791

The SENATE assembled—present as on the 5th instant,

And proceeded to consider the amendments reported by the Committee on the Bill, entitled, "An Act making appropriations for the support of government during the year one thousand seven hundred and ninety-one, and for other purposes;" to which amendments the Senate did not agree; whereupon—

ORDERED, That the Bill pass to the THIRD reading.

The report of the same Committee, on the petition of James Mathers, was considered; whereupon—

ORDERED, That the objects of this petition be included in the account of the Secretary of the Senate, when rendered, of the expence incurred in the removal of his office from New-York to Philadelphia.[17]

A message from the House of Representatives by Mr. Beckley their clerk:

"Mr. PRESIDENT,

"The House of Representatives have ordered, That the report of the Secretary of the Treasury,[18] relative to the establishment of a mint, be sent to the Senate for their information,"[19]—

And he withdrew.

ORDERED, That the report of the Secretary of the Treasury, relative to the establishment of a mint, be referred to

Mr. Morris

Mr. Izard

Mr. King

Mr. Monroe and

Mr. Schuyler, to consider and report what is proper

to be done thereon.[20]

The memorial of the Clerks in the public offices,[21] praying to be reimbursed

---

[16] This order is in Senate Simple Resolutions and Motions, Senate Records, DNA. The Senate did not consider this report.

[17] On February 8 the Appropriations Bill was read a third time and passed. The House was notified of this action.

[18] This report is in A Record of the Reports of the Secretary of the Treasury, vol. 2, House Records, DNA.

[19] This extract from the House Journal is in Messages from the House, Senate Records, DNA.

[20] This vote for committee is in Other Records: Yeas and nays, Senate Records, DNA. On March 1 this committee reported and the report was laid for consideration.

[21] This memorial is in Petitions and Memorials: Claims, Senate Records, DNA.

for losses and expences sustained by their removal from New-York to the seat of government, was read.

ORDERED, That this memorial lie on the table.

Mr. Foster, from the Committee on enrolled Bills, reported,[22] That they had examined the enrolled Bill, entitled, "An Act declaring the consent of Congress to a certain act of the State of Maryland,"[23] and had found it correct.

Mr. Morris, from the Committee appointed to consider and report on the Bill, entitled, "An Act repealing after the last day of June next, the duties heretofore laid upon distilled spirits imported from abroad, and laying others in their stead; and also upon spirits distilled within the United States, and for appropriating the same," reported the Bill amended.[24]

The amendments were read, and—

ORDERED, That they be printed for the use of the Senate.[25]

The Senate adjourned to 11 o'clock to-morrow.

TUESDAY, FEBRUARY 8, 1791

The SENATE assembled—present as yesterday, and

Proceeded to the THIRD reading of the Bill, entitled, "An Act making appropriations for the support of government during the year one thousand seven hundred and ninety-one, and for other purposes."

RESOLVED, That this Bill DO PASS.

ORDERED, That the Secretary acquaint the House of Representatives of the concurrence of the Senate therein.[26]

A message from the House of Representatives by Mr. Beckley their clerk:

"Mr. PRESIDENT,

"The Speaker of the House of Representatives having signed an enrolled Bill, I am directed to bring it to the Senate,"—

And he withdrew.

Whereupon the Vice President signed the enrolled Bill, entitled, "An Act declaring the consent of Congress to a certain act of the State of Maryland;" and it was delivered to the Committee on enrolled Bills, to be laid before the President of the United States for his approbation.[27]

---

[22] This report is in Committee on Enrolled Bills, Senate Records, DNA.

[23] The inspected enrolled bill is in Enrolled Acts, RG 11, DNA. E–23851.

[24] This report is in Various Select Committee Reports, Senate Records, DNA. E–46309, amendments only.

[25] On February 8 the amendment that the committee proposed to the fourth section of this bill was considered.

[26] On February 9 this bill was signed by both the Speaker and the Vice President and delivered to the President.

[27] The President signed this bill on February 9.

The Senate proceeded to consider the amendments reported by the Committee on the Bill, entitled, "An Act repealing after the last day of June next, the duties heretofore laid upon distilled spirits imported from abroad, and laying others in their stead; and also upon spirits distilled within the United States, and for appropriating the same;" and the amendment to the fourth section was agreed to, so that the section should be read thus:—

"SECT. IV. And be it further enacted, That the President of the United States be authorised to appoint, with the advice and consent of the Senate, such number of officers as shall appear to him necessary[28] to inspect the revenue arising under this law; and the President of the United States may in each State designate the districts and surveys in which they shall act, assigning to each district a general Inspector thereof, and as many other Inspectors to each survey therein as he shall think advisable; placing the latter under the superintendance of the former. Provided always, That it shall and may be lawful for the President, with the advice and consent of the Senate, in his discretion to appoint such and so many of the officers of the customs to be Inspectors under this act, as he shall deem advisable to employ in the execution thereof: And provided also, That if the appointment of the officers aforesaid, or any part of them, shall not be made during the present session of Congress, the President shall have power, and he is hereby empowered to make such appointments during the recess of the Senate, by granting commissions which shall expire at the end of their next session."

A motion was made to expunge the following clause of the amendment agreed to, to wit: "And provided also, That if the appointment of the officers aforesaid, or any part of them, shall not be made during the present session of Congress, the President shall have power, and he is hereby empowered to make such appointments during the recess of the Senate, by granting commissions which shall expire at the end of their next session."—On this motion,

The yeas and nays were required by one fifth of the Senators present.

Mr. Bassett		Yea
Mr. Butler		Yea
Mr. Carroll	Nay	
Mr. Dalton	Nay	
Mr. Dickinson	Nay	
Mr. Elmer	Nay	
Mr. Few	Nay	
Mr. Foster	Nay	
Mr. Gunn		Yea

---

[28] In the rough journal the remainder of this paragraph appears as a clipping from the printed amendment pasted in. The clipping begins, "to inspect the revenue, and to designate the districts. . . ." Otis made marginal corrections which conform with the text of the printed journal above.

Mr. Henry   Nay
Mr. Johnson   Nay
Mr. Johnston   Nay
Mr. Izard   Yea
Mr. King   Nay
Mr. Langdon   Yea
Mr. Maclay   Yea
Mr. Monroe   Yea
Mr. Morris   Nay
Mr. Read   Nay
Mr. Schuyler   Nay
Mr. Stanton   Yea
Mr. Strong   Nay
Mr. Wingate   Yea
Nays—14
Yeas—9[29]

So it passed in the Negative.

On motion to recommit the amendment reported on the fourth section—
It passed in the Negative.

And having made further progress in the consideration of the report[30]—
The Senate adjourned to 11 o'clock to-morrow.

WEDNESDAY, FEBRUARY 9, 1791

The SENATE assembled—present as yesterday.

Mr. Foster from the Committee on enrolled Bills, reported, That they did, on the eighth instant, lay before the President of the United States, for his approbation, the Bill, entitled, "An Act declaring the consent of Congress to a certain act of the State of Maryland."

A message from the House of Representatives by Mr. Beckley their clerk:

"Mr. PRESIDENT,

"The House of Representatives have passed the Bill sent from the Senate, entitled, 'An Act to incorporate the subscribers to the Bank of the United States.'[31]

"I am directed to acquaint the Senate, That the President of the United States has notified the House of Representatives, that he has this day approved

[29] This vote is in Other Records: Yeas and nays, Senate Records, DNA.

[30] On February 9 the Senate agreed to the amendments proposed by the committee on this bill, and the bill passed to the third reading.

[31] On February 12 both the Speaker and the Vice President signed this bill and it was given to the committee on enrolled bills for delivery to the President.

and signed the 'Act declaring the consent of Congress to a certain act of the State of Maryland.' "[32]—

And he withdrew.

The Senate proceeded to consider the report of the Committee on the Bill, entitled, "An Act repealing after the last day of June next, the duties heretofore laid upon distilled spirits imported from abroad, and laying others in their stead; and also upon spirits distilled within the United States, and for appropriating the same,"—to which report having agreed, and that the Bill be amended conformably,

ORDERED, That the Bill pass to the THIRD reading.[33]

A written message from the President of the United States, was communicated by Mr. Lear, his Secretary,—

And he withdrew.[34]

UNITED STATES, February the 9th, 1791

GENTLEMEN of the SENATE and

HOUSE of REPRESENTATIVES,

I HAVE received from the Governor of Vermont authentic documents expressing the consent of the Legislatures of New-York and of the territory of Vermont, that the said territory shall be admitted to be a distinct member of our union; and a memorial of Nathaniel Chipman and Lewis R. Morris Commissioners from the said territory, praying the consent of Congress to that admission by the name and style of the State of Vermont, copies of which I now lay before Congress, with whom the constitution has vested the object of these proceedings.

G. WASHINGTON[35]

(Copy)

"THE people of the State of New-York, by the grace of God, free and independent: To all to whom these presents shall come, greeting:—Know ye, that we having inspected the records remaining in our Secretary's office, do find there a certain original act, in the words and figures following, to wit: 'An Act appointing commissioners with power to declare the consent of the Legislature of this State, that a certain territory within the jurisdiction thereof, should be formed or erected into a new State.'—Be it enacted by the people of

---

[32] A copy of this House message is in Committee on Enrolled Bills, Senate Records, DNA.

[33] On February 10 this bill was printed in the Journal. Several motions to amend it were defeated and the fourth section was recommitted for further amendment.

[34] In the rough journal two notes in Otis's hand appear at this point: "(Here insert the Message & papers on the Vermont business)" and "See the/originals on file."

[35] The letter from the President is in the George Washington Papers, series 2, vol. 25, reel 9, Manuscript Division, DLC.

the State of New-York, represented in Senate and Assembly, and it is hereby
enacted by the authority of the same, That Robert Yates, Robert R. Livingston,
John Lansing, junior, Gulian Verplanck, Simeon De Witt, Egbert Benson,
Richard Sill, and Melancton Smith, shall be, and hereby are appointed commissioners, with full power to them, or any four or more of them, in their
discretion, as they shall judge the peace and interest of the United States in
general, and of this State in particular, to require the same, and on such terms
and conditions, and in such manner and form as they shall judge necessary and
proper, to declare the consent of the Legislature of this State, that such district
or territory within the jurisdiction, and in the north-eastern and northern parts
thereof, as the said commissioners shall judge most convenient, should be
formed and erected into a new State; and with further full power to treat, conclude, and agree with any person or persons, or any assemblies or bodies of
people, touching the premises, or touching the ceding or relinquishing the
jurisdiction of this State over such district or territory, or touching the securing or confirming of rights, titles or possessions of land within such district
or territory, held or claimed under grants from the State of New-Hampshire
while a colony, or under grants, sales or locations made by the authority of
the government or jurisdiction now existing and exercised in the north-eastern
parts of this State, under the name or style of the State of Vermont, against
persons claiming the same lands under grants from this State while a colony,
or since the independence thereof: and every act of any four or more of the
commissioners hereby appointed, in the execution of the powers aforesaid,
shall be as effectual to every purpose, as if the same were an immediate act of
the Legislature of this State: Provided such grants, sales or locations by or
under Vermont, do not extend to the westward of the towns granted, located
or occupied under the late colony of New-Hampshire, which lay in that part
of the country aforesaid, between the north boundary of the Commonwealth
of Massachusetts, continued from the north-west corner thereof, towards Hudson's River, and a parallel line extended eastward from the point of land
where Fort-Edward formerly stood, until it meets with the west bounds of any
of the said granted, located or occupied towns.—And be it further enacted by
the authority aforesaid, That whatever stipulations shall be made by the commissioners appointed by this act, with any person or persons, or any assemblies or bodies of people, touching the premises, or touching the ceding or
relinquishing the jurisdiction of this State over such district or territory, or
touching the securing of rights, titles or possessions of lands within such district, for a compensation for extinguishing the claims to lands within such
district, as derived under the late colony of New-York, shall be for the use
of such claimants, although in such stipulations such compensation should be
declared to be for the use of this State, or for the people thereof; and that

nothing in this act contained, shall be intended or construed to give any such claimant any right to any further compensation whatsoever from this State, other than such compensation which may be so stipulated as aforesaid. —And be it further enacted by the authority aforesaid, That the act entitled, 'An Act appointing commissioners with power to declare the consent of the Legislature of the State of New-York, that a certain territory within the jurisdiction thereof, should be formed or erected into a new State,' passed the sixteenth day of July, in the year one thousand seven hundred and eighty-nine, shall be, and hereby is repealed."

"STATE OF NEW-YORK, IN ASSEMBLY, February 20, 1790

"THIS Bill having been read the third time, RESOLVED, That the Bill DO PASS.

"By order of the Assembly
GULIAN VERPLANCK, Speaker"

"STATE OF NEW-YORK, IN SENATE, February 27th, 1790

"THIS Bill having been read a third time, RESOLVED, That the Bill DO PASS.

"By order of the Senate
ISAAC ROOSEVELT, President,
Pro hac vice."

"IN COUNCIL OF REVISION, 6th of March, 1790

"RESOLVED, That it does not appear improper to the Council, that this Bill, entitled, 'An Act appointing commissioners with power to declare the consent of the Legislature of this State, that a certain territory within the jurisdiction thereof, should be formed or erected into a new State,' should become a law of this State."

"GEO. CLINTON"

"All which we have exemplified by these presents. In testimony whereof, we have caused these our letters to be made patent, and the great seal of our said State to be hereunto affixed. Witness our trusty and well-beloved GEORGE CLINTON, Esquire, Governor of our said State, General and Commander in Chief of all the militia, and Admiral of the navy of the same, at our city of New-York, this first day of February, 1791, and in the fifteenth year of our independence."

"GEO. CLINTON"

(Great Seal appendant) "PASSED THE SECRETARY'S OFFICE,
2d February, 1791
ROBERT HARPUR, Dep. Sec'y."

(Copy)

"To all to whom these presents shall come:

"BE IT KNOWN, That Robert Yates, John Lansing, junior, Gulian Verplanck, Simeon De Witt, Egbert Benson, and Melancton Smith, Commissioners appointed by an act of the Legislature of the State of New-York, entitled, 'An Act appointing commissioners with power to declare the consent of the Legislature of this State, that a certain territory within the jurisdiction thereof, should be formed into a new State,' passed the sixth day of March last, do hereby, by virtue of the powers to them granted for the purpose, declare the consent of the Legislature of the State of New-York, that the community now actually exercising independent jurisdiction as the State of Vermont, be admitted into the union of the United States of America; and that immediately from such admission, all claim of jurisdiction of the State of New-York within the State of Vermont, shall cease; and thenceforth the perpetual boundary line between the State of New-York and the State of Vermont, shall be as follows, viz. Beginning at the north-west corner of the State of Massachusetts, thence westward along the south boundary of the township of Pownal, to the south-west corner thereof, thence northerly along the western boundaries of the townships of Pownal, Bennington, Shaftsbury, Arlington, Sandgate, Rupert, Pawlett, Wells and Poultney, as the said townships are now held or possessed, to the river commonly called Poultney River, thence down the same through the middle of the deepest channel thereof, to East Bay, thence through the middle of the deepest channel of East Bay, and the waters thereof, to where the same communicate with Lake Champlain, thence through the middle of the deepest channel of Lake Champlain, to the eastward of the islands called the Four Brothers, and the westward of the islands called Grand Isle and Long Isle, or the Two Heroes, and to the westward of the Isle La Motte, to the forty-fifth degree of north latitude. And the said Commissioners do hereby declare the will of the Legislature of the State of New-York, that if the Legislature of the State of Vermont shall, on or before the first day of January, in the year one thousand seven hundred and ninety two, declare that the State of Vermont shall, on or before the first day of June, in the year one thousand seven hundred and ninety-four, pay to the State of New-York, the sum of thirty thousand dollars, that immediately from such declaration by the Legislature of the State of Vermont, all rights and titles to lands within the State of Vermont, under grants from the government of the late colony of New-York, or from the State of New-York, except as herein after excepted, shall cease: Or if the Legislature of the State of Vermont shall not elect to make such declaration, then, that except in cases where the grants from New-York were intended as confirmations of grants from New-Hampshire, all rights and titles under grants from the government of the late colony of New-York, or from the State of New-York, to lands within the State of Vermont which may have been granted by the government of the colony of New-Hampshire, shall cease, and the boundaries according to which such grants from the government of the late colony of New-Hampshire have been held or possessed, shall be deemed to be the true boundaries. And the said Commissioners do hereby further declare the will of the Legislature of the State of New-York, that all rights and titles to lands within the State of Vermont, under grants from the government of the late colony of New-York, or from the State of New-York, and not granted by the government of the late colony of New-Hampshire, shall be suspended until the expiration of three years after the Governor of the State of Vermont for the time being, shall have been notified that a commissioner to be appointed by the State of New-York, after the first day of January, in the year one thousand seven hundred and ninety-two, and to reside and hold a public office at the city of Albany, shall have entered upon the execution of his office. And if within one year after such notification there shall be delivered to such commissioner, either the original, or a certified abstract, containing the date, the names of the grantees, and the boundaries of a grant from New-York, and if thereupon, at any time before the expiration of the said term of three years above mentioned, there shall be paid to such commissioner, at the rate of ten cents per acre for the whole or any parcel of the lands contained in such grant from New-York, all right and title under such grant shall, in respect to the lands for which payment shall so be made, cease; and a receipt under the hand and seal of such commissioner, specifying the land for which payment shall be made, shall be evidence of the payment: and in default of delivering the original, or such certified abstract of the grant to the commissioner, within the said term of one year for that purpose above limited, all right and title under the grant in respect of which there shall be such default of delivery, shall cease; but where the original, or certified abstract of the grant, shall be duly delivered to the commissioner, and if thereupon payment shall not be duly made to the commissioner, the right and title under the grant in respect to the lands for which payment shall not be made, shall remain; and suits for the recovery of such lands may be prosecuted in the ordinary course of law: Provided the suit be commenced within ten years after the State of Vermont shall have been admitted into the union of the United States, otherwise the right and title under the grant from New-York, shall in such case also cease.—In testimony whereof, the said Commissioners have hereunto set their hands and affixed their seals, the seventh day of October, in the fifteenth year of the independence of the United States of America, 1790.

EGBERT BENSON   (L.S.)

GULIAN VERPLANCK (L.S.)

ROBERT YATES (L.S.)
MELANCTON SMITH (L.S.)
SIMEON DE WITT (L.S.)
JOHN LANSING, jun. (L.S.)

Witnesses
RICHARD VARICK
ALEXANDER HAMILTON
SAMUEL JONES
ROBERT BENSON"

"An ACT directing the payment of thirty thousand dollars to the State of New-York, and declaring what shall be the boundary line between the State of Vermont and State of New-York, and declaring certain grants therein mentioned, extinguished

"WHEREAS Robert Yates, John Lansing, junior, Gulian Verplanck, Simeon De Witt, Egbert Benson, and Melancton Smith, Esquires, Commissioners appointed by an Act of the Legislature of the State of New-York, entitled, 'An Act appointing commissioners with power to declare the consent of the Legislature of the State of New-York, that a certain territory within the jurisdiction thereof, should be formed into a new State,' passed the fifth day of March, in the year of our Lord one thousand seven hundred and ninety, did, by their certain act, on the seventh day of October instant, at New-York, by virtue of the powers to them granted for that purpose, among other things declare the consent of the Legislature of the State of New-York, that the State of Vermont be admitted into the union of the United States of America; and that immediately from such admission, all claims of jurisdiction of the State of New-York, within the State of Vermont, should cease, and thenceforth the perpetual boundary line between the State of New-York and the State of Vermont, should be as follows, viz. Beginning at the north-west corner of the State of Massachusetts, thence westward along the south boundary of Pownal to the south-west corner thereof, thence northerly along the western boundaries of the townships of Pownal, Bennington, Shaftsbury, Arlington, Sandgate, Rupert, Pawlet, Wells and Poultney, as the said townships are now held or possessed, to the river commonly called Poultney River, thence down the same through the middle of the deepest channel thereof to East Bay, thence through the middle of the deepest channel of East Bay, and the waters thereof, to where the same communicate with Lake Champlain, thence through the middle of the deepest channel of Lake Champlain, to the eastward of the islands called the Four Brothers, and the westward of the islands called the Grand Isle and Long Isle, or the Two Heroes, and to the westward of the Isle La Motte, to the forty-fifth degree of north latitude. And the said Commissioners, by virtue of the powers to them granted, did declare the will of the Legislature of the State of New-York, that if the Legislature of the State of Vermont should, on or before the first day of January, one thousand seven hundred and ninety-two, declare, that on or before the first day of June, one thousand seven hundred and ninety-four, the said State of Vermont would pay to the State of New-York, the sum of thirty thousand dollars; that immediately from such declaration by the Legislature of the State of Vermont, all rights and titles to lands within the State of Vermont, under grants from the government of the late colony of New-York, or from the State of New-York, except as is therein excepted, should cease: Wherefore—

"It is hereby enacted by the General Assembly of the State of Vermont, That the State of Vermont shall, on or before the first day of June, one thousand seven hundred and ninety-four, pay the State of New-York thirty thousand dollars; and the Treasurer of this State, for and in behalf of this State, and for the purposes mentioned in the act of the Commissioners aforesaid, shall pay to the State of New-York the sum of thirty thousand dollars, on or before the first day of June, one thousand seven hundred and ninety-four.— And it is hereby further enacted, That the said line described in the said act of the said Commissioners, shall henceforth be the perpetual boundary line between the State of Vermont and the State of New-York: and all grants, charters or patents of land lying within the State of Vermont, made by or under the government of the late colony of New-York, except such grants, charters or patents as were made in confirmation of grants, charters or patents made by or under the government of the late province or colony of New-Hampshire are hereby declared null and void, and incapable of being given in evidence in any court of law within this State."

"STATE of VERMONT, SECRETARY'S OFFICE
"BENNINGTON, January 21st, 1791
"THE preceding is a true copy of an Act passed by the Legislature of the State of Vermont, the twenty-eighth day of October, in the year of our Lord one thousand seven hundred and ninety.
"Attest.
"ROSWELL HOPKINS, Sec'ry of State"

"An ACT to authorise the people of this State to meet in convention, to deliberate upon and agree to the constitution of the United States
"WHEREAS in the opinion of this Legislature, the future interest and welfare of this State render it necessary that the constitution of the United States of America, as agreed to by the convention at Philadelphia, on the 17th day of September, in the year of our Lord one thousand seven hundred and eighty-

seven, with the several amendments and alterations, as the same has been since established by the United States, should be laid before the people of this State, for their approbation,—

"It is hereby enacted by the General Assembly of the State of Vermont, that the first constable in each town, shall warn the inhabitants who by law are entitled to vote for representatives in General Assembly, in the same manner as they warn freemans meetings to meet in their respective towns, on the first Tuesday of December next, at ten o'clock in the forenoon, at the several places fixed by law for holding the annual election; and when so met, they shall proceed in the same manner as in the election of representatives, to chuse some suitable person from each town, to serve as a delegate in a State convention, for the purpose of deliberating upon and agreeing to the constitution of the United States as now established. And the said Constable shall certify to the State convention, the person so chosen in manner aforesaid,—and,

"It is hereby further enacted by the authority aforesaid, That the persons so elected to serve in State convention, as aforesaid, do assemble and meet together on the first Thursday of January next, at Bennington, in the county of Bennington, then and there to deliberate upon the aforesaid constitution of the United States, and if approved of by them, finally to assent to, and ratify the same, in behalf and on the part of the people of this State, and make report thereof to the Governor of this State for the time being, to be by him communicated to the President of the United States, and the Legislature of this State."

"STATE of VERMONT, SECRETARY's OFFICE,
"BENNINGTON, January 21, 1791
"THE preceding is a true copy of an Act passed by the Legislature of the State of Vermont, the twenty-seventh day of October, the year of our Lord one thousand seven hundred and ninety."

"Attest. ROSWELL HOPKINS, Sec'ry of State"

"IN CONVENTION of the DELEGATES of the People of the State of Vermont
"WHEREAS, by an Act of the Commissioners of the State of New-York, done at New-York the seventh day of October, in the fifteenth year of the independence of the United States of America, and in the year of our Lord one thousand seven hundred and ninety, every impediment, as well on the part of the State of New-York as on the part of the State of Vermont, to the admission of the State of Vermont into the union of the United States of America, is removed, in full faith and assurance that the same will stand approved and ratified by Congress.

"This convention having impartially deliberated upon the constitution of the

United States of America, as now established, submitted to us by an Act of
the General Assembly of the State of Vermont, passed October twenty-seventh,
one thousand seven hundred and ninety, do, in virtue of the power and authority to us given for that purpose, fully and entirely approve of, assent to,
and ratify the said constitution; and declare, that immediately from and after
this State shall be admitted by the Congress into the union, and to a full par-
ticipation of the benefits of the government now enjoyed by the States in the
union, the same shall be binding on us, and the people of the State of Vermont for ever.

> "Done at Bennington, in the county of Bennington, the tenth day of
> January, in the fifteenth year of the independence of the United
> States of America, one thousand seven hundred and ninety-one.
> In testimony whereof, we have hereunto subscribed our names.
> (Signed)   "THOMAS CHITTENDEN, President"

"Signed by one hundred and five Members—dissented, four.

> "Attest. ROSWELL HOPKINS, Sec'ry of Conv."

"STATE of VERMONT, SECRETARY'S OFFICE
> "BENNINGTON, January 21st, 1791

"THE preceding is a true copy of the original Act of the convention of the
State of Vermont, done at Bennington the tenth day of January, one thousand
seven hundred and ninety-one.

> "Attest. ROSWELL HOPKINS, Sec'ry of State"

"By his Excellency THOMAS CHITTENDEN, Esquire, Captain-General,
Governor and Commander in Chief in and over the State of
Vermont

(L.S.)

"THIS certifies, That Roswell Hopkins, Esquire, is Secretary to the
State of Vermont, and that all due faith and credence ought to be given to
attestations by him officially made.

> "In testimony hereof, we have caused the seal of this State to be
> affixed in Council, this twenty-second day of January, one thou-
> sand seven hundred and ninety-one.
> (Signed)   "THOMAS CHITTENDEN

"By his Excellency's command
"JOSEPH FAY, Sec'ry."

> "BENNINGTON, January 22d, 1791

"SIR,

"I HAVE the honor to transmit to you copies of two Acts of the Legislature
of this State; the one directing the payment of thirty thousand dollars to the
State of New-York, and declaring the boundary line between the State of Vermont and the State of New-York, and extinguishing certain grants therein

mentioned; the other, an Act authorising the people of this State to meet in convention, to deliberate upon and agree to the constitution of the United States; and also a copy of the proceeding of the convention.

"This will be delivered by the Honorable Nathaniel Chipman and Lewis R. Morris, Esquires, who are appointed Commissioners to apply to the Congress of the United States for the admission of this State into the union, whom I beg leave to recommend to your favorable notice.

"I have the honor to be, &c.

(Signed)   "THOS. CHITTENDEN

"The PRESIDENT of the
  United States" }

※   ※ "By his Excellency THOMAS CHITTENDEN, Esquire, Captain-General,
(L.S.)   Governor and Commander in Chief in and over the State of
※___※   Vermont

"To the Honorable Nathaniel Chipman, Esquire, and Lewis R. Morris, Esquire, greeting:

"YOU being elected by the Legislature of this State, Commissioners to the Congress of the United States, to apply for the admission of the State of Vermont into the union, are hereby authorised and empowered to proceed to the Congress of the United States, now in session at the city of Philadelphia, and negociate on behalf of this State, agreeable to your said appointment.

"In testimony whereof, we have caused the seal of this State to be affixed in Council, at Bennington, this twenty-fourth day of January, one thousand seven hundred and ninety-one, and in the fifteenth year of the independence of this State.

(Signed)   "THOMAS CHITTENDEN

"By his Excellency's command
  "JOSEPH FAY, Sec'ry."

"The PRESIDENT and CONGRESS of the UNITED STATES of AMERICA

"Nathaniel Chipman and Lewis R. Morris, Commissioners, authorised and appointed by the State of Vermont, most respectfully represent, that the citizens of that State having shared in common with those of the other States, in the hazards and burthens of establishing the American revolution, have long anxiously desired to be united with them, under the same general government. They have seen, with great satisfaction, a new and more perfect union of the people of America, and the unanimity with which they have recently approved the national constitution, manifests their attachment to it, and the zeal with which they desire to participate its benefits.

"Questions of interfering jurisdiction between them and the State of New-York, have heretofore delayed this application; these points being now happily adjusted, the memorialists, on behalf of their constituents, most respectfully petition, that the Congress will consent to the admission of the State of Vermont, by that name and style, as a new and entire member of the United States.

"They have the honor to accompany this memorial with such papers and documents as have relation to the same, and with the highest deference for the wisdom of Congress, the memorialists repeat their solicitations, that during their present session, they would be pleased to adopt such measures as will include within the national government, a people zealous to support and defend it."

(Signed) "NATHANIEL CHIPMAN
"LEWIS R. MORRIS

"Philadelphia, Feb. 7th, 1791"[36]

ORDERED, That the message from the President of the United States of this date, with the papers accompanying it, be referred to

Mr. King
Mr. Monroe
Mr. Ellsworth
Mr. Langdon and
Mr. Hawkins, to consider and report what is proper

to be done thereon.[37]

Mr. Foster, from the Committee on enrolled Bills, reported that they had examined the enrolled Bill, entitled, "An Act making appropriations for the support of government during the year one thousand seven hundred and ninety-one, and for other purposes,"[38] and that they found it correct.[39]

A message from the House of Representatives by Mr. Beckley their clerk:

"Mr. PRESIDENT,

"The Speaker of the House of Representatives having signed an enrolled Bill, I am directed to bring it to the Senate, for the signature of the Vice President,"—

And he withdrew.

The Vice President signed the enrolled Bill, entitled, "An Act making appropriations for the support of government during the year one thousand

---

[36] The enclosures are not located in the Senate files.

[37] This vote for committee is in Other Records: Yeas and nays, Senate Records, DNA. On February 10 this committee reported a bill which was printed in the Journal, read a first time, and passed to the second reading.

[38] The inspected enrolled bill is in Enrolled Acts, RG 11, DNA. E–23860.

[39] The smooth journal includes the following paragraph at this point: "Ordered, that the Secretary to certify to the auditor of the Treasury the number of days that James Mathers was employed in the service of the United States during the last recess of Congress." This paragraph also appears in the rough journal with the notation "not printed" in Otis's hand.

seven hundred and ninety-one, and for other purposes;" and it was delivered to the Committee on enrolled Bills, to be laid before the President of the United States for his approbation.[40]

The petition of Stephen Drayton,[41] praying compensation for supplies to the army during the late war, was read, and—

ORDERED, That it lie on the table.[42]

The Senate adjourned to 11 o'clock to-morrow.

THURSDAY, FEBRUARY 10, 1791

The SENATE assembled—present as yesterday.

Mr. Foster, from the Committee on enrolled Bills, reported that they did yesterday lay before the President of the United States for his approbation, the Bill, entitled, "An Act making appropriations for the support of government during the year one thousand seven hundred and ninety-one, and for other purposes."[43]

Mr. King, from the Committee to whom was referred the message from the President of the United States of the 9th instant, relative to the State of Vermont, with the papers therein contained, reported a Bill as follows,[44] "An Act for the admission of the State of Vermont into this union."

1   "SECT. I. THE State of Vermont having petitioned the Con-
2   gress to be admitted a member of the United States, be it enac-
3   ted by the Senate and House of Representatives of the United
4   States of America in Congress assembled, and it is hereby enac-
5   ted and declared, That on the fourth day of March, one thou-
6   sand seven hundred and ninety-one, the said State, by the name
7   and style of 'the State of Vermont,' shall be received and
8   admitted into this union, as a new and entire member of the
9   United States of America.
1   "SECT. II. And be it further enacted, That until the Repre-
2   sentatives in Congress shall be appointed, according to an actual
3   enumeration of the inhabitants of the United States, the said
4   State shall be entitled to choose two Representatives."

This Bill was read the FIRST time.

---

[40] On February 11 the President signed this bill and the Senate was notified.

[41] This petition is in Petitions and Memorials: Claims, Senate Records, DNA.

[42] The House referred this petition to the Secretary of War.

[43] The smooth journal includes the following paragraph at this point: "ORDERED, That all Bills and Resolutions sent from the House of Representatives for concurrence be entered at large on the Journals of Senate." This paragraph also appears in the rough journal with the notation "not printed" in Otis's hand.

[44] This bill is in Senate Bills, Senate Records, DNA.

ORDERED, That this Bill pass to the SECOND reading.[45]

The Senate proceeded to the THIRD reading of the Bill, entitled,[46] "An Act repealing, after the last day of June next, the duties heretofore laid upon distilled spirits imported from abroad, and laying others in their stead; and also upon spirits distilled within the United States; and for appropriating the same."

1   "SECT. I.   BE it enacted by the Senate and House of Repre-
2   sentatives of the United States of America, in Congress assem-
3   bled, That after the last day of June next, the duties laid on
4   distilled spirits by the Act, entitled, 'An Act making further
5   provision for the payment of the debts of the United States,'
6   shall cease; and that upon all distilled spirits which shall be im-
7   ported into the United States after that day, from any foreign
8   port or place, there shall be paid for their use the duties fol-
9   lowing; that is to say—
10 "For every gallon of those spirits more than ten percent.
11 below proof, according to Dycas's hydrometer, twenty cents.
12 "For every gallon of those spirits under five, and not more
13 than ten per cent. below proof, according to the same hydro-
14 meter, twenty-one cents.
15 "For every gallon of those spirits of proof, and not more than
16 five per cent. below proof, according to the same hydrometer,
17 twenty-two cents.
18 "For every gallon of those spirits above proof, but not ex-
19 ceeding twenty per cent. according to the same hydrometer,
20 twenty-five cents.
21 "For every gallon of those spirits more than twenty, and not
22 more than forty per cent. above proof, according to the same
23 hydrometer, thirty cents.
24 "For every gallon of those spirits more than forty per cent.
25 above proof, according to the same hydrometer, forty cents.
1   "SECT. II.   And be it further enacted, That the said duties
2   shall be collected in the same manner, by the same persons, un-
3   der the same regulations, and subject to the same forfeitures and
4   other penalties, as those heretofore laid; the Act concerning
5   which shall be deemed to be in full force for the collection of

---

[45] On February 11 this bill was read a second time; the second section was expunged; and the bill passed to the third reading.

[46] At this point the rough journal includes Otis's instructions to the copyist: "Excise Bill (Here the Bill as from the H of R) but in inverted commas numbering the lines of each section."

6 the duties herein before imposed, except as to the alterations
7 contained in this Act.
1   "SECT. III. And be it further enacted, That the said duties,
2 when the amount thereof shall not exceed fifty dollars, shall be
3 immediately paid; but when the said amount shall exceed fifty
4 dollars, may, at the option of the proprietor, importer or con-
5 signee, be either immediately paid, or secured by bond, with
6 condition for the payment of one moiety thereof in three
7 months, and the other moiety thereof in six months: which
8 bond, at the like option of the proprietor, importer or con-
9 signee, shall either include one or more sureties to the satisfac-
10 tion of the Collector, or person acting as such, or shall be ac-
11 companied with a deposit in the custody of the said Collector,
12 or person acting as such, of so much of the said spirits as shall
13 in his judgment be a sufficient security for the amount of the
14 duties for which the said bond shall have been given, and the
15 charges of the safe-keeping and sale of the spirits so deposited;
16 which deposit shall and may be accepted in lieu of the said
17 surety or sureties, and shall be kept by the said Collector, or
18 person acting as such, with due and reasonable care, at the
19 expence and risque of the party or parties on whose account
20 the same shall have been made, until the first of the said moie-
21 ties shall become due; at which time, if such moiety shall not
22 be paid, so much of the said deposited spirits as may be neces-
23 sary, shall be sold at public sale, and the proceeds thereof, after
24 deducting the charges of keeping and sale, shall be applied to the
25 payment of the whole sum of the duties for which such deposit
26 shall have been made, rendering the overplus of the said pro-
27 ceeds, and the residue of the said spirits, if any there be, to
28 the person or persons by whom such deposit shall have been
29 made, or to his, her or their representatives; and in case the se-
30 cond moiety shall not be paid when it shall become due, then
31 the like proceedings shall be had as are directed in case of failure
32 in the payment of the first moiety.
1   "SECT. IV. And be it further enacted, That the President of
2 the United States, be authorised to appoint, with the advice and
3 consent of the Senate, such number of officers as shall appear to
4 him necessary, to be denominated Inspectors of the Revenue;
5 and to assign to them respectively such districts or limits for the
6 exercise of their respective offices, as he shall judge best adapted
7 to the execution thereof; dividing the districts, if he shall think

8 it advisable, into general and particular, and placing the Inspec-
9 tors of the latter under the superintendance of the former, with-
10 in the limits whereof they shall be respectively comprehended.

1 "SECT. V. And be it further enacted, That the Inspector or
2 Inspectors of the revenue for each district, shall establish one or
3 more offices within the same, as may be necessary; and in order
4 that the said offices may be publicly known, there shall be pain-
5 ted or written, in large legible characters upon some conspicuous
6 part outside and in front of each house, building or place in
7 which any such office shall be kept, these words, 'OFFICE
8 OF INSPECTION;' and if any person shall paint or write,
9 or cause to be painted or written, the said words, upon any
10 other than such house or building, he or she shall forfeit and
11 pay for so doing, one hundred dollars.

1 "SECT. VI. And be it further enacted, That within forty-
2 eight hours after any ship or vessel, having on board any dis-
3 tilled spirits brought in such ship or vessel from any foreign
4 port or place, shall arrive within any port of the United States,
5 whether the same be the first port of arrival of such ship or
6 vessel, or not, the master or person having the command or
7 charge thereof, shall report to the Inspector or other chief
8 officer of inspection of the port at which he shall so arrive, the
9 place from which she last sailed, with her name and burthen,
10 and the quantity and kinds of the said spirits on board of her,
11 and the casks or cases containing them, with their marks and
12 numbers; on pain of forfeiting the sum of five hundred dollars.

1 "SECT. VII. And be it further enacted, That the Collector
2 or other officer, or person acting as Collector, with whom
3 entry shall have been made of any of the said spirits, pursu-
4 ant to the act, entitled, 'An Act to provide more effectually
5 for the collection of the duties imposed by law on goods,
6 wares and merchandizes imported into the United States, and
7 on the tonnage of ships or vessels,' shall forthwith after such
8 entry certify and transmit the same, as particularly as it shall
9 have been made with him, to the Inspector of the revenue, or
10 other proper officer of inspection, of the port where it shall be
11 intended to commence the delivery of the spirits so entered, or
12 any part thereof: for which purpose, every proprietor, impor-
13 ter or consignee, making such entry, shall deliver two manifests
14 of the contents (upon one of which the said certificate shall be
15 given) and shall at the time thereof declare the port at which

16 the said delivery shall be so intended to be commenced, to the
17 Collector or officer with whom the same shall be made. And
18 every permit granted by such Collector, for the landing of any
19 of the said spirits, shall previous to such landing, be produced
20 to the said officer of inspection, who shall make a minute in
21 some proper book, of the contents thereof, and shall indorse
22 thereupon the word 'INSPECTED,' the time when, and
23 his own name; after which he shall return it to the person by
24 whom it shall have been produced; and then, and not other-
25 wise, it shall be lawful to land the spirits therein specified; and
26 if the said spirits shall be landed without such indorsement upon
27 the permit for that purpose granted, the master or person hav-
28 ing charge of the ship or vessel from which the same shall have
29 been so landed, shall for every such offence forfeit the sum of
30 five hundred dollars.

1 "SECT. VIII. And be it further enacted, That whenever it
2 shall be intended that any ship or vessel shall proceed with the
3 whole or any part of the spirits which shall have been brought
4 in such ship or vessel from any foreign port or place, from one
5 port in the United States to another port in the said United States,
6 whether in the same or in different districts, the master or per-
7 son having the command or charge of such ship or vessel, shall
8 previous to her departure, apply to the proper officer of inspec-
9 tion for the port from which she is about to depart, for a certifi-
10 cate of the quantity and particulars of such of the said spirits as
11 shall have been certified to him to have been entered as imported
12 in such ship or vessel, and of so much thereof as shall appear to
13 him to have been landed out of her at such port; which certifi-
14 cate the said officer shall forthwith grant without fee or charge.
15 And the master or person having the command or charge of such
16 ship or vessel, shall within twenty-four hours after her arrival
17 at the port to which she shall be bound, deliver the said certifi-
18 cate to the proper officer of inspection of such last mentioned
19 port. And if such ship or vessel shall proceed from one port to
20 another within the United States, with the whole or any part
21 of the spirits brought in her as aforesaid, without having first ob-
22 tained such certificate; or if within twenty-four hours after her
23 arrival at such other port, the said certificate shall not be deli-
24 vered to the proper officer of inspection there, the master or
25 person having the command or charge of the said ship or vessel,
26 shall in either case forfeit the sum of five hundred dollars; and

27 the spirits on board of her at her said arrival, shall be forfeited,
28 and may be seized by any officer of inspection.

1   "SECT. IX.   And be it further enacted, That all spirits which
2   shall be imported as aforesaid, shall be landed under the inspec-
3   tion of the officer or officers of inspection for the place where
4   the same shall be landed, and not otherwise, on pain of forfei-
5   ture thereof: for which purpose the said officer or officers shall,
6   at all reasonable times, attend: Provided that this shall not be
7   construed to exclude the inspection of the officers of the customs
8   as now established and practised.

1   "SECT. X.   And be it further enacted, That the officers of
2   inspection under whose survey any of the said spirits shall be
3   landed, shall upon landing thereof, and as soon as the casks and
4   cases containing the same shall be gauged or measured, brand
5   or otherwise mark in durable characters, the several casks or
6   cases containing the same, with progressive numbers; and also
7   with the name of the ship or vessel wherein the same was or
8   were imported, and of the port of entry, and with the proof
9   and quantity thereof; together with such other marks, if any
10 other shall be deemed needful, as the respective Inspectors of
11 the revenue may direct. And the said officer shall keep a book,
12 wherein he shall enter the name of each vessel in which any of
13 the said spirits shall be so imported, and of the port of entry and
14 of delivery; and of the master of such vessel, and of each im-
15 porter, and the several casks and cases containing the same, and
16 the marks of each; and if not an Inspector or the chief officer
17 of inspection for the place, shall as soon as may be thereafter,
18 make an exact transcript of each entry, and deliver the same
19 to such Inspector of chief officer, who shall keep a like book
20 for recording the said transcripts.

1   "SECT. XI.   And be it further enacted, That the Inspector of
2   the revenue, or other chief officer of inspection within whose
3   survey any of the said spirits shall be landed, shall give to the
4   proprietor, importer or consignee thereof, or his or her agent,
5   a certificate to remain with him or her, of the whole quantity
6   of the said spirits which shall have been so landed; which cer-
7   tificate besides the said quantity, shall specify the name of such
8   proprietor, importer or consignee, and of the vessel from on
9   board which the said spirits shall have been landed, and of the
10 marks of each cask or case containing the same. And the said
11 Inspector or other chief officer of inspection, shall deliver to the

12 said proprietor, importer or consignee, or to his or her agent,
13 a like certificate for each cask or case; which shall accompany
14 the same wherever it shall be sent, as evidence of its being
15 lawfully imported. And the officer of inspection granting the
16 said certificates, shall make regular and exact entries in the
17 book to be by him kept as aforesaid, of all spirits for which the
18 same shall be granted, as particularly therein described. And
19 the said proprietor, importer or consignee, or his or her agent,
20 upon the sale and delivery of any of the said spirits, shall deli-
21 ver to the purchaser or purchasers thereof, the certificate or
22 certificates which ought to accompany the same; on pain of
23 forfeiting the sum of fifty dollars for each cask or case with which
24 such certificate shall not be delivered.

1   "Sect. XII.   And be it further enacted, That every importer
2   of distilled spirits, shall enter in a book to be kept for that pur-
3   pose, the name or names of every person or persons to whom
4   any of the said spirits shall be sold or delivered, and the mark
5   or marks which according to the provisions of this act, are di-
6   rected to be put upon the casks or cases containing the same;
7   and the said importer shall, as often as required, produce the
8   said book to the officer of inspection requiring the same, who
9   may take a copy of such entries, and compare the deliveries and
10 the spirits then on hand, with the original entry thereof; and
11 if any importer or importers of distilled spirits, shall neglect or
12 refuse to keep such book of entries, or shew the same and the
13 spirits on hand, to the proper officer, when required, he, she
14 or they so neglecting or refusing, shall forfeit for every such
15 neglect or refusal a sum not exceeding one hundred dollars.

1   "Sect. XIII.   And be it further enacted, That upon all spirits
2   which after the said last day of June next, shall be distilled within
3   the United States, wholly or in part from molasses, sugar, or
4   other foreign materials, there shall be paid for their use the du-
5   ties following; that is to say—

6   "For every gallon of those spirits more than ten per cent.
7   below proof, according to Dycas's hydrometer, eleven cents.

8   "For every gallon of those spirits under five, and not more
9   than ten per cent. below proof, according to the same hydro-
10 meter, twelve cents.

11   "For every gallon of those spirits of proof, and not more than
12 five per cent. below proof, according to the same hydrometer,
13 thirteen cents.

14   "For every gallon of those spirits above proof, and not ex-
15 ceeding twenty per cent. according to the same hydrometer,
16 fifteen cents.

17   "For every gallon of those spirits more than twenty, and not
18 more than forty per cent. above proof, according to the same
19 hydrometer, twenty cents.

20   "For every gallon of those spirits more than forty per cent.
21 above proof, according to the same hydrometer, thirty cents.

1   "SECT. XIV.   And be it further enacted, That upon all spirits
2 which after the said last day of June next, shall be distilled within
3 the United States, from any article of the growth or produce of
4 the United States, in any city, town or village, there shall be
5 paid for their use the duties following; that is to say—

6   "For every gallon of those spirits more than ten per cent.
7 below proof, according to Dycas's hydrometer, nine cents.

8   "For every gallon of those spirits under five and not more
9 than ten per cent. below proof, according to the same hydro-
10 meter, ten cents.

11   "For every gallon of those spirits of proof, and not more
12 than five per cent. below proof, according to the same hydro-
13 meter, eleven cents.

14   "For every gallon of those spirits above proof, but not ex-
15 ceeding twenty per cent. according to the same hydrometer,
16 thirteen cents.

17   "For every gallon of those spirits more than twenty and
18 not more than forty per cent. above proof, according to the
19 same hydrometer, seventeen cents.

20   "For every gallon of those spirits more than forty per cent.
21 above proof, according to the same hydrometer, twenty-five
22 cents.

1   "SECT. XV.   And be it further enacted, That the said duties
2 on spirits distilled within the United States, shall be collected
3 under the management of the Inspectors of the revenue.

1   "SECT. XVI.   And be it further enacted, That the said du-
2 ties on spirits distilled within the United States, shall be paid or
3 secured previous to the removal thereof from the distilleries at
4 which they are respectively made. And it shall be at the option
5 of the proprietor or proprietors of each distillery, or of his, her
6 or their agent having the superintendance thereof, either to pay
7 the said duties previous to such removal, with an abatement at
8 the rate of two cents for every ten gallons, or to secure the
9 payment of the same, by giving bond quarter yearly, with one

10 or more sureties, to the satisfaction of the officer of inspection
11 within whose survey such distillery shall be, and in such sum as
12 the said officer shall direct, with condition for the payment of
13 the duties upon all such of the said spirits as shall be removed
14 from such distillery, within three months next ensuing the date
15 of the bond, at the expiration of nine months from the said date.

1   "SECT. XVII. And be it further enacted, That the Inspec-
2   tor or Inspectors of each district, shall appoint a proper officer
3   to have the charge and survey of each distillery within his or
4   their district, who shall attend such distillery at all reasonable
5   times, for the execution of the duties by this act enjoined on him.

1   "SECT. XVIII. And be it further enacted, That previous
2   to the removal of any of the said spirits from any distillery, the
3   officer of inspection within whose survey the same may be, shall
4   brand or otherwise mark each cask containing the same, in dura-
5   ble characters, and with progressive numbers, and with the name
6   of the acting owner or other manager of such distillery, and of
7   the place where the same was situate, and with the quantity
8   therein, to be ascertained by actual gauging, and with the proof
9   thereof. And the duties thereupon having been first paid, or
10 secured, as above provided, the said officer shall grant a certi-
11 ficate for each cask of the said spirits, to accompany the same
12 wheresoever it shall be sent, purporting that the duty thereon
13 hath been paid or secured, as the case may be, and describing
14 each cask by its marks; and shall enter in a book for that purpose
15 to be kept, all the spirits distilled at such distillery, and removed
16 from the same; and the marks of each cask, and the persons for
17 whose use, and the places to which removed, and the time of each
18 removal, and the amount of the duties on the spirits so removed.
19 And if any of the said spirits shall be removed from any such
20 distillery without having been branded or marked as aforesaid,
21 or without such certificate as aforesaid, the same, together with
22 the cask or casks containing, and the horses or cattle, with the
23 carriages, their harness and tackling employed in removing them,
24 shall be forfeited, and may be seized by any officer of inspection.
25 And the superintendant or manager of such distillery shall also
26 forfeit the full value of the spirits so removed, to be computed
27 at the highest price of the like spirits in the market.

1   "SECT. XIX. And be it further enacted, That no spirits
2   shall be removed from any such distillery at any other times
3   than between sun rising and sun setting.

1   "SECT. XX. And be it further enacted, That upon stills

2   which after the last day of June next, shall be employed in
3   distilling spirits from materials of the growth or production of
4   the United States, in any other place than a city, town or vil-
5   lage, there shall be paid for the use of the United States, the
6   yearly duty of sixty cents for every gallon, English wine mea-
7   sure, of the capacity or content of each and every such still,
8   including the head thereof.

1   "SECT. XXI. And be it further enacted, That the evidence
2   of the employment of the said stills shall be, their being erected
3   in stone, brick or some other manner whereby they shall be in
4   a condition to be worked.

1   "SECT. XXII. And be it further enacted, That the said
2   duties on stills shall be collected under the management of the
3   Inspectors of the revenue, who, in each district shall appoint
4   and assign proper officers for the surveys of the said stills and the
5   admeasurement thereof, and the collection of the duties there-
6   upon; and the said duties shall be paid half yearly, within the
7   first fifteen days of January and July, upon demand, of the pro-
8   prietor or proprietors of each still, at his, her or their dwelling,
9   by the proper officer charged with the survey thereof: And in
10   case of refusal or neglect to pay, the amount of the duties so
11   refused or neglected to be paid, may either be recovered with
12   costs of suit in an action of debt in the name of the Inspector or
13   Inspectors of the district within which such refusal shall happen,
14   for the use of the United States, or may be levied by distress and
15   sale of goods of the person or persons refusing or neglecting to
16   pay, rendering the overplus (if any there be after payment of
17   the said amount and the charges of distress and sale) to the said
18   person or persons.

1   "SECT. XXIII. And be it further enacted, That if the pro-
2   prietor of any such still, finding himself or herself aggrieved by
3   the said rates, shall enter or cause to be entered in a book or on
4   a paper to be kept for that purpose, from day to day when such
5   still shall be employed, the quantity of spirits distilled therefrom,
6   and the quantity from time to time sold or otherwise disposed of,
7   and to whom and when, and shall produce the said book or pa-
8   per to the proper officer of inspection within whose survey such
9   still shall be, and shall make oath (or affirmation) that the same
10   doth contain to the best of his or her knowledge and belief, true
11   entries made at their respective dates, of all the spirits distilled
12   within the time to which such entries shall relate, from such still,
13   and of the disposition thereof; and shall also declare upon such

14 oath or affirmation, the quantity of such spirits then remaining
15 on hand, it shall be lawful in every such case for the said officer
16 to whom the said book or paper shall be produced, and he is
17 hereby required to estimate the duties upon such still, accord-
18 ing to the quantity so stated to have been actually made there-
19 from at the rate of nine cents per gallon, which, and no more,
20 shall be paid for the same: Provided, That if the said entries
21 shall be made by any person other than the said proprietor, a
22 like oath or affirmation shall be made by such person.

1   "And the more effectually to prevent the evasion of the du-
2   ties hereby imposed, to the no less injury of the fair trader than
3   of the revenue:

4   "Sᴇᴄᴛ. XXIV.   Be it further enacted, That every person
5   who shall be a dealer or trader in distilled spirits (except as an
6   importer, maker or distiller thereof) in the original casks or cases
7   in which they shall be imported, or in quantities of twenty-five
8   gallons at one sale, shall be deemed a wholesale dealer in spirits,
9   and shall write or paint, or cause to be written or painted, in
10 large, legible and durable characters, upon some conspicuous
11 part outside and in front of each house or other building or place,
12 and upon the door or usual entrance of each vault, cellar or
13 apartment within the same in which any of the said spirits shall
14 be at any time by him or her deposited or kept, or intended so
15 to be, the words 'wholesale dealer in spirits;' and shall also,
16 within three days at least before he or she shall begin to keep or
17 sell any of the said spirits therein, make a particular entry in
18 writing at the nearest office of inspection, of the district in which
19 the same shall be situate, if within ten miles thereof, of every
20 such house or other building or place, and of each cellar, vault or
21 apartment within the same, in which he or she shall intend to put
22 or keep any of the said spirits; and if any such dealer shall omit
23 to write or paint, or cause to be written or painted, the words
24 aforesaid, and in manner aforesaid, upon any such house or other
25 building or place, or vault, cellar or apartment thereof, in which
26 he or she shall so have or keep any of the said spirits, or shall in
27 case the same be situated within the said distance of ten miles of
28 any office of inspection, omit to make entry thereof as aforesaid,
29 such dealer shall for every such omission or neglect forfeit the
30 sum of five hundred dollars, and all the spirits which he or she
31 shall have or keep therein, or the value thereof, to be computed
32 at the highest price of such spirits in the market.

1   "Sᴇᴄᴛ. XXV.   And be it further enacted, That every person

2 who shall be a maker or distiller of spirits within any city, town
3 or village, shall write or paint, or cause to be written or painted
4 upon some conspicuous part outside and in front of each house
5 or other building or place made use of, or intended to be made
6 use of by him or her for the distillation or keeping of spirituous
7 liquors, and upon the door or usual entrance of each vault, cel-
8 lar or apartment within the same, in which any of the said liquors
9 shall be at any time by him or her distilled, deposited or kept,
10 or intended so to be, the words 'Distiller of spirits;' and
11 every such distiller shall within three days before he or she shall
12 begin to distil therein, make a particular entry in writing, at
13 the nearest office of inspection, if within ten miles thereof, of
14 every such house, building or place, and of each vault, cellar and
15 apartment within the same, in which he or she shall intend to
16 carry on the business of distilling, or to keep any spirits by him
17 or her distilled. And if any such distiller within any city, town
18 or village, shall omit to paint or write, or cause to be painted
19 or written the words aforesaid, in manner aforesaid, upon any
20 such house or other building or place, or vault, cellar or apart-
21 ment thereof, or shall, in case the same be situate within the said
22 distance of ten miles of any office of inspection, omit to make
23 entry thereof as aforesaid, such distiller shall for every such omis-
24 sion or neglect, forfeit one hundred dollars, and all the spirits
25 which he or she shall keep therein, or the value thereof, to be
26 computed at the highest price of such spirits in the market; to be
27 recovered by action, with costs of suit, in any court proper to
28 try the same, in the name of the Inspector of the district within
29 which such omission or neglect shall be, for the use of the United
30 States: Provided always, and be it further enacted, That the
31 said entry, to be made by persons who shall be dealers in or
32 distillers of spirits, on the first day of July next, shall be made
33 on that day, or within three days thereafter, accompanied (ex-
34 cept where the duties hereby imposed are charged on the still)
35 with a true and particular account or inventory of the spirits,
36 on that day and at the time, in every or any house, building or
37 place by him or her entered; and of the casks, cases and vessels
38 containing the same, with their marks and numbers, and the
39 quantities and qualities of the spirits therein contained, on pain
40 of forfeiting for neglecting to make such entry, or to deliver
41 such account, the sum of one hundred dollars, and all the spirits
42 by him or her had or kept in any such house, building or place;

43 to be recovered as aforesaid: And provided also, that nothing
44 herein contained shall be construed to exempt any such distiller,
45 who shall be, besides his dealing as a distiller, a dealer or trader
46 in distilled spirits as described in the twenty-fourth section of
47 this act, from the regulations therein prescribed; but every such
48 distiller, so being also a dealer or trader in distilled spirits, shall
49 observe and be subject to all the rules, regulations and penalties
50 therein specified.

1   "SECT. XXVI. And be it further enacted, That the In-
2   spector or Inspectors of the revenue for the district wherein any
3   house, building or place shall be situate, whereof entry shall be
4   made as last aforesaid, shall as soon as may be thereafter, visit
5   and inspect or cause to be visited and inspected by some proper
6   officer or officers of inspection, every such house or other build-
7   ing or place within his or their district, and shall take or cause
8   to be taken, an exact account of the spirit therein respectively
9   contained, and shall mark or cause to be marked in durable cha-
10 racters, the several casks, cases or vessels containing the same,
11 with progressive numbers, and also with the name of each dealer
12 or distiller to whom the same may belong, or in whole custody
13 the same may be, and the quantities, kinds and proofs of spirits
14 therein contained, and these words 'Old Stock.' And the said
15 Inspector or Inspectors shall keep a book wherein he or they
16 shall enter the name of every such dealer or distiller within his
17 or their district, and the particulars of such old stock in the pos-
18 session of each, designating the several casks and cases containing
19 the same, and their respective quantities, kinds, proofs and
20 marks. And he or they shall also give a certificate to every
21 such dealer or distiller, of the quantity and particulars of such
22 old stock in his or her possession, and a separate certificate for
23 each cask, case or vessel, describing the same, according to its
24 marks; which certificates shall accompany the same wheresoever
25 it shall be sent. And in case there shall be no officer of inspec-
26 tion within the said distance of ten miles of any such house or
27 other building or place, then it shall be the duty of such dealer
28 to whom the same may belong, to mark with the like durable
29 characters the several casks containing the spirits therein, and
30 in like manner as above directed to be done by the said Inspec-
31 tor or Inspesctors. And the said dealer shall make entry thereof
32 in some proper book or on some proper paper to be by him or
33 her kept for that purpose, specifying particularly each cask, case

34 or vessel, and its marks, and the quantity and quality of the
35 spirits therein contained (of which entry he or they shall, upon
36 request, deliver an exact copy to the Inspector or Inspectors of
37 the revenue for the district) and if required by him or them, shall
38 attest the same by oath, or affirmation. And the said dealer,
39 with every such cask, case or vessel which shall be delivered out
40 of his or her house or other building or place, shall give a certi-
41 ficate or permit, signed by himself or herself, of the like im-
42 port of that above directed to be given by the said Inspector or
43 Inspectors; which certificate shall in like manner accompany the
44 same wheresoever it may be sent. And if any such dealer shall
45 in the said case omit to mark the said several casks, cases or ves-
46 sels containing the said spirits, or to make entry thereof in some
47 proper book, or on some proper paper as aforesaid, he or she
48 shall forfeit and pay for every such neglect the sum of one hun-
49 dred dollars. And if in the same case he or she shall deliver
50 out or send away any of the said spirits, without such certificate
51 by him or her directed to be furnished as aforesaid, the said spi-
52 rits so delivered out or sent away, shall be forfeited, and may
53 be seized by any officer of inspection; and the said dealer shall
54 also forfeit the full value thereof: Provided always that nothing
55 herein contained shall be construed to extend to casks, capable
56 of containing two hundred gallons or upwards, and which are
57 not intended to be removed; but in order to prevent the abuse
58 of this exemption, it shall be necessary whenever any of the
59 said dealers shall have occasion to put any spirits into any cask of
60 the capacity of two hundred gallons or upwards, he or she shall
61 give notice in writing of his or her intention so to do, to the
62 officer of inspection nearest the building or place in which such
63 cask shall be (if there shall be an officer of inspection within one
64 mile of such house or building) specifying the time when he or
65 she intends to commence the putting such spirits into such cask,
66 to the end that the officer of inspection may by himself or de-
67 puty, attend the doing thereof; but in case of non-attendance
68 by the officer or his deputy, such dealer may nevertheless pro-
69 ceed therein according to his or her notification.

1   "SECT. XXVII.   And be it further enacted, That every im-
2   porter of distilled spirits, who, on the first day of July next,
3   shall have in his or her possession any distilled spirits, shall, within
4   three days thereafter, make due entry thereof with the officer
5   of inspection within whose district the same shall then be; who

6 shall mark the casks or cases containing such spirits, in like man-
7 ner as is herein directed for spirits in possession of wholesale
8 dealers; and all the casks or cases marked, and the spirits therein
9 contained, shall be under the like rules, regulations and forfei-
10 tures in all things respecting the delivery thereof, and the cer-
11 tificate which shall accompany the same, as is by the 24th section
12 of this act provided for distilled spirits in the possession of whole-
13 sale dealers; and if any such importer or importers shall refuse
14 or neglect to make such entry at the time and in the manner
15 herein directed, all such spirits as shall not be so entered shall
16 be forfeited, and the importer or importers in whose custody
17 the same shall be found, shall moreover forfeit the sum equal to
18 the full value thereof, according to the highest price of such
19 spirits in the market.

1 "SECT. XXVIII. And be it further enacted, That when any
2 such wholesale dealer in spirits, shall bring into his or her entered
3 house, building or place, any of the said spirits, if such house,
4 building or place be within two miles of any office of inspection,
5 he or she shall within twenty-four hours after the said spirits
6 shall be brought into such house, building or place, send notice
7 thereof in writing to the said office, specifying therein the quan-
8 tity and kinds of the spirits so brought in, and the marks of the
9 cask or casks, case or cases containing the same, on pain of for-
10 feiting, for every neglect to give such notice, fifty dollars. And
11 it shall be the duty of the officer to whom such notice shall be
12 given, forthwith thereafter to inspect and take an account of
13 such spirits.

1 "SECT. XXIX. And be it further enacted, That if any dis-
2 tilled spirits shall be found in the possession of any such dealer,
3 without the proper certificates which ought to accompany the
4 same, it shall be presumptive evidence that the same are liable
5 to forfeiture, and it shall be lawful for any officer of inspection
6 to seize them as forfeited; and if upon the trial, in consequence
7 of such seizure, the owner or claimant of the spirits seized, shall
8 not prove that the same were imported into the United States
9 according to law, or were distilled as mentioned in the thirteenth
10 and fourteenth sections of this act, and the duties thereupon
11 paid, or were distilled at one of the stills mentioned in the
12 twentieth section of this act, they shall be adjudged to be for-
13 feited.

1 "SECT. XXX. And be it further enacted, That it shall be

2 lawful for the officers of inspection of each district, at all times
3 in the day time, upon request, to enter into all and every the
4 houses, store-houses, ware-houses, buildings, and places which
5 shall have been entered by the said wholesale dealers in manner
6 aforesaid, and by tasting, gauging, or otherwise, to take an
7 account of the quantity, kinds and proofs of the said spirits
8 therein contained; and also to take samples thereof, paying for
9 the same the usual price.

1   "SECT. XXXI. And be it further enacted, That every such
2 dealer shall keep the several kinds of spirits in his or her enter-
3 ed ware-house building or place, separate and apart from each
4 other, on pain of forfeiting upon every conviction of neglect,
5 fifty dollars; and shall also, upon request, shew to the officers
6 of inspection of the district wherein he or she is so a dealer, or
7 to any of them, each and every cask, vessel and case in which
8 he or she shall keep any distilled spirits, and the certificates
9 which ought to accompany the same, upon pain of forfeiting
10 every such cask, vessel or case, as shall be shewn, together with
11 the spirits therein contained.

1   "SECT. XXXII. And be it further enacted, That if any per-
2 son or persons shall rub out or deface any of the marks set upon
3 any cask or case pursuant to the directions of this act, such per-
4 son or persons shall for every such offence, forfeit and pay the
5 sum of one hundred dollars.

1   "SECT. XXXIII. And be it further enacted, That no cask,
2 barrel, keg or case, marked as "Old stock," shall be made use
3 of by any dealer or distiller of spirits, for putting or keeping
4 therein any spirits other than those which were contained
5 therein when so marked, on pain of forfeiting the sum of one
6 hundred dollars for every cask, barrel, keg, vessel or case wherein
7 any such spirits shall be so put or kept; neither shall any such dea-
8 ler have or keep any distilled spirits in any such cask, barrel, keg,
9 vessel or case, longer than for the space of one year from the said
10 last day of June next, on pain of forfeiting the said spirits.

1   "SECT. XXXIV. And be it further enacted, That in case
2 any of the said spirits shall be fraudulently deposited, hid or
3 concealed in any place whatsoever, with intent to evade the
4 duties hereby imposed upon them, they shall be forfeited: And
5 for the better discovery of any such spirits so fraudulently depo-
6 sited, hid or concealed, it shall be lawful for any Judge of any
7 Court of the United States, or either of them, or for any Jus-

8   tice of the Peace, upon reasonable cause of suspicion, to be
9   made out to the satisfaction of such Judge or Justice, by the oath
10   or affirmation of any person or persons, by special warrant or
11   warrants under their respective hands and seals, to authorise any
12   of the officers of inspection, by day, in the presence of a Con-
13   stable or other officer of the peace, to enter into all and every
14   such place or places in which any of the said spirits shall be sus-
15   pected to be so fraudulently deposited, hid or concealed, and to
16   seize and carry away any of the said spirits which shall be there
17   found so fraudulently deposited, hid or concealed, as forfeited.

1   "SECT. XXXV. And be it further enacted, That after the
2   last day of June next, no spirituous liquors shall be brought from
3   any foreign port or place, in casks of less capacity than fifty
4   gallons at the least, on pain of forfeiting of the said spirits, and
5   of the ship or vessel in which they shall be brought: Provided
6   always, that nothing in this act contained shall be construed to
7   forfeit any spirits for being imported or brought into the United
8   States, in other casks or vessels than as aforesaid, or the ship or
9   vessel in which they shall be brought, if such spirits shall be for
10   the use of the seamen on board such ship or vessel, and shall not
11   exceed the quantity of four gallons for each such seaman.

1   "SECT. XXXVI. And be it further enacted, That in every
2   case in which any of the said spirits shall be forfeited by virtue
3   of this act, the casks, vessels and cases containing the same, shall
4   also be forfeited.

1   "SECT. XXXVII. And be it further enacted, That every
2   dealer by wholesale, or distiller of spirits, on which the duty
3   is hereby charged by the gallon, shall keep or cause to be kept,
4   an exact account of the said spirits which he or she shall sell,
5   send out or distil, distinguishing their several kinds and proofs;
6   and shall every day make a just and true entry in a book or on
7   a paper to be kept for that purpose, of the quantities and par-
8   ticulars of the said spirits by him or her sold, sent out or dis-
9   tilled on the preceding day; specifying the marks of the several
10   casks in which they shall be so sold or sent out, and the person
11   to whom and for whose use they shall be so sold or sent out:
12   which said books and papers shall be prepared for the making
13   such entries, and shall be delivered upon demand, to the said
14   dealers and distillers, by the Inspectors of the revenue of the
15   several districts, or by such person or persons as they shall re-
16   spectively for that purpose appoint, and shall be severally re-

17 turned or delivered at the end of each year, or when the same
18 shall be respectively filled up, (which shall first happen, to the
19 proper officers of inspection; and the truth of the entries made
20 therein shall be verified upon the oath or the affirmation of the
21 person by whom those entries shall have been made, and as
22 often as the said books and papers shall be furnished upon like
23 demand by the proper officers of inspection, to the said dealers
24 and distillers respectively. And the said books and papers shall
25 from time to time, while in the possession of the said dealers
26 and distillers, lie open for the inspection of, and upon request
27 shall be shewn to the proper officers of inspection under whose
28 survey the said dealers and distillers shall respectively be, who
29 may take such minutes, memorandums, or transcripts thereof,
30 as they may think fit. And if any such dealer or distiller, shall
31 neglect or refuse to keep such book or books, paper or papers,
32 or to make such entries therein, or to shew the same upon re-
33 quest, to the proper officer of inspection, or not return the same
34 according to the directions of this act, he or she shall forfeit for
35 every such refusal or neglect, the sum of one hundred dollars.

1 "SECT. XXXVIII. And be it further enacted, That the pe-
2 nalties by this act imposed on distillers for neglecting to make
3 report to the Inspectors, of their intentions of distilling spirits,
4 or for neglecting to mark the houses, apartments or vessels to be
5 employed, or for neglecting to enter in books or on paper the
6 quantity of spirits distilled, shall not extend to any person who
7 shall employ one still only, and that of a capacity not exceeding
8 fifty gallons, including the still head.

1 "SECT. XXXIX. And be it further enacted, That the seve-
2 ral kinds of proof herein before specified, shall in marking the
3 casks, vessels and cases containing any distilled spirits, be distin-
4 guished corresponding with the order in which they are men-
5 tioned by the words FIRST PROOF—SECOND PROOF—THIRD
6 PROOF—FOURTH PROOF—FIFTH PROOF—SIXTH PROOF: which
7 words may be expressed by their respective initials. And that
8 it be the duty of the Secretary of the Treasury, to provide and
9 furnish to the officers of inspection and of the customs, proper
10 instruments for ascertaining the said several proofs.

1 "SECT. XL. Be it further enacted, That in any prosecution
2 or action which may be brought against any Inspector or other
3 officer of inspection, for any seizure by him made, it shall be
4 necessary for such Inspector or officer to justify himself by mak-

5 ing it appear that there was probable cause for making the said
6 seizure; upon which, and not otherwise, a verdict shall pass in
7 his favor. And in any such action or prosecution, or in any
8 action or prosecution which may be brought against such In-
9 spector or other officer, for irregular or improper conduct in
10 the execution of his duty, the trial shall be by jury. And in any
11 action for a seizure, in which a verdict shall pass for such In-
12 spector, the jury shall nevertheless assess reasonable damages for
13 any prejudice or waste (according to the true amount in value
14 thereof) which shall be shewn by good proof to have happened
15 to the spirits seized, in consequence of such seizure; and also
16 for the detention of the same, at the rate of six per cent. per
17 annum, on the true value of the said spirits at the time of such
18 seizure, from that time to the time of restoration thereof; which
19 shall be paid out of the Treasury of the United States: Provided
20 that no damages shall be assessed when the seizure was made for
21 want of the proper certificate or certificates, or by reason of a
22 *refusal* to shew any officer of inspection, upon his request, the
23 spirits in any entered house, or other building or place.

1 "SECT. XLI. And be it further enacted, That if any Inspec-
2 tor or other officer of inspection, in any criminal prosecution
3 against him, shall be convicted of oppression or extortion in the
4 execution of his office, he shall be fined not exceeding five hun-
5 dred dollars, or imprisoned not exceeding six months, or both,
6 at the discretion of the court; and shall also forfeit his office.

1 "SECT. XLII. And be it further enacted, That no fee shall
2 be taken for any certificate to be issued or granted pursuant to
3 this act.

1 "SECT. XLIII. And be it further enacted, That if any of
2 the said Inspectors or other officers of inspection, shall neglect to
3 perform any of the duties hereby enjoined upon them respec-
4 tively, according to the true intent and meaning of this act,
5 whereby any person or persons shall be injured or suffer damage,
6 such person or persons shall and may have an action founded
7 upon this act, against such Inspector or other officers, and shall
8 recover full damages for the same, together with costs of suit.

1 "SECT. XLIV. And be it further enacted, That any action
2 or suit to be brought against any person or persons, for any thing
3 by him or them done in pursuance of this act, shall be com-
4 menced within three months next after the matter or thing done,
5 *and shall be laid in the proper county* in which the cause of action

6 shall have arisen; and the defendant or defendants in any such
7 action or suit may plead the general issue, and on the trial there-
8 of give this act and the special matter, in evidence; and if a
9 verdict shall pass for the defendant or defendants, or the plaintiff
10 or plaintiffs become nonsuited, or discontinue his, her or their
11 action or prosecution, or judgment shall be given against such
12 plaintiff or plaintiffs, upon demurrer or otherwise, then such
13 defendant or defendants shall have costs awarded to him, her or
14 them, against such plaintiff or plaintiffs.

1 "SECT. XLV. And in order that all persons who may have
2 incurred any of the penalties of this act, without wilful negli-
3 gence or intention of fraud, may be relieved from such penalties,
4 "Be it further enacted, That it shall be lawful for the Judge
5 of the district within which such penalty or forfeiture shall have
6 been incurred, upon petition of the party who shall have incur-
7 red the same, to enquire in a summary manner into the cir-
8 cumstances of the case, first causing reasonable notice to be given
9 to the person or persons claiming such penalty or forfeiture,
10 and to the Attorney of such district; to the end that each may
11 have an opportunity of shewing cause against the mitigation or
12 remission thereof: and if upon such enquiry it shall appear to
13 the said Judge that such penalty or forfeiture was incurred
14 without wilful negligence, or any design or intention of fraud,
15 it shall be lawful for him to remit the same, and to cause
16 any spirits which may have been seized, to be restored to the
17 proprietor or proprietors, upon such terms and conditions as
18 shall appear to him reasonable. And the decision of the Judge
19 (if the terms and conditions prescribed by him be complied with)
20 shall be conclusive to the parties: Provided that such penalty,
21 or the value of the spirits forfeited, does not exceed five hun-
22 dred dollars; but if the amount of such penalty or forfeiture
23 exceeds five hundred dollars, the person or persons claiming the
24 same, may, within three days after such decision shall be pro-
25 nounced, appeal from the same to the circuit court of the district;
26 which court shall summarily hear the parties, and either confirm
27 or reverse the decision of the district Judge, as shall appear to
28 them proper: Provided always, that after the first day of July
29 in the year one thousand seven hundred and ninety-two, such
30 remission shall in no case exceed one half the penalty, or half
31 the spirits forfeited, or the value thereof.

1 "SECT. XLVI. And be it further enacted, That the one half

2   of all penalties and forfeitures incurred by virtue of this act,
3   except as above provided, shall be for the benefit of the person
4   or persons who shall make a seizure, or who shall first discover
5   the matter or thing whereby the same shall have been incurred;
6   and the other half to the use of the United States. And such
7   penalty and forfeiture shall be recoverable with costs of suit, by
8   action of debt, in the name of the person or persons intitled,
9   thereto, or by information, in the name of the United States
10   of America; and it shall be the duty of the Attorney of the
11   district wherein any such penalty or forfeiture may have been
12   incurred, upon application to him, to institute or bring such
13   information accordingly: Provided always, that no officer of
14   inspection other than chief officer, or officers of a district, shall
15   be intitled to the benefit of any forfeiture unless notice of the
16   seizure by him made, shall be by him given within forty-eight
17   hours next after such seizure, to the said chief officer or officers;
18   but in such case the United States shall have the entire benefit
19   of such forfeiture.

1   "SECT. XLVII.   And be it further enacted, That if any per-
2   son or persons shall counterfeit or forge, or cause to be coun-
3   terfeited or forged any of the certificates herein before directed
4   to be given, or shall knowingly or willingly accept or receive
5   any false or untrue certificate with any of the said spirits, or
6   shall fraudulently alter or erase any such certificate, after the
7   same shall be given, or knowingly or willingly publish or make
8   use of such certificate so counterfeited,[47] forged, false, untrue,
9   altered or erased, every person so offending, shall for each and
10   every offence, severally forfeit and pay the sum of five hundred
11   dollars.

1   "SECT. XLVIII.   And be it further enacted, That any person
2   or persons that shall be convicted of wilfully taking a false oath
3   or affirmation, in any of the cases in which oaths or affirmations
4   are required to be taken by virtue of this act, shall be liable to
5   the pains and penalties to which persons are liable for wilful and
6   corrupt perjury.

1   "SECT. XLIX.   And be it further enacted, That if any person
2   or persons shall give, or offer to give any bribe, recompence or
3   reward whatsoever, to any Inspector or officer of inspection of
4   the revenue, in order to corrupt, persuade or prevail upon such
5   officer, either to do any act or acts contrary to his duty in the

---

[47] The smooth journal substitutes the word "countersigned" for "counterfeited."

6 execution of this act, or to neglect or omit to do any act or
7 thing which he ought to do in the execution of this act, or to
8 connive at or to conceal any fraud or frauds relating to the
9 duties hereby imposed on any of the said spirits, or not to dis-
10 cover the same, every such person or persons shall, for such
11 offence, whether the same offer or proposal be accepted or not,
12 forfeit and pay a sum not exceeding five hundred dollars.

1 "SECT. L. And be it further enacted, That if any person or
2 persons shall forcibly obstruct or hinder any Inspector or officer
3 of inspection, in the execution of this act, or of any of the pow-
4 ers or authorities hereby vested in him, or shall forcibly rescue,
5 or cause to be rescued any of the said spirits after the same shall
6 have been seized by any such Inspector or officer, or shall attempt
7 or endeavour so to do, all and every person and persons so of-
8 fending, shall for every such offence for which no other penalty
9 is particularly provided by this act, forfeit and pay a sum not
10 exceeding two hundred dollars.

1 "SECT. LI. And be it further enacted, That if any such In-
2 spector or officer, shall enter into any collusion with any person
3 or persons, for violating or evading any of the provisions of this
4 act, or the duties hereby imposed, or shall fraudulently concur in
5 the delivery of any of the said spirits out of any house, building
6 or place wherein the same are deposited without payment, or
7 security for the payment of the duties thereupon, or shall falsely
8 or fraudulently mark any cask, case or vessel, contrary to any of
9 the said provisions, or shall embezzle the public money, or other-
10 wise be guilty of fraud in his office, such Inspector or officer shall
11 for every such offence forfeit the sum of one thousand dollars,
12 and upon conviction of any of the said offences, shall forfeit his
13 office, and shall be disqualified for holding any other office under
14 the United States.

1 "SECT. LII. And be it further enacted, That it shall be law-
2 ful for the Inspectors of the revenue, and when requested by
3 any such dealer, they are hereby required to provide blank cer-
4 tificates, in such form as shall be directed by the Secretary of the
5 Treasury, and in the cases in which certificates are hereby direc-
6 ted to be issued or granted by the said dealers, to furnish them
7 therewith the blanks in which certificates shall be filled up by
8 such dealers, according to the nature and truth of each particu-
9 lar case, subject to the penalty heretofore declared for granting
10 or using false or untrue certificates. And every such dealer

11 shall from time to time, when thereunto requested, account with
12 such Inspectors respectively, for the number of certificates recei-
13 ved by him, and for the disposition of such of them as may have
14 been disposed of, and shall produce and shew the residue thereof
15 to the said Inspector, and shall pay for every certificate for which
16 he cannot satisfactorily account, the sum of fifty cents.

1   "SECT. LIII.   And be it further enacted, That in every case
2   in which an oath or affirmation is required by virtue of this act,
3   it shall be lawful for the Inspectors of the revenue, or any of
4   them, or their lawful deputy, or the lawful deputy of one of
5   them, where not more than one in a district, to administer and
6   take such oath or affirmation; and that wherever there are more
7   than one Inspector for one district, a majority of them may exe-
8   cute all and any of the powers and authorities hereby vested in
9   the Inspectors of the revenue: Provided, that this shall not be
10 construed to make a majority necessary in any case in which,
11 according to the nature of the appointment or service, and the
12 true intent of this act, the authority is or ought to be several.

1   "SECT. LIV.   And for the encouragement of the export trade
2   of the United States,

3   "Be it further enacted, That if any of the said spirits (where-
4   upon any of the duties imposed by this act shall have been paid
5   or secured to be paid) shall after the last day of June next, be
6   exported from the United States to any foreign port or place,
7   there shall be an allowance to the exporter or exporters thereof,
8   by way of drawback, equal to the duties thereupon, according
9   to the rates in each case by this act imposed, deducting therefrom
10 half a cent. per gallon, and adding to the allowance upon spi-
11 rits distilled within the United States, from molasses, which shall
12 be so exported, three cents per gallon, as an equivalent for the
13 duty laid upon molasses by the said act making further provision
14 for the payment of the debts of the United States: Provided
15 always, that the said allowance shall not be made, unless the said
16 exporter or exporters shall observe the regulations herein after
17 prescribed: and provided further, that nothing herein contained
18 shall be construed to alter the provisions in the said former act,
19 concerning drawbacks or allowances, in nature thereof, upon
20 spirits imported prior to the first day of July next.

1   "SECT. LV.   And be it further enacted, That in order to
2   intitle the said exporter or exporters to the benefit of the said
3   allowance, he, she or they, shall previous to putting or lading

4   any of the said spirits on board of any ship or vessel for expor-
5   tation, give twenty-four hours notice at the least, to the proper
6   officer of inspection of the port from which the said spirits shall
7   be intended to be exported, of his, her or their intention to ex-
8   port the same, and of the number of casks and cases, or either of
9   them, containing the said spirits so intended to be exported, and
10 of the respective marks thereof, and of the place or places where
11 the said spirits shall be then deposited, and of the place to which,
12 and ship or vessel in which they shall be so intended to be expor-
13 ted: whereupon it shall be the duty of the said officer to inspect,
14 by himself or deputy, the casks and cases so noticed for expor-
15 tation, and the quantities, kinds and proofs of the spirits therein,
16 together with the certificates which ought to accompany the same
17 according to the directions of this act, which shall be produced
18 to him for that purpose; and if he shall find that the said casks
19 and cases have the proper marks according to the directions of
20 this act, and that the spirits therein correspond with the said
21 certificates, he shall thereupon brand each cask or case with the
22 word 'Exportation;' and the said spirits shall, after such in-
23 spection, be laden on board the same ship or vessel of which notice
24 shall have been given, and in the presence of the same officer
25 who shall have examined the same, and whose duty it shall be
26 to attend for that purpose. And after the said spirits shall be
27 laden on board such ship or vessel, the certificates aforesaid shall
28 be delivered to the said officer, who shall certify to the Collector
29 of the said district, the amount and particulars of the spirits so
30 exported, and shall also deliver the said certificates which shall
31 have been by him received, to the said Collector, which shall be
32 a voucher to him, for payment of the said allowance.

1   "SECT. LVI. Provided nevertheless, and be it further enacted,
2   That the said allowance shall not be made, unless the said expor-
3   ter or exporters shall make oath, or affirmation, that the said
4   spirits so noticed for exportation, and laden on board such ship
5   or vessel, are truly intended to be exported to the place whereof
6   notice shall have been given, and are not intended to be re-landed
7   within the United States; and that he or she doth verily believe
8   that the duties thereupon charged by this act, have been duly
9   paid; and shall also give bond to the Collector, with two sure-
10 ties, one of whom shall be the master, or other person having
11 the command or charge of the ship or vessel in which the said
12 spirits shall be intended to be exported; the other, such sufficient

13 person as shall be approved by the said Collector, in the full
14 value, in the judgment of the said Collector, of the said spirits
15 so intended to be exported; with condition that the said spirits
16 (the dangers of the seas and enemies excepted) shall be really
17 and truly exported to, and landed in some port or place with-
18 out the limits of the United States, according to the late treaty
19 of peace with Great-Britain, and that the said spirits shall not
20 be unshipped from on board of the said ship or vessel, whereupon
21 the same shall have been laden for exportation, within the said
22 limits, or any ports or harbours of the United States, or re-landed
23 in any other part of the same (shipwreck or other unavoidable
24 accident excepted).

1   "SECT. LVII. Provided also, and be it further enacted, That
2   the said allowance shall not be paid until six months after the
3   said spirits shall have been so exported: And provided also, that
4   whenever the owner of any ship or vessel, on board of which
5   any such spirits are laden for exportation, shall make known
6   to the Collector, previous to the departure of such ship or vessel
7   from the port where such spirits are laden, that such ship or
8   vessel is not going to proceed the voyage intended, or the voyage
9   is altered; it shall be lawful for the Collector to grant a permit
10 for the re-landing the same.

1   "SECT. LVIII. And be it further enacted, That if any of the
2   said spirits, after the same shall have been shipped for exporta-
3   tion, shall be unshipped for any purpose whatever, either within
4   the limits of any part of the United States, or within four
5   leagues of the coast thereof, or shall be re-landed within the
6   United States, from on board the ship or vessel wherein the
7   same shall have been laden for exportation, unless the voyage
8   shall not be proceeded on, or shall be altered as aforesaid, or
9   unless in case of necessity or distress to save the ship and goods
10 from perishing, which shall be immediately made known to the
11 principal officer of the customs, residing at the port nearest to
12 which such ship or vessel shall be at the time such necessity or
13 distress shall arise; then, not only the spirits so unshipped, toge-
14 ther with the casks and cases containing the same, but also the
15 ship or vessel in or on board which the same shall have been so
16 shipped or laden, together with her guns, furniture, ammuni-
17 tion, tackle and apparel; and also the ship, vessel or boat into
18 which the said spirits shall be unshipped or put, after the un-
19 shipping thereof, together with her guns, furniture, ammuni-

20 tion, tackle and apparel, shall be forfeited, and may be seized
21 by any officer of the customs, or of inspection, unless the voyage
22 shall not be proceeded on or be altered as aforesaid.

1   "SECT. LIX. And be it further enacted, That the said al-
2   lowance shall not be made when the said spirits shall be expor-
3   ted in any other than a ship or vessel of the burthen of thirty
4   tons and upwards, to be ascertained to the satisfaction of the
5   Collector of the district from which the same shall be intended
6   to be exported.

1   "SECT. LX. And be it further enacted, That the bonds to be
2   given as aforesaid, shall and may be discharged by producing
3   within one year from the respective dates thereof (if the same
4   be shipped to any part of Europe or America, and within two
5   years if shipped to any part of Asia or Africa, and if the de-
6   livery of the spirits in respect to which the same shall have been
7   given, be at any place where a Consul, or other Agent of the
8   United States resides) a certificate of such Consul or Agent, and
9   if there be no such Consul or Agent, then a certificate of any
10 two known and reputable American merchants residing at the
11 said place; and if there be not two such merchants residing at
12 the said place, then a certificate of any other two reputable
13 merchants, testifying the delivery of the said spirits, at the said
14 place. Which certificate shall in each case be confirmed by
15 the oath or affirmation of the master and mate, or other like
16 officer of the vessel in which the said spirits shall have been ex-
17 ported; and when such certificate shall be from any other than
18 a Consul or Agent, or merchants of the United States, it shall
19 be a part of the said oath or affirmation, that there were not
20 upon diligent enquiry, to be found two merchants of the United
21 States, at the said place: Provided always, that in the case of
22 death, the oath or affirmation of the party dying, shall not be
23 deemed necessary: And provided further, that the said oath
24 or affirmation, taken before the chief civil Magistrate of the
25 place of the said delivery, and certified under his hand and seal,
26 shall be of the same validity as if taken before a person qualified
27 to administer oaths within the United States; or such bonds
28 shall and may be discharged upon proof that the spirits so ex-
29 ported, were taken by enemies or perished in the sea, or de-
30 stroyed by fire; the examination and proof of the same being
31 left to the judgment of the Collector of the customs, naval
32 officer, and chief officer of inspection, or any two of them,

33 of the place from which such spirits shall have been exported.
34 And in cases where the certificates herein directed cannot be
35 obtained, the exporter or exporters of such spirits, shall never-
36 theless be permitted to offer such other proof as to the delivery
37 of the said spirits without the limits of the United States, as he
38 or they may have; and if the same shall be deemed sufficient
39 by the said Collector, he shall allow the same, except when the
40 drawback to be allowed shall amount to one hundred dollars or
41 upwards; in all which cases the proofs aforesaid shall be referred
42 to the Comptroller of the Treasury, whose decision thereon shall
43 be final.

1   "SECT. LXI.   And be it further enacted, That the prosecu-
2   tion for all fines, penalties and forfeitures incurred by force of
3   this act, and for all duties payable in virtue thereof, and which
4   shall not be duly paid, shall and may be had before any Justice
5   of the Peace, or court of any State of competent jurisdiction,
6   or court of the United States of the district in which the cause
7   of action shall arise, with an appeal as in other cases: Provided,
8   that where the cause of action shall exceed in value fifty dollars,
9   the same shall not be cognizable before a Justice of the Peace
10 only.

1   "SECT. LXII.   And be it further enacted, That this act shall
2   commence and take effect as to all matters therein contained, in
3   respect to which no special commencement is hereby provided
4   (except as to the appointment of officers and regulation of the
5   districts) from and immediately after the last day of June next.

1   "SECT. LXIII.   And be it further enacted, That the net pro-
2   duct of the duties herein before specified, which shall be raised,
3   levied and collected by virtue of this act, or so much thereof as
4   may be necessary, shall be, and they are hereby pledged and
5   appropriated for the payment of the interest of the several and
6   respective loans which had been made in foreign countries, prior
7   to the fourth day of August last; and also upon all and every
8   the loan and loans which have been made, and shall be made and
9   obtained pursuant to the act, entitled, 'An Act making pro-
10 vision for the debt of the United States;' and according to the
11 true intent and meaning of the said act, and of the several pro-
12 visions and engagements therein contained and expressed, and
13 subject to the like priorities and reservations as are made and
14 contained in and by the said act, in respect to the monies therein
15 appropriated, and subject to this further reservation, that is to

16 say,—of the net amount or product during the present year, of
17 the duties laid by this act, in addition to those heretofore laid
18 upon spirits imported into the United States, from any foreign
19 port or place, and of the duties laid by this act on spirits distilled
20 within the United States, and on stills;[48] to be disposed of in the
21 first place to the discharge of the debts of the United States,
22 arising since the first day of September last, and unprovided for
23 by any prior appropriations; and the residue to be applied to-
24 wards sinking the principal of the stock and loans above men-
25 tioned. And to the end that the said monies may be inviolably
26 applied in conformity to the appropriation hereby made, and
27 may never be diverted to any other purpose until the final re-
28 demption or reimbursement of the loans or sums for the pay-
29 ment of the interest whereof they are appropriated, an account
30 shall be kept of the receipts and disposition thereof, separate
31 and distinct from the product of any other duties, impost, excise
32 and taxes whatsoever, except those heretofore laid and appro-
33 priated to the same purposes: Provided always, that nothing
34 herein contained, shall be construed to prevent the Legislature
35 of the United States, from substituting other duties or taxes of
36 equal value to any or all of the said duties and imposts.

1   "SECT. LXIV. And be it further enacted, That the unap-
2   propriated surplus, if any there shall be, of the revenue arising
3   under this act, at the end of each year, shall be applied to the
4   reduction of the public debt in like manner as is directed by the
5   act, entitled, 'An Act making provision for the reduction of
6   the public debt;' and provided by the act, entitled, 'An Act
7   making provision for the debt of the United States;' unless the
8   said surplus, or any part thereof, shall be required to the public
9   exigencies of the United States, and shall by special acts of Con-
10 gress, be appropriated thereto.

1   "SECT. LXV. And be it further enacted, That the several
2   duties imposed by this act, shall continue to be collected and paid
3   until the debts and purposes for which they are pledged and
4   appropriated, shall be fully discharged and satisfied, and no
5   longer."

"Jan. 27th, 1791, Passed the House of Representatives."

Jan. 28th, 1791, Before the Senate for concurrence:
On motion to expunge the sixty-fifth section—
                        It passed in the Negative.

---

[48] The smooth journal inserts the word "or."

On motion "to amend the thirteenth section, line 7th, by expunging '*eleven*,' and inserting '*eight*;' and that in the fourteenth section, in the 7th line, the word '*nine*' be struck out, and '*six*' inserted; and that the duties proposed to be raised by this Bill from spirits distilled in the United States, be conformed to this ratio in the different grades mentioned in the Bill, keeping the same rate of difference in each,"—

It passed in the Negative.

On motion "to amend section thirteenth, line 7th, by striking out eleven, and inserting nine,"—

It passed in the Negative.

On motion "to amend section first, line 11th, by inserting '*one*' between 'twenty,' and 'cents,' and to make a proportionable addition upon all the different grades of imported spirits mentioned in the Bill; and in like proportion to reduce the duty on distilled spirits manufactured within the United States,"—

It passed in the Negative.

ORDERED, That the fourth section of the Bill be re-committed for further amendment.[49]

The Senate adjourned to 11 o'clock to-morrow.

F R I D A Y, FEBRUARY 11, 1791

The SENATE assembled—present as yesterday.

A message from the House of Representatives by Mr. Beckley their clerk:

"Mr. PRESIDENT,

"The House of Representatives have passed a Bill, entitled, 'An Act authorising the President of the United States, to cause the debt due to foreign officers, to be paid and discharged,'[50]—

"Also the Bill, entitled, 'An Act to continue in force for a limited time, an Act passed at the first session of Congress, entitled, "An Act to regulate processes in the courts of the United States," '[51] in which they desire the concurrence of the Senate,—

"I am directed to inform the Senate that the President of the United States has notified the House of Representatives, that he has this day approved and signed 'An Act making appropriations for the support of government during

---

[49] On February 11 the committee reported a further amendment to section four of this bill which was agreed to. The bill and the committee report were recommitted for the purpose of conforming the bill to the amendments that were passed.

[50] This bill is in Engrossed House Bills, House Records, DNA.

[51] This bill has not been located.

the year one thousand seven hundred and ninety-one, and for other purposes,' "[52]—

And he withdrew.

The Senate proceeded to the FIRST reading of the Bill sent from the House of Representatives, for concurrence, as follows:

"An ACT to continue in force for a limited time, an Act passed at the first session of Congress, entitled, 'An Act to regulate processes in the courts of the United States ' "

1   "BE it enacted by the Senate and House of Representatives
2   of the United States of America, in Congress assembled, That
3   an Act passed on the twenty-ninth day of September, in the year
4   one thousand seven hundred and eighty-nine, entitled, 'An Act
5   to regulate processes in the courts of the United States,' shall be,
6   and the same hereby is continued in force until the end of the
7   next session of Congress, and no longer."

"1791, Feb. 11th, Passed the House of Representatives."

ORDERED, That this Bill pass to the SECOND reading.[53]

The Senate proceeded to the FIRST reading of the Bill sent from the House of Representatives, for concurrence, as follows:

"An ACT authorising the President of the United States, to cause the debt due to foreign officers, to be paid and discharged "

1   "BE it enacted by the Senate and House of Representatives
2   of the United States of America, in Congress assembled, That
3   the President of the United States, be, and he hereby is reques-
4   ted to cause the debt, including principal and interest, due by
5   the United States to the officers of the late army thereof, the
6   interest whereof is payable in Paris, in the kingdom of France,
7   to be paid and discharged, out of any monies which shall have
8   been borrowed pursuant to the second section of the Act, enti-
9   tled, 'An Act making provision for the debt of the United
10   States:' Provided that such payment do not in anywise interfere
11   with the purposes therein specified and provided for."

"1791, Feb. 11th, Passed the House of Representatives."

ORDERED, That this Bill pass to the SECOND reading.[54]

A message from the House of Representatives by Mr. Beckley their clerk:

---

[52] This message is in Committee on Enrolled Bills, Senate Records, DNA.
[53] On February 12 this bill was read a second time and passed to the third reading.
[54] On February 12 this bill was read a second time and committed.

"Mr. PRESIDENT,

"The House of Representatives have passed the Bill, entitled, 'An Act to alter the time of the next meeting of Congress,'[55] in which they desire the concurrence of the Senate,"—

And he withdrew.

The Senate proceeded to the FIRST reading of the Bill sent from the House of Representatives, for concurrence, as follows:

"An ACT to alter the time of the next meeting of Congress "

1   "BE it enacted by the Senate and House of Representatives of
2   the United States of America, in Congress assembled, That after
3   the close of the present session of Congress, the next meeting
4   shall be on the first Monday of November next."

    "1791, Feb. 11th, Passed the House of Representatives."

ORDERED, That this Bill pass to the SECOND reading.[56]

"The Bill for the admission of the State of Vermont into this union," was read the SECOND time, and—

On motion it was agreed that the second section should be expunged.

ORDERED, That this Bill pass to the THIRD reading.[57]

On motion, it was agreed by unanimous consent, to dispense with the rule so far as to permit Mr. King, at this time, to bring in "a Bill regulating the number of Representatives to be chosen by the States of Kentucky and Vermont;"[58] which Bill was read the FIRST time, as follows:

"An ACT regulating the number of Representatives to be chosen by the States of Kentucky and Vermont "

1   "BE it enacted by the Senate and House of Representatives
2   of the United States of America, in Congress assembled, That
3   until the Representatives in Congress shall be apportioned ac-
4   cording to an actual enumeration of the inhabitants of the United
5   States, the States of Kentucky and Vermont shall each be inti-
6   tled to choose two Representatives."

It was agreed by unanimous consent, that the rule be so far dispensed with as that this Bill be now read the SECOND time.

ORDERED, That this Bill pass to the THIRD reading.[59]

---

[55] The bill is in Engrossed House Bills, House Records, DNA.

[56] On February 12 this bill was read a second time, and consideration of it was postponed.

[57] On February 12 this bill was read a third time, passed, and sent to the House for concurrence.

[58] This bill is in Senate Bills, Senate Records, DNA.

[59] On February 12 this bill was read a third time, passed, and sent to the House for concurrence.

Mr. Morris reported from the Committee instructed to consider the fourth section of the Bill, entitled, "An Act repealing after the last day of June next, the duties heretofore laid upon distilled spirits imported from abroad, and laying others in their stead; and also upon spirits distilled within the United States, and for appropriating the same," a further amendment;[60] and the report was adopted.

ORDERED, That the Report and the Bill be re-committed, and that the Committee be instructed to conform the Bill to the several amendments agreed on.[61]

The Senate adjourned to 11 o'clock to-morrow.

SATURDAY, FEBRUARY 12, 1791

The SENATE assembled—present as yesterday, and

Agreeably to the order of the day, proceeded to the THIRD reading of the Bill, "for the admission of the State of Vermont into this union."

RESOLVED, That this Bill DO PASS, and that the title of it be "An Act for the admission of the State of Vermont into this union."[62]

ORDERED, That the Secretary carry this Bill to the House of Representatives, and desire concurrence therein.[63]

The Senate proceeded to the THIRD reading of the "Bill regulating the number of Representatives to be chosen by the States of Kentucky and Vermont."

RESOLVED, That this Bill DO PASS, and that the title thereof be "An Act regulating the number of Representatives to be chosen by the States of Kentucky and Vermont."[64]

ORDERED, That the Secretary carry this Bill to the House of Representatives, and desire concurrence therein.[65]

The Senate proceeded to the consideration of the report of the joint Committee appointed "to confer on and report what time will be proper for the commencement of the next session of Congress," and—

ORDERED, That the further consideration hereof be postponed to this day se'nnight.

---

[60] This report is in Various Select Committee Reports, Senate Records, DNA.

[61] On February 12 this committee reported. A motion to amend the bill was defeated. The bill was then passed by a roll-call vote with amendments which were printed in the Journal. The House was notified of this action.

[62] The resolve, noted on the engrossed bill, is in Engrossed Senate Bills and Resolutions, Senate Records, DNA.

[63] On February 12 the House read this bill the first and second times. On February 14 it was considered in the committee of the whole, read a third time, and passed. The Senate was notified of this action.

[64] The resolve, noted on the engrossed bill, is in Engrossed Senate Bills and Resolutions, Senate Records, DNA.

[65] The House received this bill on this date and read it the first and second times. On February 19 the House considered it in the committee of the whole, passed it, and notified the Senate.

The resolution of the House of Representatives of the 28th January, on the report of the joint Committee on this subject, was read.

ORDERED, That the consideration thereof be postponed to the same time.[66]

Mr. Foster, from the Committee on enrolled Bills, reported, That they had examined the enrolled Bill, entitled, "An Act to incorporate the subscribers to the bank of the United States,"[67] and that it was correct.

A message from the House of Representatives by Mr. Beckley their clerk:

"Mr. PRESIDENT,

"The Speaker of the House of Representatives having signed an enrolled Bill, I am directed to bring it to the Senate, for the signature of the Vice President,"—

And he withdrew.

The Vice President signed the enrolled Bill, entitled, "An Act to incorporate the subscribers to the bank of the United States," and it was delivered to the Committee on enrolled Bills, to be laid before the President of the United States for his approbation.[68]

The Bill, entitled, "An Act to alter the time of the next meeting of Congress," was read the SECOND time, and—

ORDERED, That the further consideration hereof be postponed to this day se'nnight.[69]

The Bill, entitled, "An Act authorising the President of the United States to cause the debt due to foreign officers, to be paid and discharged," was read the SECOND time, and

ORDERED, That this Bill be committed to

> Mr. Maclay
> Mr. Dickinson and
> Mr. Wingate, to consider and report what is proper

to be done thereon.[70]

The Bill, entitled, "An Act to continue in force for a limited time, an Act passed at the first session of Congress, entitled, 'An Act to regulate processes in the courts of the United States,' " was read the SECOND time.

ORDERED, That this Bill pass to the THIRD reading.[71]

Mr. Morris reported from the Committee to whom was re-committed the

---

[66] On February 19 this report and resolution were again postponed.

[67] The inspected enrolled bill is in Enrolled Acts, RG 11, DNA. E–23875.

[68] On February 14 the committee on enrolled bills reported that it had delivered this bill to the President.

[69] On February 19 consideration of this bill was postponed.

[70] This vote for committee is in Other Records: Yeas and nays, Senate Records, DNA. On February 22 this committee reported and the report was laid for consideration.

[71] On February 14 this bill was read a third time and passed, and the House was notified.

Bill, entitled, "An Act repealing after the last day of June next, the duties heretofore laid upon distilled spirits imported from abroad, and laying others in their stead; and also upon spirits distilled within the United States, and for appropriating the same."[72]

On motion, "That the rates of duties on imported spirits be so increased as that the sums payable on imported spirits shall be one third higher than the duties payable on spirits of similar proof, distilled within the United States, from foreign materials,"[73]—

It passed in the Negative.

On the question, shall this Bill pass as amended? the yeas and nays were required by one fifth of the Senators present:

Mr. Bassett	Yea	
Mr. Butler	Yea	
Mr. Carroll	Yea	
Mr. Dalton		Nay
Mr. Dickinson	Yea	
Mr. Ellsworth	Yea	
Mr. Elmer	Yea	
Mr. Few	Yea	
Mr. Foster		Nay
Mr. Gunn		Nay
Mr. Hawkins	Yea	
Mr. Henry	Yea	
Mr. Johnson	Yea	
Mr. Johnston	Yea	
Mr. Izard	Yea	
Mr. King	Yea	
Mr. Langdon	Yea	
Mr. Maclay		Nay
Mr. Monroe	Yea	
Mr. Morris	Yea	
Mr. Read	Yea	
Mr. Schuyler	Yea	
Mr. Stanton	Yea	
Mr. Strong		Nay
Mr. Wingate	Yea	

Yeas—20
Nays—5[74]

So it was,

---

[72] This report has not been located.
[73] This motion is in Various Select Committee Reports, Senate Records, DNA.
[74] This vote is in Other Records: Yeas and nays, Senate Records, DNA.

RESOLVED, That this Bill PASS, with the following amendments:

SECT. III. Line 3d, after "fifty," insert "and shall not amount to more than five hundred."

Lines 6, 7, expunge "of one moiety thereof in three months, and the other moiety thereof in six months," and substitute "thereof in four months; and if the amount of the said duties shall exceed five hundred dollars, the same may be immediately paid or secured by bond, with condition for the payment thereof in six months."

Line 8, after "bond," insert "in either case."

Line 20, expunge from the word "made," to the word "shall," in the 23d line, and substitute "and if at the expiration of the time mentioned in the bond for the payment of the duties thereby intended to be secured, the same shall not be paid, then the said deposited spirits."

Line 29, expunge from the word "Representatives," to the end of the section.

SECT. IV. Expunge the whole section, and substitute—

"In order to a due collection of the duties imposed by this Act, *Be it further enacted*, That the United States shall be divided into thirteen districts, each consisting of one State, but subject to alteration by the President of the United States, from time to time, by adding to the smaller such portion of the greater as shall in his judgment best tend to secure and facilitate the collection of the revenue; which districts it shall be lawful for the President of the United States to sub-divide into surveys of inspection, and the same to alter at his discretion.

"That the President be authorised to appoint, with the advice and consent of the Senate, a Supervisor to each district, and as many Inspectors to each survey therein as he shall judge necessary, placing the latter under the direction of the former: *Provided always*, that it shall and may be lawful for the President, with the advice and consent of the Senate, in his discretion to appoint such, and so many officers of the customs to be Inspectors, in any survey of inspection, as he shall deem advisable to employ in the execution of this Act: *Provided also*, that where in the judgment of the President, a Supervisor can discharge the duties of that office, and also that of Inspector, he may direct the same: *And provided further*, that if the appointment of the Inspectors of surveys, or any part of them, shall not be made during the present session of Congress, the President may, and he is hereby empowered to make such appointments, during the recess of the Senate, by granting commissions, which shall expire at the end of their next session."

SECT. ———. *And be it further enacted*, That the Supervisors, Inspectors and officers to be appointed by virtue of this Act, and who shall be charged to take bonds for securing the payment of the duties upon spirits distilled within the United States, and with the receipts of monies in discharge of such duties, shall keep fair and true accounts and records of their transactions in their respective offices, in such manner and form as may be directed by the proper department or officer having the superintendance of the collection of the revenue, and shall at all times submit their books, papers and accounts to the inspection of such persons as are or may be appointed for that purpose; and shall at all times pay to the order of the officer who is or shall be authorised to direct the payment thereof, the whole of the monies which they may respectively receive by virtue of this Act; and shall also once in every three months, or oftener if they shall be required, transmit their accounts for settlement, to the officer or officers whose duty it is or shall be to make such settlement.

SECT. ———. *And be it further enacted,* That all officers and persons to be appointed pursuant to this act, before they enter on the duties of their respective offices, shall take an oath or affirmation, diligently and faithfully to execute the duties of their said offices respectively, and to use their best endeavours to prevent and detect frauds in relation to the duties on spirits imposed by this Act: which oath or affirmation may be taken before any Magistrate authorised to administer oaths, within the district or survey to which he belongs, and being certified under the hand and seal of the Magistrate by whom the same shall have been administered, shall within three months thereafter, be transmitted to the Comptroller of the Treasury; in default of taking which oath or affirmation, the party failing shall forfeit and pay two hundred dollars to the use of the United States, to be recovered with costs of suit.

SECT. V. Lines 1, 2, expunge "Inspector or Inspectors;" substitute "Supervisor."

SECT. VI. Line 7, after the word "to," insert "one of;" add "s" to "Inspector."

Lines 7, 8, expunge "or other chief officer of inspection."

SECT. VII. Lines 9, 10, expunge "Inspector of the revenue or other."

SECT. VIII. Line 8, expunge "proper."

Line 9, after "inspection," insert "to whom report was made."

Line 11, after "certified," insert "or reported."

Line 14, expunge "without fee or charge."

SECT. X. Lines 3, 5, and 15, after "casks," insert "vessels."

Line 16, after "each," expunge to the end of the section, and substitute "and if such officer is not the chief Inspector within the survey, he shall as soon as may be thereafter, make an exact transcript of each entry, and deliver the same to such chief Inspector, who shall keep a like book for recording the said transcripts."

SECT. XI. Lines 1, 2, expunge "Inspector of the revenue or other."

Line 11, expunge "Inspector or other chief;" also expunge "of inspection."

Line 15, expunge "of inspection."

Line 18, after "particularly," insert "as."

SECT. XII. expunge the whole section.

SECT. XVI. Line 10, before "officer," insert "chief."

SECT. XVII. Line 1, expunge from the word "the," to the word "who," in the 4th line, and substitute "Supervisor of each district shall appoint proper officers to have the charge and survey of the distilleries within the same, assigning to each, one or more distilleries as he may think proper."

SECT. XVIII. Line 3, expunge "of inspection," and after "whose," insert "charge and."

Line 23, after "tackling," insert "and the vessel or boat, with its tackle and apparel."

SECT. XIX. At the end of the section, add, "except by consent and in presence of the officer having the charge and survey thereof, on pain of forfeiture of such spirits, or the value thereof, at the highest price in the market; to be recovered with costs of suit, from the acting owner or manager of such distillery."

SECT. XXII. Line 3, expunge "Inspector of the revenue who;" substitute "Supervisor."

Line 3, after "district," insert "who."

Lines 12, 13, expunge "Inspector or Inspectors;" substitute "Supervisors."

SECT. XXIII. Lines 3, 4, expunge "or on a paper."

Lines 7, 8, expunge "or paper."

Line 8, expunge "proper."

Line 16, expunge "or paper."

SECT. XXIV. Line 2, expunge from the preamble, after the word "imposed," and also the whole section; and after the said word "imposed," add "on spirits distilled within the United States."

SECT. XXV. Line 1, expunge "and."

Lines 2, 3, expunge "within any city, town or village," and substitute "from molasses, sugar, or other foreign materials, or from materials the growth or production of the United States."

Lines 17, 18, expunge "within any city, town or village."

Line 28, expunge "Inspector;" substitute "Supervisor."

Line 31, expunge "dealers in or."

Line 43, after the word "aforesaid," expunge to the end of the section.

SECT. XXVI. Lines 1, 2, expunge "Inspector or Inspectors;" substitute "Supervisor."

Line 7, expunge "or their."

Lines 11, 12, expunge "dealer or."

Line 14, after "stock," expunge the remainder of the section, and substitute "and the Inspector of each survey shall keep a book, wherein he shall enter the name of every distiller, and the particulars of such old stock in the possession of each, designating the several casks, cases and vessels containing the same, and their respective quantities, kinds, proofs and marks; and shall also give a certificate to every such distiller, of the quantity and particulars of such old stock in his or her possession, and a separate certificate for each cask, case or vessel, describing the same; which certificate shall accompany the same wheresoever it shall be sent. And such distiller, his or her agent or manager, upon the sale and delivery of any of the said spirits, shall deliver to the purchaser or purchasers thereof, the certificate or certificates that ought to accompany the same, on pain of forfeiting fifty dollars for each cask, case or vessel with which such certificate shall not be delivered."

SECT. XXVII. Line 5, expunge "within whose district;" substitute "at the port where."

Line 7, expunge from the word "herein," to the word "and," in the 13th line, and substitute "before directed, touching such spirits as shall be in the possession of distillers on the first day of July next, and shall grant the like certificates therefor as for such spirits; which certificates shall accompany the respective casks, cases and vessels to which they shall relate, wheresoever they shall be sent; and such importer, his or her agent, upon the sale and delivery of any of the said spirits, shall deliver to the purchaser or purchasers thereof, the certificate or certificates which ought to accompany the same, on pain of forfeiting fifty dollars for each cask, case or vessel with which such certificate shall not be delivered."

SECT. XXVIII. Expunge the whole section.

SECT. XXIX. Line 1, expunge from the word "any," to the word "it," in the 4th line, and substitute "cask, case or vessel containing distilled spirits, which by the foregoing provisions of this act, ought to be marked and accompanied with a certificate, shall be found in the possession of any person, unaccompanied with such marks and certificate."

SECT. XXX. Line 2, expunge "district," substitute "survey."

Line 5, expunge "by the said wholesale dealers."

SECT. XXXI. Expunge the whole section.

SECT. XXXIII. Line 3, expunge "dealer or."

Lines 7, 8, expunge "dealer," substitute "distiller." At the end of the section, add, "Provided that nothing in this section contained shall be construed to extend to casks or vessels capable of containing two hundred gallons and upwards, and which are not intended to be removed."

SECT. XXXIV. Lines 12, 13, expunge "in the presence of a Constable or other officer of the peace."

SECT. XXXV. Line 2, after "liquors," insert "except gin or cordials in cases, jugs or bottles."

Line 11, expunge "such."

SECT. XXXVII. Line 2, expunge "dealer by wholesale, or."

Lines 6, 7, expunge "or on a paper."

Line 12, expunge "and papers."

Line 14, expunge "dealers and;" expunge "Inspectors," substitute "Supervisors."

Line 22, expunge "and papers."

Lines 23, 24, expunge "dealers and."

Line 24, expunge, "and papers."

Lines 25, 26, expunge "dealers and."

Line 28, expunge "dealers and."

Line 30, expunge "dealer or."

Line 31, expunge "paper or papers."

SECT. XXXIX. Lines 6, 7, expunge "which words may be expressed by their respective initials."

SECT. XL. Line 2, expunge "Inspector," insert "Supervisor."

Line 11, expunge "Inspector," substitute "officer."

Line 23, expunge "or other."

At the end of the section, add, "*And provided also,* That if it shall appear from the verdict of the jury, that any such prejudice or waste was sustained by the negligence of the officer, he shall be responsible therefor to the United States."

SECT. XLI. Line 1, expunge "Inspector," substitute "Supervisor."

SECT. XLIII. Line 2, expunge "Inspector," substitute "Supervisors."

SECT. XLIV. Line 5, after the word "and," insert "unless brought in a court of the United States."

Line 5, expunge the word "proper."

SECT. XLV. Line 1, expunge the word "all."

Line 6, after the word "incurred," insert "at any time within one year after the last day of June next."

Line 7, expunge "manner," insert "way."

Line 12, after the word "thereof," expunge to the end of the section, and substitute "and shall cause the facts which shall appear upon such enquiry, to be stated and annexed to the petition, and direct their transmission to the Secretary of the Treasury of the United States, who shall thereupon have power to mitigate or remit such penalty or forfeiture, if it shall appear to him that such penalty or forfeiture was incurred without wilful negligence, or any design or intention of fraud, and to cause any spirits which may have been seized, to be restored to the proprietor or proprietors, upon such terms and conditions as shall appear to him reasonable."

SECT. XLVI. Line 14, expunge "direct," substitute "survey."

SECT. XLIX. Line 3, expunge "Inspector or;" substitute "Supervisor or other."

SECT. L. Line 2, expunge "Inspector or;" substitute "Supervisor or other." Line 6, the same amendment.

SECT. LI. Lines 1, 2, expunge "such Inspector or;" substitute "Supervisor or other."

Line 10, expunge "Inspector;" substitute "Supervisor or other."

SECT. LII. Expunge the whole section.

SECT. LV. Line 8, after "casks," insert "vessels."

Line 14, the same.

Lines 18, 19, the same.

Line 21, after "cask," insert "vessel."

SECT. LVI. Line 9, after "paid," insert "or secured to be paid."

Lines 18, 19, expunge "according to the late treaty of peace with Great-Britain."

SECT. LVIII. Line 21, from the word "inspection," expunge the remainder of the section.

SECT. LXI. Line 4, expunge "any Justice of the Peace, or court of any State of competent jurisdiction or;" substitute the word "the." Expunge the proviso.

SECT. ———. After section LXI. insert "*And be it further enacted,* That it shall and may be lawful for the President, from time to time to make such allowances to the said Supervisors, Inspectors, and to the deputies and officers by them to be appointed and employed, for their respective services in the execution of this act, to be paid out of the product of the said duties, as he shall deem reasonable and proper: *Provided always,* that the aggregate amount of the allowance to all the said Supervisors, Inspectors, deputies, and other officers, shall not exceed five per cent. of the said product computed throughout the United States; and such allowances shall continue to be paid until altered by law."

SECT. LXII. Line 5, after "districts," insert "and surveys."

SECT. LXIII. Line 4, expunge "they are," substitute "is."

Line 20, after the first word "of," expunge to the word "and," in the 25th line, and substitute "towards such purposes for which appropriations shall be made during the present sessions." Expunge the proviso, and add it to sixty-fifth section.

SECT. LXIV. Line 3, expunge "each," insert "this and every succeeding."

Line 8, expunge "to," insert "for."

The sections to be numbered to correspond with the amendments.

ORDERED, That the Secretary carry this Bill to the House of Representatives, and desire their concurrence in the amendments.[75]

A message from the House of Representatives by Mr. Beckley their clerk:

"Mr. PRESIDENT,

"The House of Representatives have passed a Bill, entitled, 'An Act for raising and adding another regiment to the military establishment of the United States, and for making further provision for the protection of the frontiers,' "[76]—

And he withdrew.

The Bill was read the FIRST time, as follows:[77]

"An ACT for raising and adding another regiment to the MILITARY ESTAB-
LISHMENT of the UNITED STATES, and for making further provision for
the PROTECTION of the FRONTIERS "

1   "SECT. I. *Be it enacted by the* SENATE *and House of* REPRESEN-
2   TATIVES *of the United States of America in Congress assembled,* That
3   there shall be raised an additional regiment of infantry, which,
4   exclusive of the commissioned officers, shall consist of nine hun-
5   dred and twelve non-commissioned officers, privates and musicians.

1   "SECT. II. *And be it further enacted,* That the said regiment
2   shall be organized in the same manner as the regiment of infan-
3   try described in the Act, entitled, 'An Act for regulating the
4   military establishment of the United States.'

1   "SECT. III. *And be it further enacted,* That the troops aforesaid
2   by this Act to be raised, including the officers, shall receive the
3   same pay and allowances, be subject to the same rules and regu-
4   lations, and be engaged upon the same conditions, in all respects,
5   excepting the bounty herein after-mentioned, as are stipulated for
6   the troops of the United States, in the before-mentioned act.

---

[75] The House committed these amendments to the committee of the whole which discharged them on February 17. On that date some of the Senate amendments were agreed
to. On February 18 the Senate amendments were considered again and more of them
were agreed to. On February 19 the House agreed to all the Senate amendments—
except the amendment to the thirty-fourth section—with amendments, and the Senate
was notified on February 21. On the same day the Senate receded from its amendment
to the thirty-fourth section and agreed to all the House amendments except one following the sixty-first section, which it amended. Several wording amendments were agreed
to, and the House was notified of these actions.

[76] This printed bill is in House Bills, Senate Records, DNA.

[77] The text of the bill does not appear in the rough journal, but there is a note to
the copyist in Otis's hand: "(Here insert the Bill)."

1   "SECT. IV. *And be it further enacted*, That all non-commissioned
2   officers, privates and musicians, who have inlisted or shall inlist
3   upon the terms prescribed in the aforesaid act, shall be entitled to
4   receive six dollars as a bounty.

1   "SECT. V. *And be it further enacted*, That for defraying the
2   expence of the aforesaid additional troops by this act to be raised
3   for the term of one year, there be appropriated a sum not ex-
4   ceeding one hundred and twenty thousand two hundred and
5   seventy-six dollars and twenty cents, to be paid out of the mo-
6   nies which, prior to the first of January next, shall arise from
7   the duties imposed by the act passed during the present session of
8   Congress, entitled, 'An Act repealing, after the last day of
9   June next, the duties heretofore laid upon distilled spirits impor-
10   ted from abroad, and laying others in their stead; and also upon
11   spirits distilled within the United States, and for appropriating
12   the same.'

1   "SECT. VI. *And be it further enacted*, That in case the Presi-
2   dent of the United States should deem the employment of a
3   Major-General, Brigadier-General, a Quarter-Master and Chap-
4   lain, or either of them, essential to the public interest, that he
5   be, and he hereby is empowered, by and with the advice and con-
6   sent of the Senate, to appoint the same accordingly. And a
7   Major-General so appointed, may chuse his Aid-de-Camp, and a
8   Brigadier-General his Brigade-Major, from the Captains or Su-
9   balterns of the line.

1   "SECT. VII. *And be it further enacted*, That in case a Major-
2   General, Brigadier-General, Quarter-Master, Aid-de-Camp, Bri-
3   gade-Major and Chaplain should be appointed, their pay and
4   allowances shall be, respectively, as herein mentioned. The
5   Major-General shall be entitled to one hundred and twenty-
6   five dollars monthly pay, twenty dollars allowance for forage,
7   monthly, and for daily subsistence fifteen rations, or money in
8   lieu thereof, at the contract price. The Brigadier-General shall
9   be entitled to ninety-four dollars monthly pay, with sixteen dol-
10   lars allowance for forage, monthly, and for daily subsistence
11   twelve rations, or money in lieu thereof at the contract price.
12   That the Quarter-Master shall be entitled to the same pay, ra-
13   tions and forage, as the Lieutenant-Colonel Commandant of a
14   regiment. That the Aid-de-Camp be entitled, including all al-
15   lowances, to the same pay, rations and forage, as a Major of a

16 regiment. That the Brigade-Major be entitled, including all
17 allowances, to the same pay, rations and forage as a Major of
18 a regiment. That the Chaplain be entitled to fifty dollars per
19 month.

1 "SECT. VIII. *And be it further enacted,* That if, in the opinion
2 of the President, it will be conducive to the good of the service,
3 to engage a body of militia to serve as cavalry, they furnishing
4 their own horses, arms and provisions, it shall be lawful for him
5 to offer such allowances to encourage their engaging in the service
6 for such time, and on such terms, as he shall deem it expedient to
7 prescribe. *Provided,* That such allowances shall not exceed the
8 sum herein after appropriated.

1 "SECT. IX. *And be further enacted,* That to enable the Pre-
2 sident, in virtue of the powers vested in him by law, to call into
3 the service of the United States, such number of the militia as he
4 shall deem necessary for the public service, there be appropriated
5 a sum not exceeding one hundred and ninety-two thousand four
6 hundred and ten dollars, as well to defray the expence of such
7 militia, whether cavalry or infantry, or of such military opera-
8 tions as he may direct, and also of such posts as he may think it
9 expedient to establish, to be paid out of the monies which, prior
10 to the first day of January next, shall arise from the duties im-
11 posed by the aforesaid act of the present session of Congress.

1 "SECT. X. *Provided nevertheless, and be it further enacted,* That
2 if the President should be of opinion, that it would be more con-
3 ducive to the public service to employ troops inlisted under the
4 denomination of levies, than militia, it shall be lawful for him
5 to raise, for a term not exceeding four months, a corps of two
6 thousand non-commissioned officers, privates, and musicians, with
7 a suitable number of commissioned officers: *Provided,* That the
8 expenses thereof shall not exceed the sum heretofore appropri-
9 ated in the ninth section of this act.

1 "SECT. XI. *And be it further enacted,* That the President be,
2 and he hereby is empowered to organize the said levies, and
3 alone to appoint the commissioned officers thereof, in the man-
4 ner he may judge proper.

1 "SECT. XII. *And be it further enacted,* That the commissioned
2 and non-commissioned officers, privates, and musicians of the
3 militia, or said corps of levies, shall, during the time of their
4 service, be subject to the rules and articles of war; and they

5 shall be entitled to the same pay, rations, and forage, and in
6 cases of wounds and disability in the line of their duty, to the
7 same compensation as the troops of the United States.
1   "SECT. XIII. *And be it further enacted*, That the non-commis-
2 sioned officers, privates and musicians of the said corps of levies,
3 shall be entitled to receive such proportional quantity of cloth-
4 ing, as their time of service shall bear to the annual allowance
5 of clothing to the troops of the United States, subject however,
6 to a proportional deduction from their pay.
1   "SECT. XIV. *And be it further enacted*, That the non-commis-
2 sioned officers, privates and musicians of the said levies, shall be
3 entitled to receive three dollars as a bounty."
1791, February the 12th—Passed the House of Representatives.

ORDERED, That this Bill pass to the SECOND reading, and that it be printed[78] for the use of the Senate.[79]

The Senate adjourned to Monday next, at 11 o'clock.

M O N D A Y, FEBRUARY 14, 1791

The SENATE assembled—present as on the 12th instant.

A message from the House of Representatives by Mr. Beckley their clerk:

"Mr. PRESIDENT,

"The House of Representatives have passed the Bill sent from the Senate, entitled, 'An Act for the admission of the State of Vermont into this union,'[80]—

"I am directed to bring to the Senate, the resolution of the House of Representatives, on the petition of Andrew Brown, with the report of the Secretary of State thereon,"[81]—

And he withdrew.

Mr. Foster, from the Committee on enrolled Bills, reported, That they had this day laid before the President of the United States, for his approbation, the Bill, entitled, "An Act to incorporate the subscribers to the bank of the United States."[82]

---

[78] The rough journal adds the phrase "under injunctions of Secrecy."

[79] On February 14 this bill was read a second time and committed.

[80] On February 16 this bill was signed by both the Speaker and the Vice President and given to the committee on enrolled bills for delivery to the President.

[81] This resolve is in Messages from the House, Senate Records, DNA. The report is in A Record of the Reports of the Secretary of State, vol. 1, House Records, DNA.

[82] On February 25 the President signed this bill. On the same day the bill was printed in the Journal.

On motion,

ORDERED, That the resolutions of the Assembly of Virginia, upon the claims of sundry individuals, with the papers accompanying them, be referred to the Committee appointed the thirty-first of January, to take into consideration the extract of a letter from governor Randolph, relative to the bounty lands to the officers and soldiers of the Virginia line, on continental establishment.[83]

The Senate proceeded to the THIRD reading of the Bill sent from the House of Representatives for concurrence, entitled, "An Act to continue in force for a limited time an Act passed at the first session of Congress, entitled, 'An Act to regulate processes in the courts of the United States.'"

RESOLVED, That this Bill PASS.

ORDERED, That the Secretary acquaint the House of Representatives, with the concurrence of the Senate in this Bill.[84]

The Senate proceeded to the SECOND reading of the Bill sent from the House of Representatives, entitled, "An Act for raising and adding another regiment to the military establishment of the United States, and for making further provision for the protection of the frontiers."

ORDERED, That this Bill be committed to

Mr. Gunn
Mr. Schuyler
Mr. Dickinson
Mr. Hawkins and
Mr. Strong[85]

The resolution of the House of Representatives, of the 12th inst. upon the petition of Andrew Brown, printer, was read as follows:

"The House proceeded to consider the report of the Secretary of State, on the petition of Andrew Brown; whereupon—

1   "RESOLVED, That Andrew Brown, or any other printer,
2   be permitted, under the direction of the Secretary of State, to
3   collate with and correct by the original rolls, the laws, resolu-
4   tions and treaties of the United States, to be by him printed;
5   and that a certificate of their having been so collated and cor-
6   rected, be annexed to the said edition.

---

[83] This motion is in Senate Simple Resolutions and Motions, Senate Records, DNA. On March 3 this committee reported, and the report, which was printed in the Journal, was agreed to.

[84] On February 16 this bill was signed by both the Speaker and the Vice President and given to the committee on enrolled bills for delivery to the President.

[85] This vote for committee is in Other Records: Yeas and nays, Senate Records, DNA. On February 17 this committee reported amendments to the bill, and consideration was postponed.

7   "Provided that such collation and correction be at the ex-
8   pense of the said Andrew Brown, or such other printer, and
9   that the person or persons to be by him or them employed in
10   that service, be approved by the Secretary of State."

ORDERED, That the consideration of this resolution be deferred until to-morrow.[86]

A written message from the President of the United States, was communicated by Mr. Lear his Secretary,—

And he withdrew.

UNITED STATES, February the 14th, 1791

GENTLEMEN of the SENATE and of the

    HOUSE of REPRESENTATIVES

SOON after I was called to the administration of the government, I found it important to come to an understanding with the court of London, on several points interesting to the United States, and particularly to know whether they were disposed to enter into arrangements, by mutual consent, which might fix the commerce between the two nations on principles of reciprocal advantage: for this purpose I authorised informal conferences with their ministers, and from these I do not infer any disposition, on their part, to enter into any arrangements merely commercial. I have thought it proper to give you this information, as it might at some time have influence on matters under your consideration.

G. WASHINGTON[87]

ORDERED, That the message from the President of the United States, lie for consideration.

The Senate adjourned to 11 o'clock to-morrow.

TUESDAY, FEBRUARY 15, 1791

The SENATE assembled—present as yesterday, and

The Honorable Richard Henry Lee, from the State of Virginia, attended.

The petition of Donald Campbell,[88] praying compensation for services during the late war, was read.

ORDERED, That it be committed to

        Mr. Langdon

        Mr. King and

        Mr. Dickinson, to consider and report thereon.[89]

---

[86] On February 15 this resolution was considered and concurred in.

[87] The message is in the George Washington Papers, series 2, vol. 25, reel 9, Manuscript Division, DLC.

[88] This petition is in Petitions and Memorials: Claims, Senate Records, DNA.

[89] This vote for committee is in Other Records: Yeas and nays, Senate Records, DNA. On February 18 this committee reported and the report was disagreed to. The petition of Donald Campbell was dismissed.

The Senate proceeded to the consideration of the resolution of the House of Representatives of the 12th inst. on the petition of Andrew Brown, printer,[90] and—

RESOLVED, That they concur in the said resolution.

ORDERED, That the Secretary acquaint the House of Representatives, with the concurrence of the Senate in this resolution.[91]

Mr. Foster, from the Committee on enrolled Bills, reported, That they had examined the enrolled Bill, entitled, "An Act for the admission of the State of Vermont into this union,"[92] and had found it correct.

The Senate adjourned to 11 o'clock to-morrow.

WEDNESDAY, FEBRUARY 16, 1791

The SENATE assembled—present as yesterday.

Mr. Carroll gave notice, that to-morrow he intended to move for leave to bring in a Bill to amend the act, entitled, "An Act for establishing the temporary and permanent seat of the government of the United States," pursuant to the plan suggested in the President's message of the 24th of January last.[93]

On motion,

ORDERED, That the Secretary of the Treasury cause a statement of the exports of the United States for one year, to be laid before the Senate; enumerating therein the articles of export, the value thereof, and the countries to which the same shall have been exported.[94]

The petition of the Masters of American vessels in the port of Charleston, South-Carolina,[95] praying some further regulations for the encouragement of the carrying trade to Europe, was read.

ORDERED, That this petition lie on the table.

Mr. Foster, from the Committee on enrolled Bills, reported, That they had examined the enrolled Bill, entitled, "An Act to continue in force for a limited time, an Act passed at the first session of Congress, entitled, 'An Act to regulate processes in the courts of the United States;' "[96] and the enrolled

---

[90] In the rough journal this paragraph reads: "The Senate consideration of the Resolution of the House of Represents of the 12th instant, on the petition of Andrew Brown, printer was resumed."

[91] On February 16 this resolve was signed by both the Speaker and the Vice President and given to the committee on enrolled bills for delivery to the President.

[92] The inspected enrolled bill is in Enrolled Acts, RG 11, DNA. E–23856.

[93] This motion is in Senate Simple Resolutions and Motions, Senate Records, DNA. On February 17, after a vote on whether or not to allow the bill to be brought in, Mr. Carroll introduced an amendatory Residence Bill which was read the first time, printed in the Journal, and passed to the second reading.

[94] This motion is in Senate Simple Resolutions and Motions, Senate Records, DNA.

[95] This petition is in Petitions and Memorials: Various subjects, Senate Records, DNA.

[96] The inspected enrolled bill is in Enrolled Acts, RG 11, DNA. E–23872.

"Resolution authorising Andrew Brown, printer, to publish the laws of the
United States;"[97] and that they were duly enrolled.

A message from the House of Representatives by Mr. Beckley their clerk:

"Mr. PRESIDENT,

"The House of Representatives have passed a Bill, entitled, 'An Act to
establish offices for the purpose of granting lands within the territories of the
United States,'[98] in which they desire the concurrence of the Senate,—

"The Speaker of the House of Representatives having signed two enrolled
Bills, and an enrolled Resolution, I am directed to bring them to the Senate
for the signature of the Vice President,"—

And he withdrew.

The Vice President signed the enrolled Bill, entitled, "An Act to continue
in force for a limited time, an Act passed at the first session of Congress, entitled, 'An Act to regulate processes in the courts of the United States.' "—The
enrolled Bill, entitled, "An Act for the admission of the State of Vermont into
this union."—And the enrolled "Resolution authorising Andrew Brown,
printer, to publish the laws of the United States;" and they were delivered to
the Committee on enrolled Bills, to be laid before the President of the United
States, for his approbation.[99]

The Bill sent from the House of Representatives for concurrence, entitled,
"An Act to establish offices for the purpose of granting lands within the
territories of the United States," was read the FIRST time, as follows:[100]

"An ACT to establish OFFICES for the purpose of granting LANDS within the
    territories of the UNITED STATES."

1   "SECT. I. *Be it enacted by the* SENATE *and House of* REPRESEN-
2   TATIVES *of the United States of America in Congress assembled,* That
3   an office shall be established at the seat of the government of the
4   United States, for the purpose of granting Lands within the terri-
5   tories of the United States: And that two subordinate offices shall
6   be established for the same purpose—one in the territory north-
7   west of the Ohio, and the other in the territory south of the Ohio.
8   That no lands shall be sold or granted, except those to which the
9   titles of the Indian tribes shall have been previously extinguished.

---

[97] The inspected enrolled resolve is in Enrolled Acts, RG 11, DNA. E–23878.

[98] This bill is in Engrossed House Bills, House Records, DNA. A printed copy is in
the Broadside Collection. RBkRm, DLC. E–46310.

[99] On February 17 this committee reported that it had presented these bills and the
resolve to the President.

[100] The text of the bill does not appear in the rough journal, but two notes to the
copyist are included:

 here recite the
Bill. (S)   /   This Bill in
                                          part printed

10 That the seven ranges of townships already surveyed, shall be
11 sold in lots as they are laid out. That any quantities of other
12 land may be sold by special contract. That convenient tracts
13 from time to time be set apart for the purpose of locations by
14 actual settlers. That the Superintendants of each subordinate
15 office, shall have the management of all sales, and the issuing of
16 warrants for all locations in the tracts to be set apart for the
17 accommodation of individual settlers, subject to the direction of
18 the Superintendant of the general land-office, who may also com-
19 mit to them the management of any other sales or locations,
20 which it may be found expedient to place under their direction.

1 "SECT. II. *And be it further enacted*, That the price of all land
2 sold or granted by the United States, shall be twenty-five cents
3 per acre, except such as may be sold by special contract, and
4 such as may be granted as bounties for military services; the
5 warrants for which last mentioned lands shall be located, survey-
6 ed and patented, in the same manner as warrants issuing from
7 the land-office, in consideration of the payment of money, and
8 the exclusive right of locating such warrants in districts, set apart
9 for the army, shall cease from and after the first day of May,
10 one thousand seven hundred and ninety-four: *Provided always*,
11 That any purchaser of lands, when the payment thereof shall be
12 due, may proffer in payment any of the certificates of the funded
13 debt of the United States, at the same rates as the Treasurer
14 shall have allowed for such certificates, respectively, in the last
15 purchase which he shall have made thereof prior to such pay-
16 ment.

1 "SECT. III. *And be it further enacted*, That no credit shall be
2 given for any quantity of land less than twenty-three thousand
3 acres; and no credit shall be given for any quantity, unless one
4 quarter part of the price shall be paid down, and sufficient se-
5 curity (other than the land sold) given for the payment of the
6 residue within two years. And that no patent shall issue, or
7 title be made for any part of a tract of land purchased, beyond
8 the proportion for which the money shall be actually paid.

1 "SECT. IV. *And be it further enacted*, That all persons who have
2 really and bona fide settled on unappropriated land, in either of
3 the said territories, and have made improvements thereon,
4 the titles to which lands are not, or might not have been se-
5 cured by the governments of those territories, or by the acts or
6 ordinances of Congress, shall be entitled to six hundred and forty

7   acres each, including their respective improvements. *Provided*
8   that such settlers shall, within twelve months after the passing
9   of this act, pay to the Secretary of the territory, in which the
10 settlement hath been made, the stated price for the land to which
11 such settler is entitled by virtue of his improvement, or for so
12 much thereof as he shall incline to take, and prove by the oath
13 or affirmation of two or more credible persons, their residence
14 and improvements; a certified copy of which oath or affirma-
15 tion shall be produced to the said Secretary, to be by him filed in
16 his office.

1   "SECT. V.   *And be it further enacted*, That a Surveyor of lands
2   shall be appointed in each of the said territories, who may ap-
3   point as many Deputy-Surveyors as may be necessary to assist
4   them in executing all warrants to them respectively directed,
5   which warrants shall be signed by the Superintendant of the res-
6   pective offices, and directed to the Surveyor of the territory in
7   which the land to be located lies. The priority of location of
8   warrants shall be determined by the time of application to the
9   Surveyor, and in case of two applications at the same time for
10 the same land, the priority shall be determined by lot.

1   "SECT. VI.   *And be it further enacted*, That the Treasurer of
2   the United States shall be the receiver of all monies to be paid
3   for lands granted at the general land-office, and that the Secre-
4   taries of the government established in the said territories, shall
5   be the receivers of all monies arising from the sales or grants of
6   land at the offices of their respective territories. And that any
7   person paying into his, or their hands, a sum of money for the
8   purchase of land, shall be entitled to a receipt expressing the sum
9   paid, and the quantity of land to be granted in consideration
10 thereof; on producing of which receipt to the Superintendant
11 of the proper office, and lodging the same with him to be record-
12 ed, the Superintendant shall issue a warrant directed to the Sur-
13 veyor of the territory, specifying the quantity of land purchased,
14 and authorizing him to cause the same to be surveyed agreeably
15 to the established rules of the land-office. And where the money
16 shall be paid for a settlement-right, the receipt shall so express;
17 on producing which receipt to the Superintendant of the land-
18 office of the territory in which the land may be, a warrant shall
19 issue, and the same proceedings be had thereon, as in cases of
20 money paid to the Treasurer of the United States for the like
21 quantity.

1   "SECT. VII. *And be it further enacted*, That the Superinten-
2   dant of the general land-office, the Surveyor, and the Superin-
3   tendants of the land-offices in each of the said territories, shall
4   not purchase any public lands, and shall be incapable of holding
5   any such lands as may be purchased by them, or by any person
6   for their use, during their continuance in office.

1   "SECT. VIII. *And be it further enacted*, That all patents shall
2   be signed by the President of the United States, and shall be
3   recorded in the office of the Secretary of State.

1   "SECT. IX. *And be it further enacted*, That all officers to be
2   appointed by virtue of this act, shall take an oath or affirmation,
3   before some judge or magistrate of the United States, that they
4   will faithfully discharge the duties of their respective offices; a
5   certificate of which oath or affirmation, shall be returned to the
6   general land-office, or to the land-office of the territory in which
7   the duties are to be performed, previous to their entering upon
8   the execution of their offices.

1   "SECT. X. *And be it further enacted*, That the Secretaries of
2   the said governments shall give bond, with sufficient sureties, in
3   the sum of ten thousand dollars each, for the faithful discharge
4   of their duty, as receivers of the money arising from the sale
5   of land at their respective offices.

1   "SECT. XI. *And be it further enacted*, That the Superintendant
2   of the general land-office may agree with any person or persons
3   for the sale of any quantity of land, not less than twenty-three
4   thousand acres, to be located in one body, and particularly de-
5   scribed by natural boundaries, or by lines to be run and plainly
6   marked by the Surveyor of the district or territory in which the
7   land may lie, at the expence of the purchaser or purchasers,
8   provided the price be not less than twenty cents per acre.

1   "SECT. XII. *And be it further enacted*, That the Superintend-
2   ant of the general land-office shall have power to establish all
3   such rules and regulations as he shall judge necessary, respecting
4   the form, time, and manner of locating warrants for lands, of
5   making and returning surveys, issuing patents thereupon, enter-
6   ing caveats and proceedings preparatory to the trial thereof, and
7   all such other rules and regulations as shall be necessary to carry
8   this act into effect, according to the true intent and meaning
9   thereof; which rules he shall cause to be published, in one ga-
10   zette at least, in each of the United States, and in each of the
11   said territories in which there may be a gazette.

1   "SECT. XIII. *And be it further enacted*, That controversies
2   concerning rights to patents or grants shall be determined by the
3   Superintendant of that office, under whose immediate direction
4   or jurisdiction the locations in respect to which they may arise,
5   shall have been made: *Provided*, That no determination of such
6   Superintendants shall be construed to prevent either of the par-
7   ties from bringing their action or actions, suit or suits, in law or
8   equity, for the final decision of their rights to the lands in dis-
9   pute, or for recovering damages for waste or trespass committed
10   thereon.

1   "SECT. XIV. *And be it further enacted*, That the Attorney-
2   General of the United States shall, by virtue of his office, be Su-
3   perintendant of the general land-office; and that the Governors
4   of the said territories shall, by virtue of their offices, be Super-
5   intendants of the subordinate land-offices within their respective
6   governments.

1   "SECT. XV. *And be it further enacted*, That a separate account
2   shall be kept at the Treasury, of the monies arising from the sale
3   of the aforesaid lands; and the said monies shall be, and they are
4   hereby appropriated to the purchase of the debt of the United
5   States, according to the terms of the 'Act making provision
6   for the reduction of the public debt.' "

1791, February the 16th,—Passed the House of Representatives, and sent to
the Senate for concurrence.

ORDERED, That this Bill pass to the SECOND reading, and that in the mean
time it be printed for the use of the Senate.[101]

The Senate adjourned to 11 o'clock to-morrow.

THURSDAY, FEBRUARY 17, 1791

The SENATE assembled—present as yesterday, and

Proceeded in the SECOND reading of the Bill, entitled, "An Act to establish
offices for the purpose of granting lands within the territories of the United
States."

ORDERED, That the further consideration hereof be postponed.[102]

Agreeably to notice given yesterday, leave was requested to bring in a Bill
to amend an Act, entitled, "An Act for establishing the temporary and
permanent seat of the government of the United States,"—

[101] On February 17 this bill was read a second time and postponed.
[102] On February 18 this bill was considered again.

And on the question, shall leave be given to bring in the Bill moved for?
The yeas and nays were required by one fifth of the Senators present.

Mr. Butler		Yea
Mr. Carroll		Yea
Mr. Dalton	Nay	
Mr. Dickinson		Yea
Mr. Ellsworth	Nay	
Mr. Elmer		Yea
Mr. Few		Yea
Mr. Foster	Nay	
Mr. Gunn		Yea
Mr. Hawkins		Yea
Mr. Henry		Yea
Mr. Johnson	Nay	
Mr. Johnston		Yea
Mr. Izard		Yea
Mr. King	Nay	
Mr. Langdon		Yea
Mr. Lee		Yea
Mr. Maclay	Nay	
Mr. Monroe		Yea
Mr. Morris		Yea
Mr. Read		Yea
Mr. Stanton		Yea
Mr. Strong		Yea
Mr. Wingate	Nay	

Yeas—17
Nays—7[103]

So it passed in the Affirmative—

And the Bill was accordingly brought in and read the FIRST time as
follows:[104]

"An ACT to amend 'An Act for establishing the temporary and permanent
SEAT of the GOVERNMENT of the UNITED STATES ' "

1   *Be it enacted by the* SENATE *and House of* REPRESENTATIVES *of*
2   *the United States of America in Congress assembled,* That so much of
3   the Act, entitled, "An Act for establishing the temporary and
4   permanent seat of the government of the United States," as
5   requires that the whole of the district of territory not exceeding
6   ten miles square to be located on the river Potowmac, for the

---

[103] This vote is in Other Records: Yeas and nays, Senate Records, DNA.
[104] Two annotated copies of this bill are in Senate Bills, Senate Records, DNA.

7 permanent seat of the government of the United States, shall
8 be located above the mouth of the eastern branch, be and is here-
9 by repealed; and that it shall be lawful for the President of the
10 United States to make any part of the territory below the said
11 limit and above the mouth of the Hunting Creek, a part of the
12 said district, so as to include a convenient part of the eastern
13 branch and of the lands lying on the lower side thereof, and also
14 the town of Alexandria; and the territory so to be included shall
15 form a part of the district not exceeding ten miles square, for the
16 permanent seat of the government of the United States, in like
17 manner and to all intents and purposes as if the same had been
18 within the purview of the above recited Act: *Provided*, That
19 nothing herein contained shall authorize the erection of the
20 public buildings otherwise than on the Maryland side of the river
21 Potowmac, as required by the aforesaid Act.

ORDERED, That this Bill pass to the SECOND reading.[105]

Mr. Schuyler from the Committee appointed to take into consideration the Bill sent from the House of Representatives for concurrence, entitled, "An Act for raising and adding another regiment to the military establishment of the United States, and for making further provision for the protection of the frontiers," reported the Bill amended.[106]

ORDERED, That the amendments be printed for the consideration of the Senate.[107]

Mr. Foster from the Committee on enrolled Bills, reported, That they had this day laid before the President of the United States, the Bill, entitled, "An Act for the admission of the State of Vermont into this union." The Bill, en-titled, "An Act to continue in force for a limited time, an Act passed at the first session of Congress, entitled, 'An Act to regulate processes in the courts of the United States.' " And the resolution authorizing Andrew Brown to print the laws of the United States.[108]

The Senate adjourned to 11 o'clock to-morrow.

---

[105] On February 18 this bill was read a second time and consideration of it was post-poned by a roll-call vote.

[106] A list of amendments attached to the bill probably was from this committee and is located in House Bills, Senate Records, DNA.

[107] On February 19 the Senate agreed to the first section of this bill and amended the tenth section. The committee reported amendments which were adopted. The bill then passed to the third reading.

[108] On February 18 the President signed these bills and this resolve, and the Senate was notified.

FRIDAY, FEBRUARY 18, 1791

The SENATE assembled—present as yesterday.

A message from the President of the United States, by Mr. Lear his Secretary:

"Mr. PRESIDENT,

"The President of the United States has this day approved and signed 'The Act for the admission of the State of Vermont into this union,'—

"He also delivered the following written message from the President of the United States,"—

And he withdrew.

UNITED STATES, February 18, 1791

GENTLEMEN of the SENATE and
HOUSE of REPRESENTATIVES,

I HAVE received from the Secretary of State, a report on the proceedings of the Governor of the north western territory at Kaskaskia, Kahokia and Prairie, under the resolution of Congress of August 29th 1788, which containing matter proper for your consideration, I lay the same before you.

G. WASHINGTON[109]

ORDERED, That the message and papers therein referred to, lie for consideration.

ORDERED, That the Secretary acquaint the House of Representatives, that the President of the United States has this day approved and signed "The Act for the admission of the State of Vermont into this union."

Mr. Langdon from the Committee appointed to take into consideration the petition of Donald Campbell, reported,[110] "That he be allowed six hundred and ninety-five dollars, and twenty three ninetieths, that sum being the difference between two and a half per cent. heretofore allowed, and five per cent. on the transactions of his department, to which he is entitled by the resolutions of Congress; together with interest thereon from the time of performing the said service: The foregoing allowance to be in full of all claims and demands of the said Donald Campbell, against the United States."

To which report the Senate did not agree; and on motion—

ORDERED, That the memorial of Donald Campbell be dismissed, his claims having been fully and repeatedly stated and decided on.[111]

Agreeably to the order of the day, the Senate proceeded in the SECOND

---

[109] This message, including documents, is in President's Messages: Transmitting reports from the Secretary of State, Senate Records, DNA.

[110] This report is in Various Select Committee Reports, Senate Records, DNA.

[111] This motion is in Senate Simple Resolutions and Motions, Senate Records, DNA.

reading of the Bill, entitled, "An Act to establish offices for the purpose of granting lands within the territories of the United States."

ORDERED, That the consideration thereof be postponed.[112]

A message from the House of Representatives by Mr. Beckley their clerk:

"Mr. PRESIDENT,

"The President of the United States has notified the House of Representatives that he has this day approved and signed 'The Act to continue in force for a limited time, an Act passed at the first session of Congress, entitled, "An Act to regulate processes in the courts of the United States." '—

"Also the resolution of Congress granting permission to Andrew Brown, or any other printer, to print the laws of the United States, under certain regulations therein contained."[113]—

And he withdrew.

The Senate proceeded to the SECOND reading of "The Bill to amend an Act, entitled, 'An Act for establishing the temporary and permanent seat of the government of the United States,' "—

And on motion to postpone the consideration thereof to this day se'nnight, the yeas and nays were required by one fifth of the Senators present:

Mr. Butler	Nay	
Mr. Carroll	Nay	
Mr. Dalton		Yea
Mr. Dickinson		Yea
Mr. Ellsworth		Yea
Mr. Elmer		Yea
Mr. Few	Nay	
Mr. Foster		Yea
Mr. Gunn	Nay	
Mr. Hawkins	Nay	
Mr. Henry	Nay	
Mr. Johnson		Yea
Mr. Johnston	Nay	
Mr. Izard	Nay	
Mr. King		Yea
Mr. Langdon		Yea
Mr. Lee	Nay	
Mr. Maclay		Yea
Mr. Monroe	Nay	

[112] On February 21 this bill was considered again and committed.

[113] A copy of this House message from Tobias Lear is in Committee on Enrolled Bills, Senate Records, DNA.

Mr. Morris	Yea
Mr. Read	Yea
Mr. Schuyler	Yea
Mr. Stanton	Yea
Mr. Strong	Yea
Mr. Wingate	Yea

Yeas—15

Nays—10[114]

So it passed in the Affirmative.[115]

The Senate adjourned to 11 o'clock to-morrow.

SATURDAY, FEBRUARY 19, 1791

The SENATE assembled—present as yesterday, and

Resumed the consideration of the Bill, entitled, "An Act for raising and adding another regiment to the military establishment of the United States, and for making further provision for the protection of the frontiers," reported by the Committee, with amendments, and—

On motion to adopt the first section of the Bill as sent from the House of Representatives and reported by the Committee of the Senate, the yeas and nays were required by one fifth of the Senators present.

Mr. Butler	Nay	
Mr. Carroll		Yea
Mr. Dalton		Yea
Mr. Dickinson		Yea
Mr. Ellsworth		Yea
Mr. Elmer		Yea
Mr. Few	Nay	
Mr. Foster		Yea
Mr. Gunn	Nay	
Mr. Henry		Yea
Mr. Johnson		Yea
Mr. Johnston		Yea
Mr. Izard		Yea
Mr. King		Yea
Mr. Langdon		Yea
Mr. Lee	Nay	
Mr. Maclay	Nay	
Mr. Monroe	Nay	

[114] This vote is in Other Records: Yeas and nays, Senate Records, DNA.

[115] On February 25 the Senate considered this bill and a section of the first clause was agreed to. The bill then passed to the third reading.

Mr. Schuyler	Yea
Mr. Stanton	Yea
Mr. Strong	Yea
Mr. Wingate	Nay

Yeas—15

Nays—7[116]

So it passed in the Affirmative.

On motion to add after the tenth section agreed to, with an amendment reported by the Committee—

"*And be it further enacted*, That if the President of the United States should be of opinion that the service for which the aforesaid regiment is intended, can be performed by the militia or troops under the denomination of levies, he is fully authorized, any thing heretofore to the contrary notwithstanding, to substitute levies or militia accordingly, to continue in pay during such term only as the President of the United States in his discretion shall deem it requisite for the public service, or until the next session of Congress."[117]—

It passed in the Negative.

Other amendments were reported by the Committee, and adopted, and it was agreed to amend the Bill accordingly.

ORDERED, That this Bill pass to the THIRD reading.[118]

The SECOND reading of the Bill, entitled, "An Act to alter the time of the next meeting of Congress," was postponed until Tuesday next.[119]

It was agreed further to postpone the report of the Committee appointed to consider and report what time will be proper for the commencement of the next Congress, together with the resolution of the House of Representatives thereon.[120]

A message from the House of Representatives by Mr. Beckley their clerk:

"Mr. PRESIDENT,

"The House of Representatives have passed the Bill sent from the Senate, entitled, 'An Act, regulating the number of Representatives to be chosen by the States of Kentucky and Vermont.' "[121]—

And he withdrew.

The Senate adjourned to Monday next, at 11 o'clock.

---

[116] This vote is in Other Records: Yeas and nays, Senate Records, DNA.

[117] This motion is in Senate Simple Resolutions and Motions, Senate Records, DNA.

[118] On February 21 an amendment to this bill was defeated, and the bill was read a third time and passed with amendments, which were printed in the Journal.

[119] On February 22 a motion to amend this bill was defeated and the Senate voted not to read this bill a third time.

[120] The Senate did not consider this report and resolution again.

[121] On February 22 this bill was signed by both the Speaker and the Vice President and given to the committee on enrolled bills for delivery to the President.

MONDAY, FEBRUARY 21, 1791

The SENATE assembled—present as on the 19th.

The petition of Joseph Tatlow,[122] for compensation for a vessel said to be lost in the service of the United States, was read.

ORDERED, That this petition lie on the table.[123]

A message from the House of Representatives by Mr. Beckley their clerk:

"Mr. PRESIDENT,

"The House of Representatives have agreed to the amendments of the Senate to the Bill, entitled, 'An Act repealing after the last day of June next, the duties heretofore laid upon distilled spirits imported from abroad, and laying others in their stead; and also upon spirits distilled within the United States, and for appropriating the same,' with amendments;[124] in which amendments the House of Representatives desire the concurrence of the Senate.—

"I am directed to inform the Senate, that in the 10th, 11th, 40th, and 43d sections of the Bill, there appear to be sundry omissions of corresponding amendments, which are rendered necessary in consequence of other amendments to the same section."[125]—

And he withdrew.

The Senate proceeded to consider the resolutions of the House of Representatives of the 17th of February, on the amendments of the Senate to the Bill last mentioned.—Which amendments are as follow:

"RESOLVED, That this House doth disagree to the amendment to the 34th section, and doth agree to the amendments to all the other sections, as far as the 58th section inclusive, with amendments to several of the said amendments, as follow:

"SECT. III. First amendment—transpose it, so as to come in after the word 'fifty,' in the third line of the section.

"SECT. IV. In the first of the three sections proposed by the Senate to be inserted in lieu of the fourth section, and in the third line, strike out 'thirteen,' and insert 'fourteen.'

"SECT. XXVII. First amendment—in the words proposed by the Senate to be substituted in lieu of the words stricken out, strike out 'at the port where;' insert 'within whose survey.'

"RESOLVED, That this House doth agree to the amendment to the 61st section, with an amendment, by striking out, in addition to the words pro-

---

[122] This petition is in Petitions and Memorials: Claims, Senate Records, DNA.

[123] The House referred this petition to the Secretary of the Treasury.

[124] These amendments have not been located.

[125] A draft of some amendments to these sections is in Various Select Committee Reports, Senate Records, DNA.

posed to be stricken out by the Senate, the whole of the said section without any substitute.

"RESOLVED, That this House doth agree to all the other amendments proposed by the Senate to the before mentioned Bill, with an amendment to the section which is proposed to follow the 61st section, as followeth: Strike out from the word 'exceed,' in the ninth line, and insert 'seven per cent. of the whole product of the duties arising from the spirits distilled within the United States; and such allowances shall continue to be paid for the space of two years, unless sooner altered by law.' "

Whereupon—

RESOLVED, That the Senate do recede from their amendments disagreed to by the House of Representatives, and agree to those of that House, except to the amendment proposed to follow the 61st section, to which the Senate agree, amended as follows: "Seven per cent. of the whole product of the duties arising from spirits distilled within the United States; and such allowances shall continue to be paid until altered by law."[126]

RESOLVED, That the Senate do agree to the corresponding amendments suggested by the House of Representatives, as necessary in the 10th, 11th, 40th and 43d sections of the Bill, to wit:

SECT. X. Line 10, expunge "Inspectors," substitute "Supervisors."

In the fourth amendment of the Senate, to section tenth, line 4th, after "chief," expunge "Inspector," and substitute "officer."

SECT. XI. Lines 10, 13, and 23d, after "cask" insert "vessel."

SECT. XL. Line 4, expunge "Inspector," substitute "Supervisor."

Line 9, insert before "officer," "Supervisor or other."

SECT. XLIII. Line 7, expunge "Inspector," substitute "Supervisors."[127]

And the Senate agree to such other amendments of a similar nature, as may occur.

ORDERED, That the Secretary acquaint the House of Representatives with the proceedings of the Senate on their amendments to the amendments of the Senate, on the above mentioned Bill.[128]

The Bill sent from the House of Representatives for concurrence, entitled, "An Act for raising and adding another regiment to the military establishment of the United States, and for making further provision for the protection of the frontiers," was read the THIRD time.

---

[126] This resolve has not been located.

[127] A draft of some amendments is attached to the committee report located in Various Select Committee Reports, Senate Records, DNA.

[128] On February 22 the House agreed to all but one of the Senate changes in the bill; it insisted upon its amendment to the section following the sixty-first section. The Senate was notified of this action on February 23 and insisted upon the amendment that the House disagreed to. The Senate requested a conference on the amendment which the House agreed to on the same day.

On motion to amend the first section of the Bill, so as to limit the number of the regiment to six hundred and eight, instead of nine hundred and twelve non-commissioned officers, privates and musicians,—the yeas and nays were required by one fifth of the Senators present.

Mr. Bassett	Nay	
Mr. Butler		Yea
Mr. Carroll	Nay	
Mr. Dalton	Nay	
Mr. Dickinson	Nay	
Mr. Ellsworth	Nay	
Mr. Elmer	Nay	
Mr. Few		Yea
Mr. Foster	Nay	
Mr. Gunn		Yea
Mr. Hawkins	Nay	
Mr. Henry	Nay	
Mr. Johnson	Nay	
Mr. Johnston	Nay	
Mr. Izard	Nay	
Mr. King	Nay	
Mr. Langdon	Nay	
Mr. Lee		Yea
Mr. Maclay		Yea
Mr. Monroe		Yea
Mr. Morris	Nay	
Mr. Read	Nay	
Mr. Schuyler	Nay	
Mr. Stanton		Yea
Mr. Strong	Nay	
Mr. Wingate		Yea

Nays—18
Yeas—8[129]

So it passed in the Negative.

RESOLVED, That this Bill pass with the following amendments.

SECT. III. Line 3, after "engaged," insert "for the like term and."

SECT. IV. Line 1, expunge from the word "That," to the word "shall," in the third line, and insert "each non-commissioned officer, private and musician who has inlisted or shall inlist pursuant to the Act aforesaid, or who shall inlist pursuant to this Act."

SECT. V. Expunge the whole section.

---

[129] This vote is in Other Records: Yeas and nays, Senate Records, DNA.

SECT. VI. At the end, add *"Provided always,* That the Major-General and Brigadier-General, so to be appointed, shall respectively continue in pay during such term only as the President of the United States, in his discretion shall deem it requisite for the public service."

SECT. VII. Line 19, at the end, add "including pay, rations and forage."

SECT. VIII. Line 7, strike out the proviso.

SECT. IX. Expunge the whole section.

1   SECT. X. Line 1, expunge *"Provided nevertheless."*
2   Line 4, expunge from "militia," to the end of the section,
3   and insert "which in virtue of the powers vested in him by law,
4   he is authorised to call into the service of the United States, it
5   shall be lawful for him to raise, for a term not exceeding six
6   months, (to be discharged sooner if the public service will per-
7   mit) a corps of two thousand non-commissioned officers, privates
8   and musicians, with a suitable number of commissioned officers.
9   And in case it shall appear probable to the President that the re-
10   giment directed to be raised by the aforesaid Act, and by this Act,
11   will not be compleated in time to prosecute such military opera-
12   tions as exigencies may require, it shall be lawful for the Pre-
13   sident to make a substitute for the deficiency, by raising such fur-
14   ther number of levies, or by calling into the service of the United
15   States, such a body of militia as shall be equal thereto."

1   SECT. XIV. Line 1, after "that," insert "each of."

1   SECT. ——— *"And be it further enacted,* That in case the nature
2   of the service upon which the troops of the United States may
3   be employed, should require a greater number of Surgeons-mates
4   than are provided for in the before mentioned Act, the President
5   of the United States may engage from time to time such addi-
6   tional number of Surgeons-mates as he shall judge necessary."

1   SECT. ——— *"And be it further enacted,* That the commis-
2   sioned officers who shall be employed to recruit men for the said
3   regiments, shall be entitled to receive for every recruit who shall
4   be duly enlisted and mustered, the sum of two dollars."

1   SECT. ——— *"And be it further enacted,* That for defraying
2   the expense of one year of the additional regiment to be raised
3   by virtue of this Act: for defraying the expense for a like term,
4   of the officers mentioned in the sixth section of this Act: for de-
5   fraying the expense of the said militia horse, militia foot, and
6   levies, which may be called into or engaged for the service of the
7   United States, pursuant to this Act: for defraying the expense of
8   such Surgeon's-mates as may be appointed pursuant to the thir-
9   teenth section of this Act: for defraying the expense of recruiting

10 the said two regiments: and for defraying the expense of any
11 military posts which the President shall judge expedient and
12 proper to establish, there be and hereby is appropriated a sum
13 not exceeding three hundred and twelve thousand six hundred
14 and eighty-six dollars, and twenty cents. to be paid out of the
15 monies which prior to the first day of January next, shall arise
16 from the duties imposed upon spirits distilled within the United
17 States, and from stills, by the Act, entitled, 'An Act repealing
18 after the last day of June next, the duties heretofore laid upon
19 distilled spirits imported from abroad, and laying others in their
20 stead; and also upon spirits distilled within the United States,
21 and for appropriating the same;' together with the excess of
22 duties which may arise from the duties imposed by the said Act,
23 on imported spirits, beyond those which would have arisen by
24 the Act, entitled, 'An Act making further provision for the
25 payment of the debts of the United States.' "

1 Sect. ———— "And to the end that the public service may not
2 be impeded for want of necessary means—

3 *Be it further enacted*, That it shall be lawful for the President
4 to take on loan the whole sum by this Act appropriated, or so
5 much thereof as he may judge requisite, at an interest not ex-
6 ceeding six per centum per annum; and the fund established for
7 the above mentioned appropriation, is hereby pledged for the
8 re-payment of the principal and interest of any loan to be ob-
9 tained in manner aforesaid; and in case of any deficiency in the
10 said fund, the faith of the United States is hereby also pledged
11 to make good such deficiency."

And that the sections be numbered conformably to the amendments.[130]

ORDERED, That the Secretary carry this Bill to the House of Representatives, and desire their concurrence in the amendments.[131]

A message from the House of Representatives by Mr. Beckley their clerk:

"Mr. PRESIDENT,

"The House of Representatives have passed a Bill, entitled, 'An Act for giving effect to the laws of the United States within the State of Vermont,'[132] in which they desire the concurrence of the Senate."—

And he withdrew.

---

[130] The rough journal record of these amendments is made, in part, on a printed copy of the act bound into the volume.

[131] The House considered these amendments in secret sessions and notified the Senate on February 28 that it had agreed to the Senate amendments with amendments. On the same day the House amendments were printed in the Journal and considered.

[132] This bill has not been located.

The Bill was read the FIRST time as follows:

"An ACT giving effect to the LAWS of the UNITED STATES, within the State of VERMONT "

1   "SECT. I. *Be it enacted by the* SENATE *and House of* REPRE-
2 SENTATIVES *of the United States of America in Congress assembled,*
3 That from and after the third day of March next, all the laws
4 of the United States which are not locally inapplicable, ought to
5 have, and shall have, the same force and effect within the State
6 of Vermont, as elsewhere within the United States.

1   "SECT. II. And to the end that the Act, entitled, 'An Act
2 to establish the judicial courts of the United States,' may be duly
3 administered within the said State of Vermont—
4 *Be it further enacted*, That the said State shall be one district,
5 to be denominated Vermont district; and there shall be a district
6 court therein, to consist of one Judge, who shall reside within the
7 said district, and be called a district Judge, and shall hold annu-
8 ally four sessions; the first to commence on the first Monday in
9 May next, and the three other sessions progressively on the like
10 Monday of every third calendar month afterwards. The said
11 district court shall be held alternately at the towns of Rutland
12 and Windsor, beginning at the first.

1   "SECT. III. *And be it further enacted*, That the said district
2 shall be, and the same hereby is annexed to the eastern circuit;
3 and there shall be held annually in the said district one circuit
4 court: the first session shall commence on the seventeenth day of
5 June next, and the subsequent sessions on the like day of June
6 afterwards, except when any of the said days shall happen on a
7 Sunday, and then the session shall commence on the day follow-
8 ing; and the said sessions of the said circuit court shall be held at
9 the town of Bennington.

1   "SECT. IV. *And be it further enacted*, That there shall be al-
2 lowed to the Judge of the said district court, the yearly compen-
3 sation of eight hundred dollars, to commence from the time of his
4 appointment, and to be paid quarter yearly, at the Treasury of
5 the United States.

1   "SECT. V. *And be it further enacted*, That all the regulations,
2 provisions, directions, authorities, penalties, and other matters
3 whatsoever (except as herein afterwards is expressly provided)
4 contained and expressed in and by the Act, entitled, 'An Act
5 providing for the enumeration of the inhabitants of the United
6 States,' shall have the same force and effect within the said State

7　of Vermont, as if the same were, in relation thereto, repeated
8　and re-enacted in and by this present Act.

1　　"SECT. VI. *And be it further enacted*, That the enumeration
2　of the inhabitants of the said State, shall commence on the first
3　Monday of April next, and shall close within five calendar months
4　thereafter.

1　　"SECT. VII. *And be it further enacted*, That the Marshal of the
2　district of Vermont shall receive, in full compensation for all the
3　duties and services confided to, and enjoined upon him in and by
4　this Act in taking the enumeration aforesaid, two hundred dollars.

1　　"SECT. VIII. And that the Act, entitled, 'An Act to pro-
2　vide more effectually for the collection of the duties imposed by
3　law on goods, wares and merchandize imported into the United
4　States, and on the tonnage of ships and vessels,' may be carried
5　into effect in the said State of Vermont—
6　*Be it further enacted*, That for the due collection of the said
7　duties, there shall be in the said State of Vermont, one district:
8　and a Collector shall be appointed, to reside at Allburgh, on
9　Lake Champlain, which shall be the only port of entry or delivery
10　within the said district, of any goods, wares or merchandize,
11　not the growth or manufacture of the United States."

1791, February the 21st,—Passed the House of Representatives.

───────────

ORDERED, That this Bill pass to the SECOND reading.[133]

The Senate resumed the SECOND reading of the Bill, entitled, "An Act to establish offices for the purpose of granting lands within the territories of the United States."

ORDERED, That this Bill be committed to

　　　　Mr. Strong
　　　　Mr. Ellsworth
　　　　Mr. Foster
　　　　Mr. King and
　　　　Mr. Monroe, to consider and report what is proper
to be done thereon.[134]

───────────

[133] On February 22 this bill was read a second time, amended, and passed to the third reading.

[134] This vote for committee is in Other Records: Yeas and nays, Senate Records, DNA. On February 26 this committee reported that consideration of the bill should be postponed until the next session of Congress. The report was postponed, and the bill was recommitted.

Mr. Schuyler gave notice that to-morrow he intended to move for leave to bring in "A Bill to provide for the payment of balances due to the United States, in certain cases."[135]

The Senate adjourned to 11 o'clock to-morrow.

TUESDAY, FEBRUARY 22, 1791

The SENATE assembled—present as yesterday, and

Proceeded in the SECOND reading of the Bill sent from the House of Representatives for concurrence, entitled, "An Act for giving effect to the laws of the United States, within the State of Vermont," and having agreed to an amendment[136]—

ORDERED, That this Bill pass to the THIRD reading.[137]

The SECOND reading of the Bill sent from the House of Representatives for concurrence, entitled, "An Act to alter the time of the next meeting of Congress," was resumed:

On motion to insert "the second Monday in September," in place of the "first Monday of November,"—

It passed in the Negative.

And on the question, Shall this Bill be read the THIRD time?—

It passed in the Negative.[138]

A message from the House of Representatives by Mr. Beckley their clerk:

"Mr. PRESIDENT,

"The House of Representatives have passed a Bill, entitled, 'An Act to explain and amend an Act, entitled, "An Act making further provision for the payment of the debts of the United States," '[139] in which they desire the concurrence of the Senate."—

And he withdrew.

The Bill was read the FIRST time, as follows:

"An ACT to EXPLAIN and AMEND an ACT, entitled, 'An Act making further PROVISION for the payment of the DEBTS of the UNITED STATES ' "

    1   "SECT. I. *Be it enacted by the* SENATE *and House of* REPRE-

    2   SENTATIVES *of the United States of America in Congress assembled,*

    3   That the duty of one cent. per pound, laid by 'The Act making

---

[135] On February 26 this bill was introduced, read the first time, printed in the Journal, and passed to the second reading.

[136] This amendment is in House Bills, Senate Records, DNA.

[137] On February 23 this bill was read a third time, passed with an amendment, and returned to the House for concurrence in the amendment.

[138] The resolve for postponement is in Engrossed House Bills, House Records, DNA. On February 24 the House passed the Time of Meeting Bill [HR–132], and sent it to the Senate.

[139] This bill has not been located.

4 further provision for the payment of the debts of the United
5 States,' on bar and other lead, shall be deemed and taken to ex-
6 tend to all manufactures wholly of lead, or in which lead is the
7 chief article, which shall hereafter be brought into the United
8 States, from any foreign port or place.
1   "SECT. II. *And be it further enacted*, That the duty of seven
2 and a half per cent. *ad valorem*, laid by the Act aforesaid on
3 chintzes and coloured callicoes, shall be deemed and taken to ex-
4 tend to all printed, stained and coloured goods, or manufactures
5 of cotton or of linen, or of both, which hereafter shall be brought
6 into the United States from any foreign port or place.
1   "*Provided always*, That nothing in this Act shall in anywise
2 affect the true construction or meaning of the Act aforesaid, in
3 relation to any of the above described articles brought into the
4 United States before the passing of this Act."
  "1791, February 22d,—Passed the House of Representatives."

ORDERED, That this Bill pass to the SECOND reading.[140]

Mr. Maclay reported from the Committee appointed to consider the Bill sent from the House of Representatives for concurrence, entitled, "An Act authorising the President of the United States, to cause the debt due to foreign officers, to be paid and discharged."[141]

ORDERED, That the report lie for consideration.[142]

On motion—

RESOLVED *by the* SENATE *and House of* REPRESENTATIVES *of the United States of America in Congress assembled*, That the President of the United States be requested to cause to be communicated to the National Assembly of France, the peculiar sensibility of Congress, to the tribute paid to the memory of BENJAMIN FRANKLIN, by the enlightened and free Representatives of a great nation, in their decree of the eleventh day of June, one thousand seven hundred and ninety.[143]

ORDERED, That the Secretary carry this resolution to the House of Representatives, and desire their concurrence.[144]

Mr. Foster from the Committee on enrolled Bills, reported, That they had

---

[140] On February 23 this bill was read a second time and passed to the third reading.
[141] This report is in Various Select Committee Reports, Senate Records, DNA.
[142] On February 23 the House resolved not to read this bill a third time.
[143] This resolve is in Senate Joint and Concurrent Resolutions, Senate Records, DNA. A draft of the resolution is in Senate Simple Resolutions and Motions, Senate Records, DNA.
[144] On February 23 the House notified the Senate that it concurred in this resolution of thanks.

examined the enrolled Bill, entitled, "An Act regulating the number of Representatives to be chosen by the States of Kentucky and Vermont,"[145] and that it was correct.

The Senate adjourned to 11 o'clock to-morrow.

WEDNESDAY, FEBRUARY 23, 1791

The SENATE assembled—present as yesterday, and

Proceeded to the SECOND reading of the Bill sent from the House of Representatives for concurrence, entitled, "An Act to explain and amend an Act, entitled, 'An Act making further provision for the payment of the debts of the United States.' "

ORDERED, That this Bill pass to the THIRD reading.[146]

The Bill sent from the House of Representatives for concurrence, entitled, "An Act for giving effect to the laws of the United States, within the State of Vermont," was read the THIRD time.

RESOLVED, That this Bill PASS, with the following amendment:

At the end of the Bill, add—

"*Provided nevertheless,* That the exception contained in the sixty-ninth section of the Act last above mentioned, relative to the district of Louisville, shall be, and is hereby extended to the said port of Allburgh.'

ORDERED, That the Secretary desire the concurrence of the House of Representatives, in this amendment.[147]

The Senate proceeded to the consideration of the report of the Committee on the Bill sent from the House of Representatives for concurrence, entitled, "An Act authorising the President of the United States, to cause the debt due to foreign officers to be paid and discharged:"

Whereupon—

RESOLVED, That this Bill do not pass to the THIRD reading.[148]

A message from the House of Representatives by Mr. Beckley their clerk:

"Mr. PRESIDENT,

"The House of Representatives insist on their amendment to the last clause of the section proposed by the Senate to follow section sixty-first, of the Bill, entitled, 'An Act repealing after the last day of June next, the duties heretofore laid upon distilled spirits imported from abroad, and laying others in

---

[145] The inspected enrolled bill is in Enrolled Acts, RG 11, DNA. E–23863.

[146] On February 24 this bill was read the third time and passed, and the House was notified. On the same day a motion to reconsider the passage of the bill was defeated.

[147] On February 4 the House notified the Senate that it had concurred in this amendment.

[148] This simple resolution, attached to the House bill, is in Engrossed House Bills, House Records, DNA. This bill was not considered again.

their stead; and also upon spirits distilled within the United States, and for appropriating the same'—

"The Speaker of the House of Representatives having signed an enrolled Bill, I am directed to bring it to the Senate, for the signature of the Vice President—

"The House of Representatives have agreed to the resolution, requesting the President of the United States, to cause a communication to be made to the National Assembly of France, respecting the late Benjamin Franklin[149]—

"They have passed a Bill, entitled, 'An Act supplementary to the Act, entitled, "An Act to incorporate the subscribers to the bank of the United States," '[150] in which they desire the concurrence of the Senate"—

And he withdrew.

The Senate proceeded to consider the resolution of the House of Representatives, insisting on their amendment to the last clause of the section proposed by the Senate, to follow section sixty-first, of the Bill, entitled, "An Act repealing after the last day of June next, the duties heretofore laid upon distilled spirits imported from abroad, and laying others in their stead; and also upon spirits distilled within the United States, and for appropriating the same;" and—

On motion,

That the Senate insist on their amendment to the amendment of the House of Representatives to the said clause, the yeas and nays were required by one fifth of the Senators present.

Mr. Bassett	Yea	
Mr. Butler	Yea	
Mr. Carroll		Nay
Mr. Dalton	Yea	
Mr. Dickinson	Yea	
Mr. Ellsworth	Yea	
Mr. Elmer	Yea	
Mr. Few		Nay
Mr. Foster	Yea	
Mr. Hawkins		Nay
Mr. Henry		Nay
Mr. Johnson	Yea	
Mr. Johnston		Nay
Mr. Izard	Yea	
Mr. Lee		Nay

---

[149] On February 4 this resolution was signed by both the Speaker and the Vice President and given to the committee on enrolled bills for delivery to the President.
[150] This bill has not been located.

Mr. Maclay		Nay
Mr. Monroe		Nay
Mr. Morris	Yea	
Mr. Read	Yea	
Mr. Schuyler	Yea	
Mr. Stanton	Yea	
Mr. Strong	Yea	
Mr. Wingate		Nay

Yeas—14
Nays—9

So it was—

RESOLVED, That the Senate insist on their amendment to the amendment of the House of Representatives, in the clause of the section to follow section sixty-first of the Bill last mentioned.

RESOLVED, That a conference be desired with such managers as the House of Representatives may appoint on their part, on the subject of disagreement; and that   Mr. Ellsworth

Mr. King and

Mr. Morris, be the managers at the conference proposed,[151] on the part of the Senate.

ORDERED, That the Secretary communicate this resolution to the House of Representatives, and desire the conference, and the appointment of managers on their part.

The Bill sent from the House of Representatives for concurrence, entitled, "An Act supplementary to the Act, entitled, 'An Act to incorporate the subscribers to the bank of the United States,' " was read the FIRST time, and is as follows:

"An ACT supplementary to the Act, entitled, 'An Act to incorporate the subscribers to the BANK of the UNITED STATES ' "

I   "SECT. I.   *Be it enacted by the* SENATE *and House of* REPRE-
2   SENTATIVES *of the United States of America, in Congress assembled,*
3   That the subscriptions to the stock of the Bank of the United
4   States, as provided by the Act, entitled, 'An Act to incorporate
5   the subscribers to the Bank of the United States,' shall not be
6   opened until the first Monday in July next.

I   "SECT. II.   *And be it further enacted,* That so much of the first
2   payment, as by the said Act is directed to be in the six per cent.
3   certificates of the United States, may be deferred until the first
4   Monday in January next.

---

[151] This vote for committee is in Other Records: Yeas and nays, Senate Records, DNA.

1   "SECT. III. *And be it further enacted*, That no person, cor-
2   poration or body politic, except in behalf of the United States,
3   shall for the space of three months after the said first Monday in
4   July next, subscribe in any one day, for more than thirty shares.

1   "SECT. IV. *And be it further enacted*, That every subscriber
2   shall, at the time of subscribing, pay into the hands of the persons
3   who shall be appointed to receive the same, the specie propor-
4   tion required by the said Act to be then paid. And if any such
5   subscriber shall fail to make any of the future payments, he shall
6   forfeit the sum so by him first paid, for the use of the corpo-
7   ration.

1   "SECT. V. *And be it further enacted*, That such part of the
2   public debt, including the assumed debt, as is funded at an in-
3   terest of three per cent. may be paid to the Bank, in the like
4   manner with the debt funded at six per cent. computing the
5   value of the former at one half the value of the latter, and re-
6   serving to the subscribers who shall have paid three per cent.
7   stock, the privilege of redeeming the same with six per cent.
8   stock, at the above rate of computation, at any time before the
9   first day of January, one thousand seven hundred and ninety-
10   three; unless the three per cent. stock shall have been previously
11   disposed of by the Directors."

"February 23d, 1791—Sent from the House of Representatives for
concurrence."

ORDERED, That this Bill pass to the SECOND reading, and that in the mean
time it be printed for the use of the Senate.[152]

The Vice President signed the enrolled Bill, entitled, "An Act regulating
the number of Representatives to be chosen by the States of Kentucky and
Vermont," and it was delivered to the Committee on enrolled Bills, to be laid
before the President of the United States, for his approbation.[153]

Mr. Monroe gave notice, that to-morrow he intended to move that the
doors of the Senate Chamber be opened, to the end that the citizens of the
United States, may be admitted to hear the debates of the Senate.[154]

A message from the House of Representatives by Mr. Beckley their clerk:

"Mr. PRESIDENT,

"The House of Representatives have agreed to the proposed conference on

---

[152] On February 24 this bill was read a second time and passed to the third reading.
[153] On February 25 the President signed this bill and the Senate was notified. The bill
is printed in the Journal on the same date.
[154] On February 24 two resolutions on this subject were introduced and debated.

the amendment to the amendment of the Senate on the Bill, entitled, 'An Act repealing after the last day of June next, the duties heretofore laid upon distilled spirits imported from abroad, and laying others in their stead; and also upon spirits distilled within the United States, and for appropriating the same,' and have appointed managers on their part"[155]—

And he withdrew.

A motion was made that the Senate agree to the following Resolution—

"Whereas the duties imposed by law on the Attorney-General of the United States, require the aid of clerks, and are attended with other expenses, for which no provision hath been made—

"RESOLVED, That for the space of one year from the date hereof, and from thence to the end of the succeeding session of Congress, there be allowed to the said Attorney-General, at the rate of   dollars per annum, for the purposes aforesaid."[156]

ORDERED, That the consideration of this motion be postponed until tomorrow.[157]

The Senate adjourned to 11 o'clock to-morrow.

THURSDAY, FEBRUARY 24, 1791

The SENATE assembled—present as yesterday.

The Bill sent from the House of Representatives for concurrence, entitled, "An Act supplementary to the Act, entitled, 'An Act to incorporate the subscribers to the bank of the United States,' " was read the SECOND time; and on the question, shall this Bill pass to the THIRD reading? the yeas and nays were required by one fifth of the Senators present.

Mr. Bassett	Yea	
Mr. Butler	Yea	
Mr. Carroll		Nay
Mr. Dalton	Yea	
Mr. Dickinson	Yea	
Mr. Ellsworth	Yea	
Mr. Elmer	Yea	
Mr. Few	Yea	
Mr. Gunn		Nay
Mr. Hawkins	Yea	
Mr. Henry	Yea	

---

[155] On February 25 the conference committee reported, and the House receded from its disagreement to the amendment with an amendment. The Senate was notified of this action on February 26, and concurred in the House resolution.

[156] This motion is in Senate Simple Resolutions and Motions, Senate Records, DNA.

[157] On February 24 the Senate committed these resolutions.

Mr. Johnson	Yea	
Mr. Johnston	Yea	
Mr. Izard	Yea	
Mr. King	Yea	
Mr. Langdon	Yea	
Mr. Lee	Yea	
Mr. Maclay	Yea	
Mr. Monroe		Nay
Mr. Morris	Yea	
Mr. Read	Yea	
Mr. Schuyler	Yea	
Mr. Stanton	Yea	
Mr. Strong	Yea	
Mr. Wingate	Yea	

Yeas—22

Nays—3[158]

So it was—

ORDERED, That this Bill pass to the THIRD reading.[159]

The Senate proceeded to the THIRD reading of the Bill sent from the House of Representatives for concurrence, entitled, "An Act to explain and amend an Act, entitled, 'An Act making further provision for the payment of the debts of the United States,' " and,

RESOLVED, That this Bill PASS.

ORDERED, That the Secretary acquaint the House of Representatives with the concurrence of the Senate in this Bill.

A motion was made that the Senate agree to the following Resolution[160]:

"Whereas the duties of the Treasury Department are greatly encreased by different Acts passed since the establishment of the office, insomuch as to make the salaries of the officers inadequate to the fatigue and attention requisite; and whereas the time of the present session will not admit of regulating the salaries by Bill—

"RESOLVED, That for the space of one year, the salaries of the different officers shall be advanced in the proportion of 25 per cent. on their present allowance."

ORDERED, That the foregoing motion be referred to

Mr. Ellsworth

Mr. Butler

---

[158] This vote is in Other Records: Yeas and nays, Senate Records, DNA.

[159] On February 25 this bill was read a third time and two motions to amend it were defeated. It was then passed and the House was notified.

[160] This motion and the resolution following it are in Senate Simple Resolutions and Motions, Senate Records, DNA.

Mr. Read

Mr. Strong and

Mr. King,[161] together with the motion made yesterday, respecting an additional compensation to the Attorney-General of the United States;[162] and that the Committee be instructed to consider and report generally thereon.[163]

Mr. Foster from the Committee on enrolled Bills, reported, That they had examined the enrolled "Resolution requesting the President of the United States, to cause a communiction to be made to the National Assembly of France, respecting the late Benjamin Franklin,"[164] and that they had found it correct.

A message from the House of Representatives by Mr. Beckley their clerk:

"Mr. PRESIDENT,

"The House of Representatives have passed the Bill, entitled, 'An Act fixing the time for the next annual meeting of Congress,'[165] in which they desire the concurrence of the Senate—

"The House of Representatives agree to the amendment of the Senate on the Bill, entitled, 'An Act for giving effect to the laws of the United States, within the State of Vermont'[166]—

"The Speaker of the House of Representatives having signed an enrolled Resolution, I am directed to bring it to the Senate, for the signature of the Vice President"—

And he withdrew.

On motion to re-consider the Resolution of this date, passing the Bill, entitled, "An Act to explain and amend an Act, entitled, 'An Act making further provision for the payment of the debts of the United States,' " the Bill being still in the possession of the Senate,—

It passed in the Negative.[167]

---

161 This vote for committee is in Other Records: Yeas and nays, Senate Records, DNA.

162 The rough journal includes the following canceled phrases: "to wit—Whereas the duties imposed by law on the Attr. General of the U.S. require the aid of Clerks & are attended with other expenses for which no provision hath been made:/Resolved that for the space of one year from the date hereof, and from thence to the end of the succeeding session of Congress, there be allowed to the said Attorney General."

163 On February 25 the Treasury Bill [HR–131] was referred to this committee.

164 The inspected enrolled bill is in Enrolled Acts, RG 11, DNA. E–23879.

165 This bill has not been located.

166 The note of agreement is in House Bills, Senate Records, DNA. On March 1 this bill was signed by both the Speaker and the Vice President and given to the committee on enrolled bills for delivery to the President.

167 On March 1 this bill was signed by both the Speaker and the Vice President and given to the committee on enrolled bills for delivery to the President.

The Vice President signed the enrolled "Resolution requesting the President of the United States, to cause a communication to be made to the National Assembly of France, respecting the late Benjamin Franklin," and it was delivered to the Committee on enrolled Bills, to be laid before the President of the United States for his approbation.[168]

The Bill sent from the House of Representatives for concurrence, entitled, "An Act fixing the time for the next annual meeting of Congress," was read the FIRST time, as follows:

"An ACT fixing the time for the next ANNUAL MEETING of CONGRESS"

1   "SECT. I. *Be it enacted by the* SENATE *and House of* REPRE-
2   SENTATIVES *of the United States of America, in Congress assembled,*
3   That after the third day of March next, the first annual meeting
4   of Congress shall be on the fourth Monday of October next."

"1791, February the 24th—Passed the House of Representatives."

ORDERED, That this Bill pass to the SECOND reading.[169]

Agreeably to notice given yesterday, it was moved that the Senate agree to the following Resolutions, to wit:

"RESOLVED, That it be a standing rule, that the doors of the Senate Chamber remain open whilst the Senate shall be sitting in a legislative capacity, except on such occasions as, in their judgment, may require secrecy; and that this rule shall commence and be in force on the first day of the next session of Congress"—

"RESOLVED, That the Secretary of the Senate, request the Commissioners of the city and county of Philadelphia, to cause a proper gallery to be erected for the accommodation of an audience"[170]—

And after debate hereon[171]—

The Senate adjourned to 11 o'clock to-morrow.

FRIDAY, FEBRUARY 25, 1791

The SENATE assembled—present as yesterday.

Mr. Foster from the Committee on enrolled Bills, reported, That they did on the 24th instant, lay before the President of the United States, the enrolled Bill, entitled, "An Act regulating the number of Representatives to be chosen by the States of Kentucky and Vermont."

[168] On March 1 the committee on enrolled bills delivered this bill to the President, and he signed it on the next day.

[169] On February 25 this bill was read a second time, and a motion to amend it was defeated. It then passed to the third reading.

[170] These resolutions are in Senate Simple Resolutions and Motions, Senate Records, DNA.

[171] On February 25 these resolutions were disagreed to.

The Senate proceeded to the SECOND reading of the Bill sent from the House of Representatives for concurrence, entitled, "An Act fixing the time for the next annual meeting of Congress:"

On motion to substitute "the first Monday of April," for "the fourth Monday of October," section first, line fourth—

It passed in the Negative.

ORDERED, That this Bill pass to the THIRD reading.[172]

A message from the President of the United States, by Mr. Lear his Secretary:

"Mr. PRESIDENT,

"The President of the United States has this day approved and signed two Acts which originated in the Senate; one—

'An Act to incorporate the subscribers to the bank of the United States;' the other—

'An Act regulating the number of Representatives to be chosen by the States of Kentucky and Vermont.' "—

And he withdrew.

The Act to incorporate the subscribers to the bank of the United States, (as it passed both Houses of Congress, and was approved the 25th February 1791) is as follows:

An ACT to INCORPORATE the subscribers to the BANK of the UNITED STATES

1   WHEREAS it is conceived that the establishment of a Bank
2   for the United States, upon a foundation sufficiently extensive to
3   answer the purposes intended thereby, and at the same time upon
4   the principles which afford adequate security for an upright and
5   prudent administration thereof, will be very conducive to the suc-
6   cessful conducting of the national finances; will tend to give
7   facility to the obtaining of loans for the use of the government,
8   in sudden emergencies; and will be productive of considerable
9   advantages to trade and industry in general: Therefore,

1   SECT. I. *Be it enacted by the* SENATE *and House of* REPRE-
2   SENTATIVES *of the United States of America in Congress assembled,*
3   That a bank of the United States shall be established; the capital
4   stock whereof shall not exceed Ten Millions of Dollars, divided
5   into Twenty-five Thousand shares, each share being Four Hundred
6   Dollars; and that subscriptions towards constituting the said stock,
7   shall, on the first Monday of April next, be opened at the city of
8   Philadelphia, under the superintendance of such persons, not less
9   than three, as shall be appointed for that purpose by the President

---

[172] On February 26 this bill was read a third time and passed, and the House was notified.

10 of the United States, (who is hereby empowered to appoint the said
11 persons accordingly) which subscriptions shall continue open until
12 the whole of the said stock shall have been subscribed.

1   SECT. II. *And be it further enacted,* That it shall be lawful for
2   any person, co-partnership or body politic, to subscribe for such or
3   so many shares as he, she or they shall think fit, not exceeding one
4   thousand, except as shall be hereafter directed relatively to the Uni-
5   ted States; and that the sums respectively subscribed, except on
6   behalf of the United States, shall be payable one fourth in gold
7   and silver, and three fourths in that part of the public debt, which,
8   according to the loan proposed in the fourth and fifteenth sections
9   of the Act, entitled, "An Act making provision for the debt of
10 the United States," shall bear an accruing interest at the time of
11 payment of six *per centum per annum,* and shall also be payable in
12 four equal parts in the aforesaid ratio of specie to debt, at the dis-
13 tance of six calendar months from each other; the first whereof shall
14 be paid at the time of subscription.

1   SECT. III. *And be it further enacted,* That all those who shall
2   become subscribers to the said bank, their successors and assigns,
3   shall be, and are hereby created and made a corporation and body
4   politic, by the name and style of THE PRESIDENT, DIRECTORS
5   AND COMPANY, OF THE BANK OF THE UNITED STATES, and
6   shall so continue until the fourth day of March, one thousand eight
7   hundred and eleven: And by that name shall be, and are hereby made
8   able and capable in law to have, purchase, receive, possess, enjoy
9   and retain to them and their successors, lands, rents, tenements,
10 hereditaments, goods, chattels and effects of what kind, nature or
11 quality soever, to an amount not exceeding in the whole Fifteen
12 Millions of Dollars, including the amount of the capital stock
13 aforesaid; and the same to sell, grant, demise, alien or dispose of;
14 to sue and be sued, plead and be impleaded, answer and be ans-
15 wered, defend and be defended in courts of record, or any other
16 place whatsoever: And also to make, have and use a common seal,
17 and the same to break, alter and renew at their pleasure; and also
18 to ordain, establish and put in execution such bye-laws, ordinances
19 and regulations as shall seem necessary and convenient for the go-
20 vernment of the said corporation, not being contrary to law or to
21 the constitution thereof, (for which purpose general meetings of
22 the Stockholders shall and may be called by the Directors, and in
23 the manner herein after specified) and generally to do and execute
24 all and singular acts, matters and things which to them it shall

25 or may appertain to do; subject nevertheless to the rules, regula-
26 tions, restrictions, limitations and provisions herein after prescribed
27 and declared.

1   SECT. IV. *And be it further enacted*, That for the well order-
2 ing of the affairs of the said corporation, there shall be twenty-five
3 Directors; of whom there shall be an election on the first Monday
4 of January in each year, by the Stockholders or Proprietors of the
5 capital stock of the said corporation, and by plurality of the votes
6 actually given, and those who shall be duly chosen at any election,
7 shall be capable of serving as Directors by virtue of such choice,
8 until the end or expiration of the Monday of January next ensuing
9 the time of such election, and no longer.—And the said Directors
10 at their first meeting after each election, shall choose one of their
11 number, as President.

1   SECT. V. *Provided always, and be it further enacted*, That as
2 soon as the sum of Four Hundred Thousand Dollars, in gold and
3 silver, shall have been actually received on account of the subscrip-
4 tions to the said stock, notice thereof shall be given by the persons
5 under whose superintendance the same shall have been made, in at
6 least two public gazettes printed in the city of Philadelphia; and
7 the said persons shall at the same time in like manner notify a time
8 and place within the said city, at the distance of ninety days from
9 the time of such notification, for proceeding to the election of Di-
10 rectors; and it shall be lawful for such election to be then and there
11 made, and the persons who shall then and there be chosen shall be
12 the first Directors, and shall be capable of serving by virtue of
13 such choice until the end or expiration of the Monday in January
14 next ensuing the time of making the same, and shall forthwith
15 thereafter commence the operations of the said bank, at the said
16 city of Philadelphia: *And provided further*, That in case it should
17 at any time happen that an election of Directors should not be
18 made upon any day when pursuant to this Act it ought to have
19 been made, the said corporation shall not for that cause be deemed
20 to be dissolved; but it shall be lawful on any other day to hold and
21 make an election of Directors, in such manner as shall have been
22 regulated by the laws and ordinances of the said corporation: *And*
23 *provided lastly*, That in case of the death, resignation, absence from
24 the United States, or removal of a Director by the Stockholders, his
25 place may be filled up by a new choice for the remainder of the
26 year.

1   SECT. VI. *And be it further enacted*, That the Directors for the
2 time being shall have power to appoint such officers, clerks and

3 servants under them as shall be necessary for executing the business
4 of the said corporation, and to allow them such compensation for
5 their services respectively as shall be reasonable; and shall be ca-
6 pable to exercising such other powers and authorities for the well
7 governing and ordering of the affairs of the said corporation, as shall
8 be described, fixed and determined by the laws, regulations and or-
9 dinances of the same.

1   SECT. VII. *And be it further enacted*, That the following rules,
2 restrictions, limitations and provisions, shall form and be funda-
3 mental articles of the constitution of the said corporation, viz.

1   1. The number of votes to which each Stockholder shall be
2 entitled, shall be according to the number of shares he shall hold
3 in the proportions following: That is to say, for one share and not
4 more than two shares, one vote: For every two shares above two,
5 and not exceeding ten, one vote: For every four shares above ten,
6 and not exceeding thirty, one vote: For every six shares above
7 thirty and not exceeding sixty, one vote: For every eight shares
8 above sixty, and not exceeding one hundred, one vote: And for
9 every ten shares above one hundred, one vote,—but no person, co-
10 partnership or body politic, shall be entitled to a greater number
11 than thirty votes. And after the first election, no share or shares
12 shall confer a right of suffrage which shall not have been holden
13 three calendar months previous to the day of election. Stockhol-
14 ders actually resident within the United States, and none other, may
15 vote in elections by proxy.

1   2. Not more than three fourths of the Directors in office, ex-
2 clusive of the President, shall be eligible for the next succeeding
3 year: But the Director, who shall be President at the time of an
4 election, may always be re-elected.

1   3. None but a Stockholder, being a citizen of the United States,
2 shall be eligible as a Director.

1   4. No Director shall be entitled to any emolument, unless the
2 same shall have been allowed by the Stockholders at a general meet-
3 ing. The Stockholders shall make such compensation to the Pre-
4 sident for his extraordinary attendance at the bank, as shall appear
5 to them reasonable.

1   5. Not less than seven Directors shall constitute a board for the
2 transaction of business, of whom, the President shall always be one,
3 except in case of sickness or necessary absence; in which case, his
4 place may be supplied by any other Director whom he, by writing
5 under his hand, shall nominate for the purpose.

1   6. Any number of Stockholders not less than sixty, who toge-

2   ther shall be proprietors of two hundred shares or upwards, shall
3   have power at any time, to call a general meeting of the Stock-
4   holders, for purposes relative to the institution, giving at least ten
5   weeks notice, in two public gazettes of the place where the bank
6   is kept, and specifying in such notice, the object or objects of such
7   meeting.

1   7. Every Cashier or Treasurer, before he enters upon the duties
2   of his office, shall be required to give bond, with two or more sure-
3   ties, to the satisfaction of the Directors, in a sum not less than fifty
4   thousand dollars, with condition for his good behaviour.

1   8. The lands, tenements and hereditaments which it shall be
2   lawful for the said corporation to hold, shall be only such as shall
3   be requisite for its immediate accommodation in relation to the con-
4   venient transacting of its business, and such as shall have been *bona-
5   fide* mortgaged to it by way of security, or conveyed to it in satis-
6   faction of debts previously contracted in the course of its dealings,
7   or purchased at sales upon judgments which shall have been ob-
8   tained for such debts.

1   9. The total amount of the debts which the said corporation
2   shall at any time owe, whether by bond, bill, note or other contract,
3   shall not exceed the sum of ten millions of dollars, over and above
4   the monies then actually deposited in the Bank for safe-keeping, un-
5   less the contracting of any greater debt shall have been previously
6   authorised by a law of the United States. In case of excess, the
7   Directors under whose administration it shall happen, shall be liable
8   for the same in their natural and private capacities; and an action
9   of debt may in such case be brought against them or any of them,
10   their or any of their heirs, executors or administrators, in any court
11   of record of the United States, or of either of them, by any credi-
12   tor or creditors of the said corporation, and may be prosecuted to
13   judgment and execution; any condition, covenant or agreement to
14   the contrary notwithstanding: But this shall not be construed to
15   exempt the said corporation, or the lands, tenements, goods or
16   chattels of the same from being also liable for and chargeable with
17   the said excess. Such of the said Directors who may have been
18   absent when the said excess was contracted or created, or who may
19   have dissented from the resolution or act whereby the same was so
20   contracted or created, may respectively exonerate themselves from
21   being so liable, by forthwith giving notice of the fact, and of their
22   absence or dissent, to the President of the United States, and to the
23   Stockholders, at a general meeting, which they shall have power
24   to call for that purpose.

1   10. The said corporation may sell any part of the public debt
2 whereof its stock shall be composed, but shall not be at liberty to
3 purchase any public debt whatsoever; nor shall directly or indirectly
4 deal or trade in any thing except bills of exchange, gold or silver
5 bullion, or in the sale of goods really and truly pledged for money
6 lent and not redeemed in due time; or of goods which shall be the
7 produce of its lands. Neither shall the said corporation take more
8 than at the rate of six *per centum per annum*, for or upon its loans
9 or discounts.

1   11. No loan shall be made by the said corporation for the use
2 or on account of the government of the United States to an amount
3 exceeding one hundred thousand dollars, or of any particular State
4 to an amount exceeding fifty thousand dollars, or of any foreign
5 Prince or State, unless previously authorised by a law of the United
6 States.

1   12. The stock of the said corporation shall be assignable and
2 transferable according to such rules as shall be instituted in that
3 behalf, by the laws and ordinances of the same.

1   13. The bills obligatory and of credit under the seal of the said
2 corporation, which shall be made to any person or persons, shall
3 be assignable by indorsement thereupon, under the hand or hands
4 of such person or persons, and of his, her or their assignee or assig-
5 nees, and so as absolutely to transfer and vest the property thereof
6 in each and every assignee or assignees successively, and to enable
7 such assignee or assignees to bring and maintain an action there-
8 upon in his, her or their own name or names. And bills or notes
9 which may be issued by order of the said corporation, signed by
10 the President, and countersigned by the principal Cashier or Trea-
11 surer thereof, promising the payment of money to any person or
12 persons, his, her or their order, or to bearer, though not under
13 the seal of the said corporation, shall be binding and obligatory
14 upon the same, in the like manner and with the like force and
15 effect as upon any private person or persons, if issued by him or
16 them in his, her or their private or natural capacity or capacities;
17 and shall be assignable and negotiable in like manner as if they were
18 so issued by such private person or persons,—That is to say, those
19 which shall be payable to any person or persons, his, her or their
20 order, shall be assignable by indorsement, in like manner and with
21 the like effect as foreign bills of exchange now are; and those
22 which are payable to bearer, shall be negotiable and assignable by
23 delivery only.

1   14. Half-yearly dividends shall be made of so much of the

2 profits of the bank as shall appear to the Directors adviseable; and
3 once in every three years the Directors shall lay before the Stock-
4 holders, at a general meeting, for their information, an exact and
5 particular statement of the debts which shall have remained un-
6 paid after the expiration of the original credit, for a period of
7 treble the term of that credit; and of the surplus of profit, if any,
8 after deducting losses and dividends. If there shall be a failure
9 in the payment of any part of any sum subscribed by any person,
10 co-partnership or body politic, the party failing shall lose the be-
11 nefit of any dividend which may be accrued prior to the time
12 for making such payment and during the delay of the same.

1 15. It shall be lawful for the Directors aforesaid, to establish
2 offices wheresoever they shall think fit, within the United States,
3 for the purposes of discount and deposit only, and upon the same
4 terms and in the same manner as shall be practised at the bank,
5 and to commit the management of the said offices, and the mak-
6 ing of the said discounts, to such persons, under such agreements,
7 and subject to such regulations as they shall deem proper; not
8 being contrary to law or to the constitution of the bank.

9 16. The officer at the head of the Treasury Department of the
10 United States, shall be furnished from time to time, as often as he
11 may require, not exceeding once a week, with statements of the
12 amount of the capital stock of the said corporation, and of the
13 debts due to the same; of the monies deposited therein; of the
14 notes in circulation, and of the cash in hand; and shall have a
15 right to inspect such general accounts in the books of the bank as
16 shall relate to the said statements: *Provided*, that this shall not be
17 construed to imply a right of inspecting the account of any private
18 individual or individuals with the bank.

1 SECT. VIII. *And be it further enacted*, That if the said corpo-
2 ration, or any person or persons, for or to the use of the same, shall
3 deal or trade in buying or selling any goods, wares, merchandize
4 or commodities whatsoever, contrary to the provisions of this Act,
5 all and every person or persons, by whom any order or direction
6 for so dealing or trading shall have been given, and all and every
7 person or persons who shall have been concerned as parties or
8 agents therein, shall forfeit and lose treble the value of the goods,
9 wares, merchandizes and commodities in which such dealing and
10 trade shall have been; one half thereof to the use of the informer,
11 and the other half thereof to the use of the United States, to be
12 recovered with costs of suit.

1   SECT. IX. *And be it further enacted,* That if the said corpora-
2 tion shall advance or lend any sum for the use or on account of the
3 government of the United States, to an amount exceeding one
4 hundred thousand dollars; or of any particular State, to an amount
5 exceeding fifty thousand dollars; or of any foreign Prince or State,
6 (unless previously authorised thereto by a law of the United States)
7 all and every person or persons by and with whose order, agree-
8 ment, consent, approbation or connivance such unlawful advance
9 or loan shall have been made, upon conviction thereof, shall forfeit
10 and pay for every such offence treble the value or amount of the
11 sum or sums which shall have been so unlawfully advanced or lent;
12 one fifth thereof to the use of the informer, and the residue thereof
13 to the use of the United States; to be disposed of by law, and not
14 otherwise.

1   SECT. X. *And be it further enacted,* That the bills or notes of
2 the said corporation, originally made payable, or which shall have
3 become payable on demand, in gold and silver coin, shall be re-
4 ceivable in all payments to the United States.

1   SECT. XI. *And be it further enacted,* That it shall be lawful for
2 the President of the United States, at any time or times within
3 eighteen months after the first day of April next, to cause a sub-
4 scription to be made to the stock of the said corporation, as part of
5 the aforesaid capital stock of ten millions of dollars, on behalf of
6 the United States, to an amount not exceeding two millions of
7 dollars; to be paid out of the monies which shall be borrowed by
8 virtue of either of the Acts, the one entitled, "An Act making
9 provision for the debt of the United States;" and the other enti-
10 tled, "An Act making provision for the reduction of the public
11 debt;" borrowing of the bank an equal sum, to be applied to the
12 purposes for which the said monies shall have been procured; reim-
13 bursable in ten years, by equal annual instalments; or at any time
14 sooner, or in any greater proportions that the government may
15 think fit.

1   SECT. XII. *And be it further enacted,* That no other bank shall
2 be established by any future law of the United States, during the
3 continuance of the corporation hereby created; for which the faith
4 of the United States is hereby pledged.

January 20th, 1791—Passed the Senate.

February 9th, —— Passed the House of Representatives.

For the other Act this day approved, see February 11th.

The Act for the admission of the District of Kentucky into this union, as approved February 4th, 1791, is here subjoined.

An ACT declaring the consent of CONGRESS, that a NEW STATE be formed within the jurisdiction of the Commonwealth of Virginia, and admitted into this Union by the name of the STATE of KENTUCKY.

1   WHEREAS the Legislature of the Commonwealth of Vir-
2   ginia, by an Act, entitled, "An Act concerning the erection of
3   the district of Kentucky into an independent State," passed the
4   eighteenth day of December, one thousand seven hundred and
5   eighty-nine, have consented that the district of Kentucky, within
6   the jurisdiction of the said Commonwealth, and according to its
7   actual boundaries at the time of passing the Act aforesaid, should
8   be formed into a new State: And whereas a convention of dele-
9   gates chosen by the people of the said district of Kentucky, have
10 petitioned Congress to consent, that on the first day of June, one
11 thousand seven hundred and ninety-two, the said district should
12 be formed into a new State, and received into the Union by the
13 name of the State of Kentucky:

1   SECT. I. *Be it enacted by the* SENATE *and House of* REPRE-
2 SENTATIVES *of the United States of America in Congress assembled,*
3 *and it is hereby enacted and declared,* That the Congress doth con-
4 sent that the said district of Kentucky, within the jurisdiction of
5 the Commonwealth of Virginia, and according to its actual boun-
6 daries on the eighteenth day of December, one thousand seven
7 hundred and eighty-nine, shall, upon the first day of June, one
8 thousand seven hundred and ninety-two, be formed into a new
9 State, separate from, and independent of the said Common-
10 wealth of Virginia.

1   SECT. II. *And be it further enacted and declared,* That upon the
2 aforesaid first day of June, one thousand seven hundred and
3 ninety-two, the said new State, by the name and style of the
4 State of Kentucky, shall be received and admitted into this
5 union, as a new and entire member of the United States of
6 America.

      January 4th, 1791—Originated in the Senate.

      28th, —— Passed the House of Representatives.

ORDERED, That the Secretary acquaint the House of Representatives, that the Act, entitled, "An Act to incorporate the subscribers to the bank of the United States," and the Act, entitled, "An Act regulating the number of Representatives to be chosen by the States of Kentucky and Vermont," were this day approved and signed by the President of the United States.

A communication from the Secretary of the Treasury, explaining the terms on which the loan of three millions of florins, mentioned by the President of the United States, to have been negotiated, was read as follows:

"The Secretary of the Treasury, in obedience to the orders of the President of the United States, as signified in his speech at the opening of the present session,

"Respectfully informs the SENATE and HOUSE of REPRESENTATIVES,

"That the terms of the loan of three millions of florins, mentioned by the President as having been negotiated in Holland, are as follow:

"The rate of interest is five per cent. but the charges form a deduction from the principal sum, of four and an half per cent. which will occasion the real interest to be paid on the sum actually received by the United States, to be equal to five and a quarter per cent. nearly.

"The reimbursement is to be made in six equal instalments, commencing in the year 1800, and ending in the year 1804; but it is in the option of the United States to reimburse the whole or any part of the sum borrowed, at any time they may think proper.

"That the disposition which has been made of the above mentioned sum, is as follows:

"One million five hundred thousand florins has been applied, pursuant to the directions of the President of the United States, as a payment to France.

"A further sum of about one hundred and sixty thousand florins will also have been appropriated towards a payment on account of the Dutch loans which became due on the first day of February last, including a premium of seventy thousand florins.

"The residue is in a situation to be disposed of as may be judged expedient.

"A doubt arises how far this loan may be within the meaning of the 'Act making provision for the reduction of the public debt,' on account of the limitation of the rate of interest, which, taking the charges of the loan into calculation, would be somewhat exceeded; and though it is presumed that that limitation was not intended to exclude the addition of the ordinary charges, yet a point of so much delicacy appears to require legislative explanation.

"The Secretary of the Treasury begs leave to observe, that it is in his judgment highly expedient and very important to the general operations of the Treasury, that the above mentioned loan should be deemed to be included within the meaning of the aforesaid Act. The residue may, in this case, be applied with material advantage to the purposes of that Act, and the part which has been otherwise applied, may be hereafter replaced.

"All which is humbly submitted.

"ALEXANDER HAMILTON
Secretary of the Treasury"

"TREASURY DEPARTMENT
February 24th, 1791"[173]

---

[173] This report is in A Record of the Reports of the Secretary of the Treasury, vol. 2, House Records, DNA.

ORDERED, That this report lie for consideration.[174]

The Senate resumed the consideration of the motion made yesterday, to wit:

"RESOLVED, That it be a standing rule, that the doors of the Senate Chamber remain open whilst the Senate shall be sitting in their legislative capacity, except on such occasions as, in their judgment, may require secrecy; and that this rule shall commence and be in force on the first day of the next session of Congress."

On this motion the yeas and nays were required by one fifth of the Senators present.

Mr. Bassett		Nay
Mr. Butler	Yea	
Mr. Carroll		Nay
Mr. Dalton		Nay
Mr. Dickinson		Nay
Mr. Ellsworth		Nay
Mr. Elmer		Nay
Mr. Few		Nay
Mr. Foster	Yea	
Mr. Gunn	Yea	
Mr. Hawkins	Yea	
Mr. Henry		Nay
Mr. Johnson		Nay
Mr. Johnston		Nay
Mr. Izard		Nay
Mr. King	Yea	
Mr. Langdon		Nay
Mr. Lee	Yea	
Mr. Maclay	Yea	
Mr. Monroe	Yea	
Mr. Morris		Nay
Mr. Read		Nay
Mr. Schuyler	Yea	
Mr. Stanton		Nay
Mr. Strong		Nay
Mr. Wingate		Nay

Nays—17

Yeas—9[175]

So it passed in the Negative.

---

[174] The Senate did not consider this report.

[175] This vote is in Other Records: Yeas and nays, Senate Records, DNA.

A message from the House of Representatives by Mr. Beckley their clerk:

"Mr. PRESIDENT,

"The House of Representatives have passed a Bill, entitled, 'An Act supplemental to the Act establishing the Treasury Department,'[176] in which they desire the concurrence of the Senate"—

And he withdrew.

The petition of Shubael Swain was read,[177] praying remission of a fine incurred for the breach of the revenue laws, for reasons mentioned in his petition.

ORDERED, That this petition lie on the table.

The Bill sent from the House of Representatives, for the relief of Shubael Swain, and on the sixth of January not concurred in by the Senate, is as follows:

"An ACT for the relief of SHUBAEL SWAIN "

1　"WHEREAS it appears that Shubael Swain, a prisoner in
2　the gaol of the city of Philadelphia, on account of a breach of
3　the revenue laws, is insolvent, and has suffered a long imprison-
4　ment—

1　"SECT. I. *Be it enacted by the* SENATE *and House of* REPRE-
2　SENTATIVES *of the United States of America in Congress assembled,*
3　That the right and interest of the United States in a certain judg-
4　ment for four hundred dollars, with costs of suit, recovered in
5　the district court of Pennsylvania, in the month of April, one
6　thousand seven hundred and ninety, against Shubael Swain, under
7　the Act, entitled, 'An Act to regulate the collection of the duties
8　imposed by law, on the tonnage of ships and vessels, and on
9　goods, wares and merchandizes imported into the United States,'
10　shall be, and the same is hereby remitted and released unto the
11　said Shubael Swain."

　　1791, January the 4th—Passed the House of Representatives.

Agreeably to the order of the day, the Senate resumed the SECOND reading of "The Bill to amend an Act, entitled, 'An Act for establishing the temporary and permanent seat of the government of the United States' "—

On motion that the consideration hereof be postponed, the yeas and nays were required by one fifth of the Senators present.

---

[176] An annotated printed copy of this bill is in House Bills, Senate Records, DNA.
[177] This petition is in Petitions and Memorials: Various subjects, Senate Records, DNA.

Mr. Bassett		Yea
Mr. Butler	Nay	
Mr. Carroll	Nay	
Mr. Dalton		Yea
Mr. Dickinson		Yea
Mr. Ellsworth		Yea
Mr. Elmer		Yea
Mr. Few	Nay	
Mr. Foster		Yea
Mr. Gunn	Nay	
Mr. Hawkins	Nay	
Mr. Henry	Nay	
Mr. Johnson		Yea
Mr. Johnston	Nay	
Mr. Izard	Nay	
Mr. King		Yea
Mr. Langdon	Nay	
Mr. Lee	Nay	
Mr. Maclay		Yea
Mr. Monroe	Nay	
Mr. Morris	Nay	
Mr. Read	Nay	
Mr. Schuyler	Nay	
Mr. Stanton		Yea
Mr. Strong		Yea
Mr. Wingate		Yea

Nays—14
Yeas—12[178]

So it passed in the Negative.

On motion that the first clause of this Bill be agreed to, to wit: From line first, to the word "provided," line eighteenth; the yeas and nays were required by one fifth of the Senators present.

Mr. Bassett	Nay	
Mr. Butler		Yea
Mr. Carroll		Yea
Mr. Dalton	Nay	
Mr. Dickinson	Nay	
Mr. Ellsworth	Nay	
Mr. Elmer	Nay	

[178] This vote is in Other Records: Yeas and nays, Senate Records, DNA.

Mr. Few		Yea
Mr. Foster	Nay	
Mr. Gunn		Yea
Mr. Hawkins		Yea
Mr. Henry		Yea
Mr. Johnson	Nay	
Mr. Johnston		Yea
Mr. Izard		Yea
Mr. King	Nay	
Mr. Langdon		Yea
Mr. Lee		Yea
Mr. Maclay	Nay	
Mr. Monroe		Yea
Mr. Morris		Yea
Mr. Read		Yea
Mr. Schuyler		Yea
Mr. Stanton	Nay	
Mr. Strong	Nay	
Mr. Wingate	Nay	

Yeas—14

Nays—12[179]

So it passed in the Affirmative.

ORDERED, That this Bill pass to the THIRD reading.[180]

Mr. Ellsworth reported from the managers appointed to confer with the managers on the part of the House of Representatives,[181] on the amendments to the Bill, entitled, "An Act repealing after the last day of June next, the duties heretofore laid upon distilled spirits imported from abroad, and laying others in their stead; and also upon spirits distilled within the United States, and for appropriating the same."

ORDERED, That the report lie for consideration.

The Bill sent from the House of Representatives for concurrence, entitled, "An Act supplementary to the Act, entitled, 'An Act to incorporate the sub-scribers to the bank of the United States,'" was read the THIRD time.

On motion to add the following, as a section to the Bill—

"SECT. ——— *And be it further enacted,* That the term 'Law,' used in the third section of the original Act, which requires that the bye-laws, ordinances, and regulations of the said corporation, shall not be contrary to law or the

---

[179] This vote is in Other Records: Yeas and nays, Senate Records, DNA.

[180] On February 26 this bill was read a third time, passed, and sent to the House for concurrence.

[181] This report is in Joint Committee Reports, Senate Records, DNA.

constitution thereof, shall be construed to mean the laws of the individual States, as well as of the United States,"—

It passed in the Negative.

On motion to adopt the following, as an addition to the Bill, "*And be it further enacted*, That nothing in the Act to which this is a supplement, shall restrain the Legislature of the United States from repealing the same, and abolishing the corporation thereby established, at any time after the fourth day of March, in the year one thousand eight hundred and two,"[182] the yeas and nays were required by one fifth of the Senators present.

Mr. Bassett	Nay	
Mr. Butler		Yea
Mr. Carroll		Yea
Mr. Dalton	Nay	
Mr. Dickinson	Nay	
Mr. Ellsworth	Nay	
Mr. Elmer	Nay	
Mr. Few		Yea
Mr. Foster	Nay	
Mr. Gunn		Yea
Mr. Hawkins		Yea
Mr. Henry	Nay	
Mr. Johnson	Nay	
Mr. Johnston		Yea
Mr. Izard		Yea
Mr. King	Nay	
Mr. Langdon	Nay	
Mr. Lee		Yea
Mr. Maclay	Nay	
Mr. Monroe		Yea
Mr. Morris	Nay	
Mr. Read	Nay	
Mr. Schuyler	Nay	
Mr. Stanton	Nay	
Mr. Strong	Nay	
Mr. Wingate	Nay	

Nays—17
Yeas—9[183]

So it passed in the Negative.

RESOLVED, That this Bill PASS.

---

[182] This motion is in Senate Simple Resolutions and Motions, Senate Records, DNA.
[183] This vote is in Other Records: Yeas and nays, Senate Records, DNA.

ORDERED, That the Secretary acquaint the House of Representatives with the concurrence of the Senate in this Bill.[184]

The Bill sent from the House of Representatives for concurrence, entitled, "An Act supplemental to the Act establishing the Treasury department," was read the FIRST time, as follows:

"An ACT supplemental to the Act establishing the TREASURY DEPARTMENT "

1   "SECT. I. *Be it enacted by the* SENATE *and House of* REPRE-
2   SENTATIVES *of the United States of America in Congress assembled,*
3   That the eighth section of the Act, entitled, 'An Act to establish
4   the Treasury department,' passed the second day of September,
5   one thousand seven hundred and eighty-nine, shall be, and the
6   same is hereby extended to all and every of the Clerks em-
7   ployed in the Treasury department, as fully and effectually as if
8   they and every of them were specially named therein; except
9   as to the penalty in such section mentioned, which in case of any
10   such Clerk offending against the provisions of the said section,
11   shall be five hundred dollars, and removal from office.

1   "SECT. II. *And be it further enacted,* That each and every
2   Clerk and other officer already appointed in any of the depart-
3   ments of the United States, (and who have not, since their
4   appointment, taken the oath or affirmation hereafter menti-
5   oned) shall, within fifteen days after the passing of this Act, and
6   those who shall hereafter be appointed, shall, before they enter
7   upon the duties of such appointment, take an oath or affirma-
8   tion before one of the Justices of the Supreme Court, or one of
9   the Judges of a District Court of the United States, to support
10   the Constitution of the United States; and also an oath or affir-
11   mation, well and faithfully to execute the trust committed to
12   him: which oaths or affirmations subscribed by such Clerk, and
13   certified by the person administering the same, shall be filed in
14   the office of the person employing such Clerk.

1   "SECT. III. *And be it further enacted,* That it shall and may
2   be lawful for the principal in any of the offices of the United
3   States, who is authorised by law to appoint Clerks under him,
4   to allow to each Clerk such compensation for his services as he
5   shall in the opinion of such officer deserve for the same: *Pro-*
6   *vided,* that the whole sum to be expended for Clerks, in any
7   such office (except the chief Clerk) shall not exceed a sum equal
8   to five hundred dollars for every Clerk employed therein."

"1791, February the 25th—Passed the House of Representatives."

---

[184] On March 1 this bill was signed by both the Speaker and the Vice President and given to the committee on enrolled bills for delivery to the President.

ORDERED, That this Bill pass to the SECOND reading, and that in the mean time, it be printed for the use of the Senate.[185]

The Senate adjourned to 11 o'clock to-morrow.

S A T U R D A Y, FEBRUARY 26, 1791

The SENATE assembled—present as yesterday.

Mr. Morris communicated the request of the American Philosophical Society, "that the Vice President of the United States and Senate, would attend the Eulogium to be pronounced by order of the Society, to the memory of their late worthy President BENJAMIN FRANKLIN, on Tuesday morning next, at the German Lutheran Church, at half past nine o'clock."

The Bill to amend an Act, entitled, "An Act for establishing the temporary and permanent seat of the government of the United States," was read the THIRD time.

RESOLVED, That this Bill PASS; that the title thereof be "An Act to amend an Act, entitled, 'An Act for establishing the temporary and permanent seat of the government of the United States;' " that it be engrossed,[186] and that the Secretary desire the concurrence of the House of Representatives therein.[187]

The Bill sent from the House of Representatives for concurrence, entitled, "An Act supplemental to the Act establishing the Treasury department," was read the SECOND time, and

ORDERED, That this Bill be referred to the Committee appointed the 24th[188] February, on the motions respecting the officers of the department of the Treasury and the Attorney-General.

The Bill sent from the House of Representatives for concurrence, entitled, "An Act fixing the time for the next annual meeting of Congress," was read the THIRD time.

RESOLVED, That this Bill PASS.

ORDERED, That the Secretary acquaint the House of Representatives with the concurrence of the Senate in this Bill.[189]

Agreeably to notice on the 21st instant, leave was requested to bring in "A Bill concerning the payment of balances due to the United States in certain

[185] On February 26 this bill was committed to the committee on the motions concerning the expenses of the clerks for the Attorney General. On the same day the committee reported, and several amendments to the bill were adopted.

[186] This resolve and the engrossed bill are in Engrossed Senate Bills and Resolutions, Senate Records, DNA.

[187] The House read this bill the first and second times on February 26 and committed it to the committee of the whole. On February 28 it was again considered and on March 1 the bill was read the third time and passed.

[188] The smooth journal inserts the word "of" at this point.

[189] On March 1 this bill was signed by both the Speaker and the Vice President and delivered to the President.

cases,"[190] and it being obtained, the Bill was laid on the table and read the FIRST time as follows:

An ACT concerning the PAYMENT of BALANCES due to the UNITED STATES, in certain cases

1   SECT. I. *Be it enacted by the* SENATE *and House of* REPRESEN-
2   TATIVES *of the United States of America in Congress assembled,* That
3   in every case of the settlement of an account at the Treasury
4   of the United States (in which if a balance had been or should be
5   found against the United States, such balance would have been
6   or would be liquidated by a certificate) if a balance has been or
7   shall be found in favour of the United States, it shall be lawful
8   for the person or persons from whom such balance is or shall be
9   due, to pay or satisfy the same, in certificates of debt due from
10   the United States, of the like tenor, and upon the like principles
11   as if such balance had been found against the United States.

ORDERED, That this Bill pass to the SECOND reading.[191]

Mr. Strong reported from the Committee appointed to take into consideration the Bill sent from the House of Representatives for concurrence, entitled, "An Act to establish offices for the purpose of granting lands within the territories of the United States," that the further consideration of this Bill be postponed until the next session of Congress.

On motion, it was agreed to postpone the report of the Committee, and to resume the second reading of the Bill; and after debate—

ORDERED, That this Bill be re-committed.[192]

A message from the House of Representatives by Mr. Beckley their clerk:

"Mr. PRESIDENT,

"The House of Representatives recede from their disagreement to the amendment last proposed by the Senate, to the last clause of the section to follow section sixty-first of the Bill, entitled, 'An Act repealing after the last day of June next, the duties heretofore laid upon distilled spirits imported from abroad, and laying others in their stead; and also upon spirits distilled within the United States, and for appropriating the same;' and they agree to the amendment, amended as follows: After the word 'exceed,' substitute these

---

[190] This bill is in Senate Bills, Senate Records, DNA.

[191] On February 28 this bill was read a second time and a motion to postpone it was defeated. It was then committed. On the same day the committee reported and the bill was postponed until the next session of Congress.

[192] On March 1 this committee reported a resolution which was passed and sent to the House for concurrence. Consideration of the bill was postponed until the next session of Congress.

words, 'Seven *per cent.* of the whole product of the duties arising from the spirits distilled within the United States: *And provided also,* That such allowance shall not exceed the annual amount of forty-five thousand dollars, until the same shall be further ascertained by law' "[193]—

And he withdrew.

The report from the managers appointed to confer with the managers appointed on the part of the House of Representatives, on the disagreeing votes of the two Houses, to the last clause of the section to follow section sixty-first of the last mentioned Bill, was considered,

Whereupon—

RESOLVED, That the Senate do agree to the Resolution of the House of Representatives, on the clause above referred to, and that the amendment thereon be as follows: After the word "exceed," substitute these words, "Seven *per cent.* of the whole product of the duties arising from the spirits distilled within the United States: *And provided also,* That such allowance shall not exceed the annual amount of forty-five thousand dollars, until the same shall be further ascertained by law."

ORDERED, That the Secretary communicate this Resolution to the House of Representatives.[194]

Mr. Ellsworth, from the Committee to whom was referred the Bill sent from the House of Representatives for concurrence, entitled, "An Act supplemental to the Act establishing the Treasury department," reported amendments;[195] which were adopted—and

ORDERED, That this Bill pass to the THIRD reading.[196]

The Senate adjourned to Monday next, at 11 o'clock.

MONDAY, FEBRUARY 28, 1791

The SENATE assembled—present as on the 26th, and

Proceeded to the THIRD reading of the Bill sent from the House of Representatives for concurrence, entitled, "An Act supplemental to the Act establishing the Treasury department," and—

RESOLVED, That this Bill PASS, with the following amendments:

SECT. III. Line 8, after "dollars," insert "*per annum.*"

---

[193] This House resolution and amendment are in Messages from the House, Senate Records, DNA.

[194] On February 28 this bill was signed by the Speaker. The Vice President signed it on March 1 and it was given to the committee on enrolled bills for delivery to the President.

[195] The amendments are in House Bills, Senate Records, DNA.

[196] On February 28 this bill was passed with amendments, which were printed in the Journal, and returned to the House for concurrence in the amendments.

At the end of the Bill, add

"SECT. IV. *And be it further enacted by the authority aforesaid*, That there shall be allowed, for one year, commencing with the passing of this Act, to the Register, two hundred and fifty dollars, and to the Auditor, the Comptroller of the Treasury, and the Attorney-General, four hundred dollars each, in addition to their respective salaries, and to be paid in the same manner"—

To the title add, "and for a further compensation to certain officers."[197]

ORDERED, That the Secretary desire the concurrence of the House of Representatives in these amendments.[198]

"The Bill concerning the payment of balances due to the United States, in certain cases," was read the SECOND time.

On motion that this Bill be postponed—

It passed in the Negative.

ORDERED, That this Bill be committed to

Mr. Strong

Mr. Lee and

Mr. Schuyler   to   consider   generally   and   report

thereon.[199]

A message from the House of Representatives by Mr. Beckley their clerk:

"Mr. PRESIDENT,

"The House of Representatives have passed a Bill, entitled, 'An Act concerning the rates of foreign coins,'[200] in which they desire the concurrence of the Senate—

"They agree to the amendments of the Senate, to the Bill, entitled, 'An Act for raising and adding another regiment to the military establishment of the United States, and for making further provision for the protection of the frontiers,' with amendments,[201]—in which amendments to the amendments, they desire the concurrence of the Senate"—

And he withdrew.

The amendments of the House of Representatives on the amendments of Senate, to the last mentioned Bill, are—

---

[197] The resolve on passage and a printed copy of this bill, with amendments written in for section 3 and the title, are in House Bills, Senate Records, DNA. Section 4 is omitted from the document.

[198] On March 1 the House notified the Senate that it had concurred in these Senate amendments.

[199] This vote for committee is in Other Records: Yeas and nays, Senate Records, DNA.

[200] This bill has not been located.

[201] This House resolve and the list of amendments are in House Bills, Senate Records, DNA.

"SECT. X. Second amendment. In the second line of the Bill strike out the word 'more.' In the same line, substitute 'will,' for 'would;' and in the fourth line strike out the word 'than,' and in lieu thereof insert 'in addition to or in place of the.'

"In the seventh line of the amendment of the Senate, strike out the word 'of,' and insert 'not exceeding.'

"SECT. XII. Line 6th of the Bill, make the word 'cases,' singular.

"Same line, after 'wounds,' substitute 'or' for 'and.'

"In the last of the sections proposed to be added to the Bill, line six, after annum,' insert 'or to apply any monies which he may have borrowed by virtue of any law of the United States, to the purposes of this Act.'

"Line ninth after the word 'aforesaid,' insert 'or for replacing the monies which may be so applied.'

The Bill sent from the House of Representatives for concurrence, entitled, "An Act concerning the rates of foreign coins," was read the FIRST time as follows:

"An ACT concerning the RATES of FOREIGN COINS."

1   "SECT. I. *Be it enacted by the* SENATE *and House of* REPRE-
2   SENTATIVES *of the United States of America in Congress assembled,*
3   That so much of an Act, entitled, 'An Act to provide more ef-
4   fectually for the collection of the duties imposed by law on goods,
5   wares and merchandize imported into the United States, and on
6   the tonnage of ships or vessels,' as hath rated the rix dollar of
7   Denmark at one hundred cents, be, and the same is hereby re-
8   pealed; and that this repeal shall be deemed to operate in respect
9   to all duties which have already arisen or accrued, as well as to
10   such as shall hereafter arise or accrue.

1   "SECT. II. *And be it further enacted,* That the Secretary of
2   the Treasury be authorised and directed to estimate the value of
3   the several denominations of foreign coin which are not estima-
4   ted by law, and that the Collectors of the customs, in their valu-
5   ation of such foreign coin, be required to conform to the estimate
6   thereof, which shall be made by the Secretary of the Treasury,
7   pursuant to this Act."

February the 28th, 1791—Sent from the House of Representatives for
concurrence.

ORDERED, That this Bill pass to the SECOND reading.[202]

---

[202] On March 1 this bill was read a second time and committed. On the same day this committee reported and the bill was passed with the committee's amendments, which were printed in the Journal and sent to the House for concurrence.

The Senate took into consideration the resolution of the House of Representatives, on their amendments to the amendments of the Senate, to the Bill, entitled, "An Act for raising and adding another regiment to the military establishment of the United States, and for making further provision for the protection of the frontiers," and after progress, the further consideration thereof was postponed until to-morrow.[203]

Mr. Strong reported from the Committee to whom was referred "The Bill concerning the payment of balances due to the United States, in certain cases,"[204]

Whereupon—

ORDERED, That the further consideration of this Bill be postponed to the next session of Congress.

The Senate adjourned to 11 o'clock to-morrow.

---

[203] On March 1 the Senate agreed to all the House amendments except the last two and notified the House.

[204] The rough journal adds the following canceled clause: "and the report was adopted."

TUESDAY, March 1, 1791

The Senate assembled—present as yesterday.

Mr. Foster reported from the Committee on enrolled Bills, That they had examined the following Bills, and that they are duly enrolled: The Bill, entitled, "An Act giving effect to the laws of the United States, within the State of Vermont."[1] The Bill, entitled, "An Act fixing the time for the next annual meeting of Congress."[2] The Bill, entitled, "An Act to explain and amend an Act, entitled, 'An Act making further provision for the payment of the debts of the United States.' "[3] The Bill, entitled, "An Act supplementary to the Act, entitled, 'An Act to incorporate the subscribers to the bank of the United States.' "[4] And the Bill, entitled, "An Act repealing after the last day of June next, the duties heretofore laid upon distilled spirits imported from abroad, and laying others in their stead; and also upon spirits distilled within the United States, and for appropriating the same."[5]

The Bill sent from the House of Representatives for concurrence, entitled, "An Act concerning the rates of foreign coins," was read the SECOND time, and—

Ordered, That it be committed to

Mr. Schuyler

Mr. Monroe and

Mr. Maclay, to consider generally and report thereon.[6]

The petition of John McPherson was read,[7] praying an exclusive patent, in consequence of certain inventions mentioned in his petition.

Ordered, That this petition lie on the table.

The consideration of the resolution of the House of Representatives, on the amendments of the Senate to the Bill, entitled, "An Act for raising and adding another regiment to the military establishment of the United States, and for making furher provision for the protection of the frontiers," was resumed, and—

Resolved, That the Senate agree to all the amendments of the House of Representatives, on the amendments of the Senate, except the two last, to which the Senate do not agree.

Ordered, That the Secretary communicate this resolution to the House of Representatives.[8]

---

[1] The inspected enrolled bill is in Enrolled Acts, RG 11, DNA. E–23857.

[2] The inspected enrolled bill is in Enrolled Acts, RG 11, DNA. E–23852.

[3] The inspected enrolled bill is in Enrolled Acts, RG 11, DNA. E–23974.

[4] The inspected enrolled bill is in Enrolled Acts, RG 11, DNA. E–23876.

[5] The inspected enrolled bill is in Enrolled Acts, RG 11, DNA. E–23865, E–46325.

[6] This vote for committee is in Other Records: Yeas and nays, Senate Records, DNA.

[7] This petition is in Petitions and Memorials: Various subjects, Senate Records, DNA.

[8] On March 2 the House, during a secret session, receded from the two amendments disagreed to by the Senate and notified the Senate.

Mr. Morris reported from the Committee appointed February 7th,[9] on the report of the Secretary of the Treasury, relative to the establishment of a mint; and the report was ordered to lie for consideration.[10]

Mr. Izard reported from the Committee to whom was referred the report of the Secretary of State,[11] on the subject of weights, measures and coins, "That as a proposition has been made to the National Assembly of France, for obtaining a standard of measure, which shall be invariable, and communicable to all nations, and at all times, as a similar proposition has been submitted to the British Parliament, in their last session; as the avowed object of these is, to introduce an uniformity in the measures and weights of the commercial nations; as a coincidence of regulation, by the government of the United States, on so interesting a subject, would be desirable, your Committee are of opinion, that it would not be eligible, at present, to introduce any alteration in the measures and weights which are now used in the United States"—

And the report was adopted.

A message from the House of Representatives by Mr. Beckley their clerk:

"Mr. PRESIDENT,

"The Speaker of the House of Representatives has signed several enrolled Bills, which I am directed to bring to the Senate for the signature of the Vice President"—

And he withdrew.

Whereupon the Vice President signed the following enrolled Bills, and they were delivered to the Committee, to be laid before the President of the United States for his approbation, to wit: The Bill, entitled, "An Act giving effect to the laws of the United States, within the State of Vermont." The Bill, entitled, "An Act fixing the time for the next annual meeting of Congress," The Bill, entitled, "An Act to explain and amend an Act, entitled, 'An Act making further provision for the payment of the debts of the United States.' " The Bill, entitled, "An Act supplementary to the Act, entitled, 'An Act to incorporate the subscribers to the bank of the United States.' " And the Bill, entitled, "An Act repealing after the last day of June next, the duties heretofore laid upon distilled spirits imported from abroad, and laying others in their stead; and also upon spirits distilled within the United States, and for appropriating the same."[12]

---

[9] This report is in Various Select Committee Reports, Senate Records, DNA.

[10] On March 2 this report was considered and the Senate resolved that a mint should be established and resolved to empower the President to carry this resolve into effect. The House was notified of this action.

[11] This report is in Various Select Committee Reports, Senate Records, DNA.

[12] On March 2 the committee on enrolled bills reported that it had laid these bills before the President on the preceding day. On March 1 the President had signed all these bills except the Duties on Distilled Spirits Bill, which was signed on March 3.

On motion that it be "Resolved that a Committee be appointed, to join with a Committee of the House of Representatives, to wait on the President of the United States, and communicate to him the desire of both Houses of Congress, that he would cause every proper means to be used, to bring about a peace between the United States and the Wabash and Miami Indians, previous to further hostilities on those nations; and that Congress will make provision to defray the necessary expence thereof"—

A motion was made to add to the motion as follows: "And likewise to obtain from such tribes a relinquishment of their claims to the territory of the United States, wherein it can be accomplished, so as to make the same a more productive fund for the payment of the public debt"[13]—

And the consideration hereof was postponed until to-morrow.[14]

Mr. Schuyler from the Committee on the Bill sent from the House of Representatives for concurrence, entitled, "An Act concerning the rates of foreign coins," reported amendments,[15] and it was agreed to amend the Bill accordingly.

It was agreed by unanimous consent, so far to dispense with the rule, as that this Bill be now read the THIRD time; and the Bill having been read accordingly—

RESOLVED, That this Bill PASS, with the following amendments:

Expunge the whole of the second section.

In the title, after the word "Act," expunge the whole, and substitute "relative to the rix dollar of Denmark."[16]

ORDERED, That the Secretary desire the concurrence of the House of Representatives, in these amendments.[17]

A message from the House of Representatives by Mr. Beckley their clerk:

"Mr. PRESIDENT,

"The House of Representatives have passed the Bill sent from the Senate for concurrence, entitled, 'An Act to amend "An Act for establishing the temporary and permanent seat of the government of the United States" '[18]—

"They agree to the amendments of the Senate on the Bill, entitled, 'An Act supplemental to the Act establishing the Treasury department, and for a further compensation to certain officers'[19]—

---

[13] Drafts of these motions are in Senate Simple Resolutions and Motions, Senate Records, DNA.

[14] On March 3 these motions were postponed until the next session of Congress.

[15] These amendments are in Various Select Committee Reports, Senate Records, DNA.

[16] These amendments have not been located.

[17] On March 2 the House notified the Senate that it had concurred in these amendments.

[18] On March 2 this bill was signed by both the Speaker and the Vice President and given to the committee on enrolled bills for delivery to the President.

[19] This message is in Messages from the House, Senate Records, DNA. On March 2 this bill was signed by both the Speaker and the Vice President and given to the committee on enrolled bills for delivery to the President.

"They have passed the Bill, entitled, 'An Act for making compensations to the Commissioners of loans, for extraordinary expenses,'[20] and the Bill, entitled, 'An Act providing compensations for the officers of the judicial courts of the United States, and for jurors and witnesses, and for other purposes;'[21] in which two last mentioned Bills they desire the concurrence of the Senate"—

And he withdrew.

The Bill sent from the House of Representatives for concurrence, entitled, "An Act for making compensations to the Commissioners of loans for extraordinary expenses," was read the FIRST time as follows:

"An ACT for making COMPENSATIONS to the COMMISSIONERS of LOANS, for
    extraordinary expenses "

1   "SECT. I. *Be it enacted by the* SENATE *and House of* REPRESEN-
2   TATIVES *of the United States of America in Congress assembled,* That
3   the Commissioners of loans in the several States, shall be allowed
4   in the settlement of their accounts, such sums as shall appear to
5   have been necessarily expended by them in the purchase of stati-
6   onary for the use of their several offices, from the commencement
7   of the same to the first day of October next.

1   "SECT. II. *And be it further enacted,* That the Commissioners
2   of loans in the several States, shall be allowed in the settlement of
3   their several accounts, such sums as they shall have necessarily
4   expended for the hire of Clerks to assist in executing the duties
5   of their several offices, from the commencement of the same to
6   the first day of October next, excepting only the hire of one
7   Clerk for the several Commissioners in the States of Massachu-
8   setts, New-York, Pennsylvania and Virginia."

    "March the 1st, 1791—Passed the House of Representatives."

ORDERED, That this Bill pass to the SECOND reading.[22]

The Bill sent from the House of Representatives for concurrence, entitled, "An Act providing compensations for the officers of the judicial courts of the United States, and for jurors and witnesses, and for other purposes," was read the FIRST time as follows:

"An ACT providing compensations for the OFFICERS of the JUDICIAL COURTS
    of the United States, and for JURORS and WITNESSES, and for other
    purposes "

1   "SECT. I. *Be it enacted by the* SENATE *and House of* REPRE-

---

[20] This bill has not been located.
[21] An annotated printed copy of this bill is in House Bills, Senate Records, DNA.
[22] On March 2 this bill was read a second time and committed. On the same day the committee reported an amendment which was agreed to.

2   SENTATIVES *of the United States of America in Congress assembled,*

3   That there be allowed to the several officers following, in addi-

4   tion to the fees (except mileage to the Marshals) to which they

5   are otherwise by law entitled, and also to jurors and witnesses,

6   in the courts of the United States, the following respective com-

7   pensations; that is to say, To the Attorney of the United States

8   for the district, for his expenses and time in travelling from the

9   place in the State where the office of the Clerk of the district

10   court is kept, to the other place in the district where a circuit

11   court is directed to be held, at the rate of ten cents per mile

12   going, and the same allowance for returning.

13   "To the Clerk of the district court, for attending in the district

14   or circuit court, five dollars per day, and the like compensation

15   for travelling as is above allowed to the Attorney for the district.

16   "To the Clerk of the supreme court, for attending in court,

17   eight dollars per day.

18   "To the Marshal of the district, for attending the supreme

19   circuit or district courts, five dollars per day; for summoning a

20   grand jury three dollars, and for summoning a petit jury two

21   dollars, and for serving a writ five cents per mile from the place

22   where the office of the Clerk of the district court is kept, to the

23   place where the writ shall be served, but there shall not in any

24   case be an allowance of mileage to the Marshals exceeding one

25   hundred miles; to the grand and petit jurors, each fifty cents

26   per day, for attending in court, and for travelling, at the rate

27   of fifty cents for every ten miles, from their respective places

28   of abode, to the place where the court is held, and the like al-

29   lowance for returning; to witnesses summoned on the part of

30   the United States, or in behalf of any prisoner to be tried for

31   any capital offence in any of the courts thereof, the same com-

32   pensation as is above allowed to grand and petit jurors. That

33   the several officers above specified, shall be deemed to have

34   been entitled to the above respective compensations, from the

35   time of their respective appointments, and that the grand and

36   petit jurors and witnesses who have heretofore attended, shall

37   also be deemed entitled to the above compensation, in like man-

38   ner as those who shall hereafter attend.

39   "That there shall also be paid to the Marshal the amount of

40   the expense for fuel, candles and other reasonable contingencies

41   for holding a court, as hath accrued or shall accrue, and the

42 compensations to the grand and petit jurors, and witnesses, shall
43 be included in the account of, and paid to the Marshal, to the
44 use of and be by him accordingly paid over to the several persons
45 entitled to the same: And the accounts of the several officers for
46 the compensations aforesaid (except mileage to the Marshal, for
47 the service of writs in civil causes) having been previously exa-
48 mined and certified by the Judge of the district, shall be passed
49 in the usual manner at, and the amount thereof paid out of the
50 Treasury of the United States. And a sum arising from the fines
51 and forfeitures to the United States, and equal to the amount
52 thereof, is hereby appropriated for the payment of the above
53 accounts.

1   "SECT. II. *And be it further enacted*, That instead of the pro-
2 visions in that respect heretofore made, the first session of the
3 circuit courts in the Eastern Circuit, after the passing of this
4 Act, shall commence at the times following; That is to say,—
5 in New-York district, on the fifth, and in Connecticut district,
6 on the twenty-fifth days of April next; in Massachusetts district,
7 on the twelfth, and in New-Hampshire district, on the twenty-
8 fourth days of May next; and in Rhode-Island district, on the
9 seventh day of June next; and the subsequent sessions in the re-
10 spective districts, on the like days of every sixth calendar month
11 thereafter, except when any of those days shall happen on a Sun-
12 day, and then the sessions shall commence on the next day fol-
13 lowing. And the sessions of the said circuit court shall be held in
14 New-Hampshire district, at Portsmouth and Exeter alternately,
15 beginning at the first; in Massachusetts district, at Boston; in
16 Rhode-Island district, at New-Port and Providence alternately,
17 beginning at the first; in Connecticut district, at Hartford and
18 New-Haven alternately, beginning at the last; and in New-York
19 district, at the city of New-York only.

1   "SECT. III. *And be it further enacted*, That from and after the
2 passing of this Act, instead of the provisions in the Act for that
3 purpose, the sessions of the circuit court for the district of Virginia,
4 shall be holden in the city of Richmond only.

1   "SECT. IV. *And be it further enacted*, That this Act shall con-
2 tinue in force until the end of the next session of Congress, and
3 no longer."

"March the 1st, 1791—Passed the House of Representatives."

ORDERED, That this Bill pass to the SECOND reading, and that in the mean time it be printed for the use of the Senate.[23]

ORDERED, That   Mr. Schuyler

Mr. Ellsworth and

Mr. Butler, be a Committee to revise the laws of the United States,[24] to report such as are expired or are about to expire; and a Bill or Bills, for the revival of such as may be deemed necessary.[25]

Mr. Langdon from the Committee appointed to consider that part of the speech of the President of the United States which relates to the commerce of the Mediterranean, and to whom was referred the message from the President of the United States of the 30th December, and papers, together with his message of 22d February, reported a Bill, which was read the FIRST time as follows:[26]

An ACT making an APPROPRIATION for the purposes therein mentioned

1   SECT. I. *Be it enacted by the* SENATE *and House of* REPRESEN-
2   TATIVES *of the United States of America in Congress assembled,* That
3   for the purpose of effecting a recognition of the treaty of the
4   United States, with the new Emperor of Morocco, there be, and
5   hereby is appropriated a sum not exceeding twenty thousand
6   dollars; to be paid out of the monies which, prior to the first
7   day of January next, shall arise from the duties imposed upon
8   spirits distilled within the United States, and from stills, by the
9   Act, entitled, "An Act repealing after the last day of June next,
10   the duties heretofore laid upon distilled spirits imported from
11   abroad, and laying others in their stead; and also upon spirits dis-
12   tilled within the United States, and for appropriating the same;"
13   together with the excess of duties which may arise from the du-
14   ties imposed by the said Act on imported spirits, beyond those
15   which would have arisen by the Act, entitled, "An Act making
16   further provision for the payment of the debts of the United
17   States;" and the President is hereby authorised to take on loan
18   the whole sum of this Act appropriated, or so much thereof as
19   he may judge requisite, at an interest not exceeding six per cent.
20   per annum, and the fund established for the above mentioned
21   appropriation is hereby pledged for the payment of the principal
22   and interest of any loan to be obtained in manner aforesaid; and
23   in case of any deficiency in the said fund, the faith of the United

---

[23] On March 2 this bill was read a second time and committed.

[24] This vote for committee is in Other Records: Yeas and nays, Senate Records, DNA.

[25] On March 2 this committee presented the Mitigation of Forfeitures Bill which was read for the first time and printed in the Journal.

[26] This bill has not been located.

24   States is hereby also pledged to make good such deficiency.[27]
March the 2d, 1791—Passed the Senate.

It was agreed by unanimous consent, so far to dispense with the rule, as that this Bill be now read the SECOND time.

On motion to commit the Bill, with an instruction to augment the sum therein appropriated, to sixty thousand dollars—

It passed in the Negative.

ORDERED, That this Bill pass to the THIRD reading.[28]

Mr. Strong reported from the Committee appointed to take into consideration the Bill,[29] entitled, "An Act to establish offices for the purpose of granting lands within the territories of the United States,"

Whereupon—

RESOLVED, *By the* SENATE *and House of* REPRESENTATIVES *of the United States of America in Congress assembled,* That the President of the United States, be, and he hereby is requested to cause a return to be made to Congress, at their next session, of the quantity and situation of the lands not claimed by the Indians, nor granted to, nor claimed by any of the citizens of the United States, within the territory ceded to the United States by the State of North-Carolina, and within the territory of the United States north-west of the river Ohio.[30]

ORDERED, That the Secretary request the concurrence of the House of Representatives in this resolution.[31]

ORDERED, That the further consideration of the Bill last mentioned, be postponed until the next session of Congress.[32]

The Senate adjourned to 11 o'clock to-morrow.

WEDNESDAY, MARCH 2, 1791

The SENATE assembled—present as yesterday.

A message from the House of Representatives by Mr. Beckley their clerk:

"Mr. PRESIDENT,

"The House of Representatives recede from their two last amendments to

---

[27] The rough journal does not include a text of this act, merely the notation "here insert the Bill."

[28] On March 2 this bill was read a third time, passed, and sent to the House for concurrence. On the same day the House read this bill three times, passed it, and notified the Senate.

[29] This report is in Various Select Committee Reports, Senate Records, DNA.

[30] This resolve is in Senate Joint and Concurrent Resolutions, Senate Records, DNA.

[31] On March 3 the House notified the Senate that it had agreed to this resolution with an amendment, and the Senate agreed to the amendment.

[32] The resolve noting this order is in Engrossed House Bills, House Records, DNA.

the amendments of the Senate, to the Bill, entitled, 'An Act for raising and adding another regiment to the military establishment of the United States, and for making further provision for the protection of the frontiers,' and[33]—

"They agree to the amendments of the Senate on the Bill, entitled, 'An Act concerning the rates of foreign coin'[34]—

"The House of Representatives have passed the Bill, entitled, 'An Act to continue in force for a limited time, an Act, entitled, "An Act for the temporary establishment of the Post-Office;" '[35] the Bill, entitled, 'An Act for making compensation to the widows and orphan children of certain officers who were killed, or who died in the service of the United States, during the late war; and for the relief of certain invalids, and other persons therein mentioned;'[36] and the Bill, entitled, 'An Act supplementary to the Act making provision for the reduction of the public debt,'[37] in which three last mentioned Bills they desire the concurrence of the Senate—

"I am directed to bring to the Senate several enrolled Bills, which are signed by the Speaker of the House of Representatives, for the signature of the Vice President"—

And he withdrew.

Mr. Foster reported from the Committee on enrolled Bills, That they did yesterday, lay before the President of the United States, the following enrolled Bills, for his approbation:

The Bill, entitled, "An Act giving effect to the laws of the United States, within the State of Vermont"—

The Bill, entitled, "An Act fixing the time for the next annual meeting of Congress"—

The Bill, entitled, "An Act to explain and amend an Act, entitled, 'An Act making further provision for the payment of the debts of the United States' "—

The Bill, entitled, "An Act supplementary to the Act, entitled, 'An Act to incorporate the subscribers to the bank of the United States' "—

The Bill, entitled, "An Act repealing after the last day of June next, the duties heretofore laid upon distilled spirits imported from abroad, and laying

---

[33] On March 1 this bill was signed by both the Speaker and the Vice President and given to the committee on enrolled bills for delivery to the President.

[34] An abbreviated statement relating to John Beckley's message is in Messages from the House, Senate Records, DNA. On March 3 this bill was signed by the Speaker, the Vice President, and the President.

[35] This bill has not been located. On this day the bill was read the first time and printed in the Journal. Later during the same day the rules were dispensed with, the bill was read a second time, and the second section was expunged. The bill then passed to the third reading.

[36] This bill has not been located. On this day the bill was read the first and second times, printed in the Journal, and committed.

[37] This bill has not been located. On this day the Senate read this bill the first and second times, and it was printed in the Journal.

others in their stead; and also upon spirits distilled within the United States, and for appropriating the same"—

And the Resolution, "requesting the President of the United States to cause to be communicated to the National Assembly of France, the peculiar sensibility of Congress to the tribute paid to the memory of BENJAMIN FRANKLIN"—

He also reported from the same Committee, that they had examined the following Bills, and that they were duly enrolled:

The Bill, entitled, "An Act for raising and adding another regiment to the military establishment of the United States, and for making further provision for the protection of the frontiers"[38]—

The Bill, entitled, "An Act supplemental to the Act establishing the Treasury department, and for a further compensation to certain officers,"[39] and—

The Bill, entitled, "An Act to amend 'An Act for establishing the temporary and permanent seat of the government of the United States.'"[40]

A message from the President of the United States, by Mr. Lear his Secretary:

"Mr. PRESIDENT,

"The President of the United States has this day approved and signed a Resolution which originated in the Senate, requesting that the President of the United States would cause to be communicated to the National Assembly of France, the sense which Congress have, of the tribute paid to the memory of BENJAMIN FRANKLIN"[41]—

And he withdrew.

Mr. Schuyler from the Committee appointed to revise the laws of the United States, reported a Bill,[42] which was read the FIRST time as follows:

An ACT to continue in force the Act therein mentioned, and to make further provision for the payment of PENSIONS to INVALIDS, and for the support of Light-Houses, Beacons, Buoys and public Piers

   1   SECT. I. *Be it enacted by the* SENATE *and House of* REPRESEN-
   2   TATIVES *of the United States of America in Congress assembled,* That
   3   the Act, entitled, "An Act to provide for mitigating or remit-
   4   ting the forfeitures and penalties accruing under the revenue laws,
   5   in certain cases therein mentioned," shall be, and is hereby con-
   6   tinued in force until the end of the next session of Congress, and
   7   no longer.

---

[38] The inspected enrolled bill is in Enrolled Acts, RG 11, DNA. E–23855.
[39] The inspected enrolled bill is in Enrolled Acts, RG 11, DNA. E–23866.
[40] The inspected enrolled bill is in Enrolled Acts, RG 11, DNA. E–23869.
[41] This message is in Committee on Enrolled Bills, Senate Records, DNA.
[42] This bill is in Senate Bills, Senate Records, DNA.

1   SECT. II. *And be it further enacted*, That the yearly pensions
2   which have been allowed by or in pursuance of any Act or Law
3   of the United States, to persons who were wounded and disabled
4   during the late war, shall for the space of one year from the 4th
5   day of March next, be paid out of the Treasury of the United
6   States, under such regulations as the President of the United
7   States may direct.

1   SECT. III. *And be it further enacted*, That all expenses which
2   shall accrue from the first day of July next, inclusively, for the
3   necessary support, maintenance and repairs of all light-houses,
4   beacons, buoys and public piers, shall continue to be defrayed by
5   the United States, until the first day of July, in the year one
6   thousand seven hundred and ninety-two, notwithstanding such
7   light-houses, beacons, buoys or public piers, with the lands and
8   tenements thereunto belonging, and the jurisdiction of the same,
9   shall not in the mean time, be ceded to, or vested in the United
10   States, by the State or States respectively, in which the same may
11   be; and that the said time be further allowed to the States re-
12   spectively, to make such cession.

March the 2d, 1791—Originated in Senate.

ORDERED, That this Bill pass to the SECOND reading.[43]
The Bill sent from the House of Representatives for concurrence, entitled,
"An Act for making compensation to the widows and orphan children of
certain officers, who were killed or who died in the service of the United
States, during the late war; and for the relief of certain invalids and other
persons therein mentioned," was read the FIRST time as follows:

"An ACT for making compensation to the WIDOWS and ORPHAN CHILDREN
of certain OFFICERS who were killed, or who died in the service of the
United States, during the late war; and for the relief of certain INVALIDS,
and other persons therein mentioned "

1   "SECT. I. *Be it enacted by the* SENATE *and House of* REPRESEN-
2   TATIVES *of the United States of America in Congress assembled*, That
3   the Register of the Treasury shall, and he hereby is required to
4   grant to the orphan children of the late captain Robert Lewis,
5   who died while in the service of the United States, a certificate to
6   entitle them to a sum equal to an annuity of seven years half pay
7   of a Captain; to commence the twenty-second day of March,
8   one thousand seven hundred and seventy-seven, in conformity to

---

[43] On March 3 this bill was read a second time and committed. On the same day the
committee reported and the bill was passed with an amendment and sent to the House.

9 the Act of the late Congress, passed on the twenty-fourth day of
10 August, one thousand seven hundred and eighty; that the said
11 certificate be liquidated, and granted upon similar principles with
12 the other debts of the United States. That the said Register
13 grant in like manner, to Hannah Douglass, widow of the late
14 colonel William Douglass, who died in the service of the United
15 States, a certificate to entitle her to a sum equal to an annuity
16 of seven years half pay of a Colonel; to commence the fifteenth
17 day of May, one thousand seven hundred and seventy-seven.
18 That the said Register grant in the like manner, and upon
19 similar principles, to Anne Roberts, widow of the late colonel
20 Owen Roberts, who was killed while in the Service of the United
21 States, a certificate to entitle her to a sum equal to an annuity of
22 seven years half pay of Colonel of Artillery; to commence as
23 from the twentieth day of June, one thousand seven hundred and
24 seventy-nine: *Provided*, it shall first be made to appear that the
25 said annuity or seven years half pay, or any part thereof, has not
26 been paid by the State of South-Carolina; and in case any part
27 of the said annuity shall have been paid by the said State, the said
28 Register shall grant a certificate only for the balance which re-
29 mains unpaid. That the said Register grant in like manner, to
30 the orphan children of the late major Andrew Leitch, who was
31 killed while in the service of the United States, a certificate to
32 entitle them to a sum equal to an annuity of seven years half pay
33 of a Major; to commence as from the sixteenth day of Septem-
34 ber, one thousand seven hundred and seventy-six. That the said
35 Register grant in like manner, to the orphan children of the late
36 captain William White, who was killed while in the service of
37 the United States, a certificate to entitle them to a sum equal to
38 an annuity of seven years half pay of a Captain; to commence
39 as from the fifteenth day of October, one thousand seven hun-
40 dred and eighty-one. That the said Register grant in like man-
41 ner, to the orphan children of the late lieutenant John Harris,
42 who was killed while in the service of the United States, a cer-
43 tificate to entitle them to a sum equal to an annuity of seven
44 years half pay of a Lieutenant; to commence as from the fif-
45 teenth day of December, one thousand seven hundred and seventy-
46 seven.

1 "SECT. II. *And be it further enacted*, That the Secretary for the
2 department of war, be, and he hereby is required to place on the
3 invalid list, Timothy Mix, disabled in the late war, by the loss

4 of his right hand, while in the service of the United States, at the
5 rate of the half pay of a Lieutenant of Artillery; to commence
6 on the fourth day of November, one thousand seven hundred and
7 eighty-three: *Provided*, That the said Timothy Mix shall first
8 return the amount of the commutation of the half pay for life,
9 which he has received. That the said Secretary place on the
10 invalid list, Abel Turney, mariner, disabled while in the service
11 of the United States, at the rate of one dollar per month; to
12 commence on the first day of January, one thousand seven hun-
13 dred and eighty-one.

1 "SECT. III. *And be it further enacted*, That the arrears of the
2 said pensions be paid as the laws direct in similar cases.

1 "SECT. IV. *And be it further enacted*, That the Comptroller of
2 the Treasury, be, and he hereby is directed to adjust the accounts
3 of Joseph Pannil, a lieutenant-colonel in the service of the United
4 States, during the late war, and to allow him the usual commu-
5 tation of the half pay for life, of a Lieutenant-Colonel; and that
6 the Register of the Treasury be, and he hereby is required to
7 grant a certificate for the amount thereof accordingly. That the
8 said Comptroller adjust the account of the late brigadier-general
9 De Haa's, admitting to the credit of the said account, such sums
10 as by evidence shall appear to have been advanced for the public
11 service; and that the said Register do grant a certificate for the
12 balance due on such settlement. That the said Comptroller ad-
13 just the account of Thomas McIntire, a captain in the service of
14 the United States, during the late war, and allow him the usual
15 commutation of the half pay for life, of a Captain; and that the
16 said Register grant a certificate for the amount thereof accord-
17 ingly.

1 "SECT. V. *And be it further enacted*, That the Comptroller of
2 the Treasury, be, and he is hereby required to adjust the account
3 of Francis Suzor Debevere, a surgeon's-mate, in the service of the
4 United States during the late war, and who remained in captivity
5 to the end thereof; and that the Register of the Treasury be, and
6 he hereby is required to grant a certificate for the amount which
7 shall be found due for the services of the said Francis Suzor De-
8 bevere. That the said Comptroller adjust the account of Robert
9 King, as a lieutenant deranged upon the principles of the Act of
10 the late Congress, passed the twenty-fourth day of November,
11 one thousand seven hundred and seventy-eight; and that the said
12 Register grant a certificate accordingly. That the said Comp-

13   troller adjust the account of Lemuel Sherman, as a sailing-master
14   of a galley on Lake Champlain, and as such taken prisoner; and
15   that the said Register grant a certificate accordingly.
 1   "Sect. VI. *And be it further enacted*, That there be granted
 2   to Nicholas Ferdinand Westfall, who left the British service, and
 3   joined the army of the United States, during the late war, one
 4   hundred acres of unappropriated land in the western territory of
 5   the United States, free of all charges; and also the sum of three
 6   hundred and thirty-six dollars, out of any money appropriated
 7   to the contingent charges of government."
     "March the 2d, 1791—Passed the House of Representatives."

It was agreed by animous consent, that the rule be so far dispensed with, as
that this Bill be now read the SECOND time.
     ORDERED, That this Bill be committed to
                    Mr. Wingate
                    Mr. Strong and
                    Mr. Carroll, to consider and report thereon.[44]
The Bill sent from the House of Representatives for concurrence, entitled,
"An Act supplementary to the Act making provision for the reduction of the
public debt," was read the FIRST time as follows:
"An ACT supplementary to the Act making provision for the REDUCTION of
     the PUBLIC DEBT "
 1   "WHEREAS it hath been made known to Congress that the
 2   President of the United States, in consequence of the several Acts,
 3   the one entitled, 'An Act making provision for the debt of the
 4   United States;' the other, entitled, 'An Act making provision for
 5   the reduction of the public debt;' or one of them, hath caused a
 6   certain loan to be made in Holland, on account of the United
 7   States, to the amount of three millions of florins, bearing an
 8   interest of five per centum per annum; and reimbursable in six
 9   yearly instalments, commencing in the year one thousand eight
10   hundred, and ending in the year one thousand eight hundred and
11   six, or at any time sooner, in whole or in part, at the option of
12   the United States—
 1   "And whereas it hath been also stated to Congress, that the
 2   charges upon the said loan have amounted to four and a half per
 3   centum, whereby a doubt hath arisen whether the said loan be

---

[44] This vote for committee is in Other Records: Yeas and nays, Senate Records, DNA.
On March 3 this committee reported and consideration of the bill was postponed until
the next session.

4 within the meaning of the said last mentioned Act, which limits
5 the rate of interest to five per centum per annum—
1   "And whereas it is expedient that the said doubt be removed:
1   "SECT. I. *Be it enacted and declared by the* SENATE *and House*
2 *of* REPRESENTATIVES *of the United States of America in Congress*
3 *assembled,* That the loan aforesaid shall be deemed and construed
4 to be within the true intent and meaning of the said Act, entitled,
5 'An Act making provision for the reduction of the public debt;'
6 and that any further loan, to the extent of the principal sum
7 authorised to be borrowed by the said Act, the interest whereof
8 shall be five per centum per annum, and the charges whereof shall
9 not exceed the said rate of four and a half per centum, shall, in
10 like manner be deemed and construed to be within the true intent
11 and meaning of the said Act."
     "March the 1st, 1791—Passed the House of Representatives."

It was agreed by unanimous consent, so far to dispense with the rule, as that
this Bill pass to the SECOND reading at this time; and after progress, the further consideration of this Bill was postponed until to-morrow.[45]

The Bill sent from the House of Representatives for concurrence, entitled,
"An Act to continue in force for a limited time, an Act, entitled, 'An Act for
the temporary establishment of the Post Office,' " was read the FIRST time as
follows:

"An ACT to continue in force for a limited time, an Act, entitled, 'An Act for
     the temporary establishment of the POST OFFICE ' "

1   "SECT. I. *Be it enacted by the* SENATE *and House of* REPRESEN-
2 TATIVES *of the United States of America in Congress assembled,* That
3 the Act passed the first session of Congress, entitled, 'An Act for
4 the temporary establishment of the Post Office,' be, and the same
5 is hereby continued in full force until the end of the next session
6 of Congress, and no longer.

1   "SECT. II. *And be it further enacted,* That no law of any State
2 shall operate to impede or obstruct the stage carriages which shall
3 be employed by virtue of this Act, in conveying the mail of the
4 United States, or to prevent passengers being carried in such
5 carriages, or to subject the owners or drivers of such carriages
6 to any penalty or tax on account of such employment.

---

[45] On March 2 this bill was read a third time, passed with amendments, and returned
to the House for concurrence in the amendments. The House agreed to the amendments
on the same date and notified the Senate.

1   "SECT. III. *And be it further enacted,* That all letters to and
2   from the Treasurer, Comptroller and Auditor of the Treasury,
3   and the Assistant of the Secretary of the Treasury, on public ser-
4   vice, shall be received and conveyed by the post, free of postage."
"1791, March the 1st—Passed the House of Representatives."

ORDERED, That this Bill pass to the SECOND reading.

The Vice President signed the following enrolled Bills, and they were delivered to the Committee, to be laid before the President of the United States,
for his approbation.

The Bill, entitled, "An Act for raising and adding another regiment to the
military establishment of the United States, and for making further provision
for the protection of the frontiers"—

The Bill, entitled, "An Act supplemental to the Act establishing the Treasury department, and for a further compensation to certain officers," and—

The Bill, entitled, "An Act to amend 'An Act for establishing the temporary and permanent seat of the government of the United States.' "[46]

The Bill, entitled, "An Act making an appropriation for the purpose therein
mentioned," was read the THIRD time.

RESOLVED, That this Bill PASS, that the title thereof be "An Act making an
appropriation for the purpose therein mentioned," that the Bill be engrossed,[47]
and that the Secretary desire the concurrence of the House of Representatives
therein.

The Bill sent from the House of Representatives for concurrence, entitled,
"An Act for making compensations to the Commissioners of loans for extraordinary expenses," was read the SECOND time.

ORDERED, That this Bill be committed to

> Mr. Langdon,
> Mr. Schuyler and
> Mr. Ellsworth, to consider and report thereon.[48]

A message from the House of Representatives by Mr. Beckley their clerk:

"Mr. PRESIDENT,

"The House of Representatives have passed the Bill sent from the Senate
for concurrence, entitled, 'An Act concerning Consuls and Vice-Consuls,' with
amendments,[49] in which amendments they desire the concurrence of the
Senate—

---

[46] On March 3 the President signed all these bills and the Senate was notified.
[47] The engrossed bill and the resolve are in Engrossed Senate Bills and Resolutions,
Senate Records, DNA.
[48] This vote for committee is in Other Records: Yeas and nays, Senate Records, DNA.
[49] The amendments are in Senate Bills, Senate Records, DNA.

"They have passed the Bill, entitled, 'An Act in addition to an Act, entitled, "An Act for establishing the salaries of the executive officers of government, with their assistants and clerks," '[50] in which they desire the concurrence of the Senate—

"The President of the United States has notified the House of Representatives that he has this day approved and signed several Acts which originated in that House; a list of which I am directed to bring to the Senate"—

And he withdrew.

The Acts this day approved and signed by the President of the United States, are—

"An Act giving effect to the laws of the United States within the State of Vermont."

"An Act to explain and amend an Act, entitled, 'An Act making further provision for the payment of the debts of the United States.' "

"An Act supplementary to the Act, entitled, 'An Act to incorporate the subscribers to the bank of the United States,' " and

"An Act fixing the time for the next annual meeting of Congress."

The Bill, entitled, "An Act in addition to an Act, entitled, 'An Act for establishing the salaries of the executive officers of government, with their assistants and clerks,' " was read the FIRST time, as follows:

"An ACT in addition to an Act, entitled, 'An Act for establishing the SALARIES of the executive OFFICERS of GOVERNMENT, with their Assistants and Clerks ' "

1   "SECT. I. *Be it enacted by the* SENATE *and House of* REPRE-
2   SENTATIVES *of the United States of America in Congress assembled,*
3   That from and after the passing of this Act, there shall be allowed
4   to the chief clerk of the Auditor, the annual sum of two hundred
5   dollars, in addition to the salary allowed to him by the Act, en-
6   titled, 'An Act establishing the salaries of the executive officers
7   of government, with their assistants and clerks;' to be paid at
8   the Treasury of the United States, in quarterly payments; and
9   from like appropriations as may be assigned for the payment of
10   the other salaries mentioned in the above recited Act."

"1791, March the 2d—Passed the House of Representatives."

It was agreed by unanimous consent, so far to dispense with the rule, as that this Bill have the SECOND reading at this time.

---

[50] This bill has not been located.

ORDERED, That this Bill pass to the THIRD reading.[51]

The amendments of the House of Representatives, proposed in their resolution of March 2d, on the Bill sent from the Senate for concurrence, entitled, "An Act concerning Consuls and Vice-Consuls," was taken into consideration.

The Bill, as it passed the Senate, is as followeth:

An ACT concerning CONSULS and VICE-CONSULS

1   FOR carrying into full effect the convention between his Most
2   Christian Majesty and the United States of America, entered into
3   for the purpose of defining and establishing the functions and
4   privileges of their respective Consuls and Vice-Consuls,

1   SECT. I. *Be it enacted by the* SENATE *and House of* REPRE-
2   SENTATIVES *of the United States of America, in Congress assembled,*
3   That where in the seventh article of the said convention, it is
4   agreed that when there shall be no Consul or Vice-Consul of the
5   Most Christian King, to attend to the saving of the wreck of any
6   French vessel stranded on the coasts of the United States, or that
7   the residence of the said Consul or Vice-Consul (he not being at
8   the place of the wreck) shall be more distant from the said place
9   than that of the competent Judge of the county, the latter shall
10   immediately proceed to perform the office therein prescribed;
11   the nearest District Judge of the United States shall proceed
12   therein according to the tenor of the said article. The District
13   Judges of the United States shall also, within their respective dis-
14   tricts, be the competent judges for the purposes expressed in the
15   ninth article of the said convention, and it shall be incumbent
16   on them to give aid to the Consuls and Vice-Consuls of his Most
17   Christian Majesty, in arresting and securing deserters from vessels
18   of the French nation, according to the tenor of the said article.
19   And where by any article of the said convention, the Consuls
20   and Vice-Consuls of his Most Christian Majesty are entitled to
21   the aid of the competent executive officers of the country, in the
22   execution of any precept, the Marshals of the United States, and
23   their deputies, shall, within their respective districts, be the com-
24   petent officers, and shall give their aid according to the tenor of
25   the stipulations.
26   And whenever commitments to the gaols of the country shall
27   become necessary, in pursuance of any stipulation of the said
28   convention, they shall be to such gaols within the respective dis-

---

[51] On March 3 this bill was read a third time, passed with amendments, and returned to the House for concurrence in the amendments. On the same day the House concurred in the amendments.

29 tricts as other commitments under the authority of the United
30 States are by law made.
1   SECT. II.   And for the direction of the Consuls and Vice-Con-
2 suls of the United States, in certain cases,
3   *Be it enacted by the Authority aforesaid,* That they shall have right
4 in the ports or places to which they are or may be severally ap-
5 pointed, of receiving the protests or declarations, and all other acts
6 which such captains, masters, crews, passengers and merchants, as
7 are citizens of the United States, may respectively chuse to make
8 there; and also their testaments and other disposals by last will:
9 and the copies of the said acts duly authenticated by the said Consuls
10 or Vice-Consuls, under the seal of their consulates, respectively,
11 shall be evidence in all courts of justice of the United States. It
12 shall be their duty, in case of the absence of the legal represen-
13 tative, and where the laws of the country permit, to take pos-
14 session of the personal estate left by any citizen of the United
15 States, who shall die within their consulate; they shall inventory
16 the same, with the assistance of two merchants of the United
17 States, or for want of them, of any others at their choice; shall
18 collect the debts due to the deceased, in the country where he
19 died, and pay the debts due from his estate, which he shall have
20 there contracted; shall sell such part of the estate as shall be of a
21 perishable nature, and such further part, if any, as shall be ne-
22 cessary for the payment of his debts, and at the expiration of one
23 year from his decease, the residue; and the balance of the estate
24 they shall transmit to the Treasury of the United States, to be
25 holden in trust for the legal claimants. But if at any time before
26 such transmission, the legal representative of the deceased shall
27 appear and demand his effects in their hands, they shall deliver
28 them up, being paid their fees, and shall cease their proceedings.
29   For the information of the representative of the deceased, it
30 shall be the duty of the Consul or Vice-Consul, authorised to
31 proceed as aforesaid in the settlement of his estate, immediately
32 to notify his death in one of the gazettes published in the consu-
33 late, and also to the Secretary of State, that the same may be
34 notified in the State to which the deceased shall belong; and he
35 shall also as soon as may be, transmit to the Secretary of State,
36 an inventory of the effects of the deceased, taken as before
37 directed.
1   SECT. III.   *And be it further enacted,* That the said Consuls and
2 Vice-Consuls, in cases where ships or vessels of the United States

3 shall be stranded on the coasts of their consulates respectively,
4 shall, as far as the laws of the country will permit, take proper
5 measures, as well for the purpose of saving the said ships or ves-
6 sels, their cargoes and appurtenances, as for storing and securing
7 the effects and merchandize saved, and for taking an inventory
8 or inventories thereof; and the merchandize and effects saved,
9 with the inventory or inventories thereof taken as aforesaid,
10 shall, after deducting therefrom the expense, be delivered to the
11 owner or owners: *Provided*, That no Consul or Vice-Consul
12 shall have authority to take possession of any such goods, wares,
13 merchandize or other property, when the master, owner, or
14 consignee thereof is present or capable of taking possession of the
15 same.

1 SECT. IV. *And be it further enacted*, That it shall and may be
2 lawful for every Consul and Vice-Consul of the United States to
3 take and receive the following fees of office, for the services
4 which he shall have performed:

5 For authenticating under the consular seal, every protest, de-
6 claration, letter of attorney, last will and testament, deposition
7 or other act, which such captains, masters, mariners, seamen,
8 passengers, merchants or others as are citizens of the United
9 States, may respectively chuse to make, the sum of two dollars.

10 For the taking into possession, inventorying, selling and finally
11 settling and paying, or transmitting as aforesaid, the balance due
12 on the personal estate left by any citizen of the United States,
13 who shall die within the limits of his consulate, five *per centum*
14 on the gross amount of such estate.

15 For taking into possession and otherwise proceeding on any
16 such estate which shall be delivered over to the legal represen-
17 tative before a final settlement of the same, as is herein before
18 directed, two and a half *per centum* on such part delivered over
19 as shall not be in money, and five *per centum* on the gross amount
20 of the residue.

21 And it shall be the duty of the Consuls and Vice-Consuls of
22 the United States, to give receipts for all fees which they shall
23 receive by virtue of this Act, expressing the particular services
24 for which they are paid.

1 SECT. V. *And be it further enacted*, That in case it be found
2 necessary for the interest of the United States, that a Consul
3 or Consuls be appointed to reside on the coast of Barbary, the
4 President be authorised to allow an annual salary, not exceeding

5   two thousand dollars to each person so to be appointed: *Provided,*
6   That such salary be not allowed to more than one Consul for any
7   one of the States on the said coast.
1   SECT. VI. *And be it further enacted,* That every Consul and
2   Vice-Consul, shall, before they enter on the execution of their
3   trusts, or if already in the execution of the same, within one year
4   from the passing of this Act, or if resident in Asia, within two
5   years, give bond, with such sureties as shall be approved by the
6   Secretary of State, in a sum not less than two thousand, nor
7   more than ten thousand dollars, conditioned for the true and
8   faithful discharge of the duties of his office according to law, and
9   also for truly accounting for all monies, goods, and effects which
10 may come into his possession by virtue of this Act: And the said
11 bond shall be lodged in the office of the Secretary of the Trea-
12 sury.
1   SECT. VII. *And be it further enacted,* That to prevent the mari-
2   ners and seamen, employed in vessels belonging to citizens of the
3   United States, in cases of shipwreck, sickness or captivity, from
4   suffering in foreign ports, it shall be the duty of the Consuls and
5   Vice-Consuls respectively, from time to time, to provide for them
6   in the most reasonable manner, at the expense of the United
7   States, subject to such instructions as the Secretary of State shall
8   give, and not exceeding an allowance of twelve cents to a man
9   *per diem.* and all masters and commanders of vessels belonging
10 to citizens of the United States, and bound to some port of the
11 same, are hereby required and enjoined to take such mariners or
12 seamen on board of their ships or vessels, at the request of the said
13 Consuls or Vice-Consuls respectively, and to transport them to
14 the port in the United States to which such ships or vessels may
15 be bound, free of cost or charge; but that the said mariners or
16 seamen shall, if able, be bound to do duty on board such ships or
17 vessels, according to their several abilities: *Provided,* that no
18 master or captain of any ship or vessel, shall be obliged to take
19 a greater number than two men to every one hundred tons
20 burthen of said ship or vessel, on any one voyage: And if any
21 such captain or master shall refuse the same on the request or
22 order of the Consul or Vice-Consul, such captain or master shall
23 forfeit and pay the sum of thirty dollars for each mariner or sea-
24 man so refused; to be recovered for the benefit of the United
25 States, by the said Consul or Vice-Consul, in his own name, in
26 any court of competent jurisdiction.

1   SECT. VIII. *And be it further enacted,* That citizens of the
2   United States appointed to reside in foreign ports and places as
3   Consuls or Vice-Consuls of the United States, shall be enabled to
4   own any ships or vessels in their own names respectively, or in
5   partnership with any other citizen or citizens of the United
6   States, residing within the said States, and be entitled to all the
7   privileges and advantages in regard to such ships or vessels, as
8   if such Consuls or Vice-Consuls owning said ships or vessels, ac-
9   tually resided within any port or place within the United States;
10   any law to the contrary notwithstanding.

1   SECT. IX. *And be it further enacted,* That where a ship or ves-
2   sel belonging to citizens of the United States, is sold in a foreign
3   port or place, the master, unless the crew are liable by their
4   contract, or do consent to be discharged there, shall send them
5   back to the State where they entered on board, or furnish them
6   with means sufficient for their return, to be ascertained by the
7   Consul or Vice-Consul of the United States, having jurisdiction
8   of the port or place. And in case of the master's refusal, the
9   said Consul or Vice-Consul may (if the laws of the land permit
10   it) cause his ship, goods and person, to be arrested and held until
11   he shall comply with his duty herein.

1   SECT. X. *And be it further enacted,* That the specification of
2   certain powers and duties in this Act, to be exercised or per-
3   formed by the Consuls and Vice-Consuls of the United States,
4   shall not be construed to the exclusion of others resulting from
5   the nature of their appointments, or any treaty or convention
6   under which they may act.

January 27th, 1791—Passed the Senate.

The amendments of the House of Representatives are,—

"Strike out all the Bill, except the first section—and

"Amend the title, to read thus—'An Act for carrying into effect the con-vention between his Most Christian Majesty and the United States, respecting Consuls and Vice-Consuls.' "

RESOLVED, That the Senate do not agree to the amendments of the House of Representatives, on the last mentioned Bill.[52]

ORDERED, That the Secretary communicate this resolution to the House of Representatives.

---

[52] The House resolve with amendments and the Senate resolve are in Senate Bills, Senate Records, DNA.

A message from the House of Representatives by Mr. Beckley their clerk:

"Mr. PRESIDENT,

"The House of Representatives have passed the Bill sent from the Senate for concurrence, entitled, 'An Act making an appropriation for the purpose therein mentioned' "[53]—

And he withdrew.

It was agreed by unanimous consent to dispense with the rule so far as that the Bill sent from the House of Representatives for concurrence, entitled, "An Act to continue in force for a limited time, an Act, entitled, 'An Act for the temporary establishment of the Post-Office,' " be now read the SECOND time—

And it was agreed to expunge the second section of the said Bill.

ORDERED, That this Bill pass to the THIRD reading.[54]

A message from the House of Representatives by Mr. Beckley their clerk:

"Mr. PRESIDENT,

"The House of Representatives have passed the Bill sent from the Senate for concurrence, entitled, 'An Act for granting lands to the inhabitants and settlers at Vincennes and the Illinois Country, in the territory north-west of the Ohio, and for confirming them in their possessions,' with amendments,[55] in which amendments they desire the concurrence of the Senate"—

And he withdrew.

The Bill sent from the Senate to the House of Representatives for concurrence, is as follows:

An ACT for granting LANDS to the inhabitants and settlers at VINCENNES and the ILLIONOIS COUNTRY, in the territory north-west of the OHIO, and for confirming them in their possessions

1   SECT. I. *Be it enacted by the* SENATE *and House of* REPRE-
2   SENTATIVES *of the United States of America in Congress assembled,*
3   That four hundred acres of land be given to each of those persons
4   who, in the year one thousand seven hundred and eighty-three,
5   were heads of families at Vincennes, or in the Illinois Country,
6   on the Mississippi, and who since that time have removed from
7   one of the said places to the other; and the Governor of the
8   territory north-west of the Ohio, is hereby directed to cause the
9   same to be laid out for them, at their own expense, either at

---

[53] On March 3 this bill was signed by the Speaker, the Vice President, and the President.

[54] On March 3 this bill was read a third time, amended, and passed. On the same day the House agreed to the Senate amendments.

[55] These amendments are in Engrossed Senate Bills and Resolutions, Senate Records, DNA.

10 Vincennes, or in the Illionois Country, as they shall severally
11 elect.

1   SECT. II. *And be it further enacted and declared,* That the
2 heads of families at Vincennes, in the year one thousand seven
3 hundred and eighty-three, who afterwards removed without the
4 limits of the said territory, are notwithstanding entitled to the
5 donation of four hundred acres of land, made by the resolve of
6 Congress of the twenty-ninth of August, one thousand seven
7 hundred and eighty-eight.

1   SECT. III. *And be it further enacted,* That one hundred and
2 fifty acres of land, heretofore in possession of the Piankeshaw
3 Indians, and now under actual improvement, and constituting a
4 part of the village of Vincennes, be given to the persons who are
5 severally in possession of the said land.

1   SECT. IV. *And be it further enacted,* That where lands have
2 been actually improved and cultivated at Vincennes, or in the
3 Illionois Country, under a supposed grant of the same by any
4 commandant or court claiming authority to make such grant,
5 the Governor of the said territory be, and he hereby is empow-
6 ered to confirm to the persons who made such improvements,
7 their heirs or assigns, the lands supposed to have been granted
8 as aforesaid, or such parts thereof as he in his discretion may
9 judge reasonable, not exceeding to any one person four hundred
10 acres.

1   SECT. V. *And be it further enacted,* That a tract of land, con-
2 taining about five thousand four hundred acres, which for many
3 years has been fenced and used by the inhabitants of Vincennes
4 as a common, be and the same is hereby confirmed to the said
5 inhabitants, to be used as a common, until a division thereof in
6 severalty among the said inhabitants shall be directed by law.

1   SECT. VI. *And be it further enacted,* That the Governor of the
2 said territory be authorised to make a grant of land, not exceed-
3 ing one hundred acres to each person, who hath not obtained any
4 donation of land from the United States, and who on the first
5 day of August, one thousand seven hundred and ninety, was
6 enrolled in the militia at Vincennes, and has done militia duty;
7 the said land to be laid out at the expense of the grantees, and
8 in such form and place as the said Governor shall direct.

   January 11th, 1791—Passed the Senate.

The amendments of the House of Representatives to the last mentioned Bill, are as follow:

"SECT. II. Line 2, after the word 'Vincennes,' add 'or in the Illionois Country.'

"Line 7th, after the word 'eight,' add 'and the Governor of the said territory, upon application to him for that purpose, is hereby directed to cause the same to be laid out for such heads of families or their heirs, and shall also cause to be laid off and confirmed to such persons, the several tracts of land which they may have possessed, and which, before the year one thousand seven hundred and eighty-three, may have been allotted to them, according to the laws and usages of the government under which they had respectively settled: *Provided nevertheless*, That if such persons or their heirs, do not return and occupy the said lands within five years, such lands shall be considered as forfeited to the United States.'

"SECT. V. Line 4, after the word 'common,' insert 'also a tract of land including the villages of Chohos and Prairie du Pont, and heretofore used by the inhabitants of the said villages as a common.'

"Same line, after the word 'same,' strike out to the end of the clause, and add 'are hereby appropriated to the use of the inhabitants of Vincennes and of the said villages respectively, to be used by them as a common, until otherwise disposed of by law.'

"SECT. VI. Line 6, after the word 'Vincennes,' insert 'or in the Illionois Country;' and to end of the same line add '*Provided nevertheless*, That no claim founded upon purchase or otherwise, shall be admitted within a tract of land heretofore occupied by the Kaskaskia nation of Indians, and including their village, which is hereby appropriated to the use of the said Indians.'

"To the end of the Bill, add—

"SECT. VII. *And be it further enacted*, That two lots of land heretofore in the occupation of the Priests at Cahokia, and situated near that village, be, and the same is hereby granted in fee, to P. Gibault; and that a tract of land at Kaskaskia, formerly occupied by the Jesuits, be laid off and confirmed to St. Jame Beouvais, who claims the same in virtue of a purchase thereof."

"SECT. VIII. *And be it further enacted,* That so much of the Act of Congress of the twenty-eighth day of August, one thousand seven hundred and eighty-eight, as refers to the locations of certain tracts of land, directed to be run out and reserved for donations to the ancient settlers in the Illinois country, be, and the same is hereby repealed; and the Governor of the said territory is directed to lay out the same agreeably to the Act of Congress of the twentieth day of June, one thousand seven hundred and eighty-eight."

ORDERED, That these amendments be referred to the Committee who were originally appointed to bring in the Bill, to consider and report thereon.[56]

A message from the House of Representatives by Mr. Beckley their clerk:

"Mr. PRESIDENT,

"The House of Representatives have passed a Bill, entitled, 'An Act to compensate George Gibson,'[57] in which they desire the concurrence of the Senate"—

And he withdrew.

The Bill, entitled, "An Act providing compensations for the officers of the judicial courts of the United States, and for jurors and witnesses, and for other purposes," was read the SECOND time.

ORDERED, That this Bill be committed to

> Mr. Ellsworth
> Mr. Henry and
> Mr. King, to consider and report thereon.[58]

A message from the House of Representatives by Mr. Beckley their clerk:

"Mr. PRESIDENT,

"The House of Representatives insist on their amendments to the Bill sent from the Senate for concurrence, entitled, 'An Act concerning Consuls and Vice-Consuls'[59]—

"They have passed the Bill, entitled, 'An Act making further provision for the collection of duties by law imposed on teas, and to prolong the term for the payment of the duties on wines,'[60] in which they desire the concurrence of the Senate"—

And he withdrew.

The Senate resumed the consideration of the report of the Committee on the subject of the Mint, which was agreed to:

---

[56] On March 3 this committee reported, and the Senate approved the House amendments with an amendment which was concurred in by the House on the same day. The Speaker, the Vice President, and the President signed this bill on March 3.

[57] This bill is in Engrossed House Bills, House Records, DNA.

[58] On March 3 this committee reported amendments to the bill which were agreed to. The bill was then read a third time, passed with amendments, and returned to the House for concurrence in the amendments. On the same day the House agreed to some of these amendments and disagreed to others. The Senate then receded from the amendments disagreed to and the bill was signed by the Speaker, the Vice President, and the President that day.

[59] This House message is in Senate Bills, Senate Records, DNA. On March 3 the Senate adhered to its disagreement to the House amendments and the House adhered to them. This bill was not passed.

[60] This bill has not been located.

Whereupon—

RESOLVED, *by the* SENATE *and House of* REPRESENTATIVES *of the United States of America in Congress assembled,* That a Mint shall be established under such regulations as shall be directed by law.

RESOLVED, That the President of the United States be, and he is hereby authorised to cause to be engaged such artists and workmen as shall be necessary to carry the preceding resolution into effect, and to stipulate the terms and conditions of their service, and also to cause to be procured such apparatus as shall be requisite for the same purpose.[61]

ORDERED, That the Secretary carry this resolution to the House of Representatives, and desire their concurrence.[62]

Mr. Langdon from the Committee on the Bill, entitled, "An Act for making compensations to the commissioners of loans for extraordinary expenses," reported the Bill with an amendment[63]—

And the report was agreed to.

ORDERED, That this Bill pass to the THIRD reading.[64]

The Senate took into consideration the resolution of the House of Representatives, insisting on their amendments to the Bill, entitled, "An Act concerning Consuls and Vice-Consuls:"

Whereupon—

RESOLVED, That the Senate do adhere to their disagreement to the amendments of the House of Representatives on the said Bill.[65]

ORDERED, That the Secretary acquaint the House of Representatives therewith.

The Bill sent from the House of Representatives for concurrence, entitled, "An Act making further provision for the collection of the duties by law imposed on teas, and to prolong the term for the payment of the duties on wines," was read the FIRST time as follows:

"An ACT making further provision for the collection of the DUTIES by law
    imposed on TEAS, and to prolong the term for the payment of the
    DUTIES on WINES

        I   WHEREAS it is conceived that the following regulations

---

[61] These resolves are in Senate Joint and Concurrent Resolutions, Senate Records, DNA.

[62] On March 3 the House notified the Senate that it had agreed to these resolutions with amendments. The Senate agreed to these amendments on the same day and notified the House. That evening the resolves were signed by the Speaker, the Vice President, and the President.

[63] This report has not been located.

[64] On March 3 this bill was read a third time and passed with an amendment. The House disagreed to this amendment and the Senate adhered to it. The House then receded from its disagreement to the amendment. On the same date the bill was signed by the Speaker, the Vice President, and the President.

[65] The Senate resolution is in Senate Bills, Senate Records, DNA.

2   concerning teas, may be conducive both to the accommodation
3   of the importers thereof, and to the security of the revenue—
1   "SECT. I. *Be it enacted by the* SENATE *and House of* REPRESEN-
2   TATIVES *of the United States of America in Congress assembled,* That
3   in addition to the provisions contained in the fortieth and forty-
4   first sections of the Act, entitled, 'An Act to provide more effec-
5   tually for the collection of the duties imposed by law on goods,
6   wares and merchandize imported into the United States, and on
7   the tonnage of ships or vessels,' as they regard the payment, or
8   securing the payment of the duties on teas, it shall be lawful for
9   every importer of teas, if he or she shall elect so to do, to give his
10 or her bond to the Collector of the district in which any of the said
11 teas shall be landed, in double the amount of the duties thereupon,
12 with condition for the payment of the said duties, in two years
13 from the date of such bond; which bond shall be accepted by such
14 Collector, without surety, upon the terms following; that is to say,
15 The teas, for the duties whereof the said bond shall be accepted,
16 shall be deposited at the expense and risk of the said importer, in
17 one or more store-house or store-houses, as the case may require,
18 to be agreed upon between the said importer and the Inspector,
19 or other officer of inspection of the revenue, for the port where
20 the said teas shall be landed; and upon every such store-house,
21 the said Inspector or officer of inspection, shall cause to be affixed
22 two locks, the key of one of which locks shall be kept by such
23 importer, his or her agent, and the key of the other of which
24 locks shall be kept by the said Inspector, or by such other person
25 as he shall depute and appoint in that behalf, whose duty it shall
26 be to attend at all reasonable times, for the purpose of deliver-
27 ing the said teas out of the said store-house or store-houses; but
28 no delivery shall be made of any of the said teas, without a per-
29 mit, in writing, under the hand of the said Inspector or officer of
30 inspection. And in order to the obtaining of such permit, it shall
31 be necessary that the duties upon the teas, for which the same
32 shall be required, be first paid, or, at the option of the party or
33 parties applying for the same, secured to be paid in manner fol-
34 lowing; that is to say—The said party or parties shall give bond
35 with one or more surety or sureties, to the satisfaction of the said
36 Inspector, in double the amount of the duties upon the quantity
37 of teas in each case to be delivered, with condition for the pay-
38 ment of the said duties, if the same shall not exceed one hundred
39 dollars, in four months; or, if the same shall exceed one hundred

40 dollars, and shall not exceed five hundred dollars, in eight months;
41 or, if the same shall exceed five hundred dollars, in twelve months:
42 *Provided always*, That the time to be allowed for the payment
43 of the duties upon any parcel of teas to be delivered, shall not be
44 such as to extend the credit for such duties beyond the term of
45 two years originally allowed upon the depositing of the said teas.
1   "SECT. II.   *And be it further enacted*, That if the duties on any
2   parcel of teas, which shall have been deposited as aforesaid, shall
3   not have been paid or secured to be paid in manner last specified,
4   within the term of two years, according to the condition of the
5   obligation to be given to the Collector of the district within which
6   the same shall have been landed, it shall be the duty of the said
7   Collector, to cause so much of the said teas as may be necessary,
8   to be sold at public auction, and retaining the sum which shall
9   have been so paid or secured of the said duties, together with the
10 expenses of safekeeping, and sale of the said teas, shall return
11 the overplus, if any, to the owner or owners thereof, his, her or
12 their agent or lawful representative.
1   "SECT. III.   *And be it further enacted*, That the bonds which
2   have been or shall be directed to be given, by this or any other
3   Act, for monies or duties to be paid or performed to the United
4   States, shall be taken in the name of the United States of Ame-
5   rica, unless special direction shall have been given to take them
6   in some other name. And the bonds to be taken, as aforesaid,
7   by any Inspector of the revenue, shall be delivered by him forth-
8   with to the Collector of the district within which the teas, to which
9   they may relate, shall have been landed, in order to the collection
10 of the monies therein specified. And the permits which shall
11 have been granted by such Inspector, for the delivery of any
12 teas out of any store-house wherein they shall have been depo-
13 sited, shall be received by such Collector, towards satisfying any
14 bond which shall have been in the first instance, taken by the said
15 Collector, touching the said teas; which permits shall therefore
16 specify the amount of the duties which shall have been paid or
17 secured, upon the teas to be delivered in virtue thereof; and the
18 name of the ship or vessel in which they shall have been imported,
19 and of the importer or importers thereof.
1   "SECT. IV.   *And be it further enacted*, That all teas, which
2   after the first day of April next, shall be imported into the United
3   States from any foreign port or place, shall be landed under the
4   care of the Inspectors of the revenue for the ports where the

5 same shall be respectively landed; and for that purpose, every
6 permit which shall be granted by any Collector, for landing the
7 same, shall, prior to such landing, be produced to the said In-
8 spector, who by an indorsement thereupon under his hand, shall
9 signify the production thereof to him, and the time when; after
10 which, and not otherwise, it shall be lawful to land the teas men-
11 tioned in such permit. And the said Inspector shall make an
12 entry of all such permits, and of the contents thereof; and each
13 chest, box or package containing any teas, shall be marked by
14 the officer, under whose immediate inspection the same shall be
15 landed, in legible and durable characters, with progressive num-
16 bers, and with the name of the vessel in which the same shall have
17 been imported. And the said officer shall grant a certificate for
18 each such chest, box or package, specifying therein the name or
19 names of the importer or importers, the ship or vessel in which
20 the same shall have been imported, and the number thereof, to
21 accompany the same wheresoever it shall be sent.

1 "And whereas for the payment of the duties accruing on Ma-
2 deira wines, and which may be secured by bond, the term of
3 twelve months is allowed, and it is proper to extend, in like
4 manner, the payment of the duties accruing on other wines;
5 Therefore—

1 "SECT. V. *Be it enacted*, That for the payment of the duties on
2 other than Madeira wines, and which shall be secured by bond,
3 such bond shall be taken with condition for the payment of the
4 duties in twelve months, in like manner as by law is directed for
5 the payment of the duties on Madeira wines."

"March the 2d, 1791—Passed the House of Representatives."

It was agreed by unanimous consent, that the rule should be so far dispensed with, as that this Bill pass to the SECOND reading at this time.

ORDERED, That this Bill be referred to

      Mr. Morris,
      Mr. Langdon and
      Mr. Schuyler, to consider and report thereon.[66]

The Bill sent from the House of Representatives for concurrence, entitled,
"An Act to compensate George Gibson," was read the FIRST time as follows:

---

[66] This vote for a committee is in Other Records: Yeas and nays, Senate Records,
DNA. On March 3 this committee reported, and the bill was read a third time and
passed without amendments.

"An ACT to compensate GEORGE GIBSON "

1   "SECT. I. *Be it enacted by the* SENATE *and House of* REPRE-
2   SENTATIVES *of the United States of America, in Congress assembled,*
3   That there be allowed and paid to George Gibson, the sum of
4   one thousand dollars for extraordinary services by him rendered
5   to the United States during the year one thousand seven hundred
6   and seventy-six."

   "1791, March the 2d—Passed the House of Representatives."

ORDERED, That this Bill pass to the SECOND reading.[67]

The Senate adjourned to 10 o'clock to-morrow.

T H U R S D A Y, MARCH 3, 1791

The SENATE assembled—present as yesterday.

Mr. Foster reported from the joint Committee on enrolled Bills,[68] That they had this day laid before the President of the United States, for his approbation, the enrolled Bill, entitled, "An Act for raising and adding another regiment to the military establishment of the United States, and for making further provision for the protection of the frontiers"—

An enrolled Bill, entitled, "An Act to amend an Act for establishing the temporary and permanent seat of the government of the United States,"—

And an enrolled Bill, entitled, "An Act supplemental to the Act establishing the Treasury department, and for a further compensation to certain officers."

He further reported, that the joint Committee had examined the enrolled Bill, entitled, "An Act making an appropriation for the purpose therein mentioned."[69] Also the enrolled Bill, entitled, "An Act relative to the rix dollar of Denmark;"[70] and that they were duly enrolled.

Mr. Morris from the Committee appointed to take into consideration the Bill, entitled, "An Act making further provision for the collection of the duties by law imposed on teas, and to prolong the term for the payment of the duties on wines," reported the Bill without amendment, and—

The Bill was read the THIRD time.

RESOLVED, That this Bill PASS.

---

[67] On March 3 this bill was read a second time and postponed until the next session of Congress.

[68] This report is in Committee on Enrolled Bills, Senate Records, DNA.

[69] The inspected enrolled bill is in Enrolled Acts, RG 11, DNA. E–23859.

[70] The inspected enrolled bill is in Enrolled Acts, RG 11, DNA. E–23964.

ORDERED, That the Secretary acquaint the House of Representatives of the concurrence of the Senate in this Bill.[71]

Mr. Strong reported from the Committee appointed to consider the amendments of the House of Representatives to the Bill sent by the Senate to that House for concurrence, entitled, "An Act for granting lands to the inhabitants and settlers at Vincennes, and the Illionois country, in the territory north-west of the Ohio, and for confirming them in their possessions:"[72]

Whereupon—

RESOLVED, That the Senate concur with the House of Representatives in the amendments, with an amendment to the amendment proposed in the sixth section, to wit: "Insert the Proviso at the end of the sixth section."[73]

ORDERED, That the Secretary desire the concurrence of the House of Representatives herein.

The Senate proceeded in the THIRD reading of the Bill sent from the House of Representatives for concurrence, entitled, "An Act for making compensations to the Commissioners of loans for extraordinary expenses"—

RESOLVED, That this Bill PASS, with an amendment—

Strike out these words "excepting only the hire of one Clerk for the several Commissioners in the States of Massachusetts, New-York, Pennsylvania and Virginia."

ORDERED, That the Secretary desire the concurrence of the House of Representatives in the amendment.

A message from the House of Representatives by Mr. Beckley their clerk:

"Mr. PRESIDENT,

"The Speaker of the House of Representatives having signed two enrolled Bills, I am directed to bring them to the Senate, for the signature of the Vice President—

"The House of Representatives adhere to their amendments on the Bill, entitled, 'An Act concerning Consuls and Vice-Consuls'[74]—

"They disagree to the amendment of the Senate on the Bill, entitled, 'An Act for making compensations to the Commissioners of loans, for extraordinary expenses'—

"They agree to the Resolution sent from the Senate, for concurrence, 'requesting the President of the United States to cause a return to be made to Congress, of the lands not claimed by the Indians,' with an amendment,[75] to

---

[71] During the March 3 evening session, this bill was signed by the Speaker, the Vice President, and the President.

[72] The report on concurrence is in Senate Bills, Senate Records, DNA.

[73] This resolve is in Engrossed Senate Bills and Resolutions, Senate Records, DNA.

[74] This message, with slight word variations, is in Senate Bills, Senate Records, DNA.

[75] An abbreviated statement of this House resolve is in Senate Joint and Concurrent Resolutions, Senate Records, DNA.

wit: Lines 3 and 4, strike out 'a return to be made to,' and insert 'an estimate to be laid before.'—In which amendment they desire the concurrence of the Senate"—

And he withdrew.

The Senate took into consideration the last recited message from the House of Representatives:

Whereupon—

RESOLVED, That they adhere to their amendment on the Bill, entitled, "An Act for making compensations to the Commissioners of loans, for extraordinary expenses."

RESOLVED, That the Senate agree to the amendment of the House of Representatives on "The Resolution requesting the President of the United States, to cause an estimate to be laid before Congress, of the lands not claimed by the Indians."[76]

ORDERED, That the Secretary acquaint the House of Representatives with these Resolutions.

The Vice President affixed his signature to the Bill, entitled, "An Act relative to the Rix Dollar of Denmark;" and to the Bill, entitled, "An Act making an appropriation for the purpose therein mentioned," and they were delivered to the Committee on enrolled Bills, to be laid before the President of the United States, for his approbation.

Mr. Foster reported from the Committee on enrolled Bills, That they did this day, lay before the President of the United States, for his approbation, the Bill, entitled, "An Act relative to the Rix Dollar of Denmark." And the Bill, entitled, "An Act making an appropriation for the purpose therein mentioned."

The Senate proceeded to the THIRD reading of the Bill, entitled, "An Act in addition to an Act, entitled, 'An Act for establishing the salaries of the executive officers of government, with their assistants and clerks,' " and the Bill being amended[77]—

On the question, shall this Bill pass as amended? The yeas and nays were required by one fifth of the Senators present:

Mr. Bassett		Nay
Mr. Butler	Yea	
Mr. Carroll	Yea	
Mr. Dalton		Nay
Mr. Dickinson	Yea	
Mr. Ellsworth		Nay

[76] This resolve is in Senate Joint and Concurrent Resolutions, Senate Records, DNA. On the evening of March 3 this resolve was signed by the Speaker, the Vice President, and the President.

[77] These amendments are in House Bills, Senate Records, DNA.

Mr. Elmer		Nay
Mr. Foster		Nay
Mr. Hawkins	Yea	
Mr. Henry	Yea	
Mr. Johnson		Nay
Mr. Johnston	Yea	
Mr. Izard	Yea	
Mr. King	Yea	
Mr. Langdon	Yea	
Mr. Lee	Yea	
Mr. Monroe	Yea	
Mr. Morris	Yea	
Mr. Read	Yea	
Mr. Schuyler	Yea	
Mr. Stanton		Nay
Mr. Strong		Nay
Mr. Wingate		Nay

Yeas—14
Nays—9[78]

So it was—

RESOLVED, That this Bill PASS, with the following amendments:

To the end of the Bill add,

"*And be it further enacted,* That there be allowed to the Clerks employed in the several offices attached to the seat of government, in addition to their respective salaries, their reasonable and necessary expenses incurred by the removal of Congress from the city of New-York to the city of Philadelphia."

"*And be it further enacted,* That there be allowed to the assistant Secretary of the Treasury, in addition to his salary, for one year, commencing with the passing of this Act, four hundred dollars, to be paid in the same manner as his salary."

ORDERED, That the Secretary carry this Bill to the House of Representatives, and request their concurrence in the amendments.

The Senate proceeded to the SECOND reading of the Bill, entitled, "An Act to compensate George Gibson," and—

RESOLVED, That this Bill be postponed until the next session of Congress.[79]

Mr. Ellsworth from the Committee appointed to take into consideration the Bill, entitled, "An Act providing compensations for the officers of the judicial courts of the United States, and for jurors and witnesses, and for other

---

[78] This vote is in Other Records: Yeas and nays, Senate Records, DNA.

[79] Notation of this resolve is attached to the House bill located in Engrossed House Bills, House Records, DNA.

purposes," reported the Bill with amendments;[80] and it was agreed to amend the Bill accordingly.

ORDERED, That this Bill be now read the THIRD time.

RESOLVED, That this Bill PASS, with the following amendments:

SECT. I. Line 9, strike out from the word "place," to the word "at," line 11th, and insert "of his abode, to any court of the United States, on which his attendance shall be requisite."

Lines 21 to 25, strike out from the word "serving," to the word "to," and insert "and returning a writ, five cents per mile, for his necessary travel."

Strike out from the word "jurors," in the 25th line, to the word "to," in the 29th line, and insert "such compensations respectively as they would by law be entitled to for attending the courts of the State of which they are citizens."

Strike out from the word "thereof," in the 31st line, to the word "that," in the 32d line, and insert "each fifty cents per day for attending in court, and for travelling five cents per mile, from their respective places of abode to the place where the court is held, and the like allowance for returning."

ORDERED, That the Secretary desire the concurrence of the House of Representatives in these amendments.

The Bill, entitled, "An Act to continue in force for a limited time, the Act, entitled, 'An Act for the temporary establishment of the Post Office,' " was read the THIRD time:

On motion, it was agreed further to amend this Bill.

RESOLVED, That this Bill PASS, with the following amendments:[81]

Strike out the second section, and add at the end of the Bill—

"*And be it further enacted*, That the Postmaster-General shall be, and he hereby is authorised to extend the carrying of the mail from Albany, in the State of New-York, to Bennington, in the State of Vermont."

ORDERED, That the Secretary desire the concurrence of the House of Representatives in the amendments to this Bill.

Mr. Monroe from the Committee appointed the 31st of January, to take into consideration the extract of a letter from governor Randolph, to the President of the United States, containing a copy of the resolution of the Commonwealth of Virginia, relative to the bounty lands to the officers and soldiers of the Virginia line; and to whom was also referred the resolutions of the Assembly of Virginia, upon the claims of sundry individuals, with the papers accompanying them, reported[82]—

---

[80] The amendments and an amended printed copy of the bill are in House Bills, Senate Records, DNA.

[81] One amendment is in House Bills, Senate Records, DNA.

[82] This report is in Various Select Committee Reports, Senate Records, DNA.

"That it appears to your Committee, that the provisions made by the Act, entitled, 'An Act to enable the officers and soldiers of the Virginia line, on continental establishment, to obtain titles to certain lands lying north-west of the river Ohio, between the Little Miami and Sciota,' are, in the opinion of your Committee, sufficiently extensive to enable the said officers and soldiers, or their legal representatives, to obtain patents for the bounty lands promised them by Acts of the United States, and by the laws of the Commonwealth of Virginia, and that further legislative interference seems unnecessary"—

And the report was agreed to.

Mr. Monroe also reported from the same Committee[83]—

"That the claims alluded to, may be classed as follows:

"1st. Ten claims for pay and depreciation of pay, by persons who had left the service of the United States, previous to the tenth of April one thousand seven hundred and eighty.

"2d. Ten claims for pay and depreciation of pay, by persons who left the service subsequent to the tenth of April, one thousand seven hundred and eighty.

"3d. One claim for depreciation of pay, by a person who was not inlisted for three years, nor during the war.

"4th. Two claims for military services, by persons who do not specify the period in which they were performed.

"5th. Three claims for pensions, by persons wounded in the service of the United States.

"6th. One claim for services performed in the Quartermaster-General's department.

"7th. Ten claims for pay and depreciation of pay, by persons employed in military services under the authority of the Commonwealth of Virginia.

"That upon each of these claims the Legislature of the Commonwealth of Virginia, have passed a resolution referring some 'to the proper officer under the federal government having cognizance of such cases;' on others it has only been 'resolved that they were reasonable;' on others, 'that they were reasonable, and that the Auditor of public accounts be directed to adjust their claims and issue certificates therefor.' These last have probably been transmitted by mistake.

"That those in the first class are not entitled to depreciation by any Act of the late Congress; that if any pay is still due to them, that can only be adjusted at the proper office.

"That the States having been authorised to settle the depreciation of such as were in service on the tenth of April, one thousand seven hundred and eighty,

---

[83] This report is in Various Select Committee Reports, Senate Records, DNA.

and who were engaged for three years or during the war, those claims ought to have been adjusted by the State; that an adjustment for pay can only be had at the proper office.

"The claim mentioned in the third class, is totally unfounded.

"That those in the fourth class can only be adjusted at the proper office.

"That the claims of those in the fifth class, are foreclosed by the Act of the late Congress. That cases may however arise, in which an adherence to the foreclosing Act would be improper. That if the suggestion contained in the resolution with respect to one of those can be substantiated, legislative provision ought to be made on a proper application to Congress.

"The claim in the sixth class, can only be adjusted at the proper office.

"The claims in the seventh class, ought to have been adjusted by the State of Virginia, and might have been a proper charge in its account with the United States, but cannot now be allowed by Congress.

"That only thirteen of the thirty-seven claims, are accompanied with any kind of vouchers, and these very deficient.

"That it appears to your Committee, if any person has a demand against the United States, so circumstanced as that a legislative provision is requisite to obtain an adjustment, the claimant, his assignee or legal representative, ought to prefer an immediate application to Congress. That a decision on a claim against the United States, by the Legislature of any State, tends to create embarrassments, and ought not to be countenanced by Congress.

"That therefore it would be proper to permit the resolution of the Legislature of Virginia, of the 28th of December last, with the particular resolutions and claims accompanying it, to be withdrawn."

On motion, that the papers reported on by the Committee, be withdrawn—
It passed in the Negative.

And on motion, it was agreed that the report of the Committee be accepted.

A message from the President of the United States, by Mr. Lear his Secretary:

"Mr. PRESIDENT,

"The President of the United States has this day approved and signed the following Acts:

'An Act to amend an Act for establishing the temporary and permanent seat of the government of the United States,'—and

'An Act making an appropriation for the purpose therein mentioned' "[84]—

And he withdrew.

ORDERED, That the Secretary acquaint the House of Representatives that the

---

[84] This message is in Committee on Enrolled Bills, Senate Records, DNA.

President of the United States has approved and signed the last mentioned Bills.

Mr. Wingate reported from the Committee appointed on the Bill, entitled, "An Act for making compensation to the widows and orphan children of certain officers who were killed, or who died in the service of the United States, during the late war; and for the relief of certain invalids, and other persons therein mentioned:"

Whereupon—

RESOLVED, That the further consideration of this Bill be postponed until the next session of Congress.

The Senate resumed the SECOND reading of the Bill, entitled, "An Act supplementary to the Act making provision for the reduction of the public debt," which was amended,[85] and,

It was agreed by unanimous consent, that this Bill be now read the THIRD time.

RESOLVED, That this Bill PASS, with the following amendments:

In the preamble, line 2, expunge from the word "of," to the word "an," in the 4th line.

Line 5, expunge these words, "or one of them."

ORDERED, That the Secretary desire the concurrence of the House of Representatives in the amendments.

A message from the House of Representatives by Mr. Beckley their clerk:

"Mr. PRESIDENT,

"The House of Representatives agree to the amendment of the Senate, to their amendments on the Bill sent from the Senate for concurrence, entitled, 'An Act for granting lands to the inhabitants and settlers at Vincennes and the Illionois Country, in the territory north-west of the Ohio, and for confirming them in their possessions'—

"They agree to the Resolution sent from the Senate for concurrence, respecting the establishment of a Mint, with an amendment,[86] to wit:

"Insert, line 5, after 'principal,' 'such.'—

"Expunge, line 5, 'and workmen.'—

"The House of Representatives recede from their disagreement to the amendment of the Senate on the Bill sent from the House of Representatives for concurrence, entitled, 'An Act for making compensations to the Commissioners of loans, for extraordinary expenses'[87]—

---

[85] This amendment is in House Bills, Senate Records, DNA.

[86] The amendments, with slight word variations, are in Senate Joint and Concurrent Resolutions, Senate Records, DNA.

[87] During the March 3 evening session, this bill was signed by the Speaker, the Vice President, and the President.

"They agree to the amendments of the Senate, on the Bill sent from the House of Representatives for concurrence, entitled, 'An Act to continue in force for a limited time, an Act, entitled, "An Act for the temporary establishment of the Post-Office" '[88]—

"They also agree to the amendments of the Senate, on the Bill sent from the House of Representatives for concurrence, entitled, 'An Act in addition to an Act, entitled, "An Act for establishing the salaries of the executive officers of government, with their assistants and clerks" '[89]—

"The President of the United States has notified the House of Representatives that he has this day approved and signed the following Acts—

"An Act for raising and adding another regiment to the military establishment of the United States, and for making further provision for the protection of the frontiers"[90]—

"An Act repealing, after the last day of June next, the duties heretofore laid upon distilled spirits imported from abroad, and laying others in their stead; and also upon spirits distilled within the United States, and for appropriating the same"—

"An Act supplemental to the Act establishing the Treasury department, and for a further compensation to certain officers," and—

"An Act relative to the Rix Dollar of Denmark"[91]—

And he withdrew.

The Senate proceeded to consider the amendments of the House of Representatives to the Resolution sent from the Senate for concurrence, relative to the establishment of a Mint; and—

RESOLVED, That the Senate agree to the amendments on the said Resolution.[92]

ORDERED, That the Secretary acquaint the House of Representatives therewith.

A message from the House of Representatives by Mr. Beckley their clerk:

"Mr. PRESIDENT,

"The House of Representatives agree to the amendments of the Senate on the Bill sent from the House of Representatives for concurrence, entitled, 'An Act supplementary to the Act making provision for the reduction of the public debt'[93]—

---

[88] During the March 3 evening session, this bill was signed by the Speaker, the Vice President, and the President.

[89] An abbreviated statement of John Beckley's message is in Messages from the House, Senate Records, DNA.

[90] This message is in Committee on Enrolled Bills, Senate Records, DNA.

[91] This message is in Committee on Enrolled Bills, Senate Records, DNA.

[92] This resolve, with slight word variations, including the House amendments, is in Senate Joint and Concurrent Resolutions, Senate Records, DNA.

[93] On the evening of March 3 this bill was signed by the Speaker, the Vice President, and the President.

"They agree to some, and disagree to other amendments of the Senate, on the Bill sent from the House of Representatives for concurrence, entitled, 'An Act providing compensations for the officers of the judicial courts of the United States, and for jurors and witnesses, and for other purposes' "—

And he withdrew.

The Senate proceeded to consider their amendments disagreed to by the House of Representatives, on the Bill last mentioned; which are—

Amendment the 3d, line 25 to 29.

Amendment the 4th, line 31 to 32.

RESOLVED, That the Senate recede from the amendments disagreed to by the House of Representatives, on the Bill last mentioned.

ORDERED, That the Secretary deliver a message to the House of Representatives accordingly.

The Senate agreed by unanimous consent, so far to dispense with the rule, as that the Bill, entitled, "An Act to continue in force the Act therein mentioned, and to make further provision for the payment of pensions to invalids, and for the support of light-houses, beacons, buoys and public piers," be now read the SECOND time.

ORDERED, That this Bill be committed to

> Mr. King
> Mr. Ellsworth and
> Mr. Read, to consider and report thereon.[94]

A message from the House of Representatives by Mr. Beckley their clerk:

"Mr. PRESIDENT,

"The House of Representatives have agreed shortly to adjourn to 6 o'clock this evening"—

And he withdrew.

Mr. Foster from the Committee on enrolled Bills, reported, That they have this day examined the enrolled Bill, entitled, "An Act making compensation to the Commissioners of loans, for extraordinary expenses;"[95] and the enrolled Bill, entitled, "An Act in addition to an Act, entitled, 'An Act for establishing the salaries of the executive officers of government, with their assistants and clerks;' "[96] also the enrolled "Resolution respecting the establishment of a Mint;"[97] and the enrolled "Resolution requesting the President of the United States to cause an estimate to be laid before Congress, of the quantity and situation of lands not claimed by the Indians,"[98] and that they are duly enrolled.

---

[94] The vote for committee is in Other Records: Yeas and nays, Senate Records, DNA.
[95] The inspected enrolled bill is in Enrolled Acts, RG 11, DNA. E–23854.
[96] The inspected enrolled bill is in Enrolled Acts, RG 11, DNA. E–23858.
[97] The inspected enrolled resolve is in Enrolled Acts, RG 11, DNA. E–23880.
[98] The inspected enrolled resolve is in Enrolled Acts, RG 11, DNA.

Mr. King from the Committee appointed to take into consideration "The Bill to continue in force the Act therein mentioned, and to make further provision for the payment of pensions to invalids, and for the support of light-houses, beacons, buoys and public piers," reported an amendment;[99] which was adopted—whereupon,

It was agreed by unanimous consent, so far to dispense with the rule, as that this Bill be now read the THIRD time.

RESOLVED, That this Bill PASS, with the following amendment:

At the end of the Bill, add—

"*Provided*, That nothing in the said Act shall be construed to limit or restrain the power of the President of the United States, to grant pardons for offences against the United States"[100]—

That the title of the Bill be "An Act to continue in force the Act therein mentioned, and to make further provision for the payment of pensions to invalids, and for the support of light-houses, beacons, buoys and public piers;" that it be engrossed, and that the Secretary desire the concurrence of the House of Representatives therein.[101]

ORDERED, That the motion made the first instant, respecting a treaty with the Wabash and Miami Indians, together with the motion for amendment, be postponed.[102]

The Senate adjourned to 6 o'clock this evening.

THURSDAY EVENING, MARCH 3, 1791

The SENATE assembled agreeably to adjournment—
present as in the morning.

A message from the House of Representatives by Mr. Beckley their clerk:

"Mr. PRESIDENT,

"The House of Representatives have passed 'A Resolve making a temporary provision for the safe-keeping of prisoners committed under the authority of the United States,'[103] in which they desire the concurrence of the Senate—

---

[99] This report has not been located.

[100] The engrossed bill, with a notation of passage, and the amendment are in Engrossed Senate Bills and Resolutions, Senate Records, DNA. In the rough journal this amendment appears on a separate slip, pasted in at this point.

[101] During the March 3 evening session, this bill was passed by the House and signed by the Speaker, the Vice President, and the President.

[102] The following resolution appears in the rough journal at this point with the marginal notation "not print": "Ordered that James Mathers be & he is hereby, authorized to take the care of the rooms appropriated for the use of the Senate, until the next Session of Congress, and also to make the necessary provision of fire wood for the next Session." The resolve is in Senate Simple Resolutions and Motions, Senate Records, DNA.

[103] This resolve has not been located.

"The Speaker of the House of Representatives having signed several enrolled Bills and Resolves, I am directed to bring them to the Senate, for the signature of the Vice President"—

And he withdrew.

The Vice President affixed his signature to the following enrolled Bills and Resolves:

The Bill, entitled, "An Act for making compensations to the Commissioners of loans for extraordinary expenses."

The Bill, entitled, "An Act in addition to an Act, entitled, 'An Act for establishing the salaries of the executive officers of government, with their assistants and clerks.' "

"The Resolve requesting the President of the United States to cause an estimate to be laid before Congress, of the lands not claimed by the Indians," and,

The Resolve providing for the establishment of a Mint.

And they were delivered to the Committee on enrolled Bills, to be laid before the President of the United States, for his approbation.

The Senate took into consideration "The Resolve providing for the safe-keeping of prisoners committed under the authority of the United States," sent from the House of Representatives for concurrence, which is as follows:

1 "WHEREAS Congress did by a Resolution of the twenty-
2 third day of September, one thousand seven hundred and eighty-
3 nine, recommend to the several States to pass laws making it
4 expressly the duty of the keepers of their jails, to receive and
5 safe-keep therein all prisoners committed under the authority of
6 the United States: In order therefore to ensure the administra-
7 tion of justice—

1 "RESOLVED, *By the* SENATE *and House of* REPRESENTATIVES
2 *of the United States of America in Congress assembled,* That in case
3 any States shall not have complied with the said recommendation,
4 the Marshal in such State, under the direction of the Judge of the
5 district, be authorised to hire a convenient place to serve as a
6 temporary jail, and to make the necessary provision for the safe-
7 keeping of prisoners committed under the authority of the Uni-
8 ted States, until permanent provision shall be made by law for
9 that purpose; and the said Marshal shall be allowed his reason-
10 able expenses incurred for the above purposes, to be paid out of
11 the Treasury of the United States."

And—

RESOLVED, That the Senate concur therein.

ORDERED, That the Secretary communicate this resolution of concurrence to the House of Representatives.

A message from the House of Representatives by Mr. Beckley their clerk:

"Mr. PRESIDENT,

"The House of Representatives have passed a Bill, entitled, 'An Act for carrying into effect the convention between his Most Christian Majesty and the United States,'[104] in which they desire the concurrence of the Senate"—

And he withdrew.

The Bill was read the FIRST time as follows:

"An ACT for carrying into full effect the CONVENTION between his MOST CHRISTIAN MAJESTY and the UNITED STATES of AMERICA "

1 "FOR carrying into full effect the convention between his
2 Most Christian Majesty and the United States of America, entered
3 into the purpose of defining and establishing the functions and
4 privileges of their respective Consuls—

1 "SECT. I. *Be it enacted by the* SENATE *and House of* REPRE-
2 SENTATIVES *of the United States of America in Congress assembled,*
3 That where, in the seventh article of the said convention, it is
4 agreed 'that when there shall be no Consul or Vice-Consul of the
5 Most Christian King, to attend to the saving of the wreck of any
6 French vessels stranded on the coasts of the United States, or that
7 the residence of the said Consul or Vice-Consul (he not being at
8 the place of the wreck) shall be more distant from the said place
9 than that of the competent Judge of the country, the latter shall
10 immediately proceed to perform the office therein prescribed,'
11 the nearest district Judge of the United States, shall proceed
12 therein according to the tenor of the said article. The district
13 Judges of the United States, shall also, within their respective
14 districts, be the competent Judges for the purposes expressed in
15 the ninth article of the said convention; and it shall be incum-
16 bent on them to give aid to the Consuls and Vice-Consuls of his
17 Most Christian Majesty, in arresting and securing deserters from
18 the French nation, according to the tenor of the said article.
19 And where by any article of the said convention, the Consuls and
20 Vice-Consuls of his Most Christian Majesty are entitled to the aid
21 of the competent executive officers of the country, in the execu-
22 tion of any precept, the Marshals of the United States, and their
23 deputies shall, within their respective districts, be the competent
24 officers, and shall give their aid according to the tenor of the

---

[104] This bill is in Engrossed House Bills, House Records, DNA.

25   stipulations; and whenever commitments to the jails of the coun-
26   try shall become necessary in pursuance of any stipulation of the
27   said convention, they shall be to such jails within the respective
28   districts as other commitments under the authority of the United
29   States are by law made."

March the 3d, 1791—Passed the House of Representatives.

On the question, shall this Bill pass to the SECOND reading at this time?
The yeas and nays were required by one fifth of the Senators present:

Mr. Bassett		Nay
Mr. Carroll	Yea	
Mr. Dalton	Yea	
Mr. Ellsworth		Nay
Mr. Foster	Yea	
Mr. Hawkins	Yea	
Mr. Henry	Yea	
Mr. Johnson		Nay
Mr. Johnston	Yea	
Mr. Izard	Yea	
Mr. King		Nay
Mr. Langdon	Yea	
Mr. Lee	Yea	
Mr. Maclay	Yea	
Mr. Monroe	Yea	
Mr. Morris		Nay
Mr. Schuyler		Nay
Mr. Stanton	Yea	
Mr. Strong	Yea	

Yeas—13
Nays—6

It passed in the Negative; the rule[105] rendering it necessary, that there
should be unanimous consent for reading a Bill the second time, on the same
day.

A message from the House of Representatives by Mr. Beckley their clerk:

"Mr. PRESIDENT,

"The House of Representatives concur in the Bill sent from the Senate, entitled, 'An Act to continue in force the Act therein mentioned, and to make

---

[105] The rough journal qualifies "rule" thus: "the standing Rule of conducting business in the Senate."

further provision for the payment of pensions to invalids, and for the support of light-houses, beacons, buoys and public piers' "—

And he withdrew.

Mr. Foster from the Committee on enrolled Bills, reported,[106] That they had examined the following Bills, and that they were duly enrolled:

"The Bill, entitled, 'An Act to continue in force for a limited time, an Act, entitled, "An Act for the temporary establishment of the Post-Office;" '[107] the Bill, entitled, 'An Act supplementary to the Act making provision for the reduction of the public debt;'[108] the Bill, entitled, 'An Act for granting lands to the inhabitants and settlers at Vincennes and the Illionois Country, in the territory north-west of the Ohio, and for confirming them in their possessions;'[109] and the Bill, entitled, 'An Act providing compensations for the officers of the judicial courts of the United States, and for jurors and witnesses, and for other purposes' "—[110]

Mr. Foster further reported,[111] That the Committee had laid before the President of the United States, on this day, for his approbation, the Bill, entitled, "An Act for making compensations to the Commissioners of loans, for extraordinary expenses;" the Bill, entitled, "An Act in addition to an Act for establishing the salaries of the executive officers of government, with their assistants and clerks;" "the Resolve requesting the President of the United States, to cause an estimate to be laid before Congress, of the lands not claimed by the Indians;" and "the Resolve for establishing the Mint."

A message from the House of Representatives by Mr. Beckley their clerk:

"Mr. PRESIDENT,

"The Speaker of the House of Representatives having signed several enrolled Bills, I am directed to bring them to the Senate, for the signature of the Vice President—

"The House of Representatives have passed a Bill, entitled, 'An Act for the relief of David Cook,'[112] in which they desire the concurrence of the Senate"—

And he withdrew.

The Vice President affixed his signature to the following enrolled Bills,— The Bill, entitled, "An Act for granting lands to the inhabitants and settlers at Vincennes, and the Illionois country, in the territory north-west of the Ohio, and for confirming them in their possessions;" the Bill, entitled, "An Act sup-

---

[106] This report is in Committee on Enrolled Bills, Senate Records, DNA.
[107] The inspected enrolled bill is in Enrolled Acts, RG 11, DNA. E–23871.
[108] The inspected enrolled bill is in Enrolled Acts, RG 11, DNA. E–23868.
[109] The inspected enrolled bill is in Enrolled Acts, RG 11, DNA. E–23853.
[110] The inspected enrolled resolve is in Enrolled Acts, RG 11, DNA. E–23862.
[111] This report is in Committee on Enrolled Bills, Senate Records, DNA.
[112] This bill is in Engrossed House Bills, House Records, DNA.

plementary to the Act making provision for the reduction of the public debt;" the Bill, entitled, "An Act providing compensations for the officers of the judicial courts of the United States, and for jurors and witnesses, and for other purposes;" and the Bill, entitled, "An Act to continue in force for a limited time, an Act, entitled, 'An Act for the temporary establishment of the Post-Office,'" and they were delivered to the Committee on enrolled Bills, to be laid before the President of the United States, for his approbation.

Mr. Foster from the Committee on enrolled Bills, reported,[113] That they had this day, laid the four last mentioned enrolled Bills before the President of the United States.

Mr. Foster also reported,[114] That they had examined and found duly enrolled the following Bills: The Bill, entitled, "An Act making further provision for the collection of the duties by law imposed on teas, and to prolong the time for the payment of the duties on wines;"[115] and the Bill, entitled, "An Act to continue in force the Act therein mentioned, and to make further provision for the payment of pensions to invalids, and for the support of light-houses, beacons, buoys and public piers."[116]

A message from the House of Representatives by Mr. Beckley their clerk:

"Mr. PRESIDENT,

"The Speaker of the House of Representatives having signed several enrolled Bills, I am directed to bring them to the Senate, for the signature of the Vice President"—

And he withdrew.

The Vice President affixed his signature to the Bill, entitled, "An Act making further provision for the collection of the duties by law imposed on teas, and to prolong the time for the payment of the duties on wines;" and the Bill, entitled, "An Act to continue in force the Act therein mentioned, and to make further provision for the payment of pensions to invalids, and for the support of light-houses, beacons, buoys and public piers," and they were delivered to the Committee on enrolled Bills, to be laid before the President of the United States, for his approbation.

A message from the President of the United States, by Mr. Lear his Secretary:

"Mr. PRESIDENT,

"The President of the United States has this day approved and signed 'The Resolve for establishing the Mint;' and 'The Resolve requesting the

---

[113] This report is in Committee on Enrolled Bills, Senate Records, DNA.
[114] This report is in Committee on Enrolled Bills, Senate Records, DNA.
[115] The inspected enrolled bill is in Enrolled Acts, RG 11, DNA. E-23861.
[116] The inspected enrolled bill is in Enrolled Acts, RG 11, DNA. E-23873.

President of the United States to cause an estimate to be laid before Congress, of the lands not claimed by the Indians' "[117]—

And he withdrew.

ORDERED, That the Secretary communicate the purport of this message to the House of Representatives.

The Bill, entitled, "An Act for the relief of David Cook," was read the FIRST time as follows.

"An ACT for the relief of DAVID COOK."

1   "SECT. I. *Be it enacted by the* SENATE *and House of* REPRE-
2   SENTATIVES *of the United States of America in Congress assembled,*
3   That David Cook, a captain of artillery in the late war, and who
4   being shot through the body at the battle of Monmouth, is ren-
5   dered incapable to obtain his livelihood by labor, shall be placed
6   on the pension list of the United States, and shall be entitled to
7   one third of his monthly pay as a Captain of Artillery:
8   *"Provided,* That he return into the Treasury-Office two thirds
9   of his commutation of half pay, being the proportion of his pen-
10   sion to the amount of his commutation."

March the 3d, 1791—Passed the House of Representatives.

And on the question, shall this Bill be read the SECOND time?—

It passed in the Negative.[118]

Mr. Foster from the Committee on enrolled Bills, reported, That they had this day, laid before the President of the United States, for his approbation, the following enrolled Bills:—The Bill, entitled, "An Act making further provision for the collection of the duties by law imposed on teas, and to prolong the time for the payment of the duties on wines;" and the Bill, entitled, "An Act to continue in force the Act therein mentioned, and to make further provision for the payment of pensions to invalids, and for the support of light-houses, beacons, buoys and public piers"—

Mr. Foster further reported from the Committee on enrolled Bills, That they had examined "The Resolve making a temporary provision for the safe-keeping of prisoners committed under the authority of the United States,"[119] and that it was duly enrolled.

A message from the House of Representatives by Mr. Beckley their clerk:

"Mr. PRESIDENT,

"The Speaker of the House of Representatives having signed an enrolled

---

[117] This message is in Committee on Enrolled Bills, Senate Records, DNA.

[118] This simple resolve is noted on the cover sheet of the bill and is in Engrossed House Bills, House Records, DNA.

[119] The inspected enrolled resolve is in Enrolled Acts, RG 11, DNA. E–23881.

Resolve, I am directed to bring it to the Senate for the signature of the Vice President—

"The President of the United States has notified the House of Representatives, that he has this day, approved and signed several Acts which originated in that House; a list of which I am directed to bring to the Senate"—

And he withdrew.

The Acts referred to in the message, and this day approved and signed by the President of the United States, are—

"An Act for making compensations to the Commissioners of loans, for extraordinary expenses," and—

"An Act in addition to an Act, entitled, 'An Act for establishing the salaries of the executive officers of government, with their assistants and clerks.' "[120]

The Vice President signed the enrolled "Resolve making a temporary provision for the safe-keeping of prisoners committed under the authority of the United States," and it was delivered to the Committee on enrolled Bills, to be laid before the President of the United States, for his approbation.

Mr. Foster reported from the Committee on enrolled Bills, That they had this day laid the last mentioned Resolve before the President of the United States.

A message from the President of the United States, by Mr. Lear his Secretary:

"Mr. PRESIDENT,

"The President of the United States has this day, approved and signed the following Acts which originated in the Senate: 'An Act to continue in force the Act therein mentioned, and to make further provision for the payment of pensions to invalids, and for the support of light-houses, beacons, buoys and public piers;' and 'An Act for granting lands to the inhabitants and settlers at Vincennes and the Illionois country, in the territory north-west of the Ohio, and for confirming them in their possessions' "[121]—

And he withdrew.

ORDERED, That the Secretary acquaint the House of Representatives that the President of the United States has this day approved and signed the Acts last mentioned.

A message from the House of Representatives by Mr. Beckley their clerk:

"Mr. PRESIDENT,

"The President of the United States has notified the House of Representa-

---

[120] This message is in Committee on Enrolled Bills, Senate Records, DNA.
[121] This message is in Committee on Enrolled Bills, Senate Records, DNA.

tives that he has this day, approved and signed several Acts which originated in that House[122]—

"I am directed to acquaint the Senate that the House of Representatives, having completed the business before them, intend shortly to adjourn without day"—

And he withdrew.

The Acts referred to in the last message, and this day approved and signed by the President of the United States, are—

"An Act providing compensations for the officers of the judicial courts of the United States, and for jurors and witnesses, and for other purposes"—

"An Act making further provision for the collection of the duties by law imposed on teas, and to prolong the time for the payment of the duties on wines"—

"An Act to continue in force for a limited time, an Act, entitled, 'An Act for the temporary establishment of the Post-Office' "—

"An Act supplementary to the Act making provision for the reduction of the public debt," and—

"A Resolve, making a temporary provision for the safe-keeping of prisoners committed under the authority of the United States."

ORDERED, That the Secretary acquaint the House of Representatives that the Senate having compleated the legislative business before them, are about to adjourn—And having acquainted the Vice President that he had delivered the message—

The Senate adjourned without day.

Attest. SAMUEL A. OTIS, Secretary

---

[122] This message is in Committee on Enrolled Bills, Senate Records, DNA.

APPENDIX TO THE THIRD SESSION
Sundry ACTS approved, but not entered in course when the Bills were first read in the Senate.

An ACT supplementary to the Act, entitled, "An Act making further PRO-VISION for the payment of the DEBTS of the UNITED STATES"

1   WHEREAS no express provision has been made for extending
2   the Act, entitled, "An Act to provide more effectually for the
3   collection of the duties imposed by law on goods, wares and mer-
4   chandize imported into the United States, and on the tonnage
5   of ships or vessels," to the collection of the duties imposed by the
6   said "Act making further provision for the payment of the debts
7   of the United States," doubts concerning the same may arise;—
8   therefore,

1   "SECT. I. *Be it enacted by the* SENATE *and House of* REPRESEN-
2   TATIVES *of the United States of America in Congress assembled,* That
3   the Act, entitled, "An Act to provide more effectually for the
4   collection of the duties imposed by law on goods, wares and mer-
5   chandize imported into the United States, and on the tonnage of
6   ships or vessels," doth and shall extend to, and be in force for the
7   collection of the duties specified and laid, in and by the Act, en-
8   titled, "An Act making further provision for the payment of the
9   debts of the United States," as fully and effectually, as if every
10   regulation, restriction, penalty, provision, clause, matter and thing
11   therein contained, had been inserted in, and re-enacted by the Act
12   last aforesaid.

    1790, December 16th—Originated in the Senate, and passed the
                17th, and on the same day the House of Represen-
                tatives concurred without amendment.
                27th—Approved.

"An ACT to continue an Act, entitled, 'An Act declaring the assent of CON-GRESS to certain Acts of the States of MARYLAND, GEORGIA and RHODE-ISLAND and PROVIDENCE PLANTATIONS, so far as the same respects the States of Georgia, and Rhode-Island and Providence Plantations'"

1   "SECT. I. *Be it enacted by the* SENATE *and House of* REPRE-
2   SENTATIVES *of the United States of America in Congress assembled,*
3   That the Act passed the last session of Congress, entitled, 'An
4   Act declaring the assent of Congress to certain Acts of the States

5 of Maryland, Georgia, and Rhode-Island and Providence Plan-
6 tations, so far as the same respects the States of Georgia, and
7 Rhode-Island and Providence Plantations,' shall be continued,
8 and is hereby declared to be in full force for the further term of
9 one year, and from thence to the end of the then next session of
10 Congress, and no longer."

1790, December 20th—Sent from the House of Representatives for
concurrence.

1791, January 6th—The Senate amended and concurred as above.
10th—Approved.

"An ACT to provide for the unlading of SHIPS or VESSELS, in cases of obstruction by ICE."

1 "WHEREAS it sometimes happens that ships or vessels, are
2 obstructed by ice, in their passage to the ports of their destination,
3 and it is necessary that provision should be made for unlading
4 such ships or vessels:

1 "SECT. I. *Be it enacted by the* SENATE *and House of* REPRE-
2 SENTATIVES *of the United States of America in Congress assembled,*
3 That in all cases where a ship or vessel shall be prevented by ice,
4 from getting to the port at which her cargo is intended to be de-
5 livered, it shall be lawful for the Collector of the district in which
6 such ship or vessel may be so obstructed, to receive the report and
7 entry of any such ship or vessel, and with the consent of the
8 Naval Officer (where there is one) to grant a permit or permits
9 for unlading or landing the goods, wares or merchandise impor-
10 ted in such ship or vessel, at any place within his district, which
11 shall appear to him to be most convenient and proper.

1 "SECT. II. *And be it further enacted,* That the report and entry
2 of such ship or vessel and of her cargo, or any part thereof, and
3 all persons concerned therein, shall be under and subject to the
4 same rules, regulations, restrictions, penalties and provisions, as
5 if the said ship or vessel had arrived at the port of her destination,
6 and had there proceeded to the delivery of her cargo."

1791, January the 3d—Passed the House of Representatives.
5th—The Senate concurred without amendment.
7th—Approved.

"An ACT declaring the consent of CONGRESS to a certain Act of the State of
MARYLAND"

1   "SECT. I. *Be it enacted by the* SENATE *and House of* REPRE-
2   SENTATIVES *of the United States of America in Congress assembled,*
3   That the consent of Congress be, and is hereby granted and de-
4   clared to the operation of an Act of the General Assembly of
5   Maryland, made and passed at a session begun and held at the
6   city of Annapolis, on the first Monday in November last, enti-
7   tled, 'An Act to empower the wardens of the port of Baltimore
8   to levy and collect the duty therein mentioned,' until the tenth
9   day of January next, and from thence until the end of the then
10   next session of Congress, and no longer."

1791, January the 31st—Before the Senate for concurrence.

February 2d   —Passed the Senate without amendment.

9th   —Approved.

"An ACT making appropriations for the support of GOVERNMENT during the year ONE THOUSAND SEVEN HUNDRED and NINETY-ONE, and for other purposes "

1   "SECT. I. *Be it enacted by the* SENATE *and House of* REPRESEN-
2   TATIVES *of the United States of America in Congress assembled,* That
3   there be appropriated the several sums, and for the several pur-
4   poses following, to wit; A sum not exceeding two hundred and
5   ninety-nine thousand, two hundred and seventy-six dollars and
6   fifty-three cents, for defraying the expenses of the civil list, as
7   estimated by the Secretary of the Treasury, in the statement
8   number one, accompanying his report to the House of Represen-
9   tatives of the sixth instant, including the contingencies of the
10   several executive officers, and of the two Houses of Congress,
11   which are hereby authorised and granted: A sum not exceeding
12   fifty thousand, seven hundred and fifty-six dollars and fifty-three
13   cents, for satisfying the several objects specified in the statement
14   number two, accompanying the report aforesaid, all such whereof
15   as may not have been heretofore provided for by law, being
16   hereby authorised: And a sum not exceeding three hundred and
17   ninety thousand, one hundred and ninety-nine dollars and fifty-
18   four cents, for the use of the department of war, pursuant to
19   the statement number three, accompanying the report aforesaid,
20   including therein the sum of one hundred thousand dollars, for
21   defraying the expenses of an expedition lately carried on against
22   certain Indian tribes; and the sum of eighty-seven thousand, four
23   hundred and sixty-three dollars and sixty cents, being the amount

24 of one year's pensions to invalids, together with the contingen-
25 cies of the said department, which are hereby authorised: Which
26 several sums shall be paid out of the funds following, namely—
27 the sum of six hundred thousand dollars, which by the Act, en-
28 titled, 'An Act making provision for the debt of the United
29 States,' is reserved yearly for the support of the government of
30 the United States, and their common defence; The amount of
31 such surpluses as may remain in the Treasury, after satisfying
32 the purposes for which appropriations were made by the Acts
33 respectively, entitled, 'An Act making appropriations for the
34 service of the present year,' passed the twenty-ninth day of Sep-
35 tember, one thousand seven hundred and eighty-nine; 'An Act
36 making appropriations for the support of government for the
37 year one thousand seven hundred and ninety,' passed the twenty-
38 sixth day of March, one thousand seven hundred and ninety;
39 'An Act making certain appropriations therein mentioned,' pas-
40 sed the twelfth day of August, one thousand seven hundred and
41 ninety; and the product, during the present year, of such duties
42 as shall be laid in the present session of Congress."

1791, February the 2d—Sent for concurrence.

8th—Passed the Senate without amendment.

11th—Approved.

APPROPRIATION OF TEN THOUSAND DOLLARS, for the purpose of defraying
  Dr.

		For the following payments made upon orders of the President of the United States			
1790					
Aug.	17	His order in favor of Peter Maverick, for sundry seals furnished for the supreme and other courts of the United States...............	91	8	
	27	Ditto in favor of Royal Flint, agent for Jeremiah Wadsworth, being the amount of an account for apprehending the Cranes, and others concerned in counterfeiting, &c......	1061		
	31	Ditto in favor of Mark Leavenworth, agent for Amos Doolittle, for a seal made for the district court of Connecticut................	8		
Sept.	2	Ditto in favor of Peter Maverick, for a seal for the district court of Rhode-Island..........	5	50	
Oct.	5	Ditto in favor of Cyrus Griffin, judge for the district of Virginia, for cash paid by him for a seal and an iron screw, for the use of said district.................................	19	33	1184 91
		Balance subject to the orders of the President of the United States.................................			8815 9
				Dollars	10,000

the contingent charges of GOVERNMENT, by Act of 26th March, 1790

Cr.

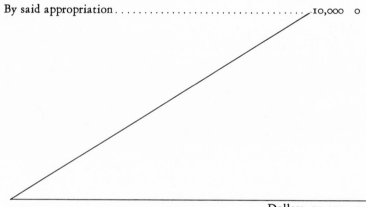

By said appropriation 10,000   0

Dollars   10,000   0

TREASURY DEPARTMENT

REGISTER's-OFFICE, January 15, 1791

JOSEPH NOURSE, Reg.

The Classes of the SENATORS of the UNITED STATES, during the first Congress

2 Years Class.	4 Years Class.	6 Years Class.
The Honorable Mr. { Carroll, Dalton, Ellsworth, Elmer, Foster, Maclay, Monroe, Read, Schuyler	The Honorable Mr. { Bassett, Butler, Dickinson, Few, Johnston, Lee, Stanton, Strong, Wingate	The Honorable Mr. { Gunn, Hawkins, Henry, Johnson, Izard, King, Langdon, Morris

March 3d, 1791

Ratifications of the ARTICLES of AMENDMENT to the CONSTITUTION of the United States, proposed by the Resolution of Congress at their first Session under the said Constitution, to wit:

The States in alphabetical order.	Ratifies the whole.	Postpone or reject.	Postpone or reject.
1 Of Delaware..........................	. . .	the 1st.	. . .
2 Maryland...........................	1 to 12	. . .	. . .
3 New-Hampshire......................	. . .	. . .	2d
4 New-Jersey..........................	. . .	. . .	2d
5 New-York...........................	. . .	. . .	2d
6 North-Carolina......................	1 to 12	. . .	. . .
7 Pennsylvania........................	. . .	the 1st.	. . .
8 Rhode-Island........................	1 to 12	. . .	. . .
9 South-Carolina......................	1 to 12	. . .	. . .

The other States have made no return.

March 3d, 1791

SUPPLEMENT TO THE APPENDIX TO THE THIRD SESSION

On the back of the title page of the Senate rough journal for the third session, the following notations were made by Otis. He outlined rules of form and procedure for making up the smooth journal, apparently for the use of his clerks.

1st Bills & Resolutions fm the H of R in Italics Amendments & motions for them &c

2d Print ~~Bills &c frm H of R & amendments in Italics~~

3d Number the lines in all bills & Sections

4th Bills originating in Senate sd reported & inserted to be numbered & inverted Commas (")
So Resolutions.

Bills and resolutions of the 2. Houses not perfected & Motions should be marked *with inverted commas* (") to shew they are copies. *NB commas only begin & end.* [*A line at this point is erased and illegible.*]
Mem. Correct the amendts & fill up references on the proof sheet

---

In the appendix insert the laws say Bills brot in this Session. Also secret bills &c.

Not printed but To be COPIED IN THE WRITTEN RECORD.

See order abt: J. Mathers   p 82.   another 181
Order abt printing laws   P 93.
Maryland act in the appendix

Mem: print the Military bill if I can—
Expunge [do] before a verb active in all cases

Appendix.

No.	Short Title	Long Title	Date Introduced	Date Signed by President

FIRST SESSION: MARCH 4, 1789–SEPTEMBER 29, 1789

No.	Short Title	Long Title	Date Introduced	Date Signed by President
1	JUDICIARY	An Act to establish the Judicial Courts of the United States	June 12	Sept. 24
2	PUNISHMENT OF CRIMES	An Act for the punishment of certain crimes against the United States	July 28	Postponed See [S–6]
3	POST OFFICE	An Act for the temporary establishment of the Post-Office	Sept. 11	Sept. 22
4	COURTS	An Act to regulate Processes in the Courts of the United States	Sept. 17	Sept. 29
5	GLAUBECK	An Act to allow the Baron de Glaubeck the Pay of a Captain in the Army of the United States	Sept. 24	Sept. 29

SECOND SESSION: JANUARY 4, 1790–AUGUST 12, 1790

No.	Short Title	Long Title	Date Introduced	Date Signed by President
6	PUNISHMENT OF CRIMES	A Bill defining the crimes and offences that shall be cognizable under the authority of the United States, and their punishment / An Act for the punishment of certain crimes against the United States	Jan. 26	Apr. 30
7	NORTH CAROLINA CESSION	An Act to accept a cession of the claims of the State of North-Carolina, to a certain district of western territory	Mar. 3	Apr. 3
8	SOUTHERN TERRITORY	An Act for the government of the territory of the United States south of the River Ohio	Apr. 9	May 26
9	COURTS	An Act to continue in force an Act passed at the last session of Congress, entitled, "An Act to regulate processes in the courts of the United States"	Apr. 23	May 26

No.	Short Title	Long Title	Date Introduced	Date Signed by President
10	NORTH CAROLINA JUDICIARY	An Act for giving effect to the Acts therein mentioned, in respect to the State of North-Carolina, and to amend the said Act	Apr. 29	Not passed See[HR–68]
11	RHODE ISLAND TRADE	An Act to prevent bringing goods, wares and merchandizes from the State of Rhode-Island and Providence Plantations, into the United States, and to authorize a demand of money from the said State	May 13	Not passed
12	RESIDENCE	A Bill to determine the permanent seat of Congress, and the government of the United States An Act for establishing the temporary and permanent seat of the Government of the United States	May 31	July 16
13	CIRCUIT COURTS	A Bill for altering the time of holding the courts in South Carolina and Georgia An Act to alter the times for holding the Circuit Courts of the United States in the districts of South-Carolina and Georgia, and providing that the District Court of Pennsylvania shall in future be held in the city of Philadelphia only	Aug. 7	Aug. 11

THIRD SESSION: DECEMBER 6, 1790–MARCH 3, 1791

No.	Short Title	Long Title	Date Introduced	Date Signed by President
14	WAYS AND MEANS	An Act supplementary to the Act, entitled, "An Act making further provision for the payment of the debts of the United States"	Dec. 16	Dec. 27
15	BANK	An Act to incorporate the subscribers to the bank of the United States	Jan. 3	Feb. 25

No.	Short Title	Long Title	Date Introduced	Date Signed by President
16	KENTUCKY STATEHOOD	An Act providing that the district of Kentucky should become an independent State, and be admitted as a member of the United States of America An Act declaring the consent of Congress that a new State be formed within the jurisdiction of the Commonwealth of Virginia, and admitted into this union by the name of the State of Kentucky	Jan. 4	Feb. 4
17	NORTHWEST TERRITORY	An Act for granting lands to the inhabitants and setlers at Vincennes and the Ilinois country, in the territory northwest of the Ohio, and for confirming them in their possessions	Jan. 7	Mar. 3
18	CONSULS AND VICE CONSULS	An Act concerning Consuls and Vice Consuls	Jan. 7	Not passed
19	VERMONT STATEHOOD	An Act for the admission of the State of Vermont into this union	Feb. 10	Feb. 18
20	KENTUCKY AND VERMONT REPRESENTATIVES	An Act regulating the number of Representatives to be chosen by the States of Kentucky and Vermont	Feb. 11	Feb. 25
21	RESIDENCE	An Act to amend an Act, entitled, "An act for establishing the temporary and permanent seat of government of the United States"	Feb. 17	Mar. 3
22	PAYMENT OF BALANCES	An Act concerning the payment of balances due to the United States in certain cases	Feb. 26	Not passed
23	MOROCCAN TREATY	An Act making an appropriation for the purposes therein mentioned [effecting a recognition of the treaty of the United States with the new Emperor of Morocco]	Mar. 1	Mar. 3

No.	Short Title	Long Title	Date Introduced	Date Signed by President
24	MITIGATION OF FORFEITURES	An Act to continued in force the Act therein mentioned [to provide for mitigating . . . forfeitures], and to make further provision for the payment of pensions to invalids, and for the support of lighthouses, beacons, buoys and public piers	Mar. 2	Mar. 3

No.	Short Title	Long Title	Date Introduced	Date Signed by President

FIRST SESSION: MARCH 4, 1789–SEPTEMBER 29, 1789

No.	Short Title	Long Title	Date Introduced	Date Signed by President
1	OATH	A Bill to regulate the taking the oath or affirmation prescribed by the sixth article of the Constitution An Act to regulate the time and manner of administering certain oaths	Apr. 14	June 1
2	IMPOST	An Act for laying a duty on goods, wares and merchandizes, imported into the United States	May 5	July 4
3	COLLECTION	A Bill for collecting duties on goods, wares, and merchandizes, imported into the United States	May 8	Tabled—HR See [HR-6]
4	No bill so numbered			
5	TONNAGE	An Act imposing duties on tonnage	May 25	July 20
6	COLLECTION	A Bill to regulate the collection of duties, imposed on goods, wares, and merchandizes, imported into the United States	May 27	No third reading— HR See [HR-11]
7	WAR DEPARTMENT	An Act to establish an Executive Department, to be denominated the Department of War	June 2	Aug. 7
8	FOREIGN AFFAIRS	An Act for establishing an Executive Department, to be denominated the Department of Foreign Affairs	June 2	July 27
9	TREASURY	A Bill to establish an Executive Department, to be denominated the Treasury Department An Act to establish the Treasury Department	June 4	Sept. 2
10	COPYRIGHT	A Bill to promote the progress of science and useful arts, by securing to authors and inventors the ex-	June 23	Postponed See [HR-39]

No.	Short Title	Long Title	Date Introduced	Date Signed by President
		clusive right to their respective writings and discoveries		
11	COLLECTION Substitute for [HR–6]	A Bill to regulate the collection of duties imposed on goods, wares and merchandizes, imported into the United States	June 29	July 31
		An Act to regulate the collection of the duties imposed by law on the tonnage of ships or vessels, and on goods, wares and merchandizes, imported into the United States		
12	LIGHTHOUSES	A Bill for the Establishment and support of lighthouses, beacons and buoys; and for authorising the several states to provide and regulate pilots	July 1	Aug. 7
		An Act for the establishment and support of Light-Houses, Beacons and Buoys		
		An Act for the Establishment and support of Light-Houses, Beacons, Buoys, and Public Piers		
13	SETTLEMENT OF ACCOUNTS	An Act for settling the accounts between the United States and individual States	July 16	Aug. 5
14	NORTHWEST TERRITORY	An Act to provide for the government of the territory north west of the River Ohio	July 16	Aug. 7
15	COMPENSATION	An Act for allowing [making] a compensation to the President and Vice President of the United States	July 22	Sept. 24
16	COASTING	A Bill for registering and clearing vessels, ascertaining their tonnage, and for	July 24	Sept. 1

No.	Short Title	Long Title	Date Introduced	Date Signed by President
		regulating the coasting trade		
		An Act for registering and clearing Vessels, regulating the Coasting Trade, and for other purposes		
17	LAND OFFICE	A Bill establishing a Land Office, in, and for the Western Territory	July 31	Postponed
18	RECORDS	A Bill to provide for the safekeeping of the acts, records, and seal of the United States; for the due publication of the acts of Congress; for the authentication of copies of records; for making out, and recording commissions, and prescribing their form, and for establishing the fees of office to be taken for making such commissions, and for copies of records and papers	July 31	Sept. 15
		An act to provide for the safekeeping of the Acts, Records, and Seal of the United States, and for other Purposes		
19	SALARIES- LEGISLATIVE	An Act for allowing compensation to the members of the Senate and House of Representatives of the United States, and to the officers of both Houses	Aug. 4	Sept. 22
20	INDIAN TREATIES	An Act providing for the Expenses which may attend Negotiations or Treaties with the Indian Tribes, and the Appointment of Commissioners for managing the same	Aug. 10	Aug. 20
21	SALARIES- EXECUTIVE	An Act for establishing the Salaries of the Executive Officers of Government, with their Assistants and Clerks	Aug. 24	Sept. 11

No.	Short Title	Long Title	Date Introduced	Date Signed by President
22	HOSPITALS AND HARBORS	A Bill providing for the establishment of hospitals for the relief of sick and disabled seamen, and prescribing regulations for for the harbours of the United States	Aug. 27	Postponed
23	COLLECTION	An Act to suspend part [obliging vessels bound up the Potomac to stop at St. Mary's or Yeocomico, to report a manifest of their cargoes] of an Act, entitled, An Act to regulate the Collection of the Duties imposed by Law on the Tonnage of Ships or Vessels, and on Goods, Wares and Merchandizes imported into the United States	Aug. 28	Sept. 16
24	TONNAGE	A Bill for suspending the operations of part of an act, entitled "An Act imposing duties on tonnage"	Sept. 9	Not passed
25	SEAT OF GOVERNMENT	An Act to establish the Seat of Government of the United States	Sept. 14	Postponed
26	COLLECTION	An Act for amending part of an Act, entitled, An Act to regulate the Collection of the Duties imposed by Law on the Tonnage of Ships or Vessels and on Goods, Wares, and Merchandizes, imported into the United States	Sept. 17	Not passed
27	TROOPS	An Act to recognize and adapt to the Constitution of the United States, the establishment of the Troops raised under the Resolves of the United States in Congress assembled, and for other Purposes therein mentioned	Sept. 17	Sept. 29

No.	Short Title	Long Title	Date Introduced	Date Signed by President
28	SALARIES-JUDICIARY	An Act for allowing certain Compensation to the Judges of the Supreme and other Courts, and to the Attorney General of the United States	Sept. 17	Sept. 23
29	INVALID PENSIONERS	An Act, providing for the payment of the invalid Pensioners of the United States	Sept. 18	Sept. 29
30	SLAVE TRADE	A Bill concerning the importation of certain persons prior to the year 1808	Sept. 19	Postponed
31	TIME OF MEETING	A Bill to alter the time of the annual meeting of Congress An Act to alter the Time for the next meeting of Congress	Sept. 21	Sept. 29
32	APPROPRIATIONS	An Act making appropriations for the service of the present year	Sept. 21	Sept. 29
33	COASTING	An Act to explain and amend an Act, entitled, "An Act for registering and clearing Vessels, regulating the Coasting Trade, and for other Purposes"	Sept. 23	Sept. 29

SECOND SESSION: JANUARY 4, 1790–AUGUST 12, 1790

No.	Short Title	Long Title	Date Introduced	Date Signed by President
34	ENUMERATION	An Act providing for the actual enumeration of the inhabitants of the United States	Jan. 18	Mar. 1
35	FOREIGN INTERCOURSE	A Bill providing the means of intercourse between the United States and foreign nations	Jan. 21	Not passed— HR See [HR-52]
36	NORTH-CAROLINA	An Act for giving effect to the several acts therein mentioned, in respect to the State of North Carolina, and other purposes	Jan. 25	Feb. 8
37	NATURALIZATION	A Bill establishing an uniform rule of naturalization	Jan. 25	Not passed— HR See [HR-40]

No.	Short Title	Long Title	Date Introduced	Date Signed by President
38	MITIGATION OF FINES	A Bill to provide for the remission or mitigation of fines, forfeitures and penalties in certain cases	Jan. 26	Not passed— HR See [HR-45]
39	COPYRIGHT	A Bill for securing the copyright of books to authors and proprietors	Jan. 28	Not passed— HR See [HR-43]
40	NATURALIZATION	A Bill to establish an uniform rule of naturalization, and to enable aliens to hold lands under certain restrictions An Act to establish a uniform rule of naturalization	Feb. 16	Mar. 26
41	PATENTS	An Act to promote the progress of useful arts	Feb. 16	Apr. 10
42	POST OFFICE	A Bill for regulating the post-office of the United States	Feb. 23	Not passed— HR See [HR-74]
43	COPYRIGHT	A Bill for the encouragement of learning, by securing the copies of maps, charts, books and other writings, to the authors and proprietors of such copies, during the times therein mentioned An Act for the encouragement of learning, by securing the copies of maps, charts, books, to the authors and proprietors of such copies, during the times therein mentioned	Feb. 25	May 31
44	BAILEY	An Act to vest in Francis Bailey, the exclusive privilege of making, using, and vending to others, punches for stamping the matrices of types, and impressing marks on plates, or any other substance, to prevent counterfeits, upon a principle by him invented, for a term of years	Feb. 26	Not passed See [HR-41]
45	MITIGATION OF FINES	An Act to provide for the remission or mitigation of	Mar. 3	See [HR-57]

No.	Short Title	Long Title	Date Introduced	Date Signed by President
		fines, foreitures, and penalties, in certain cases		
46	SALARIES OF CLERKS	An Act for encreasing the salaries of clerks in the office of the Commissioners for settling accounts, between the United States and individual states	Mar. 8	Not passed
47	APPROPRIATIONS	An Act making appropriations for the support of government for the year one thousand seven hundred and ninety	Mar. 8	Mar. 26
48	INSPECTION	An Act to prevent the exportation of goods not duly inspected according to the laws of the several States	Mar. 8	Apr. 2
49	ELY	A Bill to allow compensation to John Ely, for his services and expences as a regimental surgeon in the late army of the United States	Mar. 11	Not passed— HR See [HR–56]
50	COLLECTION	An Act further to suspend part of an Act, entitled, An Act to regulate the collection of the duties imposed by law on the tonnage of ships or vessels, and on goods, wares and merchandizes, imported into the United States An Act, further to suspend part of an Act, entitled, "An Act to regulate the collection of the duties imposed by law on the tonnage of ships or vessels, and on goods, wares, and merchandizes, imported into the United States;" and to amend the said Act	Mar. 26	Apr. 15
[50a]	MILITARY ESTABLISHMENT	An Act for regulating the military establishment of the United States	[Mar. 26, received by Senate]	Apr. 30

No.	Short Title	Long Title	Date Introduced	Date Signed by President
[50b]	INDIAN TREATY	An Act providing for holding a treaty or treaties, to establish peace with certain Indian tribes	[Mar. 29, received by Senate]	July 22
51	INDIAN TRADE	A Bill to regulate trade and intercourse with the Indian Tribes	Mar. 30	Not passed— HR See [HR–65]
52	FOREIGN INTERCOURSE	An Act providing the means of intercourse between the United States and foreign nations	Mar. 31	July 1
53	OFFICERS	An Act for the relief of a certain description of officers therein mentioned	Apr. 5	Not passed See [HR–59]
54	SALARIES- EXECUTIVE	An Act supplemental to the Act for establishing the salaries of the executive officers of government, with their assistants and clerks	Apr. 13	June 4
55	See [HR–50a]			
56	ELY	An Act to allow compensation to John Ely, for his attendance as a physician and surgeon on the prisoners of the United States	Apr. 22	Not passed
57	MITIGATION OF FORFEITURES	An Act to provide for mitigating or remitting the forfeitures and penalties accruing under the revenue laws, in certain cases therein mentioned	Apr. 27	May 26
58	AUTHENTICATION	An Act to prescribe the mode in which the public acts, records, and judicial proceedings in each State shall be authenticated, so as to take effect in every other State	Apr. 28	May 26
59	INVALID OFFICERS	An Act to authorize the issuing of certificates to a certain description of invalid officers	Apr. 30	Not passed See [HR–96]
60	STEUBEN	An Act for finally adjusting and satisfying the claims of Frederick William de Steuben	Apr. 30	June 4

No.	Short Title	Long Title	Date Introduced	Date Signed by President
61	MERCHANT SEAMEN	An Act for the government and regulation of seamen in the merchants service	May 3	July 20
62	DUTIES ON DISTILLED SPIRITS	A Bill for repealing, after the last day of ———— next, the duties heretofore laid upon distilled spirits imported from abroad, and laying others in their stead, and also upon spirits distilled within the United States, as well to discourage the excessive use of those spirits, and promote agriculture, as to provide for the support of the public credit, and for the common defence and general welfare	May 5	Not passed— HR See [HR-83]
63	FUNDING	An Act making provision for the debt of the United States	[May 6, not recorded in House Journal]	Aug. 4
64	DUTIES ON WINES	A Bill repealing, after the last day of ———— next, the duties heretofore laid upon wines imported from foreign ports or places, and laying others in their stead	May 11	Not passed— HR See [HR-83]
65	INDIAN TRADE	An Act to regulate trade and intercourse with the Indian tribes	May 14	July 22
66	TRADE AND NAVIGATION	A Bill concerning the navigation and trade of the United States	May 17	Not passed— HR
67	JENKINS	An Act for the relief of Thomas Jenkins and company	May 20	June 14
68	NORTH CAROLINA JUDICIARY	An Act for giving effect to an Act, entitled, "An Act to establish the Judicial Courts of the United States," within the State of North-Carolina	May 21	June 4

No.	Short Title	Long Title	Date Introduced	Date Signed by President
69	SETTLEMENT OF ACCOUNTS	A Bill to provide for the settlement of the accounts between the United States, and the individual States	May 27	Not passed— HR See [HR–77]
70	McCORD	An Act to satisfy the claims of John McCord, against the United States	June 2	July 1
71	RHODE ISLAND	An Act for giving effect to the several Acts therein mentioned, in respect to the State of Rhode-Island and Providence Plantations	June 2	June 14
72	TWINING	An Act for the relief of Nathaniel Twining	June 3	July 1
73	RHODE ISLAND JUDICIARY	An Act for giving effect to an Act, entitled, "An Act to establish the Judicial Courts of the United States" within the State of Rhode-Island and Providence Plantations	June 4	June 23
74	POST OFFICE	An Act to establish the Post-Office and Post-Roads within the United States	June 7	Not passed See [HR–113]
75	RHODE ISLAND ENUMERATION	An Act for giving effect to An Act, entitled, "An Act, providing for the enumeration of the inhabitants of the United States," in respect to the State of Rhode-Island and Providence Plantations	June 7	July 5
76	WEST POINT	An Act to authorize the purchase of a tract of land [at West Point] for the use of the United States	June 15	July 5
77	SETTLEMENT OF ACCOUNTS	An Act to provide more effectually for the settlement of the accounts between the United States and individual States	June 17	Aug. 5
78	TONNAGE	An Act imposing duties on the tonnage of ships or vessels	June 22	July 20
79	GOULD	An Act to satisfy the claim	June 23	Not passed

No.	Short Title	Long Title	Date Introduced	Date Signed by President
		of the representatives of David Gould, deceased, against the United States		
80	INVALID PENSIONERS	An Act further to provide for the payment of the invalid pensioners of the United States	June 29	July 16
81	MILITIA	A Bill more effectually to provide for the national defence, by establishing a uniform militia throughout the United States	July 1	Not passed— HR See [HR-102]
82	COLLECTION	An Act to provide more effectually for the collection of the duties imposed by law on goods, wares and merchandize imported into the United States, and on the tonnage of ships or vessels	July 8	Aug. 4
83	WAYS AND MEANS	An Act making further provision for the payment of the debts of the United States	July 13	Aug. 10
84	LIGHTHOUSES	An Act to amend the Act for the establishment and support of light-houses, beacons, buoys and public piers	July 14	July 22
85	VIRGINIA CESSION	An Act to enable the officers and soldiers of the Virginia line, on the continental establishment, to obtain titles to certain lands lying north-west of the river Ohio, between the Little Miami and Sciota	July 15	Aug. 10
86	CONSULS AND VICE CONSULS	A Bill for establishing the fees and perquisites to be received by Consuls and Vice-Consuls of the United States in foreign parts, and for other purposes An Act concerning consuls and vice consuls of the	July 15	Postponed See [S-18]

No.	Short Title	Long Title	Date Introduced	Date Signed by President
		United States, in foreign parts		
87	See [HR–50b]			
88	DISABLED SOLDIERS AND SEAMEN	An Act for the relief of disabled soldiers and seamen lately in the service of the United States, and of certain other persons	July 16	Aug. 11
89	COASTING	A Bill for registering ships or vessels, for regulating those employed in the coasting trade and fisheries, and for other purposes	July 22	Postponed
90	STEWART AND DAVIDSON	An Act for the relief of John Stewart and John Davidson	July 27	Aug. 4
91	BARCLAY	An Act to compensate Thomas Barclay for various public services	July 28	Not passed
92	POST OFFICE	An Act to continue in force for a limited time, an Act, entitled, "An Act for the temporary establishment of the post-office"	July 28	Aug. 4
93	NAVIGATION	An Act declaring the assent of Congress to certain Acts of the States of Maryland, Georgia, and Rhode-Island	Aug. 3	Aug. 11
94	GEORGIA	A Bill making further provision for the debt of the United States, so far as respects the assumption of the debt of the State of Georgia	Aug. 3	Not passed— HR
95	SETTLING ACCOUNTS	An Act for adding two Commissioners to the board established for settling the accounts between the United States and the individual States	Aug. 4	Not passed
96	STIRLING	An Act making an appropriation for discharging the claim of Sarah Alexander, the widow of the late Major General Lord	Aug. 4	Aug. 11

No.	Short Title	Long Title	Date Introduced	Date Signed by President
		Stirling, who died in the services of the United States		
		An Act for the relief of the persons therein mentioned or described		
97	PORTLAND HEAD LIGHTHOUSE	An Act authorizing the Secretary of the Treasury to finish the lighthouse on Portland Head in, the district of Maine	Aug. 5	Aug. 10
98	SURVEYOR GENERAL	A Bill providing for the appointment of a surveyor-general for the United States	Aug. 6	Not passed— HR
99	CALDWELL	An Act for the relief of Adam Caldwell	Aug. 6	Postponed
100	SPECIAL APPROPRIATIONS	An Act making certain appropriations therein mentioned	Aug. 9	Aug. 12
101	SINKING FUND	An Act making provision for the reduction of the public debt	Aug. 9	Aug. 12

THIRD SESSION: DECEMBER 6, 1790–MARCH 3, 1791

No.	Short Title	Long Title	Date Introduced	Date Signed by President
102	MILITIA	A Bill more effectually to provide for the national defence, by establishing a uniform militia through-the United States	Dec. 14	Not passed— HR See [HR–112]
103	NAVIGATION	An Act to continue an Act, entitled, "An Act declaring the assent of Congress to certain Acts of the States of Maryland, Georgia, and Rhode-Island and Providence Plantations"	Dec. 16	Jan. 10
104	PRESIDENCY	A Bill declaring the officer, who, in case of vacancies, both in the offices of President and Vice-President of the United States, shall act as President	Dec. 20	Not passed— HR
105	ELECTORS	A Bill declaring the respective times when the electors to vote for a President	Dec. 20	Not passed— HR

No.	Short Title	Long Title	Date Introduced	Date Signed by President
		of the United States shall be appointed or chosen, and shall give their votes		
106	PRESIDENTIAL ELECTION	A Bill directing the mode in which the lists of the votes for a President shall be transmitted to the seat of the government of the United States	Dec. 20	Not passed— HR
107	LIABILITY OF SHIPOWNERS	A Bill to ascertain how far the owners of ships and vessels shall be answerable to the freighters	Dec. 27	Not passed— HR
108	EVIDENCES OF DEBT	A Bill directing the mode in which the evidences of the debt of the United States, which have been or may be lost or destroyed, shall be renewed	Dec. 28	Not passed— HR See [HR–118]
109	COLLECTION	A Bill to provide for the delivery of goods, wares and merchandize in the state of Pennsylvania, in cases of obstruction of the river Delaware by ice An Act to provide for the unlading of ships or vessels in cases of obstruction by ice	Dec. 28	Jan. 7
110	DUTIES ON DISTILLED SPIRITS	A Bill repealing after the last day of ——— next, the duties heretofore laid upon distilled spirits imported from abroad, and laying others in their stead, and also upon spirits distilled within the United States; as well to discourage the excessive use of those spirits and promote agriculture, as to provide for the support of the public credit, and for the common defence and general welfare An Act repealing, after the last day of June next, the	Dec. 30	Mar. 3

No.	Short Title	Long Title	Date Introduced	Date Signed by President
		duties heretofore laid upon distilled spirits imported from abroad, and laying others in their stead; also upon spirits distilled within the United States, and for appropriating the same		
111	SWAIN	An Act for the relief of Shubael Swain	Dec. 31	Not passed
112	MILITIA	A Bill more effectually to provide for the national defence, by establishing a uniform militia throughout the United States	Jan. 4	Not passed— HR
113	POST OFFICE	A Bill for establishing the post-office and post-roads of the United States	Jan. 7	Not passed— HR
114	LAND OFFICE	An Act to establish offices for the purpose of granting lands within the territories of the United States	Jan. 14	Postponed
115	MARYLAND	An Act declaring the assent of Congress to a certain Act of the State of Maryland	Jan. 18	Feb. 9
116	FOREIGN OFFICERS	An Act authorizing the President of the United States, to cause the debt due to foreign officers, to be paid and discharged	Jan. 19	Rejected
117	TRANSFER OF PENSIONS	A Bill to prevent invalids who are pensioners of the United States, from selling or transferring their respective pensions before the same shall become due	Jan. 21	Not passed— HR
118	EVIDENCES OF DEBT	A Bill directing the mode in in which the evidences of the debt of the United States, which have been or may be lost or detroyed shall be renewed	Jan. 25	Not passed— HR See [HR–142]
119	SALARIES OF INSPECTORS	A Bill providing compensations for inspectors, and other officers of inspec-	Jan. 26	Not passed— HR

No.	Short Title	Long Title	Date Introduced	Date Signed by President
		tion, and for other purposes		
120	APPROPRIATIONS	An Act making appropriations for the support of government during the year one thousand seven hundred and ninety-one, and for other purposes	Jan. 31	Feb. 11
121	PATENTS	A Bill to amend an act, intituled "An act to promote the progress of useful arts"	Feb. 7	Not passed— HR
122	TIME OF MEETING	An Act to alter the time of the next meeting of Congress	Feb. 8	Rejected See [HR–132]
123	COPYRIGHT	A Bill for increasing the penalty contained in act, passed the second session of Congress, intituled, "An act for the encouragement of learning, by securing the copies of maps, charts and books, to the authors and proprietors of such copies, during the times therein mentioned"	Feb. 9	Not passed— HR
124	COURTS	An Act to continue in force for a limited time, an Act passed at the first session of Congress, entitled, "An Act to regulate processes in the courts of the United States"	Feb. 9	Feb. 18
125	BANK	An Act supplementary to the Act, entitled, "An Act to incorporate the subscribers to the bank of the United States"	Feb. 10	Mar. 2
126	JUDICIAL OFFICERS	A Bill providing compensations for clerks, marshals and jurors	Feb. 11	See [HR–133]
126A	MILITARY ESTABLISHMENT	An Act for raising and adding another regiment to the military establishment of the United States, and for making further	[Feb. 12, received by Senate]	Mar. 3

No.	Short Title	Long Title	Date Introduced	Date Signed by President
		provision for the protection of the frontiers		
127	BARNEY	A Bill to compensate Joshua Barney	Feb. 16	Rejected
128	VERMONT	An Act for giving effect to the laws of the United States, within the State of Vermont	Feb. 17	Mar. 2
129	WAYS AND MEANS	An Act to explain and amend an Act, entitled, "An Act making further provision for the payment of the debts of the United States"	Feb. 21	Mar. 2
130	DUTIES ON TEAS	A Bill making further provision for the collection of the duties imposed on teas An Act making further provision for the collection of duties by law imposed on teas, and to prolong the term for the payment of duties on wines	Feb. 22	Mar. 3
131	TREASURY	An Act supplemental to the Act establishing the Treasury Department	Feb. 22	Mar. 3
132	TIME OF MEETING	An Act fixing the time for the next annual meeting of Congress	Feb. 23	Mar. 2
133	JUDICIAL OFFICERS	A Bill providing compensations for the officers of the several courts of law, and for jurors and witnesses An Act providing compensations for the officers of the judicial courts of the United States, and for jurors and witnesses, and for other purposes	Feb. 24	Mar. 3
134	COLLECTION	A Bill repealing so much of an act [i.e., collection] as establishes the rate of the rix dollar of Denmark An Act concerning the rates of foreign coins An Act relative to the rix dollar of Denmark	Feb. 24	Mar. 3

No.	Short Title	Long Title	Date Introduced	Date Signed by President
135	COMMISSIONERS OF LOANS	An Act for making compensations to the Commissioners of loans, for extraordinary expenses	Feb. 24	Mar. 3
136	SINKING FUND	An Act supplementary to the Act making provision for the reduction of the public debt	Feb. 25	Mar. 3
136A	SALARIES	An Act in addition to an Act, entitled, "An Act for establishing the salaries of the executive officers of government with their assistants and clerks"	[Feb. 26]	Mar. 3
137	POST OFFICE	An Act to continue in force for a limited time, an Act, entitled, "An Act for the temporary establishment of the Post-Office"	Feb. 28	Mar. 3
138	GIBSON	An Act to compensate George Gibson	Feb. 28	Postponed
139	WIDOWS, ORPHANS, AND INVALIDS	An Act for making compensation to the widows and orphan children of certain officers who were killed, or who died in the service of the United States, during the late war; and for the relief of certain invalids, and other persons therein mentioned	Feb. 28	Postponed
140	COOK	An Act for the relief of David Cook	Mar. 2	Postponed
141	EVIDENCES OF DEBT	A Bill concerning certificates or evidences of the public debt	Mar. 2	Not passed— HR
142	See [HR–136A]			
143	CONSULAR CONVENTION	An Act for carrying into effect the Convention between His Most Christian Majesty and the United States	Mar. 3	Postponed

This index utilizes the short titles and numbers of bills given in the preceding List of Bills. For the full title as given in the text, the reader should consult this list.

A

Accounts of the Treasurer of the United States. *See* Treasurer of the United States, accounts of, letters and reports concerning

Acts of Congress, committee actions on, 59–60

Adams, John, 213 n; election of, 8. *See also* Vice President

Adjournment (first session), 204, 207; joint committee actions on, 107, 108, 112, 115; resolutions on, 134, 135, 194; postponement of, 184; notification of President about, joint committee actions on, 197, 199, 203

Adjournment (second session), 491; joint committees' actions on, 338, 345, 364, 372–73; resolutions on, 419, 470, 471, 480, 486–87; notification of President about, joint committee actions on, 481, 482, 484, 487, 488

Adjournment (third session), 708

Admiralty Courts, jurisdiction of, 163–64

Agriculture, 217, 220

Albany, New York, 92, 556, 694

Albemarle County, North Carolina, 233 n

Alexander, James, petition of, 496

Alexander, Sarah. *See* Stirling, Sarah, petition of

Alexandria, Virginia, 96, 539, 616

Algiers, U.S. prisoners in: documents on, 519, 537. *See also* Mediterranean Trade

Algiers and Tunis regencies, plan for truce with, 223, 228 n

Aliens. *See* Naturalization Bill [HR–40]

Allen, Thomas, petition of, 51

Allsburgh, Vermont, 627, 630

Amelung, John F., petitions of, 326, 422

Amendments, Constitutional
—House resolution on
    agreed to by House, 134
    printed, 135–38
    considered, 149, 151, 153, 154, 158–64, 166–68
  Article on
    Representation (I)
      agreed to with amendment, 150
      amended by House, 190
    Compensation (II)
      agreed to with amendment, 151
    Freedom of Religion (III)
      amendment to, 151, 166

agreed to with amendment, 151
combined with article on Freedom of Speech, Press, and Assembly (IV), 166
Freedom of Religion, Speech, Press, and Assembly (III)
  amended by House, 189
Freedom of Speech, Press, and Assembly (IV)
  amendments to, 151–52
  agreed to with amendment, 153
  combined with article on Freedom of Religion (III), 166
Right to Bear Arms (V)
  amendments to, 153, 166
  agreed to with amendment, 154
  renumbered as Article IV, 167
Quartering of Soldiers (VI)
  agreed to, 154
  renumbered as Article V, 167
Protection against Search (VII)
  agreed to, 154
  renumbered as Article VI, 167
Rights in Criminal Cases (VIII)
  agreed to with amendment, 154
  renumbered as Article VII, 167
  amendment to, 167
Speedy and Public Trial (IX)
  agreed to, 154
  renumbered as Article VIII, 167
Speedy and Public Trial (VIII)
  amended by House, 189
Trial by Jury—Criminal (X)
  agreed to with amendment, 154
  motion to strike out, 167
  motion to reconsider for amendment, 167–68
Petty Claims (XI)
  agreed to with amendment, 154–55
  combined with article on Trial by Jury—Civil (XII) and renumbered as Article IX, 167
Petty Claims and Trial by Jury—Civil (IX)
  amendment to, 167
Trial by Jury—Civil (XII)
  agreed to with amendments, 158
  amended to include article on Petty Claims (XI) and renumbered as Article IX, 167
No Cruelty nor Excessive Bail or Fines (XIII)
  agreed to, 158
  renumbered as Article X, 168

No Infringement of Rights by States (XIV)
disagreed to, 158
No Rights Denied (XV)
amendment to, 158
agreed to, 159
renumbered as Article XI, 168
Checks and Balances (XVI)
disagreed to, 159
Powers Reserved to States (XVII)
agreed to with amendment, 159
renumbered as Article XII, 168
proposed amendments to, 158–64
Preamble of, amendments to, 160
agreed to with amendments, 168
amendments to, 181, 182, 189, 192
conference actions on, 181, 182, 185–86
—resolution on, 192, 198
—proposed articles of, 208–10
—see also States by name, ratification of Constitutional amendments by
American Philosophical Society, 654
Ames, Fisher, appointed to committees on: Mitigation of Fines Bill [HR–45], 267; quorum, 215; titles, Presidential, 26
Annapolis, Maryland, 96, 711
Appropriations Bill [HR–32], 712; agreed to by House, 192; read, 192, 194, 202; committee actions on, 194, 201 n, 202; agreed to with amendments, 202; found correct and signed, 202, 203, 205
Appropriations Bill [HR–47]: agreed to by House, 259; read, 259, 262, 263, 265; committee actions on, 263, 265; agreed to with amendments, 265; amendments to, 265–66; found correct and signed, 266, 267, 268, 273
Appropriations Bill [HR–120]: agreed to by House, 545; read, 545, 546, 549; committee actions on, 546, 547, 548; agreed to, 549; found correct and signed, 562–63, 591–92
Appropriations for expenses of government, 533, 534
Arlington, Vermont, 555, 557
Armstrong, James, electoral votes cast for, 8
Army: standing, 153, 162. See also Militia
Arnold, Welcome, 58 n
Arsenals, federal, 118. See also Moore, Stephen, petition of; West Point Bill [HR–76]
Artillery. See Militia
Assumption of state debts. See Funding Bill [HR–63]; Settlement of accounts, resolution on; Settlement of Accounts Bills [HR–13], [HR–77], [HR–95]; Ways and Means Bills [HR–83], [HR–129], [S–14]
Atkinson, Captain, 293–94

Attendance, letters requesting, 3, 4, 5
Attendance and traveling expenses of Senators, 196
Attendants to Congress, petitions as. See Alexander, James, petition of; Bleecker, Leonard, petition of; Finnie, William, petition of; Maxwell, Cornelius, petition of; Mitchell, Abraham, petition of; Okee, Abraham, petition of
Attorney General, 263 n, 271 n, 614, 657; clerks for (see Clerks for Attorney General, resolution on expenses for); compensation of (see Salaries-Judiciary Bill [HR–28])
Augusta, Georgia, 400 n
Authentication Bill [HR–58]: agreed to by House, 299; read, 300, 302; agreed to, 303; found correct and signed, 304, 305, 321, 327
Avery, John, 58

B

Bailey, Francis, petition of, 235, 245, 246. See also Bailey Bill [HR–44]
Bailey Bill [HR–44]: agreed to by House, 250; read, 250; committee actions on, 251; committed to committee on Patents Bill [HR–41], 259; report on, 269
Baldwin, Abraham, appointed to committee on Compensation Bill [HR–15], 169
Baltimore, Maryland, 92, 94, 96, 131 n, 294, 385; locating permanent seat of Government at (see O'Donnell, John, and others, petitions of; Residence Bill [S-12], motions on); petitions from (see Merchants and manufacturers of Baltimore, Maryland, petition of; Shipwrights of Baltimore, Maryland, petition of); port of, collection of duties at, 533, 534; resolution on third session at, 351
Bancker, Abraham, 58 n
Bancker, Gerard, letter from, 222–23
Bank, National, report on, 514; committee to prepare bill on, 516, 522
Bank Bill [S–15]: presented, 522; read, 522, 526, 528, 530, 531, 532, 533, 534, 535; amendments to, 531–33, 534, 535; recommitted, 534; agreed to, 536, 551; found correct and signed, 595, 606, 638; printed, 638–45
Bank Bill [HR–125]: agreed to by House, 631; read, 632, 634, 635, 651; printed, 632–33; amendments to, 651–52; agreed to, 652–53; found correct and signed, 660, 661, 668, 676
Bankson, Benjamin, ix, 283 n
Barbary Coast, 679

Barbary Regencies, 228 n

Barclay Bill [HR–91]: agreed to by House, 457; read, 458, 459, 473; committee actions on, 459, 462, 469–70; agreed to with amendments, 473

Barker's Mills, petition for improvement on. *See* Montgomery, William, petition of

Barren-Point, Virginia, 93

Bartlett, Thomas, 348

Barton, Colonel William, 332

Bassett, Richard, 3 n, 16, 24 n, 283 n; attendance, 4, 5, 7, 13, 14, 88, 125, 222, 285, 309, 481, 495; classification, 46, 47, 232 n, 716; credentials, 7; salary and expenses for, 276; seated, 6; takes oath, 59; vote recorded, 85, 86, 87, 134, 142, 143, 149, 151, 157, 168, 180, 187, 188, 190, 195, 226, 311, 313, 317, 318, 323, 324, 326, 339, 340, 341, 342, 353, 365, 370, 373, 375, 377, 378, 379, 380, 383, 384, 385, 386, 387, 391, 392, 395, 396, 413, 415, 416, 417, 420, 424, 425, 426, 427, 428, 429, 430, 434, 438, 449, 450, 451, 452, 453, 454, 455, 456, 515, 531, 535, 536, 550, 596, 623, 631, 634, 648, 650, 652, 692, 703

—appointed to committees on
adjournment, 364
Appropriations Bill [HR–120], 546
Disabled Soldiers and Seamen Bill [HR–88], 457
export inspection, 248
Judiciary Bill [S–1], 11
Mitigation of Fines Bill [HR–45], 262
North Carolina act for cession of western lands, 235
rules, conference, and appointment of chaplains, 12
trade with European colonies in America, 248
vessels leaving U.S. ports, 252

Beatty, John, 476

Beaufort, South Carolina, 96

Beckley, John. *See* Clerk of the House

Beniere, letter from, 504–5

Bennets-Creek, North Carolina, 233 n

Bennington, Vermont, 555, 557, 558, 626, 694

Benson, Egbert, 553, 555, 556, 557

—appointed to committees on
Salaries-Legislative Bill [HR–19], 165
terms of federally elected officials, 299
titles, Presidential, 26, 43

Beouvais, St. Jame. *See* Northwest Territory Bill [S–17]

Bermuda Hundred, Virginia, 96

Bertier and Company, petition of, 293–94

Beverly, Massachusetts, 96

Bible printing, petition concerning. *See* Congregational clergy of Massachusetts, petition of

Bill of Rights. *See* Amendments, Constitutional

Bills. *See Bills by short titles; List of Bills*

Black Bay, North Carolina, 233 n

Blair, Dr. Samuel, 505

Blaire, Archibald, 58 n

Bland, Theodorick: appointed to committee on joint rules, 39; funeral of, resolution on, 335

Bleecker, Leonard, petition of, 20

Boardman, Seth, pension of, 476

Boston, Massachusetts, 96, 665; petition from (*see* Manufacturers of Boston, Massachusetts, petition of)

Boudinot, Elias, 74, 75; delivers message from House, 7

—appointed to committees on
Impost Bill [HR–2], 72
quorum, 496 n
Thanksgiving, 197
Tonnage Bill [HR–5], 72
Treasury Bill [HR–9], 119

Bourn, Sylvanus, 9

Bowne, George, address of, 242

Boyd's Hole, Virginia, 93

Bridgetown, New Jersey, 92

Brooke, Henry, 58 n

Brown, Andrew, petition of, 606; resolution on, 607–8, 609–10, 616, 618

Bryce, John, petition of, 12

Bucks County, Pennsylvania, 188

Burke, Aedanus, appointed to committee on Courts Bill [S–4], 196

Burlington, New Jersey, 92

Business between Houses, joint committee actions on, 297, 298, 338, 345

Butler, Pierce, 3 n, 419 n, 532 n; attendance, 4, 61, 213, 495; classification, 46, 47, 232 n, 716; credentials, 61; excused from committee on Rhode Island Trade Bill [S–11], 296; presents petitions of Colonel Henry Laurens, 519; presents Residence Bill [S–12], 330; salary and expenses for, 276; seated and takes oath, 61; vote recorded, 85, 104, 106, 124, 134, 142, 143, 149, 153, 157, 180, 187, 188, 190, 195, 226, 288 n, 311, 313, 317, 318, 323, 324, 326, 339, 340, 341, 342, 353, 365, 370, 373, 375, 376, 377, 378, 379, 380, 383, 384, 385, 386, 387, 391, 392, 395, 396, 413, 415, 416, 417, 420, 424, 425, 426, 427, 428, 429, 430, 434, 438, 449, 450, 451, 452, 453, 454, 455, 456, 515, 531, 535, 536, 550, 596, 615, 618, 619, 623, 631, 634, 648, 650, 652, 692

—appointed to committees on
Appropriation Bills [HR–32],
[HR–47], 194, 263
Bank, National, 516
Coasting Bill [HR–16], 118
Impost Bill [HR–2], 62
Indian Treaties Bill [HR–20], 121
Invalid Pensioners Bill [HR–29], 196
Jenkins Bill [HR–67], 328
Judiciary Bill [S–1], 177
laws, revision of, 666
Military Establishment Bill [HR–50a],
273
North Carolina Bill [HR–36], 230
North Carolina Judiciary Bill [S–10],
308
officers of the Treasury Department,
salaries of, 635
Post Office Bill [S–3], 170
Punishment of Crimes Bill [S–2], 67
Residence Bill [S–12], 334
Rhode Island Trade Bill [S–11], 295
settlement of accounts and the Funding
Bill [HR–63], 418
Stirling Bill [HR–96], 477
trade, 69
trade with European colonies in Amer-
ica, 241
Treasurer of the United States, accounts
of, letters and reports concerning,
372
Troops Bill [HR–27], 196
—reports for committees on
Funding Bill [HR–63], 421–22
Post Office Bill [S–3], 171
Residence Bill [S–12], 330
settlement of accounts and the Funding
Bill [HR–63], 419
trade, 82, 109

C

Cabarrus, S., 347
Cadwalader, Lambert, appointed to com-
mittee on papers of Continental Con-
gress, 29
Caldwell Bill [HR–99]: agreed to by
House, 481; read, 483, 489; post-
poned, 489
Calhorda, John, petition of, 320
Cambden, North Carolina, 233 n
Cambridge, Maryland, 92
Campbell, Donald, petitions of: committee
actions on, 421, 445, 608, 617; dis-
missed, 462, 617
Cape of Good Hope, 94
Capital Punishment, 83, 179
Carlisle, Pennsylvania, 128
Carroll, Charles, 3 n, 25 n, 609; attendance,
4, 5, 15, 258, 537; classification, 46,
47, 232 n, 716; credentials, 13; salary
and expenses for, 276; seated, 13;

takes oath, 59; vote recorded, 85, 86,
87, 104, 106, 124, 134, 142, 143, 144,
149, 151, 153, 157, 168, 180, 187,
188, 190, 195, 288 n, 311, 313, 317,
318, 323, 324, 326, 339, 340, 341,
342, 353, 365, 370, 373, 375, 376,
377, 378, 379, 380, 383, 384, 385,
386, 387, 391, 392, 395, 396, 413,
415, 416, 417, 420, 424, 425, 426,
427, 428, 429, 430, 434, 438, 449,
450, 451, 452, 453, 454, 455, 456,
550, 596, 615, 618, 619, 623, 631,
634, 648, 650, 652, 692, 703
—appointed to committees on
Acts of Congress, 59
adjournment, 108
amendments, Constitutional, 182
Appropriations Bill [HR–120], 546
classification, 42
Collection Bill [HR–11], 88
Compensation Bill [HR–15], 110
Foreign Intercourse Bill [HR–52], 299
Glaubeck, Baron de, 187
inaugural address, 33
Journal of Senate, 51
Judiciary Bill [S–1], 14
Military Establishment Bill [HR–50a],
273
newspapers, 44
Patents Bill [HR–4], 258
Post Office Bill [HR–74], 368
reception of President and Vice Presi-
dent, 17
Rhode Island Trade Bill [S–11], 294
Salaries-Legislative Bill [HR–19], 139
settlement of accounts, 398
Widows, Orphans, and Invalids Bill
[HR–139], 673
—reports for committees on
Bailey Bill [HR–44], 269
Patents Bill [HR–41], 269
Rhode Island Trade Bill [S–11], 303,
313
settlement of accounts, 406
Carroll, Daniel, appointed to committees
on: adjournment, 107, 338; terms of
federally elected officials, 299; titles,
Presidential, 27
Census. See Enumeration Bill [HR–34]
Chaillot, France, 505 n
Chaplains: appointment of, 23, 25, 35,
215, 502, 505 (see also Rules, con-
ference, and appointment of chaplains,
joint committee actions on); compensation of (see Salaries-Legislative Bill
[HR–19]); perform divine service,
33
Charleston, South Carolina, 96, 369; petitions of citizens of (see Masters of
American vessels of Charleston, South
Carolina, petition of; Prioleau, Sam-
uel, Jr., petition of)

Chesapeake Bay, 93, 102
Chester County, Pennsylvania, 188
Chester, Maryland, 92, 96
Chicahomony River, Virginia, 93
Chief Justice, compensation of. *See* Salaries-Judiciary Bill [HR–28]
Childs, Francis, 57 n
China, 62, 65, 66, 94, 95, 469
Chipman, Nathaniel, 552, 561, 562
Chittenden, Thomas, 556, 560, 561
Chohos, village of. *See* Northwest Territory Bill [S–17]
Circuit Courts. *See* Circuit Courts Bill [S–13]; Judiciary Bill [S–1]; North Carolina Judiciary Bills [S–10], [HR–68]; Rhode Island Judiciary Bill [HR–73]
Circuit Courts Bill [S–13]: read, 480, 482; agreed to, 482–83; amendments to, 483; found correct and signed, 484–85, 487, 488
Citizens of Connecticut, petition of, 91
Citizens of New Jersey and Pennsylvania, petition of, 126
Citizens of North Carolina, petitions of, 172
Citizens of Rhode Island, petitions of, 173
City Hall of New York. *See* New York City Hall
City-point, Virginia, 96
Clarkson, Mathew, and others, petition of. *See* Public creditors of United States, petition of
Classification of Senators: committee actions on, 42, 43–44, 45–46; determined, 47, 98, 231, 372
Claxton, Thomas, petition of, 11
Clayton, Joshua, letter from, 253–54
Clerk of the House, xii; attests Journal extract, 53, 55, 57, 61, 70, 75, 76; certifies Constitutional amendments, 210; compensation of (*see* Salaries-Legislative Bill [HR–19]); duties of, ix, 206 (*see also* Messages between Houses, temporary procedure for delivering; Rules, joint)
Clerks, compensation of. *See* Salaries-Legislative Bill [HR–19]
Clerks for Attorney General, resolution on expenses for, 634, 635–36
Clerks in office of Paymaster General, petition of, 153
Clerks in public offices, petitions of, 149, 548–49
Clerks of Commissioner of Army Accounts, resolution on salaries of, 437; agreed to by House, 423; committee actions on, 439, 441; agreed to, 442–43; found correct and signed, 444, 448, 463
Clinton, George, 280, 554; electoral votes cast for, 8; letter from, 279

Clymer, George, 364 n; appointed to committee on terms of federally elected officials, 299
Coasting Bill [HR–16]: agreed to by House, 112; read, 112, 118, 126, 127, 128; committee actions on, 118, 122; consideration postponed, 125; agreed to with amendments, 128, 139; amendments to, 128 n–33 n, 140, 145; signed, 147, 148, 150
Coasting Bill [HR–33], 447 n; agreed to by House, 186; read, 186, 197, 199; committee actions on, 197, 199; agreed to with amendment, 199; amendment to, 202; found correct and signed, 202–4, 205
Cobb, David, 58 n
Cockpit-point, Virginia, 93
Cod fisheries. *See* Fisheries, cod and whale, report of Secretary of State on
Cohasset, Massachusetts, 92
Coins, foreign, rate of. *See* Collection Bill [HR–134]
Coins, weights, and measures, 217, 220
—report on, 514
   committee actions on, 517–18, 661
   letter concerning, 534
Collection Bill [HR–11], 649; agreed to by House, 83–84; read, 84, 87, 88, 89, 92; committees' actions on, 88, 98–100; amendments to, 90, 92–97, 98; agreed to with amendments, 92; signed, 100, 102
Collection Bill [HR–23], 234 n; agreed to by House, 150; read, 156, 170, 172; referred to committee on Tonnage Bill [HR–24], 171; report on, 172, 173; agreed to with amendments, 173–74; signed, 174, 175, 176
Collection Bill [HR–26], 447 n; agreed to by House, 178; read, 178, 196; committee actions on, 196–97, 199; disagreed to, 199
Collection Bill [HR–50]: agreed to by House, 281; read, 282, 283; committee actions on, 282, 283; agreed to with amendments, 283; amendments to, 283 n, 284; found correct and signed, 284, 285, 286, 289
Collection Bill [HR–82], 627; agreed to by House, 423; committee actions on, 431, 439; read, 439, 441, 444, 445; papers concerning, 440; recommitted, 441; postponed, 443; amendments to, 444, 445 n–47 n, 448; agreed to with amendments, 445; found correct and signed, 460, 461, 463
Collection Bill [HR–109]: agreed to by House, 520; read, 520, 523, 524; agreed to, 524; found correct and signed, 526, 527, 528, 529
Collection Bill [HR–134]: agreed to by

House, 657; read, 658, 660, 662; printed, 658; committee actions on, 660, 662; agreed to with amendments, 662; amendments to, 668; found correct and signed, 690, 691, 692, 698

Collection of duties, petitions concerning. See Bertier and Company, petition of; Citizens of North Carolina, petitions of; Citizens of Rhode Island, petitions of; Merchants of North Carolina, petition of; Meters of New York City, petition of

Collectors. See Collection Bills in List of Bills

College of Physicians of Philadelphia, Pennsylvania, petition of concerning distilled spirits, 518

Collins, John, letter from, 230

Commerce. See Trade

Commissioners of Loans Bill [HR–135]: agreed to by House, 663; read, 663, 675, 691; printed, 663; committee actions on, 675, 686; agreed to with amendment, 691; amendment to, 691, 692, 697; found correct and signed, 699, 701, 706, 707

Communications, Presidential, joint committee actions on, 53, 54–55

Compensation, petitions for. See Clerks in office of Paymaster General, petition of; Clerks in public offices, petitions of; Mathers, James, petitions of

Compensation, Revolutionary War, petitions for. See Campbell, Donald, petitions of; Drayton, Stephen, petition of; Glaubeck, Baron de, resolution on compensation of; Jones, John, petition of; Laurens, Henry, petitions of; Officers of late U.S. Navy, petition of; Phillips, Richard, petition of; Prioleau, Samuel, Jr., petition of; Roux, Albert, petition of; Surgeons and Surgeons-Mates, petition of; Tatlow, Joseph, petition of

Compensation Bill [HR–15]: agreed to by House, 107; read, 108, 110, 157; committee actions on, 110, 114, 157; amendments to, 114, 165, 176, 182; agreed to with amendment, 157–58; conference actions on, 165, 169; found correct and signed, 183, 184, 190

Compensation for proposed use of land at West Point, petition for. See Moore, Stephen, petition of

Compensation for Senators: committee actions on (second session), 274, 276–77; schedule of (first session), 205 n

Compensation lists, resolutions on, 312–13, 315; agreed to by House, 312; committee actions on, 315, 316–17, 318; amendments to, 316–17, 318, 319;

agreed to with amendments, 318; found correct and signed, 321, 322, 329, 337

Conference rules. See Rules, conference, and appointment of chaplains, joint committee actions on

Congregational clergy of Massachusetts, petition of, 351

Congressional Reorganization Act (1946), ix

Congressional Session, fourth, commencement of: joint committee actions on, 537, 539, 542–43, 594, 595, 620. See also Time of Meeting Bills [HR–122], [HR–132]

Connecticut, 665, 714; electoral votes, 8; loan to United States, 410, 433; petition of citizens of (see Citizens of Connecticut, petition of); Senators present, 3, 7, 13, 14, 213, 214, 495, 506

Connecticut River, 118

Connogochegue River, 375, 395

Constitution: articles of, 16 n, 149, 159, 310–11, 347 (see also Classification of Senators, committee actions on); publication of, resolution on, 79; ratification of (see States by name, ratification of Constitution by)

Constitutional amendments. See Amendments, Constitutional

Consular Convention, need for, 500

Consular Convention Bill [HR–143]: agreed to by House and read, 702; printed, 702–3; disagreed to, 703

Consuls and Vice Consuls Bill [HR–86]: agreed to by House, 437; read, 438, 443–44; committee actions on, 444, 461; postponed, 461

Consuls and Vice Consuls Bill [S–18]: committee to prepare, 509; read, 528, 531, 540; committee actions on, 531, 540; agreed to with amendments, 540–41, 675; House amendments to, 677, 681, 684, 686, 691; printed, 667–81

Consuls to foreign countries, 86, 500

Continental Congress, 175, 473 n; acts of, 175, 476, 479, 508 (see also Militia, statements of; Survey of western boundary of New York; Weed, Jacob, petition of); journals of, resolution on, 54, 61; papers of, joint committee actions on, 13, 29, 42; resolutions of, 237–39, 470

Cook Bill [HR–140]: agreed to by House, 704; read, printed, and disagreed to, 706

Copyright, petition for. See Ramsay, David, petition of

Copyright Bill [HR–43]: agreed to by

House, 296–97; read, 297, 302, 309; committee actions on, 302, 309; agreed to with amendments, 309; amendments to, 310 n, 312, 321 n, 322 n; found correct and signed, 321, 322, 329, 333

Counterfeiting, prevention of, 714. *See also* Bailey, Francis, petition of; Bailey Bill [HR–44]

Courts, District and Circuit, in Portsmouth, New Hampshire, petition for. *See* Merchants and traders of Portsmouth, New Hampshire, petition of

Courts, judges of, compensation for. *See* Salaries-Judiciary Bill [HR–28]

Courts Bill [S–4]: presented, 176; read, 176, 177, 178; agreed to with amendments, 179, 192; House amendment to, 193, 194, 201, 202; conference actions on, 195, 196, 200–201; found correct and signed, 202–4, 205

Courts Bill [S–9]: committee to prepare, 223, 268; read, 292, 294; agreed to, 294, 297; found correct and signed, 304–5, 321, 322, 323

Courts Bill [HR–124]: agreed to by House, 591; read, 592, 595, 607; printed, 592; agreed to, 607; found correct and signed, 609–10, 616, 618

Cox, John, and others. *See* Citizens of New Jersey and Pennsylvania, petition of

Crane, Adonijah, 714

Crane, Francis, 714

Credentials of Senators, 7, 13, 15, 21, 51, 61, 91

Credit. *See* Public credit; Public creditors of United States, petition of

Creek Indians. *See* Indian Treaties Bill [HR–20]

Crimes, punishment of. *See* Punishment of Crimes Bills [S–2], [S–6]

Culver, Daniel, 476

Currency. *See* Coins, weights, and measures

Currituck, North Carolina, 233 n

D

Daleys, North Carolina, 233 n

Dally, Gifford, 265 n, 266

Dalton, Tristram, 3 n; attendance, 4, 16, 213, 495; classification, 46, 47, 232 n, 716; credentials, 15; salary and expenses for, 276; seated, 15; takes oath, 59; vote recorded, 85, 86, 87, 104, 106, 124, 134, 142, 143, 144, 149, 151, 153, 157, 168, 180, 187, 188, 189, 191, 195, 226, 288 n, 311, 313, 317, 318, 323, 324, 326, 339, 340, 341, 342, 353, 365, 370, 373, 375, 376, 377, 378, 379, 380, 383, 384, 385, 386, 387, 391, 392, 395, 396, 413, 415, 416, 417, 420, 424, 425, 426, 427, 428, 429, 430, 434, 438, 449, 450, 451, 452, 453, 454, 455, 456, 515, 535, 536, 550, 596, 615, 618, 619, 623, 631, 634, 648, 650, 652, 692, 703

—appointed to committees on
Appropriations Bill [HR–120], 546
attendance and traveling expenses of Senators, 196
Coasting Bills [HR–16], [HR–33], 118, 197
Collection Bills [HR–11], [HR–26], [HR–50], [HR–82], 88, 197, 282, 431
export inspection, 247
Impost Bill [HR–2], 62
inaugural ceremony, 26
Jenkins Bill [HR–67], 328
Lighthouses Bill [HR–12], 90
Merchant Seamen Bill [HR–61], 394
oath, Presidential, 24
Punishment of Crimes Bill [S–2], 44
reception of President and Vice President, 17
Residence Bill [S–12], 334
Stewart and Davidson Bill [HR–90], 458
titles, Presidential, 24
Tonnage Bills [HR–24], [HR–78], 171, 382
trade, 69
trade with European colonies in America, 241

—reports for committees on
Appropriations Bill [HR–120], 547
Jenkins Bill [HR–67], 331
Merchant Seamen Bill [HR–61], 402–3
Stewart and Davidson Bill [HR–90], 458

Dart, John, 58 n

Davidson, John. *See* Stewart and Davidson Bill [HR–90]

David, Jehu, 254

Dawson, Joshua. *See* White, John, resolution on petition of

Dayton, Jonathan, 521

Debevere, Francis Suzor, 672

Debt of United States. *See List of Bills;* Public creditors of United States, petition of; Public debt, provisions for

Defense (national), need for, 216, 219

De Haa's, [John Philip], 672

Delaware, 94, 131 n; electoral votes, 8; loan to United States, 410, 433; petition of citizen of (*see* Tatlow, Joseph, petition of); ratification of Constitutional amendments by, 253–54, 716; Senators present, 6, 7, 13, 14, 222, 253, 301, 495, 497; settlement of accounts of, 198

Delaware River, 127
Denmark Rix Dollar, rate of. *See* Collection Bill [HR-134]
De Saussure, Daniel, 276
De Witt, Simeon, 553, 555, 557
Dickinson, Brittingham, and others, petition of. *See* Shipwrights of Baltimore, Maryland, petition of
Dickinson, Philemon: classification, 716; credentials, 495; seated and takes oath, 495; vote recorded, 515, 531, 535, 536, 550, 596, 615, 618, 619, 623, 631, 634, 648, 650, 652, 692
—appointed to committees on
Campbell, Donald, petition of, 608
Foreign Officers Bill [HR-116], 595
Military Establishment Bill [HR-126A], 607
Di Dominico, Gaetan Drago, letter from, 223, 227–28
Dighton, Massachusetts, 446 n
Disabled Soldiers and Seamen Bill [HR-88]: agreed to by House, 448; read, 457, 458, 469; committee actions on, 458, 460, 461, 476–77; agreed to with amendments, 477; amendments to, 481–82; found correct and signed, 485, 487, 490
Distillers of Philadelphia, Pennsylvania, petition of, 63
District Courts, 653. *See also* Judiciary Bill [S-1]; North Carolina Judiciary Bills [S-10], [HR-68]; Rhode Island Judiciary Bill [HR-73]
Dobson, Thomas, letter from, 303
Doolittle, Amos, 714
Doorkeeper: compensation of (*see* Salaries-Legislative Bill [HR-19]); elected, 11; order for, 207 n. *See also* Mathers, James
Double jeopardy, 154
Douglass, Hannah, 671
Douglass, William, 671
Drayton, Stephen, petition of, 563
Duane, James. *See* New York City, mayor of
Dumfries, Virginia, 93, 96
Dutch loan. *See* Loan from Holland
Duties, 65–66, 87, 172, 463–67, 468–69, 629; collection of, in Maryland (*see* Maryland, act of); on distilled spirits, 65, 67, 131 n–33 n, 291, 464; on distilled spirits, petitions concerning (*see* College of Physicians of Philadelphia, Pennsylvania, petition of concerning distilled spirits; Inhabitants of Lancaster County, Pennsylvania, petition of concerning liquors); foreign (*see* Rhode Island, foreign duties of, committee actions on letter on); on molasses, 67, 569, 585, 599; on rum, 67, 131 n, 133 n, 172, 291 n; on sugars,

172, 464, 569, 599; on teas, 65, 464. *See also* List of Bills
Duties on Distilled Spirits Bill [HR-110], 666; agreed to by House, 541–42; read, 542, 543, 545, 549, 564; committee actions on, 545–46, 549, 550–51, 552, 590–91, 594, 595–96; printed, 564–90; amendments to, 590–91, 596, 597–603, 621–22, 630–32, 655–56; recommitted, 591, 594; agreed to with amendments, 597; conference actions on, 632, 633–34, 651, 656; found correct and signed, 660, 661, 668–69, 698
Duties on Teas Bill [HR-130]: agreed to by House, 685; read, 686, 690; printed, 686–89; committee actions on, 689, 690; agreed to, 690–91; found correct and signed, 705, 706, 707–8

E

East Greenwich, Rhode Island, 446 n
East Windsor, Connecticut, 283 n
Edenton, North Carolina, 233 n–34 n, 445
Election of President and Vice President: certificates of, and letters concerning, 9–11; electoral votes, 8; letter concerning, 26
Elections, regulation of, 164
Electoral votes, 7, 8
Eliot, David, petition of, 11 n
Ellicott, Andrew, petition of, 121. *See also* Gorham, Nathaniel, petition of; Survey of western boundary of New York, resolution on
Ellsworth, Oliver, 14 n, 16 n, 33 n, 34 n, 40 n, 168 n, 348, 515 n; attendance, 4, 5, 7, 13, 14, 88, 99, 214, 495; classification, 46, 47, 232 n, 716; credentials, 7; delivers message to House, 7; presents resolution on settlement of accounts, 352; salary and expenses for, 276; seated, 3; takes oath, 59; vote recorded, 85, 87, 104, 106, 124, 134, 142, 143, 144, 149, 151, 153, 157, 168, 180, 187, 188, 189, 191, 195, 226, 288 n, 311, 313, 317, 318, 323, 324, 327, 339, 340, 341, 342, 353, 365, 373, 375, 376, 377, 378, 379, 380, 383, 385, 386, 387, 391, 392, 395, 396, 413, 415, 416, 417, 420, 424, 425, 426, 427, 428, 429, 430, 434, 438, 449, 450, 451, 452, 453, 454, 455, 456, 515, 531, 535, 536, 596, 615, 618, 619, 623, 631, 634, 648, 650, 652, 692, 703
—appointed to committees on
adjournment, 108
amendments, Constitutional, 182

Appropriations Bill [HR–32], 194
Bailey Bill [HR–44], 251
Bank, National, 516
classification, 42
Collection Bill [HR–50], 282
Commissioners of Loans Bill [HR–135], 675
Compensation Bill [HR–15], 110
compensation for Senators (second session), 274
compensation lists, 315
Congressional session, fourth, 537
Consuls and Vice Consuls Bill [S–18], 509, 531
Courts Bills [S–4], [S–9], 195, 223
Duties on Distilled Spirits Bill [HR–110], 545, 632
election of President and Vice President, 9
Enumeration Bill [HR–34], 242
Executive Journal, 538
export inspection, 248–49
Foreign Intercourse Bill [HR–52], 299
Funding Bill [HR–63], 347
Impost Bill [HR–2], 62, 73
Indian Trade Bill [HR–65], 412
Indian Treaties Bill [HR–20], 121
Invalid Officers Bill [HR–59], 303
Invalid Pensioners Bill [HR–29], 196
Journal of Senate, 15
Judicial Officers Bill [HR–133], 685
Judiciary Bill [S–1], 11, 177
Land Office Bill [HR–114], 627
laws, revision of, 666
Mediterranean trade, 508
messages between Houses, 34
Military Establishment Bill [HR–50a], 273
Mitigation of Fines Bill [HR–45], 262, 267
Mitigation of Forfeitures Bill [S–24], 699
Morris, Robert, petition of, 240
Naturalization Bill [HR–40], 256
New York City Hall, communications on, 14
North Carolina act for cession of western lands, 235
North Carolina Bill [HR–36], 230
North Carolina Cession Bill [S–7], 246
North Carolina Judiciary Bill [S–10], 222
Northwest Territory Bill [S–17], 519
Officers Bill [HR–53], 292
officers of the Treasury Department, salaries of, 635
Post Office Bills [HR–74], [S–3], 170, 407
Punishment of Crimes Bill [S–6], 227
reception of President and Vice President, 17
Rhode Island Trade Bill [S–11], 295

rules, conference, and appointment of chaplains, 12
Salaries-Executive Bill [HR–54], 299
settlement of accounts, 398
settlement of accounts and the Funding Bill [HR–63], 418
Settlement of Accounts Bills [HR–72], [HR–77], 394, 402, 413
Southern Territory Bill [S–8], 281
State of the Union Address, 501
Steuben Bill [HR–60], 306
terms of federally elected officials, 300
titles, Presidential, 40, 41
Tonnage Bills [HR–5], [HR–24], 73, 171
trade, 110
trade with European colonies in America, 241
Troops Bill [HR–27], 196
unfinished business of first session, 224
Vermont Statehood Bill [S–19], 562
Virginia Cession Bill [HR–85], 437
Ways and Means Bills [HR–83], [S–14], 437, 509
—reports for committees on
amendments, Constitutional, 185
compensation for Senators (second session), 276
compensation lists, 316
Consuls and Vice Consuls Bill [S–18], 528, 540
Duties on Distilled Spirits Bill [HR–110], 651
Judicial Officers Bill [HR–133], 693–94
Judiciary Bill [S–1], 179
North Carolina Cession Bill [S–7], 251
North Carolina Judiciary Bill [S–10], 295
Post Office Bill [HR–74], 442
Punishment of Crimes Bill [S–6], 227
Settlement of Accounts Bill [HR–77], 439
Southern Territory Bill [S–8], 283
State of the Union Address, 505, 507
terms of federally elected officials, 309
Treasury Bill [HR–131], 656
unfinished business of first session, 225
Elmer, Jonathan, 3 n; attendance, 4, 5, 7, 13, 14, 52, 70, 221, 259, 274, 481, 497; classification, 46, 47, 232 n, 716; credentials, 7; salary and expenses for, 276; seated, 6; takes oath, 71; vote recorded, 85, 86, 87, 105, 106, 124, 134, 142, 143, 144, 149, 151, 153, 157, 226, 288 n, 311, 313, 323, 324, 327, 339, 340, 341, 342, 353, 370, 373, 375, 376, 377, 378, 379, 380, 383, 384, 385, 386, 387, 391, 392, 395, 396, 414, 415, 416, 417, 420, 424, 425, 426, 427, 428, 429, 430, 434, 438, 449, 450, 451, 452, 453,

454, 455, 456, 515, 531, 535, 536,
550, 596, 615, 618, 619, 623, 631,
634, 648, 650, 651, 652, 693
—appointed to committees on
Campbell, Donald, petition of, 421
clerks of Commissioner of Army Accounts, 439
Compensation Bill [HR–15], 110
Ely Bill [HR–56], 302
Gould Bill [HR–79], 382
McCord Bill [HR–70], 337
Mentges, Francis, petition of, 457
Punishment of Crimes Bill [S–2], 44
Ely Bill [HR–56]: agreed to by House,
299; read, 300, 301; committee actions on, 301–2, 307; disagreed to,
307
Emoluments for Navy Officers, petition for.
See Officers of late U.S. Navy, petition of
Emperor of Morocco. See Moroccan Treaty
Bill [S–23]
Encyclopedia, American edition. See Dobson, Thomas, letter from
Endorsement of bills, order for, 37
England. See Great Britain
Enrolled bills, joint committees on: appointed and instructed, 102, 103, 236,
488, 514; reports of, 110, 139, 148,
169, 174, 175, 177, 178, 183, 202,
203–4, 206–7, 236, 237, 247, 266,
268, 274, 275, 282, 284, 285–86, 292,
295, 304–5, 321, 328–29, 331, 335,
344, 352, 354, 366, 381, 388, 397,
407, 408, 421, 431, 437, 443, 444,
447–48, 460, 461–62, 481, 484, 489,
490, 516, 517, 526, 528, 530, 542,
546, 549, 551, 562, 563, 595, 606,
609, 610, 616, 629–30, 636, 637, 660,
668, 690, 692, 699, 704, 705, 706, 707
Enrollment of bills. See Rules, joint
Enumeration Bill [HR–34], 626; agreed
to by House, 240; read, 240, 241, 243;
amendments to, 241 n–42 n, 243 n–
44 n, 245; committee actions on, 242,
243; agreed to with amendments, 243;
found correct and signed, 247, 248,
250
European colonies in America. See Trade
with European colonies in America,
committee actions on
Eveleigh, Nicholas, 513
Execution of criminals, 500
Executive business, 240, 256, 258, 273,
295, 296, 545
Executive Journal of Senate, 536, 537, 538
Executive officers, compensation of. See
Salaries-Executive Bill [HR–21]
Exeter, New Hampshire, 665
Export inspection, committee actions on,
247, 248–49
Exports of United States, 609

F

Fairfield, Connecticut, 96
Falmouth, Massachusetts, 96, 445 n
Fauchet, L'Abbe of Paris. See Franklin,
Benjamin, civic eulogy to
Fay, Joseph, 561
Federal Building, carriages prevented from
passing during session, 12 n
Federal district. See Seat of Government
Fenner, Arthur, 193–94, 332, 389
Fenno, John, x, 57 n
Few, William, 14 n, 21 n, 25 n; attendance,
4, 5, 7, 13, 15, 148, 213, 495; classification, 46, 47, 232 n, 716; credentials,
7; salary and expenses for, 276;
seated, 3; takes oath, 59; vote recorded, 85, 86, 87, 105, 106, 124, 134,
142, 143, 144, 226, 288 n, 317, 318,
323, 324, 327, 339, 340, 341, 342,
353, 365, 370, 373, 375, 376, 377,
378, 379, 380, 383, 384, 385, 386,
387, 391, 392, 395, 396, 414, 415,
416, 417, 420, 424, 425, 426, 427,
428, 429, 430, 435, 438, 449, 450,
451, 452, 453, 454, 455, 456, 515,
532, 535, 536, 550, 596, 615, 618,
619, 623, 631, 634, 648, 650, 651, 652
—appointed to committees on
Appropriations Bill [HR–47], 263
Bailey Bill [HR–44], 251
classification, 42
Collection Bill [HR–11], 99
Compensation Bill [HR–15], 110
compensation for Senators (second session), 274
export inspection, 248
Foreign Intercourse Bill [HR–52], 299
Indian Trade Bill [HR–65], 398
Indian Treaties Bill [HR–20], 121
Judiciary Bill [S–1], 11
Military Establishment Bill [HR–50a],
273
New York City Hall, communications
on, 14
New York City Hall, use of, 41
North Carolina act for cession of western
lands, 235
Patents Bill [HR–41], 258
reception of President and Vice President, 12
Salaries-Executive Bill [HR–54], 299
trade with European colonies in America, 248
votes, 246
Ways and Means Bill [HR–83], 437
—reports for committees on
Military Establishment Bill [HR–50a],
281, 289–90
Salaries-Executive Bill [HR–54], 328
Financial accounts, publication of, 162
Finnie, William, petition of, 23

Fisheries, 133 n; cod and whale, report on, 547–48

Fitch, John, petitions of, 264, 265, 397. *See also* Patents Bill [HR–41]

Fitzsimons, Thomas, appointed to committees on: Impost Bill [HR–2], 72; Tonnage Bill [HR–5], 72; Treasury Bill [HR–9], 119

Flint, Royal, 714

Floyd, William, appointed to committees on: communications, Presidential, 53; Oath Bill [HR–1], 52

Foreign Affairs Bill [HR–8]: agreed to by House, 71–72; read, 73, 78, 83, 84, 85, 86; amendments to, 84, 87, 88; agreed to with amendments, 87; committee to present to President, 89, 90; signed, 90, 92

Foreign intercourse, provisions for, 216–17

Foreign Intercourse Bill [HR–52]: agreed to by House, 297; read, 297, 299, 322; committee actions on, 299, 305, 320; recommitted, 305; agreed to with amendment, 322; amendment to, 322 n, 328, 329; conference actions on, 329–30, 333, 367, 371–72; found correct and signed, 381, 382, 388, 394–95

Foreign Officers Bill [HR–116]: agreed to by House, 591; read, 592, 595; printed, 592; committee actions on, 595, 629; disagreed to, 630

Fort Harmar, 123

Foster, Abiel, appointed to committee on North Carolina Judiciary Bill [S–10], 308

Foster, Theodore: attendance, 509; classification, 372, 716; credentials, 371; seated and takes oath, 371; vote recorded, 373, 375, 376, 377, 378, 379, 380, 383, 384, 385, 386, 387, 391, 392, 395, 396, 414, 415, 416, 417, 420, 424, 425, 426, 427, 428, 429, 430, 435, 438, 449, 450, 451, 452, 453, 454, 455, 456, 515, 532, 535, 536, 550, 596, 615, 618, 619, 623, 631, 648, 650, 651, 652, 693, 703

—appointed to committees on
  Collection Bill [HR–82], 431
  enrolled bills, 488, 514
  Land Office Bill [HR–114], 627
  Navigation Bill [HR–93], 473
  Stewart and Davidson Bill [HR–90], 458

—reports for committees on
  enrolled bills, 489, 490, 516, 517, 526, 528, 530, 542, 546, 549, 551, 562, 563, 595, 606, 609, 616, 629, 636, 637, 660, 668, 690, 692, 699, 704, 705, 706, 707
  Navigation Bill [HR–93], 482

France, 470; Dauphin of, 204

—National Assembly of, 540, 661
  tribute of (*see* Franklin, Benjamin, tribute to)

Franklin, Benjamin: civic eulogy to, 505; eulogium for, 654; letter from, 242; memorial of, 242

—tribute to, 540
  resolution on, 629, 631, 636, 637, 669

Frederica, Georgia, 93

Frontiers, 200 n; prospects of hostilities on, 541; statement on, 538

Frontiers (southern and western), need for protection of, 216, 220

Funding Act [HR–63]: resolution on, 513, 514–16; petition relating to (*see* Publice creditors of Pennsylvania, petition of)

Funding Bill [HR–63], 639, 673, 674, 712; agreed to by House, 334; read, 334, 335, 337, 344, 345, 367, 423; committee actions on, 347, 354, 355, 362, 363, 364–65, 366; special committee actions on, 417; second committee actions on, 418, 419–20, 422, 423; recommitted, 420–21; amendments to, 423–30, 432–35, 438, 444, 445, 448–57; postponed, 431; agreed to with amendments, 439; found correct and signed, 460, 461–62, 463

G

Genoa, Italy, 228 n

Georgetown, Maryland, 96, 539; to be permanent seat of government (*see* Peters, Robert, and others, petition of; Residence Bill [S–12], message from President on)

George-town, South Carolina, 96

Georgia: electoral votes, 8; holding of Circuit Courts in (*see* Circuit Court Bill [S–13]); loan to United States, 410, 433; Senators present, 3, 7, 13, 15, 21, 213, 284, 495, 533. *See also* Indian Treaties Bill [HR–20]

Germantown, Pennsylvania, 128, 188, 191

Gerry, Elbridge, appointed to committee on Foreign Intercourse Bill [HR–52], 333

Geyer, Andrew, 497

Gibault, P. *See* Northwest Territory Bill [S–17]

Gibson Bill [HR–138]: agreed to by House, 685; read, 689, 693; printed, 690; postponed, 693

Gilman, Nicholas, appointed to committees on: adjournment, 199, 481; enrolled bills, 236; quorum, 215

Gilpin, Joseph, 57 n

Glasgow, James, 346, 347

Glasshouse buildings, petition for land

grant for. *See* Amelung, John F., petition of

Glass Manufacture Aid, petition for. *See* Amelung, John F., petition of

Glaubeck, Baron de, resolution on compensation of, 186, 187, 190

Glaubeck Bill [S–5]: read, 190, 198–99, 206; agreed to, 206; found correct and signed, 207

Gloucester, Massachusetts, 96

Goddard, Mary Katherine, petition of, 243

Goodhue, Benjamin, appointed to committee on Compensation Bill [HR–15], 169

Gorham, Nathaniel, petition of, 121. *See also* Ellicott, Andrew, petition of; Survey of the western boundary of New York, resolution on

Gould Bill [HR–79]: agreed to by House, 371; read, 372, 381; committee actions on, 381, 382, 399; disagreed to, 401–2

Governor of Northwest Territory, reports of, 175, 617. *See also* Northwest Territory Bill [S–17]

Governors. *See* Chittenden, Thomas [Vermont]; Clayton, Joshua [Delaware]; Clinton, George [New York]; Collins, John [Rhode Island]; Fenner, Arthur [Rhode Island]; Howard, John E. [Maryland]; Martin, Alexander [North Carolina]; Pinckney, Charles [South Carolina]; Randolph, Beverley [Virginia]; Sullivan, John [New Hampshire]

Grayson, William, 3 n, 83; attendance, 4, 5, 114; classification, 46, 47, 232 n, 716; credentials, 51; seated, 51; takes oath, 59; vote recorded, 85, 86, 87, 105, 106, 149, 151, 153, 168, 180, 187, 188, 189, 191, 195
—appointed to committees on
 Glaubeck, Baron de, 187
 Punishment of Crimes Bill [S–2], 51

Great Britain: commercial relations with, 608; Parliament of, 661

Greenleaf, Thomas, x, 49 n, 57 n; petition of, 49

Greenwich, New Jersey, 92

Griffin, Cyrus, 714

Gunn, James, 3 n; attendance, 4, 284, 533; classification, 46, 47, 232 n, 716; credentials, 21; seated, 21; takes oath, 59; vote recorded, 85, 86, 87, 105, 106, 124, 134, 142, 143, 144, 149, 152, 153, 157, 168, 180, 187, 188, 189, 191, 195, 288 n, 311, 317, 318, 323, 324, 327, 339, 340, 341, 342, 353, 365, 370, 383, 384, 385, 386, 387, 391, 392, 395, 396, 415, 416, 417, 420, 424, 425, 426, 428, 429, 430, 435, 438, 449, 450, 451, 452, 453, 454, 455, 456, 535, 536, 550, 596, 615, 618, 619, 623, 634, 648, 650, 651, 652
—appointed to committees on
 Disabled Soldiers and Seamen Bill [HR–88], 458
 Executive Journal, 538
 Indian Treaty Bill [HR–50b], 406
 Military Establishment Bill [HR–126A], 607
 Navigation Bill [HR–93], 473
 Punishment of Crimes Bill [S–2], 44
 West Point Bill [HR–76], 363

H

Hamilton, Alexander, 11 n, 557. *See also* Secretary of Treasury

Hampton, Virginia, 93, 94

Hancock, John, electoral votes cast for, 8

Hancock-Town, Maryland, 395

Hand, Edward, letter from, 128

Harmar, Josiah, 117

Harper, John, 477

Harpur, Robert, 554

Harris, John, 671

Harrisburg, Pennsylvania, 128

Harrison, Robert H., electoral votes cast for, 8

Hartford, Connecticut, 665

Hartley, Thomas, appointed to committees on: adjournment, 107, 338; unfinished business of first session, 225

Harwood, William, 350

Hawkins, Benjamin, 270 n; attendance, 495; classification, 231, 232 n, 716; credentials, 221; presents copy of North Carolina act for cession of western lands, 233; salary and expenses for, 277; seated and takes oath, 221; vote recorded, 226, 288 n, 314, 317, 318, 323, 324, 325, 327, 339, 340, 341, 342, 353, 365, 373, 375, 376, 377, 378, 379, 380, 381, 385, 386, 387, 391, 392, 395, 396, 414, 415, 416, 417, 420, 424, 425, 426, 427, 428, 429, 430, 435, 438, 449, 450, 451, 452, 453, 454, 455, 456, 515, 532, 535, 536, 596, 615, 618, 623, 631, 634, 648, 650, 651, 652, 693, 703
—appointed to committees on
 Bailey Bill [HR–44], 251
 Consuls and Vice Consuls Bill [S–18], 509, 531
 Enumeration Bill [HR–34], 242
 Indian Trade Bill [HR–65], 398
 Invalid Officers Bill [HR–59], 303
 Military Establishment Bill [HR–126A], 607
 Navigation Bill [HR–103], 510

North Carolina Bill [HR–36], 230
North Carolina Judiciary Bill [S–10], 222, 308
Officers Bill [HR–53], 292
Punishment of Crimes Bill [S–6], 227
Settlement of Accounts Bill [HR–72], 394
Swain Bill [HR–111], 525
trade with European colonies in America, 248
Vermont Statehood Bill [S–19], 562
votes, 246
Ways and Means Bill [S–14], 509
—reports for committees on
Indian Trade Bill [HR–65], 404
Navigation Bill [HR–103], 518, 525
North Carolina Bill [HR–36], 233
votes, 247
Hay, Charles, 58 n
Henry, John, 3 n, 21 n, 25 n; attendance, 4, 5, 213, 528; classification, 45, 47, 232 n, 716; credentials, 21; salary and expenses for, 276; seated, 21; takes oath, 59; vote recorded, 85, 86, 87, 105, 106, 124, 134, 142, 143, 144, 149, 152, 153, 157, 168, 180, 187, 188, 189, 191, 195, 226, 288 n, 311, 314, 317, 318, 323, 324, 325, 327, 339, 340, 341, 342, 353, 365, 370, 373, 375, 376, 377, 378, 379, 380, 381, 383, 384, 385, 386, 387, 391, 392, 395, 396, 414, 415, 416, 417, 420, 424, 426, 427, 428, 429, 430, 435, 438, 449, 450, 451, 452, 453, 454, 455, 456, 532, 551, 596, 615, 618, 619, 623, 631, 634, 648, 650, 651, 652, 693, 703
—appointed to committees on
attendance and traveling expenses of Senators, 196
Bailey Bill [HR–44], 251
Collection Bill [HR–82], 431
Courts Bill [S–9], 233
export inspection, 248
Judicial Officers Bill [HR–133], 685
Mitigation of Fines Bill [HR–38], 257
Morris, Robert, petition of, 239
Naturalization Bill [HR–40], 250
Navigation Bill [HR–92], 473
North Carolina act for cession of western lands, 234
Oath Bill [HR–1], 28
Punishment of Crimes Bill [S–2], 44
Residence Bill [S–12], 334
rules, joint, 40
Stewart and Davidson Bill [HR–90], 458
trade with European colonies in America, 248
unfinished business of first session, 224
—reports for committees on

Naturalization Bill [HR–37], 258
North Carolina act for cession of western lands, 243
Hereditary office, 161
Heysham, Robert, ix
Hillsborough, North Carolina, 312, 314, 315
Holland, 470, 673; loan from (see Loan from Holland)
Hopkins, Roswell, 558, 559, 560
Howard, John E., 350; letters from, 326, 351
Howard, Samuel Harvey, 350
Hudson, New York, 92
Hudson River, 118, 553
Hunting Creek, 615
Huntington, Benjamin, appointed to committees on: Mitigation of Fines Bill [HR–45], 267; terms of federally elected officials, 299
Huntington, Samuel, electoral votes cast for, 8
Hutchins, Thomas. See Western territories, resolution on survey of

I

Illinois County and Vincennes, land grants to settlers at. See Northwest Territory Bill [S–17]
Impeachment of Senators, 164
Impost Bill [HR–2]: agreed to by House, 49; read, 49, 51, 58, 60, 62, 63, 64; considered, 52, 53, 56, 58; committees' actions on, 62, 77; agreed to with amendments, 64, 67; amendments to, 60 n, 61 n, 63 n, 64–67, 69–70, 72–73, 74–75; conference actions on, 72, 73, 74; signed, 78, 79; petition for relief from (see Tanners of Philadelphia, Pennsylvania, petition of)
Imposts, petitions concerning. See Distillers of Philadelphia, Pennsylvania, petition of; Merchants and traders of Portland, Massachusetts, petition of
Inaugural address, 30–33; committee actions on, 33, 37–39, 40 n, 43, 46, 47; answer to, 48–49
Inaugural ceremony: attended by members of Congress, 29; description of, 29–30; joint committee actions on, 26, 27, 28, 29, 33
—divine service following
resolution on, 27, 35
attended by members of Congress, 33
India, 62, 65, 66, 94, 95, 469
Indian Department, 221
Indians, 115, 200 n, 216, 219, 291 n, 499, 506, 610; letter from Secretary of War on, 504; messages from President on, 113–14, 120, 175, 507–8. See also

Lands in North Carolina cession and Northwest Territory, resolution on; Wabash and Miami Indians, motion on

Indian Town, North Carolina, 233 n

Indian Trade Bill [HR–65]: agreed to by House, 368; read, 368–69, 398, 404; committee actions on, 398, 404; agreed to with amendments, 404; amendments to, 404 n, 407, 408, 423; conference actions on, 409, 412; found correct and signed, 431, 432, 437, 440

Indian Treaties Bill [HR–20]: agreed to by House, 120; read, 120, 121, 123, 124; committee actions on, 121, 122–23; amendments to, 122–23, 124, 126; agreed to with amendment, 125; signed, 126, 127

Indian Treaty Bill [HR–50b]: agreed to by House, 269; read, 270, 278, 302, 406, 421; committee actions on, 406, 419; agreed to with amendment, 421; amendment to, 421 n, 423; found correct and signed, 431, 432, 437, 440

Infantry. See Militia

Inhabitants of Lancaster County, Pennsylvania, petition of concerning liquors, 541

Inspection Bill [HR–48]: agreed to by House, 269; read, 270, 273; agreed to, 273; found correct and signed, 274–75, 277

Inspectors of Revenue. See Duties on Distilled Spirits Bill [HR–110]

Invalid Officers Bill [HR–59]: agreed to by House, 302; read, 302, 303, 403; committee actions on, 303, 403; disagreed to, 403

Invalid Pensioners Bill [HR–29]: agreed to by House, 193; read, 196, 200; committee actions on, 196, 200; agreed to, 200; found correct and signed, 202, 203–4, 205

Invalid Pensioners Bill [HR–80]: agreed to by House, 394; read, 397, 402; agreed to with amendment, 402; amendment to, 402 n, 406; found correct and signed, 407, 409, 419

Inventions, need to encourage, 217, 220

Investigation of financial record of Robert Morris. See Morris, Robert, petition of

Irvine, General William, 364 n

Irwin, Mathew, 261

Izard, Ralph, 3 n, 16 n, 27 n, 34 n, 213 n; attendance, 4, 15, 213, 495; classification, 46, 47, 232 n, 716; credentials, 13; seated, 13; takes oath, 59; vote recorded, 85, 86, 87, 105, 106, 124, 134, 142, 143, 144, 149, 152, 157, 168, 180, 187, 188, 189, 191, 195, 226, 288 n, 311, 314, 317, 318, 323,

324, 325, 327, 339, 340, 341, 342, 353, 365, 370, 373, 375, 376, 377, 378, 379, 380, 381, 383, 384, 385, 386, 387, 391, 392, 393, 395, 396, 414, 415, 416, 417, 420, 424, 426, 427, 428, 429, 430, 435, 438, 449, 450, 451, 452, 453, 454, 455, 456, 515, 532, 535, 536, 551, 596, 615, 618, 619, 623, 631, 635, 648, 650, 651, 652, 693, 703

—appointed to committees on
adjournment, 197, 487
Appropriations Bill [HR–47], 263
Bailey, Francis, petition of, 235
business between Houses, 298
coins, weights, and measures, 517
communications, Presidential, 53
Compensation Bill [HR–15], 110, 165
compensation lists, 315
Congressional session, fourth, 537
Continental Congress, papers of, 14
export inspection, 247
Foreign Intercourse Bill [HR–52], 330
Glaubeck, Baron de, 187
inaugural ceremony, 26
Judiciary Bill [S–1], 14
messages between Houses, 17
mint, 548
Mitigation of Fines Bill [HR–38], 257
Morris, Robert, petition of, 239
North Carolina act for cession of western lands, 234
North Carolina Cession Bill [S–7], 246
oath, Presidential, 24
quorum, 214
reception of President and Vice President, 21
Rhode Island Trade Bill [S–11], 295
Salaries-Executive Bill [HR–54], 299
Salaries-Legislative Bill [HR–19], 139, 166
State of the Union Address, 218, 501
Steuben Bill [HR–60], 306
Stirling Bill [HR–96], 477
Thanksgiving, 197
titles, Presidential, 24
vessels leaving U.S. ports, 252
Ways and Means Bill [HR–83], 437
West Point Bill [HR–76], 363

—reports for committees on
adjournment, 488
coins, weights, and measures, 661
Morris, Robert, petition of, 240
vessels leaving U.S. ports, 253
West Point Bill [HR–76], 370

J

Jackson, James, appointed to committees on: Continental Congress, papers of, 29; Courts Bill [S–4], 196; Mitiga-

tion of Fines Bill [HR–45], 267; unfinished business of first session, 225
James River, 93
James Town, Rhode Island, 445 n
Jay, John: delivers messages from President, 193, 204; electoral votes cast for, 8
Jefferson, Thomas. *See* Secretary of State
Jekyl Island, Georgia, 93
Jenkins Bill [HR–67]: agreed to by House, 319; read, 319, 325, 328; committee actions on, 328; agreed to, 331; found correct and signed, 335, 336, 352, 353
Jesuits, 684
Johnson, Charles, 347
Johnson, Thomas, Jr., 350
Johnson, William Samuel, 13 n, 14 n, 16 n, 33 n, 35 n; attendance, 4, 5, 7, 13, 14, 213, 506; classification, 45, 47, 232 n, 716; credentials, 7; salary and expenses for, 277; seated, 3; takes oath, 59; vote recorded, 85, 86, 87, 105, 106, 124, 134, 142, 143, 144, 149, 152, 153, 157, 168, 180, 187, 188, 189, 191, 195, 226, 288 n, 311, 314, 317, 318, 323, 324, 325, 327, 339, 340, 341, 342, 353, 365, 370, 373, 375, 376, 377, 378, 379, 380, 381, 383, 384, 385, 386, 387, 391, 392, 395, 414, 415, 416, 417, 420, 435, 438, 515, 532, 535, 536, 551, 596, 615, 618, 619, 623, 631, 635, 648, 650, 651, 652, 693, 703
—appointed to committees on
adjournment, 197
Continental Congress, papers of, 14
Copyright Bill [HR–43], 302
Courts Bill [S–9], 223
election of President and Vice President, 9
Enumeration Bill [HR–34], 242
inaugural address, 33
Kentucky Statehood Bill [S–16], 508
Naturalization Bill [HR–40], 256
Oath Bill [HR–1], 28
Patents Bill [HR–41], 258
Punishment of Crimes Bills [S–2], [S–6], 44, 227
reception of President and Vice President, 12, 17
Thanksgiving, 197
titles, Presidential, 40, 41
Treasury Bill [HR–9], 119
—reports for committees on
adjournment, 203
Punishment of Crimes Bill [S–2], 98
Thanksgiving, 203
Treasury Bill [HR–9], 121
Johnston, Samuel, 270 n, 336; attendance, 495; classification, 231, 232 n, 716; credentials, 231; letter from, 219; presents North Carolina act for cession of western lands, 233; salary and expenses for, 277; seated and takes oath, 231; vote recorded, 288 n, 311, 314, 315, 317, 323, 324, 325, 327, 339, 340, 341, 342, 353, 365, 370, 373, 375, 376, 377, 378, 379, 380, 381, 383, 384, 385, 386, 387, 391, 392, 393, 395, 414, 415, 416, 417, 420, 424, 426, 427, 428, 429, 430, 435, 438, 449, 450, 451, 452, 453, 454, 455, 456, 515, 532, 536, 551, 596, 615, 618, 619, 623, 631, 635, 648, 650, 651, 652, 693, 703
—appointed to committees on
adjournment, 487
Appropriations Bill [HR–47], 263
compensation lists, 315
export inspection, 247
North Carolina Judiciary Bill [S–10], 308
Post Office Bill [HR–74], 368
Residence Bill [S–12], 334
Southern Territory Bill [S–8], 281
Steuben Bill [HR–60], 306
—reports for committees on
North Carolina Judiciary Bill [S–10], 314
Post Office Bill [HR–74], 393
Joint rules. *See* Rules, joint
Jones, John, petition of, 546
Jones, Samuel, 557
Journal of Senate, 84; committee actions on, 15–16, 25, 34 n, 48, 50, 51
Journal of Senate, Executive. *See* Executive Journal of Senate
Journals of Congress: House order to send to states, 206; publication of, 162
Journals of Continental Congress. *See* Continental Congress, journals of
Judges, salaries of, 164. *See also* Salaries-Judiciary Bill [HR–28]
Judicial officers, oath of, 36
Judicial Officers Bill [HR–133]: agreed to by House, 663; read, 663, 666, 685, 694; printed, 663–65; committee actions on, 685, 693–94; agreed to with amendments, 694; amendments to, 694, 699; found correct and signed, 704, 705, 706, 707–8
Judiciary. *See Courts Bills in List of Bills*
Judiciary Bill [S–1], 626; committee to prepare, 11, 14; presented, 67; read, 67, 71, 74, 75, 76, 77, 78, 79, 80–82; amendments to, 80–83; recommitted, 83; agreed to with amendments, 85, 88, 176; House amendments to, 177, 179, 180; found correct and signed, 183, 184, 190
Judiciary system, need for improvements in, 500, 506
Justice, right to, 161

K

Kahokia, 617. *See also* Northwest Territory Bill [S–17]
Kammerer, Joseph, 57 n
Kaskaskia, 617. *See also* Northwest Territory Bill [S–17]
Kentucky: district court of, 307
—statehood for, 498, 505
　documents relating to, and message from President on, 502–4
Kentucky and Vermont Representatives Bill [S–20]: presented, 593; read, 593, 594; printed, 593; agreed to, 594, 620; found correct and signed, 629–30, 631, 633, 637, 638
Kentucky Statehood Bill [S–16]: committee actions on, 508, 522–23; presented, 523–24; read, 524–25, 528, 530; agreed to, 530–31, 542; title of corrected, 542; found correct and signed, 542, 543, 546, 547; printed, 646
King, Robert, 672
King, Rufus, 487 n; attendance, 213, 495; classification, 98, 232 n, 716; credentials, 91; presents Kentucky and Vermont Representatives Bill [S–20], 593; salary and expenses for, 277; seated and takes oath, 91; vote recorded, 105, 106, 124, 135, 142, 143, 144, 149, 152, 153, 157, 168, 180, 187, 188, 189, 191, 195, 226, 288 n, 311, 314, 317, 318, 323, 324, 325, 327, 339, 340, 341, 342, 353, 365, 370, 373, 375, 376, 377, 378, 379, 380, 381, 383, 384, 385, 386, 387, 391, 392, 393, 395, 396, 414, 415, 416, 417, 420, 424, 426, 427, 428, 429, 430, 435, 438, 449, 450, 451, 452, 453, 454, 455, 456, 515, 532, 535, 536, 551, 596, 615, 618, 619, 623, 635, 648, 650, 651, 652, 693, 703
—appointed to committees on
Appropriations Bill [HR–32], 194
Barclay Bill [HR–91], 459
Campbell, Donald, petition of, 608
Coasting Bill [HR–16], 118
Compensation Bill [HR–15], 165
compensation lists, 315
Consuls and Vice Consuls Bills [HR–86], [S–18], 444, 531
Courts Bills [S–4], [S–9], 195, 223
Duties on Distilled Spirits Bill [HR–110], 632
Executive Journal of Senate, 538
export inspection, 248
Foreign Intercourse Bill [HR–52], 330
Funding Bill [HR–63], 347
Indian Treaties Bill [HR–20], 121
Invalid Pensioners Bill [HR–29], 196

Judicial Officers Bill [HR–133], 685
Land Office Bill [HR–114], 627
Mediterranean trade, 508
mint, 548
Mitigation of Forfeitures Bill [S–24], 699
Naturalization Bill [HR–40], 256
North Carolina Judiciary Bill [S–10], 308
officers of the Treasury Department, salaries of, 636
Post Office Bill [HR–74], 408
Records Bill [HR–18], 148
Salaries-Legislative Bill [HR–19], 138, 166
settlement of accounts and the Funding Bill [HR–63], 418
Settlement of Accounts Bills [HR–72], [HR–77], 394, 402, 413
State of the Union Address, 218, 501
terms of federally elected officials, 300
trade, 110
trade with European colonies in America, 248
Troops Bill [HR–27], 196
Vermont Statehood Bill [S–19], 562
—reports for committees on
Barclay Bill [HR–91], 462
Consuls and Vice Consuls Bill [HR–86], 461
Foreign Intercourse Bill [HR–52], 367
Mitigation of Forfeitures Bill [S–24], 700
Records Bill [HR–18], 152
Salaries-Legislative Bill [HR–19], 138
Settlement of Accounts Bill [HR–77], 399
State of the Union Address, 219, 221
Vermont Statehood Bill [S–19], 563
Kinnimicut, Rhode Island, 445 n
Kinsale, Virginia, 93
Klock, Jacob, 477
Knox, Henry, 114; delivers message from President, 113, 115; signs statement on Army, 118. *See also* Secretary of War
Koch, Severnus, pension of, 477

L

Lake Champlain, 555, 557, 627, 673
Lancaster, Pennsylvania, 128
Lancaster County, Pennsylvania, petition of inhabitants of. *See* Inhabitants of Lancaster County, Pennsylvania, petition of concerning liquors
Land bounty for officers and soldiers, of the Virginia line. *See* Virginia, resolutions and petition from
Land grant for glasshouse buildings, petition for. *See* Amelung, John F., petition of

Land Office Bill [HR–114]: agreed to by House, 610; read, 610, 614, 617–18, 627, 655; printed, 610–14; committee actions on, 627, 655, 667; recommitted, 655; postponed, 667

Lands in North Carolina cession and Northwest Territory, resolution on, 667, 691–92, 699, 701, 704, 705–6

Langdon, John, 58 n; address of, 21; administers oath, 59; attendance, 4, 5, 7, 13, 14, 139, 213, 481, 495; classification, 45, 46, 47, 232 n, 716; credentials, 7; elected president *pro tempore*, 7, 8, 113; salary and expenses for, 277; seated, 3; signs documents, 9, 10, 11; takes oath, 59; vote recorded, 85, 86, 87, 105, 106, 124, 135, 226, 288 n, 311, 314, 317, 318, 323, 324, 325, 327, 339, 340, 341, 342, 353, 365, 370, 373, 375, 376, 377, 378, 379, 380, 381, 383, 384, 385, 386, 387, 391, 392, 393, 395, 396, 414, 415, 416, 417, 420, 424, 426, 427, 428, 429, 430, 435, 438, 449, 450, 451, 452, 453, 454, 455, 515, 532, 535, 536, 551, 596, 615, 618, 619, 623, 635, 648, 650, 651, 652, 693, 703

—appointed to committees on
Acts of Congress, 59
Appropriations Bill [HR–47], 263
Bailey, Francis, petition of, 235
Barclay Bill [HR–91], 459
Campbell, Donald, petition of, 608
Coasting Bill [HR–16], 118
coins, weights, and measures, 518
Collection Bills [HR–11], [HR–50], [HR–82], 88, 282, 431
Commissioners of Loans Bill [HR–135], 675
Compensation Bill [HR–15], 110
Consuls and Vice Consuls Bill [HR–86], 444
Duties on Distilled Spirits Bill [HR–110], 545
Duties on Teas Bill [HR–130], 689
export inspection, 247
Indian Treaty Bill [HR–50b], 406
Jenkins Bill [HR–67], 328
Lighthouses Bill [HR–12], 90
Mediterranean trade, 508
Merchant Seamen Bill [HR–61], 394
Military Establishment Bill [HR–50a], 273
Mitigation of Fines Bill [HR–38], 257
Navigation Bill [HR–103], 510
newspapers, 44
North Carolina Judiciary Bill [S–10], 308
Post Office Bill [HR–74], 368
Punishment of Crimes Bill [S–2], 44
quorum, 496–97

reception of President and Vice President, 12, 17
rules, joint, 39
Swain Bill [HR–111], 525
trade, 69
trade with European Colonies in America, 241
Twining Bill [HR–72], 355
Vermont Statehood Bill [S–19], 562
votes, 246
West Point Bill [HR–76], 363
—reports for committees on
Campbell, Donald, petition of, 617
Collection Bill [HR–50], 282–83
Commissioners of Loans Bill [HR–135], 686
Mediterranean trade, 526, 544, 666
quorum, 497
Twining Bill [HR–72], 366

Lansing, John, Jr., 553, 555, 557
Laurens, Francis Eleanor, pension of. *See* Stirling Bill [HR–96], committee actions on
Laurens, Henry, petitions of, 519, 520
Laurens, John, 479, 519 n, 520 n
Lawrence, Elisha, 474, 475
Lawrence, John, appointed to committee on quorum, 496 n
Laws of United States: committee to revise, 666, 669; printing of (*see* Brown, Andrew, petition of)
Lear, Tobias, 58 n, 219; certifies document, 254, 261, 279, 281, 332, 347, 349, 350, 351, 356, 362; delivers messages from President (*see* President, messages from)
Leavenworth, Mark, 714
Lee, Richard Bland, appointed to committee on adjournment, 199
Lee, Richard Henry, 3 n, 16 n, 20 n, 23 n, 24 n, 27 n, 28 n, 34 n, 40 n, 45 n, 83, 338 n; attendance, 4, 5, 7, 13, 283, 608; classification, 46, 47, 232 n, 716; credentials, 7; seated, 6; takes oath, 59; vote recorded, 85, 86, 87, 105, 124, 135, 142, 143, 144, 149, 152, 153, 157, 168, 180, 187, 188, 189, 191, 195, 288 n, 314, 317, 318, 323, 324, 325, 327, 339, 340, 341, 342, 353, 365, 370, 373, 375, 376, 377, 378, 379, 380, 381, 383, 384, 385, 386, 387, 388, 391, 392, 393, 395, 396, 414, 415, 416, 417, 420, 424, 426, 427, 428, 429, 430, 435, 438, 449, 450, 451, 452, 453, 454, 455, 456, 615, 618, 619, 623, 631, 635, 648, 650, 651, 652, 693, 703

—appointed to committees on
Acts of Congress, 59
business between houses, 298
Collection Bill [HR–11], 88
communications, Presidential, 53

Compensation Bill [HR–15], 110
compensation lists, 315
election of President and Vice President, 9
Funding Bill [HR–63], 347
Impost Bill [HR–2], 62, 73
inaugural ceremony, 26
Indian Treaties Bill [HR–20], 121
Journal of Senate, 15
Judiciary Bill [S–1], 11
messages between houses, 17, 34
New York City Hall, communications on, 14
oath, Presidential, 24
Oath Bill [HR–1], 49–50
Payment of Balances Bill [S–22], 657
Residence Bill [S–12], 334
rules, conference, and appointment of chaplains, 12
Salaries-Legislative Bill [HR–19], 139
settlement of accounts, 398
settlement of accounts and the Funding Bill [HR–63], 418
Settlement of Accounts Bill [HR–77], 402, 413
titles, Presidential, 24, 40, 41
Tonnage Bill [HR–5], 73
trade, 69
trade with European colonies in America, 294
Treasury Bill [HR–9], 119
Virginia Cession Bill [HR–85], 437
Ways and Means Bill [HR–83], 437
—reports for committees on
business between houses, 338, 344–45
Courts Bill [S–4], 176
Funding Bill [HR–63], 354
inaugural ceremony, 29
Judiciary Bill [S–1], 67
Virginia Cession Bill [HR–85], 440
Ways and Means Bill [HR–83], 461
Leitch, Andrew, 671
Lewis, Robert, 670
Library of Philadelphia, Pennsylvania, resolution of, 534
Licenses for trading. See Coasting Bills [HR–16], [HR–33]
Lighthouses Bill [HR–12]: agreed to by House, 88; read, 89, 90, 98, 99, 100, 102; committee actions on, 90, 91; agreed to with amendments, 102, 104; amendments to, 102–3, 107; found correct and signed, 110, 112, 114
Lighthouses Bill [HR–84]: agreed to by House, 418; read, 419, 421, 422; agreed to, 422; found correct and signed, 431, 432, 437, 440
Lincoln, Benjamin, 508; electoral votes cast for, 8
Liquors. See College of Physicians of Philadelphia, petition of concerning distilled spirits; Duties, on distilled spirits; Duties, on rum; Duties on Distilled Spirits Bill [HR–110]; Duties on Teas Bill [HR–130]; Inhabitants of Lancaster County, Pennsylvania, petition of concerning liquors
Literature, promotion of, 217, 220
Little Rivers, North Carolina, 233 n
Livermore, Samuel, appointed to committees on: Compensation Bill [HR–15], 169; North Carolina Judiciary Bill [S–10], 308
Livingston, Robert R., 553. See also New York, Chancellor of
Livingston, William, 475
Lloyd, Peter Zachary, 261
Loan from Holland, 498; report of Secretary of Treasury on, 646–48
London, England, 608
Long, Thomas, and others, petition of. See Merchants and manufacturers of Baltimore, Maryland, petition of
Loudon, Samuel, petition of, 49 n
Louis XVI, 204, 676, 702
Louisville, Kentucky, 630
Louisville, Massachusetts, 447 n
Louisville, Virginia, 93 n
Lynn [Linn], William, 35

M

McClellan, John, petition of. See Merchants and traders of Portland, Massachusetts, petition of
McCord Bill [HR–70]: agreed to by House, 336; read, 336–37, 363; committee actions on, 337, 363; agreed to with amendment, 364; amendment to, 364 n, 367; found correct and signed, 381, 382, 388, 395
McIntire, Thomas, 672
McKean, Thomas, and others, petition of. See Public creditors of Pennsylvania, petition of
Maclay, William, 13 n, 14 n, 23 n, 24 n, 128; attendance, 4, 5, 7, 13, 89, 213, 443, 495; classification, 46, 47, 232 n, 716; credentials, 7; nominates sites for seat of government, 128; salary and expenses for, 277; seated, 3; takes oath, 59; vote recorded, 85, 86, 87, 124, 135, 142, 143, 144, 180, 187, 188, 189, 191, 226, 288 n, 311, 314, 317, 318, 323, 324, 325, 327, 339, 341, 342, 353, 365, 370, 373, 375, 376, 377, 378, 379, 380, 381, 383, 384, 385, 386, 387, 388, 391, 392, 393, 395, 396, 414, 415, 416, 417, 420, 424, 426, 427, 428, 429, 430,

435, 438, 515, 532, 535, 536, 551, 596, 615, 618, 619, 623, 632, 635, 648, 650, 651, 652, 703
—appointed to committees on
Campbell, Donald, petition of, 421
clerks of Commissioner of Army Accounts, 439
Collection Bill [HR–134], 660
Continental Congress, papers of, 14
Ely Bill [HR–56], 301
Foreign Intercourse Bill [HR–52], 299
Foreign Officers Bill [HR–116], 599
Funding Bill [HR–63], 347
Gould Bill [HR–79], 382
Judiciary Bill [S–1], 11
McCord Bill [HR–70], 337
New York City Hall, use of, 41
Northwest Territory Bill [S–17], 519
Patents Bill [HR–41], 258
Post Office Bill [HR–74], 368
rules, conference, and appointment of chaplains, 12
Steuben Bill [HR–60], 306
Twining Bill [HR–72], 355
unfinished business of first session, 224
—reports for committees on
Ely Bill [HR–56], 307
Foreign Officers Bill [HR–116], 629
Steuben Bill [HR–60], 319
McLean, Archibald, petition of, 44
McPherson, John, petition of, 660
Madison, James: delivers message from House, 9
—appointed to committees on
amendments, Constitutional, 181
Impost Bill [HR–2], 72
titles, Presidential, 26, 43
Tonnage Bill [HR–5], 72
Treasury Bill [HR–9], 119
Manufacturers of Boston, Massachusetts, petition of, 62
Manufacturers of New York City, petition of, 62
Manufactures, need to promote, 217, 220
Marblehead, Massachusetts, 96
Martin, Alexander, letters from, 234, 346
Maryland, 539, 616; act of, 533, 534; electoral votes, 8; loan to United States, 410, 433; petitions of citizens of (see Amelung, John F., petition of; Goddard, Mary K., petition of; Merchants and manufacturers of Baltimore, Maryland, petition of; O'Donnell, John, and others, petition of; Peters, Robert, and others, petition of; Shipwrights of Baltimore, Maryland, petition of; White, John, petition of); ratification of Constitutional amendments by, 226, 227, 716; Senators present, 13, 15, 21, 213, 258, 528, 537; settlement of accounts of, 98

Maryland Bill [HR–115]: agreed to by House, 541; read, 543, 545; agreed to, 545; found correct and signed, 549, 551–52
Massachusetts, 553, 555, 663, 665, 691; electoral votes, 8; loan to United States, 410, 432; petitions of citizens of (see Congregational clergy of Massachusetts, petition of; Gorham, Nathaniel, petition of; Manufacturers of Boston, Massachusetts, petition of; Merchants and traders of Portland, Massachusetts, petition of; Tracy, Nathaniel, petition of); Senators present, 3, 7, 13, 14, 213, 495, 497
Masters of American vessels of Charleston, South Carolina, petition of, 609
Mathers, James, 265 n, 266; elected doorkeeper of Senate, 11; orders concerning, 562 n, 700 n; petitions of, 11 n, 262, 263, 546, 547–48
Maurice River, New Jersey, 92
Maverick, Peter, 714
Maxwell, Cornelius, petition of, 12
Measures, 500. See also Coins, weights, and measures
Medford, Massachusetts, 92
Mediterranean trade: committee actions on, 508, 519, 526–27, 537, 544, 666; report on, 520; status of, 499, 506
Mentges, Francis, petition of, resolution on, 448, 457, 462, 473–74
Merchants, petition for relief of. See Tracy, Nathaniel, petition of
Merchants and manufacturers of Baltimore, Maryland, petition of, 62
Merchants and traders of Portland, Massachusetts, petition of, 63
Merchants and traders of Portsmouth, New Hampshire, petition of, 268
Merchant Seamen Bill [HR–61]: agreed to by House, 374; read, 374, 394, 403; committee actions on, 394, 402–3; agreed to with amendments, 403; amendments to, 403 n, 407, 408; found correct and signed, 421, 422, 432
Merchants of North Carolina, petition of, 320
Merchants of Philadelphia, Pennsylvania, petition of, 537–38
Meredith, Samuel, 513. See also Treasurer of United States
Meriwether, J., 58 n
Messages between Houses: joint committee actions on, 17–18, 23–25, 28–29, 34; motion to adopt procedure of delivering, committee actions on, 34, 36, 37, 41; temporary procedure for delivering, 34
Messenger of Senate, election of, 12

Meters of New York, petition of, 87

Miami Indians, peace with. *See* Wabash and Miami Indians

Middletown, Connecticut, 446 n; petition concerning (*see* Citizens of Connecticut, petition of)

Military Establishment Bill [HR–50a]: agreed to by House, 268; read, 269, 270, 285, 288, 290; committee actions on, 278, 281, 289–90; amendments to, 288 n, 290 n–91 n, 293; recommitted, 289; motion on, 289 n; agreed to with amendments, 290; signed, 295, 300

Military Establishment Bill [HR–126A]: agreed to by House, 603; read, 603, 607, 622; printed, 603–6; committee actions on, 607, 616, 619, 620; amendments to, 623–25, 657–58, 659, 660, 667–68; agreed to with amendments, 623; found correct and signed, 668, 669, 675, 690, 698

Militia, 163, 401 n; maintenance of, 216, 219; need for establishment of, 500; plan for, 224; rations of, 117; statements of, 113–14, 115–18, 175. *See also* Military Establishment Bills [HR–50a], [HR–126A]; Troops Bill [HR–27]

Milton, John, electoral votes cast for, 8

Mint, establishment of, 500; report on committee actions on, 548, 661, 685–86; resolutions on, 686, 697, 698, 699, 701, 704, 705

Mississippi River, 682

Mitchell, Abraham, petition of, 12

Mitchell, George, 254

Mitigation of Fines Bill [HR–45]: agreed to by House, 255; read, 255–56, 257, 259, 262; committee actions on, 257, 258, 259, 262; special committee actions on, 262, 263; agreed to with amendment, 263; amendment to, 263 n, 267, 268, 283, 284–85; conference actions on, 267, 278

Mitigation of Forfeitures Bill [HR–57]: agreed to by House, 297; read, 298, 301; agreed to with amendments, 301; amendments to, 301 n, 304; found correct and signed, 304, 305, 321, 327

Mitigation of Forfeitures Bill [S–24]: presented, 669; read, 669, 699, 700; printed, 669–70; committee actions on, 699, 700; agreed to, 700, 703–4; amendment to, 700; found correct and signed, 705, 706, 707

Mix, Timothy, 671, 672

Monmouth, Battle of, 706

Monmouth County, New Jersey. *See* New Jersey, act of

Monroe, James, 633; classification, 716; credentials, 495; presents resolutions and memorial from Virginia, 531; reports for committee on Virginia, resolutions and petition from, 694–95; seated and takes oath, 495; vote recorded, 532, 535, 536, 551, 596, 615, 618, 619, 623, 632, 635, 648, 650, 651, 652, 693, 703

—appointed to committees on

coins, weights, and measures, 517

Collection Bill [HR–134], 660

Kentucky Statehood Bill [S–16], 508

Land Office Bill [HR–114], 627

mint, 548

Vermont Statehood Bill [S–19], 562

Virginia, resolutions and petition from, 543

Montgomery, William, petition of, 222, 362

Moore, Andrew, appointed to committee on terms of federally elected officials, 299

Moore, Stephen, petition of, committed to committee on West Point Bill [HR–76], 363

Morgan, Jacob, and others, petition of. *See* Distillers of Philadelphia, Pennsylvania, petition of

Moroccan Treaty Bill [S–23]: presented, 666; read, 666, 667, 675; printed, 666–67; motion to commit, 667; agreed to, 675, 682; found correct and signed, 690, 691, 692, 696

Morocco, 470

Morris, Lewis R., 552, 561, 562

Morris, Robert, 128, 320 n; attendance, 4, 5, 7, 42, 104, 224, 269, 288, 495; classification, 45, 47, 232 n, 716; credentials, 7; salary and expenses for, 277; seated, 3; takes oath, 59; vote recorded, 85, 86, 87, 105, 106, 124, 135, 142, 143, 144, 149, 152, 157, 168, 180, 187, 188, 189, 191, 195, 226, 311, 314, 317, 318, 323, 324, 325, 327, 339, 341, 342, 353, 365, 370, 373, 375, 376, 377, 378, 379, 380, 381, 383, 384, 385, 386, 387, 388, 391, 392, 393, 395, 396, 414, 415, 416, 417, 420, 424, 426, 427, 428, 429, 430, 435, 438, 449, 450, 451, 452, 453, 454, 455, 456, 515, 532, 535, 536, 551, 596, 615, 619, 623, 632, 635, 648, 650, 651, 652, 693, 703

—appointed to committees on

Acts of Congress, 59

Appropriations Bill [HR–32], 194

Bailey, Francis, petition of, 235

Bank, National, 516

Barclay Bill [HR–91], 459

Coasting Bills [HR–16], [HR–33], 118, 197

coins, weights, and measures, 517
Collection Bills [HR–11], [HR–26], [HR–82], 88, 197, 431
Compensation Bill [HR–15], 110, 165
Consuls and Vice Consuls Bills [HR–86], [S–18], 444, 531
Duties on Distilled Spirits Bill [HR–110], 545, 632
Duties on Teas Bill [HR–130], 689
export inspection, 247
Impost Bill [HR–2], 62, 73
Invalid Pensioners Bill [HR–29], 196
Lighthouses Bill [HR–12], 90
McCord Bill [HR–70], 337
Mediterranean trade, 508
Merchant Seamen Bill [HR–61], 394
mint, 548
Mitigation of Fines Bill [HR–45], 257, 262
Navigation Bill [HR–103], 518
Post Office Bill [S–3], 170
Punishment of Crimes Bill [S–2], 44
quorum, 496, 497
Rhode Island Trade Bill [S–11], 295
Salaries-Legislative Bill [HR–19], 138, 166
Settlement of accounts and the Funding Bill [HR–63], 418
Settlement of Accounts Bill [HR–77], 402
Swain Bill [HR–111], 525
terms of federally elected officials, 300
Tonnage Bills [HR–5], [HR–24], [HR–78], 73, 171, 382
trade, 69
trade with European colonies in America, 241
Treasurer of United States, accounts of, 372
Troops Bill [HR–27], 196
Ways and Means Bill [HR–83], 437
—petition of, 237–39
committee actions on, 239, 240–41
—presents
American Philosophical Society, request of, 654
Bailey, Francis, petition of, 235
College of Physicians of Philadelphia, Pennsylvania, petition of concerning distilled spirits, 518
Dobson, Thomas, letter from, 303
merchants of Philadelphia, Pennsylvania, petition of, 538
Pennsylvania, General Assembly resolution of, 181
surgeons and surgeons-mates, petition of, 534
—reports for committees on
Bailey, Francis, petition of, 245
Coasting Bill [HR–16], 121–22
Collection Bill [HR–82], 439

Compensation Bill [HR–15], 114
Duties on Distilled Spirits Bill [HR–110], 549, 594, 595
Duties on Teas Bill [HR–130], 690
Impost Bill [HR–2], 74
McCord Bill [HR–70], 363
mint, 661
Mitigation of Fines Bill [HR–38], 258
Rhode Island Trade Bill [S–11], 309
Settlement of Accounts Bill [HR–77], 404
Swain Bill [HR–111], 526
Tonnage Bills [HR–5], [HR–24], 74, 172
Muhlenberg, Frederick Augustus. See Speaker of the House
Murpheysborough, North Carolina, 233 n
Muter, George, letter from, 502–3, 504

N

Nantucket, Massachusetts, 96
National Assembly of France. See France, National Assembly of
National Bank. See Bank, National
Naturalization, need for uniform rule of, 217, 220
Naturalization Bill [HR–40]: agreed to by House, 252; read, 252, 255, 256, 262, 264; amendments to, 255 n, 264; committee actions on, 256, 258, 259, 262; agreed to with amendment, 264; found correct and signed, 266, 267, 268, 273
Naval Officers. See Collection Bills
Navigation: encouragement of, 499, 506; laws of, 162
Navigation Bill [HR–93]: agreed to by House, 463; read, 468, 473, 482; committee actions on, 473, 482; agreed to with amendments, 482; amendment to, 483; found correct and signed, 485, 487–88, 490
Navigation Bill [HR–103]: agreed to by House, 510; read, 510, 525, 526; committee actions on, 510, 518, 525; recommitted, 518; amendments to, 525, 527; agreed to with amendments, 526; found correct and signed, 528–29, 530
Navy of United States. See Officers of late U.S. Navy, petition of
Negroes, 244 n
Nelson, Thomas, Jr., 295
New Bedford, Massachusetts, 446 n
Newbern, North Carolina, 234 n, 314, 315
New-Biggen Creek, North Carolina, 233 n
Newbury-Port, Virginia, 96
Newcastle, Delaware, 92, 94
New Hampshire, 553, 665; district court of, 314; electoral votes, 8; loan to

United States, 410, 432; petition of citizens of (*see* Merchants and traders of Portsmouth, New Hampshire, petition of); ratification of Constitutional amendments, 348–49, 716; Senators present, 3, 7, 13, 14, 213, 495

New Haven, Connecticut, 96, 665

New Jersey, 17; act of, 520, 521–22; electoral votes, 8; loan to United States, 410, 433; petition of citizens of (*see* Citizens of New Jersey and Pennsylvania, petition of); ratification of Constitutional amendments by, 474–76, 716; Senators present, 5, 6, 7, 13, 14, 43, 70, 113, 214, 221, 274, 322, 497

Newkirk, Jacob, pension of, 477

New London, Connecticut, 96, 283 n

Newport, Rhode Island, 665

Newport, Virginia, 93

Newspapers, 224, 507; joint committee actions on, 44, 48, 49, 50, 51, 54, 56–57, 58

New York, 238, 663, 665, 691; acts of, 278; Chancellor of, 26, 29; laws of, revised copy of, 223; legislature of, 125; loan to United States, 410, 433; petitions of citizens of (*see* Bleecker, Leonard, petition of; Bryce, John, petition of; Campbell, Donald, petitions of; Clerks in office of Paymaster General, petition of; Clerks in public office, petition of; McLean, Archibald, petition of; McPherson, John, petition of; Manufacturers of New York City, petition of; Meters of New York, petition of; Officers of late U.S. Navy, petition of; Okee, Abraham, petition of; Stirling, Sarah, petition of; Weed, Jacob, petition of); ratification of Constitutional amendments by, 278, 279, 281, 716; Senators present, 91, 213, 495, 507; Western boundary of, survey of (*see* Ellicott, Andrew, petition of; Gorham, Nathaniel, petition of; Survey of western boundary of New York). *See also* Vermont, statehood for

New York City, 190, 665; letter to, 290–91; mayor of, 11, 69 n, 491; petitions from (*see* Manufacturers of New York City, petition of; Meters of New York, petition of); resolution of thanks to, 490. *See also* Residence Bill [S–12], motions on

New York City Hall, 207; communications on, 11, 14, 15; joint committee actions on use of, 41, 42–43, 69, 70–71

Nixinton, North Carolina, 233 n

Norfolk, Virginia, 96

North Carolina, 436 n; act for cession of western lands, 233, 234; committee actions on act for cession of western lands, 234, 243, 244, 245; impost laws affecting, 172; loan to United States, 410, 433; pay of soldiers of (*see* Compensation lists); petitions of citizens of (*see* Citizens of North Carolina, petition of; Merchants of North Carolina, petition of; Moore, Stephen, petition of); ratification of Constitution by, 216, 219; ratification of Constitutional amendments by, 192, 198, 345–46, 716; Senators present, 221, 231, 495; trade of (*see* Collection Bill [HR–23])

North Carolina Bill [HR–36]: agreed to by House, 229; read, 229, 230, 233; committee actions on, 230, 233; agreed to with amendments, 233; amendments to, 233 n–34 n, 235–36; found correct and signed, 236, 237, 240

North Carolina cession, lands in. *See* Lands in North Carolina cession and Northwest Territory, resolution on

North Carolina Cession Bill [S–7]: committee to prepare, 246; presented, 251; read, 251, 252; agreed to, 252–53; House amendment to, 269, 270, 272; found correct and signed, 274, 275–76

North Carolina Judiciary Bill [S–10]: committee to prepare, 222; presented, 295; read, 295, 296, 300; agreed to, 300, 305; House amendments to, 306–7, 312, 314–15, 316; conference actions on, 308, 314, 315

North Carolina Judiciary Bill [HR–68]: agreed to by House, 319; read, 319, 325–26, 328; agreed to, 328; found correct and signed, 331, 333, 335, 337

North River, North Carolina, 233 n

Northwest Territory: governor of (*see* Governor of Northwest Territory); land grants in, 516–17. *See also* Lands in North Carolina cession and Northwest Territory, resolution on

Northwest Territory Bill [HR–14]: agreed to by House, 89; read, 89, 91, 103, 105; amendments to, 105, 106, 108; agreed to with amendments, 106; found correct and signed, 110, 112, 114

Northwest Territory Bill [S–17]: committee to prepare, 519, 526, 691; read, 527, 528, 529; agreed to with amendments, 529, 682; printed, 682–83; House amendments to, 684, 685, 691, 697; found correct and signed, 704, 705, 707

Nourse, Joseph, 513, 715

O

Oath, Presidential: administered, 29–30; committee actions on, 24, 26
Oath Bill [HR–1], 58; agreed to by House, 28; read, 28, 35, 36; committees' actions on, 28, 35, 50, 52; amendments to, 35–36, 39; agreed to with amendments, 36–37; signed, 51–52, 56
Oath of office administered, 59, 61, 71, 91
O'Donnell, John, and others, petition of, 373
Officers Bill [HR–53]: agreed to by House, 291; read, 291, 292; committee actions on, 292, 293; disagreed to, 293
Officers of late U.S. Navy, petition of, 268
Officers of Treasury Department, committee on resolution on salaries of, 635–36
O'Hara, Thomas, petition of, 153
Ohio River, 118, 175, 610
Okee, Abraham, petition of, 12
Olyphant, David, petition of, 256
Open sessions of Senate, 632; motion for, 296, 298; resolutions on, 637, 648–49
Orders, standing. See Rules, Senate
Osgood, Samuel, 17. See also Postmaster General
Otis, Samuel: elected Secretary of Senate, 12. See also Secretary of Senate
Otis, Samuel, Jr., ix
Owen, Abraham, petition of. See Montgomery, William, petition of
Owen, Daniel, 359, 362; letter from, 332, 355–56
Oxford, Maryland, 92, 96

P

Page, John, appointed to committee on titles, Presidential, 43
Pagen, William Samuel, 364 n
Pannil, Joseph, 672
Papers of Continental Congress. See Continental Congress, papers of
Paris, France, 505, 592
Partridge, George, 54
—appointed to committees on
communications, Presidential, 53
enrolled bills, 102
Impost Bill [HR–2], 77
Oath Bill [HR–1], 52
Pasquotank, North Carolina, 233 n
Passamaquoddy, Massachusetts, 447 n
Patents, petitions for. See Bailey, Francis, petition of; Fitch, John, petition of; McPherson, John, petition of

Patents Bill [HR–41]: agreed to by House, 257; read, 257, 258, 271; committee actions on, 258, 269; agreed to with amendments, 271; amendments to, 271–72, 277–78; signed, 282, 284
Paterson, William, 3 n, 20 n, 25 n, 28 n, 34 n, 274 n; appointed to count electoral votes, 8; attendance, 4, 5, 7, 13, 14, 16, 43, 92, 113, 214, 304, 322; classification, 46, 47, 232 n, 716; credentials, 7; letters from, 495, 521; reports for committee on Enumeration Bill [HR–34], 242, 243; salary and expenses for, 277; seated, 5; signs New Jersey act, 522; takes oath, 59; vote recorded, 85, 86, 87, 135, 142, 143, 149, 152, 153, 157, 168, 180, 187, 188, 189, 191, 195, 226, 288 n, 323, 324, 325, 327, 339, 341, 342, 353, 365, 370, 373, 375, 376, 377, 378, 379, 380, 381, 383, 384, 385, 386, 387, 388, 391, 392, 393, 395, 396, 414, 415, 416, 417, 420, 424, 426, 427, 428, 429, 430, 435, 438, 449, 450, 451, 452, 453, 454, 455, 456
—appointed to committees on
amendments, Constitutional, 182
Copyright Bill [HR–43], 302
election of President and Vice President, 9
Enumeration Bill [HR–34], 242
export inspection, 248
Funding Bill [HR–63], 347
inaugural address, 33
Journal of Senate, 51
Judiciary Bill [S–1], 11, 177
North Carolina Judiciary Bill [S–10], 222
Oath Bill [HR–1], 28
Patents Bill [HR–41], 258
Punishment of Crimes Bill [S–6], 227
Records Bill [HR–18], 148
settlement of accounts, 398
State of the Union Address, 218
trade with European colonies in America, 248
Pawlett, Vermont, 555, 557
Paymaster General, clerks in office of, petition of. See Clerks in office of Paymaster General, petition of
Payment of Balances Bill [S–22]: presentation of, 628, 654–55; read, 655, 657; printed, 655; motion to postpone, 657; committee actions on, 657, 659; postponed, 659
Pearson, Joseph, 58, 349
Pemberton, James, letter from, 242
Pennsylvania, 187, 188, 191, 201, 473 n, 663, 691; district court of, 307, 649; electoral votes, 8; General Assembly

of, resolution of, 181; legislature of, 188; loan to United States, 410, 433; militia of, 175; petitions of citizens of (see Bailey, Francis, petition of; Bertier and Company, petition of; Citizens of New Jersey and Pennsylvania, petition of; College of Physicians of Philadelphia, Pennsylvania, petition of concerning distilled spirits; Distillers of Philadelphia, Pennsylvania, petition of; Fitch, John, petitions of; Franklin, Benjamin, memorial of; Inhabitants of Lancaster County, Pennsylvania, petition of concerning liquors; Jones, John, petition of; Mathers, James, petitions of; Merchants of Philadelphia, Pennsylvania, petition of; Mitchell, Abraham, petition of; Morris, Robert, petition of; Public creditors of Pennsylvania, petition of; Public creditors of United States, petition of; Shipwrights of Philadelphia, Pennsylvania, petition of; Swain, Shubael, petitions of; Tanners of Philadelphia, Pennsylvania, petition of); proposed sites for seat of government in (see Hand, Edward, letter from); ratification of Constitutional amendments by, 259–60, 716; Senators present, 3, 7, 13, 42, 213, 224, 288, 495; settlement of accounts of, 198

Pennsylvania Abolition Society, petition of. See Franklin, Benjamin, letter from

Pensions, petition for. See Laurens, Henry, petitions of; List of Bills; Roberts, Ann, petition of; Stirling, Sarah, petition of; Stirling Bill [HR–90]

Perth-Amboy, New Jersey, 96

Peters, Richard, 260, 261

Peters, Robert, and others, petition of, 374

Philadelphia Commissioners, letters to and from, 497, 500–502

Philadelphia County, Pennsylvania, 188

Philadelphia, Pennsylvania, 96, 128, 131 n, 188, 307, 364 n, 637, 640, 649; library of (see Library of Philadelphia, Pennsylvania); petitions from (see Distillers of Philadelphia, Pennsylvania, petition of; Shipwrights of Philadelphia, Pennsylvania, petition of); proposed site of third session of Congress (see Residency [third session], resolutions on; Residence Bill [S–12], motions on); resolution concerning, as seat of government (see Pennsylvania, General Assembly of, resolution of)

Phillips, Richard, petition of, 68, 90

Piankeshaw Indians, 683

Pickering, Timothy, 210

Pilots, regulation of. See Lighthouses Bill [HR–12]

Pinckney, Charles, letter from, 275

Plankbridge, North Carolina, 233 n

Plymouth, Massachusetts, 96

Plymouth, North Carolina, 233 n

Port Elizabeth, New Jersey, 92

Portland, Massachusetts, 96; petition from (see Merchants and traders of Portland, Massachusetts, petition of)

Portland Head Lighthouse Bill [HR–97]: agreed to by House, 470; read, 471, 477; agreed to, 477–78; found correct and signed, 481, 482, 484, 485

Port Penn, Delaware, 94

Ports, regulation of. See Coasting Bills [HR–16], [HR–33]

Portsmouth, New Hampshire, 96, 314

Portsmouth, Virginia, 93, 94, 96

Port Washington, North Carolina, 445 n

Post, Anthony, and others, petition of. See Manufacturers of New York City, petition of

Postmaster General, 243 n, 400 n–401 n

Postmistress of Baltimore, Maryland, petition of. See Goddard, Mary Katherine, petition of

Post Office, 217, 220, 500; House resolution on, 169, 170, 171

Post Office Bill [S–3]: committee to prepare, 170; presented, 171; read, 171, 173, 174; agreed to, 174, 175, 176; found correct and signed, 177, 178, 184

Post Office Bill [HR–74]: agreed to by House, 364; read, 366, 368, 399; committee actions on, 368, 393, 398, 399; agreed to with amendments, 399; amendments to, 399 n–401 n, 406, 441, 442; conference actions on, 407–8, 409

Post Office Bill [HR–92]: agreed to by House, 457; read, 457–58, 459; agreed to, 459; found correct and signed, 460, 461–62, 463

Post Office Bill [HR–137]: agreed to by House, 669; read, 674, 682, 694; printed, 674–75; amendments to, 682, 694, 698; agreed to with amendments, 694; found correct and signed, 704, 705, 707–8

Post Roads, 217, 220, 500

Potomac River, 93, 94, 188, 375, 539, 615, 616; locating permanent seat of government on (see Residence Bill [S–12], message from President on; motions on)

Poultney, Vermont, 555, 557

Poultney River, 555, 557

Pownal, Vermont, 555, 557

Prairie, 617. *See also* Northwest Territory Bill [S–17]

Prairie du Pont. *See* Northwest Territory Bill [S–17]

President: attends divine service, 33; bills signed by (*see* Bills by name); compensation of (*see* Compensation Bill [HR–15]); election of (*see* Election of President and Vice President; Inaugural address; Reception of President and Vice President); messages from, 184, 185, 190, 205, 207, 218, 226, 230, 234, 259, 278, 322, 331, 345, 348, 355, 388, 418, 474, 502, 505, 507, 517, 518, 520, 533, 538, 540, 541, 547, 552, 608, 617, 638, 669, 696, 705, 707 (*see also* Communications, Presidential); notified of date of adjournment, 203; replies to Senate addresses, 48–49, 222, 507; requested to proclaim day of thanksgiving, 203; takes oath, 30; term of, 163; title of (*see* Titles, Presidential)

President of Delaware. *See* Clayton, Joshua, letter from

President of New Hampshire. *See* Sullivan, John

President of Senate. *See* Langdon, John; Vice President

President *pro tempore*. *See* Langdon, John

Printers and stationers: letters from, 57 n; petitions concerning (*see* Allen, Thomas, petition of; Bryce, John, petition of; Greenleaf, Thomas, petition of; Loudon, Samuel, petition of; McLean, Archibald, petition of; Newspapers)

Printing, orders for (*see* Journal of Senate, committee actions on)

Prioleau, Samuel, Jr., petition of, 508

Prisoners, safe-keeping of: New York State law concerning, 278; resolutions on (first session), 183, 184, 185, 186, 190; (third session), 700, 701, 706, 707, 708

Pritchard, Paul, petition of. *See* Shipwrights of South Carolina, petition of

Providence, Rhode Island, 665

Provoost, Samuel, 33; appointed chaplain, 25, 215; letter of, 27

Public credit, 218, 220, 498, 505

Public creditors of Pennsylvania, petition of, 510, 515

Public creditors of United States, petition of, 145

Public debt, provisions for, 500

Public offices, clerks in. *See* Clerks in public offices, petition of

Public sessions of Senate. *See* Open sessions of Senate

Punishment of Crimes Bill [S–2]: committee to prepare, 44, 51, 67; presented, 98; read, 98, 104, 120, 125, 139; agreed to, 147; postponed, 177

Punishment of Crimes Bill [S–6]: committee to prepare, 223, 227; read, 227, 229; agreed to with amendment, 230, 231; agreed to by House with amendments, 234; House amendments to, 284, 285, 286–87, 289; found correct and signed, 292, 295, 296

Q

Quakers, petition of. *See* Franklin, Benjamin, memorial of

Quorum, 3, 4, 6, 7, 213, 495, 496; joint committees' actions on, 214–15, 496–97; message from President on, 213 n

R

Ramsay, David, petition of, 18

Randolph, Beverley, 543

Read, George, 3 n; attendance, 4, 5, 14, 253, 497; classification, 46, 47, 232 n, 716; credentials, 13; salary and expenses for, 277; seated, 13; takes oath, 59; vote recorded, 85, 86, 87, 105, 106, 124, 135, 142, 143, 144, 149, 152, 154, 157, 168, 180, 187, 188, 189, 191, 195, 288 n, 311, 314, 317, 318, 323, 324, 325, 327, 339, 341, 342, 353, 365, 373, 375, 376, 377, 378, 379, 380, 381, 383, 384, 385, 386, 387, 388, 391, 392, 393, 395, 396, 414, 415, 416, 417, 420, 424, 426, 427, 428, 429, 430, 435, 438, 449, 450, 451, 452, 453, 454, 455, 456, 515, 532, 535, 536, 551, 596, 615, 619, 623, 632, 635, 648, 650, 651, 652, 693

—appointed to committees on
Acts of Congress, 59
Appropriations Bill [HR–32], 194
Coasting Bill [HR–33], 197
Collection Bill [HR–26], 197
Compensation Bill [HR–15], 110
Copyright Bill [HR–43], 302
Courts Bill [S–4], 195
Foreign Intercourse Bill [HR–52], 330
Invalid Pensioners Bill [HR–29], 196
Journal of Senate, 15
messages between Houses, 34
Mitigation of Fines Bill [HR–45], 262, 267
Mitigation of Forfeitures Bill [S–24], 699
Navigation Bill [HR–103], 510

Oath Bill [HR–1], 28
officers of the Treasury Department, salaries of, 636
Punishment of Crimes Bill [S–2], 44
Records Bill [HR–18], 148
rules, joint, 39
settlement of accounts and the Funding Bill [HR–63], 418
Settlement of Accounts Bill [HR–72], 394
Tonnage Bill [HR–78], 382
trade, 110
Troops Bill [HR–27], 196
Virginia, resolutions and petition from, 543
—reports for committees on
Appropriations Bill [HR–32], 201
Coasting Bill [HR–33], 199
Collection Bill [HR–26], 199
Copyright Bill [HR–43], 308
Invalid Pensioners Bill [HR–29], 200
Mitigation of Fines Bill [HR–45], 263
Tonnage Bill [HR–78], 408
Troops Bill [HR–27], 200
Read, Jacob, 58 n, 275
Reading, Pennsylvania, 128
Reception of President and Vice President: committees' actions on, 12, 14, 16–17, 21, 29
Records Bill [HR–18]: agreed to by House, 140; read, 146–47, 148, 155; committee actions on, 148, 152; agreed to with amendments, 155–56; amendments to, 155, 165; found correct and signed, 169–70, 174, 176
Records of Congress, preservation of, ix–xi
Reed, Bowes, 475, 476
Registration of ships. See Coasting Bills [HR–16], [HR–33]
Rehobeth, Massachusetts, 172
Remsen, Henry, 58 n
Residence Bill [S–12]: 480; presented, 330; read, 330, 331, 334, 374, 382, 390, 395; committee actions on, 334, 336, 337, 340, 341; motions on, 340–43, 371, 374–75, 376–81, 382–88, 390–92, 395–96; agreed to, 397, 407; found correct and signed, 407, 409, 418; message from President on, 539
Residence Bill [S–21]: request to present, 609, 614–15; read, 615, 618, 649–50, 654; printed, 615–16; postponed, 619; considered, 650–51; agreed to, 654, 662; found correct and signed, 668, 669, 675, 690, 696
Residency (third session): resolutions on, 320, 325, 328, 333, 334, 339, 351, 374
Revenue Bills. See List of Bills
Revenue Law Fine, petition for remission of. See Swain, Shubael, petitions of
Rhode Island, 234 n, 430 n, 665, 714; for-

eign duties of, committee actions on letter on, 230–31; Governor of, letters of, 193–94, 230–31; impost laws affecting, 172; loan to United States, 410, 433; petition of citizens of (see Citizens of Rhode Island, petition of); provisions concerning (see Rhode Island Trade Bill [S–11]); ratification of Constitution by, 230, 331–32, 355–62; ratification of Constitutional amendments by, 192, 198, 388–90, 716; Senators present, 371, 508, 509; trade of (see Collection Bill [HR–23])
Rhode Island Bill [HR–71]: agreed to by House, 336; read, 336, 337, 343; agreed to with amendment, 343; found correct and signed, 344, 352, 353
Rhode Island Enumeration Bill [HR–75]: agreed to by House, 382; read, 382, 393, 394; agreed to, 394; found correct and signed, 397, 398, 404
Rhode Island Judiciary Bill [HR–73]: agreed to by House, 338; read, 344, 347–48, 352; agreed to with amendments, 352; amendment to, 354; found correct and signed, 354, 355, 366, 368
Rhode Island Trade Bill [S–11]: committee to prepare, 294–95, 296, 303, 305–6, 307; presented, 309; read, 309, 311, 312, 313; recommitted, 312; committee actions on, 313; agreed to, 314
Richmond, Virginia, 665
Ridgely, H[enry], 350
Rix dollar of Denmark, rate of. See Collection Bill [HR–134]
Roberts, Ann[e], 671; petition of, 508
Roberts, Colonel Owen, 508, 671
Rock Landing, Georgia. See Indian Treaties Bill [HR–20], amendments to
Rogers, Thomas, 346
Roosevelt, Isaac, 280, 554
Ross, John, petition of, 29 n
Rouen, France, 505 n
Roux, Albert, petition of, 540
Rules, conference, and appointment of chaplains, joint committee actions on, 12, 16, 20
Rules, joint: joint committee actions on, 39–40, 42, 46; resolution on, 107, 108, 111–12, 114
Rules, Senate, 637; committee actions on, 12, 13, 15, 17, 18–20; resolutions on, 20, 51, 100, 248 n; motion on, 84
Rules, standing, ix
Rumsey, James. See Montgomery, William, petition of
Rupert, Vermont, 555, 557
Rutland, Vermont, 626
Rutledge, John, electoral votes cast for, 8
Ryans, North Carolina, 233

S

St. Clair, Arthur. *See* Governor of Northwest Territory

St. Paul's Chapel, 27, 33, 35

Salaries Bill [HR–136A]: agreed to by House, 676; read, 676–77, 692; printed, 676; agreed to with amendments, 692–93; amendments to, 693, 698; found correct and signed, 699, 701, 704, 707

Salaries-Executive Bill [HR–21]: agreed to by House, 147; read, 147, 148–49, 156; agreed to with amendments, 156; amendments to, 156 n, 165–66, 169; found correct and signed, 169, 170, 174

Salaries-Executive Bill [HR–54]: agreed to by House, 296; read, 297, 299, 328; committee actions on, 299, 328; agreed to, 328; found correct and signed, 331, 333, 335, 337

Salaries-Judiciary Bill [HR–28]: agreed to by House, 179; read, 179, 180, 181; amendments to, 180, 183; agreed to with amendments, 181; found correct and signed, 183, 184, 185

Salaries-Legislative Bill [HR–19]: agreed to by House, 115; read, 119, 120, 138, 140, 145; committee actions on, 138, 139, 140–42, 143, 144; resolution on, 142; agreed to with amendments, 146, 148; amendments to, 144–45, 146, 150, 157, 171–72; conference actions on, 165, 166; signed, 174, 175, 185

Salaries of Clerks Bill [HR–46]: agreed to by House, 257; read, 257–58, 270, 271; disagreed to, 271

Salem, Massachusetts, 96

Salem, New Jersey, 92

Salisbury, Maryland, 92

Sandgate, Vermont, 555, 557

Sandwich, Massachusetts, 445 n

Sandy-Hook. *See* New Jersey, act of; New York, acts of

Savannah, Georgia, 96, 369, 400 n

Savannah River, 525

Sawyers Creek, 233 n

Schell, George, pension of, 476

Schuykill River, Pennsylvania, 128

Schuyler, Philip, 508 n, 628; attendance, 91, 213, 507; classification, 98, 232 n, 716; credentials, 91; salary and expenses for, 277; seated, 91; takes oath, 91; vote recorded, 105, 106, 124, 135, 142, 143, 144, 149, 154, 157, 168, 180, 187, 188, 189, 191, 195, 226, 311, 314, 317, 318, 323, 324, 325, 327, 339, 341, 342, 353, 365, 370, 373, 375, 376, 377, 378, 379, 380, 381, 383, 384, 385, 386, 387, 388, 391, 392, 393, 395, 396, 414, 415, 416, 417, 420, 424, 426, 427, 428, 429, 430, 435, 438, 449, 450, 451, 452, 453, 454, 455, 456, 515, 532, 535, 536, 551, 596, 619, 620, 623, 632, 635, 648, 650, 651, 652, 693, 703

—appointed to committees on

Bank, National, 516

coins, weights, and measures, 518

Collection Bill [HR–134], 660

Commissioners of Loans Bill [HR–135], 675

Compensation Bill [HR–15], 110

Consuls and Vice Consuls Bill [S–18], 509, 531

Disabled Soldiers and Seamen Bill [HR–88], 458

Duties on Distilled Spirits Bill [HR–110], 546

Duties on Teas Bill [HR–130], 689

Indian Trade Bill [HR–65], 398, 412

Indian Treaty Bill [HR–50b], 406

Invalid Officers Bill [HR–59], 303

Kentucky Statehood Bill [S–16], 508

laws, revision of, 666

Military Establishment Bills [HR–50a], [HR–126A], 273, 607

mint, 548

Navigation Bill [HR–103], 518

Officers Bill [HR–53], 292

Payment of Balances Bill [S–22], 657

Settlement of Accounts Bill [HR–77], 402

Stirling Bill [HR–96], 477

Virginia, resolutions and petition from, 543

Ways and Means Bill [S–14], 509

—reports for committees on

Collection Bill [HR–134], 662

Disabled Soldiers and Seamen Bill [HR–88], 461

Indian Treaty Bill [HR–50b], 419

Invalid Officers Bill [HR–59], 403

Kentucky Statehood Bill [S–16], 520

laws, revision of, 669

Military Establishment Bill [HR–126A], 616

Officers Bill [HR–53], 293

Stirling Bill [HR–96], 478

Ways and Means Bill [S–14], 509

Science, promotion of, 217, 220

Scott, Edward, pension of, 476

Scott, Lewis A., 280

Scott, Thomas, appointed to committee on New York City Hall, use of, 43

Seals of Supreme and Circuit Courts, 714; resolution on, 441, 442, 443, 444–45, 448, 463

Seat of Government: letter concerning site of (*see* Hand, Edward, letter from); petitions concerning (*see* Citizens of New Jersey and Pennsylvania, petition of; O'Donnell, John, petition of; Peters, Robert, petition of); proposed sites of, in Pennsylvania, 128. *See also* Pennsylvania, General Assembly of, resolution of; Residence Bill [S–12]

Seat of Government Bill [HR–25]: read, 184, 185, 187, 190, 194; amendments to, 187, 190, 191, 201, 203; agreed to with amendments, 195; postponed, 203

Secretary of Continental Congress. *See* Continental Congress, papers of

Secretary of Senate, ix, x, xii, 85, 505 n, 548; attests Senate Journal, 207, 213 n, 491, 708; certifies Constitutional amendments, 210; compensation of (*see* Salaries-Legislative Bill [HR–19]); duties of, ix, x–xi, 206 (*see also* Messages between Houses, temporary procedure for delivering; Rules, joint); elected, 12; order to, 562 n; takes oath, 59

Secretary of State, 263 n, 271 n, 520 n, 678, 680; letters from, 533–34, 537; petition referred to, 362; reports of, 514, 547; resolution concerning (*see* Statutes-at-large of states)

Secretary of Treasury, 11 n, 93, 128 n, 129 n, 156 n, 191, 263 n, 301 n, 313, 420, 436, 446 n, 484, 498, 680, 711; ordered to prepare statement on exports of United States, 609; petitions referred to, 245, 461; reports of, 246, 514, 548, 647–48. *See also* Treasury Bill [HR–9]

Secretary of War, 114, 202 n, 271 n, 499; delivers message from President, 175; letter from, 504; petition referred to, 540; report of, 221

Secretary to President. *See* Lear, Tobias

Senate: open sessions of. *See* Open sessions of Senate

Senate Resolution No. 99, ix–x

Senators. *See Individual names*

Seney, Joshua, appointed to committee on quorum, 215

Separation of powers, 161

Sergeant-at-arms: appointment of postponed, 42 n; compensation of (*see* Salaries-Legislative Bill [HR–19])

Sessions of Senate, open. *See* Open sessions of Senate

Settlement of accounts: petitions concerning (*see* Olyphant, David, petition of; Weed, Jacob, petition of); notice of intention to present bill on, 348; committees' actions on resolution on, 352, 397–98, 406, 409–12, 413–16, 417, 418, 419–21

Settlement of Accounts Bill [HR–13]: agreed to by House, 92; read, 92, 99;

agreed to, 99; found correct and signed, 107, 108

Settlement of Accounts Bill [HR–77]: agreed to by House, 367; read, 367, 369, 371, 393, 394, 402, 405; committees' actions on, 394, 399, 401, 402, 404; agreed to with amendments, 405; amendments to, 405 n, 413, 439–41; conference actions on, 413, 439; found correct and signed, 443, 447–48, 468

Settling Accounts Bill [HR–95]: agreed to by House, 468; read, 469; disagreed to, 471

Shaftsbury, Vermont, 555, 557

Sharp, Gibbons, and others, petition of. *See* Manufacturers of Boston, Massachusetts, petition of

Sherman, Lemuel, 673

Sherman, Roger, appointed to committees on: amendments, Constitutional, 181; business between Houses, 297; Salaries-Legislative Bill [HR–19], 165; Thanksgiving, 197; titles, Presidential, 27, 43; unfinished business of first session, 225

Shipwrights of Baltimore, Maryland, petition of, 62

Shipwrights of Philadelphia, Pennsylvania, petition of, 62

Shipwrights of South Carolina, petition of, 49

Shuttlief, Joseph, 476

Sickles, Robert, petition of. *See* Meters of New York, petition of

Sill, Richard, 553

Silvester, Peter, appointed to committees on: newspapers, 48; Thanksgiving, 197

Sinking Fund Act [HR–101], report on, 510–13

Sinking Fund Bill [HR–101]: agreed to by House, 483; read, 484, 486; amendments to, 486, 488; agreed to with amendments, 486; found correct and signed, 489, 490

Sinking Fund Bill [HR–136]: agreed to by House, 668; read, 673, 674, 697; printed, 673–74; agreed to with amendments, 697; amendments to, 697–98; found correct and signed, 704, 705, 707–8

Skaats, 15

Skewarkey, North Carolina, 333 n

Slavery, abolition of, society for. *See* Franklin, Benjamin, memorial of

Smith, Melancton, 553, 555, 557

Smith, William (South Carolina), appointed to committees on: adjournment, 481; business between Houses, 297; newspapers, 48; quorum, 496 n

Smith's Point, Virginia, 93

Snow Hill, Maryland, 93

Soldiers, enlistment term, 163

Sorbonne, University of, 505 n

South Carolina: electoral votes, 8; holding of Circuit Courts in (*see* Circuit Courts Bill [S–13]); loan to United States, 410, 433; pay of soldiers of (*see* Compensation lists, resolutions on); petitions of citizens of (*see* Drayton, Stephen, petition of; Laurens, Henry, petition of; Masters of American vessels of Charleston, South Carolina, petition of; Olyphant, David, petition of; Prioleau, Samuel, Jr., petition of; Ramsay, David, petition of; Roberts, Ann[e], petition of; Roux, Albert, petition of, Shipwrights of South Carolina, petition of); ratification of Constitutional amendments by, 275, 276, 716; Senators present, 13, 15, 61, 213, 495

Southern frontiers, appropriations for defense of, 122–23

Southern Territory Bill [S–8]: committee to prepare, 281; presented, 283; read, 283, 285, 286; agreed to with amendments, 286, 297; House amendments to, 301, 304; found correct and signed, 305, 321, 322

South Quay, Virginia, 445 n

Southwest frontiers and Indian Department, 221

Speaker of the House: bills signed by (*see* *Individual bills*); office of, expenses of (*see* Salaries-Legislative Bill [HR–19]); signs Constitutional amendments, 210

Special Appropriations Bill [HR–100], 712; agreed to by House, 485; read, 487, 488, 489; agreed to with amendment, 488–89; found correct and signed, 489, 490

Springfield, Massachusetts, 118

Standing orders. *See* Rules, Senate

Stanton, Joseph, Jr.: appointed to committee on Mentges, Francis, petition of, resolution on, 457; attendance, 508; classification, 372, 716; credentials, 371; seated and takes oath, 371; vote recorded, 373, 375, 376, 377, 378, 379, 380, 381, 383, 384, 385, 386, 387, 388, 391, 392, 393, 395, 396, 414, 415, 416, 417, 420, 424, 426, 427, 428, 429, 430, 435, 438, 449, 450, 451, 452, 453, 454, 455, 456, 515, 535, 536, 551, 596, 615, 619, 620, 623, 632, 635, 648, 650, 651, 652, 693, 703

State, Department of. *See* Foreign Affairs Bill [HR–8]

State, Secretary of. *See* Secretary of State

State Legislatures, oath of, 36

State of the Union Addresses, 216–18, 498–501

—answer to (second session), 221
committee to prepare, 218, 219–20
reply to, 222

—answer to (third session)
committee to prepare, 500, 505–6
reply to, 507

Statutes-at-large of states, 267 n; resolution on, 177, 178, 183, 184, 185

Steele, John, appointed to committee on North Carolina Judiciary Bill [S–10], 308

Steuben Bill [HR–60]: agreed to by House, 306; read, 306, 326; committee actions on, 306, 319, 321, 323; amendments to, 323, 326, 329; agreed to with amendments, 327; found correct and signed, 331, 333, 335, 337

Stewart and Davidson Bill [HR–90]: agreed to by House, 448; read, 457, 458; committee actions on, 458; agreed to, 458; found correct and signed, 460, 461–62, 463

Stillwell's Landing, 92

Stirling, Earl of. *See* Stirling, Sarah, petition of

Stirling, Sarah, petition of, 336

Stirling Bill [HR–96]: agreed to by House, 470; read, 471, 477, 480; committee actions on, 477, 478–80; agreed to with amendments, 480; amendments to, 481; found correct and signed, 485–86, 488, 490

Stoner, Charles, petition of, 9 n

Stonington, Connecticut, 446 n

Stout, Harman, and others, petition of. *See* Clerks in public offices, petition of

Strong, Caleb, 214 n; attendance, 4, 5, 7, 13, 14, 126, 213, 481, 497; classification, 46, 47, 232 n, 716; credentials, 7; salary and expenses for, 277; seated, 3; takes oath, 59; vote recorded, 85, 86, 87, 105, 106, 124, 226, 288 n, 311, 314, 317, 318, 323, 324, 325, 327, 339, 341, 342, 353, 365, 370, 373, 375, 376, 377, 378, 379, 381, 383, 384, 385, 386, 387, 388, 391, 392, 393, 395, 396, 414, 415, 416, 417, 420, 424, 426, 427, 428, 429, 430, 435, 438, 449, 450, 451, 452, 453, 454, 455, 456, 515, 532, 535, 536, 551, 596, 615, 619, 620, 623, 632, 635, 648, 650, 651, 652, 693, 703

—appointed to committees on
adjournment, 108, 364
Bailey Bill [HR–44], 251
Bank, National, 516
business between Houses, 298

Compensation Bill [HR–15], 110
Congressional session, fourth, 537
Courts Bill [S–9], 223
Duties on Distilled Spirits Bill [HR–110], 546
Enumeration Bill [HR–34], 242
Foreign Affairs Bill [HR–8], 89
Foreign Intercourse Bill [HR–52], 299
Indian Trade Bill [HR–65], 412
Judiciary Bill [S–1], 11
Land Office Bill [HR–114], 627
Mediterranean trade, 508
messages between Houses, 17
Military Establishment Bills [HR–50a], [HR–126A], 273, 607
Mitigation of Fines Bill [HR–45], 257, 262, 267
Naturalization Bill [HR–40], 256
newspapers, 44
New York City Hall, use of, 41
North Carolina Cession Bill [S–7], 246
Northwest Territory Bill [S–17], 519
Oath Bill [HR–1], 28
officers of Treasury Department, salaries of, 636
Payment of Balances Bill [S–22], 657
Post Office Bill [HR–74], 368, 408
Punishment of Crimes Bill [S–6], 227
quorum, 214
reception of President and Vice President, 21
Rhode Island Trade Bill [S–11], 296
rules, conference, and appointment of chaplains, 12
settlement of accounts, 398
settlement of accounts and the Funding Bill [HR–63], 418
Settlement of Accounts Bill [HR–72], 394
Southern Territory Bill [S–8], 281
Steuben Bill [HR–60], 306
Treasury Bill [HR–9], 119
vessels leaving U.S. ports, 252
Virginia Cession Bill [HR–85], 437
Widows, Orphans, and Invalids Bill [HR–139], 673
—reports for committees on
adjournment, 115, 372–73
Bailey Bill [HR–44], 251
Bank Bill [S–15], 522, 534
Congressional session, fourth, 539
Courts Bill [S–9], 292
Foreign Affairs Bill [HR–8], 90
Foreign Intercourse Bill [HR–52], 304, 320
Land Office Bill [HR–114], 655, 667
Mitigation of Fines Bill [HR–45], 278
Northwest Territory Bill [S–17], 526, 527
Oath Bill [HR–1], 35
Payment of Balances Bill [S–22], 659

quorum, 215
Sturges, Jonathan, appointed to committee on New York City Hall, use of, 43
Sullivan, John, 58 n; letter from, 349
Superintendent of Indian Affairs, 122, 156 n
Supreme and Circuit Court Seals, expenses of. See Seals of Supreme and Circuit Courts
Supreme Court, 271 n, 301 n, 653; jurisdiction of, 163–64; justices of, compensation of (see Salaries-Judiciary Bill [HR–28]). See also Judiciary Bill [S–1]
Surgeons and surgeons-mates, petition of, 534
Survey of western boundary of New York: petitions on (see Ellicott, Andrew, petition of; Gorham, Nathaniel, petition of); resolution on, 119, 121, 125–26, 134, 138, 140
Surveyors. See Collection Bills
Susquehanna River, 128, 187, 188
Swain, Shubael, petitions of, 523, 649. See also Swain Bill [HR–111]
Swain Bill [HR–111]: agreed to by House, 523; read, 523, 525, 526; committee actions on, 525, 526; disagreed to, 526; printed, 649
Swaine, John, 57 n

T

Talcott, Matthew, and others, petition of. See Citizens of Connecticut, petition of
Tanners of Philadelphia, Pennsylvania, petition of, 345
Tappahannock, Virginia, 93
Tatlow, Joseph, petition of, 621
Taxation, direct, 158
Telfair, Edward, electoral votes cast for, 8
Terms of federally elected officials, joint committee actions on, 299, 300, 309, 310–11, 315–16
Thanksgiving: resolution on, 192, 197; joint committee actions on, 192, 197, 203
Thatcher, George, appointed to committees on: communications, Presidential, 53; unfinished business of first session, 225
Thomas, Evan, 497
Thomson, Charles, letters to and from, 9, 26
Thomson, William, 364 n
Time of Meeting Bill [HR–31]: agreed to by House, 186; read and agreed to, 193; found correct and signed, 202–4, 205
Time of Meeting Bill [HR–122]: agreed

to by House, 593; read, 593, 595, 620, 628; printed, 593; postponed, 595; amendment to, 628; disagreed to, 628

Time of Meeting Bill [HR–132]: agreed to by House, 636; read, 637, 638, 654; printed, 637; amendment to, 638; agreed to, 654; found correct and signed, 660, 661, 668, 676

Titles, foreign, 159

Titles, Presidential: joint committee actions on, 24, 26, 37, 40, 41; committee actions on, 40, 41–42, 45; conference actions on, 41, 43, 44, 45; resolution on, amendment to, 45

Todd, Thomas, 505

Tonnage Bill [HR–5]: agreed to by House, 54; ordered for consideration, 55; read, 63, 67, 68; agreed to with amendments, 68; amendments to, 68–69, 72, 73, 75–76, 77; conference actions on, 72, 73, 74, 76; committee to present to President, 79–80; signed, 80, 88

Tonnage Bill [HR–24]: agreed to by House, 170; read, 170, 171; committee actions on, 171, 172, 173; disagreed to, 173

Tonnage Bill [HR–78]: agreed to by House, 369; read, 369, 382, 408; committee actions on, 382, 408; agreed to, 408; found correct and signed, 421, 422, 432

Tracy, Nathaniel, petition of, 264

Trade, 162; committees actions on, 69, 82–83, 109–10; encouragement and protection of, petition for (see Merchants of Philadelphia, Pennsylvania, petition of); need to promote, 217, 220; regulation of, 159 (see also Manufacturers of Boston, Massachusetts, petition of; Manufacturers of New York City, petition of; Masters of American vessels of Charleston, South Carolina, petition of; Merchants and manufacturers of Baltimore, Maryland, petition of; Merchants of Philadelphia, Pennsylvania, petition of; Merchants and traders of Portsmouth, New Hampshire, petition of; Shipwrights of Baltimore, Maryland, petition of; Shipwrights of Philadelphia, Pennsylvania, petition of; Shipwrights of South Carolina, petition of); status of, 498. See also Foreign Intercourse Bill [HR–52]

Trade with European colonies in America, committee actions on, 241, 248–49, 268, 294

Trade with Great Britain. See Great Britain, commercial relations with

Treasurer of United States, 364 n, 511; accounts of, letters and reports concerning, 231, 372, 461, 524

Treasury, Secretary of. See Secretary of Treasury

Treasury Bill [HR–9]: agreed to by House, 78; read, 78, 89, 99, 100; amendments to, 100–101, 108–9, 112, 134, 135; agreed to with amendments, 101, 103; conference actions on, 118–19, 121; found correct and signed, 139, 140, 145, 148, 150

Treasury Bill [HR–131]: agreed to by House, 649; read, 653, 654, 656; printed, 653; committee actions on, 654, 656; agreed to with amendments, 656; amendments to, 656–57, 662; found correct and signed, 668, 669, 675, 690, 698

Treasury Department, 94, 239

Treaties: commercial, 162; publication of, resolution on, 334, 344, 352–53

"Trial by jury" clause, petition for. See Fitch, John, petitions of

Troops. See Militia

Troops Bill [HR–27]: agreed to by House, 185; read, 185, 196, 200; committee actions on, 196, 200; agreed to with amendments, 200; amendments to, 205, 206; found correct and signed, 206, 207

Trumbull, Jonathan, appointed to committees on: Continental Congress, papers of, 29; rules, joint, 39; titles, Presidential, 43

Tucker, Thomas Tudor, appointed to committee on Salaries-Legislative Bill [HR–19], 165

Tunis. See Algiers and Tunis Regencies, plan for truce with

Turney, Abel, 672

Twining, Nathaniel, petition of, 362

Twining Bill [HR–72]: agreed to by House, 354; read, 354, 371; committee actions on, 354–55, 366, 369; agreed to, 371; found correct and signed, 381, 382, 388, 395

U

Unfinished business of first session: committee actions on, 224, 225; resolution on, 226, 227

University (national), need for establishment of, 217

Updike, Daniel, 359, 362

V

Van Staphorst (ship), 293–94

Van Woort, Lewis, 477

Varick, Richard, 557. *See also* New York
City, mayor of
Vermont: ratification of Constitution by,
558–60; statehood for, 552–62
Vermont Bill [HR–128]: agreed to by
House, 625; read, 626, 628, 630;
printed, 626–27; agreed to with
amendment, 630; amendment to, 628,
630, 636; found correct and signed,
660, 661, 668, 676
Vermont Statehood Bill [S–19]: committee to prepare, 562, 563; printed, 563;
read, 563–64, 593, 594; amendment
to, 593; agreed to, 594, 606; found
correct and signed, 609, 610, 616, 617
Verplanck, Gulian, 280, 553, 554, 555–56,
557
Vessels leaving U.S. ports, clearance of:
motion on, 251, 252; resolution on,
253
Vice President, 231, 505 n; addresses to
and from, 21–23; adjourns Senate,
207, 491; administers oath, 59, 61, 71,
221, 293, 495; attendance, 3, 113,
495; attends divine service, 33; bills
signed by (*see Individual bills*); certifies salaries and expenses for Senators, 277; compensation of (*see* Compensation Bill [HR–15]); delivers
Senate answer to inaugural address,
39, 48; election of (*see* Election of
President and Vice President; Reception of President and Vice President);
reports for commissioners on Sinking
Fund Act [HR–101], 510; signs
Constitutional amendments, 210;
signs letter to Philadelphia commissioners, 502; takes oath, 59; titles of
(*see* Titles, Presidential); vote recorded, 86, 135, 181, 189, 318, 324,
325, 327, 341, 385, 387, 388, 449,
450, 456; voting procedure, order on,
85
Vienna, Maryland, 92
Vincennes and the Illinois Country, settlers
at, land grants to. *See* Northwest Territory Bill [S–17]
Vining, John, appointed to committees on:
adjournment, 199; amendments, Constitutional, 181; business between
Houses, 297; rules, joint, 39
Virginia, 216, 663, 665, 691, 714; electoral
votes, 8; loan to United States, 410,
433; militia of, 175; pay of soldiers
of (*see* Compensation lists); petition
of citizen of (*see* Finnie, William,
petition of); resolutions and memorial
from, 531; Senators present, 6, 7, 13,
51, 283, 293, 608. *See also* Kentucky,
statehood for; Kentucky Statehood
Bill [S–16]

—resolutions and petition from, 533, 534
letter concerning, committee actions on,
543–44, 694–95
committed to committee on letter concerning, 607
Virginia Cession Bill [HR–85]: agreed to
by House, 431; read, 436–37, 442,
447, 471; committee actions on, 437,
440, 478; recommitted, 448; amendments to, 462, 471–73, 481; agreed to
with amendments, 478; found correct
and signed, 481, 482, 484, 485
Votes, committee actions on, 246, 247, 248

W

Wabash and Miami Indians, motion on,
662, 700
Wabash Indians, 175
Wadsworth, Jeremiah, 714; appointed to
committees on adjournment, 107, 338,
364
Wagner, John. *See* Tanners of Philadelphia, Pennsylvania, petition of
Walker, John: credentials, 293; replaced
in Senate, 495; seated and takes oath,
293; vote recorded, 311, 314, 317,
318, 323, 324, 325, 327, 339, 341,
342, 353, 365, 370, 373, 375, 376,
377, 378, 379, 380, 381, 383, 384,
385, 386, 387, 388, 391, 392, 393,
396, 397, 414, 416, 417, 420, 424,
426, 427, 428, 429, 430, 435, 438,
449, 450, 451, 452, 453, 454, 455,
456
Waln, Nicholas, address of, 242
War, Secretary of. *See* Secretary of War
War Department Bill [HR–7]: read, 78,
89, 104; amendments to, 104–5, 108;
agreed to with amendments, 105;
found correct and signed, 110, 112,
114
Ward, Henry, 389, 390
Washington, George, 9, 473 n; election of,
8. *See also* President
Washington, North Carolina, 234 n
Ways and Means Bill [HR–83]: 666;
agreed to by House, 423; read, 436,
437, 468; committee actions on, 437,
461, 462, 463–67, 468; amendments
to, 468–69, 478; agreed to with
amendments, 469; found correct and
signed, 481, 482, 484, 485
Ways and Means Bill [S–14]: presented
and read, 509; agreed to, 509, 513;
found correct and signed, 516, 517
Ways and Means Bill [HR–129]: agreed
to by House, 628; printed, 628–29;
read, 628, 630, 635; agreed to, 635;
motion to reconsider, 636; found correct and signed, 660, 661, 668, 676

Weaver, David, pension of, 476

Weed, Jacob, petition of, 460; committee actions on, 461

Weights, 500. See also Coins, weights, and measures

Wells, Vermont, 555, 557

Western lands of North Carolina, cession of. See North Carolina act for cession of western lands

Western territories, survey of, resolution on, 483, 484, 489, 490

Westfall, Nicholas Ferdinand, 673

West Indies, trade with. See Trade, committee actions on

West Point, New York, 118; petition for compensation for land at (see Moore, Stephen, petition of)

West Point Bill [HR–76]: agreed to by House, 362; read, 362, 370, 373; committee actions on, 363, 370; agreed to, 370, 373; found correct and signed, 397, 398, 404

Whale fisheries. See Fisheries, cod and whale, report of Secretary of State on

Wharton, John, and others, petition of. See Shipwrights of Philadelphia, Pennsylvania, petition of

White, Alexander, appointed to committees on: adjournment, 481; Courts Bill [S–4], 196; enrolled bills, 102, 236; Foreign Intercourse Bill [HR–52], 333; Impost Bill [HR–2], 77; New York City Hall, use of, 43; North Carolina Judiciary Bill [S–10], 308; unfinished business of first session, 225

White, John, resolution on petition of, 193, 198, 205, 207

White, William (chaplain), 502, 671

White, William, pension of, 477

Widows, Orphans, and Invalids Bill [HR–139]: agreed to by House, 668; read, 670, 673; printed, 670–73; committee actions on, 673, 697; postponed, 697

Willard, Reverend Joseph, and others, petition of. See Congregational clergy of Massachusetts, petition of

Williams, Colonel, 477

Williams, William, 58 n

Williamsburg, Virginia, 473 n

Williams' Digest, 267 n

Williamson, Hugh, appointed to committees on: Foreign Intercourse Bill [HR–52], 333; North Carolina Judiciary Bill [S–10], 308

Willing, Morris and Company, 238

Wilmington, Delaware, 94, 96, 446 n; motion to locate permanent seat of government at (see Residence Bill [S–12], motions on)

Wilmington, North Carolina, 234 n, 320

Windsor, Connecticut, 283 n

Windsor, Vermont, 626

Wingate, Paine, 16 n, 24 n; attendance, 4, 5, 7, 13, 14, 213, 488, 495; classification, 46, 47, 232 n, 716; credentials, 7; salary and expenses for, 277; seated, 3; takes oath, 59; vote recorded, 85, 86, 87, 105, 106, 124, 135, 142, 143, 144, 149, 152, 154, 157, 168, 180, 187, 188, 189, 191, 195, 226, 288 n, 311, 314, 317, 318, 323, 324, 325, 327, 339, 341, 342, 353, 365, 370, 373, 375, 376, 377, 378, 379, 380, 381, 383, 384, 385, 386, 387, 388, 391, 392, 393, 396, 397, 414, 416, 417, 420, 424, 426, 427, 428, 429, 430, 435, 438, 449, 450, 451, 452, 453, 454, 455, 456, 515, 532, 535, 536, 551, 596, 615, 619, 620, 623, 632, 635, 648, 650, 651, 652, 693

—appointed to committees on

attendance and traveling expenses of Senators, 196

Campbell, Donald, petition of, 421

clerks of the Commissioner of Army Accounts, salaries of, 439

compensation of Senators during second session, 274

Ely Bill [HR–56], 302

enrolled bills, 102, 236

Foreign Officers Bill [HR–116], 595

Gould Bill [HR–79], 382

Impost Bill [HR–2], 77

Journal of Senate, 51

Judiciary Bill [S–1], 11

Mentges, Francis, petition of, 457

Tonnage Bill [HR–5], 79

Treasurer of United States, accounts of, 372

Twining Bill [HR–72], 355

Widows, Orphans, and Invalids Bill [HR–139], 673

—reports for committees on

Campbell, Donald, petition of, 445

clerks of the Commissioner of Army Accounts, salaries of, 441

enrolled bills, 110, 139, 148, 169, 174, 175, 177, 178, 183, 202, 236, 237, 247, 266, 268, 274–75, 282, 284, 285–86, 292, 295, 304–5, 321, 328–29, 331, 335, 344, 352, 354, 366, 381, 388, 397, 407, 408–9, 421, 431, 437, 443, 444, 447–48, 460, 461–62, 481, 484

Gould Bill [HR–79], 399

Impost Bill [HR–2], 77

Mentges, Francis, petition of, 462

Tonnage Bill [HR–5], 79–80

Widows, Orphans, and Invalids Bill [HR–139], 697

Winsor, North Carolina, 233 n
Winton, North Carolina, 233 n
Wiscasset, Massachusetts, 400 n
Wolcott, Oliver, Jr., signs report on Sinking Fund Act [HR–101], 512
Wright, John. See White, John, petition of
Wrights Ferry, Pennsylvania, 128
Wynkoop, Henry, appointed to committee on newspapers, 48

Y

Yates, Robert, 553, 555, 557
Yeocomico River, Virginia, 93
York River, Virginia, 93
Yorktown, Pennsylvania, 128
Yorktown, Virginia, 96
Younglove, John, pension of, 477

THE JOHNS HOPKINS UNIVERSITY PRESS

This book was composed in Garamond text and display
by Monotype Composition Company from a design by
Gerard A. Valerio. It was printed by Universal Lithographers,
Inc. on 50-lb. Sebago Regular and bound in Arrestox cloth by
L. H. Jenkins, Inc.